Secret Intelligence

This Reader in the field of intelligence studies focuses on policy, blending classic works on concepts and approaches with more recent essays dealing with current issues and the ongoing debate about the future of intelligence.

The subject of secret intelligence has never enjoyed a higher profile. The terrorist attacks of 9/11, Madrid and London, the conflicts in Iraq and Afghanistan, the missing WMD, public debates over prisoner interrogation and new domestic security regulations have all contributed to make this a 'hot' subject over the past decade.

Aiming to be more comprehensive than existing books, and to achieve truly international coverage of the field, this book provides key readings and supporting material for students and course convenors. It is divided into four main sections, each of which includes full summaries of each article, further reading suggestions and student questions:

- The intelligence cycle
- Intelligence, counter-terrorism and security
- Ethics, accountability and control
- Intelligence and the new warfare

Comprising essays by leading scholars in the field, *Secret Intelligence* will be essential reading for students of intelligence studies, strategic studies, international security and political science in general, and of interest to anyone wishing to understand the current relationship between intelligence and policy-making.

Christopher Andrew is a Fellow and President of Corpus Christi College, Cambridge, Professor of Modern and Contemporary History and former Chair of the Faculty of History at Cambridge University.

Richard J. Aldrich is Professor of International Security at the University of Warwick.

Wesley K. Wark is an Associate Professor in the Department of History of the University of Toronto, a Fellow of Trinity College and an Associate of the Munk Centre for International Studies.

Secret Intelligence

A Reader

**Edited by
Christopher Andrew, Richard J. Aldrich
and Wesley K. Wark**

Routledge
Taylor & Francis Group

LONDON AND NEW YORK

First published 2009
by Routledge
2 Park Square, Milton Park, Abingdon, Oxon, OX14 4RN

Simultaneously published in the USA and Canada
by Routledge
270 Madison Avenue, New York, NY 10016

Reprinted 2009, 2010 (twice)

Routledge is an imprint of the Taylor and Francis Group, an informa business

Typeset in Baskerville by
RefineCatch Limited, Bungay, Suffolk
Printed and bound in Great Britain
by TJ International, Padstow, Cornwall

British Library Cataloguing in Publication Data
A catalogue record for this book is available from the British Library

Library of Congress Cataloging-in-Publication Data
Secret intelligence : a reader / edited by Christopher Andrew, Richard J. Aldrich
and Wesley K. Wark.
    p. cm.
  1. Intelligence service—United States.   2. Intelligence service—Great
Britain.   3. Secret service—United States.   4. Secret service—Great Britain.
5. Terrorism—Prevention.   6. Military intelligence.   7. Peacekeeping forces.
I. Andrew, Christopher M.   II. Aldrich, Richard J. (Richard James), 1961–
III. Wark, Wesley K., 1952–
    JK468.I6S394 2009
    327.1273—dc22   2008029007

ISBN10: 0–415–42023–7 (hbk)
ISBN10: 0–415–42024–5 (pbk)

ISBN13: 978–0–415–42023–5 (hbk)
ISBN13: 978–0–415–42024–2 (pbk)

Contents

The analysis of intelligence

Intelligence at the top: Producer-consumer linkage

Liaison: Intelligence co-operation

PART 2
INTELLIGENCE, COUNTER-TERRORISM AND SECURITY

Intelligence and 9/11

Intelligence and WMD

Security intelligence and counter-terrorism

Counter-intelligence

PART 3
ETHICS, ACCOUNTABILITY AND CONTROL

The problems of oversight and accountability

The problem of surveillance and civil liberties

Intelligence and ethics

The editors

Christopher Andrew is one of the world's leading intelligence scholars. His 14 books include studies of the British, US and Soviet intelligence services. He is a Fellow and President of Corpus Christi College, Cambridge, Professor of Modern and Contemporary History and former Chair of the Faculty of History at Cambridge University. He has been a visiting Professor at Harvard, Toronto and the Australian National University. He is a frequent broadcaster, holds an honorary doctorate in strategic intelligence from the Joint Military Intelligence College in Washington, DC, and is Honorary Air Commodore of 7006 Squadron (Intelligence) in the Royal Auxiliary Air Force. His authorised history of MI5, the UK Security Service, will be published by Allen Lane/Penguin in 2009.

Richard J. Aldrich is Professor of International Security at the University of Warwick and is the author of several books including *The Hidden Hand: Britain American and Cold War Secret Intelligence* which won the Donner Book prize in 2002 and was short-listed for the Westminster Medal. More recently he has co-ordinated an international programme of research into diaries of the Second World War. He has held a Fulbright fellowship at Georgetown University in Washington DC and more recently has spend time in Canberra and Ottawa as a Leverhulme fellow. A regular media commentator on war and espionage, he is currently completing a book examining the impact of globalization upon intelligence services.

Wesley K. Wark is an Associate Professor in the Department of History of the University of Toronto, a Fellow of Trinity College and an Associate of the Munk Centre for International Studies. His recent publications include *Twenty-First Century Intelligence* (2004). He is an expert of Canadian and international intelligence and security issues, and has published numerous books and articles on this subject. He is the Past-President of the Canadian Association for Security and Intelligence Studies and organized the Association's September 2000 conference held in Ottawa on the 'Future of Intelligence'. For many years he was co-editor of the journal, *Intelligence and National Security*. He has served as a consultant to the Privy Council Office of Canada on intelligence policy.

The contributors

Matthew M. Aid, a native of New York City, holds a Bachelor's degree in International Relations from Beloit College, Wisconsin. He has served as a senior executive with several large international financial research and investigative companies for more than 15 years. The author of many articles on the history of signals intellgence, he is was also the co-editor with Cees Wiebes of *Secrets of Signals Intelligence During the Cold War and Beyond* (2001). His most recent publication is *Secret Sentinel: A History of the National Security Agency* (2009).

R. K. Betts is Director of the Saltzman Institute of War and Peace Studies at Columbia University and Co-editor of Paradoxes of Strategic Intelligence. He previously served on the staff of the Senate's Church Committee investigation of U.S. intelligence agencies and as a consultant in the intelligence community. His most recent publication is *Enemies of Intelligence: Knowledge and Power in American National Security* (2007).

Bradley W.C. Bamford is from Monkton NB and is completing a Ph.D. at the University of Toronto. He serves with the 8th Canadian Hussars and has also written on current aspects of the UK's war on terrorism.

Daniel Byman is Associate Professor and Director of the Security Studies Program and the Center for Peace and Security Studies at Georgetown University's Edmund A. Walsh School of Foreign Service. He is also a non-resident Senior Fellow at the Saban Center for Middle East Policy at the Brookings Institution. Dr. Byman has served as a Professional Staff Member with both the National Commission on Terrorist Attacks on the United States (The 9–11 Commission) and the Joint 9/11 Inquiry Staff of the House and Senate Intelligence Committees. He has also worked as the Research Director of the Center for Middle East Public Policy at the RAND Corporation and as an analyst of the Middle East for the U.S. intelligence community. His latest book is *Deadly Connections: States that Sponsor Terrorism* (2005).

Philip H. J. Davies is a Senior Lecturer in Politics at Brunel University, Uxbridge, Middlesex, England. A political sociologist specializing in the institutional development of national intelligence agencies and communities, he is the author of *MI-6 and the Machinery of Spying* (2004) the most detailed study of the management of a British intelligence organization published to date. With Professor Anthony Glees, he is coauthor of *Spinning the Spies: Intelligence, Open Government and the Hutton Inquiry* (2004). He is currently researching a comparative study of British and American intelligence institutions, to be published by Greenwood Press.

John Ferris is a Professor of History at the University of Calgary. He has written widely on the history of intelligence, diplomacy, strategy and war. Among his publications are *Men, Money and Diplomacy: The Evolution of British Strategic Policy 1919–1926* (1989); *The British Army and Signals Intelligence During the First World War* (1992); (with Christon Archer, Holger Herwig and Tim Travers) *A World History of Warfare* (2002) and *Intelligence and Strategy: Selected Essays* (2005).

K.L. Gardiner is a retired CIA officer with thirty years service, half of it on the analytic side. His last job was as deputy director of the Analytic Group of the National intelligence Council. In the 1990s he was a consultant to the agency on its programme to train analysts at the John F. Kennedy School of Government at Harvard University.

Peter Gill is Professor of Intelligence Studies at Salford University. He is the author of *Policing Politics: Security Intelligence and the Liberal Democratic State* (1994) and has recently co-authored (with Mark Pythian) *Intelligence in an Insecure World* (2006). He continues to research issues involving the democratization of intelligence and the impact on intelligence of the 'war on terror.'

Michael Herman served in Government Communications Headquarters (GCHQ) 1952–87 and also spent a period as Secretary of the Joint Intelligence Committee. Since retirement has been associated with Oxford and other universities in writing extensively about intelligence. He is renowned for his contributions to the general theory of intelligence is best known writings are *Intelligence Power in Peace and War* (1996) and *Intelligence Services in the Information Age* (2001).

Robert Jervis is Adlai E. Stevenson professor of international affairs at Columbia University. He has also held professorial appointments at the University of California at Los Angeles and Harvard University. In 2000–2001, he served as the President of the American Political Science Association. He is a fellow of the American Association for the Advancement of Science and of the American Academy of Arts and Sciences. In 1990 he received the Grawemeyer Award for his book *The Meaning of the Nuclear Revolution*. He has published widely on intelligence and strategy. He serves on the board of nine scholarly journals and has authored over 70 publications.

Garrett Jones is currently a senior fellow of the Foreign Policy Research Institute and a 1993 graduate of the U.S. Army War College. He served as a case officer with the CIA in Africa, Europe, and the Middle East. He retired from the CIA in 1997 and now lives in the Northwestern United States. The material that is reprinted here has been reviewed by the CIA. That review neither constitutes CIA authentication of information nor implies CIA endorsement of the author's views.

Jennifer D. Kibbe is an Assistant Professor of Government at Franklin & Marshall College. She holds a Master's in Foreign Service from Georgetown University and a Ph.D. in Political Science from UCLA. She has also worked on South African politics for a number of years at a research organization in Washington. Immediately prior to coming to Franklin & Marshall, she returned to D.C. for a two-year post-doctoral fellowship at The Brookings Institution. Her research and teaching interests include U.S. foreign policy, intelligence and covert action, international relations and political psychology.

Sir Stephen Lander is the Chair of the Serious Organised Crime Agency and is also a Non-Executive Director of Northgate Informational Solutions. He was previously Director General of the Security Service (MI5) 1996–2002 having served in that counterintelligence and counterterrorism. The analysis and opinions expressed in this article are solely those of the author and do not necessarily reflect the view of any agency of the United States Government.

James J. Wirtz holds a doctorate from Columbia University and is associate professor of national security affairs at the Naval Postgraduate School, Monterey, California. He was a John M. Olin Fellow at the Center for International Affairs, Harvard University, and his work on the subjects of national security and intelligence has been published in many journals. He is the author *of The Tet Offensive: Intelligence Failure in War* (1994) and *Rockets' Red Glare: National Missile Defense and the Future of World Politics* (2001) with Jeffrey Larsen.

Preface

Intelligence, history and policy

> Alice: 'I can't remember things before they happen.'
> The Queen: 'it's a poor sort of memory that only works backwards.'[1]

Few people who know their intelligence history can have lived through the early years of the twenty-first century without a disturbing sense of déjà vu. Most of the current intelligence problems, whether they relate to predicting surprise attack, the politicisation of intelligence, or questions of ethics and privacy, are old conundrums. Equally, many of the suggested solutions are ideas that have been tried before. However, it is hard to escape the feeling that closer attention to obvious lessons from the past would have assisted us in avoiding or mitigating some of the more obvious pitfalls of the last decade. Indeed, one of the greatest challenges for intelligence studies is to connect intelligence history and current policy. Policy makers are inclined to talk about 'new threats' and certainly some threats, especially those related to globalization, are innovative. However, talk of newness is sometimes an excuse to ignore important and inconvenient lessons from the recent past.

The events of 9/11 quickly brought forth public assertions that this was 'another Pearl Harbor'. Yet the important lessons that intelligence studies has patiently distilled through the close analysis of many historic surprise attacks were soon lost on politicians, policy-makers and the public. Even a brief consultation of the burgeoning intelligence studies literature would have revealed that surprise attacks are hard to avoid and, within complex societies, they often constitute what Charles Perrow has called 'normal accidents'.[2] Moreover, a cursory review of the efforts of Western intelligence to estimate stocks of Weapons of Mass Destruction (WMD) held by authoritarian states during the Cold War would have reminded us that this is a difficult task and that we have often got it wrong in the past. In the realm of WMD, more than on any other subject, intelligence produces 'estimates', not certainties. As Michael Hayden famously remarked during his tenure as Director of the NSA, 'if it were fact, it wouldn't be intelligence'.[3]

It is not only policy-makers but also intelligence agencies themselves who have paid too little attention to history and historians. The major intelligence failure since the end of the Cold War was not 9/11 or the wayward estimates of Iraqi WMD, or indeed even the failure to spot the end of the Cold War itself. Instead, it was the startling lack of attention given to the rise of irregular warfare – including insurgency, warlordism and the 'new terrorism', which in fact resembled groups from previous centuries. Transnational violence by non-state groups was the emerging future threat in the 1990s. Academics such as Bruce Hoffman and Brian Jenkins spotted this trend as early as 1989 and warned of it repeatedly in the 1990s, but the intelligence agencies were oblivious. Instead, they spent the early 1990s focused on the state-based threat of economic espionage. Remarkably, in 1993, during his confirmation hearings, the new DCI, James Woolsey, told Congress that economic espionage was 'the hottest current topic in intelligence policy'.[4]

Policy-makers and intelligence aristocrats alike bought into fashionable theories about 'democratic peace' and the 'end of history'. They were convinced that they were entering a new and tranquil era, and promptly set about cutting their intelligence budgets by a quarter. Had they given some attention to the more historically grounded work of Bruce Hoffman and Brian Jenkins, they would have realised that terrorism was returning to its familiar past whence it had been more violent and dangerous. A longer perspective on the history of terrorism would have underlined that the sorts of terrorist groups we encountered in the 1970s and 1980 were an aberration. History also shows that fanaticism is dangerous because it often combines obsession conspiracy theories about its opponents with great tactical and operational skill, a combination which intelligence analysts have traditionally found difficult to comprehend.[5]

Politicians and policy-makers have displayed a woefully poor comprehension of intelligence, but we also need improved public understanding. No public organisation succeeds in every enterprise that it attempts, yet the public persist in setting absurdly high standards for intelligence. Every surprise is deemed to be an intelligence failure. Some of the distortions here are even more extreme. One of the many historical parallels between 9/11 and previous surprise attacks is the steady rise of increasingly bizarre and paranoid explanations of intelligence-related events. The 'parallel narratives of the twin towers' recall Richard Hofstadter's famous essay in which he outlined what he called 'the paranoid style'. Although matters of intelligence are very different in democratic and authoritarian states, one of the tendencies that seems to transcend all human societies and all historical epochs is a tendency to associate secret intelligence with vast international conspiracies of a menacing kind. Hofstadter correctly noted that this was an infectious mentalité and a persistent way of seeing the world at moments of crisis.[6]

If history underlines continuity, what has genuinely changed? Since 1989 it has become progressively easier to write about current intelligence. This reflects contradictory trends over two decades. Amid the optimism of the early 1990s, the emphasis was upon democratisation, regulation and greater transparency. A treasure trove of new historical archives began to flow from Eastern Europe and many European secret services placed their secret services on the statute books. As a result, the regulatory reports of more than two dozen European intelligence and security services can now be read on an annual basis. Underpinning these developments in the 1990s was perhaps a misplaced sense that we could say more about intelligence because it was becoming less important.

Since 9/11, a torrent of information has entered the public domain about intelligence, but for quite different reasons. Together, Osama bin Laden and Saddam Hussein managed to completely transform the policy of the UK government on the public use of intelligence to support policy. Over six months in late 2002 and early 2003, the Blair government released two much-discussed dossiers on Iraq, both of which incorporated some intelligence material. Tony Blair was correct to say that it was unprecedented for the Government to produce full documents of this kind for the public and the press. If his hope was to draw public attention towards intelligence matters then – in one sense at least – he was successful. Intelligence is now firmly under the spotlight and the amount of media coverage given to debates about intelligence is certainly quite unprecedented.

The opening-up of intelligence has followed the law of unintended consequences. In Washington, Whitehall and indeed Canberra, governments only intended to place selected morsels of intelligence in the public domain. They did not intend to encourage a free-for-all. Indeed, if anything, in the wake of 9/11 some hoped for a tightening up of security. In Washington, the authorities had already begun a bizarre process of re-classifying many archival documents from the 1950s that had been opened to historians in the National Archives more than a decade before. It has been estimated that over the last decade the US government has typically spent $16 billion dollars a year and has employed 31,000 full time officials to safeguard classified documents.[7] But to no avail. Such has been the intelligence controversy since 9/11 that documents that were top secret on Tuesday have sometimes made the pages of *The Washington Post* by Thursday.

One result of this efflux has been the rapid development of the literature on current intelligence. This material often incorporates one of the abiding strengths of intelligence studies, a pleasingly inter-disciplinary mix of history and policy, together with an ability to view present issues in long perspective. These virtues are in part accidental. In the 1980s, when intelligence studies was developing as a relatively new field, the historical dimension was dominant because current information was relatively sparse. This has ensured that those most scholars working in the field of intelligence studies are imbued with a strong sense of the past. More recently, many intelligence historians have turned their attention to more current issues and we have seen the emergence of a synthetic literature that blends the nuanced use of history with policy prescription. Ernest May and Richard Neustadt have characterised this as 'thinking in time'. Much of the writing in this present volume is of that character.[8]

Although many of the core problems in the realm of intelligence display historical continuity, the nature of real world intelligence operations is undoubtedly changing. Many of our opponents are now more transnational and intelligence agencies have had to adapt their activities to follow their elusive quarry. As a result, international intelligence co-operation is now of the first importance. It is also different in character, involving new and improbable partners, together with non-state actors and private companies, for example civilian airlines. More than ever before, intelligence is now something conducted with allies. In 2005, the CIA's Deputy Director of Operations reportedly told a closed committee session on Capitol Hill that 'virtually every capture or killing of a suspected terrorist outside Iraq since the Sept. 11, 2001, attacks – more than 3,000 in all – was a result of foreign intelligence services' work alongside the agency.'[9]

The intelligence literature is having to run to keep up. Although there has been a proliferation of fine textbooks and readers on intelligence over the last five years, the landscape is changing. The growth of intelligence co-operation or 'liaison' is symptomatic of this. Despite its overwhelming importance in the real world of intelligence, it is one of the intelligence subjects that is conspicuous by its absence within textbooks and handbooks. Equally, intelligence support to peacekeeping is a neglected subject in student texts. The United Nations now has more military forces on active operations than any nation-state other than the United States. The growing role of intelligence in assisting peacekeeping – and indeed peacemaking activities – demands closer attention in our mainstream writing. The same might be said of intelligence support for counter-insurgency. Equally, the controversial matter of the interrogation of detainees has rarely been out of newspapers in recent years, yet this too seems absent from most of the teaching literature. One of the ambitions of this volume is to bring together some of the classic literature with writings on new developments.

Once lurking in the shadows of academe, this subject of intelligence is now centre-stage. Accordingly, the academic study of intelligence in universities is now a more mainstream subject. We are conscious that recent events have prompted academics in departments of history, politics and international relations to contemplate teaching intelligence for the first time. Therefore we have also sought to provide substantial suggestions for additional reading, together with possible seminar and essay questions. In compiling this suggested reading we have taken a holistic approach, seeking to draw on essays from areas such as criminology, psychology, law and sociology. Hidden in journals with improbable titles there are some neglected treasures and we have sought to bring them to light in the reading lists. We have also attempted to broaden the range of national examples.

This volume emerges in part out of our most enjoyable experiences in teaching intelligence at the Universities of Cambridge, Nottingham, Toronto and Warwick. It has been a particular pleasure to be able to teach jointly with our research students. The volume also reflects our efforts to share that experience with colleagues in other universities and amongst the growing numbers of centres for the study of intelligence. The development of postgraduate and undergraduate degrees in intelligence at the Universities of Aberystwyth, Birmingham, Brunel, Edinburgh, Kings London and Salford has been especially heartening. We are particularly indebted to Philip Davies, Robert Jervis and others for comments on our selection of material together with anonymous readers. We would like to thank Andrew Humphrys and Emily Kindleysides at Taylor and Francis for their patient support during the long gestation of this project. Most importantly we would like to express our profound thanks to the authors, editors and publishers whose work we republish in this volume.

Christopher Andrew
Richard J. Aldrich
Wesley K. Wark

Notes

1 Lewis Carroll, *Through the Looking-Glass*, Ch. 5, Wool and Water.
2 Charles Perrow, *Normal Accidents: Living with High-Risk Technologies* (Princeton: Princeton University Press, 1999).
3 Evan Thomas, 'I Haven't Suffered Doubt', *Newsweek*, 26 April 2004, pp. 22–6.
4 R. Jeffrey Smith, 'Administration to Consider Giving Spy Data to Business,' *Washington Post*, 3 February 1993.
5 Christopher Andrew, 'Intelligence analysis needs to look backwards before looking forward', *History and Policy*, June 2004 http://www.historyandpolicy.org/papers/policy-paper-23.html
6 Richard Hofstadter, 'The Paranoid Style in American Politics', *Harper's Magazine*, November 1964, pp. 77–86.
7 Michael Perelman, *Class Warfare in the Information Age* (NY: St Martin's, 1998) p. 77.
8 Richard E. Neustadt and Ernest R. May, *Thinking in Time: The Uses of History for Decision-Makers* (NY: Free Press 1986).
9 Dana Priest, 'Foreign Network at Front of CIA's Terror Fight: Joint Facilities in Two Dozen Countries Account for Bulk of Agency's Post-9/11 Successes,' *Washington Post*, 18 November 2005.

Acknowledgments

The publisher would like to thank the following for permission to reprint their material:

Studies in Intelligence, for Michael Warner, 'Wanted: A Definition of "Intelligence" ' *Studies in Intelligence*, 46, 3 (2002) pp.15–23.

Harvard International Review, for Philip Davies, 'Ideas of Intelligence: Divergent National Concepts and Institutions', *Harvard International Review* 24, 3 (2002) pp.62–66.

Elsevier Limited on behalf of Foreign Policy Research Institute, for Garrett Jones, *Orbis: A Journal of World Affairs*, 50, Jones et al, 'It's a Cultural Thing: Thoughts on a Troubled CIA', pp.25–41, © Elsevier (2006).

Taylor and Francis for Matthew Aid, 'All Glory Is Fleeting: Sigint and the Fight against International Terrorism', *Intelligence and National Security* 18/4 (Winter 2003) pp.72–120.

Studies in Intelligence, for Stephen Mercado, 'A Venerable Source in a New Era: Sailing the Sea of OSINT in the Information Age', *Studies in Intelligence* 48/3 (2004) pp.45–55.

The Academy of Political Science, for R.K. Betts, 'Surprise Despite Warning: Why Sudden Attacks Succeed', *Political Science Quarterly* 95/4 (1980) pp.551–72

Studies in Intelligence, for Carmen Medina, 'What To Do When Traditional Models Fail', *Studies in Intelligence* 46/3 (2002) pp.23–9.

Taylor and Francis, for C.M. Andrew, 'American Presidents and their Intelligence Communities', *Intelligence and National Security* 10/4 (1995) pp.95–113.

Taylor and Francis, for K.L. Gardiner, 'Squaring the Circle: Dealing with Intelligence-Policy Breakdowns', *Intelligence and National Security* 6/1 (1991) pp.141–152.

Taylor and Francis, for S. Lander, 'International Intelligence Co-operation: An Inside Perspective', *Cambridge Review of International Affairs* 17/3 (2004) pp.481–93.

Annual Reviews, for Daniel Byman, 'Strategic Surprise And The September 11 Attacks', *Annual Review of Political Science*, 8 (2005) pp.145–170. Reprinted, with permission, from the *Annual Review of Political Science*, volume 8, © 2005 by Annual Reviews www.annualreviews.org

Harvard International Review, for James J. Wirtz, 'Deja Vu? Comparing Pearl Harbor and September 11', *Harvard International Review* 24/3 (2002) pp.73–77.

Taylor and Francis, for Robert Jervis, 'Reports, Politics, and Intelligence Failures: The Case of Iraq', *Journal of Strategic Studies*, 29/1 (2006) pp.3–52.

Royal Irish Academy, for Richard J. Aldrich, 'Whitehall and the Iraq War: The UK's Four Intelligence Enquiries', *Irish Studies in International Affairs*, 16 (2005) pp.73–88.

Elsevier Limited on behalf of Foreign Policy Research Institute, for John R Schindler, Orbis: A Journal of World Affairs, 49, Schindler et al, 'Defeating the Sixth Column: Intelligence and Strategy in the War on Islamist Terrorism', pp.695–712 © Elsevier (2005).

Taylor and Francis, for B. Bamford, 'The Role and Effectiveness of Intelligence in Northern Ireland', *Intelligence and National Security*, 20/4 (2005) pp.581–607.

Taylor and Francis, for Frederick L Wettering, 'Counterintelligence: The Broken Triad,' *International Journal of Intelligence and Counterintelligence* 13/3 (2000) pp.265–300.

Taylor and Francis, for M.C. Ott, 'Partisanship and the Decline of Intelligence Oversight.' *International Journal of Intelligence and Counterintelligence*, Spring 2003, 16/1, pp.69–94.

Taylor and Francis, for Mark Phythian, 'The British experience with intelligence accountability', *Intelligence and National Security* 22/1 (2007) pp.75–99.

The Johns Hopkins University Press, for Kate Martin, 'Domestic Intelligence and Civil Liberties', *SAIS Review* 24/1 (2004) pp.7–21. © The Johns Hopkins University Press.

Oxford University Press, for James Sheptycki, 'High Policing in the Security Control Society', *Policing* 1/1 (2007) pp.70–79.

Taylor and Francis, for Michael Herman, 'Ethics and Intelligence after September 2001', in L.V. Scott and P.D. Jackson, (eds.) *Understanding Intelligence in the Twenty-First Century: Journeys in Shadows* (London: Routledge 2004), pp. 180–194.

Taylor and Francis, for Sir David Omand, 'Ethical Guidelines in Using Secret Intelligence for Public Security', *Cambridge Review of International Affairs* 19/4 (2006) pp.613–28.

Taylor and Francis, for Maureen Ramsay, 'Can the torture of terrorist suspects be justified?', *The International Journal of Human Rights*, 10/2 (2006) pp.103–19.

Taylor and Francis, for Jennifer D. Kibbe, 'Covert action and the Pentagon', *Intelligence and National Security*, 22/1 (2007) pp.57–74.

Taylor and Francis, for John Ferris, 'Netcentric Warfare, C4ISR and Information Operations: Towards a revolution in Military Intelligence?' in L.V. Scott and P.D. Jackson, (eds.) *Understanding Intelligence in the Twenty-First Century: Journeys in Shadows*, (London: Routledge 2004), pp.54–77.

Taylor and Francis, for Peter Gill, 'Securing the Globe: Intelligence and the Post-9/11 Shift from "Liddism" to "Drainism"', *Intelligence and National Security* 19/3 (2004) pp.467–489

The International Institute for Strategic Studies, for Hugh Smith, 'Intelligence and UN Peacekeeping', *Survival* 36/3 (1994) pp.177–97 (c) The International Institute for Strategic Studies.

Het Spinhuis, for Joop van Reijn, 'Germany and the Netherlands in the Headquarters of the International Security assistance Force in Afghanistan (ISAF): An Intelligence perspective', in Beatrice de Graaf, Ben de Jong & Wies Platje (eds.) *Battleground Western Europe: Intelligence Operations in Germany and the Netherlands in the Twentieth Century* (Apeldoorn: Het Spinhuis 2007) pp. 217–33.

Taylor and Francis, for Wesley K. Wark, 'Learning to Live with Intelligence', *Intelligence and National Security*, 18/4 (Winter 2003) pp.1–14.

Every effort has been made to contact copyright holders for their permission to reprint material in this book. The publishers would be grateful to hear from any copyright holder who is not here acknowledged and will undertake to rectify any errors or omissions in future editions of this book.

Introduction

What is intelligence?

'Intelligence has never been more important in world politics than it is now at the opening of the twenty-first century'.

Len Scott and Peter Jackson[1]

What do we mean by intelligence? How does it differ from mere information? The Chinese do not have words in their vocabulary that makes this distinction, while the French prefer to talk of reseignment or 'research'. Mark Lowenthal, the distinguished American scholar of intelligence, offers a useful taxonomy, arguing that we can think about intelligence in three ways. First, as process, through which intelligence is requested by policy-makers or operational commanders, then collected, analysed and fed to the consumers. This is often referred to as the intelligence cycle. Second, we can define it as product, once upon a time circulated as paper, but now increasingly distributed through multi-level secure electronic databases. Finally, we can talk of intelligence services and intelligence communities as institutions. However, as their name implies, these organisations that provide an intelligence service to government also conduct activities that go far beyond the mere collection of information, as we shall discover in this volume.[2]

Historically, definitions of intelligence have been shaped by patterns of state development. Most ancient religious texts make reference to espionage and Sun Tzu is eloquent upon the subject. However, the emergence of sophisticated intelligence systems often accompanied the deployment of military-technical challenges to the state. From the mid-nineteenth century, the ability of commanders to move and control military force at speed, facilitated by the telegraph and the railway, presented a new kind of challenge. This manifested itself as a surprise attack – surely the sternest test for the modern state. Unsurprisingly, the same period saw the emergence of more modern intelligence bureaux that sought to counter this threat. Famously, at the beginning of the nineteenth century, Carl von Clausewitz had offered a cavalier dismissal of the value of intelligence, remarking that it merely added to the fog of war. However, by the end of the same century, technology has ensured that the disregard of intelligence was no longer possible. The next few decades witnessed a revolution in methods of war and diplomacy during which intelligence would be produced on an industrial scale.

Recent developments have made the task of defining intelligence no easier. Non-state actors are more important. Since the 1970s, the emergence of the market state has meant that larger and larger parts of national infrastructure are also in private hands. The most obvious examples are telecom and ISP providers who are now required by law to work with government as intelligence collectors. The growing emphasis on protecting national infrastructure ensures that businesses such as airlines are not only collectors of intelligence, but also important consumers. Even state intelligence and security agencies have turned to contracting out a surprising range of their activities. The requirement to surge intelligence capacity since 9/11 has accelerated this process and in 2003 approximately a third of CIA employees were private contractors. We can no longer claim that intelligence is a predominantly state-based activity.[3]

The growth of the importance of 'open source' intelligence, has also blurred traditional distinctions between intelligence and information and the barrier between secret and non-secret. Historically, open source intelligence has always been present, but the ability to comb this material instantly ensures that it is now more important than ever. Information technology has also subverted the familiar intelligence cycle, allowing policy-makers to become their own DIY analysts. Meanwhile, the challenges of counter-terrorism mean that, quite often, intelligence services have become key consumers of their own product. This is because they are often the lead elements in acting against terrorism as well as watching it. As they are asked to undertake more disruption and enforcement they have become more activist. Intelligence services are increasingly supported rather than supporting elements in what has become an interactive network. However, we choose to define intelligence, we can be sure that it has never been more important than now at the beginning of the twenty-first century.

Notes

1 L.V. Scott and P. Jackson, Preface to *Understanding Intelligence in the Twenty-First Century: Journey in Shadows* (London: Routledge, 2004), xi.
2 Mark M. Lowenthal, *Intelligence: From Secrets to Policy* (Washington DC: CQ Press, 2002), p. 8.
3 Walter Pincus and Stephen Barr, 'CIA Plans Cutbacks, Limits on Contractor Staffing', *Washington Post*, 11 June 2007.

1 Wanted

A definition of 'intelligence'

Michael Warner

This essay offers a classical definition of intelligence that emphasises the use of secret information and methods for full effectiveness. It also argues for a state-based conception of intelligence in terms of both its collectors and customers. More controversially, it views intelligence as being reports about foreign powers, or at least matters overseas, arguing that the surveillance of domestic citizens is more to do with law enforcement or governance. It also embraces what intelligence services do, and does not see intelligence merely as a process or a product, suggesting this may involve influencing overseas by 'means that are unattributable'. In conclusion, Warner offers the definition that: 'Intelligence is secret, state activity to understand or influence foreign entities'.

> . . . all attempts to develop ambitious theories of intelligence have failed.
>
> Walter Laqueur[1]

In a business as old as recorded history, one would expect to find a sophisticated understanding of just what that business is, what it does, and how it works. If the business is 'intelligence,' however, we search in vain. As historian Walter Laqueur warned us, so far no one has succeeded in crafting a theory of intelligence.

I have to wonder if the difficulty in doing so resides more in the slipperiness of the tools than in the poor skills of the craftsmen or the complexity of the topic. Indeed, even today, we have no accepted definition of intelligence. The term is defined anew by each author who addresses it, and these definitions rarely refer to one another or build off what has been written before. Without a clear idea of what intelligence is, how can we develop a theory to explain how it works?

If you cannot define a term of art, then you need to rethink something. In some way you are not getting to the heart of the matter. Here is an opportunity: a compelling definition of intelligence might help us to devise a theory of intelligence and increase our understanding. In the hope of advancing discussions of this topic, I have collected some of the concise definitions of intelligence that I deem to be distinguished either by their source or by their clarity.[2] After explaining what they do and do not tell us, I shall offer up my own sacrificial definition to the tender mercies of future critics.

Official solutions

The people who write the laws that govern intelligence, and administer the budgets and resources of intelligence agencies, deserve the first word. The basic charter of America's intelligence services – the National Security Act of 1947 with its many amendments – defines the kind of intelligence that we are seeking in this manner:

> The term 'foreign intelligence' means information relating to the capabilities, intentions, or activities of foreign governments or elements thereof, foreign organizations, or foreign persons.[3]

Study commissions appointed to survey the Intelligence Community have long used similar language. The Clark Task Force of the Hoover Commission in 1955 decided that:

> Intelligence deals with all the things which should be known in advance of initiating a course of action.[4]

An influential report from the mid-1990s (produced by the Brown-Aspin Commission) provides this definition:

> The Commission believes it preferable to define 'intelligence' simply and broadly as information about 'things foreign' – people, places, things, and events – needed by the Government for the conduct of its functions.[5]

The Joint Chiefs of Staff qualify as both employers and consumers of intelligence, so they deserve a say as well. Their latest Dictionary of Military and Associated Terms defines intelligence as:

1. The product resulting from the collection, processing, integration, analysis, evaluation and interpretation of available information concerning foreign countries or areas.
2. Information and knowledge about an adversary obtained through observation, investigation, analysis, or understanding.[6]

And finally, the Central Intelligence Agency has weighed in with the following sentence:

> Reduced to its simplest terms, intelligence is knowledge and foreknowledge of the world around us – the prelude to decision and action by US policymakers.[7]

All of these definitions stress the 'informational' aspects of intelligence more than its 'organizational' facets – an ironic twist given that all of them come from organizations that produce and use intelligence, and which thereby might be expected to wax poetic on the procedural aspects of the term as well.

Private attempts

Authors writing about intelligence for commercial publication might seem to enjoy a little more freedom and flexibility than the drafters of official government statements. Nonetheless, many outside authorities also say that intelligence is basically 'information.' Here are some examples, beginning with one of the earliest theorists in the field, CIA's re-doubtable senior analyst, Sherman Kent:

> Intelligence, as I am writing of it, is the knowledge which our highly placed civilians and military men must have to safeguard the national welfare.[8]

Former Deputy Director of Central Intelligence Vernon Walters published a chatty memoir of his long and eventful public career, *Silent Missions*, that offers a more detailed definition:

> Intelligence is information, not always available in the public domain, relating to the strength, resources, capabilities and intentions of a foreign country that can affect our lives and the safety of our people.[9]

Another high-ranking CIA officer, Lyman Kirkpatrick, was a true student of the business while he served in the Agency and enjoyed a second career as a respected commentator on intelligence topics. He contributes the following:

> [Intelligence is] the knowledge – and, ideally, foreknowledge – sought by nations in response to external threats and to protect their vital interests, especially the well-being of their own people.[10]

And last but not least, a study of the American intelligence establishment commissioned by the Council on Foreign Relations in 1996 noted:

> Intelligence is information not publicly available, or analysis based at least in part on such information, that has been prepared for policymakers or other actors inside the government.[11]

What is wrong with 'information'?

Nothing is wrong with 'information' *per se*. Policymakers and commanders need information to do their jobs, and they are entitled to call that information anything they like. Indeed, for a policymaker or a commander, there is no need to define intelligence any further.

For producers of intelligence, however, the equation 'intelligence = information' is too vague to provide real guidance in their work. To professionals in the field, mere data is not intelligence; thus these definitions are incomplete. Think of how many names are in the telephone book, and how few of those names anyone ever seeks. It is what people do with data and information that gives them the special quality that we casually call 'intelligence.'

With all due respect to the legislators, commanders, officials, and scholars who drafted the definitions above, those definitions let in far more than they screen out. After all, foreign policy decisionmakers all need information, and they get it from many sources. Is each source of information, and each factual tidbit, to be considered intelligence? Obviously not, because that would mean that newspapers and radio broadcasts and atlases are intelligence documents, and that journalists and geographers are intelligence officers. The notion that intelligence is information does not say who needs the information, or what makes the information needed in the first place. Intelligence involves information, yes, but obviously it is far more.

Let us begin again. The place for definitions is a dictionary. A handy one found in many government offices (Webster's Ninth New Collegiate) tells us that intelligence is:

. . . information concerning an enemy or possible enemy or an area, also: an agency engaged in obtaining such information.

Of course, one should hardly consult just any dictionary on such an important matter. The dictionary – the Oxford English Dictionary – defines intelligence as follows:

> 7a. Knowledge as to events, communicated by or obtained from one another; information, news, tidings, spec. information of military value . . . b. A piece of information or news . . . c. The obtaining of information; the agency for obtaining secret information; the staff of persons so employed, secret service . . . d. A department of a state organization or of a military or naval service whose object is to obtain information (esp. by means of secret service officers or a system of spies).

Sherman Kent expressed something similar in a 1946 article on the contemporary direction of intelligence reform:

> In the circumstances, it is surprising that there is not more general agreement and less confusion about the meaning of the basic terms. The main difficulty seems to lie in the word 'intelligence' itself, which has come to mean both what people in the trade do and what they come up with. To get this matter straight is crucial: intelligence is both a process and an end-product.[12]

This seems to be getting somewhere, but it is hardly concise. We need something punchy. At this point, the same Walter Laqueur who complained above about the lack of a coherent theory of intelligence uncannily proved his own point by rendering Kent's point in a sentence that contains no new insight but economizes on words:

> On one hand, it [intelligence] refers to an organization collecting information and on the other to the information that has been gathered.[13]

Professors Kent and Laqueur recognized that intelligence is both information and an organized system for collecting and exploiting it. It is both an activity and a product of that activity.

National Intelligence Council officer Mark Lowenthal reminds us that intelligence is something broader than information and its processing for policymakers and commanders, even when that information is somehow confidential or clandestine. His useful primer on intelligence contains this definition:

> Intelligence is the process by which specific types of information important to national security are requested, collected, analyzed, and provided to policymakers; the products of that process; the safeguarding of these processes and this information by counter-intelligence activities; and the carrying out of operations as requested by lawful authorities.[14]

Lowenthal is on to something important. Intelligence is several things: It is information, process, and activity, and it is performed by 'lawful authorities' – i.e., by nationstates. But he still has too much freight loaded on his definition. Information that is 'important to national security' could include intelligence, all right, but also many other things, such as the number of American males of age to bear arms, the weather conditions in Asia, and the age of a politburo member. Indeed, almost anything 'military' can be subsumed under Dr. Lowenthal's definition, and many things diplomatic fit as well. He has the right categories, but he has made them too broad. In addition, his definition is partly tautological in saying that intelligence is that which is protected by counterintelligence.

Nonetheless, one senses that we have found the right road. Lowenthal adds that interesting clause at the end: 'the carrying out of operations.' Why did he associate operations with information processing? My guess is that is he is a good observer who draws what he sees. He knows that information agencies using secret information have been – and very often still are – intimately associated with agencies that conduct secret operations.

In ancient times that coincidence might have occurred because the agent and the operative were the same man. In many cases, the operation and the information are one and the same; the product of espionage could only be known to its collector (for fear of compromising the source) and thus the collector becomes the analyst. This is how the KGB worked, and no one can say that the KGB lacked sophistication in the intelligence business. Other nations, however, have differentiated analysis and operations and placed them in separate offices, sometimes with and sometimes without a common director. Funny, though, that both the analytical and the operational offices are commonly described as 'doing' intelligence.

The missing ingredient

Why is it that the word 'intelligence' is used to describe the work of analytical committees *and* covert action groups? Of signals collectors *and* spies? Why do so many countries – Western and Eastern, democratic and despotic – tend to organize their intelligence offices in certain patterns around their civilian leaders and military commanders?

Another good observer, Abram Shulsky, has noticed this aspect of the intelligence business. Looking at this wide variety of intelligence activities, he laments, 'it seems difficult to find a common thread tying them together.' But soon he picks up the scent again: 'They all, however, have to do with obtaining or denying information.' Furthermore, Shulsky explains, these activities are conducted by organizations, and those organizations have something in common: they have as one of their 'most notable characteristics . . . the secrecy with which their activities must be conducted.' Secrecy is essential because intelligence is part of the ongoing 'struggle' between nations. The goal of intelligence is truth, but the quest for that truth 'involves a struggle with a human enemy who is fighting back.'[15]

Shulsky thus emphasizes the need for secrecy in intelligence activities and organizations. Indeed, he comes close to calling secrecy a constitutive element of intelligence work, saying 'the connection between intelligence and secrecy is central to most of what distinguishes intelligence from other intellectual activities.' But then he retreats when confronted with the problem of explaining how it is that covert action (clandestine activity performed to influence foreign countries in unattributable ways) always seems to be assigned to intelligence agencies, rather than to military services or diplomatic corps. Why did it happen in the United States, for example, that the covert action mission was assigned to the Central Intelligence Agency despite the Truman administration's initial impulse to give it to either the State Department or the Secretary of Defense? Shulsky notices the pattern, but wonders whether it means anything:

> Even if, for practical bureaucratic reasons, intelligence organizations are given the responsibility for covert action, the more fundamental question – from a theoretical, as

well as a practical, viewpoint – of whether covert action should be considered a part of intelligence would remain.[16]

The institutional gravitation that tends to pull intelligence offices toward one another has been observed by others as well. In 1958 a CIA operations officer noticed the same tendency that puzzled Shulsky. Rather than setting it aside, however, he attempted to explain it. Writing under the pen-name R. A. Random in the CIA's then-classified journal Studies in Intelligence, he suggested that intelligence, by definition, always has something secret about it:

> Intelligence is the official, secret collection and processing of information on foreign countries to aid in formulating and implementing foreign policy, and the conduct of covert activities abroad to facilitate the implementation of foreign policy.[17]

This is getting somewhere. It calls intelligence an activity and a product, says it is conducted in confidential circumstances on behalf of states so that policymakers can understand foreign developments, and that it includes clandestine operations that are performed to cause certain effects in foreign lands. There is really little to quibble with in Random's definition. It includes many things that it needs, but without incorporating much or anything that it does not need.

Notwithstanding the quality of Random's definition, it drew a rejoinder six months later in *Studies in Intelligence* from a CIA counterintelligence officer pen-named Martin T. Bimfort, who complained that Random had neglected the discipline of counterintelligence in describing the constituent parts of intelligence. Bimfort amended Random:

> Intelligence is the collecting and processing of that information about foreign countries and their agents which is needed by a government for its foreign policy and for national security, the conduct of non-attributable activities abroad to facilitate the implementation of foreign policy, and the protection of both process and product, as well as persons and organizations concerned with these, against unauthorized disclosure.[18]

This does not seem to help. Bimfort has added bells and whistles to Random, but the addition of 'counterintelligence' hints that Bimfort has missed one of the essential elements of Random's definition: its assertion that intelligence is a state activity that involves secrecy. If Bimfort had grasped that point, he should have conceded that an activity that is official and secret ipso facto implies subsidiary activities to keep it secret. Thus Bimfort's addition – 'the protection of both process and product, as well as persons and organizations concerned with these, against unauthorized disclosure' – is not only ponderous, it is superfluous. It is, moreover, unhelpful, because it reaches beyond counterintelligence and subsumes all sorts of ordinary security functions common to many government offices and private enterprises.

This criticism of Bimfort's critique brings us willy-nilly to something important. What is the difference between security (and the law enforcement aspects of catching and prosecuting security risks) and counterintelligence? I would argue that the difference is secrecy. Plenty of agencies and businesses have security offices; many also perform investigative work. But not all of those organizations are thereby intelligence agencies. Security and investigative work against foreign spies becomes 'counter-intelligence' when it has to be done secretly for fear of warning the spies or their parent service.

Indeed, secrecy is the key to the definition of intelligence, as Random hinted. Without secrets, it is not intelligence. Properly understood, intelligence is that range of activities – whether analysis, collection, or covert action – performed on behalf of a nation's foreign policy that would be negated if their foreign 'subjects' spotted the hand of another country and acted differently as a consequence.[19]

Toward a solution

A comprehensive definition of intelligence – one that says what it is, without also including all sorts of things that it is not – would have several elements. We can say now that 'intelligence' is that which is:

- Dependent upon confidential sources and methods for full effectiveness
- Performed by officers of the state for state purposes (this implies that those officers receive direction from the state's civilian and military leaders).
- Focused on foreigners – usually other states, but often foreign subjects, corporations, or groups (if its objects are domestic citizens, then the activity becomes a branch of either law enforcement or governance).
- Linked to the production and dissemination of information.
- Involved in influencing foreign entities by means that are unattributable to the acting government (if the activities are open and declared, they are the province of diplomacy; if they utilize uniformed members of the armed forces, they belong to the military).

Random's definition has come the closest to date to incorporating all of these elements. I can make him more elegant, but I cannot supplant him. Here is my definition:

Intelligence is secret, state activity to understand or influence foreign entities.

Conclusion

Plato's *Republic* is an extended dialogue between Socrates and his students on the nature of justice. As their discussion begins, Socrates addresses the distinguished father of one of his young admirers, seeking the elder's opinion on the topic. As might be expected, the father replies in utterly conventional terms, and soon leaves Socrates and the young men to their theorizing, which takes off in several directions in turn. Toward the end of the Republic, however, Socrates has led his students to an understanding of justice that looks remarkably like what the old gentleman had offered in the beginning. Convention often holds a wisdom that is not lightly set aside.

Perhaps something similar has happened with our definition of intelligence. The typical American, asked to define 'intelli-gence,' is likely to evoke an image of some shadowy figure in a fedora and trenchcoat skulking in a dark alley. We intelligence officers know that stereotype is silly; intelligence is something far more sophisticated than a 'Spy v. Spy' cartoon. And yet the popular caricature possesses a certain wisdom, for it intuits that secrecy is a vital element – perhaps the key element – of intelligence. Intelligence involves information, yes, but it is secrecy, too. For producers of intelligence, it is more about secrecy than information. Convention holds a wisdom for us as well.

Why does this matter? Various agencies have gotten along well enough for many years, thank you, without a suitable-for-framing definition of intelligence. One can add, moreover, that providing them with such a thing is hardly likely to revolutionize their work. And yet, the definition I just proposed could assist the growing number of scholars who study the field and might ultimately help the Intelligence Community in several respects. It could provide a firmer institutional footing for covert action, which has long been a step-child in CIA – in no small part because some Agency leaders and policymakers downtown have regarded it as not really 'intelligence' at all, but rather something that the White House happened to tack on to the Agency's list of missions. A better definition of intelligence might also guide declassification policy by clarifying just what are and are not the 'sources and methods' that the DCI is obliged by statute to protect. And finally, a stress on secrecy as the defining characteristic of intelligence should help future oversight staffs and study commissions to sort the various activities performed in the Intelligence Community with an eye toward husbanding that which they and they alone can do – and leaving the remainder to be performed by other parts of the government.

Notes

1 Walter Laqueur, *A World of Secrets: The Uses and Limits of Intelligence* (New York, NY: Basic Books, 1985), p. 8.
2 I credit Nicholas Dujmovic, Directorate of Intelligence, and his fine compilation of intelligence quotations for many of the definitions recorded here.
3 50 USC 401a.
4 Commission on Organization of the Executive Branch of the Government [the Hoover Commission], 'Intelligence Activities,' June 1955, p. 26. This was an interim report to Congress prepared by a team under the leadership of Gen. Mark Clark.
5 Commission on the Roles and Capabilities of the United States Intelligence Community, Preparing for the 21st Century: An Appraisal of US Intelligence [the 'Brown-Aspin Report'] (Washington, DC: Government Printing Office, 1996), p. 5.
6 Joint Chiefs of Staff, Department of Defense Dictionary of Military and Associated Terms, Joint Publication 1–02, 12 April 2001, p. 208.
7 Central Intelligence Agency (Office of Public Affairs), *A Consumer's Guide to Intelligence*, (Washington, DC: Central Intelligence Agency, 1999), p. vii.
8 Sherman Kent, *Strategic Intelligence for American Foreign Policy* (Princeton, NJ: Princeton University Press, 1949), p. vii.
9 Vernon Walters, Silent Missions (Garden City, NY: Doubleday, 1978), p. 621.
10 Lyman B. Kirkpatrick, Jr., 'Intelligence,' in Bruce W. Jentelson and Thomas G. Paterson, (eds.) *Encyclopedia of US Foreign Relations*, Volume 2 (New York: Oxford University Press, 1997), p. 365.
11 Council on Foreign Relations [Richard N. Haass, project director], *Making Intelligence Smarter: Report of an Independent Task Force* (New York, NY: Council on Foreign Relations, 1996), p. 8.
12 Sherman Kent, 'Prospects for the National Intelligence Service,' *Yale Review*, 36 (Autumn 1946), p. 117. Emphases in original.
13 Laqueur, p. 12.
14 Mark M. Lowenthal, *Intelligence: From Secrets to Policy* (Washington, DC: Congressional Quarterly Press, 2002 [second edition]), p. 8.
15 Abram N. Shulsky (revised by Gary J. Schmitt), *Silent Warfare: Understanding the World of Intelligence* (Washington, DC: Brassey's (US), 2002 [third edition]), pp. 1–3, 171–176.
16 Ibid.
17 H. A. Random, 'Intelligence as a Science,' *Studies in Intelligence*, Spring 1958, p. 76. Declassified.
18 Martin T. Bimfort, 'A Definition of Intelligence,' *Studies in Intelligence*, Fall 1958, p. 78. Declassified.
19 The notion that people act differently when watched is a familiar one to social scientists, who long ago dubbed it the 'Hawthorne Effect.' The Western Electric Company's Hawthorne Works in the 1920s hosted a team of researchers interested in the effects of lighting on factory workers. The team, in sight of the employees, fiddled with the illumination levels and learned to its surprise that both brighter and dimmer settings increased output. Employees worked harder even when they mistakenly thought the lights had been adjusted. Did they just like the attention, or did they worry about the potential consequences of not increasing their output? As long as the workers knew they

were being watched, the research team could not answer that question – or learn which light levels workers liked best. F. J. Roethlisberger and William J. Dickson, *Management and the Worker* (Cambridge, MA: Harvard University Press, 1956 [1939]), pp. 14–18

Reprinted with permission from Michael Warner, 'Wanted: A Definition of "Intelligence" ' *Studies in Intelligence*, 46, 3 (2002) pp.15–23.

2 Ideas of intelligence

Divergent national concepts and institutions

Philip Davies

This essay argues that in seeking a catch-all definition for intelligence we may be 'barking up the wrong tree'. By seeking to explore the divergence of British and US concepts of intelligence he suggests that we can learn a great deal about intelligence culture, drawing parallels with debates about the value of the concept of 'strategic culture'. It is suggested here that the cornerstone of any comprehensive theory of intelligence culture has to be a recognition that there are many competing national ideas of intelligence, and that these have both institutional and operational consequences.

Since World War II, much effort has gone into defining 'intelligence.' This effort has even given rise to what is sometimes called intelligence theory, which can be traced to Sherman Kent's desire to see intelligence programmatically examined, addressed, and subsumed by the mainstream social science tradition. During World War II Kent served in the Bureau of Analysis and Estimates of the US Office of Strategic Services, and later headed the Office of National Estimates of the US Central Intelligence Agency (CIA). Virtually all intelligence theory could be considered a footnote to Kent. His conviction that intelligence should be a broad-based analytical discipline is embodied in his maxim 'intelligence is knowledge,' which has set the precedent for most subsequent debate.

Since Kent's day, many alternative approaches to intelligence have been suggested by a succession of authors. In his 1996 *Intelligence Power in Peace and War*, British scholar and former intelligence officer Michael Herman tried to present the range of conceptualizations of intelligence as a spectrum, ranging from the broad definitions that approach intelligence primarily as 'all-source analysis' (typified by Kent's view) to narrow interpretations that focus on intelligence collection, particularly covert collection. Herman notes in passing that the broader interpretations tend to be favored by US writers and narrow approaches by the British. What Herman does not pursue, however, is the fundamental difference this matter of definition effects in the British and US approaches to intelligence and how those conceptual differences have been reflected in their respective intelligence institutions and in legislation. It is entirely possible that by asking 'what is intelligence?' we may be barking up the wrong intellectual tree. The real questions should perhaps be 'How do different countries and institutions define intelligence?' and 'What are the consequences of those different definitions?'

A study in contrast

Conceptual divergences in the concept of intelligence are particularly worth keeping in mind when comparing Britain and the United States. The 1995 US Congressional Aspin/Brown Commission examined the British national intelligence machinery. Likewise, one of the first actions of the British Parliamentary Intelligence and Security Committee after its creation under the 1994 Intelligence Services Act was a similar evaluation of US methodologies. Neither side found anything to incorporate from the other's methods, and yet neither seemed to detect that they were talking – and hence thinking – about entirely different things when they were talking about intelligence. To a large degree, transatlantic dialogue on the subject of intelligence has tended to be conducted at cross-purposes.

In current usage, 'intelligence' in US parlance tends to refer to 'finished' intelligence that has been put through the all-source analysis process and turned into a product that can provide advice and options for decision makers. Perhaps the classic US definition comes from a past edition of the Dictionary of United States Military Terms for Joint Usage, which states that intelligence is 'the product resulting from the collection, evaluation, analysis, integration, and interpretation of all available information which concerns one or more aspects of foreign nations or areas of operation which is immediately or potentially significant for planning.' This definition includes the collection of raw information, but the end result does not become 'intelligence' as such until it has been thoroughly analyzed. Hence, in the US context, intelligence production means analytical production.

This very broad sense of the term intelligence was used as far back as 1949 when Kent argued that intelligence consists of three 'substantive' elements: first, descriptive background; second, reportorial current information and threats, the 'most important complicated element of strategic intelligence'; and third, the 'substantive-evaluative' analytical process of evaluation and 'extrapolation.' In 1967, Harold Wilensky approached intelligence as 'the problem of gathering, processing, interpreting, and communicating the technical and political information needed in the decision process.' At the start of the 1980s Roy Godson provided the 'elements of intelligence' scheme, describing intelligence as the sum total of collection, analysis, counter-intelligence, and covert action, a set of criteria whose breadth leaves behind even the official government rhetoric. The United States is therefore evidently oriented toward a broad notion of intelligence that is shared by both government practitioners and scholars.

It is more difficult to locate a formally constituted idea of 'intelligence' in British thinking. In part this is because British official practice has more of what might be termed a civil law orientation toward procedures and terminology, driven by precedent and convention rather than by formalized exactitude. The behavoralist undercurrent in political and policy thinking has also always been stronger in the United States than in Britain, where the traditions of political thought owe more to political history and political philosophy than to political science. It is, however, possible to identify indicative or typical expressions of the British approach to intelligence.

While US intelligence analysis is professionalized, in British practice it is really no more than the ordinary work of government departments and ministries. Former Foreign and Commonwealth Office (FCO) official Reginald Hibbert has argued that the FCO 'is itself a huge assessment machine.' He breaks down the total spectrum of available raw information sources fed into the FCO into being '50 percent . . . drawn from published sources,' another 10 percent to 20 percent from 'privileged material which is not strictly speaking classified,' and 20 percent to 25 percent from classified material available from the 'normal product of diplomatic activity,' leaving 10 to 15 percent from secret sources. The FCO then 'chews the cud of this material day by day, reacts to it as it becomes available, and applies it in the decision-taking and policy-forming process which is the end product.'

Hence, in British practice, raw intelligence moves straight into policymaking circles without passing through a separate, intervening analytical stage. This is not because there is no assessment process but because all-source analysis is subsumed by the civil service employees who, in their role as advisors to ministers of the crown, take ultimate responsibility for the policies and actions of their departments before Parliament. As a result, intelligence as such tends to refer more narrowly to those kinds of information not available from the 'normal product' of departmental activity. British intelligence officials are fond of intoning the mantra that 'intelligence is about secrets, not mysteries.' British intelligence scholar Ken Robertson has captured this sentiment succinctly by defining intelligence as 'the secret collection of other people's secrets,' a phrase that closely parallels former Secret Intelligence Service (SIS) officer Nicholas Elliott's description of the SIS role as being 'to find out by clandestine means what the overt organs of government cannot find out by overt means.' In British usage, then, 'intelligence production' means raw intelligence collection.

Institutionalizing intelligence

In more concise terms, the difference between British and US concepts of intelligence is that the United States approaches information as a specific component of intelligence, while Britain approaches intelligence as a specific type of information. Of the two, the British conception is unsurprisingly of greater antiquity, and it can probably be argued that the US usage of the term was closer to the British one prior to World War II. Despite institutional and constitutional differences between the two governments, US intelligence institutions such as the US Navy's Signals Intelligence Service were geared mainly toward producing raw intelligence for departmental exploitation. The contemporary US approach to intelligence can, however, be traced fairly directly to the nation's experience of the 1941 Japanese attack on Pearl Harbor. By comparison, if the British had any comparable formative trauma it was probably the disastrous South African campaign of 1899–1903, commonly known as the Boer War. These two experiences were catastrophic for different reasons, and the diagnoses of these failures provided the intellectual foundations for the two countries' respective institutions as well as their conceptions of intelligence.

At the turn of the century, the British went into South Africa ignorant not merely about the geography but also about the demographics, economy, and social organization of the region. They knew little about the transportation and raw materials in South Africa, had little or no insight into the Afrikaans settlers, and were surprised by the Afrikaaners' guerrilla tactics and ability to live off the land. The surviving papers of the post-Boer War Special Section of the War Office reveal how deeply the failings in South Africa affected British military intelligence officers. The lessons of the campaign were crucial contributing factors in establishing and maintaining an extensive and effective theater-level human intelligence system.

By 1910, years of saber-rattling arms races both on and around the European continent combined with a widespread, xenophobic 'spy scare' (partly fomented by popular novelists like William Le Queux) to force the Committee of Imperial Defence to convene a subcommittee of inquiry into the threat of foreign espionage known as the Haldane Committee. During deliberations, the Admiralty and the War Office complained that 'our organization for acquiring information of what is taking place in foreign ports and dockyards is defective' and furthermore that they were 'in a difficult position when dealing with foreign spies who may have information to sell, since their dealings have to be direct and not through intermediaries.' The resulting report had a series of recommendations, including the creation of a new Secret Service Bureau (SSB) to take over the tasks of the Special Section at a national rather than just War Office level. Although the SSB arose out of an inquiry into foreign espionage against Britain, two of its three proposed functions were directed toward British espionage against foreign states, i.e. to 'act as a screen' between the War Office and Admiralty and foreign agents with information they wished to sell and as an intermediary between those same two departments of state and 'agents we employ in foreign countries.'

In due course, the SSB fragmented along domestic and foreign lines into what became the Security Service (formerly MI5) and the SIS (formerly MI6). After World War I, the central role of demand for raw intelligence was reinforced by what has been called the '1921 Arrangement,' in which departments attached sections of their own intelligence branches to SIS headquarters to articulate their departmental requirements directly to the service's operational personnel. The same 1921 Arrangement set the requirements for the predecessor of Government Communications Headquarters until that agency gained independence after World War II. At that point, an analogous body called Z Division was set up within the Directorate of Signal Intelligence Plans and Production. In all of this, the role of the 'intelligence community,' such as it may have been, was to provide raw intelligence to be factored into the ruminations of the overt machinery of the British central government.

The foundations of the contemporary US intelligence community similarly arose out of a public inquiry, the joint congressional committee that investigated the causes of the Pearl Harbor attack. Unlike the British experience in South Africa, the post-Peal Harbor diagnosis was not that the United States lacked raw intelligence. The appraisal adopted by the joint committee stated that 'the coordination and proper evaluation of intelligence in times of stress must be insured by continuity of service and centralization of responsibility in competent officials,' although it added darkly that 'only partial credence, however, can be extended this conclusion inasmuch as no amount of coordination and no system could be effected to compensate for lack of alertness and imagination' on the part of commanders and decision makers. In part as a consequence of the joint committee, the administration of US President Harry Truman passed the 1947 National Security Act, which created the National Security Council (NSC) to coordinate national security policy and the CIA to centralize intelligence assessment.

The original mandate of the CIA, though in part managerial, was most significantly analytical, framed in words strikingly close to the joint committee's final report: 'to correlate and evaluate the intelligence relating to the national security and to provide for the appropriate dissemination of such intelligence.' The CIA was originally intended to collate and assess information provided by other departments of government, chiefly the State and Defense departments. Its operational assets were acquired as something of a retrofit or afterthought, justified by an umbrella clause in the 1947 National Security Act allowing the CIA to perform 'other functions and duties related to intelligence affecting the national security' under the direction of the NSC. To a degree well beyond the British case, there was a public debate about the US need for intelligence in peace time, culminating in Kent's 1949 *Strategic Intelligence for US World Policy*, in which Kent took up the notion of intelligence as collection plus all-source assessment. Because of the post-Pearl Harbor reflections on intelligence in the United States, intelligence came to be considered and defined in terms of the analytical process. To be sure, purely collection-oriented agencies such as the National Reconnaissance Office and the National Security Agency exist, but agencies like the CIA, the Defense Department's Defense Intelligence Agency, and the State Department's Bureau of Intelligence and Research define their roles and responsibilities primarily in analytical terms.

Theory in practice

The tendency of countries to employ differing definitions of intelligence has both conceptual and substantive implications. Substantively, it provides a particularly telling insight into how and why intelligence institutions take shape in specific ways. It is not, of course, the whole story; governmental, institutional, and even constitutional factors come into play but are significant in terms of why intelligence is conceived one way or another as well as in terms of what architectures are created and in what form. The decentralization of power in the British cabinet system is undoubtedly a factor in the decentralization of all-source analysis, much as executive centralization under the US presidency influenced the centralization of analysis – except that the impetus toward central collation and analysis in the United States came from the US Congress while the decentralized power interests of the British system opted for centralized, covert collection. Key traumatic events that demonstrate the failures of intelligence in each country have driven national perceptions of what intelligence ought to be. And such normative concepts are crucial in how we think we ought to go about building an intelligence community, much as key normative concepts provide an intellectual framework for other activities.

Different US and British conceptions of intelligence also have been an underlying factor in the differences in the history of public debate and legislation on intelligence in the two countries. The CIA was established by legislative will in 1947 while the SIS and GCHQ had no equivalent legal standing until the Conservative administration of John Major passed enabling legislation in 1994. Similarly, there has been a vigorous and well informed public debate over the role and functions of intelligence in the United States since the late 1940s, but no equivalent open discussion in Britain happened until the late 1980s. These differences have generally been attributed to the greater openness of the US political system. However, it is also far easier to talk publicly about intelligence analysis, even all-source analysis, than it is to speak openly about the sensitive and competitive sphere of covert intelligence collection. Both the 1947 act and the concurrent public debate dealt primarily with analysis and policy and relatively little with the role and content of collection, especially covert collection. Likewise, although official acknowledgment of the existence of Britain's foreign intelligence services had to wait until the 1980s, the first officially attributable references to the Joint Intelligence Subcommittee and the Joint Intelligence Bureau appear in a Royal Institute of Public Administration study of the machinery of British central government published in 1957. It appears that having a broad definition of intelligence makes it easier to be open about intelligence institutions, legislation, and policy.

And yet these profound divergences emerge within two closely related and closely integrated intelligence communities, which also share a common language and political culture. If Britain and the United States differ so widely and so fundamentally, what about systems that are less cognate? Where there is little or no common cultural and institutional heritage, the divergences run deeper, increasing the risk that decision makers and intelligence practitioners may misunderstand what foreign agencies are essentially about. Non-democratic states typically define their agencies as security services rather than intelligence services. This is often not least because agencies of revolutionary regimes like the old Soviet KGB and the Chinese Department of Public Security and Department of State Security have their roots in the pursuit of counter-revolutionary and dissident forces at home and abroad. John Dziak has categorized states like the Soviet Union as 'counter-intelligence states' in which intelligence agencies evolve out of an almost paranoid concern about threats to regime survival rather than policy needs for information.

The way 'intelligence' services of non-democratic societies view themselves differs fundamentally from the self-perception of intelligence services in open societies. Intelligence was eventually consolidated in Nazi Germany under RSHA (Reich's Chief Security Department) and Communist East Germany relied on its MFS (Ministry of Security). But Federal Germany's 'Gehlen' organization was formally the BND (Federal Information Service). Of course, there are odd transitional cases like France, whose foreign intelligence service is categorized as DGSE (Directorate-General of External Security), but the French agency has often been criticized for an aggressive, even brutal paramilitary orientation. The French visualize their service less as a national information provider than as the first and last line of defense for France.

Thinking and doing

The key conceptual implication of the divergence of British and US concepts is that there is an advantage to thinking seriously about formulating and articulating a theory of intelligence culture. In recent years, a great deal has been made of the theoretical value of the concept of 'strategic culture' as a means of reconstructing national thinking on defense and strategic policy. That concept itself has owed much to the longer-standing and more extensive literature on 'political culture' as a means for understanding governmental institutions and policies. It would seem natural, even inevitable, to conclude that how we define what it is we think we are doing when we think we are doing intelligence shapes how we do intelligence. And the cornerstone of any theory of intelligence culture has to be the idea of intelligence, or more accurately, the many different ideas of intelligence and their institutional and operational consequences.

Reprinted with permission from Philip Davies, 'Ideas of Intelligence: Divergent National Concepts and Institutions', *Harvard International Review* 24, 3 (2002) pp.62–66.

WHAT IS INTELLIGENCE

Further reading: Books and reports

Peter Gill and Mark Pythian, *Intelligence in an Insecure World* (Cambridge: Polity 2006), chapters 1 & 2.

P. Gill, S. Marrin and M. Pythian (eds.) *Intelligence Theory Key Questions and Debates* (London: Routledge, 2008).

Michael Herman, *Intelligence Power in Peace and War* (Cambridge: Cambridge University Press 1996) chapters 1–3 & 21.

Michael Herman, *Intelligence Services in the Information Age* (London: Frank Cass 2001) chapter 1.

Sherman Kent, *Strategic Intelligence for American Foreign Policy* (Princeton: Princeton University Press 1949), chapter 1.

L. Krizan, *Intelligence Essentials for Everyone*, Joint Military Intelligence College, Occasional Paper No.6 (Washington DC: GPO 1999).

Loch K. Johnson & James J. Wirtz, *Intelligence and National Security: The Secret World of Spies* (NY: Oxford UP, 2nd ed. 2007).

Walter Laqueur, *World of Secrets: The Uses and Limits of Intelligence* (NY: Basic Books, 1985) pp.4–70.

Mark Lowenthal, *Intelligence: From Secrets to Policy* (Washington D.C.: CQ Press, 3rd Ed 2006), chapter 1.

Abram N. Shulsky and Gary J. Schmitt, *Silent Warfare: Understanding the World of Intelligence* (Dulles, VA: Brassey's Inc., 2002) chapter 1.

G. F. Treverton, Seth G. Jones, Steven Boraz & Phillip Lipscy, *Toward a Theory of Intelligence Workshop Report*, (Santa Monica, CA: Rand 2006 0-8330-3911-3).

Further reading: Essays and articles

Christopher Andrew, 'Intelligence, International Relations and "Under-theorisation" ' in L.V. Scott & P.D. Jackson, (eds.), *Understanding Intelligence in the Twenty-First Century: Journeys in Shadows*, (London: Routledge 2004), pp.29–41.

Aspin-Brown Commission, 'The Need to Maintain an Intelligence Capability', in *Preparing for the 21st Century: An Appraisal of U.S. Intelligence* (Washington DC: GPO 1996) chapter 1.

James Der Derian, 'Anti-diplomacy: Intelligence theory and surveillance practice', *Intelligence and National Security* 8/3 (1993): 29–51.

Stuart Farson, 'Schools of thought: National perceptions of intelligence', *Conflict Quarterly* 9/2 (1989) pp.52–104.

M.R.D. Foot, 'What Use Are Secret Services?' in Hayden B. Peake and Samuel Halpern (eds.) *In the Name of Intelligence: Essays in Honor of Walter Pforzheimer* (Washington, DC: NIBC Press, 1994) pp.277–282.

Loch K. Johnson, 'Bricks and Mortar for a Theory of Intelligence', *Comparative Strategy* 22/1 (2003): 1–28.

Loch K. Johnson, 'Preface to a Theory of Strategic Intelligence,' *International Journal of Intelligence and Counterintelligence* 16/4 (2003): 638–663.

David Kahn, 'An Historical Theory of Intelligence,' *Intelligence and National Security* 16/3 (2001): 79–92.

David Omand, 'Reflections on Secret Intelligence' in Peter Hennessy (ed.), *The New Protective State* (London: Continuum 2007) pp.97–122.

Andrew Rathmell, 'Towards Postmodern Intelligence', *Intelligence and National Security* 17/3 (2002) pp.87–104.

Len Scott and Peter Jackson, 'The Study of Intelligence in Theory and Practive', in L.V. Scott and P.D. Jackson, (eds.), *Understanding Intelligence in the Twenty-First Century: Journeys in Shadows*, (London: Routledge 2004) pp.139–69.

Len Scott and Peter Jackson, 'Journeys in Shadows', in L.V. Scott and P.D. Jackson, (eds.), *Understanding Intelligence in the Twenty-First Century: Journeys in Shadows*, (London: Routledge 2004), pp.1–28.

Jennifer Sims, 'What Is Intelligence? Information for Decision Makers', in Roy S. Godson et al., (eds.), *U.S. Intelligence at the Crossroads: Agendas for Reform*, (Washington, D.C.: Potomac Books Inc. 1995).

T.F. Troy, 'The "Correct" Definition of Intelligence', *International Journal of Intelligence and Counterintelligence* 5/4 (1991–1992) pp.433–54.

Essay or seminar questions

- To what extent does the nature and value of 'intelligence' differ from 'information'?
- Compare and contrast the intelligence cultures and styles of the UK and the USA.
- How far do you accept Michael Herman's contention that it is useful to talk about secret intelligence as a form of 'state power', akin to economic or military power?
- How far do you accept Michael Warner's assertion that 'Intelligence is secret, state activity to understand or influence foreign entities.'?

Part 1

The intelligence cycle

'In this "intelligence cycle", much can go wrong . . .'
Loch Johnson [1]

SUMMARY

The 'intelligence cycle' is a phrase used to capture the idea of a seamless process by which states manage the vast knowledge-intensive industries which constitute their intelligence communities. The traditional cycle begins with the targeting of collection assets, be they human spies or satellites. Once raw intelligence has been collected it is processed, validated, analysed and discussed. Thereafter, a much reduced selection of material is passed to the hard-pressed policy-maker in order to inform their decisions. Either in the backwash of a major crisis, or as part of a routine review, the target list is then re-assessed, and the cycle begins again. This classical concept of an intelligence cycle shaped the early policy-orientated literature on intelligence, which tended to reflect the functional elements of the cycle. The notion remains useful because it captures and connects the majority of activities undertaken by intelligence services and emphasises how they inform the wider business of government. In this sense, intelligence services do what their name suggests, they provide an information service to government that assists both policy-formation and action.[2]

Yet the intelligence cycle is now a questionable concept. Even during the Cold War, it was increasingly clear that the cycle could often run in reverse, with dirigiste policy-makers telling their collectors to scurry away and seek evidence to support pre-determined policies, rather then responding to objective information that arrived on their desks. Over the last decade, new challenges, especially terrorism, have shortened the decision cycle. The Cold War landscape in which committees of analysts engaged in leisurely debate over the numbers of enemy missiles now seems far distant. Technology has also eroded the intelligence cycle, since secure multi-level databases means that policy-makers can act as their own analysts. Indeed, there is some uncertainty as to exactly whom the customer is, since some intelligence might be placed in the public domain to justify pre-emption. Moreover, as intelligence services undertake more enforcement, disruption and covert action – acting as hunters as well as gatherers – they have become consumers of their own product. Gregory Treverton and David Omand have both spoken of the 'real intelligence cycle' which incorporates these many cross-cutting connections. Notwithstanding this, the intelligence cycle remains the appropriate place to begin any understanding of intelligence.[3]

Collection

The intelligence scholar Ken Robertson once described intelligence as 'the secret collection of someone else's secrets'[4]. This notion captures the essence of traditional intelligence collection as one of the black arts of statecraft. It underlines, not only the fact that our opponents have information that they do not want us to know, it also reminds us that the value of discovering those secret things is increased if our opponents believe that their secrets have not been compromised. Partly for this reason, the last half-century has seen the emergence of a range of security processes, including rigid compartmentalisation, that accompany the distribution of secret intelligence. This in turn makes the intelligence product difficult to use flexibly, especially in the context of counter-terrorism or counter-insurgency. Providing timely intelligence to customers from secret sources, without comprising those sources, remains one of the great challenges of intelligence management.

Traditional espionage using human agents is as old as time and exhortations such as 'go spy out the land' are recorded in many ancient religious texts. The human spy, as both watcher and saboteur, figures prominently in ancient Indian texts. Kautiliya's *Arthasastra*, a Sanskrit work on statecraft of the c. 4th century B.C., discusses intelligence agencies or 'institutes of espionage' (samsthásvarpayeyuh) and offers a typology of no less than nine different types of spy.[5] When Clausewitz was writing in the early nineteenth century intelligence, collection was still largely about human spies. Thereafter, it evolved rapidly alongside military technology and accordingly the first modern intelligence departments together with railways and the telegraph. The advent of airpower and wireless networks during the First World War allowed the emergence of technical intelligence that soon assumed an industrial scale. This took the form of large-scale interception, code-breaking and airborne photo-reconnaissance. The end result was not just more intelligence but 'real-time intelligence' that exerted a transformative influence on military operations.

After 1945, the emergence of atomic weapons increased this trend. Nuclear arsenals were accompanied by a vast panoply of satellites that simultaneously watched and targeted strategic systems. The great leviathans of intelligence collection remain satellites that collect both imagery and signals. In common with nuclear weapons, states that possess these systems belong to a premier league of information superpowers and so they have symbolic as well as real value. The developing ability to push this information forward to front line echelons, witnessed recently in Iraq and Afghanistan, continues to revolutionise the deployment of military forces. Alongside the satellite revolution has been the computer revolution. Although initially affecting only analysis, the advent of the desktop computer and the internet has ushered in the age of the computer as a collection tool in its own right.

Ironically, despite the vast sums spent on secret collection, the majority of intelligence, and indeed often the best intelligence, now comes from open sources. The decline of closed societies, wherein even basic information was hard to obtain, together with the information technology revolution, has ensured that a great deal of information that was hitherto secret is now accessed cheaply and easily. The increasing use of open source intelligence has facilitated greater co-operation between governments and NGOs. Yet at the same time the level of resource and the degree of thought devoted to open source remains small compared to its potential. The aristocrats of the intelligence world are perhaps justifiably anxious about the relegation of secret intelligence to the category of 'mere information'.[6]

Analysis

The former Soviet Union stands testament to the fact that good intelligence collection is not enough. Often brilliant human source operations by the Soviet intelligence services were wasted as a result of poor tasking, analysis and consumption by an absurd and rigid hierarchy. Soviet ideology, together with a marked tendency amongst Soviet leaders towards conspiracy theory, fatally undermined their ability to make use of excellent raw intelligence. Therefore, despite a track record of impressive intelligence collection there were remarkably few dividends for foreign policy. The former Soviet Union presents a useful model of all that can go wrong with the intelligence cycle.[7]

The term 'analysis' covers a wide variety of processes. This can involve early evaluation of the reliability of intelligence – sometimes called 'validating' – which can involve comparing and contrasting many different pieces of information. This can be complex. During the Cuban Missile crisis the CIA was bewildered by hundreds of conflicting human source reports. More recently, on the subject of Iraq, analysts were bedevilled by the problem of the single source. Either way, evaluation is a serious challenge. Some intelligence requires sophisticated technical processing or translation. Thereafter, the business of high-level interpretation begins. This can require the reconciliation of contradictory pieces of information from different types of sources and from competing agencies. Most importantly, it is about deciding upon the small selection of material that will end up on the desk of a Prime Minster or a President.

The United States has perhaps given more attention to intelligence analysis than any other country. Large components of the so-called collection agencies are in fact given over to collation, processing and analysis. Underpinning this is a conviction that thinking analytically is an important skill that adds value to the information that has been gathered. One of the main achievements of intelligence studies over the last thirty years has been to demonstrate that intelligence failures rarely result from failures in intelligence collection. Instead they tend to occur due to problems in the processing of information, or as a result of poor responses by the decision-makers. By contrast the Soviet Union, and now Russia, has invested relatively little resource in processing and analysing intelligence. In the UK, the Butler Report of 2004 also exhorted Whitehall to professionalise its analytical service.

For several decades, the majority of writing on analysis has focused on the problem of strategic surprise, which is often interpreted as 'intelligence failure'. This reflects the shock created by the scale of surprise inflicted upon Israel by the Arab states in October 1973, and thereafter academics gave this problem increasing attention. The field has been dominated by the writings of Michael Handel and Richard K. Betts. Commentators have tended to identify two different types of problems in the realm of high-level analysis. The first is *cognitive bias*, the kind of error that result from using models, theories and analytical assumptions. To some extent all organisations dealing with large amounts of information must make assumptions about how the world works and these models are usually helpful. However when the behaviour of an adversary confounds the assumptions and stereotypes, surprise results. Therefore one of the great challenges for analysts is self-awareness. Preconceptions are inevitable but intelligence analysts strive for objectivity by trying to make their making basic assumptions explicit. The second barrier to effective analysis is often the vast bureaucracy of the analytical machine itself that must seek to converge the hundreds of contributions. The result is often comprise and a mediocre analysis can emerge despite much time devoted to examination and argument.[8]

The policy-maker

Politicians and indeed most senior policy-makers rarely understand the realm of intelligence. For this reason, the most difficult task is managing the interface between the analyst and the consumer. On the one hand, the analysts must be sufficiently immersed in the world of politics to be able to support current policy or operations. On the other hand, the analysts needs to avoid simply telling the customer what they wish to hear and pandering to their preferences. The challenge is to be policy-relevant, while at the same time avoiding the incipient dangers of politicisation.

Closely linked to this conundrum is the question of exactly how much intelligence analysis should be placed in the public domain. The desire of legislative bodes and their specialist committees to become legitimate customers of the intelligence services is understandable. Indeed, some would argue that a genuinely democratic foreign policy demands it. However, efforts to disseminate intelligence more widely can quickly spark charges that intelligence has become a slave to public relations. The animated debate over WMD intelligence preceding the invasion of Iraq in 2003 has focused attention on the issue of 'public intelligence'. Each generation tends to discover these issues anew and much of the debate over Iraq replays similar controversies that arose over intelligence and its role in policy towards Vietnam in the late 1960s.

Increasingly, intelligence services support customers at every level. One of the notable changes in intelligence since 2001 has been the increased emphasis on 'forward leaning' intelligence that assists operations on the battlefield. Hard lessons learned in Iraq and Afghanistan have forced a major rethink about how to deliver intelligence in real-time to tactical customers. This idea is encapsulated in the phrase 'a single intelligence battlespace' that emphasises that intelligence is not something that should reside only in rear head-quarters. No less important has been the need to supply intelligence to areas of government and indeed – even commercial entities – that are developing resilience against terrorist attack. Commercial airlines are just one example of the new customers in the intelligence cycle. In an era of globalization, these customers include an ever-growing range of international partners.

Co-operation or 'liaison'

International co-operation between intelligence services helps to underline the complexity of the 'real intelligence cycle' – since it may well occur at each or every stage of the cycle. Intelligence co-operation, which is often termed, 'liaison', can be placed in two clear categories. Most obviously, countries engage in formal liaison with a range of chosen partners and these relationships are often regulated by a range of agreements and treaties. In their most elaborate form these agreements can look remarkably like the treaties that are concluded between states. Major intelligence agencies have their own 'ambassadors' stationed in embassies abroad that are designated 'liaison officers'. The vast majority of intelligence treaties are bilateral and even so-called multilateral sharing arrangements, such as the fabled UKUSA communications intelligence agreement concluded in the late 1940s, consist mostly of a complex series of bilateral letters and memoranda of understanding. Major intelligence powers typically enjoy agreements with upwards of fifty formal intelligence partners. However, wider sharing occurs informally with other countries and non-state groups.[9]

Since the 1990s, the pressures of globalization have driven a gradual change in intelligence culture that embraces wider co-operation. Elusive transnational threats including terrorism and organised crime have encouraged a migration from a culture of 'need to know' to 'need to share'. This trend accelerated markedly after 9/11. The challenges here are immense. Major actors such as the United States are not only sharing sensitive data with tried and trusted partners but also with local police forces in far flung countries. Key operations might now conducted with the assistance of unexpected partners including Syria, Jordan and Egypt. Perhaps the most dramatic change has been the expansion of liaison between internal security services. The internal security services of foreign countries often have most to contribute to either the global war on terror or the equally gruelling struggle against organised crime. Accordingly the FBI now has as many overseas liaison officers serving abroad as the CIA. This erosion of the distinction between what is inside and what is outside is a perhaps symptom of the growing impact of globalization upon intelligence services.

Notes

1 Loch K. Johnson, Analysis for a new age', *Intelligence and National Security*, 11/4 (1996) p.657.
2 See for example, Roy Godson (ed.), *Intelligence Requirements for the 1980s: Elements of Intelligence* (Washington, DC: National Strategy Information Centre, 1979).
3 G. Treverton, *Reshaping national intelligence in an age of information* (NY: Cambridge University Press, 2001), p.106.
4 K.G. Robertson, 'Intelligence, Terrorism and Civil Liberties', *Conflict Quarterly*, 7/2 (1987) p. 46.
5 Kautiliya, *Arthasastra*, Book 1, Chapters 11–12, 'The Institution of Spies' (Delhi: Pengunin, 1992).
6 Tom Hyland, 'Open secret: spy agencies reject essential sources', *Melbourne Age*, 2 March 2008.
7 Christopher Andrew & Julie Elkner, 'Stalin and Foreign Intelligence', *Totalitarian Movements and Political Religions* 4/1 (2003) pp.69–94.
8 The classic account is R.K. Betts, *Surprise Attack: Lessons for Defense Planning* (Washington DC: Brookings Institution 1982).
9 The first extended study of liaison is probably Alfred Vagts, *The Military Attaché* (Princeton: Princeton University Press, 1967).

3 It's a cultural thing

Thoughts on a troubled CIA

Garrett Jones

The Central Intelligence Agency has been subjected to commissions and enquiries looking at both individual operations or the possibility of reform. Although these reports have often asserted that the Agency must change its 'culture' in fact they tend to focus on superficial issues of organisation. This article examines deeper remedies for cultural problems in the two directorates, the Directorate of Intelligence (which undertakes analysis) and the Directorate of Operations (which undertakes collection). He also reminds us that the once sacrosanct boundaries between collection and analysis have been eroded over recent years.

Since retiring from the CIA in 1997 after almost twenty years as a case officer ("spy runner," "asset handler," or "agent recruiter"), I have followed the Agency's failures and successes through the media. The Agency has never been as close to termination as it is now. Numerous presidential commissions and Congressional committees are currently engaged in fault-and fact-finding about recent Agency missions. These groups by their nature are concerned either with the details of individual operations or with sweeping reforms in structure and organization.

The director of the CIA (DCIA) will need to address these specific issues as the Agency tries to move forward, but one of the repeated themes in these reports is that the Agency must change its "culture"—the day-to-day details of its operation. Much of the Agency's culture is positive and a normal outcome of the nature of its business. Even some of the culture that outsiders find hard to understand may be healthy and useful. But some of the Agency's culture does have to change: a few features that were always counterproductive have now become intolerable. This article identifies some of these cultural problems and offers possible remedies.[1]

Directorate of intelligence

The Directorate of Intelligence (DI) is where the intelligence analysts live in the CIA. The intelligence analysts' job is to take all-source raw intelligence reports (human, satellite, communications intercepts, etc.) and open-source information and then to distill this mass of information into a finished intelligence product. The finished product should provide the U.S. policy-maker with the best information and interpretations of the foreign policy issues that confront him or her. The DI's failure to properly evaluate and process the intelligence information on Iraqi WMD illustrates several problems that recur in DI products. These recurring practices are sources of continuing confusion and unhappiness for the DI's intelligence consumers.

Far too many DI products simply summarize publicly available information and/or attach so many caveats in answering policymakers' questions that the answers are effectively without value. It may be useful for busy policymakers to have a summary of publicly available information, but such a summary is not an analytical judgment on current intelligence. Neither is answering a specific question with an array of equally possible outcomes. While it may be human nature and bureaucratically wise for the DI to try to give an extensive answer to every question posed, it is also intellectually dishonest and a disservice to the policymaker. "We don't know" can be a valuable answer, even if it is not what the questioner wants to hear. The DI should be required to change its processes to require it to make an accountable affirmation that it has sufficient intelligence reporting available to make a meaningful analytical judgment on any question posed to it.

Words of estimative probability

When writing analytical judgments, a DI analyst can use any word he or she wishes— "likely," "possibly," etc.—to estimate the probability of an event's occurring. This imprecision could easily be overcome by acting on a proposal made by Sherman Kent, the inventor of the intelligence analyst profession, which the DI rejected at the time it was first made. He observed that my "maybe" might be your "probably," and someone else's "certainly" may be my "probably." To prevent confusion, only certain words describing probability should be permitted in intelligence reporting. These allowed words would be defined on a numeric scale of 1–10 or 0–100. The words and their numeric values would be made known to the consumer, so that the analyst and the consumer can communicate precisely. The simplicity and clarity of the idea should refine both the analyst's intent and the consumer's understanding of analytical judgments.[2]

Analysts in operations

The CIA formed the Counterterrorist Center in the mid 1980s to bring together case officers collecting information on a terrorist target and DI analysts with specialized knowledge of a subject matter. It was originally an effort to better identify and exploit assets across the traditional geographic boundaries of the Directorate of Operations. (For the most part, the DO is broken down along geographic lines, such as the Middle East, Africa, etc.) This was a good idea that worked well as originally conceived, and since then there have been a number of intelligence centers set up to cover several different multinational subjects.

From its founding in 1947, one of the CIA's cardinal rules was that intelligence should be collected by a different group of people than those who analyzed what the intelligence meant and its value. The CIA's founders understood that a collector of intelligence invested far too much professional and personal energy into a source or a method to be able to evaluate the resulting intelligence in an unbiased manner. In fact, when the old CIA headquarters was first opened, the hallway doors between the DI and the DO were permanently locked. DI and DO personnel were not to mix. The DI had no stake in how much time and money the DO had expended in collecting a piece of intelligence. Their only task was to evaluate the accuracy and importance of the collected intelligence.

Unfortunately, it has become common practice in many intelligence centers for analysts to both direct the collection of intelligence and, because of their training, make the first cut on the meaning and value of the intelligence. When it comes time for the DI to produce a formal product, among the first people it sounds out on what the intelligence means are the analysts responsible for its collection. This is a fundamental error and may be at least partially responsible for the failures surrounding the Iraqi WMD question. This is not to say that collectors' opinions on the intelligence should not be considered: they often have subtle and meaningful insight into the situation. However, their opinions should be one data-point among many, not the first draft of a National Intelligence Estimate.

The current practice is a profound violation of analytical tradecraft. If you are going to collect, collect; if you are going to analyze, analyze. Having analysts involved in the collection process is a good idea, but once they have invested themselves in collection, they must not be involved in the subsequent analysis.

Reports officers

Report Officers (ROs), sometimes called Collection Management Officers, work for the DO, but their primary job is to interface between the DO collectors and the first-line intelligence consumers, usually DI analysts. ROs are the intermediaries between collectors and consumers.[3] While they are not required to have experience or specialization in the given subject or geographical area, they are tasked to give the DO collectors feedback from the intelligence consumers on the value of the raw intelligence reports, identify possible gaps in coverage, and discern new areas of interest. Conversely, ROs are to tell the consumers of the reliability and past performance of the DO sources and provide them a general sense of the access the source has to the intelligence targets. ROs are also supposed to ensure that the clerical details of a raw intelligence report are handled correctly: checking that the correct addresses are on the report, verifying that an up-to-date source description is used, and serving as the last editorial check, seeing to it that the report's wording conforms to Agency style.

Based on what we have learned about the Iraqi WMD issue, it appears that the interface role of the ROs is completely broken and that neither analysts nor case officers are being well served.[4] It is time to start over and redesign the RO function. The interface role between the collectors and the consumer has to be performed differently. The clerical component of the RO's job is non-controversial, and the DO should retain it. The interface component of the job, however, should be shifted to the DI or to a new independent review panel. If due regard is given to the collector/analyst problem, the RO interface function may be an excellent task for DI analysts to take on when they are seconded to the DO.

Not invented here and not used either: what is intelligence after 9/11 and who gets it?

During the Cold War, the DI produced a limited number of finished intelligence products. The average DI analyst knew exactly who his consumers were and in what information they were interested. Consumers were usually policymakers at the Department of State, the Pentagon, and the White House. Occasionally, the Departments of Commerce and Treasury were involved in certain economic reporting, but the audience for finished reporting was small.

Since 9/11, intelligence consumers have run the gamut from policy-makers to local police chiefs, and from combat commanders at the unit level to FBI agents trying to get a search warrant. Some of the consumers want masses of data sifted through, while others insist on receiving a real-time flow of the raw data. A DI analyst may no longer be able even to identify his consumers, much less grasp their individual needs for intelligence. The DI has met this new challenge by largely ignoring its existence. Finished intelligence products are delivered to consumers in more or less the same format and by more or less the same methods as they did during the Cold War, and they address more or less the same questions.

This is not good enough. For a start, the DI needs to identify all of its consumers and find out who needs what information and in what format. A second step might be to find out what other parts of the U.S. government have already amassed large amounts of raw information that could benefit DI consumers. The Drug Enforcement Agency, for instance, has an enormous amount of raw information on the operational details of drug cartels. Do the operations of drug cartels mirror in any way the operations of terrorist cells? Does the multiyear hunt for drug lord Pablo Escobar have any lesson that could aid in the hunt for Osama bin Laden?

Performing analysis no longer means just pulling together written documents of various pedigrees and condensing their meaning. There is no public indication that the DI is researching recent developments in computer data-mining of both classified and open-source databases looking for counterintuitive or nonlinear relationships. (An example of a nonlinear or counterintuitive relationship would be dress hemlines and the U.S. stock market, which rise and fall with each other. No one knows why, but the relationship seems real and predictive over time.)

Another new challenge not yet addressed by the DI is that the intelligence analysis function can change over time, even for the same consumer. While policymakers may require the traditional "secret information"—i.e., plans, intentions, and capabilities—to define an emerging situation, their needs can change once an initial policy has been formed. Determining that a chemical weapon plant exists is an example of the traditional "secret stealing"; finding out who is being bribed to sell illicit equipment and by means of what bank accounts is new to the Agency, which has not even explored how to do something covert to effectively end the bribery. Historically, the default is to go to the diplomats and see if a strongly worded démarche can achieve anything; if a diplomatic resolution is not possible, then it's "send in the Marines." There has to be something in between—perhaps compromising the existence of secret international bank accounts, starting civil suits against the various players operating through deniable fronts, mounting direct-action missions against material in transit, or rerouting shipments by compromising computer systems. The information, or intelligence analysis, needed to carry out any of these nontraditional efforts in no way resembles traditional intelligence analysis. Shipping schedules are rarely classified, and Swiss bankers may fear public disclosure more than covert action. Those who carry out these nontraditional activities, whether collection or covert action, require intelligence analysis. Are the collectors going to do this, analysts working with the collectors, or a new branch of the DI?

Liaison services 101: none are friendly and many are not competent

There have been repeated calls in the media and Congress for the CIA to increase its cooperation with "friendly" foreign intelligence liaison services to obtain better reporting on terrorism and other vital intelligence targets. This could be valuable, but there are a few features of liaison services to bear in mind. First, there are no "friendly" liaison services, not even among those allies who are historically, philosophically, and economically closest to us. There are several liaison services whose own national interests often coincide with U.S. interests and with whom we often cooperate to some degree. But they are not on our side: they are on their own side. They report to their own governments, and what is good for their governments is not always good for the United States. The intelligence the CIA receives from a foreign service may be reliable, partly accurate, or completely false, depending on how that service sees its own national interest on a particular subject.

A second factor is whether the foreign service is any good at reporting on the intelligence subject in question. Besides the CIA, perhaps two or three other national intelligence services are worldwide in scope. There are then perhaps a baker's dozen of good regional services that can accurately report on their neighbors or some specific region of the world. The rest, including a number of wealthy and sophisticated countries, would be better served by subscribing to the *New York Times* for foreign intelligence reporting.

However, the liaison services' internal reporting abilities are often outstanding. Inside their own borders, most liaison services have an excellent grasp on what is going on and who is involved. Their powers normally exceed anything the FBI can do, and if they are willing to share the information, it is usually more accurate and detailed than anything the CIA can hope to obtain unilaterally.

All these factors must be considered in evaluating liaison service reporting. As the Iraqi WMD fiasco demonstrates, they are not. The CIA's Counterintelligence Center remains the primary component that performs a regular evaluation of the foreign liaison services. The Center is chiefly focused on evaluating how much of a counterintelligence threat the liaison service might pose to U.S. interests. Evaluating the service's foreign intelligence reporting creditability is outside the Center's scope. Logically, the ROs could pick up the slack, but as noted above, that role appears to be completely broken.

Whatever component is finally drafted to take on this task is going to have to tell the intelligence consumer a few things upfront when disseminating a liaison service's intelligence report. Does the service have credibility? Has it ever reported on the given intelligence subject? What percentage of its reports were correct? It will also need to inform the consumer about the liaison service's own agenda. Are its internal politics such that it will tell us everything it knows or only some of what it knows? Will they embellish what information they might have in order to influence U.S. policy? Making these evaluations will be a full-time job, not something that can be done some slow afternoon. Too much is at stake.

Directorate of operations

In the DO, some things have been broken for years, and it is time they were fixed. Despite a widespread knowledge among Agency officers of these dysfunctional artifacts, senior officers cling to them with a sense of entitlement, a *droit du seigneur* that borders on the edge of "power corrupts, but absolute power is pretty neat."

The not-so-meritorious promotion system

In a bureaucracy such as the DO, the promotion system is supposed to do two things well: reward past superior performance and select the people who will advance through the organization and become the future senior officers. In the DO, it works this way: until grade scale 13, it is pretty much pass/fail. (This is for case officers in the DO; it varies over other directorates and job titles.) There is no competition to speak of; if you show up and do the job, the promotions will come. (The DO had to do this for retention reasons, given how expensive it is for a family to live in the Washington, D.C. area.)

From GS-14 on up, it becomes competitive, "sort of." There are two lists: one of everyone who is eligible for promotion and recommended for promotion by their respective component chiefs, and the other listing everyone else who is eligible for promotion. Both lists are ranked by merit. The first list is then matched to the number of available promotions, and those folks are promoted. Generally, the recommended list is roughly the same size as the available number of promotions. If there are any positions left after the first list has been promoted, then starting with number one, folks on the second list are promoted until all the promotions are filled. Promotions to the Senior Intelligence Service (SIS, the grades above GS-15) do not even go through the motions of a merit system. The component chiefs take their picks to the DDO (Deputy Director for Operations); ultimate decisions are generally governed by who has the most influence with the DDO that week.

Where there are competitive lists (GS-14 and GS-15), the two lists are not ranked against each other. The first dozen or so folks on the not-recommended list may be as good as or better than anyone on the recommended list, but they will not be considered for promotion until the recommended list has been promoted. This often happens. This is unfair, but that is not the worst part of this system. The real problem with this system is, especially at the SIS level, that whatever kind of management and leadership you have had before, you will have again. Not one of the many articles written about the CIA and the DO over the last few years has called for more of the same, but more of the same is what the DO's promotion system fosters. If you liked the past, you are going to love the future.

The quickest way to change things is to have one list for promotions above GS-13, including the SIS levels. Everyone is ranked by merit on the same list and the top performers on the list are promoted. A few folks with new ideas, uncomfortable and threatening ideas to the status quo, may be just what the DO needs. At this point, it cannot hurt to try.

"They did what?" how the agency does not learn from its mistakes

Whether you call them after-action reports or lessons-learned studies,[5] these usually have two main components: identify what your organization has done well or poorly, and then disseminate what you think you have learned to everyone involved. This is inarguably a good idea, but the CIA—and the DO in particular—has yet to buy into it. The DO does not require lessons-learned studies, has no guidelines on how to produce them, no personnel responsible for preparing them, and no mechanism for routinely disseminating such products if they were produced. When an outside body such as the Inspector General does undertake a review or investigation, the results are normally shared with only a few high-ranking individuals. These select readers are often the people responsible for the failure in the first place and have the most at stake in concealing their errors.[6]

If an organization is neither trying to learn from its mistakes nor circulating information organization-wide on how to do better, it cannot improve performance. True, such a standardized review will require a commitment of resources and may embarrass otherwise good people. Consider, however, the resources it will take to repair a disaster. Isn't a little constructive criticism good for everyone? Perhaps one could begin by reviewing generally acknowledged mistakes as a normal course of business. If that proves useful, then the practice could be extended. As far as potential security problems in such a process, since everyone in the DO has high-level security clearances, posting a suitably redacted report available to all in the DO on a classified system is a trivial problem.[7] This is a simple idea that should have been implemented a long time ago.

Worldwide presence vs. Worldwide capability

Within the Agency in the early 1990s, two contrasting schools of thought arose about the number of overseas stations the DO should maintain. One school of thought, the *worldwide presence* advocates, is that the DO should be on the ground as a permanent presence in as many different locations as possible. Another school, those favoring simply a *worldwide capability*, believed the DO should conserve its resources, have a permanent presence in only a few key locations, and then be prepared to surge into other geographical locations on a temporary, as-needed basis. These competing premises are ones upon which reasonable people can disagree. The Agency opted for the worldwide-capability model, and over the years, many DO stations were closed overseas. I believe there is a qualitative difference in the effectiveness and reliability of collection operations that are based on a permanent presence.

I have participated in "surge" operations to cover breaking intelligence targets, and they are inherently risky, from both counterintelligence and reliability standpoints. They are also very expensive in personnel and money. In a "surge," operation you are trying to create in days what would normally take years of careful work. This is done by throwing money and personnel at the problem. You can get away with this some of the time, but eventually it will undo you. Better is taking the long view and carefully vetting collection operations. Intelligence collection is about quality, and quality operations take time and preparation.

A second reason a worldwide presence is preferable is the fact that many of the Agency's best sources over the years have been volunteers. It is human to believe in talent and hard work, but sometimes you can also get lucky. In the past, simply put, the Agency was not very hard to find. Most embassies had a DO officer immediately available and extensive preparations had been set in place to securely handle the genuine volunteer with valuable intelligence. With the closure of many stations, this is simply no longer the case in many places. To win the lottery, you have to buy a ticket. In this case, the price of a ticket is a station on the ground.

Toxic people and due diligence

The Agency used to have a reputation for attracting and retaining some very "different" people. I have worked with a few of them. They ran the gamut from individuals who were astonishingly creative and a joy to be around to those who cause one to wonder how they made it to adulthood. In the Agency, this second group are known as "toxic people." The Agency has a history of tolerating them in positions of authority. The theory has always been that despite the damage they do to those around them, these "toxic" individuals are brilliant and the results they produce justify their retention and promotion.

The Agency may have been strong enough at one time to tolerate "toxic" people and the damage they caused to careers and morale, but I do not believe that this is any longer the case. The current DO workforce will no longer suffer in silence what they perceive as arbitrary and abusive treatment by senior officers. With Congress looking over their shoulders more than ever before, the DCIA and the DDO must demonstrate "due diligence" in their selections of individuals to fill senior positions. The days of senior DO officers with poor people skills and contempt for subordinates are over. If the DCIA does not take note of this change, it will come back to haunt him.

Management vs. Leadership

Never in senior officers' entire careers within the DO will they be evaluated on their *leadership* ability. There is no leadership training. The Agency's position is that it evaluates and trains its senior officers in *management* ability, but there is a substantial difference between the two concepts: leadership requires inspiring people, while management involves stewardship of resources. The U.S. military observes this distinction: their doctrine is that one leads people and manages non-human resources. Managing, instead of leading, people is to treat them as commodities.

Case officers are often called upon to do dangerous and difficult things in dangerous and unpleasant places. The senior officer who wrote a particularly effective memo on reducing the costs associated with the use of rental cars may be a wonderful person, but he may not be the person to call the shots when officers' lives are endangered in some far-off place among hostile people.

Leadership can be taught. The military academies do it every year with 18-year-olds. Leadership can be objectively evaluated, the easiest way being to look back and see if anyone is following you. Intelligence work in the field demands extraordinary things in difficult circumstances. Those performing this work need to be led by senior officers who know the difference between leadership and management. The Agency's senior officers should be evaluated on their leadership abilities before they are promoted.

Jointness: on being purple

Squabbles over resource allocations began as soon as the U.S. military services were founded. After World War II, Congress attempted to force the various services to adopt the concept of "Jointness," where the needs of all the services are placed before the individual needs of each service. (In the military services, this is known as "being purple," purple being the color one ostensibly gets when one mixes all the uniform colors of the various services.) Congress was largely unsuccessful. Finally, in 1986, a frustrated Congress mandated that no officer could be promoted to general officer unless he/she had served in a "joint tour of duty," loosely defined as two years working with other services, in which role you are not to represent your own service's parochial interests. The effort worked. Faced with career-ending restrictions, the U.S. professional officer corps embraced the Jointness concept and translated the concept into the superb military machine that now dominates the world military scene.

Since 9/11, Congress and the executive branch have attempted to promote the concept of Jointness within the intelligence community, but with little success. The bureaucratic inertia and foot-dragging they have encountered mirror the resistance of the military services when they were first confronted with the idea of Jointness. If Congress and the president want Jointness to be implemented in the intelligence community, they are going to have to force the issue. They could begin by mandating that no one within the IC can advance beyond the level of GS-14 (about equivalent to the military's lieutenant colonel) without serving in a "joint tour." The intelligence community may not embrace the Jointness concept, but it will have to give it attention.

Retirees and contractors

When I first joined the Agency in the late 1970s, I noticed a few older folks in the halls sporting green badges instead of the normal staff badge. When I asked about them I was told that they were retired staffers who had come back to work on contract to help with liaison visits or temporary workforce shortages, or because they had unusual language or area skills. At the time, I thought this was a good system: experienced, cleared people could help when there was a workload surge or temporarily plug the gaps until things could be sorted out permanently. Over the years this practice expanded as the Agency's workload and responsibilities increased. By the early 1990s it was largely out of control, with the contracting process in effect being used to fill the gap left by the lower number of employees authorized by Congress. The Agency could not hire new employees at the rate it needed, but it could bring back retirees.

After 9/11, the practice of contracting retirees exploded. Today, the DO would grind to a halt if the retirees were removed. RUMINT[8] has it that about 30 percent of DO employees are retirees. DO employees can retire, join a firm that is contracting with the Agency, and resume their old job within weeks, with a 25-percent increase in salary. This practice could be justified as a short-term measure and a "necessary evil," but in the war on terror, there are adverse long-term effects.

Apart from the usual abuse that can come from having this kind of money sloshing around, widespread retiree-contracting distorts the workforce by siphoning off workers to early retirement. Contract retirees are not in the DO chain of command. As more experienced employees are enticed into retirement, the pool of experience is reduced at the command levels. The practice also tends to separate core functions and skills from staff employees. Several components within the DO are for all intents and purposes completely staffed by retirees, with one staff employee in the front office. The practice creates two workforces, paid significantly different amounts to do the same work. This is becoming a morale problem for staff employees.

This is not to criticize the retired employee contractors, who more than earn their salary and do an excellent job in the process. But Agency management has to assess the long-term impact of the contracting process and how it impacts the hiring and training of tomorrow's leaders.

Agency-wide reforms and problems

Counterintelligence and connectivity

Since 9/11, both the executive and the Congress have mandated that all elements within the intelligence community must be interconnected and must share information about possible terrorist threats. This is a reasonable reaction to the information fragmentation that was the norm among the intelligence community before 9/11. Unfortunately, there has not been any consideration of the unintended effects of the mandated change in procedures. In the intelligence business, information security equals inefficiency. Raise the efficiency with which you can share information and you automatically increase the possibility that information can be compromised.

This has always been a conflict in the intelligence profession: sharing information risks revealing its existence and endangering the source of the intelligence. The arrival of interconnected networks and computer databases has exponentially raised the damage a hostile mole can do to the intelligence community. It used to be that a hostile mole could steal the papers on his desk; now he can steal his own work and everyone else's that is in the various databases to which he has access. To paraphrase Paul Redmond, one of the CIA's counterintelligence gurus: "It is an actuarial certainty that there is a hostile mole operating within the intelligence community at any given time." The next mole is going to clean the intelligence community out because of interconnectivity. There are some computer security steps that can be taken, but to put it bluntly, they are hard to do, expensive, and do not work well. This is a cost and an unforeseen consequence of interconnectivity within the intelligence community. It is a matter of when, not if. If the policymakers are not warned early and often, then the intelligence community leadership will deserve the outraged criticism it will receive.

Falling through the cracks

Since 9/11, all the components of the intelligence community have significantly redirected their efforts towards counterterrorism. Informed RUMINT has it that of the FBI's 12,000 or so special agents, only 4,600 are working criminal cases, with the rest working against counterterrorism, domestic security, and counterintelligence targets. One can wonder whether keeping the FBI out of the criminal enforcement business to such an extent is a good thing. It was comforting having the bureau focusing on organized crime, international gangs, and white-collar crime.

The classified personnel numbers at the CIA no doubt reflect a similar shift of resources. This means that subjects and areas to which the CIA used to devote resources have been downgraded in coverage. This means we are going to be surprised. No government handles surprise well, and national intelligence agencies are always found to be guilty. Neither the public nor Congress are going to understand it when the inevitable surprise happens. The CIA has taken some bad hits recently in this regard, and a few more may be fatal. Generally, the public handles the truth fairly well, even if it is not what they want to hear. The DCIA or the new National Intelligence Director needs to craft a program of informing the public of what it can reasonably expect in the short-and medium-term from the CIA. No intelligence service wants to tell the world where it is weak, and it will have to be a careful performance by whoever assumes the task. The alternative to reasonable expectations may well be a complete loss of public trust and a subsequent crippling of the CIA and the intelligence community.

You could always ask them

The DCIA may want to survey employees on what they perceive to be problems within the Agency. This sort of survey has been done before at the Agency; a particularly large-scale survey was conducted under Director William Casey in the late 1980s, but the results were never released to the employees or the public. RUMINT has it that the results of these inquiries are so embarrassing, Agency leadership has refused to release the results. Agency employees have in fact consistently pointed to the same problems over the years. This may be the right moment to conduct a survey, and one with some degree of transparency for employees.

Staff relations

Not unlike some parts of government, the military, and the private sector, there has been a long-standing tradition at the CIA of senior officials' engaging in sexual relations with newly hired and/or junior officers who work for them. In the early 1980s, the practice became so disruptive at the Agency's main training facility, The Farm, that it was made a firing offense.

The perception of favoritism as a result of such relationships, especially in promotions and assignments, is extremely corrosive to employee morale. The DCIA needs to take a position on the problem for his senior staff: if you get caught doing it, you are fired.

"Palsied by Lawyers"

While I do not always agree with Michael Scheuer,[9] he certainly got it right with that phrase. Having your own lawyer has become as necessary as having top-secret clearances at anything above the lowest level of CIA management. Each level of management has its own lawyer, fundamentally tasked with keeping that level of management out of trouble. Getting something done comes in a distant second priority. This is not an unreasonable response by CIA managers. Since the Boland Amendment in the 1980s, Congress has levied a series of formal and informal requirements on the CIA. Not even their authors agree on exactly what they mean. Couple this with ambiguous guidance from successive administrations, a "gotcha" political climate, and reluctance on the part of CIA directors to back their own people, and the various managers are left looking for cover.

In the CIA as in any other agency, things roll downhill. Starting at the top, at each level a lawyer tries to identify where the "bright line" is that either Congress or the White House does not want the CIA to cross. Having identified where s/he thinks that line is, they then subtract 5 percent to ensure a safety margin for their management level. After a dozen or so levels of management, a lethal-action order turns into a request to speak harshly in bin Laden's general direction. An exaggeration, but not by much.

The lawyers should be pulled out of the unit level and put back with the Office of General Counsel at the director's level, where they belong. Then, a policy can be established of "one issue, one lawyer, and one legal opinion." You have a legal question. The General Counsel has assigned one lawyer to that issue, and that lawyer tells you what the director's guidance is. One interpretation, one safety margin, and one place for Congress or the White House to go, at the highest level of the Agency, if they are not happy with how the policy is implemented. Rooting around at the branch level trying to hold some GS-12 accountable for interpreting guidance originating at the highest levels of the government is ridiculous. Short of malfeasance or criminal intent, the buck stops at the director's office, or at least it should.

Internal affairs

The CIA has no Internal Affairs Unit or Office of Professional Responsibility to handle violations of Agency regulations or procedures. Depending on what the offense might be, an individual can be investigated for wrongdoing by any or all of the Office of Security, the Counterintelligence Center, the Office of the Inspector General, the individual's work component (for example, the DO for a case officer), and the General Counsel (to determine whether to refer the matter to the Justice Department for prosecution). Each of these has its own procedures and standards, and each reports its results to different authorities. It is entirely possible for multiple components to investigate the same set of facts at the same time and come to different results.[10] The process is so arbitrary, the "powers that be" can decide who is going to be the designated scapegoat for a particular incident and then convene an investigation to obtain evidence to support their decision.

For reasons of efficiency and fairness, this has to change. Employee investigations, other than criminal acts, need to be conducted by a single investigative office within the CIA, with uniform standards and procedures. The Inspector General has certain statutorily required duties, but perhaps this task could be added to its purview. The Office of Security might be another place to consolidate this function. Wherever the function is located, the results of these investigations should then be reported to a single place, where a consistent standard of accountability can be applied. At the moment, the employee's component chief decides what penalty, if any, is appropriate based on the various findings—that is, unless the higher-ups have become involved, and then the component chief does what they are told. The entire procedure or lack thereof serves neither the employee nor the Agency.

9/11 and accountability

Shortly after 9/11, an Agency-wide investigation was instituted to hold individuals account-able for failures that may have resulted in the events of 9/11, and on August 26, 2005, the CIA sent the Inspector General's report on CIA performance leading up to 9/11 to the House and Senate Intelligence Oversight Committees.[11] Clearly, if it requires nearly four years to hold someone accountable, an agency's procedures are broken.

Even more troubling, this report is not being released in either a classified form for use within the CIA or in an unclassified form for release to the public. On October 6, Director Goss confirmed that he would neither release the report nor hold any CIA officer account-able for intelligence failures prior to 9/11.[12]

The *Washington Post*, reporting based on interviews with persons who had seen the report, characterized the report as harsh, since it named the CIA officers responsible for the Agency's failures before 9/11 and called for disciplinary action against them. In the same article, "an unidentified official" stated that Director Goss was inclined to shelve the entire report with-out action, claiming that many of the retired officials involved could not be disciplined by the CIA. Additionally, those retired officers who were still working at the Agency were leading the CIA's efforts against terrorism and did not need to be distracted from their current jobs. There seems to be more than a whiff of *après moi, le deluge* in this—"We may have been in error, but it does not matter, for we are irreplaceable!"

This was the most significant intelligence failure since Pearl Harbor, yet the CIA just wants to move on. That the DCIA and the senior officers of the CIA should even harbor such thoughts signals that the CIA's leadership has lost touch with the thinking and mood of the American public, and that it is unmindful of the partisan political war that will be started if the CIA tries to go forward with this position. For now, both the public and the political classes are distracted by recovery efforts after Hurricane Katrina. One observes that in the case of that disaster, a natural one in which bin Laden had no part, the clamor to hold accountable the officials responsible for mishandling the disaster was immediate and has not abated even with the removal of FEMA's Michael Brown. Hoping the 9/11 report goes away is "group-thinking" of the first order. To quote the originator of the term "group-think" in describing small, insular groups with a homogeneous worldview: "These kinds of groups share the illusion of invulnerability, a willingness to rationalize away possible coun-terarguments and a conviction that dissent is not useful."[13]

The CIA's desire to deflect the American public's obsession to blame someone, anyone, is understandable to a degree. There probably was not sufficient information available to the CIA or anyone else before 9/11 to stop the attacks. In all likelihood the intelligence com-munity had not collected enough "dots" to be able to do any connecting. That, however, is not the point. Policies and practices employed long before 9/11 led the intelligence com-munity in general and the CIA in particular to the situation where they could not protect the United States from a terrorist attack. Identifying those policies and practices is fair game. If the organization does not know how it fell into the hole, it is unlikely to be able to crawl out. If the CIA does not learn from mistakes made before 9/11 and is not seen to be holding people accountable for what they did or did not do, it has no future.

Whomever the senior retired officials named in the report are, the CIA in fact has significant leverage over them. One can be reasonably sure that most of these senior officials have maintained their security clearances and are enjoying a second career consulting on homeland security and intelligence matters for major corporations involved with government contracts. Security clearances are like gold: with them, you are a highly paid consultant and "beltway bandit"; without them, you are just another retiree. Security clearances are not a right; they are completely discretionary. The DCIA can revoke security clearances for any reason or no reason, and he does not have to explain his actions. If the DCIA wishes to express how unhappy he is with how you did your job before you retired, this falls well within his authority. This is exactly what happened to former Director John Deutch.[14] One cannot appeal the DCIA's decision. One could sue, but federal case law is on the side of the DCIA.

The mid-level people who may be culpable for their behavior before 9/11 are now the senior people in charge of the counterterrorism effort. If there is another terrorist attempt on the United States, then the people who may have been culpable for 9/11 will be responsible for averting the new attack. Where I am from, allowing something like that to occur will get you hunted down by people with dogs.

If one believes that the process of holding people accountable might distract officials within the CIA, think how distracted they will be if an angry Congress abolishes the CIA and they have to start over from scratch building a new intelligence apparatus. For the CIA as an agency to put 9/11 behind it, everything needs to be made public that can be made public. Trying to stall this subject is going to lead to a disaster in short order.

Conclusion

This article endeavors to draw attention to some of the cultural artifacts at the CIA that have failed to change with the times. Whatever utility these practices may have had when they originated, they have become liabilities in the current environment. A unifying theme among them is that in each instance, there is a marked tendency on the part of senior levels of the CIA not to tolerate criticism, but instead to staunchly defend the status quo. In my experience, working-level Agency employees would welcome substantive change, not just meaningless reorganizations. Additionally, a distorted selection/promotion system has led the Agency to become top heavy with risk-averse "careerists."

Another event such as 9/11 or the Iraqi WMD fiasco could lead to the break-up of the CIA as it is currently known: the ice is that thin. That said, there are some great people working their hearts out at the CIA. With a modicum of enlightened leadership and support, there is nothing that is beyond their reach. The clock is ticking.

Notes

1 See also Richards Heuer, "Limits of Intelligence Analysis," and Peter R. Neumann and Michael L. R. Smith, "Missing the Plot? Intelligence and Discourse Failure," *Orbis*, Winter 2005.
2 *Sherman Kent and the Board of National Estimates: Collected Essays*, edited by Donald P. Steury, Center for the Study of Intelligence, 1994, p. 127.
3 Sherman Kent, *Strategic Intelligence for American World Policy*, Princeton University Press, 1949, pp. 170–73. Kent uses the term "middleman" for the RO function.

4 Steven R. Weisman, "Powell Calls His U.N. Speech A Lasting Blot on His Record," *New York Times*, Sept. 9, 2005, discusses the CIA's failure on the WMD issue.
5 Robert Johnston, Analytic Culture in the U.S. Intelligence Community: An Ethnographic Study, Center for the Study of Intelligence (Washington D.C.: Central Intelligence Agency, 2005).
6 See Burton Gerber, "Managing Humint: The Need for a New Approach," in Jennifer E. Sims and Burton Gerber, eds., *Transforming U.S. Intelligence* (Washington, D.C.: Georgetown University Press, 2005).
7 See Dan Baum, "Battle Lessons," *New Yorker*, Jan. 17, 2005, for the Army's mechanisms to share "lessons learned."
8 RUMINT, or rumor intelligence, is an informal term in common use within the intelligence community. It is the only form of human communication alleged to travel faster than the speed of light.
9 Michael Scheuer, *Imperial Hubris: Why the West is Losing the War on Terror* (Potomac Books, 2004).
10 Richard Holm, *The American Agent: My Life in the CIA* (St. Ermin Press, 2004). Three different components were conducting simultaneous investigations on the same set of facts. None of the investigating components interviewed the person in charge at the time of the alleged incident.
11 Katherine Shrader, "CIA Panel: 9/11 Failure Warrants Action," *Washington Post*, Aug. 26, 2005.
12 Katherine Shrader, "Lawmakers Ask CIA to Open Sept. 11 Report," *Las Vegas Sun*, Sept. 16, 2005; "DCIA's statement on the Inspector General's 9/11 report," Oct. 6, 2005, at www.cia.gov.
13 Irving Janis, *Groupthink: Psychological Studies of Policy Decisions and Fiascoes* (Boston: Houghton Mifflin, 1982), quoted in James Surowiecki, *The Wisdom of Crowds* (New York: Anchor Books, 2005), pp. 36–37.
14 "CIA suspends former Director's security clearances," CNN.com, Aug. 21, 1999; see also CIA Press Release on former Director John Deutch, Aug. 20, 1999, at www.cia.gov.

Reprinted with permission from Garrett Jones, 'It's a Cultural Thing: Thoughts on a Troubled CIA', *Orbis* 50/1 (2006) pp.25–41.

4 All glory is fleeting

SIGINT and the fight against international terrorism

Matthew Aid

Matthew Aid reviews the lessons learned from the performance of U.S. signals intelligence prior to 9/11. He argues for more clandestine or unconventional SIGINT collection activity and for the reduction of barriers between Humint agencies and SIGINT services. He also emphasises the need to improve analysis of the volume of communications traffic that is collected and to do this at higher speed. Finally he emphasises the importance of broader co-operation among national SIGINT agencies.

'The impact of terrorism is currently far more limited by the failure or unwillingness of terrorists to exploit new technologies and complex vulnerabilities than by the inherent difficulty in conducting much more lethal attacks. The problem is not a lack of credible means to an end, but rather the lack of a real-world Doctor No or Professor Moriarity.'

Anthony Cordesman

Despite more than five years having passed since the deadly terrorist attacks of September 11, 2001, it is still extremely difficult to objectively discuss the important role that Signals Intelligence (SIGINT) has played, and must necessarily continue to play, in the war against terrorism. Naturally, the single largest impediment to an educated discussion of the subject is the secrecy that surrounds virtually all aspects of contemporary SIGINT operations. The U.S. government and its partners have released virtually no primary documentation about the role played by intelligence in the events leading up to the bombings in New York City and Washington, D.C., and the congressional public hearings on the performance of the U.S. intelligence community prior to September 11th left much unsaid because of security considerations.

As such, much of the discussion in the American press and other public forums about the so-called 'intelligence failure of 9–11' have taken place in an information vacuum without the benefit of hard information other than what has been leaked to the press, and it is the author's opinion, based on discussions with U.S. intelligence officials, that the veracity of much that has been published must necessarily be viewed with scepticism. This chapter, therefore, seeks to set out what is known or can be authoritatively established about the role that SIGINT played in the events leading up to the terrorist attacks on September 11, 2001, especially the performance of America's SIGINT organization, the National Security Agency (NSA), and discuss what the potential future role of SIGINT in the war on terrorism on a going-forward basis.

SIGINT and the changing war on terrorism in the 1990s

In order to understand the role that SIGINT played in the war against international terrorism in the 1990s, and more specifically NSA's intelligence collection operations against Osama bin Laden and the al Qaeda organization, it is essential to understand the global context within which SIGINT had to operate in the early 1990s.

The Cold War, which had marked world politics for more than 40 years, came to an abrupt end with the dismantling of the Berlin Wall in 1989–1990, and the subsequent collapse of the Soviet Union in 1991. With the end of the Cold War, virtually all Western intelligence services, including virtually every agency comprising the U.S. intelligence community, were pared down to 'peacetime levels.' Between 1991 and 1998, Congressionally ordered budget cuts forced the U.S. intelligence community to reduce its size by 22.5%, meaning that more than 20,500 men and women lost their jobs, and the U.S. intelligence budget was slashed from about $34 billion to $27 billion. NSA, which was the single largest and most expensive component of the U.S. intelligence community, lost one-third of its staff between 1991 and 1996, and its budget was slashed by 35% from $5.2 billion to less than $3.5 billion.[1] We now know that these cuts, especially the loss of so many of the Agency's most talented managers, had a devastating impact on NSA's ability to perform its mission. According to a declassified congressional study: 'One of the side effects of NSA's downsizing, outsourcing and transformation has been the loss of critical program management expertise, systems engineering, and requirements definition skills.'[2]

NSA was not the only SIGINT service feeling the pinch. The British SIGINT organization, the Government Communications Headquarters (GCHQ), was also forced to pair down its operations and reorganize itself in the early 1990s in order to deal with the new geostrategic threats and changes in global telecommunications technology.[3] In 1992, GCHQ director Sir John Adye informed his staff that he had ordered a three-year study into a 'redirection of effort' for the agency, which led to the closure of a number of GCHQ stations, and GCHQ's civilian staff of 7,000 was cut by about 10%.[4] Another study completed in 1995 revealed that GCHQ was still over manned, inefficient and cost more than it was producing in the way of hard intelligence.[5] This study resulted in further substantial cuts in the size and budget of GCHQ. Between 1995 and 2000, GCHQ's staff was cut from 5,500 to only 4,600 civilian and military personnel.[6]

The intelligence struggle against international terrorism also changed dramatically with the end of the Cold War. In the fall of 1991, Yasser Arafat and the leadership of the Palestinian Liberation Organization (PLO) agreed to participate for the first time in political dialog with Israel. This dialog, which was brokered by the Norwegian government, led to the signing of the so-called Oslo Accord on the front lawn of the White House on September 13, 1993. With the creation in 1995 of an autonomous Palestinian governing entity, the Palestinian Authority, on the West Bank and the Gaza Strip, acts of international terrorism by Palestinian terrorists fell dramatically in the early 1990s. With the support of virtually all of the frontline Arab states, including Saudi Arabia, the PLO ceased its sponsorship of terrorist activities and recognized the State of Israel. The Oslo Accord also effectively emasculated the more radical Palestinian organizations who opposed reconciliation with Israel, such as those led by George Habash and Abu Nidal, who fell into disfavor with the countries which previously supported them. As a result, their terrorist activities came to an almost complete standstill as they lost their relevance on the international stage.

As a result of the dramatic decline in Middle Eastern terrorism, the size of the intelligence resources dedicated to monitoring worldwide terrorist activities by the U.S. and other Western intelligence agencies, especially in the area of SIGINT, fell precipitously in the first half of the 1990s as more pressing intelligence targets ate up a higher percentage of the available collection resources.[7] This did not mean, however, that terrorist activities completely disappeared, which meant that NSA and other Western SIGINT services continued to work the problem without respite, albeit with significantly fewer resources than before.[8]

Western intelligence services had to adapt and readjust the nature and extent of their collection activities to deal with the changing and more diffuse global terrorist threat. For example, NSA's counter-terrorist SIGINT mission in the early to mid-1990s was complicated by the wide geographic dispersion and disparate nature of the new terrorist targets that it was being asked to cover. There was the continued threat posed by state-sponsored terrorism, especially from Iran. For instance, SIGINT intercepts of Iranian government message traffic between Teheran and the Iranian embassies in Paris, France and Berne, Switzerland confirmed that Iranian secret agents operating from the Iranian embassy in Berne had murdered former Iranian prime minister Shahpour Bakhtiar on August 8, 1991 in Paris.[9] Muammar Quaddafi's Libyan regime was also still periodically active trying to eliminate his political opponents living outside of Libya. In 1993, SIGINT intercepts strongly indicated that Libyan intelligence may have been behind the disappearance of the prominent Libyan dissident Mansur Kikhia, who radio intercepts indicated was abducted from his residence in Cairo by Libyan intelligence operatives.[10] According to press reports, NSA SIGINT intercepts, together with HUMINT provided by the CIA station in Khartoum, led to the August 14, 1994 arrest in the Sudan of the Venezuelan-born terrorist Ilyich Ramirez Sanchez, better known as 'Carlos' or 'The Jackal', and his subsequent extradition to France to stand trial for murder. In 1997, 'Carlos' was sentenced to life imprisonment by a French court for the 1975 killing of two French security officers and a Lebanese national.[11]

Then NSA had to devote SIGINT collection resources to monitoring the activities of the new generation of smaller but more violent terrorist organizations, including the Iranian-backed Shi'ite organization Hezbollah (Party of God) based in Lebanon, the Egyptian group Islamic Jihad, the Palestinian terrorist organization Hamas, the Shining Path in Peru, Abu Saayef in the Philippines, and the tiny 50-man 'November 17' organization in Greece. Probably the most important terrorist target for the U.S. intelligence community, including NSA, during the early and mid-1990s was the Iranian-backed Shi'ite organization Hezbollah in Lebanon because of its previous attacks on American targets in Lebanon during the 1980s and its close ties to the Iranian government.[12] NSA SIGINT intercepts dating as far back as 1983 revealed that the Iranian ambassador in Damascus, Mohammed Mohtashami-Pur, managed and financed a significant portion of the terrorist activities of Hezbollah.[13] On June 17, 1987, an American journalist with ABC News named Charles Glass, the son of the Lebanese Defense Minister, Ali Osserian, and their Lebanese driver, were kidnaped by members of Hezbollah on the road between Sidon and Beirut in southern Lebanon. After pressure was brought to bear on the kidnappers by the Syrian government, the two Lebanese men were released, but Glass was not let go until two months later. According to press reports, GCHQ's listening post at Ayios Nikolaos on Cyprus intercepted the communications traffic between the Iranian ambassador in Damascus and the Iranian Foreign Ministry in Teheran as they debated what to do with Glass, strongly suggesting that the Iranian government was behind the kidnaping.[14] NSA and GCHQ were reportedly able to successfully listen to the tactical radio communications of Hezbollah forces in Lebanon because they sometimes used insecure walkie talkies to coordinate their operations against Israel from bases in southern Lebanon.[15] Intercepts of diplomatic communications traffic in July 1991 revealed that a number of Arab states were pressuring Hezbollah to release the remaining American and British hostages then being held by the organization in eastern Lebanon.[16] SIGINT intercepts reportedly implicated Hezbollah in the March 1992 bombing of the Israeli embassy in Buenos Aires, Argentina, which killed 29 people. The intercepts reportedly showed that Iranian officials had acquired the plastic explosives used by Hezbollah in the attack.[17]

The new generation of Palestinian terrorist organizations, such as Hamas, posed an entirely different set of problems for SIGINT in the 1990s, especially for the Israeli intelligence services. Arguably, no country has more experience with SIGINT monitoring of terrorist organizations than Israel. Over the past decade, Israel's national SIGINT organization, Unit 8200, has developed highly sophisticated techniques for monitoring Palestinian terrorist activities in the Gaza Strip and on the West Bank, using both conventional and unconventional SIGINT collection systems fuzed together with HUMINT. At the same time that the Oslo Accord was being signed in Washington in September 1993, Unit 8200, then commanded by Brigadier General Hanan Gefen, began secretly constructing a network of intercept sites adjacent to the West Bank and the Gaza Strip to spy on the soon-to-be-created Palestinian Authority.[18] Israeli intercepts of telephone transmissions led Israeli agents to Hamas' principal bomb maker, Yehia Ayyash, who was popularly known as 'The Engineer.' Ayyash was the mastermind behind seven terror bombings inside Israel during 1994 and 1995 that killed 55 Israelis. Using a combination of intelligence gathered by both SIGINT and HUMINT, the Israelis eventually caught up with Ayyash, tracking him down to a hideout in the Gaza Strip. The 29 year old Ayyash was killed in Gaza in January 1996 by an exploding cell phone planted on him by Israeli intelligence.[19] In 1996, at the height of the *Intifadah* in the Palestinian territories, Unit 8200 spent millions of dollars to build a network of special intercept antennas located within Israeli hilltop settlements throughout the West Bank to intercept cellular telephone calls coming from the Palestinian-controlled territories. Naturally, the cell phone numbers of key Palestinian Authority (PA) and terrorist suspects were monitored around-the-clock. Computers at Unit 8200's headquarters north of Tel Aviv scan the calls looking for key words of intelligence significance, as well as track the locations of the cell phones of PA officials.[20] In 1999, Palestinian Authority security officials discovered that the Israelis had planted miniature listening devices inside the cellular telephones used by Palestinian Authority officials, which enabled Israeli eavesdroppers to listen to everything the phone's owner said, even when the phone was switched off.[21]

During the wave of fighting between Israel and the Palestinian Authority in 2002, Israel used its electronic eavesdropping prowess to try and prevent terrorist attacks, as well as proactively attack key officials of the Palestinian Authority who they held responsible for the violence. Press reports indicate that Israeli SIGINT has for years intercepted all of the telephone calls, FAXes and e-mails coming in and out of Yasser Arafat's headquarters complex in Ramallah. According to Israeli intelligence officials cited in these reports, the intercepts reportedly prove that Arafat has financed the terrorist arm of his Fatah organization, the Al-Aqsa Martyr's Brigade, knowing that this unit would conduct terrorist attacks inside Israel.[22] Israeli newspapers have alleged that Israel has intercepted telephone calls from the PA Preventive Security Service chief in Gaza, Mohammed Dahlan, or his deputy, Rashid Abu-Shibak, where they reportedly ordered terrorist attacks on Israeli targets. The Israeli newspapers have alleged that the recordings were made by the CIA, although this would seem unlikely given the political sensibilities involved.[23] Palestinian Authority security officials quickly determined that the success of Israeli attacks on their leadership was due in large part to Unit 8200's ability to monitor their cell phone conversations. This led PA officials to ban the use of cell phones among their senior members on the

West Bank in the spring of 2002 during the height of the fighting between Palestinian and Israeli troops in and around Jenin.[24]

Countries other than the U.S. also extensively used SIGINT to combat terrorism in the 1990s. Historically, Britain's foreign intelligence service (MI-6) and security service (MI-5) have always devoted a greater percentage of their intelligence collection resources to countering the terrorist threat than Britain's SIGINT organization, the Government Communications Headquarters (GCHQ) because of the Irish Republican Army's minimal international presence. But beginning in the early 1990s, GCHQ began devoting a small but increasing amount of intercept and processing resources to monitoring international terrorist activities around the world, but relative to other targets, terrorism was certainly not one of GCHQ's priority targets.[25] A section within GCHQ's K Division produced a weekly Top Secret Codeword document called the 'Travel Digest,' which detailed the movements as reflected in SIGINT of individuals on watch lists prepared by MI-5, MI-6 and other law enforcement bodies in Britain, including international terrorists.[26]

NSA and the new international terrorists

Despite the marked decline in Palestinian and Middle Eastern state-sponsored terrorism in the 1990s, there were clear signs that a new and more dangerous actor in the terrorism arena was beginning to take form. On February 26, 1993, a powerful bomb hidden inside a rented truck blew up in the basement parking garage of the World Trade Center's North Tower in New York City, killing six people and injuring more than a thousand others. Unlike the terrorist attacks of the previous three decades, the World Trade Center bombing was carried out by a small group of Muslim extremists living in the U.S. led by Ramzi Ahmed Yousef, a 36-year old Pakistani national who had studied electronics and chemical engineering in England. What made this group unique is that they planned and executed the bombing without the benefit of any discernible support from a state sponsor or overseas parent organization other than ties to radical organizations based in the Pakistani city of Peshawar.[27]

Following the 1993 World Trade Center bombing, NSA and the rest of the U.S. intelligence community was ordered to increase the level of intelligence coverage of terrorism, with emphasis on the host of Muslim extremist organizations then known to be operating with impunity in Peshawar.[28] How much in the way of additional SIGINT collection and processing resources NSA dedicated to this new target cannot be definitively determined, but a former senior NSA official indicated that the SIGINT collection and processing resources dedicated to the terrorist problem by the Agency at the time were relatively modest when compared with the substantially larger collection resources being devoted to higher-priority transnational intelligence targets, such as trying to stem the flow of illegal narcotics from Latin America and countering the proliferation of weapons of mass destruction around the world.[29]

By all accounts, NSA and its partners reacted slowly to the changing terrorist threat. Part of the reason that NSA experienced difficulty focusing on terrorist activities at the time was that the Agency was experiencing considerable internal turmoil. Thousands of NSA's employees were in the process of either retiring early or being let go as part of the previously mentioned 'reduction in force' of the Agency. Among the casualties were many of NSA's most experienced senior managers, analysts and technical personnel, including a number of key analysts who had specialized in international terrorism.[30] As part of an effort to reduce duplication of effort and improve the efficiency of the Agency's global SIGINT effort, in February 1992

NSA drastically reorganized its Operations Directorate (DDO), which managed the Agency's worldwide SIGINT collection, processing, analysis and reporting activities. The Directorate's largest component, A Group, which previously had covered the Soviet Union and the Communist states of Eastern Europe, was reorganized and reoriented towards intelligence gathering on Europe as a whole. B Group, which intercepted the communications of Asian communist nations absorbed G Group, which had handled the rest of the world, including terrorism. From the merger came a new organizational entity called B Group, which essentially was tasked with intelligence coverage of the world except for Europe and Central Asia, including international terrorism. A new G Group was created, which was designated as the Collection Operations Group and assigned the mission of managing NSA's worldwide SIGINT collection operations. Finally, a new group, the Cryptanalysis Group (Z Group), was created to centralize NSA's codebreaking activities under one roof.[31]

The emergence of al-Qaeda as a threat

Despite the slightly greater effort being devoted to monitoring terrorist activities in the mid-1990s, it was to take several years before Osama bin Laden and al Qaeda was to resonate loudly within the U.S. intelligence community. According to former U.S. intelligence officials, Osama bin Laden did not become a viable target entity as far as the U.S. intelligence community was concerned until sometime in 1994, when intelligence reports began to circulate indicating that bin Laden's organization, al Qaeda (which in Arabic means 'The Base'), was providing financial support to a number of Muslim extremist organizations in the Middle East and elsewhere around the world.[32]

Unfortunately, getting timely and accurate intelligence information about bin Laden's activities proved to be an extremely difficult proposition for the U.S. intelligence community, with a recent U.S. congressional report admitting that al Qaeda 'proved an exceptionally difficult target for U.S. intelligence.'[33]

In general, spying on terrorist organizations historically has always has been an extremely difficult proposition. Ron Bonighton, a senior Australian intelligence official told reporters in December 2004: 'Let me say that in the 37 years I have worked in the intelligence business this is the toughest target I have come across.'[34] A 1997 study by the U.S. Defense Department's Defense Science Board stated that 'Because of the very high security consciousness of transnational groups, there is generally insufficient, verifiable information available about transnational adversary operations, membership, and other important details. Moreover, these groups often come from countries in which the United States has no human intelligence capabilities.'[35]

SIGINT collection against al Qaeda was a particularly difficult task given the unorthodox nature of the organization. First, al Qaeda is, from an organizational standpoint, a much different actor than the Palestinian and Lebanese-based terrorist organizations that U.S. intelligence and its partners had previously spied on. Unlike the rigidly organized and bureaucratic Palestinian terrorist organizations of the 20th Century, all of whom were state-sponsored to one degree or another, al Qaeda was a truly transnational phenomena in that it was not dependent on support from state sponsors. With a reported net worth of about $250 million, Osama bin Laden did not have to depend on the largesse of state sponsors for his survival or ability conduct terrorist operations.[36] Vincent Cannistraro, the former head of the CIA's Counterterrorism Center, went so far as to describe al Qaeda in an interview as representing 'the privatization of international terrorism.'[37]

Second, al Qaeda has depended on unconventional sources of financing over the last decade to fund its worldwide operations. There is no question that bin Laden has dug deep into his own personal fortune over the last ten years to finance al Qaeda. But available information suggests that bin Laden has largely gone through his personal inheritance over the last ten years, and today his personal net worth is nowhere near the $250 million that has been reported previously in the press.[38] Prior to September 11, 2001, evidence suggests that al Qaeda depended on a combination of extortion and voluntary donations from wealthy Arab businessmen for most of their financing. The unconventional nature of al Qaeda's financial operations made it an extremely difficult organization to monitor since it is not dependent on conventional bank accounts and wire transfers as previous state-sponsored terrorist organizations were.[39]

Third, al Qaeda has remained since its inception a relatively small, loosely-knit confederation of a number of Islamic fundamentalist terrorist organizations from all over North Africa, the Middle East, the former Soviet Union, and Asia, with Osama bin Laden acting as the organization's nominal titular head or 'Sheik.' More properly stated, al Qaeda is 'a network of networks of networks, in which terrorists from various organizations and cells pool their resources and share their expertise. This loose and amorphous confederation of disparate organizations did not have the clear lines of communication or a centralized command structure, such as that provided by an army general or a corporate chief executive officer. The network is, instead, a "combination of convenience," with groups joining or departing, depending on their interests and the needs of their particular operations,' with bin Laden acting as a facilitator, financier and source of training and logistical support for these organizations.[40] The unstructured nature of al Qaeda made SIGINT collection against it extremely difficult since, as two intelligence scholars have correctly observed: 'The problem with clandestine organizations is that, unlike governments or conventional military [forces], they very rarely have an organized operational communications network.'[41]

Fourth, from a Human Intelligence (HUMINT) perspective, trying to penetrate the al Qaeda organization was, and remains a difficult proposition given its unusual internal makeup. Al Qaeda is a religious, non-political organization which views the U.S. and its friends and allies as intractable and implacable foes. As such, its members tend to be fervent followers of the politico-religious dogma espoused by bin Laden despite their relative lack of higher education and intellectual sophistication. Traditional espionage recruiting lures for potential agents, such as financial inducements and sexual favors, generally do not work with Muslim fundamentalists, who comprise the vast majority of al Qaeda. As demonstrated by the behavior of al Qaeda prisoners being held at the U.S. naval base at Guantanamo Bay, Cuba, interrogators have learned the hard lesson that the fanatical disposition of al Qaeda members has meant that it is near impossible to 'turn' these individuals into American spies, much less get useful and reliable intelligence information from them. A natural predisposition to distrust outsiders has also made it extremely difficult to penetrate al Qaeda with agents from the outside.[42]

And fifth, compartmentalization of information within the organization meant that even if agents were successfully planted inside al Qaeda, the likelihood that they would be able to produce high-level intelligence information was very low unless the source held a very high-ranking post within the organization who was also close to bin Laden.[43] A recently released congressional report confirmed, based on a review of available classified intelligence information, that only a select few individuals within the upper echelons of al Qaeda knew the details of the organization's terrorist operations.[44] For example, it would appear based on videotaped admissions by Osama bin Laden himself that the al Qaeda operatives who participated in the September 11, 2001 terrorist attacks in the U.S. did not know what their target was until just before they boarded their aircraft. In a November 2001 videotape captured by U.S. forces in Afghanistan and released to the public on December 13, 2001, bin Laden told his associates: 'The brothers who conducted the operation, all they knew was that they have a martyrdom operation and we asked each of them to go to America, but they didn't know anything about the operation, not even one letter. But they were trained and we did not reveal the operation to them until they are there and just before they boarded the planes.'[45]

SIGINT and al Qaeda

For reasons explained in greater detail by other papers in this volume, but in large part due a combination of the factors cited above, the documentation available to date strongly suggests that the CIA's clandestine service was unable to to penetrate al Qaeda. The inherent difficulty of spying on an organization such as al Qaeda was compounded by the fact that the CIA failed to mount an agressive effort to infiltrate bin Laden's organization in Afghanistan prior to the September 11, 2001 bombings. The almost complete absence of American HUMINT sources within al Qaeda, recently declassified studies have determined, left the U.S. intelligence community largely blind as to bin Laden and his lieutenants' intentions prior to 9–11. The absence of HUMINT sources also left the U.S. intelligence community largely dependent on information of varying reliability received from foreign intelligence services and SIGINT in the period prior to 9–11.[46] Because of the historic tendency on the part of American intelligence analysts to be skeptical of the reliability of intelligence reporting from foreign intelligence services, by the mid-1990s SIGINT had become by far the most important source of intelligence about bin Laden and al Qaeda within the U.S. intelligence community.[47]

Much of NSA's SIGINT emphasis on bin Laden during the early 1990s was directed at trying to trace the sources of al Qaeda's finances, since bin Laden was widely suspected by the U.S. intelligence community at the time of being nothing more than a financier of international terrorist activities.[48] The thinking inside the U.S. intelligence community at the time was that NSA was well suited to perform this task because of the Agency's success in the 1980s tracking terrorist finances. In 1981, NSA began intercepting financial data transmissions concerning money transfers that were being carried by three large international wire transfer clearinghouses: the Clearing House Interbank Payments Systems (CHIPS), which was a worldwide computer network run from New York City that was used by 139 member banks in 35 countries to transfer money in U.S. Dollars from one bank to another; the CHAPs network based in London, which handled wire transfers paid in the British Pound Sterling; and the SIC financial network in Basel, Switzerland, which handled wire transfers that were based on the Swiss Franc.[49]

By monitoring these international banking clearinghouses, NSA was able to develop much useful intelligence during the 1980s concerning terrorist activities, as well as information about the financing of illegal drug trafficking, money laundering, illegal technology transfer to Soviet Bloc countries, nuclear proliferation, and international debt issues in the Third World.[50]

For example, according to Dr. Norman Bailey, the Special Assistant for National Security Planning in the National Security Council from 1981 to 1983, after the La Belle Disco bombing in West Berlin on April 5, 1986, NSA analysts reviewed thousands of intercepted money wire transfers carried by the three banking clearinghouses and discovered that the Libyan government was financing Palestinian and other international terrorist organizations.

The intercepted wire transfers revealed that in 1985, the Libyan government had wired $60 million to bank accounts controlled by a number of international terrorist and guerrilla organizations, including $20 million apiece to the Red Brigades in West Germany, the Irish Republican Army (IRA), and the M-16 guerrilla organization in Columbia.[51]

According to Western intelligence analysts, from an intelligence standpoint al Qaeda's weakness has always been its finances, which could be tracked, albeit with difficulty, by monitoring the electronic movement of bin Laden's money around the world.[52] As early as 1994, NSA intercepts began to indicate that bin Laden was involved in financing a broad range of terrorist activities around the world. For example, SIGINT intercepts in the mid-1990s revealed that a number of wealthy Saudi Arabian businessmen were directly involved in financing terrorist operations, such as al Qaeda and Muslim insurgents in the southern Philippines. Among the intelligence collected were electronic wire transfers moving large sums of money from bank accounts in Europe to the Philippines.[53] In December 1995, the British were able to track electronic wire transfers from the bank accounts of a number of bin Laden companies in Khartoum to a London-based cell of a fundamentalist Muslim terrorist organization called the Algerian Armed Islamic Group (GIA).[54] According to a October 2001 news account, NSA SIGINT intercepts revealed that beginning in 1996, the Saudi Arabian government secretly began sending large sums of money to al Qaeda, reportedly to ensure that bin Laden kept his terrorist activities out of Saudi Arabia.[55] All of these intelligence reports were based on intercepts of electronic wire transfers from bank accounts in the Middle East and South Asia known to be controlled by bin Laden or his operatives.[56]

It would appear that NSA and its partners focused their efforts on monitoring bin Laden's telephone traffic being carried by the Umm Haraz satellite ground station outside the Sudanese capital of Khartoum, which handled all international telephone traffic coming in and out of the Sudan being relayed by Intelsat or Arabsat communications satellites in orbit over the Indian Ocean. Beginning in 1995, NSA analysts identified a series of telephone numbers belonging to telephones that were used by Osama bin Laden or his key lieutenants. By monitoring these telephone numbers around-the-clock, especially calls coming in and out of bin Laden's office at his ranch outside Khartoum, NSA analysts began to slowly derive some very useful intelligence information about bin Laden and the activities of his fledgling al Qaeda organization.[57]

Despite these successes, it would appear that NSA was experiencing considerable difficulty monitoring bin Laden. A July 1, 1996 CIA report lamented that 'We have no unilateral sources close to bin Laden, nor any reliable way of intercepting his communications . . . We must rely on foreign intelligence services to confirm his movements and activities.'[58]

As noted above, spying on terrorist organizations is inherently difficult, and the same holds true for SIGINT. Testifying before Congress in 2002, NSA Director General Michael Hayden admitted that 'cracking into these targets is hard – very hard – and SIGINT operations require considerable patience – sometimes over years – before they mature.'[59] Interviews with former U.S. intelligence officials suggests that the difficulties that NSA was experiencing in the mid-1990s trying to monitor bin Laden's communications was due to a combination of technical factors. The first of these was the fact that al Qaeda operatives only sporadically spoke about operational matters over the phone, and even then they used word codes or phrases which NSA linguists and analysts found difficult to understand much less interpret. NSA's SIGINT collectors also had a difficult time trying to identify the telephone lines that bin Laden and his chief lieutenants were using to communicate with each other on operational matters other than the phone at bin Laden's ranch outside

Khartoum. Intensive efforts were made to search the telecommunications spectrum looking for other communications links being used by al Qaeda members, but with little success. Despite not using encryption to protect its communications, al Qaeda utilized a crude but effective communications security procedure of rarely using the same communications mean twice. A former intelligence analyst recalled being exhilarated after identifying a particular telephone number being used by an al Qaeda operative in Southwest Asia, only to be disappointed when it was not used again. The analyst recalled going home one night and being confronted by his teenage daughter, who was distraught because her boyfriend had not called her. All he could tell her was that he knew exactly what she was going through, but couldn't tell her why.[60]

The fallacy of high-tech terrorism

But in 1996, Osama bin Laden was forced out of the Sudan by the Sudanese government, moving his base of operations to Afghanistan, where he was protected by the fundamentalist Taliban regime. Former U.S. intelligence officials confirm that bin Laden's move to Afghanistan turned out to be a godsend from an intelligence point of view, since it made SIGINT coverage of his activities significantly easier than it had been when he was living in the Sudan.[61]

Afghanistan, which was Osama bin Laden's principal base of operations between 1996 and 2001, was a particularly difficult environment for American HUMINT collectors to operate in. Afghanistan was a closed society controlled by a fundamentalist regime that did not brook dissent of any kind, with public execution being a typical punishment for even the slightest infraction of the Taliban regime's numerous strictures. The U.S. government had no embassy in Kabul, and therefore no on-the-ground intelligence presence inside Afghanistan throughout the 1990s. This forced the CIA to depend on the generosity of neighboring Pakistan and its intelligence service, the Inter-Service Intelligence (ISI), for much of the HUMINT intelligence available to the U.S. intelligence community, whose reliability was fair at best given ISI's deep ties to the Taliban regime in Kabul. It should therefore come as no surprise that a 1996 American congressional study recognized that insofar as intelligence coverage of so-called 'rogue states' was concerned, and Afghanistan qualified as such, HUMINT 'played a secondary role to SIGINT' as the primary source of intelligence information for American intelligence analysts.[62]

A detailed review of available information clearly demonstrates that despite its very public operational accomplishments over the last decade, al Qaeda was nowhere near as professional, disciplined or as sophisticated as the Palestinian terrorist organizations of the 1960s, 1970s and 1980s, or even the secretive Hezbollah in Lebanon and Hamas in Gaza and the West Bank. Unlike their Palestinian counterparts, many of whom received advanced training in intelligence and security procedures in East Germany and the Soviet Union during the Cold War, most of al Qaeda's senior officials and operatives have had little if any prior professional training or experience. As such, Western intelligence analysts found that many of the operational procedures and tactics employed by al Qaeda bordered on the amateurish, such as the abysmally poor communications security discipline exhibited by the organization's members throughout the 1990s.[63]

The public record shows that over the last decade bin Laden and his operatives broke virtually every basic tenant of good spying tradecraft, the most important commandment of which was and remains never to speak about one's operations using communications means that can be intercepted. As will be demonstrated below, this cardinal rule, which is beaten into every junior intelligence officer around the world in the first week of their beginners training course, was repeatedly violated by bin Laden and his operatives throughout much of the 1990s. Not surprisingly, NSA and its partners quickly discovered this chink in bin Laden's armor and exploited it to best advantage over a period of many years prior to September 11, 2001. British author Philip H.J. Davies has written that during an 'off-the-record' February 1996 briefing given to British academics by a senior British intelligence officer, a question was asked as to whether SIGINT had declined in importance in the years since the end of the Cold War. The intelligence officer stated that exactly the opposite was true, adding that 'If anything it is even more important. More terrorists and drug barons are using cellular phones and satellites to talk to each other than ever before.'[64]

It took years of mind-numbing research to identify phone numbers used by bin Laden's operatives, but once identified American SIGINT analysts found that al Qaeda operatives in Europe and elsewhere tended to talk ceaselessly on their phones, sometimes referring to pending operations and even identifying fellow operatives. One of the fallacies that writers and commentators in the West have latched on to since the attacks of September 11, 2001 is the concept that Osama bin Laden and al Qaeda were significant users of high technology, including encryption and high-tech telecommunications technology. Some pundits have even suggested that al Qaeda used extremely advanced technology such as steganography (hiding textual information in pictures) in order to convey orders to operatives around the world. It turns out that nothing could be further from the truth. Instead, al Qaeda operatives used simple word codes or disguised their meaning using 'flowery language' when referring to their operations on the telephone.[65] When captured in Karachi in September 2002, Ramzi Binalshibh, allegedly one of the planners of the September 11, 2001 terrorist attacks, had in his possession a laptop computer containing reams of valuable information about al Qaeda activities, none of which he had apparently bothered to encrypt.[66]

One does not have to dig very deep to discern that the telecommunications options available to Osama bin Laden and his operatives in Afghanistan prior to the U.S.-led invasion in late 2001 were few and far between. One could make the argument that if one was to choose a place best suited from which to run a global terrorist network, Afghanistan would probably rate near the bottom of available choices. The impoverished state of the country and the backwardness of the Taliban regime which ruled it meant that the country had virtually no telecommunications infrastructure. As of late 2001, conventional landline telephone service in Afghanistan was practically nonexistent except in a small number of government offices in Kabul. Most of the Soviet-made telecommunications equipment installed during the 1980s had been allowed to fall into disrepair during the civil strife in Afghanistan during the 1990s. According to data compiled by the United Nations, Afghanistan had only 29,000 telephones in the entire country, which equates to 0.14 phones per every inhabitant of the country (22 million inhabitants in 1999), almost all of which were located in the cities of Kabul and Kandahar. This placed Afghanistan near dead last in the UN rankings, with Afghanistan possessing fewer telephones per capita then even impoverished Bangladesh. It should therefore come as no surprise that there were virtually no FAX machines in Afghanistan, no fibre-optic cable telecommunications lines, nor was there any cellular telephone service whatsoever prior to the U.S.-led invasion.[67] Moreover, in July 2001 the Taliban regime declared the Internet 'unholy' and banned its use throughout Afghanistan because it carried 'obscenity, vulgarity and anti-Islamic content.' Even Afghan government departments were banned from using the Internet. It should be noted that there was practically no Internet usage in Afghanistan prior to the ban because of an almost total lack of computers in the country. This meant, of course, that e-mail connections in and out of Afghanistan were non-existent prior to September 2001.[68]

Without these tools, people living in Afghanistan were forced to use satellite telephones to communicate with the outside world, including al Qaeda members, who were among the few people in impoverished Afghanistan who could afford these relatively expensive tele-communications systems. Naturally, this led NSA to monitor virtually all satellite phone calls coming in and out of Afghanistan beginning in the mid-1990s.[69]

In November 1996, one of bin Laden's operatives living in the U.S. named Ziyad Khalil, purchased a *Inmarsat Compact M* satellite telephone and more than 3,000 hours of prepaid satellite time from a company in Deer Park, New York for $7,500.[70] The sat-phone worked by bouncing phone calls off an Inmarsat communications satellite parked in orbit over the Indian Ocean. The sat-phone was assigned the international telephone number 00873 682 505 331.[71] Khalil purchased the telephone and satellite time using the credit card of Dr. Saad al-Fagih, a 45-year old Saudi-born surgeon who headed the Movement for Islamic Reform in Arabia, which is headquartered in London. This satellite phone was shipped to another bin Laden sympathizer living in Herndon, Virginia named Tariq Hamdi, who sent the set to Dr. al-Fagih in England. Al-Fagih arranged for the satellite phone to be transported to bin Laden in Afghanistan.[72] For two years, this satellite phone was the primary means of communications for Osama bin Laden and his military operations chief, Mohammed Atef, who used it to keep in touch with their operatives and sympathizers around the world.[73]

Former NSA officers recall that many of the bin Laden telephone intercepts were, at best, banal and of relatively low intelligence value. For instance, many of the calls to and from bin Laden's satellite phone dealt with repeated attempts by the publicity-driven exiled Saudi financier to generate favorable press coverage of al Qaeda from influential Arabic-language newspapers and television broadcast networks in England and Yemen.[74] But other intercepts helped foil a number of bin Laden terrorist plots around the world. In 1997, information in part developed from NSA communications intercepts allowed the CIA to disrupt two terrorist attacks on American embassies overseas, as well as foil three terrorist plots that were in the initial stages of planning.[75] In 1998 SIGINT was credited with helping foil seven potential attacks by al Qaeda terrorists on American diplomatic or military establishments overseas, including a planned terrorist attack on American forces stationed at Prince Sultan Air Base in Saudi Arabia.[76] Also in 1998, intelligence obtained from SIGINT as well as human sources allowed the CIA to prevent the hijacking of an American airliner.[77] In August 1998, the U.S. intercepted a number of telephone conversations between Osama bin Laden in Afghanistan and a number of his senior operatives around the world as they plotted a series of terrorist attacks against American targets.[78]

Access to these highly sensitive intercepts was a fierce bone of contention between NSA and the CIA. According to Michael Scheuer, then the head of the CIA's 'Bin Laden Station' at CIA headquarters, in December 1996 a CIA officer seconded to an NSA overseas station learned about the existence of the bin Laden sat phone calls, which apparently NSA was not yet fully exploiting. According to Scheuer, NSA '. . . refused to exploit the conduit and threatened legal action against the Agency officer who advised of its existence.' After a series of conferences failed to yield a satisfactory solution, the CIA mounted its own independent SIGINT collection operation to intercept and exploit the bin Laden sat phone calls. In the end, the CIA managed to intercept half of the sat phone traffic, and NSA succeeded in getting the rest, but refused to share its take with the CIA.[79]

In August 1998, NSA intercepted messages among bin Laden operatives which confirmed that al Qaeda was directly involved in the bombings of the American embassies in Nairobi, Kenya and Dar es Salaam, Tanzania on August 7, 1998, which killed 224 people (12 of whom were Americans) and injured thousands more. One intercepted conversation among a number of bin Laden operatives in Africa, which took place just before the bombings, caught one of the operatives saying that 'something bad was going to happen' and that the operatives were 'going to get out of the area.' After the attack, NSA intercepted another conversation among bin Laden officials, wherein one angry operative stated that the attack had killed too many Kenyans and Tanzanians, and not enough Americans. Another intercept revealed that bin Laden and a number of his senior commanders were to have a meeting at a training camp outside the town of Khost in southeastern Afghanistan on August 20, 1998.[80]

U.S. retaliation for the attacks was not long in coming. On August 20, 1998, the al Qaeda Kili al-Badr training camp at Khost and five other facilities in eastern Afghanistan were leveled by 66 Tomahawk cruise missiles fired by U.S. Navy warships operating in the Arabian Sea. A few hours earlier, NSA had intercepted a satellite phone call made by bin Laden from the Kili al-Badr camp, which helped determine the target for the retaliatory strike (Clinton Administration officials later denied that bin Laden was the target of the attack). Bin Laden survived the attack unscathed. Another 13 cruise missiles fired by U.S. Navy warships cruising in the Red Sea destroyed the El Shifa pharmaceutical plant outside of the Sudanese capital of Khartoum, which a soil sample obtained by a CIA operative reportedly indicated was manufacturing precursor chemicals for VX nerve gas. A postmortem examination of intelligence information showed, however, that the plant was making nothing more harmful than a generic form of the drug ibuprofen for headaches.[81]

After news reports in August 1998 revealed that NSA and its partners were listening to his phone conversations, bin Laden reportedly ceased using his satellite telephone to communicate with his subordinates and sympathizers outside of Afghanistan, although he may not have completely ceased using his sat phone until February 1999.[82] According to Indian government intelligence reports, after the fall of 1998 bin Laden conveyed his orders to his operatives around the world by sending operatives across the border to Peshawar, Pakistan, where they used public telephones at hotels and other commercial establishments in the city to transmit bin Laden's orders to his operatives around the world.[83] Bin Laden finally was forced to realize that the mounting toll of failed or blown operations were caused by his own poor operational security practices and those of his senior lieutenants.[84]

The days of wine and roses

In his October 2002 testimony before Congress, NSA Director General Michael Hayden cryptically stated: 'You are also well aware that the nation's SIGINT effort has successfully thwarted numerous terrorist attacks in the past. While our successes are generally invisible to the American people, *everyone* knows when an adversary succeeds. NSA *has had* many successes, but these are even *more* difficult to discuss in open session.'[85] What General Hayden was referring was the fact that while Osama bin Laden may have ceased using his satellite telephone shortly after the 1998 East Africa bombings, evidence shows that his lieutenants and operatives around the world did not follow his example, and continued talking openly about their activities on satellite and cellular phones and other telecommunications means. As a result of these operations, between 1998 and September 2001, 'some notable successes' were achieved against al Qaeda, including the thwarting of planned attacks on American targets in the U.S., Europe and the Middle East.[86]

Part of the reason for the improvement in results coming out of NSA was a reorganization of NSA's management structure. In 1997, responsibility for managing and coordinating NSA's global SIGINT efforts against international terrorism was moved to a newly created operations analysis organization called the Global Issues and Weapons Systems Group, or W Group, then headed by Michael S. Green. W Group was responsible for SIGINT collection on a host of transnational issues, including international terrorism, as well as counterintelligence issues, international drug trafficking, international organized crime, and illegal alien smuggling communications traffic.[87] A unit within W Group, designated W9B, was the NSA Terrorism Customer Service Center, which served as the primary interface between NSA's collectors and analysts and the Agency's intelligence consumers.[88] Concurrent with these organizational changes, NSA dedicated more SIGINT intercept and processing resources to monitoring al-Qaeda activities following the August 1998 East African bombings.[89]

One of the SIGINT sources that proved to be of high intelligence value for NSA were intercepts of calls to a telephone number in Yemen that belonged to an al Qaeda operative named Ahmed al-Hada.[90] U.S. intelligence had identified this number after interrogating one of the captured planners of the August 1998 East Africa bombings, Muhammed Rashed Daoud al-Owhali. SIGINT coverage of al-Hada's telephone calls began in the fall of 1998. Intercepts of calls coming in and out of al-Hada's home in Sana'a revealed that he acted as an information clearing house, relaying messages between bin Laden and his lieutenants in Afghanistan and al Qaeda operatives around the world. Al-Hada's home was also used to plan terrorist operations, including the October 2000 attack on the destroyer USS Cole, as well as serve as an al Qaeda logistics center.[91]

Also in 1999, a team of CIA operatives working for the Special Collection Service (SCS), the joint CIA-NSA clandestine SIGINT collection unit, slipped into southeastern Afghanistan to emplace a remote-controlled SIGINT collection system near a series of al Qaeda camps near the town of Khost.[92]

According to publicly-available information, these and other SIGINT sources generated reams of actionable intelligence during the years 1999 and 2000. In early 1999 the British intercepted telephone calls from a senior Osama Bin Laden operative named Said Mokhles to cohorts in Britain, indicating that Bin Laden's terrorist organization was examining the possibility of attacking the British embassy in Brussels, Belgium.[93] In June 1999, the U.S. State Department temporarily closed six American embassies in Africa after intelligence reports, including COMINT intercepts, revealed the bin Laden operatives were in the final stages of preparing an attack on an American diplomatic target in Africa. The intercepts of conversations by bin Laden operatives revealed that bomb-making materials had been transported to Africa for the attack.[94] By early July 1999, intercepted al Qaeda communications traffic revealed that bin Laden operatives were preparing another operation, this time in Western Europe. Other intercepts reportedly showed that Saudi billionaire Sheikh Khalid bin Mahfouz, owner of the National Commercial Bank, and the Dubai Islamic Bank were hiding and moving bin Laden's money.[95] In mid-July 1999, communications intercepts indicated that bin Laden was planning to hit a major American 'target of opportunity' in Albania. As a result, planned trips to Albania by Secretary of State Madeleine Albright and Secretary of Defense William Cohen were hastily canceled.[96]

In late 1999, NSA intercepted telephone calls to al-Hada's home in Yemen (described in the 9/11 Commission's final report as a 'suspected terrorist facility in the Middle East'), which revealed that an 'operational cadre' of al Qaeda operatives intended to travel to Kuala Lumpur, Malaysia in January 2000. The call identified only the first names of the 'cadre' as 'Nawaf,' 'Salem' and 'Khalid.' Based on the context and wording of the conversation, NSA analysts concluded that 'Salem' was most likely the younger brother of 'Nawaf', which as it turned out, was correct. 'Salem' was Salem al Hazmi, the younger brother of Nawaf al Hazmi. A CIA analyst who reviewed the transcript and accompanying NSA report surmised that: 'Something more nefarious [was] afoot' given the link not only with al Qaeda, but with a target known to have been involved in the 1998 East Africa bombings.[97]

Despite the successes of the previous two years, it was only a matter of time before al Qaeda finally succeeded. On October 12, 2000, al Qaeda suicide bombers attacked the U.S. Navy destroyer USS Cole as it lay at anchor in the port of Aden, Yemen. Seventeen sailors were killed in the blast and another 39 wounded. On the same day that the attack on the USS Cole occurred, NSA issued an intelligence report based on COMINT intercepts (the intercepts were most likely calls coming in and out of Ahmed al-Hada's home in Yemen) warning that terrorists were planning an attack in the region. However, the NSA warning message was not received by consumers until well after the attack had taken place.[98]

SIGINT and the September 11, 2001 terrorist attacks

We now know that in the year prior to the September 11, 2001 bombings, NSA did intercept an increasing volume of al Qaeda messages which indicated that Osama bin Laden was planning a major operation against American targets. Most U.S. intelligence analysts concluded that the threat was primarily to U.S. military or diplomatic installations overseas, particularly in the Middle East and Persian Gulf. In late 2000, NSA intercepted a message, wherein an al Qaeda operative reportedly boasted over the phone that bin Laden was planning to carry out a 'Hiroshima' against the U.S.[99] Beginning in May and continuing through early July 2001, NSA intercepted at least 33 messages indicating that al Qaeda intended to conduct in the near-term future one or more terrorist operations against U.S. targets.[100] In some of the intercepted message traffic, bin Laden operatives reportedly referred to an upcoming operation using a series of codewords and double talk to disguise what they were talking about, but no specifics of the operation were revealed in the messages. But the intercepts did reveal increased activity levels, including the movement of key al Qaeda operatives.[101]

During the summer of 2001, the volume of NSA intercepts of al Qaeda communications traffic continued to surge, with the nature of threats implied in these intercepts suggesting that an operation against one or more American targets was imminent, although no specifics as to date, time and place of the threatened attacks was reportedly ever given. But some of these intercepts were so threatening that they forced the U.S. government to take drastic measures to protect American personnel stationed overseas. In June 2001, SIGINT intercepts led to the arrest of two bin Laden operatives in the Middle East who were planning to attack U.S. military installations in Saudi Arabia. At about the same time, another al Qaeda agent was captured with the help of SIGINT, who was planning an attack on U.S. diplomatic facilities in Paris.[102] On June 22, 2001, U.S. military forces in the Persian Gulf were placed on alert after NSA intercepted a conversation between two al Qaeda operatives in the region which indicated that 'a major attack was imminent,' although no specifics as to the date, time or place of the attack were given in the intercept. But as a result, all U.S. forces in the Middle East were placed on the highest state of alert, a military exercise in Jordan was cut short, and all U.S. Navy ships docked in Bahrain, homeport of the U.S. Fifth Fleet, were ordered to put to sea immediately.[103] In July 2001, advanced warning provided by SIGINT intercepts allowed American and allied intelligence services to disrupt planned al Qaeda terrorist attacks in Paris, Rome and Istanbul.[104] In August 2001, either NSA or GCHQ reportedly intercepted a telephone call from one of bin Laden's chief lieutenants, Abu Zubaida, to an al Qaeda associate believed to be in Pakistan. According to press reports, the conversation centered on an operation that was to take place in September, as well as the possible ramifications stemming from the operation. About the same time, bin Laden telephoned another associate inside Afghanistan and discussed the upcoming operation. Bin Laden reportedly praised the other party to the conversation for his role in planning the operation. For some reason, the intercepts were reportedly never forwarded to intelligence consumers, although this contention is strongly denied by NSA officials.[105] Just prior to the September 11, 2001 bombings, several European intelligence services reportedly intercepted a telephone call that Osama bin Laden made to his wife who was living in Syria, asking her to return to Afghanistan immediately.[106]

Finally, on September 10, 2001, the day before the U.S. attacks too place, either NSA or GCHQ intercepted two messages involving a telephone number in Afghanistan known to be used by senior al Qaeda officials. Buried within the intercept transcripts were hints which, although extremely vague, indicated that an al Qaeda terrorist attack was going to occur in the immediate future. In the middle of the first conversation one of the speakers reportedly said that 'The big match is about to begin.' In the second intercept, another unknown speaker was overhead saying that 'Tomorrow was "zero hour."' NSA translated the messages on September 12, 2001, the day after the terrorist attacks in New York City and Washington, D.C. took place.[107] According to a congressional report, "These intercepts did not provide any indication of where, when or what activities might occur. Taken in their entirety, it is unclear whether they were referring to the September 11 attacks."[108]

Evaluation of NSA's counterterrorist intelligence activities

Given what we know now, what judgements can one make about NSA's performance in the war against terrorism prior to the attacks of September 11, 2001? As will be shown below, SIGINT's performance against international terrorism in the 1990s can only be described as mixed.

NSA and the 9–11 attacks

In the more than five years since the terrorist bombings of September 11, 2001, government officials, legislators and pundits around the world have tried to determine if the bombings could have been prevented by better intelligence work. The preliminary conclusion to be drawn from the information available to date appears to be that the U.S. intelligence community did not possess any information which individually, or taken together, would have given any warning as to the timing, location or nature of the September 11 attacks. In short, the U.S. intelligence community apparently did not miss any so-called 'red flags' indicating that terrorist attacks on New York and Washington were imminent. In a July 12, 2002 statement to the press, then Congressman Saxby Chambliss of the House Permanent Select Committee on Intelligence, stated: 'This was such a closely held, compartmentalized act of devastation that was carried out by the terrorist community that we don't know of any way that it could have been prevented.'[109] Congressman Chambliss' evaluation is confirmed by the June 2002 annual report of the British Parliament's Intelligence and Security

Committee, who after taking testimony from British intelligence officials and reviewing the classified documentary record, concluded: 'The [intelligence] Agencies have told us that they had no intelligence forewarning . . . specifically about the 11 September attacks on the USA. A subsequent re-examination of material across the intelligence community did not find any that, with the wisdom of hindsight, could have given warning of the attacks.'[110]

Does NSA itself and/or its SIGINT partners bear any responsibility for the alleged intelligence failure leading up to the terrorist attacks of Septembers 11, 2001? Some commentators in the U.S. and Europe have chosen to blame NSA in part or in whole for the intelligence failures leading up to the bombings of September 11, 2001. Is the criticism of NSA, and SIGINT in general, deserved? What primary source material that is available suggests that NSA did not commit any egregious errors in the days and months leading up to the attacks. A recently released congressional report concluded that: 'Prior to 11 September 2001, NSA had no specific information indicating the date, time, place, or participants in an attack on the United States.'[111] Moreover, it would appear that NSA performed better than the rest of the U.S. intelligence community prior to September 11, 2001, although this judgement is not universally shared within the U.S. intelligence community.[112]

A July 2002 report prepared by a subcommittee of the House Permanent Select Committee on Intelligence was critical of NSA's performance prior to the September 11, 2001 attacks, stating that NSA failed: '. . . to provide tactical and strategic warning' of the attacks.[113] NSA's response to this criticism was that it collected no intelligence upon which it could have provided a warning of the attacks. Despite all of the 'indications' that an impending al Qaeda attack that were appearing in SIGINT prior to the September 11, 2001 attacks, NSA officials candidly admitted that 'NSA had no SIGINT suggesting that al-Qaida was specifically targeting New York and Washington, D.C., or even that it was planning an attack on U.S. soil. Indeed, NSA had no knowledge before September 11th that any of the attackers were in the United States.'[114]

A U.S. intelligence official quoted in a newspaper interview neatly summarized the conundrum surrounding NSA's performance prior to the September 11, 2001 attacks, stating 'The good news is we didn't miss it. The bad news is it wasn't there to be missed.'[115]

Over-dependence on SIGINT

Some pundits have argued that prior to September 11, 2001, the U.S. intelligence community was too dependent on SIGINT and placed too little emphasis on Human Intelligence (HUMINT). Ephraim Halevy, the former head of the Israeli foreign intelligence service, the Mossad, has harshly criticized the U.S. intelligence community's heavy dependence on SIGINT, arguing that 'SIGINT has turned into the ultimate judge of reality, and the power of the other disciplines are used to confirm, cross-reference, and supplement [SIGINT]. SIGINT has become the high priest of intelligence and . . . blinded those deciphering the signs.'[116]

This is a legitimate criticism of the overall performance of the U.S. counterterrorist intelligence effort, and raises important questions about why the Central Intelligence Agency (CIA) and the Pentagon's Defense HUMINT Service (DHS) did not attack al Qaeda and other terrorist targets with greater gusto prior to September 2001. The Israeli military's experience fighting Hezbollah in southern Lebanon during the 1990s only serves to reinforce the notion that SIGINT is no substitute for good HUMINT in counterterrorist operations, especially when the terrorist groups in question limit their use of telecommunications in order to preserve operational security.[117] For almost a decade, government and congressional officials, senior American intelligence officers, and a host of public commentators have pressed for greater emphasis on HUMINT. For example, in 1998 former CIA director James Woolsey told a subcommittee of the U.S. Senate Committee on the Judiciary that HUMINT was essential for combating terrorism. He and others who testified before the committee acknowledged that HUMINT collection on terrorism was expensive, hard to achieve, and oftentimes involved the recruitment of 'unsavory individuals.'[118]

One overall conclusion that can be derived from the available documentation is that SIGINT was the U.S. intelligence community's principal source of 'actionable' information about terrorist activities prior to September 11, 2001. Available evidence indicates that the performance of the CIA's clandestine service's against international terrorist activities began to markedly deteriorate in the mid-1990s, just as Osama bin Laden and al Qaeda were becoming increasingly important intelligence targets. An internal CIA assessment conducted in 1994 found that HUMINT was 'the most important source of intelligence' on international terrorism.[119] But by the end of the 1990s, internal U.S. intelligence community assessments showed that SIGINT had surpassed, if not supplanted HUMINT as the primary source of intelligence reporting on international terrorism. In 2001, a former senior Pentagon official told Congress that since the early 1990s, SIGINT '... has provided decisionmakers with the lion's share of operational counterterrorism intelligence.'[120] Another document indicates that by the end of the 1990s SIGINT had become the most consistent producer of hard intelligence against the so-called transnational targets, i.e. international terrorism, narcotics trafficking, arms control compliance, weapons proliferation, and international economics.[121] A Congressionally-funded report issued in June 2000 stated that 'The National Security Agency (NSA) is America's most important asset for technical collection of terrorism information.'[122]

SIGINT as a passive collector

On the negative side, SIGINT was used solely as a passive collection source, and not as an active means by which terrorists could be rooted out and destroyed by other intelligence and security agencies. An American counterintelligence official complained that 'NSA's position was that it was solely an intelligence collector, and that it was the responsibility of the CIA and the FBI to use the SIGINT it was producing to get the [terrorists].'[123]

NSA's reluctance to become more actively involved in the counterterrorism fight stemmed from the Agency's traditional culture as an intelligence collector. In the past, NSA officials have taken the position that it was more important to collect intelligence on the targets being monitored than to disrupt or destroy them, which would result in the loss of the source.[124] For example, in 1997 Pentagon officials complained that NSA still was reluctant to give the military the intelligence information that they needed to do their job because of concerns about compromising the security of the Agency's sources. This led one Pentagon official to charge that 'long-entrenched civilian NSA employees are still fighting the Cold War and are more worried about maintaining security than improving tactical warfighting capabilities.'[125] These restrictions have placed extreme burdens on the counterterrorist action agencies and effectively prevented them from using the intelligence gathered by NSA to go after terrorist organizations.

There were officers within NSA who, prior to September 11th, strongly advocated making SIGINT more freely available to those tasked with combating al Qaeda, but existing policy and security considerations prevented this policy from being acted upon. Moreover, a former NSA official argued that since NSA is only an intelligence collection agency, it is the responsibility of the Agency's military and civilian consumers to use the information to attack terrorist groups and their members. Only since the September 11, 2001 attacks have 'the gloves come off,' and SIGINT is now actively being used to destroy al Qaeda cells around the world.[126]

Strategic direction

Former and current U.S. intelligence officials complain, probably with some justification, that the guidance that they received over the last decade from the Director of Central Intelligence (DCI) SIGINT Committee in terms of priorities regarding SIGINT collection on international terrorism were oftentimes and vague and ambiguous. It was left to NSA to try to interpret the consumers' will into concrete tasking directives to NSA's SIGINT collectors. Moreover, many of the tasking requests received from U.S. law enforcement agencies on terrorism, such as from the FBI and U.S. Secret Service, conflicted with mission tasking received from U.S. intelligence community members.[127] This lack of clearly defined set of counterterrorism tasking requirements from the DCI SIGINT Committee resulted in NSA being swamped by some 1,500 formal tasking requirements from dozens of intelligence consumer agencies, many of which were non-specific in nature (one consumer agency tasked NSA with 'all intelligence on Middle East terrorist groups') which the agency could not cover with the limited resources at its disposal.[128]

Part of the reason for this anomaly is that the tasking guidance received from NSA's consumers through the DCI SIGINT Committee in Washington, D.C. was oftentimes contradictory or confusing, leaving it up to NSA officials to determine how best to cover specific terrorist targets and what resources to dedicate to the problems at hand.[129] The tasking conundrum was due to the fact that by 1997 the number of federal agencies involved in one way or another in counterterrorism had jumped from only a handful to more than 40 government departments and agencies, each of whom had their own parochial interests that was reflected in the tasking they levied on NSA through the DCI SIGINT Committee.[130]

Resource allocation to the counter-terrorism mission

A pointed criticism of NSA's counterterrorist SIGINT effort raised in a July 2002 report by the House Permanent Select Committee on Intelligence (HPSCI) is that in the years prior to September 11, 2001, NSA did not dedicate enough SIGINT collection and processing resources to the counterterrorist mission. This raises the obvious question as to whether NSA SIGINT officials gave counterterrorism a sufficiently high priority given the high level of consumer interest in the subject.[131] Past and present NSA officials have admitted that there is some truth to this charge insofar as they believe that NSA could have devoted more resources to monitoring worldwide terrorist threats. But the officials stated that this could only have been accomplished by diverting precious SIGINT intercept and processing resources from other equally important targets which were competing with international terrorism for the attention of NSA's interceptors and analysts.[132]

A related criticism levelled by some members of Congress is that NSA paid insufficient attention to al Qaeda. Congressman Saxby Chambliss (R-Georgia) of the House Permanent Select Committee on Intelligence has stated that though NSA monitored 'large volumes of phone calls from the part of the world where al Qaeda was located . . . the problem was, they didn't focus on al Qaeda' to the degree that intercepts were not being identified and processed quickly enough.[133] In testimony before Congress in October 2002, NSA Director General Michael Hayden rejected this criticism, stating that NSA did, in fact, focus its efforts and resources on al Qaeda after DCI George Tenet 'declared war' on Osama bin Laden in 1998.[134]

The truth probably lies somewhere in between these two positions. According to the final report of the joint congressional inquiry into the handling of intelligence prior to the 9–11 attacks: 'NSA and other agencies learned valuable information from intercepting terrorist communications and prevented several planned attacks. Indeed. Numerous officials throughout the policy and Intelligence Community told the Joint Inquiry that SIGINT was a valuable source of information on al-Qaida. Exploitation of terrorist communications, however, was uneven at best and suffered from insufficient investment. Al-Qaida was only one of several high priority targets and a difficult one.'[135]

It is true that two significant problems that NSA faced when it came to SIGINT collection on international terrorists were money and resources. Three independent government commissions that examined the terrorist threat in the late 1990s all concluded that the U.S. intelligence community needed to devote more resources to intelligence coverage of terrorism, which naturally required that the priority assigned to intelligence coverage of international terrorism needed to be elevated.[136] But somehow, these public calls for a higher priority to be placed on intelligence on international terrorism got muddled in the transmission to NSA. Moreover, the House and Senate intelligence committees did not allocate to NSA increased funding for more resources to dedicate to international terrorism. According to U.S. intelligence officials, NSA did not have sufficient resources to conduct a comprehensive, large-scale global counterterrorism target development program, i.e. dedicating a certain number of collection and processing resources to find and development new terrorist communications targets beyond those that were already known and being exploited.[137]

This issue is potentially the most troubling since it raises the spectre that NSA and other SIGINT services may not be able to sustain the current level of effort against terrorism targets for anything more than the duration of the current crisis. Since September 11, 2001, NSA, GCHQ and other SIGINT services have succeeded in increasing the level of resources dedicated to coverage of international terrorism only by stripping personnel, equipment and other collection and processing resources away from other critical targets, such as the Balkans.[138] The British Parliament's Intelligence and Security Committee in its June 2003 annual report warned that the shift of precious intelligence collection resources from other targets to counter-terrorism was creating a dangerous situation, stating that: 'These reductions are causing intelligence gaps to develop, which may mean over time unacceptable risks will arise in terms of safeguarding national security and in the prevention and detecting of Serious Organised Crime.'[139] Among the NSA SIGINT targets which have suffered in recent years are monitoring of the former Soviet Union, China, North Korea, Bosnia, Kosovo, and the national counternarcotics program. NSA's inability to dedicate sufficient resources to monitoring narcotics trafficking in the Western Hemisphere has forced the DEA to take over a significant part of this responsibility.[140] The danger is that this level of effort cannot be sustained indefinately because of financial considerations and the likelihood of another crisis breaking outsomewhere else in the world, requiring another reapportionment of finite SIGINT resources away from the international terrorism mission. The fear in some quarters is that once the current crisis abates, the services will quietly return to their pre-September 11th target coverage.[141]

The difficulty of the new terrorist targets

Intelligence coverage of the new generation of terrorist organizations has become more difficult because of the geographic changes in the global battlefield. The new terrorist hideouts are no longer the traditional terrorist sanctuaries of the past, such as Libya, Syria and Lebanon, but rather smaller and more obscure countries in the Middle East and South Asia which previously American and other Western intelligence services have paid little heed to, such as Afghanistan, Yemen and Somalia. These countries have little in the way of modern infrastructure, such as robust telecommunications systems, which makes SIGINT collection on targets inside these countries extremely difficult.

In addition, intercepted terrorist communications are also extremely difficult to understand because they are oftentimes fragmentary in nature. A senior American intelligence official has been quoted as saying that 'You rarely get a SIGINT smoking gun. It's usually very fragmentary . . . Very often you don't even know who you're listening to.'[142] This problem continues to this day. Over a two year period prior to the terrorist attacks of September 11, 2001, NSA intercepted hundreds of telephone calls made by bin Laden and members of his al Qaeda organization, generating tens of thousands of pages of transcripts. But analysts who have reviewed the transcripts of al Qaeda intercepts confirm that these materials are extremely difficult to understand, much less accurately interpret, given the propensity of the speakers to 'talk around' sensitive subjects on the telephone. A U.S. intelligence official who has listened to some of the al Qaeda intercepts confirmed that NSA's best linguists found the intercepts difficult to understand, adding that 'a lot of it is crap.'[143] The FBI's former counterterrorism chief recalled that these intercepts '. . . did little good. U.S. officials often didn't know who was speaking to whom. This wasn't like Mafia wiretaps, where you know who's calling the boss; who's all the way down through the organization. These were just voices. And in most cases they were talking in code. It only became clear to us after the [September 11] bombings.'[144] This problem is not unique to NSA. Commenting on the Israeli SIGINT effort, a former United Nations official said that 'Israeli signals intelligence in the Middle East was second to none. They can hear a pin drop anywhere. But the trouble is that they don't always know what it means.'[145]

SIGINT collection issues

Although the evidence is spotty at best, there are indications that terrorist organizations around the world began shifting some of their communications to the newer forms of computer and telecommunications technology that became widely available to the public in the 1990s. In March 2000, CIA director George J. Tenet warned that a number of international terrorist organizations, including al Qaeda, were 'using computerized files, e-mail and encryption to support their operations.'[146]

While factually correct, Tenet's statement perhaps overstates the problem. For example, all available evidence suggests that the use of sophisticated encryption technology by international terrorist organizations over the last decade has been extremely rare. A 1997 study found only five instances where individuals engaged in terrorist activities had used encryption to communicate or protect information concerning their operational plans on their computers, including the planner of the 1993 World Trade Center bombing, Ramzi Yousef, who encrypted the files in his laptop computer to conceal his plan to blow up 11 American airliners in the Far East. As the authors of the study point out, however, virtually all of the same planning information was available elsewhere on Yousef's computer in unencrypted form.[147]

There is some evidence that a small number of terrorist organizations have used some of the new telecommunications technologies that became widely available on the commercial market in the 1990s. Pakistani-backed guerrillas operating in the state of Kashmir, calling themselves the Hizbul Mujahideen, have used frequency-hopping radios, burst transmission technology, citizen-band radios, satellite telephones and even sophisticated encryption technology (presumably with Pakistani assistance), which has made it increasingly difficult for the Indian government's SIGINT services to monitor, much less exploit, their communications traffic.[148] In Sri Lanka, the Liberation Tigers of Tamil Elam (LTTE) guerrilla organization used commercially available Japanese walkie talkie sets to handle much of their tactical communications. These sets could operate on ten different preset frequencies, which made it extremely difficult to locate these transmitters using the older Soviet-made direction finding equipment then used by the Indian military's SIGINT units.[149]

SIGINT processing problems

It is now widely recognized that SIGINT agencies around the world are being stretched to the limit by what can only be described as 'information overload.' According to the International Telecommunications Union (ITU), in the last five years, the volume of international communications traffic has doubled from 61.7 billion minutes in 1995 to 120.9 billion minutes in the year 2000.[150] By the year 2002, it was estimated that international telephone traffic would have grown to 157.1 billion minutes, which equates to a growth rate of 15% per annum.[151] Moreover, SIGINT collection technology has improved to the point where it is indeed possible to gain access to much of this worldwide communications traffic. As of 1995, the various SIGINT collection systems owned by NSA were capable of intercepting the equivalent of the entire collection of the U.S. Library of Congress (1 quadrillion Bits of information) every three hours.[152]

But as the volume of worldwide communications traffic has increased, and the efficiency of the SIGINT collections systems have concurrently improved, the result has been that it has become increasingly difficult for even the largest and best funded of the world's SIGINT organizations to process, analyze and disseminate the vast amount of incoming data.[153] This is not a new phenomena. During Operation Desert Storm in 1990–1991, the volume of Iraqi intercepts being collected by NSA's SIGINT satellites alone reportedly surpassed the ability of NSA's computers, analysts and linguists to process.[154] According to news reports, during the 1999 military operations in Kosovo, NSA experienced great difficulty processing and getting to its consumers the huge volumes of perishable SIGINT data that it was collecting on the operations of the Yugoslav Army.[155]

What this means is that in reality, the primary problem facing SIGINT today and in the near-future is not collection, but rather the processing, analysis and reporting of this information. A 1996 U.S. congressional report delineated the problem this way: 'The ability to filter through the huge volumes of data and to extract the information from the layers of formatting, multiplexing, compression, and transmission protocols applied to each message is the biggest challenge of the future.'[156] In addition, it is becoming harder to find the few nuggets of intelligence gold amidst the growing amount of material being intercepted every day.[157] A 1999 study commissioned by the U.S. Senate Permanent Select Committee on Intelligence described the problem as being comparable to trying to find 'needles in the haystack, but the haystack is getting larger and larger.'[158]

The implication is that SIGINT's ability to perform its counterterrorist mission may be in jeopardy. A June 2000 congressional report stated that the National Security Agency was unable to 'translate the rising volume of terrorist traffic into intelligence, putting the U.S. at increased risk for attacks.' The report also noted that NSA falling further and further behind in its ability to 'target and exploit' the advanced technology that terrorists around the world are using.[159]

One example of this problem will suffice. In April 1996, Germany's foreign intelligence agency, the Bundesnachrichtendienst (BND), began a massive signals intercept program to try and find information about international terrorism and narcotics trafficking based on monitoring communications traffic coming in and out of Germany. As one might imagine, this was not an easy task since about 8 million domestic and international telephone calls and FAX or telex transmissions come in or out of Germany every day. Over the course of the two-year program, BND analysts plugged a total of 856 search terms into a computer database, which was supposed to help the collectors identify which intercepted messages might contain information of intelligence value. Between April 1996 and April 1998, out of the tens of millions of telephone calls and transmissions monitored, only 2,494 messages were filtered out which contain one or more of the search terms concerning international terrorism. After reviewing these messages, the BND analysts determined that only 21 of the intercepts in fact contained information of intelligence value. In effect, the BND program was a massive and very expensive failure. At the same time, the BND was searching through all German communications traffic for information about international narcotics trafficking. According to BND statistics, between September 1996 and May 1998 only 600 messages were intercepted which contained one or more of the search terms that flagged it as of potential intelligence value. The information gained was of some intelligence value, but the operation did not yield a single clue which would have allowed the German police to make an arrest.[160]

Personnel shortages

Another serious failing identified by the House Permanent Select Committee on Intelligence in its July 2002 report was NSA's critical shortage of intelligence analysts specializing in terrorism and linguists who understood critical Middle Eastern and South Asian languages in the years leading up to the terrorist bombings of September 11, 2001.[161] The final report of the congressional Joint Inquiry into the 9–11 intelligence failures found that 'personnel employed in the [NSA] counterterrorism organization were largely static over several years, despite repeated efforts by local managers to increase the number of linguists and analysts. General Hayden testified that in hindsight he would have liked to have doubled his resources against al-Qaida.'[162]

Post-mortem examinations following every foreign crisis have consistently found that the U.S. intelligence community's linguistic resources were grossly deficient. In a letter to the *Washington Post*, former Illinois Senator Paul Simon stated that 'In every national crisis from the Cold War through Vietnam, Desert Storm, Bosnia and Kosovo, our nation has lamented its foreign language shortfalls. But then the crisis goes away, and we return to business as usual. One of the messages of Sept. 11 is that business as usual is no longer an acceptable option.'[163]

Analytic shortcomings

NSA officials also found that NSA's W Group, the operations analysis group at Ft. Meade which handles, amongst other subjects, international terrorism, has consistently suffered from pervasive shortages of intelligence analysts and area specialists to adequately handle the reams of intercepts being produced on terrorist targets.[164] A declassified congressional report revealed that throughout 2001, NSA's counterterrorism office had a standing request for dozens of additional analysts, but because of tight purse strings the report revealed that 'there was little expectation that such a large request would be satisfied.'[165] These shortages of analysts and linguists clearly hindered the collection and processing of SIGINT relating to international terrorism over the last decade. Thousands of intercepts piled up unread by analysts at NSA headquarters because there were not enough qualified linguists to translate them. This meant of course that NSA's analysts never got to see the vast majority of the products that NSA's intercept platforms were forwarding to Ft. Meade.[166]

Moreover, the shortage of experienced analysts in W Group at Ft. Meade meant that much of what the translators did reduce to English never was read, analyzed or reported to intelligence consumers. According to a report prepared by the House Permanent Select Committee on Intelligence, 'At the NSA and CIA, thousands of pieces of data are never analyzed, or are analyzed "after the fact," because there are too few analysts; even fewer with the necessary language skills.'[167]

Problems with dissemination

Historically, because of the need to protect sensitive intelligence sources, NSA's SIGINT intercepts were given extremely limited distribution within the highest levels of government and the military, and even then, only on a need-to-know basis.[168] The 2004 9/11 Commission final report noted that NSA continues to suffer from: 'An almost obsessive protection of sources and methods . . .'[169] FBI and other law enforcement officials have complained repeatedly that when they did receive SIGINT reports from NSA, the restrictions placed on their use by NSA were so onerous that they could not be used. For example, NSA has historically forbidden the FBI and other U.S. law enforcement agencies from using SIGINT if such use would compromise NSA's sources and methods. As one might imagine, these restrictions have frustrated FBI and U.S. Department of Justice officials since the end of World War II.[170] Within the U.S. intelligence community SIGINT intercepts relating to international terrorist organizations were deemed to be some of the most sensitive materials then being produced by NSA. For instance, during the 1980s counter-terrorist SIGINT being produced by NSA was deemed so sensitive that the U.S. intelligence community assigned this specific category of COMINT intercept the codename Spectre, which severely limited access to this compartment of intelligence information to a very select few high-level intelligence customers in Washington, D.C.[171]

Prior to the September 11, 2001 terrorist attacks, access to SIGINT on terrorism within the U.S. intelligence community was circumscribed by the high classification levels assigned to these materials, which restricted the number of personnel who could have access to this intelligence as well as how it could be used. A congressional staff study found that: 'Poor information systems and the high level of classification prevented FBI field officers from using NSA and CIA data.' In other words, many of the intelligence consumers who needed the information the most were not able to see it because they had no access to computer systems carrying the NSA materials, or were not cleared for access to SIGINT.[172]

Problems with inter-agency cooperation and coordination

During congressional hearings held in October 2002, witnesses from the CIA and FBI openly complained about NSA's 'unwillingness' to share information with its customers.[173]

As before, there would appear to be some truth to these accusations. The crux of the problem seems to center on NSA's unwillingness to engage in any form of SIGINT collection against targets in the U.S. According to the July 2004 final report of the 9/11 Commission: 'NSA had the technical capability to report on communications with suspected terrorist facilities in the Middle East, the NSA did not seek FISA Court warrants to collect communications between individuals in the United States and foreign countries, because it believed that this was an FBI role. It also did not want to be viewed as targeting persons in the United States and possibily violating laws that governed NSA's collection of foreign intelligence.[174]

Although NSA's adherence to the word of the law is admirable, its uncompromising position on this issue created no end of problems with its counterparts within the U.S. intelligence community. FBI officials have alleged that NSA occasionally refused to accept mission tasking requests from the FBI if the request did not specify that the information was needed for 'foreign intelligence' purposes only, earning NSA a reputation for being generally unresponsive to requests for information from American law enforcement agencies.[175] A congressional report found that because of legal restrictions on the dissemination of intelligence information to law enforcement agencies, NSA: 'began to indicate on all its reporting that the content could not be shared with law enforcement personnel without the prior approval of the FISA Court.'[176] For example, every NSA SIGINT report relating to international terrorism in the 1990s contained the following caveat on its cover: 'This information is provided for intelligence purposes in an effort to develop potential investigative leads. It cannot be used in affidavits, court proceedings, subpeonas, or for other legal or judicial purposes.'[177]

NSA's response to these accusations was that it routinely provided significant amount of intelligence information to U.S. law enforcement agencies. In the early 1990s, NSA expanded the size and scope of its inter-agency cooperation with other U.S. intelligence and law enforcement organizations in the field of terrorism. Beginning in 1992, NSA intelligence analysts began spending multi-year tours of duty at the Federal Bureau of Investigations (FBI) helping the bureau fight terrorism.[178] As of the fall of 2002 alone, the FBI alone received some 200 SIGINT reports a day from NSA.[179] After the 1993 World Trade Center bombings, a sizeable number of NSA intelligence analysts were posted for the first time with the CIA's Counterterrorist Center (CTC) at CIA headquarters in Langley, Virginia, where they helped direct intelligence collection against terrorist targets and analyzed SIGINT materials forwarded to CTC from NSA concerning international terrorist groups.[180] But NSA Director General Michael V. Hayden also was forced to admit that 'We have been able to be more agile in sharing information with some customers (like the Department of Defense) than we have with others (like the Department of Justice),' adding that Congressional and court-imposed legal restrictions did in fact impede his ability to freely convey intelligence information to law enforcement agencies such as the FBI.[181]

NSA had its own set of problems in working with the FBI. Congressional reports indicate that a poor defined division of labor between NSA and other U.S. intelligence services and law enforcement agencies hindered the counterterrorism effort prior to the September 11, 2001 attacks. NSA officials were particularly critical of the FBI, which failed to coordinate its efforts with NSA in order to identify and find Islamic militants associated with al Qaeda and other terrorist organizations operating in the U.S. As a result of the lack of cooperation between NSA and the FBI, according to a congressional report, NSA did not use a particularly sensitive SIGINT collection resource that would have been particularly useful in locating al Qaeda operatives working in the U.S. This no doubt is related to the above-mentioned NSA unwillingness to engage in any form of collection against targets in the U.S. proper.[182]

Commenting on the overall state of relations between NSA and the FBI, one senior American intelligence official stated that 'Our cooperation with our foreign allies is a helluva lot better than with the FBI.'[183]

Regardless of the veracity of the conflicting accusations, it is clear that these inter-agency conflicts hampered the free-flow of intelligence information between NSA and the U.S. law enforcement community, and impaired the U.S. counterterrorist effort. As a 1996 congressional report aptly put it, 'These internecine squabbles between agencies seriously undermine the country's ability to combat global crime in an effective manner and must be ended.'[184]

Hunters rather than gatherers

What has changed since the September 11, 2001 attacks is that NSA's counterterrorist SIGINT program has been transformed from a purely passive intelligence collection effort to an interactive source that is being used to hunt down and destroy terrorist cells around the world. NSA's Director, General Michael Hayden, described his agency's new doctrine as 'hunters rather than gatherers.'[185]

One does not have to look far to find evidence that SIGINT is now being actively used to locate al Qaeda terrorists. Shortly after the U.S. began supporting the Northern Alliance forces in Afghanistan in October 2001, NSA and its partners apparently began intercepting all satellite telephone calls coming in and out of Pakistan, where U.S. intelligence officials believed most of the fugitive Al Qaeda and Taliban officials had fled. It did not take long before this collection program began to yield results. On the night of March 27, 2002, Pakistani security forces captured one of Osma bin Laden's chief lieutenants, Abu Zubaida, along with 19 other al Qaida operatives in the eastern Pakistani city of Faisalabad. The house where Abu Zubaida was hiding was located when American intelligence operators in Pakistan intercepted a series of satellite phone calls from Afghanistan to the al Qaida leader's hideout in Faisalabad.[186] In July 2002, an intercepted satellite telephone conversation led Pakistani security forces to a shanty town outside Karachi, where they arrested a 33-year old Kenyan named Sheikh Ahmed Salim, who was wanted by U.S. authorities for his role in the 1998 embassy bombings in Kenya and Tanzania.[187] In September 2002, an intercepted satellite phone call led Pakistani paramilitary police to the hideout in a suburb of the Pakistani port city of Karachi of Yemeni national Ramzi Binalshibh, who was one of the al Qaeda planners of the September 11, 2001 terrorist bombings in the U.S.[188] In what has been described publicly as an important intelligence coup, in February 2003 intercepted e-mails and satellite telephone communications led U.S. and Pakistani security officials to the hideout in the Pakistani city of Rawalpindi of reputed September 11 mastermind Khalid Shaikh Mohammed. At 4:00 AM on the morning of March 1, 2003, heavily armed Pakistani security forces burst into Mohammed's hideout and arrested him and another key al-Qaeda operative, Mohammed Ahmed al-Hawsawi, while they slept.[189]

Lessons learned

The future of SIGINT in the fight against terrorism can, in large part, be sketched by delineating the key lessons learned by American intelligence officials from their review of U.S. intelligence performance prior to the September 11, 2001 terrorist attacks.

One of the lessons learned is that there is an urgent need for more clandestine or unconventional SIGINT collection resources, because these collection resources can get better intelligence by getting closer to targets than most other sources. With the advent of new wireless communications technologies, such as cellular telephones and wireless paging systems, 'close-in' SIGINT collection has become increasingly important in the last decade, while more conventional SIGINT collection systems have diminished in value. Gregory F. Treverton, the former vice chairman of the U.S. National Intelligence Council, wrote in the fall of 2001 that: 'SIGINT will need to get closer to the signals in which it is interested. During the high Cold War, the Soviet Union sent many of its phone calls through microwave relay stations. Since private telephones were relatively few, intercepting those conversations with satellites yielded important insights into economic production and sometimes into military movements or lines of command. Now, though, with hundreds of communications bundled into fibre optic lines, there is less for satellites to intercept. If SIGINT is to intercept those signals, it will have to tap into particular communications lines in specific places. It will have to collect keystrokes straight from a personal computer, before software encrypts the message.'[190]

One of the premier practitioners of this arcane intelligence art-form is the joint CIA-NSA clandestine SIGINT collection unit, the Special Collection Service (SCS).[191] Headquartered in Beltsville, Maryland, the SCS has become an increasingly important intelligence collection resource in the last decade, intercepting foreign political, military and internal security telecommunications traffic from within American diplomatic establishments abroad, or by unconventional clandestine means in unfriendly 'denied area environments' where the U.S. has no diplomatic representation.[192] For example, in January 1999 the Boston Globe and the Washington Post revealed that the SCS had created a covert SIGINT system to help U.N. weapons inspectors locate and destroy Iraqi weapons of mass destruction. This clandestine SIGINT collection program began in February 1996, and consisted of commercially-available VHF radio intercept receivers provided by the CIA being secretly placed inside UNSCOM headquarters at Al-Thawra in the suburbs of Baghdad. In addition, sophisticated radio scanners hidden inside backpacks and the UNSCOM mobile ambulance were also used by the U.N. inspection teams when they operated in the field.[193]

Another lesson of the September 11, 2001 attacks is that it would seem to be imperative that intelligence services break down the barriers that have historically existed between HUMINT agencies and SIGINT services. It is widely recognized that the deeply ingrained partisan attitudes among the differing intelligence and security agencies will be difficult to breakdown. For example, a former head of the Federal Bureau of Investigation's domestic counterterrorist unit was recently quoted in the press as saying 'I'll take a live source any day over an electronic intercept.'[194] Regardless of whether intelligence consumers have personal preferences for HUMINT, SIGINT or any other intelligence source, it is absolutely essential that intelligence analysts and consumers accept that all sources of intelligence fused together into an 'all source' intelligence product will be the only way to effectively combat terrorism.[195]

Partisans of HUMINT and SIGINT must recognize and accept that there has always existed a synergistic cross-dependency between these two longtime competitors, and that this cross-dependency continues to exist today. One could even make the argument that in increasingly fractured post 9–11 world, one intelligence discipline cannot survive without the other. The logic of greater cooperation between HUMINT and SIGINT operators would seem to be obvious. Former CIA director John Deutch wrote in the journal *Foreign Policy* that: 'Cooperation between human and technical intelligence, especially communications intelligence, makes both stronger. Human sources . . . can provide access to valuable signals intelligence . . . Communications intercepts can validate information provided by a human source.'[196] Agreement on this point transcends international borders. Former British Foreign

Secretary Robin Cook told Parliament in June 2000 that: 'The collection of signals intelligence and of human intelligence often bears its greatest fruit and best results when the two are put together.'[197] The former vice chairman of the U.S. National Intelligence Council, Gregory Treverton, perhaps makes the strongest argument for greater inter-disciplinary cooperation, writing: '[I]n the future spying will focus less on collecting information than facilitating its collection by technical means. The clandestine service will gather secrets less through what its own spies hear than through the sensors those spies can put in place . . . The United States probably breaks more codes by stealing code books than by breaking the codes with the National Security Agency's supercomputers and brainy mathematicians.'[198]

There is precedent for this sort of inter-disciplinary cooperation between HUMINT and SIGINT collectors. During the 1980s, the U.S. Army operated a clandestine intelligence unit called the U.S. Army Intelligence Support Activity (ISA), which successfully combined SIGINT and HUMINT intelligence collection resources into a single integrated organization that was capable of acting instantly on the information gathered by these collection assets.[199] In January 1982, SIGINT technicians from ISA took part in the search for Brigadier General James Dozier, the highest ranking American officer in Italy, who had been kidnapped from his home in Verona, Italy by Italian Red Brigade terrorists on December 17, 1981. ISA operatives used helicopters equipped with sophisticated direction finding gear to locate the Red Brigades terrorists holding General Dozier, who was rescued unharmed.[200]

Then there is the critical need to improve SIGINT's ability handle the ever increasing volume of communications traffic being intercepted. Publicly-available sources suggest that partial technological solutions to these problems are available, albeit at considerable cost. Technology is presently available which allow computers to screen large volumes of communications for items of potential intelligence interest. Artificial intelligence algorithms, such as those used in today's Internet search engines, can be configured so as to identify intercepts which contain useful information based on key-word searches. This group of technologies is generically referred to as 'Text and Data Mining.'[201]

Another lesson to be derived from NSA's performance prior to September 11, 2001 is that SIGINT processing, reporting and analysis must become faster and more efficient if it is to be useful as a targeting tool against international terrorist organizations. According to the 2002 annual report of the House Permanent Select Committee on Intelligence: 'The events of September 11th highlight the critical nature of SIGINT analysis to understand the terrorist target, and moreover the need to be able to quickly exploit intercepted communications.'[202] Historically, this has not been the case. A June 2000 congressional report stated that the National Security Agency was unable to: '. . . translate the rising volume of terrorist traffic into intelligence, putting the U.S. at increased risk for attacks.' The report also noted that NSA was falling further and further behind in its ability to 'target and exploit' the advanced telecommunications technology that terrorists around the world were using.[203]

Finally, a major impediment to SIGINT's future ability to effectively combat international terrorism is the evident lack of international cooperation among national SIGINT agencies. The rationale for greater international SIGINT cooperation against terrorism is a fairly simple one. The first is that the cost of maintaining a substantive national SIGINT capability for most nations is very high, and is getting more expensive every day due to significant changes in worldwide telecommunications technology. Only a handful of the world's richest nations can afford to maintain a global SIGINT intercept and processing capability, which provides a clear incentive for smaller nations to enter into cooperative joint ventures or information-sharing relationships with the larger and richer nations in order to gain access to the intelligence information that they collect.[204]

The second attractive quality for greater transnational SIGINT cooperation is the regional expertise, technical skills and geographic access that many of the small national SIGINT services possess in those parts of the world where the larger SIGINT services heretofore have not treaded.[205] A 1996 U.S. congressional report argued that greater international intelligence cooperation was essential, stating that other countries 'provide expertise, skills, and access which U.S. intelligence does not have.'[206] For example, Russia's two SIGINT services, the GRU and FAPSI, possess intercept facilities in the region that are better situated than those 'owned' by NSA, as well as a small but capable reservoir of Pashto and Dari linguists and SIGINT analysts familiar with the region.[207] After years of fighting Pakistani-backed Muslem guerrillas in the disputed state of Kashmir and Jammu, India has developed a significant level of expertise in monitoring the communications traffic of these groups. After the September 11, 2001, the Indian government turned over to the U.S. copies of satellite phone intercepts between Muslim guerrillas in Kashmir and their agents in Afghanistan, as well as other intelligence concerning links between the guerrillas and the Taliban and al Qaeda forces in Afghanistan.[208]

This would suggest that NSA and its English-speaking partners must necessarily enter into more expansive cooperative SIGINT relationships with new partners outside of the confines of the current UKUSA membership list. A CIA officer told an interviewer that 'We've got to be serious about this: our intelligence world can't be this nice private club of English speakers any more.'[209]

The danger of broadened international SIGINT cooperation, as with all intelligence liaison relationships, is that something could potentially go wrong with the relationship that would permanently sour the parties on current future intelligence sharing and cooperation. For example, some American officials have pointed out that much of the intelligence information that the U.S. provided to Saddam Hussein's Iraq during its war with Iran in the 1980s, including SIGINT intercepts, harmed the ability of the U.S. intelligence community to monitor the Iraqi regime before, during and after Operation Desert Storm in 1990–1991.[210]

Then there is the all-important question of just how dependent the U.S. intelligence community should be on information provided by foreign intelligence services. A 2002 report issued by a congressional subcommittee was critical of what he believed to be the CIA's 'over-reliance on foreign intelligence services' for counterterrorism intelligence information.[211] Today, in the post 9–11 world, the reigning school of thought within the U.S. intelligence community is to become less reliant on liaison with foreign intelligence services, which will be a natural hindrance to further SIGINT sharing and cooperation between the U.S. and other nations.[212]

Sigint, whatever difficulties it faces, will remain an important tool for intelligence agencies in the ongoing war on terrorism. This review of the recent historical record suggests that new resource, new thinking and new ways of intra- and inter-government sharing of Sigint will be necessary. Technological obsolescence will not kill Sigint; inability to face necessary changes is the ore dangerous threat.

Notes

1 Matthew M. Aid, 'The Time of Troubles: The US National Security Agency in the Twenty-First Century,' *Intelligence and National Security*, Vol. 15, No. 3, Autumn 2000, p. 6. See also *Statement for the Record by Lt. General Michael v. Hayden, USAF, Director NSA/CSS Before the Joint Inquiry of the Senate/Select Committee on Intelligence and the House Permanent Select Committee on Intelligence*, October 17, 2002, p. 6.

2 Senate Report No. 107–351 and House Report No. 107–792, Report of the U.S. Senate Select Committee and U.S. House Permanent Select Committee on Intelligence, *Joint Inquiry Into Intelligence Community Activities Before and After the Terrorist Attacks of September 11, 2001*, 107th Congress, 2nd Session, December 2002 (declassified and released in July 2003), p. 76.

3 *Intelligence and Security Committee Annual Report 1998–99*, November 1999, para. 18, http://www.official-documents.co.uk/document/cm45/4532/4532-02.htm.

4 Richard Norton-Taylor, 'GCHQ Facing Jobs Cuts,' *Guardian*, February 4, 1992, p. 5.

5 Michael Herman, *Intelligence Power in Peace and War* (Cambridge: Cambridge University Press, 1996), p. 37 fn6, p. 38 fn8; Richard Norton-Taylor, 'Goal Posts Keep Moving in the Spying Game,' *Manchester Guardian Weekly*, January 1, 1995, p. 8; James Adams and David Leppard, 'Spy Rivals Crow as GCHQ Faces Cuts,' *Sunday Times*, March 26, 1995; 'Bad News for GCHQ,' *Intelligence Newsletter*, April 13, 1995; 'New Boss at GCHQ,' *Intelligence Newsletter*, October 12, 1995.

6 House of Commons, Select Committee on Public Accounts, *Appendix 2: Supplementary Memorandum Submitted by HM Treasury (PAC 99–00/216)*, April 2000, located at http://www.parliament.the-stationery-office.co.uk/pa/cm199900/cmselect/cmpubacc/556/556ap12.htm.

7 Confidential interview.

8 Confidential interview.

9 Louis Lief, 'Murder, They Wrote: Iran's Web of Terror,' *US News & World Report*, December 16, 1991, p. 67; Vincent Jauvert, 'Comment L'Amerique Nous Espionne,' *Nouvel Observateur*, No. 1779, December 10, 1998, p. 10.

10 CIA, DCI Counterterrorist Center, *Counterterrorist Center Commentary: The Disappearance of Libyan Oppositionist Mansur Kikhia*, December 15, 1993, CIA Electronic FOIA Reading Room, http://www.foia.cia.gov

11 Tom Bowman and Scott Shane, 'Battling High-Tech Warriors,' *Baltimore Sun*, December 15, 1995, p. 22A.

12 Testimony of Cofer Black, former chief of Counterterrorist Center, Central Intelligence Agency, before the Joint Inquiry Staff, House Permanent Select Committee on Intelligence and Senate Permanent Select Committee on Intelligence, September 26, 2002, p. 9.

13 David Martin and John Wolcott, *Best Laid Plans: The Inside Story of America's War Against Terrorism* (NY: Harper & Row, 1988), pp. 105, 133; Jack Anderson, 'U.S. Was Warned of Bombing at Beirut Embassy,' *Washington Post*, May 10, 1983, p. B15; R.W. Apple, Jr., 'U.S. Knew of Iran's Role in Two Beirut Bombings,' *New York Times*, December 8, 1986, p. A16; Stephen Engelberg, 'U.S. Calls Iranian Cleric Leading Backer of Terror,' *New York Times*, August 27, 1989, p. 16.

14 'NBC Says U.S. Intelligence Shows Iran Ordered Glass's kidnaping,' *Boston Globe*, June 2, 1987, p. 17.

15 Scott Shane and Tom Bowman, 'America's Fortress of Spies,' *Baltimore Sun*, December 3, 1995, p. 13A.

16 'Now a "Grand Swap"?,' *Newsweek*, August 19, 1991, p. 25.

17 Steven Emerson, 'Diplomacy That Can Stop Terrorism,' *Wall Street Journal*, July 22, 1994, p. A10.

18 Amir Oren, 'Meanwhile, Back at the Muqata,' *Ha'aretz*, September 27, 2002.

19 Lisa Beyer, 'Death Comes Calling,' *Time*, January 15, 1996; Stacy Perman, 'Breaking a Terror Net,' *Business 2.0 Magazine*, December 2001, located at http://www.business2.com/articles/mag/0,1640,35149,FF.html. A detailed description of the Israeli manhunt for Ayyash can be found in Samuel M. Katz, *The Hunt for the Engineer* (Guilford, CT: The Lyons Press, 2002).

20 Jamil Hamad and Ahron Klein, 'The Enemy Within,' *Time International*, August 27, 2001.

21 Kamal Qubaysi, 'Israel Accused of Spying Via Mobile Phones,' *Al-Sharq Al-Aswat*, February 22, 1999, FBIS-EAS-1999–0222.

22 Bill Saporito, 'The Scene of the Siege,' *Time*, April 8, 2002, p. 28.

23 Hagay Huberman, 'CIA Recording of Dahlan Ordering Terrorist Operations Said Passed On to Israel,' *Hatzofe*, April 13, 2001, FBIS-NES-2001–0413.

24 David Eshel, 'Israel Hones Intelligence Operations to Counter Intifada,' *Jane's Intelligence Review*, October 2002, p. 26.

25 CM 5542, Intelligence and Security Committee, *Annual Report 2001–2002*, June 2002, p. 19; Michael Evans, 'Spy Centre "Monitored Maxwell Money Deals",' *Times of London*, June 16, 1992.

26 Patrick Fitzgerald, 'All About Eavesdropping,' *New Statesman & Society*, July 29, 1994, p. 30.

27 Yousef was later arrested in February 1995 in a hotel in Islamabad, Pakistan. The month before, he had been forced to abandon his laptop computer in an apartment in Manila after he accidently

started a fire while mixing high explosives. When the NSA decrypted his hard drive, they discovered that Yousef intended to plant bombs on 11 American airliners and detonate the devices over the Pacific. In January 1998, Yousef was sentenced to life in prison.

28 Scott Shane and Tom Bowman, 'America's Fortress of Spies,' *Baltimore Sun*, December 3, 1995, p. 13A.
29 Confidential interview.
30 Matthew M. Aid, 'The Time of Troubles: The US National Security Agency in the Twenty-First Century,' *Intelligence and National Security*, Vol. 15, No. 3, Autumn 2000, p. 9.
31 Memorandum for the NSA/CSS Representative Defense, *NSA Transition Book for the Department of Defense – Information Memorandum*, December 9, 1992, Top Secret Edition, p. 22; *Naval Security Group Command Annual History 1993*, np, COMNAVSECGRU FOIA; Bill Gertz, 'Electronic Spying Reoriented at NSA', *Washington Times*, January 27, 1992, p. A4; *National Security Agency Newsletter*, August 1996, p. 2.
32 Confidential interview.
33 Joint Inquiry Staff, House Permanent Select Committee on Intelligence and Senate Permanent Select Committee on Intelligence, Eleanor Hill, Staff Director, Joint Inquiry Staff, *Joint Inquiry Staff Statement, Part I*, September 18, 2002, p. 13.
34 Patrick Walters, 'Media Leaks Jeopardise Terror Fight,' *The Australian*, December 6, 2004.
35 Office of the Under Secretary of Defense for Acquisition & Technology, *The Defense Science Board 1997 Summer Study Task Force on DoD Responses to Transnational Threats*, October 1997, Vol. I: Final Report, p. C-2.
36 Bill Gertz, 'Bin Laden's Several Links to Terrorist Units Known,' *Washington Times*, August 23, 1998, p. A1.
37 Bill Gertz, 'Bin Laden's Several Links to Terrorist Units Known,' *Washington Times*, August 23, 1998, p. A1.
38 Bruce B. Auster, Kevin Whitelaw and Lucian Kim, 'An Inside Look at Terror Inc.,' *U.S. News & World Report*, October 19, 1998, pp. 34–35.
39 Confidential interviews.
40 Frank J. Cilluffo, Ronald A. Marks, and George C. Salmoiraghi, 'The Use and Limits of U.S. Intelligence,' *The Washington Quarterly*, Winter 2002, p. 66.
41 Shlomo Gazit and Michael Handel, 'Insurgency, Terrorism and Intelligence,' in Roy Godson, ed., *Intelligence Requirements for the 1980s: Counter Intelligence* (Washington: National Strategy Information Center, 1980), p. 136.
42 Confidential interviews.
43 Glenn Zorpette, 'Making Intelligence Smarter,' *IEEE Spectrum*, January 2002; Seymour M. Hersh, 'Missed Messages,' *The New Yorker*, May 29, 2002; Thomas Patrick Carroll, 'The CIA and the War on Terror,' *Middle East Intelligence Bulletin*, Vol. 4, No. 9, September 2002, p. 2.
44 Joint Inquiry Staff, House Permanent Select Committee on Intelligence and Senate Permanent Select Committee on Intelligence, Eleanor Hill, Staff Director, Joint Inquiry Staff, *Joint Inquiry Staff Statement, Part I*, September 18, 2002, p. 13.
45 See the transcript of the November 2001 Osama bin Laden videotape, filed in Kandahar, Afghanistan on or about November 9, 2001, in 'Caught on Tape,' *ABCNews.com*, December 13, 2001, http://abcnews.go.com/sections/world/DailyNews/OBLtaperelease011213.html
46 David Johnston, 'Lack of Pre-9/11 Sources to be Cited as Intelligence Failure,' *New York Times*, July 17, 2003, p. A1.
47 Confidential interviews. See also James Risen and David Johnston, 'Little Change in a System That Failed,' *New York Times*, September 8, 2002.
48 Joint Inquiry Staff, House Permanent Select Committee on Intelligence and Senate Permanent Select Committee on Intelligence, Eleanor Hill, Staff Director, Joint Inquiry Staff, *Joint Inquiry Staff Statement, Part I*, September 18, 2002, p. 13; Senate Report No. 107–351 and House Report No. 107–792, Report of the U.S. Senate Select Committee and U.S. House Permanent Select Committee on Intelligence, *Joint Inquiry Into Intelligence Community Activities Before and After the Terrorist Attacks of September 11, 2001*, 107th Congress, 2nd Session, December 2002 (declassified and released in July 2003), p. 376.
49 Transcript, Public Broadcasting System, *Frontline: Follow The Money*, July 12, 1989; Mark Urban, *UK Eyes Alpha* (London: Faber and Faber, 1996), p. 236.
50 Alan Friedman, 'The Flight of the Condor,' *Financial Times*, November 21, 1989.

51 Transcript, PBS, *Frontline: Follow the Money*, July 12, 1989.

52 Confidential interviews.

53 Jeff Gerth and Judith Miller, 'Funds for Terrorists Traced to Persian Gulf Businessmen,' *New York Times*, August 14, 1996, p. A1.

54 Robert Windrem, 'Bin Laden's Name Raised Again,' *MSNBC*, October 18, 2000, http://www/msnbc.com/news/477832.asp.

55 Seymour M. Hersh, 'King's Ransom: How Vulnerable are the Saudi Royals?,' *The New Yorker*, October 22, 2001, p. 35.

56 Glenn Zorpette, 'Making Intelligence Smarter,' *IEEE Spectrum*, January 2002.

57 Confidential interview.

58 Bill Gertz, *Breakdown: How America's Intelligence Failures Led to September 11* (Washington, D.C.: Regenry Publishing, Inc., 2002), p. 10.

59 Senate Report No. 107–351 and House Report No. 107–792, Report of the U.S. Senate Select Committee and U.S. House Permanent Select Committee on Intelligence, *Joint Inquiry Into Intelligence Community Activities Before and After the Terrorist Attacks of September 11, 2001*, 107th Congress, 2nd Session, December 2002 (declassified and released in July 2003), p. 380.

60 Confidential interview.

61 Confidential interviews.

62 U.S. House of Representatives, Permanent Select Committee on Intelligence, *IC21: Intelligence Community in the 21st Century*, 104th Congress, 1996, p. 187.

63 Bruce B. Auster, Kevin Whitelaw and Lucian Kim, 'An Inside Look at Terror Inc.,' *U.S. News & World Report*, October 19, 1998, pp. 34–35.

64 Philip H.J. Davies, 'Information Warfare and the Future of the Spy,' *Information Communication and Society*, Vol. 2, No. 2, Summer 1999.

65 Glenn Zorpette, 'Making Intelligence Smarter,' *IEEE Spectrum*, January 2002; John Tagliabue, 'Cryptic Tapes From 2000 Hinted at Air Attacks in U.S.,' *New York Times*, May 30, 2002, p. A1.

66 'U.S. Landmarks Described,' *ABCNEWS.com*, September 17, 2002, http://abcnews.go.com/sections/world/DailyNews/pakistan020917_arrest.html

67 International Telecommunications Union, 'ITU Telecommunication Indicators,' April 2000, http://www.itu.int/ti/industryoverview/at_glance/KeyTelecom99.htm. See also Paul Kaihla, 'Weapons of the Secret War,' *Business 2.0 Magazine*, November 2001, http://www.business2.com/articles/mag/print/0,1643,17511,FF.html

68 'Taliban Outlaws Net in Afghanistan,' *Reuters*, July 17, 2001; R. Frank Lebowitz, 'Taliban Ban Internet in Afghanistan,' *Digital Freedom Network*, July 16, 2001, http://dfn.org/focus/afghanistan/internetban.htm.

69 Confidential interview.

70 Trial Transcript, May 1, 2001, p. 5290, in 98 Cr. 1028, *United States of America v. Usama bin Laden et al.*, U.S. District Court for the Southern District of New York, New York City.

71 Trial Transcript, May 1, 2001, p. 5287, in 98 Cr. 1028, *United States of America v. Usama bin Laden et al.*, U.S. District Court for the Southern District of New York, New York City.

72 Trial Transcript, May 1, 2001, pp. 5288–5292, in 98 Cr. 1028, *United States of America v. Usama bin Laden et al.*, U.S. District Court for the Southern District of New York, New York City.

73 Nick Fielding and Dipesh Gadhery, 'The Next Target: Britain?,' *The Sunday Times*, March 24, 2002, p. 1.

74 Confidential interviews.

75 Walter Pincus and Vernon Loeb, 'CIA Blocked Two Attacks Last Year,' *Washington Post*, August 11, 1998, p. A16.

76 'Terrorism Directed at America,' ERRI Daily Intelligence Report, February 24, 1999, http://www.emergency.com/1999/bnldn-pg.htm.

77 Walter Pincus, 'CIA Touts Successes in Fighting Terrorism,' *Washington Post*, November 1, 2002, p. A29.

78 'Islam Rising,' *The Atlantic Monthly*, February 17, 1999.

79 Anonymous, 'How *Not* to Catch a Terrorist,' *Atlantic Monthly*, December 2004, p. 50.

80 Mark Matthews, 'Attacks' Timing Was Driven by Threats to U.S.,' *Baltimore Sun*, August 21, 1998, p. 1A; James Risen, 'Militant Leader Was a U.S. Target Since the Spring,' *New York Times*, September 6, 1998; Tim Weiner and James Risen, 'Decision to Strike Factory in Sudan Based Partly on Surmise,' *New York Times*, September 21, 1998; Gregory L. Vistica and Daniel Klaidman,

'Tracking Terror,' *Newsweek*, October 19, 1998; Bruce B. Auster, 'An Inside Look at Terror Inc.,' *U.S. News & World Report*, October 19, 1998.

81 Vernon Loeb, 'A Dirty Business,' *Washington Post*, July 25, 1999, pp. F1, F4; Paul McGeough, 'A Teacher of Terror,' *Sydney Morning Herald*, September 22, 2001, p. 1.

82 The 9/11 Commission identified a specific *Washington Times* article as having alerted bin Laden to the fact that NSA was monitoring his phone calls. The article in question was Martin Sieff, 'Terrorist is Driven by Hatred for U.S., Israel,' *Washington Times*, August 21, 1998, p. A1. See National Commission on Terrorist Attacks Upon the United States, *The 9/11 Commission Report: Final Report of the National Commission on Terrorist Attacks Upon the United States* (NY: W.W. Norton & Company, 2004), p. 127.

83 'Indian Daily: Musharraf Unlikely to Cooperate With US Forces' Hunt for UBL,' *The Pioneer*, December 21, 2001, FBIS-NES-2001–1221.

84 Robert Windrem, 'Bin Laden's Name Raised Again,' *MSNBC*, October 18, 2000, located at http://www.msnbc.com/news/477832.asp.

85 *Statement for the Record by Lt. General Michael v. Hayden, USAF, Director NSA/CSS Before the Joint Inquiry of the Senate Select Committee on Intelligence and the House Permanent Select Committee on Intelligence*, October 17, 2002, p. 3.

86 CM 5542, Intelligence and Security Committee, *Annual Report 2001–2002*, June 2002, p. 20.

87 NSA Declassification Guidance 003–96, October 25, 1996, via Dr. Jeffrey T. Richelson.

88 U.S. Department of Defense, DoD Directive No. 2000.12, *DoD Antiterrorism/Force Protection (AT/FP) Program*, April 13, 1999, Enclosure 5, National Security Agency Responsibilities, located at http://web7.whs.osd.mil/text/d200012p.txt

89 Senate Report No. 107–351 and House Report No. 107–792, Report of the U.S. Senate Select Committee and U.S. House Permanent Select Committee on Intelligence, *Joint Inquiry Into Intelligence Community Activities Before and After the Terrorist Attacks of September 11, 2001*, 107th Congress, 2nd Session, December 2002 (declassified and released in July 2003), p. 377.

90 On February 13, 2002, al-Hada, age 25, blew himself up with a grenade in downtown Sanaà when cornered by Yemeni security forces. He was the brother-in-law of one of the 9–11 hijackers, Khalid Almihdar.

91 For a detailed examination of the role played by al-Hada, see Michael Isikoff and Daniel Klaidman, 'The Hijackers We Let Escape,' *Newsweek*, June 10, 2002.

92 Barton Gellman, 'Broad Effort Launched After '98 Attacks,' *New York Times*, December 19, 1991, p. A1.

93 'Taliban Ready to Discuss US Demands to Hand Over Osama,' *The Daily Star*, February 8, 1999, http://www.dailystarnews.com/199902/n9020813.htm.

94 'Citing Threats, Britain Joins U.S. in Closing Embassies in Africa,' CNN, June 25, 1999, http://www.cnn.com/WORLD/africa/9906/25/africa.embassies.03/; David Phinney, 'Fund-Raising for Terrorism,' *ABCNEWS.com*, July 9, 1999.

95 John McWethy, 'U.S. Tries to Get Bin Laden,' *ABCNEWS.com*, July 9, 1999.

96 Barbara Starr, 'Bin Laden's Plans,' *ABCNEWS.com*, July 16, 1999.

97 National Commission on Terrorist Attacks Upon the United States, *The 9/11 Commission Report: Final Report of the National Commission on Terrorist Attacks Upon the United States* (NY: W.W. Norton & Company, 2004), p. 181.

98 Bill Gertz, 'NSA's Warning Arrived Too Late to Save the Cole,' *Washington Times*, October 25, 2000, p. A1.

99 James Risen and Stephen Engelberg, 'Failure to Heed Signs of Change in Terror Goals,' *New York Times*, October 14, 2001, p. A1.

100 Senate Report No. 107–351 and House Report No. 107–792, Report of the U.S. Senate Select Committee and U.S. House Permanent Select Committee on Intelligence, *Joint Inquiry Into Intelligence Community Activities Before and After the Terrorist Attacks of September 11, 2001*, 107th Congress, 2nd Session, December 2002 (declassified and released in July 2003), p. 203; Joint Inquiry Staff, House Permanent Select Committee on Intelligence and Senate Permanent Select Committee on Intelligence, Eleanor Hill, Staff Director, Joint Inquiry Staff, *Joint Inquiry Staff Statement, Part I*, September 18, 2002, p. 20; *Statement for the Record by Lt. General Michael V. Hayden, USAF, Director NSA/CSS Before the Joint Inquiry of the Senate Select Committee on Intelligence and the House Permanent Select Committee on Intelligence*, October 17, 2002, p. 4.

101 James Risen, 'In Hindsight, CIA Sees Flaws that Hindered Efforts on Terrorism,' *New York Times*, October 7, 2001, p. 1.

102 Walter Pincus, 'CIA Touts Successes in Fighting Terrorism,' *Washington Post*, November 1, 2002, p. A29.

103 Mary Dejevsky, 'US Forces on High Alert After Threat of Attack,' *The Independent*, June 23, 2001, p. 15.

104 Walter Pincus, 'CIA Touts Successes in Fighting Terrorism,' *Washington Post*, November 1, 2002, p. A29.

105 'The Proof They Did Not Reveal,' *Sunday Times*, October 7, 2001, p. 2; 'Early Warnings: Pre-Sept. 11 Cautions Went Unheeded,' *ABCNews.com*, February 18, 2002.

106 Raymond Bonner and John Tagliabue, 'Eavesdropping, U.S. Allies See New Terror Attack,' *New York Times*, October 21, 2001, p. A1; Neil A. Lewis and David Johnston, 'Jubilant Calls on Sept. 11 Led to FBI Arrests,' *New York Times*, October 28, 2001, p. A1.

107 The existence of these intercepts were first disclosed in Rowan Scarborough, 'Intercepts Foretold of "Big Attack",' *Washington Times*, September 22, 2001.

108 Joint Inquiry Staff, House Permanent Select Committee on Intelligence and Senate Permanent Select Committee on Intelligence, Eleanor Hill, Staff Director, Joint Inquiry Staff, *Joint Inquiry Staff Statement, Part I*, September 18, 2002, p. 22. See also Senate Report No. 107 351 and House Report No. 107–792, Report of the U.S. Senate Select Committee and U.S. House Permanent Select Committee on Intelligence, *Joint Inquiry Into Intelligence Community Activities Before and After the Terrorist Attacks of September 11, 2001*, 107th Congress, 2nd Session, December 2002 (declassified and released in July 2003), p. 375.

109 Press briefing by Rep. Saxby Chambliss and Rep. Jane Harman, July 12, 2002.

110 CM 5542, Intelligence and Security Committee, *Annual Report 2001–2002*, June 2002, p. 21.

111 Senate Report No. 107–351 and House Report No. 107–792, Report of the U.S. Senate Select Committee and U.S. House Permanent Select Committee on Intelligence, *Joint Inquiry Into Intelligence Community Activities Before and After the Terrorist Attacks of September 11, 2001*, 107th Congress, 2nd Session, December 2002 (declassified and released in July 2003), p. 374.

112 Bill Gertz, *Breakdown: How America's Intelligence Failures Led to September 11* (Washington, D.C.: Regenry Publishing, Inc., 2002), p. 135.

113 Douglas Waller, 'The NSA Draws Fire,' *Time*, July 20, 2002, located at http://www.time.com/time/nation/article/0,8599,322587,00.html

114 *Statement for the Record by Lt. General Michael v. Hayden, USAF, Director NSA/CSS Before the Joint Inquiry of the Senate Select Committee on Intelligence and the House Permanent Select Committee on Intelligence*, October 17, 2002, p. 3.

115 John Diamond, 'Terror Group's Messengers Steer Clear of NSA Ears,' *USA Today*, October 18, 2002, p. 12A.

116 Arieh O'Sullivan, 'Mossad Head: We Need Spies, Not Just Electronics,' *Jerusalem Post*, September 25, 2001, located at http://www.jpost.com/Editions/2001/09/25/News/News.35300.html

117 See Shmuel L. Gordon, *The Vulture and the Snake: Counter-Guerrilla Air Warfare: The War in Southern Lebanon* (Jerusalem: Begin-Sadat Center for Strategic Studies, Bar-Ilan University, July 1998).

118 U.S. Senate, Committee on the Judiciary, Subcommittee on Technology, Terrorism, and Government Information, *Crime, Terror and War: National Security and Public Safety in the Information Age*, November 1998.

119 U.S. House of Representatives, Permanent Select Committee on Intelligence, *IC21: Intelligence Community in the 21st Century*, 104th Congress, 1996, p. 186.

120 Prepared statement of Dr. John J. Hamre, President and CEO, Center for Strategic and International Studies, Washington, D.C., *Defining Terrorism and Responding to the Terrorist Threat*, Hearing Before the U.S. House of Representatives, House Permanent Select Committee on Intelligence, September 26, 2001.

121 *Congressional Record*, U.S. House of Representatives, May 7, 1998, p. H2950; Neil King, Jr., 'U.S. Security Agency Defends Eavesdrop Use,' *Wall Street Journal*, April 13, 2000.

122 National Commission on Terrorism, *Countering the Changing Threat of International Terrorism*, June 2000, located at http://www.fas.org/irp/threat/commission.html.

123 Confidential interview.

124   Confidential interview.
125   David A. Fulghum, 'Computer Combat Rules Frustrate the Pentagon,' *Aviation Week & Space Technology*, September 15, 1997, p. 68.
126   Confidential interview.
127   Confidential interviews.
128   Joint Inquiry Staff, House Permanent Select Committee on Intelligence and Senate Permanent Select Committee on Intelligence, Eleanor Hill, Staff Director, Joint Inquiry Staff, *Joint Inquiry Staff Statement*, October 8, 2002.
129   Confidential interview.
130   Confidential interview for conflicting tasking on NSA. For number of federal agencies involved in counterterrorism, see U.S. General Accounting Office, GAO/T-NSIAD-98–164, *Combating Terrorism: Observations on Crosscutting Issues*, April 23, 1998, p. 4.
131   U.S. House of Representatives, House Permanent Select Committee on Intelligence, Subcommittee on Terrorism and Homeland Security, *Counterterrorism Intelligence Capabilities and Performance Prior to 9–11*, July 17, 2002, p. v.
132   Confidential interviews.
133   Douglas Waller, 'The NSA Draws Fire,' *Time*, July 20, 2002, located at http://www.time.com/time/nation/article/0,8599,322587,00.html
134   *Statement for the Record by Lt. General Michael v. Hayden, USAF, Director NSA/CSS Before the Joint Inquiry of the Senate Select Committee on Intelligence and the House Permanent Select Committee on Intelligence*, October 17, 2002, p. 9.
135   Senate Report No. 107–351 and House Report No. 107–792, Report of the U.S. Senate Select Committee and U.S. House Permanent Select Committee on Intelligence, *Joint Inquiry Into Intelligence Community Activities Before and After the Terrorist Attacks of September 11, 2001*, 107th Congress, 2nd Session, December 2002 (declassified and released in July 2003), p. 374.
136   National Commission on Terrorism, *Countering the Changing Threat of International Terrorism*, June 5, 2000, p. iv; The United States Commission on National Security/21st Century, *Road Map for National Security: Imperative for Change: The Phase III Report of the U.S. Commission on National Security/21st Century* (hereafter 'Hart-Rudman Report'), February 15, 2001, p. 85.
137   U.S. House of Representatives, House Permanent Select Committee on Intelligence, Subcommittee on Terrorism and Homeland Security, *Counterterrorism Intelligence Capabilities and Performance Prior to 9–11*, July 17, 2002, p. vi.
138   CM 5542, Intelligence and Security Committee, *Annual Report 2001–2002*, June 2002, pp. 10, 26; CM 5837, Intelligence and Security Committee, *Annual Report 2002–2003*, June 2003, p. 11.
139   CM 5837, Intelligence and Security Committee, *Annual Report 2002–2003*, June 2003, p. 20.
140   Confidential interview.
141   Confidential interviews.
142   Bob Drogin, 'Crash Jolts US e-Spy Agency,' *Los Angeles Times*, March 21, 2000, p. 1.
143   John Diamond, 'Terror Group's Messengers Steer Clear of NSA Ears,' *USA Today*, October 18, 2002, p. 12A.
144   Stephen Braun et al., 'U.S. Strikes Back Sunday Report: Haunted by Years of Missed Warnings,' *Los Angeles Times*, October 14, 2001, p. A1.
145   David Adams, 'To Fight Back, We Have to Know Why We're Hated,' *St. Petersburg Times*, September 16, 2001, p. 13.
146   Statement by Director of Central Intelligence George J. Tenet Before the Senate Committee on Armed Services, *The Worldwide Threat in 2000: Global Realities of our National Security*, February 3, 2000, p. 6.
147   Dorothy E. Denning and William E. Baugh, Jr., *Encryption and Evolving Technologies: Tools of Organized Crime and Terrorism* (Washington, D.C.: National Strategic Information Center's Working Group on Organized Crime, 1997).
148   Ramesh Vinayak, 'Wireless Wars,' *India Today*, September 14, 1998, http://www.india-today.com/itoday/14091998/war.html.
149   Confidential interview of former Indian intelligence officer.
150   'Global Traffic Review: TeleGeography 2000,' at http://www.telegeography.com.
151   'Global Traffic Review: TeleGeography 2000,' at http://www.telegeography.com.
152   Scott Shane and Tom Bowman, 'America's Fortress of Spies,' *Baltimore Sun*, December 3, 1995, p. 12A.

153 Gregory Vistica and Evan Thomas, 'Hard of Hearing,' *Newsweek*, December 13, 1999; Frank Tiboni, 'Difficulty Grows for U.S. Intelligence Gathering,' *Space News*, June 12, 2000, p. 1.

154 Major A. Andronov, 'American Geosynchrenous SIGINT Satellites,' *Zarubezhnoye Voyennoye Obozreniye*, No. 12, 1993, pp. 37–43.

155 For NSA owning the largest communications system in the federal government, see 'Prestigious Roger W. Jones Award Presented,' *NSA Newsletter*, December 1994, p. 3. For network problems, see Robert K. Ackerman, 'Security Agency Transitions From Backer to Participant,' *Signal*, October 1999, p. 23.

156 U.S. House of Representatives, Permanent Select Committee on Intelligence, *IC21: Intelligence Community in the 21st Century*, 104th Congress, 1996, p. 120.

157 Robert K. Ackerman, 'Security Agency Transitions From Backer to Participant,' *Signal*, October 1999, p. 23; Gregory Vistica and Evan Thomas, 'Hard of Hearing,' *Newsweek*, December 13, 1999; Jeffrey T. Richelson, 'Desperately Seeking Signals,' *Bulletin of Atomic Scientists*, March/April 2000, pp. 47–51.

158 *Congressional Record*, July 19, 1999, pp. S8777–S8796.

159 'Panel: Terrorists Overwelming Spy Agency,' *Bloomberg News*, June 6, 2000; Declan McCullagh, 'Feds Urged to Beef Up Spying,' *Wired News*, June 9, 2000, located at http://www.wired.com/news/politics/0,1283,36868,00.html.

160 Hans Leyendecker, 'Tapping for Trash,' *Sueddeutsche Zeitung*, August 18, 1998, FBIS-WEU-98-230.

161 U.S. House of Representatives, House Permanent Select Committee on Intelligence, Subcommittee on Terrorism and Homeland Security, *Counterterrorism Intelligence Capabilities and Performance Prior to 9–11*, July 17, 2002, p. v.

162 Senate Report No. 107–351 and House Report No. 107–792, Report of the U.S. Senate Select Committee and U.S. House Permanent Select Committee on Intelligence, *Joint Inquiry Into Intelligence Community Activities Before and After the Terrorist Attacks of September 11, 2001*, 107th Congress, 2nd Session, December 2002 (declassified and released in July 2003), p. 382.

163 Senator Paul Simon, 'Beef Up the Country's Foreign Language Skills,' *Washington Post*, October 23, 2001, p. A23.

164 Confidential interviews.

165 Senate Report No. 107–351 and House Report No. 107–792, Report of the U.S. Senate Select Committee and U.S. House Permanent Select Committee on Intelligence, *Joint Inquiry Into Intelligence Community Activities Before and After the Terrorist Attacks of September 11, 2001*, 107th Congress, 2nd Session, December 2002 (declassified and released in July 2003), p. 336.

166 Confidential interviews.

167 U.S. House of Representatives, Permanent Select Committee on Intelligence, Report 107–219, *Intelligence Authorization Act for Fiscal Year 2002*, 107th Congress, 1st Session, September 26, 2001.

168 Penelope S. Horgan, *Signals Intelligence Support to U.S. Military Commanders: Past and Present* (Carlisle Barracks, PA: U.S. Army War College, 1991), p. 84.

169 National Commission on Terrorist Attacks Upon the United States, *The 9/11 Commission Report: Final Report of the National Commission on Terrorist Attacks Upon the United States* (NY: W.W. Norton & Company, 2004), p. 88.

170 Memorandum, *To Consider Possibilities of Using Deleted Information for Prosecution*, pp. 1–3, attached to Memorandum, Belmont to Boardman, February 1, 1956, FBI Venona Files.

171 Tom Blanton, ed., *White House E-Mail: The Top Secret Computer Messages the Reagan/Bush White House Tried to Destroy* (NY: The New Press, 1995), p. 223.

172 Joint Inquiry Staff, House Permanent Select Committee on Intelligence and Senate Permanent Select Committee on Intelligence, Eleanor Hill, Staff Director, Joint Inquiry Staff, *Joint Inquiry Staff Statement*, October 8, 2002.

173 *Statement for the Record by Lt. General Michael v. Hayden, USAF, Director NSA/CSS Before the Joint Inquiry of the Senate Select Committee on Intelligence and the House Permanent Select Committee on Intelligence*, October 17, 2002, p. 10.

174 National Commission on Terrorist Attacks Upon the United States, *The 9/11 Commission Report: Final Report of the National Commission on Terrorist Attacks Upon the United States* (NY: W.W. Norton & Company, 2004), pp. 87–88.

175 Commission on the Roles and Capabilities of the United States Intelligence Community, *Preparing for the 21st Century: An Appraisal of U.S. Intelligence* (Washington, D.C.: Government Printing Office, March 1, 1996), pp. 41–42.

176 Joint Inquiry Staff, House Permanent Select Committee on Intelligence and Senate Permanent Select Committee on Intelligence, Eleanor Hill, Staff Director, Joint Inquiry Staff, *Joint Inquiry Staff Statement*, October 8, 2002.

177 Bill Gertz, *Breakdown: How America's Intelligence Failures Led to September 11* (Washington, D.C.: Regenry Publishing, Inc., 2002), p. 178.

178 National Performance Review, *Accompanying Report of the National Performance Review: The Intelligence Community* (Washingtington, D.C.: Government Printing Office, September 1993), pp. 35–36.

179 *Statement for the Record by Lt. General Michael v. Hayden, USAF, Director NSA/CSS Before the Joint Inquiry of the Senate Select Committee on Intelligence and the House Permanent Select Committee on Intelligence*, October 17, 2002, p. 10.

180 Senate Report No. 107–351 and House Report No. 107–792, Report of the U.S. Senate Select Committee and U.S. House Permanent Select Committee on Intelligence, *Joint Inquiry Into Intelligence Community Activities Before and After the Terrorist Attacks of September 11, 2001*, 107th Congress, 2nd Session, December 2002 (declassified and released in July 2003), p. 343.

181 *Statement for the Record by Lt. General Michael v. Hayden, USAF, Director NSA/CSS Before the Joint Inquiry of the Senate Select Committee on Intelligence and the House Permanent Select Committee on Intelligence*, October 17, 2002, p. 10.

182 Joint Inquiry Staff, House Permanent Select Committee on Intelligence and Senate Permanent Select Committee on Intelligence, Eleanor Hill, Staff Director, Joint Inquiry Staff, *Joint Inquiry Staff Statement*, October 8, 2002.

183 Confidential interview.

184 Commission on the Roles and Capabilities of the United States Intelligence Community, *Preparing for the 21st Century: An Appraisal of U.S. Intelligence* (Washington, D.C.: Government Printing Office, March 1, 1996), p. 38.

185 *Statement for the Record by Lt. General Michael v. Hayden, USAF, Director NSA/CSS Before the Joint Inquiry of the Senate Select Committee on Intelligence and the House Permanent Select Committee on Intelligence*, October 17, 2002, p. 8.

186 Karl Vick and Kamran Khan, 'Raid Netted Top Al Qaeda Leader,' *Washington Post*, April 2, 2002, p. A1; Aftab Ahmad, 'Osama in Faisalabad?,' *The Nation (Lahore Edition)*, April 8, 2002, FBIS-NEW-2002–0408; Ijaz Hashmat, 'US Intercepted Satellite Phone Message That Led to Raid in Faisalabad,' *Khabrain*, April 9, 2002, FBIS-NES-2002–0409.

187 Rory McCarthy and Julian Borger, 'Secret Arrest of Leading al-Qaida Fugitive,' *The Guardian*, September 4, 2002.

188 Nick Fielding, 'Phone Call Gave Away Al Qaida Hideout,' *Sunday Times*, September 15, 2001, p. 1; Rory McCarthy, 'Investigators Question Key September 11 Suspect,' *The Guardian*, September 16, 2002; Nick Fielding, 'War on Terror: Knocking on Al-Qaeda's Door,' *Sunday Times*, September 22, 2002, p. 1.

189 Kevin Johnson and Jack Kelly, 'Terror Arrest Triggers Mad Scrammble,' *USA Today*, March 2, 2003; Rory McCarthy and Jason Burke, 'Emdgame in the Desert of Death for the World's Most Wanted Man,' *The Observer*, March 9, 2003; Kevin Whitelaw, 'A Tightening Noose,' *U.S. News & World Report*, March 17, 2003.

190 Gregory F. Treverton, 'Intelligence Crisis,' *Government Executive Magazine*, November 1, 2001, http://www.govexec.com/features/1101/1101s1.htm.

191 The covername for the SCS when operating overseas is the Defense Communications Support Group.

192 Confidential interviews.

193 Colum Lynch, 'US Used UN to Spy on Iraq, Aides Say,' *Boston Globe*, January 6, 1999, p. A1; Barton Gellman, 'Annan Suspicious of UNSCOM Probe,' *Washington Post*, January 6, 1999, pp. A1, A22; Bruce W. Nelan, 'Bugging Saddam,' *Time*, January 18, 1999; Seymour M. Hersh, 'Saddam's Best Friend,' *The New Yorker*, April 5, 1999, pp. 32, 35; David Wise, 'Fall Guy,' *The Washingtonian*, July 1999, pp. 42–43.

194 Glenn Zorpette, 'Making Intelligence Smarter,' *IEEE Spectrum*, January 2002.

195 Frank J. Cilluffo, Ronald A. Marks, and George C. Salmoiraghi, 'The Use and Limits of U.S. Intelligence,' *The Washington Quarterly*, Winter 2002, p. 67.

196 John Deutch and Jeffrey H. Smith, 'Smarter Intelligence,' *Foreign Policy*, January-February 2002.

197 *House of Commons Hansard Debates*, June 22, 2000, Part 30, Column 543, located at http://

www.parliament.the-stationery-office.co.uk/pa/cm199900/cmhansrd/cm000622/debtext/00622-30.htm.

198 Gregory F. Treverton, 'Intelligence Crisis,' *Government Executive Magazine*, November 1, 2001, http://www.govexec.com/features/1101/1101s1.htm.

199 An excellent description of ISA can be found in Jeffrey T. Richelson, 'Truth Conquers All Chains: The U.S. Army Intelligence Support Activity, 1981–1989,' *International Journal of Intelligence and Counterintelligence*, Vol. 12, No. 2, Summer 1999, pp. 168–200.

200 Steven Emerson, *Secret Warriors* (NY: G.P. Putnam's Sons, 1988), p. 67.

201 Statement of the Under Secretary of Defense for Acquisition and Technology Paul G. Kaminski Before the House Permanent Select Committee on Intelligence on Enabling Intelligence Technologies for the 21st Century, October 18, 1995, located at http://www.acq.osd.mil/ousda/testimonies/inteltech.txt; Alan D. Campen, 'Intelligence is the Long Pole in the Information Operations Tent,' March 30, 2000, Infowar.com, http://www.infowar.com/info_ops/00/info_ops033000a_j.shtml..

202 U.S. House of Representatives, Permanent Select Committee on Intelligence, Report 107–592, *Intelligence Authorization Act for Fiscal Year 2003*, 107th Congress, 2nd Session, July 18, 2002.

203 'Panel: Terrorists Overwelming Spy Agency,' *Bloomberg News*, June 6, 2000; Declan McCullagh, 'Feds Urged to Beef Up Spying,' *Wired News*, June 9, 2000, located at http://www.wired.com/news/politics/0,1283,36868,00.html.

204 Commission on the Roles and Capabilities of the United States Intelligence Community, *Preparing for the 21st Century: An Appraisal of U.S. Intelligence* (Washington, D.C.: Government Printing Office, March 1, 1996), p. 127.

205 Shlomo Spiro, *Frameworks for European-Mediterranean Intelligence Sharing*, 2001, pp. 5–6, located at http://www.nato.int/acad/fellow/99–01/shpiro.pdf

206 Commission on the Roles and Capabilities of the United States Intelligence Community, *Preparing for the 21st Century: An Appraisal of U.S. Intelligence* (Washington, D.C.: Government Printing Office, March 1, 1996), p. 128.

207 Bob Drogin and Greg Miller, 'U.S. Strikes Back: Covert Moves,' *Los Angeles Times*, October 11, 2001, p. A1.

208 'India's Defense Minister Backs US in Fight Against Terrorism,' *Xinhua*, September 16, 2001, FBIS-CHI-2001–0916.

209 David Rose, 'Spy Chiefs Call for New Rules and Money to Stop Terrorists,' *The Observer*, September 16, 2001.

210 *Congressional Record*, Senate, November 7, 1991, p. S16305.

211 'Panel Urges Improving System of Intelligence,' *Agence France-Presse*, September 6, 2002.

212 Confidential interview.

Reprinted with permission from Matthew Aid, 'All Glory Is Fleeting: Sigint and the Fight against International Terrorism', *Intelligence and National Security* 18/4 (Winter 2003) pp.72–120.

5 A venerable source in a new era

Sailing the sea of OSINT in the information age

Stephen Mercado

Mercado argues that intelligence communities require better craft to navigate the vast oceans of open sources. Mercado focuses on open source radio monitoring of the kind done by FBIS (and the BBC) one of the longest-serving open source organisations. He argues that open source may be accessible but they are not necessarily easy to manage. There are not only problems of scale but also of language. Few countries have teams of appropriate linguists that are up to the task.

Our age's increasingly voluminous open-source intelligence (OSINT) sheds light on issues of the day for all-source analysts, covert collectors, and policymakers, but have we done enough to exploit its potential? My short answer is 'No,' and here's why I think so.

Collecting intelligence these days is at times less a matter of stealing through dark alleys in a foreign land to meet some secret agent than one of surfing the Internet under the fluorescent lights of an office cubicle to find some open source. The world is changing with the advance of commerce and technology. Mouse clicks and online dictionaries today often prove more useful than stylish cloaks and shiny daggers in gathering intelligence required to help analysts and officials understand the world. Combined with stolen secrets, diplomatic reports, and technical collection, open sources constitute what one former deputy director of intelligence termed the 'intricate mosaic' of intelligence.[1]

Today's commercial and technical advances are only the latest developments in a collection discipline whose pioneers began developing the field in the late 1930s. Building on early work at Princeton University to monitor foreign short-wave radio, the Foreign Broadcast Intelligence Service (FBIS) in 1941 began to turn radio into a primary intelligence source during World War II.[2] The government did not neglect the printed word either. The Inter-departmental Committee for the Acquisition of Foreign Periodicals (IDC) gathered Axis publications through a global collection network.

The men and women who labored in the OSINT fields of the day produced products that compared well in quantity and quality to those of other agencies that stamped their documents 'SECRET.' Dr. Charles B. Fah, writing in mid-1942 as chief of the Far Eastern Section, Office of Strategic Services (OSS), praised the output of FBIS as 'indispensable in our work' and 'the most extensive single source available' on developments in Japan and occupied Asia. The OSS itself fared less well, failing to establish an agent network in Japan and reporting the fabrications of an Italian 'con man' in Rome as its most valuable source on developments in Tokyo.

Publications also held up well against classified reports. John King Fairbank, the Harvard sinologist who led his field in the postwar era, recounted how, after reading an inaccurate and 'unintelligent' British report on Japanese shipbuilding, advised Col. William Donovan that better intelligence on the issue would be found in 'scrutinizing the Japanese press.'

The OSS director evidently found Dr. Fairbank's brief compelling, for he sent the young academic, literate in Chinese and Japanese, to China to help organize a publications procurement program.[3]

Navigating Cold War waters

After the guns of the Second World War fell silent, intelligence officers expert in open sources continued to help analysts and officials navigate the murky waters of the Cold War. For example, analysts in FBIS, whose acronym by then stood for the Foreign Broadcast *Information Service*, and the Foreign Document Division (FDD) led the CIA in detecting the developing estrangement between Moscow and Beijing. FBIS and FDD officers began discerning signs of the Sino-Soviet split from their readings of propaganda material in the early 1950s. In contrast, some CIA officers from the covert side of the house erred, along with many observers elsewhere, in dismissing as disinformation the open evidence well into the next decade.[4]

Throughout the Cold War, in fact, OSINT constituted a major part of all intelligence on the Soviet Union, China, and other adversaries. OSINT on the Soviet Union, for example, grew from modest beginnings to become the leading source. In the closing years of World War II, intelligence officers searched German, Japanese, and Russian documents in the Army's Special Documents Section and the joint Army-Navy Washington Document Center for clues to Soviet technical capabilities. By the late 1950s, the CIA and Air Force had discovered a 'wealth of information' in the increasing flow of books and periodicals from the Soviet Union.[5] By the early 1960s, one insider wrote that 'In aggregate, open sources probably furnish the greater part of all information used in the production of military intelligence on the Soviet Union.'[6] By the decade's end, another wrote of the 'tidal wave of publicly printed paper' that both supported and threatened 'to swamp' the Intelligence Community. He also offered an example of OSINT's value: 'Intense scrutiny of the North Vietnamese press and radio has been an essential intelligence element in support of [the] US effort' in the Indochina conflict.[7]

It is worth noting in passing that all powers exploited OSINT during World War II and the Cold War. Indeed, our adversaries used technical information from open sources in the United States and other advanced industrial nations to monitor foreign developments and to save time and money on their own projects. The US aerospace publication *Aviation Week*, dubbed 'Aviation Leak' for its scoops, was a perennial favorite. The journal was among the US technical periodicals that East German intelligence, among others, translated to monitor current developments in aerospace.[8]

By the Cold War's end, commercial and technical changes had made evident the value of OSINT. Radio, the cutting edge in the 1930s, remained a key source in the Second World War and the years thereafter. When Soviet tanks rolled into Budapest in 1956, for example, intelligence officers in Washington kept current through radio reports. One veteran of the CIA's Directorate of Operations (DO), referring to Moscow's suppression of the Hungarian uprising, wrote: 'It is a well-known phenomenon in the field of intelligence that there often comes a time when public political activity proceeds at such a rapid and fulminating pace that secret intelligence, the work of agents, is overtaken by events publicly recorded.'[9] Some 30 years later, intelligence officers at Langley and government leaders across the Potomac watched, glued to their television sets, as CNN broadcast the fall of the Berlin Wall.[10]

The world today abounds in open information to an extent unimaginable to intelligence officers of the Cold War. When the Soviet Union sent the first man into space in 1961, secretive officials revealed little and lied even about the location of the launch site. In contrast, television reports, Internet sites, and newspaper articles heralded China's first manned flight into orbit last year. Even intelligence services have emerged from the shadows to some extent. Two journalists caused a stir in 1964 by writing a landmark book on the US Intelligence Community. Today, former case officers recount their clandestine careers.[11]

OSINT, OSINT everywhere . . .

The revolution in information technology, commerce, and politics since the Cold War's end is only making open sources more accessible, ubiquitous, and valuable. Simply put, one can gather more open intelligence with greater ease and at less cost than ever before. The explosion in OSINT is transforming the intelligence world with the emergence of open versions of the covert arts of human intelligence (HUMINT), overhead imagery (IMINT), and signals intelligence (SIGINT).

The Intelligence Community has seen open sources grow increasingly easier and cheaper to acquire in recent years. The Internet's development and commercial innovation has given us Web sites, 'amazon.com,' and countless other vendors. During the Second World War, Dr. Fairbank traveled far and at great expense to gather Japanese publications in China and send them to Washington. Today, anyone, anywhere, can order Japanese media with a click of the mouse from amazon.co.jp or other online merchants and receive the orders by express air shipment. In the 'old days,' not so long ago, academics and analysts made the pilgrimage to Maryland to browse the shelves of Victor Kamkin's unmatched store for Soviet publications. In the present, one can go on line from the comfort of home to www.kamkin.com to buy from the half million Russian titles in stock or to place a custom order.

Moreover, the IT revolution extends beyond the printed word. More and more local radio and television broadcasts, for example, are found on the World Wide Web. Monitors no longer need to sit close to the broadcast source. Nor do they always need an expensive infrastructure of antennas and other equipment to listen to radio or watch television.

Beyond the usual public media, OSINT is expanding into the areas of HUMINT, IMINT, and SIGINT. In the words of one advocate with experience in both the government and private sector, 'OSINT now pervades all of the collection disciplines.' He notes that one can gather intelligence today by overtly tasking collectors to elicit information, ordering commercial satellite imagery, and using software to conduct traffic analysis.[12]

IMINT, for example, is becoming such a commercial commodity as to be in danger, in the view of one intelligence expert, of ceasing to be an 'INT.' Japan offers a fine demonstration of media exploitation of commercial IMINT. A major magazine known for its focus on North Korea, for example, prominently and frequently displays commercial imagery of such sites as the nuclear facilities at Yongbyon and the alleged residences of leader Kim Chong-il. Journalists combine the IMINT with published defector information, leaks, and other sources to analyze issues. As an example of open IMINT closer to home, the Federation of American Scientists (FAS) used Space Imaging photographs of a DPRK missile site to argue in 2000 that P'yongyang's missile threat was far less than Washington had claimed. Whatever the merits of the FAS argument, the case underscores the opening of the covert INTs.[13]

Even so, OSINT is no replacement for covert collection. Rather, open sources increasingly enhance secret collection programs. The CIA, NGA, NSA, and other actors on the classified side all benefit from the growing volume of open data serving them as collateral information. Too, OSINT allows covert collectors to marshal limited resources for the most intractable problems. Digital Globe and Space Imaging will never replace NGA, for example, but government acquisition of their commercial imagery for basic requirements can relieve NGA of mundane tasks and permit it focus on higher priorities.

In addition to their influence on collection disciplines, open sources have long played a major role in covert action. Imperial Japan, for example, employed the German, Alexander von Siebold, to influence foreign opinion in Tokyo's favor. The agent launched the journal *Ostasien* (East Asia) in 1899 with Japanese backing, contributed favorable articles to the European media, and otherwise worked to shape views on Japan. He also monitored the media, submitting his 'Baron von Siebold's Report on the Press' to inform the Japanese of foreign developments and opinion.[14] In the Cold War, covert organs of the major powers disseminated news and views through front organizations to win hearts and minds. Open sources still constitute the core of political covert action today, except that overt organizations are often conducting the campaigns.[15]

. . . Surrounding targets hard and soft . . .

Not only are open sources increasingly accessible, ubiquitous, and valuable, but they can shine in particular against the hardest of hard targets. OSINT is at times the 'INT' of first resort, last resort, and every resort in between.

To some, this assertion may represent an overselling of OSINT. Arthur Hulnick, a former CIA officer who went on to teach at Boston University has written about OSINT's importance: 'Neither glamorous nor adventurous, open sources are nonetheless the basic building block for secret intelligence.' He has also noted how OSINT, whether conveyed via FBIS or CNN, provides early warning. He has even estimated that open sources may account for 'as much as 80 percent' of the intelligence database in general. Nevertheless, Hulnick has suggested that OSINT would probably be far less useful against such tough cases as North Korea.[16]

However, open sources may often be more useful in penetrating closed borders than open societies. Because OSINT is intelligence derived from open sources, fewer sources mean greater coverage is possible with a limited number of monitors. Take the two Koreas, for example. The Democratic People's Republic of Korea (DPRK), with perhaps the world's most authoritarian government, is a relatively easy OSINT target. North Korea has only two major daily newspapers: *Nodong Sinmun* and *Minju Choson*, the newspapers of the ruling party and the government, respectively. There is no opposition newspaper in the capital and no lively provincial media to offer competing opinions or expose wrongdoing. The Republic of Korea (ROK), on the other hand, has a boisterous press, comprising over a dozen newspapers centered in Seoul, with views spanning the full spectrum of political opinion. Each day brings a flood of government statements, corporate press releases, editorials, scoops, and scandals. In relative terms, monitoring P'yongyang's media is like sipping through a straw; following Seoul's open sources is like drinking from a fire hose.

P'yongyang media, while controlled, constitute a valuable resource to anyone seeking to understand the DPRK. More than mere propaganda, as Dr. Wayne Kiyosaki, an expert literate in Korean and well-versed in the media, argued in his study of DPRK foreign relations, P'yongyang's communications are a tool of mass indoctrination. As such, they provide 'a barometer of priorities.'[17] Dr. Adrian Buzo, a former Australian diplomat with the rare experience of residing in P'yongyang, has seconded the value of DPRK media as a 'continuing record of the regime's priorities, of its ideological concerns, and of key personnel changes.' Warning readers against the common trap in the West of dismissing the media 'out of hand,' he has advised that 'Sustained exposure to the DPRK media is an essential requirement for the would-be analyst, both in itself and as an essential check on the reportage of the DPRK's adversaries.'[18]

Finally, continuing with the DPRK as an example, US analysts and policymakers often have little beyond OSINT upon which to base their judgments. The State Department has no embassy in P'yongyang. Few foreigners reside in the capital; even fewer live in the provinces. Opportunities to make contact with the rare North Koreans who reside or travel abroad have been poor. Only the trusted few may make an international telephone call, send a fax, exchange e-mails, or surf the Internet. Such restrictions reduce covert collection opportunities. The open record for HUMINT is telling. Ambassador Donald Gregg, an 'Asia hand' whose DO career included a stint in Seoul, has described the DPRK as 'one of the longest-running intelligence failures in the history of US espionage.'[19]

Other nations fare no better. One would expect the Japanese, former colonial overlords of Korea for more than 30 years, to accomplish more covert collection against their neighbors than their writings suggest. Tsukamoto Katsuichi, a retired army general with experience as defense attaché in Seoul, has confessed: 'No country is as opaque as the DPRK (North Korea). Almost no information leaks out of there. Therefore, we have no choice but to make our judgments based on the little announced in the official newspaper (*Nodong Sinmun*) and radio broadcasts (Korea Central News Agency), as well as a limited number of visitor accounts.'[20] A former officer of the Public Security Intelligence Agency (PSIA), Japan's equivalent to the FBI, has also written that analysis of 'published materials' is 'central' to analyzing the DPRK, given the absence of nearly all else. Such OSINT, he has written, is 'more important and indispensable than is generally imagined.'[21]

. . . But few to sail the sea

> Today, open source has expanded well beyond 'frosting' and comprises a large part of the cake itself. It has become indispensable to the production of authoritative analysis.
> John Gannon, former Chairman, National Intelligence Council[22]

With open sources so accessible, ubiquitous, and valuable, one would expect to see OSINT occupying a commensurately large space within the Intelligence Community. This is not the case. Too many people still reject OSINT as intelligence. Worse, too few are able to gather and exploit open sources. Worst of all, the Intelligence Community assigns only a handful of those capable people to the task.

Too many people still mistake secrets for intelligence. The enduring popularity of the fictional James Bond bears much of the blame, perhaps, for the misperception outside of the Intelligence Community that a tuxedo, pistol, and charm are the main tools of intelligence gathering. Even some insiders err in believing intelligence to be identical with covert sources and methods. The following opinion of a retired DO officer is typical: 'Despite frequent references to "open source intelligence," within the CIA this term is somewhat of an oxymoron. By definition, intelligence is clandestinely acquired information – stolen, to put it bluntly. Information from a magazine, a television broadcast, or someone's newsletter may be valuable, but it is not intelligence.'[23]

More than 40 years after Sherman Kent, the CIA's father of intelligence analysis, persuasively argued that intelligence is knowledge, some still confuse the method with the product. Sadly, such confusion is widespread. As one DPRK watcher noted: 'Much of the best political intelligence comes from careful culling of public sources, like reading reports in the North Korean media, but within the intelligence community this source is not considered as reliable as more esoteric technical means, like satellite photography and communications intercepts, or spies.'[24] However, as a staff director of the House Permanent Select Committee on Intelligence (HPSCI) once explained to a deputy director of operations, 'We don't give you brownie points for collecting intelligence by the hardest means possible.'[25]

A few examples should suffice to support Kent's definition of intelligence:

- An intelligence officer would likely have received high marks for stealing a map of the Khabarovsk area of the Soviet Far East in 1988. Drawn at a scale of 1:10,000 and running to 80 pages, the map of the General Staff's Military Topographic Headquarters would have taken a classified stamp and stayed within a secure vault, available only to those with a need to know. The map, published in 1998 and advertised as the first of this scale declassified in Russia, is for sale today.[26]
- Stanislav Levchenko, a KGB officer working under cover as a reporter in Japan, defected to the United States in 1979. In 1983, a Japanese journalist conducted more than 20 hours of interviews with him, during which the former operative named agents and discussed tradecraft. The resulting book and Levchenko's press conferences were, according to a US intelligence officer, more revealing than his CIA debriefing.[27]
- On 7 June 1942, the day after the US 'miracle' at Midway due to the top-secret breaking of Japanese communications, the *Chicago Tribune* trumpeted on its front page that the US Navy had known of Japanese plans 'several days before the battle began.' A Japanese officer reading that newspaper probably would have grasped that the naval codes were insecure.[28]

Information openly acquired, whether open from the start (say, a telephone book), declassified, or leaked, is intelligence when assessed and disseminated appropriately.[29] History abounds with examples of OSINT collection by intelligence officers:

- Military attachés have long attached magazine photographs of aircraft, ships, and tanks to their classified reports.
- Japan's Kempeitai in wartime Shanghai gathered the writings of Agnes Smedley and Edgar Snow in the course of collecting intelligence on the Chinese Communist Party.[30]
- Various services culled intelligence from the pages of the Soviet military daily *Krasnaya Zvezda* (Red Star), including the wartime Imperial Japanese Army's Harbin Special Services Agency and the postwar US Intelligence Community.[31]

Beyond the persistent dismissal of open sources as intelligence, the US Intelligence Community suffers from America's general indifference to foreign languages and ideas. Any intelligence agency reflects the society from which it comes. Americans, living in a vast country and speaking a language that has become the world's *lingua franca*, show little interest in learning other languages or, indeed, knowing what those outside their borders think. The result is an Intelligence Community recruiting officers from among a relatively small pool of Americans who, through immigration or education, possess the expertise in foreign languages and area studies required for collecting open sources.

Knowing foreign languages is the key to exploiting OSINT. An account with LexisNexis and a subscription to the *Wall Street Journal* are hardly sufficient. English is declining from the world's dominant language to merely 'first among equals.'[32] Even the Internet fails the monolingual American. Chinese is slated to surpass English as the Internet's leading language in the near future.[33] Domain names, once issued only in English or other languages with Roman letters, increasingly appear in Arabic, Chinese, Farsi, Korean, and other non-alphabet languages. Put simply, English is best for monitoring nations where English is used. But what intelligence challenges confront the United States in Australia, Britain, Canada, Ireland, or New Zealand? On the contrary, languages with which Americans are least familiar are precisely those of countries of greatest concern: Arabic (Iraq), Chinese (China), Farsi (Iran), Korean (DPRK), and Pashto (Afghanistan), to name only some examples.

Although facing such challenges, the United States lacks the education base upon which to develop tomorrow's intelligence officers. Relatively few Americans pursue a foreign language from secondary school through the university level. Worse, most university language students still study the Romance tongues or German in courses designed chiefly to produce professors of literature. The Intelligence Community must then compete with the private sector for the handful of competent linguists graduating from university. The bleak alternative is to start adults on crash courses at the Defense Language Institute (DLI) or elsewhere on some of the world's most difficult languages.

On a related issue, an indifference to foreign languages and even foreign sources in translation diminishes the OSINT value of the US mass media. American journalists on the whole have been ignorant of the countries on which they have reported. Most who have covered the nuclear dispute between P'yongyang and Washington, for example, cannot read a Korean restaurant menu, let alone the pages of *Nodong Sinmun*. Worse, as one observer noted of an earlier period of crisis: 'Reporters did not routinely read translations of the North Korean news by the Foreign Broadcast Information Service. Nor did they avail themselves of information circulating among outside experts by e-mail and fax.'[34] The resulting level of reporting has been so poor that one prominent academic who can read Korean wrote recently of having to turn to P'yongyang's 'tightly controlled press' for information on Washington-P'yongyang relations.[35]

The reluctance of US publishers to introduce foreign books in translation further lessens the flow of open sources available to Americans. For example, ROK movie star Ch'oe Un-hui and her former husband, the director Sin Sang-ok, gained extraordinary access to Kim Chong-il after he kidnapped them in 1978 in a bid to upgrade P'yongyang's film industry; they worked for him until their escape in 1986. Their account of the Dear Leader, complete with photographs, appeared in 1988 in Seoul and Tokyo. They were for years the only outsiders who had known Kim and written of their experience, but no American publisher saw fit to issue the book in translation. The same is true of numerous books in recent years from other insiders, including the architect of DPRK ideology and Kim's private sushi chef.[36]

An example closer to home is that of Dr. Emmanuel Todd's *After the Empire: The Breakdown of the American Order*. Published originally in 2003 in French, the book appeared the same year in various languages, including German, Italian, Japanese, Korean, and Spanish. The belated appearance a year later of the American edition of a book regarding what a prominent academic – who had forecast in 1976 the eventual fall of the Soviet Union – sees as Washington's futile struggle to maintain a global hegemony stands as an indictment of the US publishing industry.[37]

Compounding the problem of insufficient foreign information reaching the United States, the decline of area studies since the Cold War's end has reduced the pool of able applicants prepared to exploit foreign information in the vernacular. Russian studies, for example, have suffered grievously in funding and enrollment. Many graduates have found that US businesses prefer to send monolingual accountants to Moscow to teaching a Russian expert accounting. Area experts seeking university tenure find positions going to political scientists churning out papers on 'rational choice' regarding countries they know hardly at all. Students attending courses of area studies today are more often seeking their ethnic roots than preparing to join the Intelligence Community. For example, a German professor teaching Korean political economy at a time of high military tension between Washington and P'yongyang found that around three quarters of his students at Columbia University were Asians or Asian-Americans. He wrote, 'I was astonished by the relative lack of interest in Korea among American students, especially in such a tense situation as at present, when only deep knowledge about modern Korea can help prevent potentially disastrous policy decisions.'[38]

All of this would be bad enough, but even worse is the fact that only a handful of capable officers with language and area skills are casting their nets into the global sea of open sources for intelligence. The results have been catastrophic. In the words of one former DO officer who has argued that 'covert collectors should not be blamed' for missing Usama Bin Laden: 'It is virtually impossible to penetrate a revolutionary terrorist organization, particularly one structured and manned the way al-Qaida is. The responsibility falls on the intelligence community's overt collectors and analysts.' He suggests that the information was out there, but that analysts were simply not reading the relevant foreign media. The same lack of OSINT exploitation, he asserts, was also behind Washington's failure to comprehend the rise to power of Ayatollah Khomeini in Iran a quarter century ago.[39] Two senior CIA officers warn that things are likely to grow worse. They note how 'knowledge of culture, history, and language will be even more critical as the amount of open-source material increases.' They also admit that, 'Inadequate American foreign language skills are a mismatch for the exponential growth in foreign language materials.'[40]

Building a new 'craft' of intelligence

'The collection of foreign intelligence is accomplished in a variety of ways, not all of them either mysterious or secret. This is particularly true of overt intelligence, which is information derived from newspapers, books, learned and technical publications, official reports of government proceedings, radio and television. Even a novel or play may contain useful information about the state of a nation.'

Allen Dulles, *The Craft of Intelligence*[41]

The words of the former director of central intelligence (DCI) seem even more true today than when he published them over 40 years ago, but the Intelligence Community needs to build a better ship to sail the sea of open sources. FBIS, the largest and best equipped of the disorganized collection of offices engaged in OSINT, is too small a craft with too few hands to navigate the waters and harvest the catch. Analysts, by and large, lack the knowledge of foreign languages, media expertise, and time to do their own fishing.

What is to be done?

First, the DCI should increase the number of language officers at FBIS. Officers with knowledge of foreign languages, countries, and media are necessary to gather and analyze open sources, as photo interpreters are required to make sense of satellite imagery. The sea of open sources is arguably as large as that of covert communications, so one could argue that there should be as many open source officers surfing the Web as there are signals intelligence officers breaking secure communications. Required are college scholarships for students literate in Chinese and other innovative means of enlarging the pool of future OSINT officers.

Second, the Intelligence Community should take steps to turn the motley group of OSINT units into an organized fleet, with FBIS as the flagship. At a minimum, the Intelligence Community would do well to designate FBIS as the coordinator for OSINT. An enhanced FBIS could build on its expertise, its databases, and its longstanding role of serving the entire Intelligence Community by coordinating the output from the various embassy press translation units, military gray literature collectors, and such. An alternate, and more ambitious, plan would be to build a central agency for open intelligence based on FBIS. The new organization would be for OSINT what the DO is for HUMINT, National Reconnaissance Office is for IMINT, and the National Security Agency is for SIGINT.[42]

Third, the Intelligence Community must organize its own technical resources and tap those of the private sector to exploit the latest information technology for OSINT collection, analysis, production, and dissemination. OSINT collectors, all-source analysts, and others would benefit from smarter search engines, enhanced machine-assisted translation software, and better tools for incorporating audio and video streams into intelligence reports.

Above all, the Intelligence Community requires a sustained approach to open sources. As with other collection disciplines, one cannot conjure OSINT programs out of thin air. Assembling a substantial number of officers competent in Arabic, Chinese, Farsi, Korean, and other languages and expert in fishing in the OSINT seas, then giving them the sources and methods to do their work, would be no small feat.

Notes

1 Russell Jack Smith, *The Unknown CIA: My Three Decades with the Agency* (Washington, DC: Pergamon-Brassey's, 1989), 195.
2 Information on the Princeton Listening Center, launched in 1939, is available at http://libweb. princeton.edu:2003/libraries/firestone/rbsc/finding_aide/plc.html. For a history of FBIS during the Second World War, see Stephen C. Mercado, 'FBIS Against the Axis, 1941–1945,' *Studies in Intelligence*, Unclassified Edition no. 11 (Fall-Winter 2001): 33–43.
3 For Dr. Fah's comment, see Mercado, 41. On the Italian 'confidence trickster' who fooled James Jesus Angleton and other OSS officers, see David Alvarez, *Spies in the Vatican: Espionage and Intrigue from Napoleon to the Holocaust* (Lawrence: University Press of Kansas, 2002), 248–53. Regarding Dr. Fairbank's role in OSS, see John King Fairbank, *Chinabound: A Fifty-Year Memoir* (New York: Harper Colophon, 1983), 174–75.
4 The downgrading of the 'I' in FBIS from 'Intelligence' to 'Information' reflects the mistaken notion that only stolen secrets count as intelligence. CIA counterintelligence officers, under the leadership of James Jesus Angleton, were among those in Washington who continued to dismiss the growing evidence of the Sino-Soviet split well into the 1960s. On how OSINT officers led the way in understanding the breakup of 'monolithic communism,' see Harold P. Ford, 'Calling the Sino-Soviet Split,' Studies in Intelligence, Winter 1998–99, Unclassified Edition: 57–71. On Angleton, see also Harold P. Ford, 'Why CIA Analysts Were So Doubtful About Vietnam,' *Studies in Intelligence*, Unclassified Edition No.
5 J. J. Bagnall, 'The Exploitation of Russian Scientific Literature for Intelligence Purposes,' Studies in Intelligence (Summer 1958): 45–49. Declassified article.
6 Davis W. Moore, 'Open Sources on Soviet Military Affairs,' Studies in Intelligence (Summer 1963-declassified article): 101.
7 Herman L. Croom, 'The Exploitation of Foreign Open Sources,' *Studies in Intelligence* (Summer 1969-declassified article): 129–30.
8 Joseph Becker, 'Comparative Survey of Soviet and US Access to Published Information,' *Studies in*

Intelligence (Fall 1957-declassified article): 43; John O. Koehler, *Stasi: The Untold Story of the East German Secret Police* (Boulder, CO: Westview Press, 1999), 110. Becker's article includes a reference to Soviet reading of *Aviation Week*.

9 Peer de Silva, *Sub Rosa: The CIA and the Uses of Intelligence* (New York: Times Books, 1978), 120.

10 Antonio J. Mendez, with Malcolm McConnell, *The Master of Disguise: My Secret Life in the CIA* (New York: William Morrow & Co., 1999), 337. On the monitoring of television in the Cold War, see Maureen Cote, 'Veni, Vidi, Vid-Int,' *Studies in Intelligence*, Fall 1990. Unclassified.

11 See David Wise and Thomas B. Ross, *The Invisible Government* (New York: Random House, 1964). Notable insider accounts of recent years include Duane 'Dewey' Clarridge, *A Spy for All Seasons* (New York: Simon & Schuster, 1997) and Robert Baer, *See No Evil* (New York: Crown publishers, 2002).

12 Mark M. Lowenthal, 'OSINT: The State of the Art, the Artless State,' *Studies in Intelligence* 45, no. 3 (2001): 62.

13 On IMINT ceasing to be an 'INT,' see Gregory F. Treverton, *Reshaping National Intelligence for an Age of Information* (New York: Cambridge University Press, 2001), 87. A Japanese magazine notable for its prominent use of commercial IMINT on DPRK pol-mil issues is *SAPIO*, which advertises itself as an 'international intelligence magazine.' See *SAPIO*, 8 January 2003, for example, for use of Digital Globe imagery of alleged residences of Kim Chong-il. Regarding the FAS dispute, see *New York Times*, 11 January 2000.

14 Foreign Ministry Diplomatic Records Office and Nihon Gaikoshi Jiten Editorial Committee, eds., *Nihon Gaikoshi Jiten* [Dictionary of Japanese Diplomatic History] (Tokyo: Yamakawa Shuppansha, 1992), 361. A British historian of Japanese diplomatic history has also written of 'indications' that Von Siebold went beyond OSINT for the Japanese Foreign Ministry and Army. Ian Nish, 'Japanese Intelligence and the Approach of the Russo-Japanese War,' in Christopher Andrew and David Dilks, eds., *The Missing Dimension: Governments and Intelligence Communities in the Twentieth Century* (Urbana: University of Illinois Press, 1984), 19.

15 Frederick L. Wettering, '(C)overt Action: The Disappearing "C," ' *International Journal of Intelligence and CounterIntelligence* (Winter 2003–2004), 566–67.

16 Arthur S. Hulnick, *Fixing the Spy Machine: Preparing American Intelligence for the Twenty-First Century* (Westport, CT: Praeger, 1999), 8, 40–41.

17 Wayne S. Kiyosaki, *North Korea's Foreign Relations: The Politics of Accommodation, 1945–75* (New York, Praeger, 1976), x–xi. Dr. Kiyosaki, a graduate in Korean of the Defense Language Institute who later honed his media insights at FBIS, knew of what he wrote.

18 Adrian Buzo, *The Guerrilla Dynasty: Politics and Leadership in North Korea* (Boulder, CO: Westview Press, 1999), 284–85. On the value of DPRK media in charting personnel changes in P'yongyang, it is worth noting that the standard reference works, such as the annual *North Korea Directory* of Japan's impressive Radiopress and the online biographic compilations of the ROK's National Intelligence Service (www.nis.go.kr) are based on media monitoring. For one journalist's recognition of the value of following P'yongyang's media, see Gordon Fairclough, 'To See North Korea, Keep Your Eyes Peeled On the Official Press,' *Wall Street Journal*, 19 February 2004: 1.

19 Donald P. Gregg, 'A Long Road to P'yongyang,' *The Korea Society Quarterly*, Spring 2002: 7.

20 Tsukamoto Katsuichi, 'Kitachosen josei to Higashi Ajia no anzen hosho' *Securitarian*, July 1995: 22. General Tsukamoto, who began his career as a commissioned officer of the Imperial Japanese Army and finished it as commander of the Ground Self-Defense Force's Western Army, has written several books on Korean security issues.

21 Noda Hironari (pseud.), *CIA supai kenshu: Aru Koan Chosakan no taikenki* [CIA Spy Training: One PSIA Officer's Account] (Tokyo: Gendai Shokan, 2000): 169–170. It is interesting to note that PSIA changed its English name, but not its acronym, in 2003, replacing 'Investigation' with 'Intelligence.'

22 John Gannon, 'The Strategic Use of Open-Source Information,' *Studies in Intelligence* 45, no. 3 (2001): 67.

23 Thomas Patrick Carroll, 'The Case Against Intelligence Openness,' *International Journal of Intelligence and CounterIntelligence* (Winter 2001–2002): 561.

24 Leon V. Sigal, *Disarming Strangers: Nuclear Diplomacy With North Korea* (Princeton, NJ: Princeton University Press, 1998), 234.

25 Sherman Kent, *Strategic Intelligence for American World Policy* (Princeton, NJ: Princeton University Press, 1949). There is no more succinct definition of intelligence than the title of Part I: 'Intelligence

Is Knowledge.' For the HPSCI staff director's remark, see Mark M. Lowenthal, 'Open Source Intelligence: New Myths, New Realities,' *Defense Daily Online*, reprinted in The Intelligencer (Winter 1999): 7.

26 This and many other declassified Russian maps have been advertised on line at East View Information Services of Minneapolis, MN (www.eastview.com).

27 Levchenko's interviews, which appeared in abbreviated form in a series running in the Japanese weekly magazine *Shukan Bunshun* over five weeks in mid-1983, were issued later that year as a book. Shukan Bunshun, ed. *Refuchenko wa shogen suru* [Levchenko Testifies] (Tokyo: Bungei Shunju, 1983). Haruna Mikio, a former Washington bureau chief of Japan's Kyodo News Agency with extensive contacts in the US Intelligence Community, wrote that an unidentified CIA officer was 'surprised' at how much more detailed he found Levchenko's public revelations. See Haruna Mikio, *Himitsu no fairu: CIA no tainichi kosaku* [Secret Files: The CIA's Operations Against Japan] (Tokyo: Shinchosha Bunko, 2003), volume 2, 483. Whatever the accuracy of Haruna's purported source, Levchenko's Japanese book is more revealing than the one he published in the United States: *On the Wrong Side: My Life in the KGB* (Washington: Pergamon-Brassey's, 1988).

28 'Navy Had Word of Jap Plan To Strike at Sea,' *Chicago Tribune*, 7 June 1942. On the 'miraculous' character of the victory, see Gordon Prange *et al.*, *Miracle at Midway* (New York: McGraw-Hill, 1982).

29 Intelligence officers have long worried about the damage done through the leaks of classified intelligence and even the gathering of published information by adversaries. Leaks are an old problem. See, for example, Allen Dulles, *The Craft of Intelligence* (New York: Harper&Row, 1963), 241–43. On leaks today, see James B. Bruce, The Consequences of Permissive Neglect,' *Studies in Intelligence* 47, no. 3 (2003, Unclassified). Becker, 'Comparative Survey,' 35, noted in 1957 Soviet exploitation of US open sources and the repeated failures of the US Government from the 1940s to find a solution to the problem.

30 Tsukamoto Makoto, *Aru joho shoko no shuki* [Memoirs of an Intelligence Officer] (Tokyo: Chuo Bunko, 1998), 195. Agnes Smedley (*China's Red Army Marches*, 1934) and Edgar Snow (*Red Star Over China*, 1938) were prolific American writers with extraordinary access to Chinese communists.

31 Nakano Koyukai, ed., *Rikugun Nakano* Gakko [Army Nakano School] (Tokyo: Nakano Koyukai, 1978), 176, and Moore, 'Open Sources,' 104.

32 David Graddol, 'The Future of Language,' *Science* 303 (27 February 2004): 1329–31.

33 The prediction on Chinese Internet was made at a conference of the World Intellectual Property Organization, according to the *Financial Times*, 7 December 2001.

34 Sigal, *Disarming Strangers*, 221.

35 Bruce Cumings, *North Korea: Another Country* (New York: New Press, 2004), 47–48.

36 The architect of North Korea's Chuch'e philosophy, Hwang Chang-yop, has written a number of books, including *Na nun yoksa ui chilli rul poatta: Hwang Chang-yop hoegorok* [I Saw the Truth of History: Memoirs of Hwang Chang-yop] (Seoul: Hanul, 1999). A Japanese sushi chef in Kim's service, publishing under the pseudonym Kenji Fujimoto, wrote *Kin Seinichi no ryorinin* (Tokyo: Shinchosha, 2003). These are two of many insider accounts likely never to see the light of day in the United States.

37 Emmanuel Todd, *After the Empire: The Breakdown of the American Order* (New York: Columbia University Press, 2004), *Après l'empire: Essai sur la décomposition du système américain* (Paris: Gallimard, 2003) and *La Chute finale: Essai sur la décomposition de la sphère sovietique* (Paris: Robert Laffont, 1976).

38 Constantine Pleshakov, 'Russian Studies: A Sinking Academic Atlantis,' *Japan Times*, 15 March 1995: 17. Dr. Ruediger Frank of Humboldt-Universität zu Berlin noted the general lack of interest in 'An Interview with a Visiting Lecturer,' *Annual Report 2002–2003*, Weatherhead East Asian Institute, Columbia University, 21.

39 Robert D. Chapman, 'The Muslim Crusade,' *International Journal of Intelligence and CounterIntelligence* (Winter 2002–2003): 613–14.

40 Aris A. Pappas and James M. Simon, Jr., 'The Intelligence Community: 2001–2015,' *Studies in Intelligence* 46, no. 1 (2002): 45. For a view of how deficiencies in foreign languages hurt covert collection, see Matthew M. Aid, 'All Glory Is Fleeting: SIGINT and the Fight Against International Terrorism,' *Intelligence and National Security* 18, no. 4 (Winter 2003): 100–102.

41 Allen Dulles, *The Craft of Intelligence* (New York: Harper&Row, 1963), 55. For a similar view, see Robert D. Steele, *The New Craft of Intelligence: Personal, Public, Political* (Oakton, VA: OSS International Press, 2002). For those interested in a concrete example of literature serving as a guide to

intelligence, see how poems in the DPRK literary journal *Choson Munhak* [Korean Literature] signaled the preparation of Kim Chong-il to succeed his father. Morgan E. Clippinger, 'Kim Chong-il in the North Korean Mass Media: A Study of Semi-Esoteric Communication,' *Asian Survey* (March 1981): 291.

42 Creating a central OSINT agency is far from a novel idea. The proposal surfaced, for example, in *Studies in Intelligence* in 1969. See Croom, 'Exploitation,' 135.

Reprinted with permission from Stephen Mercado, 'A Venerable Source in a New Era: Sailing the Sea of OSINT in the Information Age', *Studies in Intelligence* 48/3 (2004) pp.45–55.

COLLECTION OF INTELLIGENCE

Further reading: books and reports

Matthew Aid, *Secret Sentry: The Top Secret History of the National Security Agency* (NY: Bloomsbury, 2008).

Christopher Andrew and Oleg Gordievsky, *KGB. The Inside Story of its Foreign Operations from Lenin to Gorbachev* (NY. Harper & Row, 1990).

Robert Baer, *See No Evil: The True Story of a Ground Soldier in the CIA's War on Terrorism* (NY: Three Rivers Press 2003).

James Bamford, *Body of Secrets: Anatomy of the Ultra-secret National Security Agency* (NY: Doubleday 2001).

Bruce Berkowitz, *The New Face of War: How War Will be Fought in the 21st Century* (NY: Free Press 2000), pp.197–218.

William E Burrow, *Deep Black: Space Espionage and National Security* (NY: Random House 1986)

D.D. Clarridge, *A Spy for All Seasons: My Life in the CIA* (NY: Scribner's, 1997). [see the detailed account of humint agent recruitment]

Roger Z. George and Robert D. Kline (eds.), *Intelligence and National Security Strategist: Enduring Issues and Challenges* (Washington DC: National Defense University Press, CSI 2004), parts IV, V & VI, pp.147–285.

Peter Gill and Mark Pythian, *Intelligence in and Insecure World* (Cambridge: Polity 2006), chapter 4.

O. Gordievsky, *Next Stop Execution* (London: Macmillan 1995). [MI6's top Cold war agent]

Thomas Graham, *Spy Satellites and Other Intelligence Technologies That Changed History* (Seattle: University of Washington Press 2007).

Michael Herman, *Intelligence Power in Peace and War* (Cambridge: Cambridge University Press 1996) chapters 4–5

Sherman Kent, *Strategic Intelligence for American Foreign Policy* (Princeton: Princeton University Press 1949).

Loch K. Johnson & James J. Wirtz, *Intelligence and National Security: The Secret World of Spies* (NY: Oxford University Press, 2nd ed 2007).

Walter Laqueuer, *World of Secrets: The Uses and Limits of Intelligence* (NY: Basic Books 1985).

David T. Lindgren, *Imagery Analysis in the Cold War* (Annapolis MD: Naval Institute Press 2000)

Mark Lowenthal, *Intelligence: From Secrets to Policy* (Washington DC: CQ Press 3rd Ed 2006), chapter 5.

Curtis Peebles *Guardians, Strategic Reconnaissance Satellites* (Novato CA: Presidio 1987) pp.1–149.

Jeffrey Richelson, *The US Intelligence Community* (Boulder CO: 5th edition Westview 2007) chapters 7–11.

Abram N. Shulsky and Gary J. Schmitt, *Silent Warfare: Understanding the World of Intelligence* (Dulles VA: Brasseys 2002) chapter 2.

Michael Smith, *Six: The Real James Bonds* (London: Lighthouse, 2009).

Robert Steele, *On Intelligence: Spies and Secrecy in an Open World* (Fairfax VA: AFCEA International Press 2000).

Bradford Westerfield (ed.), *Inside the CIA's Private World* (New Haven: Yale University Press 1995) Sections 1–3.

Further reading: essays and articles

Matthew M. Aid, 'Prometheus embattled: A post-9/11 report card on the National Security Agency', *Intelligence and National Security* 21/6 (2006) pp.980–98.

Matthew M. Aid, 'The Time of Troubles: The US National Security Agency in the Twenty-first century', *Intelligence and National Security* 15/3 (2000) pp.1–32.

Matthew M. Aid & Cees Wiebes, 'On The Importance of Signals Intelligence in the Cold War', *Intelligence and National Security* 16/1 (2001) pp.1–26.

Christopher Andrew & Julie Elkner, 'Stalin and Foreign Intelligence', *Totalitarian Movements and Political Religions* 4/1 (2003) pp.69–94.

John M Diamond, 'Re-examining problems and Prospects in US Imagery Intelligence', *International Journal of Intelligence and Counterintelligence* 14/1 (2001) pp.1–24.

Dennis D. Fitzgerald, 'Risk Management and National Reconnaissance form the Cold war up to the Global War on Terrorism,' *National Reconnaissance – A Journal of the Discipline and Practice* 1 (2005) pp.9–18

Burton Gerber, 'Managing Humint: The need for a new Approach', in Jennifer Sims & Burton Gerber (eds.) *Transforming US Intelligence* (Washington DC: Georgetown University Press, 2005) pp.180–97.

Willmoore Kendall, 'The Function of Intelligence', *World Politics* 1/6 (1949) pp.542–52.

Mark M. Lowenthal, 'OSINT: The State of the Art, the Artless State,' *Studies in Intelligence* 45/3 (2001) pp.62–66.

Patrick Riley, 'CIA and its Discontents', *International Journal of Intelligence and Counterintelligence* 11 (1998) pp.255–269.

W.C. Prillaman & M.P. Dempsey, 'Mything the Point: What's Wrong with the Conventional Wisdom about the CIA', *Intelligence and National Security* 19/1 (2004) pp.1–29.

Jeffrey T. Richelson, 'High Flyin' Spies', *Bulletin of Atomic Scientists* 52/2 (1996) pp.48–54.

Jeffrey T. Richelson, 'The Satellite Gap', *Bulletin of Atomic Scientists* 59/1 (2003) pp.48–54.

Arron Chia Eng Seng, 'MASINT: The Future of Intelligence', *DSTA Horizons* 3 (2007) pp.118–25.

Robert D. Steele, 'The Importance of Open Source Intelligence to the Military', *International Journal of Intelligence and Counterintelligence* 8/4 (Winter 1995) pp.457–70

T Trevan, 'Exploiting Intelligence in International Organisations' in RA Zilinskas (ed.) *Biological Warfare: Modern Offense and Defense* (Boulder CO: Lynne Reinner 1999) pp.207–24.

Patrick Widlake, 'National Reconnaissance Leadership for the 21st Century, Lesson from the NRO's Heritage', *National Reconnaissance – A Journal of the Discipline and Practice* 1 (2005) pp.19–34.

Essay and seminar questions

- Compare and contrast the pros and cons presented by the following types of secret intelligence collection: human (Humint), signals (Sigint), imagery (Imint).
- What are the major challenges in the realm of foreign intelligence gathering for current West European states? Illustrate with two or three examples.
- Open sources often constitute the majority of the sources of information used by government. So why is 'Opint' usually under-rated and badly resourced?
- We now know that during the Cold War the Soviet Union gathered intelligence well, but used it very poorly. How do we explain this?

6   Surprise despite warning

Why sudden attacks succeed

R.K. Betts

In this essay, Richard Betts attempts to account for why surprise attack is successful even when the victim seems to have achieved adequate raw intelligence that offers warning in advance. The role in this process of communication delays, deception, false alarms and doctrinal innovation are all explored here. This is one of two classic articles written by Betts in the 1980s that originated with a study undertaken for the CIA. It offers the first attempt to take the problem beyond poor analysis and to connect the issue of weak political response to warning. It also explores surprise in comparative perspective.

Most major wars since 1939 have begun with surprise attacks. Hindsight reveals that the element of surprise in most of these attacks was unwarranted; substantial evidence of an impending strike was available to the victims before the fact. The high incidence of surprise is itself surprising. The voluminous literature on strategic surprise, however, suffers from three fixations. One is a focus on the problem of warning, and how to improve intelligence collection, rather than on the more difficult problem of how to improve political response to ample warning indicators. Another is a common view of surprise as an absolute or dichotomous problem rather than as a matter of degree. Third is the prevalent derivation of theories from single cases rather than from comparative studies. This article puts these fixations in perspective.[1]

Intelligence and warning: The relativity of surprise

Warning without response is useless. 'Warning' is evidence filtered through perception; 'response' is action designed to counter an attack (alert, mobilization, and redeployments to enhance readiness). The linkage between the two is accurate evaluation and sound judgment, the lack of which is the source of most victims' failures to avoid the avoidable. Just as analysts of arms-control agreements distinguish between monitoring and verification (the former detects possibly discrepant indicators, the latter is political determination of what evidence constitutes satisfactory compliance), analysts of surprise attack need to distinguish more carefully between intelligence, warning, and response. The issue in most cases is not a yes-or-no question of whether there is warning or response; rather the issue is *how much* warning there is and *how soon* response begins.

For most Americans, the shock of Pearl Harbor made surprise attack seem something that comes without warning; therefore obtaining warning should avert the threat. Only if communication were instantaneous and uninhibited and judgment did not intervene between information and action would this be true, and these conditions never exist. Warning derived from intelligence gathering is a continuum in several dimensions: the amount or weight of threatening indicators detected; the ratio between these and contradictory nonthreatening indicators; and the timing of receipt, evaluation, and reaction to indicators. This is also true of the response by authorities – the intensity and duration of debate about whether and how to react, and the degree of response eventually chosen: none; some; or complete (full military readiness).

Consider five phases: data acquisition; correlation, and intelligence professionals' decision to warn; communication to decision makers; discussion, assessment, and decision to respond, by these authorities; and military commanders' implementation of the authorization to respond. These phases are logically sequential but in practice often overlap and regress. Communications between intelligence officers and policymakers produce doubt and fluctuations of certainty; officials may have second thoughts and order more search, or they may declare alerts and then cancel them. Information processing may be slower than decision time or may be unsynchronized with the deliberations. In the 1962 Cuban missile crisis, for example, a human source in Cuba reported sighting a missile on 12 September, but the report did not arrive at CIA until 21 September, two days after the meeting of the United States Intelligence Board. The time required to process such reports could have been shortened, but previously there had been no reason to invest the resources and take the necessary risks (endangering agents and communication networks) because the value of these sources had usually been minimal. Problems can be reduced by redundancy in intelligence collection, such as use of reconnaissance to complement espionage, to shrink the potential lacunae in coverage. But in this case, U-2 flights were suspended around the same time for political reasons (China had just shot down a U-2, and the State Department feared aggravation of the crisis by a similar incident over Cuba).[2]

Even if the process were orderly, the clock is ticking, and at each of the first four phases different views about whether attack is imminent (no, maybe, or yes) may prevail. Thus at each stage reactions can go wrong. Even if it takes only a reasonable time to form a consensus that war is coming, this is insufficient if it is less than the time the enemy needs to complete preparations.[3] The final tactical warnings that may congeal the consensus, as well as authorizations from the victim's leaders to their troops to move into wartime positions, can also be held up in the communication chain. This keeps the rates of speed in attack preparation and defense reaction in a ratio unfavorable to the victim. On the night of 21 June 1941, for example, Red Army commanders picked up numerous indicators that the Wehrmacht was going into motion, but reported through routine channels that delayed Moscow's receipt of the information.[4] The same night, Marshal Timoshenko delayed the alerting process by putting everything in writing rather than just telephoning his commanders – which was necessary for survival in Stalin's regime, where subordinates always knew they might need evidence that they had obeyed the dictator's orders perfectly. Transmission and decoding time further delayed military units' receipt of instructions; some did not receive them before they came under fire.[5]

Depending on his strategy, efficiency, and speed of preparation, the attacker can strike at many points along this continuum of reaction by the victim. The point determines the *degree* of surprise that prevents the defender from using his capabilities fully or effectively. Response necessarily lags behind warning. Even if recognition crystallizes perfectly before the moment of attack, the victim may still suffer the costs of surprise if alert, mobilization, and deployment to defensive positions are still getting under way. The victim may not be surprised that war breaks out, but he is still surprised in military *effect*. There is always some warning; there is usually some response; yet surprise seldom fails. For example, the night before the German assault in the West in 1940 Wehrmacht concentrations were detected. The Belgian military attaché in Berlin said the Germans would attack the next day, and Belgian military head-quarters issued warning orders and recalled men on leave.[6] But many front-line French units were standing down for training. Important staffers of the Second Army, which was in the crucial position by Sedan, had gone to see a play and were asleep when they got news the Germans were rolling through Luxembourg.[7]

Stalin also hedged against the evidence of war (by declaring a national state of emergency on 10 April 1941); in addition he increased troop readiness, assumed full power as head of the government on 1 May, and recognized the day before Operation Barbarossa that attack might be imminent. The navy was well alerted, and the army made last-minute preparations in a few places.[8] But 'the abysmal lack of contingent preparations and the cumbrous ineffi-ciency of his bureaucracy meant that even with a few hours' advance warning at the top, the system as a whole remained unwarned.'[9] German tactics also extended the surprise into the early phases of the war. Initial strikes interdicted lines of command, control, and communi-cation, preventing leaders in Moscow from discovering the scope and character of the assault during the first days and disrupting recovery by preventing the flow of instructions back to military units. As a result the cohesion of Soviet formations broke down and authority was paralyzed.[10]

By 6 December 1941 a full alert was declared for U.S. air units in the Philippines and troops took up defense positions along beaches. But the attack on Clark Field, despite the fact that it lagged behind the strike on Hawaii by nine hours, was as devastating as if it had come with no warning. The problem in the Philippines was not lack of intelligence, but deploy-ments that lacked enough flexibility to respond to short warning. MacArthur had ordered his air commander to move B-17s further south, to Del Monte, but by 7 December only half of the bombers had been transferred because the new base was not ready. B-17s and fighter planes at Clark were caught on the ground while refueling.[11]

Other notable examples of the military effect of surprise include MacArthur's testimony that even if he had received three days of warning before the North Koreans invaded in 1950, it would have made little difference since he needed three weeks to get a large body of U.S. troops from Japan to Korea;[12] General Westmoreland's miscalculations of the scope and intensity of the Tet Offensive of 1968, despite intelligence warnings three weeks prior to the attacks and despite the repositioning of U.S. forces closer to Saigon;[13] and, in October 1973, the Israelis' decision half a day before the Arabs struck that war was inevitable, which, though correct, did not allow enough time to complete mobilization; movement of ready forces into blocking positions was also incomplete by the time the Arabs struck.

Surprise is seldom absolute. Militarily, though, warning just before the fact is hardly better than no warning at all.

Obstacles to warning

To detect evidence of a threat – through reconnaissance, interception of radio transmissions, or espionage – is only the prerequisite for warning. Collected information must pass through numerous bottlenecks. It must be screened at low levels to raise initial suspicion; it must be transmitted to higher levels of the intelligence bureaucracy to be compared with data from other sources; it then has to be passed to policymakers who must judge whether the evidence warrants action. The amount and sequence of the presentation of data do much to determine how information is appreciated. But warning indicators 'are usually scattered across individuals and bureaucratic units. They are also introduced incrementally over a long period.'[14] Before Pearl Harbor the accumulation of signals was disjointed. Not all intercepts were decoded. Of those that were, some were transmitted quickly upward, others were held up at low levels, and some never got to a level where decisions could be made; 'no single person or agency ever had at any given moment all the signals existing in this vast information network.'[15] Some indicators are dismissed as false or meaningless at low levels and are never passed to decision makers.

The process of relaying intelligence can distort its meaning. Content can be altered unconsciously in transmission. Garbled data are made to appear more coherent when relayed in conversation, allowing actual disjunctions between facts to be replaced by false connections; lengthy information can be made shorter; details are suppressed subconsciously if they are not consistent with the rest of the relayer's message; and transmission errors tend to make the message sound like what the person transmitting it had been expecting to hear. Subordinates also tend to bias messages so as to minimize distress to their superiors; transmitting individuals tend toward 'closure' of incomplete images and 'confabulating detail where gaps are conspicuous'; long time periods are reported as shorter, and short ones as longer.[16] Early on the morning the Yom Kippur War began, a trusted source warned Israel that the Arabs would attack that day. Somewhere in the communication chain the time of six o'clock was added erroneously to the warning.[17] The Arabs struck over four hours sooner.

Strategic warning has come a long way since the days when one of the prime indicators was the enemy's decision to forbid the export of horses. Hundreds of bits of information pour in from technical sensors and must be digested and summarized as they are passed up to officials with progressively wider responsibilities. If done well, this may clarify the danger, but the process creates the possibility that the whole picture may be less compelling to a high-level policy-maker than it might be to a specialist spending all his time on the matter, seeing crucial connections between disparate shreds of data. George Marshall testified after Pearl Harbor, 'If I am supposed to have (had) final responsibility of the reading of all MAGIC [intercepts of Japanese diplomatic communications], I would have ceased to be Chief of Staff in practically every other respect.'[18]

Lower-level specialists, on the other hand, do not see all the collected indicators. Security mandates 'compartmentation,' and 'need-to-know' as a criterion for access to classes of data. Secrecy also complicates judgment of the credibility of information. Early in World War II the ability to decipher German communications with the 'Enigma' machine was so sensitive that decrypts sent to British intelligence staffs were disguised as espionage reports from human sources (HUMINT), which are normally much less reliable than signals intelligence (SIGINT). Analysts therefore were very skeptical about this information, which was really pure gold. Sensitivity also limited circulation of this data at field headquarters, and staffs there could not coordinate it with other, less sensitive SIGINT and field intelligence.[19] Distrust of HUMINT illustrates how possession of information does not guarantee better warning. Frequently wild, incorrect, or contradictory reports from agents in Cuba in 1961–62 led U.S. estimators to discount them in the period before missiles were discovered by aerial reconnaissance. Since protection of sources requires that the identity of agents be concealed from middle-level analysts, the analysts have no idea of how to verify the reliability of the sources. U.S. analysts of OPEC relied much more on embassy reporting than CIA clandestine service reports prior to the 1973 oil embargo and price rise, and this contributed to the failure to predict the events.[20]

The lower the level of authority, the more limited is the access; the higher the level, the more coordinated is the evaluation, but also the less time available to ponder one particular problem to the exclusion of others. Only *nine* U.S. officials were on the regular distribution list for MAGIC in late 1941, and they spent much of their time worrying about Europe in the period during which alarming evidence about Japanese moves dribbled in.

Postwar reforms in American intelligence organization have ameliorated these problems. Creation of the Watch Committee and later the Strategic Warning Staff improved the speed of communication and coordination. The need for secrecy, however, still inhibits lateral movement of information even more than in previous years because of the large variety of reconnaissance and electronic collection mechanisms.

Limits to predictability

Success in warning can be indistinguishable from failure.[21] If the defender recognizes warning, predicts war, and responds in time with defensive preparations, the attacker may cancel the operation. The prediction then appears to have been wrong. The commander of the Japanese task force en route to Pearl Harbor in 1941 had orders to abort if surprise were lost. If the Israelis had mobilized in late September 1973, as they had the previous May when threatening Arab movements were detected, Sadat might have postponed his attack. The victim's intelligence is always at the mercy of the attacker's option to change his plans. If success in prediction does not nullify itself, however, it can induce complacency. The actual occurrence of a predicted attack does not offer the best grounds on which to evaluate the quality of warning.[22]

Pure bolts-from-the-blue hardly ever occur. Sudden attacks happen after prolonged political conflict. They often do not occur at the peak of tension, but they are usually preceded by periods in which the defender's leaders believe that war is possible. And they often follow a number of false alarms. The routinization of tension desensitizes observers to the danger of imminent war. Crises are more common than the actual outbreak of war. American intelligence did not correctly assess the warnings coming from Korea in the spring of 1950 because there were similar situations all around the border areas of the Soviet Union, some of which appeared more dangerous.[23]

This simple fact of international relations makes it risky to draw political warning out of 'learning curves.' As Ezer Weizman noted ruefully after the Yom Kippur War: 'There are two popular folk sayings that are as fatal to military concepts as they are to political ones: "There is no wisdom like experience," and "History repeats itself." . . . for the man of experience who relies on the stability of history, wisdom becomes a broken reed.'[24] Historical context is of course a necessary and valuable grounding for strategic assessment, but not a reliable guide. The warnings at issue involve quick and major changes from normal behavior. Extrapolations from past behavior and from incremental changes are poor bases for anticipating such dramatic shifts.[25] Mathematical probability theory is no help in predicting one-time events when there is a small number of cases to use as the base. Forecasting is a chain of separate estimates about probability – predictions about conditions, events, or decisions that are the prerequisite to attack. Correct estimates of the probabilities in eight out of ten links in the chain is an admirable intellectual feat, but warning will nonetheless fail if the estimate in the ninth link is wrong. Great success in predicting enemy behavior under *normal* conditions of stress does not help prediction – and may hinder it – in the rare circumstances in which the stakes of the competition grow much larger.[26]

Indecision, false alerts, and fluctuations

Simple indecision by the attacker can prevent clear signals from being picked up by the defender because there *are* no clear signals.[27] Conciliatory rhetoric by the state that eventually attacks may be seen later by the victim as calculated deception, but the rhetoric may actually be innocent, reflecting genuine ambivalence within the attacker's government. While agonizing over the decision of whether to strike, decision makers want to keep options open and minimize provocation. Doves may even be temporarily ascendant and use such signals not only to reassure the eventual victim and prevent the confrontation from worsening but also to dampen the enthusiasm of the pro-war faction with whom they are contending. This possibility is greatest when the attacker's government is a collective decision-making system, or when the motivations for surprise attack are defensive, and least in an absolutist dictatorship such as Hitler's. Indecision can occur even when the attacker's motives are purely aggressive and even up to the last minute. On 25 August 1939, the Wehrmacht received orders to cross the Polish frontier the next morning. Troops and tanks approached the border that night. Later in the evening Hitler ordered a stop because negotiations with Warsaw were on again. On 1 September orders came down again to invade the next day. Commanders expected another cancellation.[28]

Whether innocent or planned, such hesitancy deceives the defender. Schedule changes and deferral of D-days are more correlated with achievement of surprise than are attacks that occur on schedule.[29] Warning officers are embarrassed by predictions that do not pan out. If their fear of being labeled a 'Chicken Little' does not lead them to hold off from a second or third such prediction, they may be derided as hysterical by decision makers tired of false alerts. An attacker able to fine-tune his plans is therefore well advised to undertake *fluctuating* preparations, to lend an up-and-down quality to strategic and tactical indicators the victim will discern. Fluctuation feeds the defender's expectation that nothing is likely to happen. The attacker may condition the victim by actually creating a *new* pattern of what is *normal*, against which subsequent actions are measured.[30] The 'cry wolf' problem is where the attacker's go-stop-go option and the danger of basing predictions on extrapolations from past behavior come together. For example, the German attack on Norway in April 1940 preserved surprise because the Norwegian foreign minister had been immunized against the indicators. Before Christmas, and again in February, he had received warnings of impending German attack, and nothing had happened.[31]

In the same period numerous false alarms poured into allied intelligence that the Germans were on the verge of striking into France. On 9 May, the day before the actual attack, French intelligence was advised 'Get ready! Attack tomorrow at dawn!' But on that day it saw no 'abnormal German movements' and British Royal Air Force reconnaissance said there was 'nothing unusual' – although German concentrations had been noted in earlier days.[32] The Dutch also failed to react to inside information. Colonel Hans Oster, deputy chief of German counterintelligence and a clandestine opponent of Hitler, had told the Dutch military attaché in Berlin each time the attack was planned. But Hitler postponed the attack numerous times between November 1939 and May 1940, so the Dutch were 'overwarned,' and Supreme Commander General I. H. Reynders ignored the reports. When Oster gave another warning ten days before the actual attack, the attaché did not even pass it on to The Hague.[33] The original German plan required six days of preparatory troop movements to attack. But the canceled attacks in November and January had accomplished most of those movements (the formations were kept in place after the cancellations), so the preparations just before

10 May were less unambiguous to the allies than they would have been had there been no previous false starts.[34]

Stalin also received numerous reports of a scheduled German attack, from March 1941 onward, which were not borne out. The Germans did delay the Barbarossa onslaught for five weeks. Soviet frontier troops grew less sensitive to evidence of threatening Wehrmacht activity in the three weeks before the attack because frequent alarms induced alert fatigue.[35]

General Short, the army commander in Hawaii, was not impressed by Washington's 27 November 1941 warning of war because he remembered the alarmism of a navy dispatch of 16 October. Short and Admiral Kimmel had also received reports several times during the year that the Japanese in Honolulu were burning their codes. The first message alarmed them, but subsequent ones seemed less serious. When they heard in the week before the attack that the Japanese were burning papers in their consulate, the commanders did not react.[36] American intelligence predictions on Korea in 1950 and Israeli assessments of Egyptian movements in late September 1973 were also hobbled by earlier false alarms.

Crying wolf decreases the decision maker's sensitivity to warning and increases the intelligence officer's sensitivity to looking foolish by raising false alarms. Thus the simple norm of 'when in doubt, *respond*' is unrealistic. And if indulged constantly, the urge to collect intelligence full-blast may be counter-productive not only politically and financially, but operationally as well. To fly 360-degree reconnaissance at Pearl Harbor with the planes available, the U.S. military would have had to reduce training, delay important shipments to the Philippines, exhaust crews, and run down the planes' airworthiness within a short time. 'An extraordinary state of alert that brings about a peak in readiness,' notes Roberta Wohlstetter, 'must be followed by a trough at a later date.'[37] (The United States today would face the same problem if it initiated airborne alert for the Strategic Air Command in response to crisis.) Readiness at the wrong time may yield unreadiness at the moment of real vulnerability.

At least in a small way, the problem of false alarm has been involved in most cases of surprise attack. To reduce the danger of relaxation induced by crying wolf, analysts and decision makers need to focus on the *differences* between previous false alarms and the enemy actions in the crisis at issue. The preparations for final attacks are usually not identical. Some exercises, deployments, and changes in communication patterns are noticeably more threatening than others. The technical nuances and details are crucial. Warning officers who are briefing decision makers, therefore, will raise the odds of response to the extent that they can show why the latest case differs from the earlier ones. If the differences are merely nuances, however, the weight of similarity may overcome suspicion. When Arye Shalev, the Israeli military spokesman in the cabinet meeting three days before the October 1973 War, interpreted new Syrian dispositions as defensive, he did note 'some exceptional aspects' in the positioning of artillery and a bridging battalion. He also said ammunition uploading by Egyptian units did not suggest a routine exercise and might be a prelude to a genuine attack. Nevertheless, Shalev concluded, the weight of reliable evidence indicated an exercise, and he ascribed the intensity of Egyptian alert to fears that Israel might seize the moment to attack.[38]

The allure of deferring decision

Because warning is a continuum, and because surprise attacks are the end products of prolonged tension rather than genuine bolts-from-the-blue, decision makers are used to living in an environment of *some* warning. The concern is how much accumulated warning warrants military reaction that will pose financial, diplomatic, and domestic political costs.

As long as the issue is how much, it is seductively easy for decision makers to wait for more. They may do this without feeling irresponsible by undertaking partial measures of response – the illusion of sufficient hedging. One 26 September 1973, for instance, Israel reacted to Syrian troop concentrations by adding an extra brigade, artillery units, antitank positions, ditches, and mines to the northern front.[39] But this was not enough to stop the Syrians immediately when the attack came over a week later.

The most basic but least helpful kinds of warning are the general political indications of enemy ambitions to change the status quo or evidence of strategic thinking and operational military objectives. On the first point, it has become a truism that allied leaders need only have read *Mein Kampf* to know Hitler would resort to subterfuge and war. On the second, for example, one post mortem notes that the allies had warning, from writings on naval strategy a decade earlier, that the Germans would feel compelled to occupy Norway.[40] Neither of these underdetermining 'facts,' however, provides any basis for guessing the certainty, moment, or location of attack; they are always a matter of at least several possibilities.

Victims sometimes recognize escalating indicators of attack yet still wait too long before mobilizing because they expect the enemy to play out more diplomatic moves before striking. When logical political possibilities remain by which the adversary could hope to achieve its goals – especially if the defender is making obvious its willingness to consider conciliation and concession – it seems reasonable to say 'the game is not up yet' and to play for time. During the Sudetenland crisis of 1939 evidence of military activity worried some in the West that the Germans might attack, but British ambassador Sir Neville Henderson was sure that Hitler would not march: 'I think it is equally possible that he will do nothing irrevocably without giving us a possibly 24-hour chance to prevent the irrevocable.'[41] And in that case Henderson was right. Two months later the Munich Conference ensued and Hitler got what he wanted without a fight. Evidence of enemy preparations to attack may be seen by a victim as a bluff, designed for diplomatic coercion. This is what Chinese warnings seemed to be between June and November 1950, before their intervention in force in Korea.

The attacker, though, can decide to skip rungs on the ladder of political escalation. Stalin, for example, expected an ultimatum before the Nazis struck and believed he still had the time in mid-1941 to temporize with economic concessions. In late 1941 the American interest was to delay conflict with Japan; despite consciousness that war might be imminent, 'the President believed he still had some time.'[42] And in mid-1945 the Japanese asked the Soviet Union to serve as an intermediary for a conditional surrender to the United States, making clear their willingness to grant Stalin substantial political and territorial concessions for this favor. Stalin deceived leaders in Tokyo, who believed he was seriously interested in negotiating. Thus they were stunned when Soviet forces, violating the Moscow-Tokyo nonaggression pact, struck in Manchuria in August.[43]

Another example of skipping stages in escalation prior to attack was highlighted by Secretary of State Dean Acheson's testimony that 'the view was generally held [before the Korean War] that since the Communists had far from exhausted the potentialities for obtaining their objectives through guerilla and psychological warfare, political pressure and intimidation, such means would probably continue to be used rather than overt military aggression.'[44] An intelligence cable from the Far East Command on 10 March 1950 noted that North Korea could be ready to attack the South by spring, but argued that plans in Korea would be contingent on Communist activities in Southeast Asia and that direct military action in Korea would 'be held in abeyance, at least until further observations made by Soviets of results of their program in such places as Indo-china, Burma, and Thailand.'[45]

Two further examples help illustrate this point. Before the 1956 Sinai Campaign some observers believed Israel would use Palestinian *fedayeen* raids as a pretext for a limited reprisal designed to provoke Egyptian counteraction, which 'would confuse the issue as to who was the aggressor, and allow Israel to launch unrestricted warfare against Egypt. . . . In fact the Israeli Government had decided to omit any intermediate steps.'[46] And, in June 1967 Israel attacked rather than wait for diplomacy to play itself out; the notion that Israel *would* wait to give diplomacy a final chance was used for deceptive purposes.[47]

Sometimes victims assume erroneously that by the logic of the situation they have the initiative, the enemy will be reacting, and therefore they read alternative explanations into tactical indicators. In 1904, just before the Japanese surprise attack on Port Arthur, the consensus among the victim's arrogant elite was that the decision for or against war would be up to Russia.[48] In early April 1940 the British were planning their own intervention in Norway, estimated the Germans would need more divisions to invade Scandinavia than were available, believed their naval superiority in itself precluded an effective German initiative in the area, and interpreted relevant indicators as evidence of German desires either to engineer another break-out of heavy ships into the Atlantic or to interdict British convoys to Norway. When information arrived via Copenhagen that Hitler would attack Narvik and Jutland with small forces, the operation seemed too daring. 'Incredulity thus was the first response in Whitehall to the Copenhagen message.'[49]

Among the most critical factors associated with the probability of recognizing signals are the perceived rewards and costs of doing so. Officials may have to make very distasteful decisions if the warning is real: 'Even a dim awareness of this prospect,' notes Alexander George, 'may subtly discourage the policy-maker from believing the warning.'[50] Officials have a natural incentive to wait as long as they think is possible because all the while that imminence of attack remains uncertain, the costs of preparing completely for it remain certain.[51] Intelligence cannot be *ignored* indefinitely. But it can be explained away. When a consumer is faced with data he prefers not to believe, he can fall back on four psychological mechanisms.

First, he can be more attentive to reassuring data. The threshold at which evidence confirming the individual's assumptions is recognized comes well before the threshold for contradictory evidence. Information that challenges reigning expectations or wishes 'is often required, in effect, to meet higher standards of evidence and to pass stricter tests to gain acceptance than new information that supports existing expectations and hypotheses.'[52] The consumer can also challenge the credibility of the source. An analyst or agency that has been chronically wrong in the past can be dismissed. Some political leaders also tend to be skeptical of advice from military sources and suspicious that professional soldiers manipulate information in order to gain authorization for desired changes in posture. A consumer's belief that the person giving him information has an ideological axe to grind, or a vested interest in changing policy, will tend to discredit the information. Third, the decision maker can appreciate the warnings, but suspend judgment and order stepped-up intelligence collection to confirm the threat, hoping to find contrary evidence that reduces the probability the enemy will strike. Finally, the consumer can rationalize. He may focus on the remaining ambiguity of the evidence rather than on the balance between threatening and reassuring data, letting his wish become father to his thought. He can explain away mounting but inconclusive threats by considering other elements of the context, or believing that enemy mobilization is precautionary and defensive. In many cases such reasoning is quite correct. The likelihood a responsible policymaker will let himself think this way varies directly with the severity of the specific costs involved in response to the warning and with the availability of reassuring evidence. There are always *some* real data to dampen alarm. Such data can also be fabricated.

Deception

Mixed signals can allow a reluctant defender to believe the worst is not yet at hand. An astute attacker can affect such a mix by injecting false indicators into the victim's view. If the intelligence *analysts* in the victimized state fail to see through the fabrication, then the efficiency of their intelligence *collection* system actually works against them. Improved observational technology hurts the victim if it monitors routine indicators that the attacker is purposely manipulating in a nonroutine way.[53] Deception can lull defenders by increasing the volume of 'noise' and thus the victim's impression that the evidence is indeterminate, as Roberta Wohlstetter suggests, or, as Barton Whaley argues, by *reducing* the apparent ambiguity of the data, reassuring the victim that favorable signs outweigh dangerous ones.

Deception is cheap. Little investment in men and material is necessary, and the return is very high.[54] It can also compensate for the erosion of secrecy that is inevitable in the extended period during which the attacker gets his ducks in a row. 'Secrecy and speed are mutually dependent on each other,' notes Erfurth. 'If secrecy cannot be maintained, speed must be increased; if speed is not practical, the enemy must be kept wholly ignorant.' He concludes, along with General Alfred Krauss, that 'confusion is the only effective method of maintaining secrecy.'[55] Deception reinforces the attacker's timing by slowing the victim's perception and keeping the pace of its preparations behind the attacker's. Defenders well versed in intrigue are not less likely to be victims of deception than are more ingenuous leaders. A comprehensive survey yielded the conclusion that 'the deceiver is almost always successful regardless of the sophistication of his victim in the same art.'[56] Stalin was alert to what he believed was British disinformation in 1940–41, but less sensitive to German deception. Paradoxically, alertness to the possibility of deception may increase susceptibility, by inhibiting revision of estimates: 'Deception provides a readily "available" explanation for discrepant evidence.'[57]

The first stage of warning is the detection of changes in normal behavior of the adversary's forces. Monitoring standard operating procedures helps to detect this, but sometimes an attacker can conceal changes in posture, provide indicators that divert the perception of threat to other sectors, or emit signals that suggest a totally innocent explanation. An example of the first possibility is the care taken by the Germans to maintain a normal pattern of radio traffic before striking into France in 1940, so as not to let a precipitous rise in the number of transmissions alert the allies;[58] an example of the second is the flow of announcements from the Wehrmacht at that time emphasizing the role of Army Group B, to reinforce the allied supposition that the principal threat was further north in Belgium, rather than Army Group A's plunge through the Ardennes;[59] an example of the third is the development of a profile of maneuver exercises similar to the movement and concentration necessary to launch an actual attack, as Egypt did in May 1973.

Deception allows the victim to retain confidence in its intelligence collection, while not raising alarm. Thus while the attacker is directing communication security and command-and-control deception procedures, the victim's leaders may be telling themselves that their own forces are alert and responsive.[60] On the other hand, an attacker might purposely increase the number of signals, by spewing out large amounts of disinformation to overload the victim's intelligence and decision system, creating confusion and encouraging delay in response; 'most information processing systems operate with little margin for coping with sudden increase in volume.'[61] This can happen even if the surge of indicators is not artificially inflated. In the crisis leading to the Soviet invasion of Czechoslovakia in 1968 the situation center at NATO headquarters was unable to handle the flow of information.[62] Sudden overload in military indicators is a warning itself. But as long as the situation still seems ambiguous, the reaction may be to wait until better sense can be made of the combined data.

Once the attack has begun, deception can still cripple the defender's response; tactical moves can amount to strategic deception. When the Germans launched the 1940 blitzkrieg it involved a strike into Belgium and the Netherlands that gave the French and British a mistaken impression of *déja vu*, suggesting a repetition of the Schlieffen Plan that began World War I. This view was reinforced by the allies' capture of the first attack plan (subsequently changed), which did resemble the 1914 operation.[63] As a result, there were no allied reserves to counter the thrust through the Ardennes.

The circumvention option: Designing around deterrence

Few defense strategies designed to deter attack are invulnerable. A determined and inventive adversary can often discover a way to avoid the strengths of a defense posture and exploit its weaknesses. Designing around the victim's strategy is most devastating when the weaknesses to be exploited are ones not fully recognized by the victim. There is usually more than one effective option for changing the status quo, and a defender who covers a dozen of those options effectively is no better off if the attacker uses a thirteenth option.[64] Most decisive are operational innovations that accomplish what the victim's leaders consider impossible, for example, crossing 'impassable' terrain, as the Germans did in the Ardennes in 1940, or as the Soviets did in the Manchurian campaign of August 1945 when they focused on the Transbaikal Front and crossed the Greater Khingan range.[65]

Some operations simply turn out to be more feasible than the defender's planners assume. So impractical did a German attack on Norway seem in 1940 that a British military intelligence official reacted to a warning by saying: 'I wish I could believe this story. German intervention in Scandinavia is just what we want.'[66] The most significant examples are innovations: those attacks that use technical or doctrinal surprises to neutralize the victim's strategy.

Technical surprise

The most militarily telling innovations are those in which the development of a new possibility is coupled quickly with an appropriate strategic and tactical concept, and is applied promptly in battle before the enemy becomes aware of, absorbs, and adapts to it. 'Every weapon is dependent not only on the strength of the opposition but also on its own willingness to make immediate, maximum use of the latest technical developments and thus to remain at the summit of its period.'[67]

American intelligence estimated that the range of Japanese fighters based on Formosa was insufficient for an attack on Clark Field in the Philippines. This *was* true until a month before Pearl Harbor, when the Japanese succeeded in increasing the range by adjusting engines and practicing rigorous fuel-conserving flight profiles.[68] There is no way to prevent intelligence failures in prediction of such short-term changes in threat if both the innovation and the attack occur in the window period before order of battle assessments are updated.

A minor innovation of this sort does not normally have massive consequences, but the chance that it will is improved if it is compounded by another such change. U.S. naval officers had grounds for complacency about the danger of attack with aerial torpedoes in Pearl Harbor, because the harbor was too shallow. They might have been alerted by the British attack on the Italian fleet in the harbor of Taranto which showed that torpedoes could be used in shallow water. Secretary of the Navy Knox noted this, but Admiral Kimmel did not worry because the torpedoes at Taranto still ran at twice the depth of Pearl Harbor. Kimmel rejected precautionary use of torpedo nets because they would tie up ship traffic. Until a month before the attack, this view was correct. Commander Minoru Genda, one of the principal planners of the operation, worried that use of torpedoes might have to be canceled. The Japanese managed, however, through a fin adjustment refined just a week before the fleet sailed, to develop torpedoes that would function even in the minimal depth of Pearl Harbor and used them with devastating effect on 7 December.[69]

A defender may know the enemy has equipment designed to accomplish certain tasks, but may assume it will not really work or can be countered easily, especially if it is simple. Israeli leaders in 1973 were impressed by the Suez Canal as a natural barrier. With little experience in wide water crossings themselves, they were not sensitive to how important such operations were in Soviet doctrine or to how well Russian advisers had trained Egyptians in the art of bridging. Arab use of infrared and other night-fighting gadgetry was also surprising.[70]

Major technical surprises are seldom absolute. Most breakthroughs are expected by some scientists or strategists in the victim nation. But there is no assurance that this awareness will be transmitted to or appreciated by enough experts to generate a new consensus of expectation in the scientific community; or enough of the highest professional military to compel a change in defensive tactics and plans; or enough political leaders to authorize changes in spending, basing, readiness, or deployment. The fact that someone in the victim's elite warns does not mean the warning will yield results. This applies particularly to the joining of technical with doctrinal innovation. Some observers assert that the blitzkrieg of 1940 was not a surprise because J.F.C. Fuller, Basil Liddell Hart, or Charles de Gaulle anticipated it. But it was a surprise because those in authority did not anticipate it.

Strictly technical surprises are frequent. Most are minor or they are recognized and hedged against with new countermeasures. They are part of the natural ebb and flow of defense modernization and procurement. The ones crucial for surprise attack are those that occur just before a war, and are not detected or evaluated, or those that facilitate not only tactical tinkering but revolution in operational strategy.

Doctrinal surprise

Purely technical surprises involve short-term ignorance by the victim; surprises in doctrinal applications of weaponry involve long-term misjudgment. The British assumed the Royal Navy would dominate engagements in the Skagerak and the North Sea and failed to assess correctly the ramifications of the development of air power. Thus the Luftwaffe was decisive in the German attack on Norway.[71] The Germans also used airborne forces (paratroops and gliders) for the first time as the vanguard of attack in the Norway operation, with novel results. (The existence of airborne forces was nothing new; the Russians had developed them as early as the 1920s.) This German novelty did not sink into the consciousness of all the western defenders. The Dutch commander did issue a preliminary alert to his forces on the German border just before the attack of 10 May, but the warning was not passed on to all units behind the line because action was not immediately expected in interior sectors. As a result the two German airborne divisions that landed at Fortress Holland came up against troops that had not been alerted, in the interest of avoiding needless fatigue.[72] The Germans also used air transport to resupply advanced armored formations with fuel and to fly in 2,000 maintenance workers to forward repair bases. 'The Allies were not thinking in such terms in May 1940,' explained Major L. F. Ellis.[73] The fact that the Egyptian army in 1973 possessed Sagger antitank missiles was no surprise to Israel, but their distribution and usage was, and caused unanticipated losses of Israeli armor. Similarly, the Egyptians' simple use of a belt of surface-to-air missiles around ground forces as a substitute for offensive air superiority, to screen the army in the Sinai, contradicted Israeli assumptions about the capacity of Israel's air force to forestall enemy advances on the ground. ('Logistical surprise' is a related possibility, as in the 1962 missile crisis, when the speed of construction of the Soviet sites in Cuba jolted American intelligence.[74] Moshe Dayan also cited Egypt's capacity to build and replace pontoon bridges as a logistical surprise in the October War.)[75]

The blitzkrieg against France is the clearest example of doctrinal surprise. The western allies knew well the strictly technical capabilities of tanks, but not their revolutionary operational potential when deployed independently of infantry and coordinated with air elements as they were by the Wehrmacht in May 1940. German success had little to do with any technical advantages per se. The allies had *both* quantitative and qualitative superiority in armored equipment.[76] The allies also had some doctrinal warning from German writings and the campaign in Poland of the 'lightning war' strategy (although Manstein's plan for deep armored penetration of France was unprecedented). In this sense the Russians, a year later, had double warning. But in both cases the victims still suffered the effects of surprise because they had not had time to digest and internalize the implications within their military organizations (the Russians had pioneered such tactics under Tukhachevsky, but abandoned them in the interim).

German development of the concepts behind the blitzkrieg strategy was explicitly motivated by the desire to capitalize on surprise. World War I had demonstrated the near impossibility of preserving surprise in operations based on frontal infantry assaults and massed indirect firepower. The vast preparations required to move artillery and ammunition took too much time and were difficult to conceal.[77] Despite the long peacetime gestation of German ideas for armored warfare, allied military leaders failed to appreciate them. Failure to absorb this doctrinal warning is not surprising because generational views of strategic reality, annealed in the experience of earlier war, are not sensitive to fragmentary, inconclusive indicators of enemy innovation; moreover, doctrinal warning *is* fragmentary and inconclusive, because a revolutionary doctrine is often resisted within the military establishment that ultimately accepts it at the last minute.

Military strategists tend to mislearn, in cyclical fashion, the lessons of war concerning the relative dominance of offensive and defensive capabilities.[78] Victors do this more than losers; having won the previous war, they see more virtue in the dominant strategies of that war. Thus the French Army, beaten by the Prussian offensive in 1870, fixated on '*l'offensive à l'outrance*' (attack to exhaustion). This prevented appreciation of intelligence collected in 1913 on German use of reserves that implied the need for French forces to stay on the defensive.[79] The war that followed was dominated by static defense and attrition. It was the German losers who reached first for strategic innovation and new offensive doctrine in 1940 when faced with the possibility of a replay of World War I. The Soviet Red Army had scant reason to be proud of its performance against Finland in 1939–40, but it did win the Winter War, and for a short but critical time learned its lessons too well. The storming of the Mannerheim Line became a model: the defense was to be ground down by gradual application of overwhelming force. 'We ceased to deal seriously with mobile combat,' Marshal Biriuzov recounted. 'We relegated to oblivion the fundamentals of combat-in-depth tactics and of combined arms maneuvers which had been widespread before the Finnish campaign. . . . [In 1941] We had to retrain ourselves under enemy fire.'[80] Biriuzov exaggerates, since the Red Army did begin to reinstitute armored formations before the onslaught, but the delay from mixed experience of the Winter War did little to help.

In light of history, we might ask whether the victors of World War II over-learned its lessons. The Warsaw Pact appears to be organized around rapid armored offensive. The United States also won World War II, but NATO's posture is more oriented to defensive operations. Some analysts, though not all, argue that the advent of highly efficient antitank guided munitions (ATGMs) heralds the pendulum's swing back toward the dominance of the defense.[81] There is ambiguous evidence that since the October War in the Middle East the Soviets have recognized the problems this creates for their strategy and have responded with even greater interest in the value of preemption and surprise. Yet it will be difficult for American observers to anticipate sea-changes in Soviet doctrine.

Doctrinal innovation may be a surprise when it unfolds on the battlefield because it is almost a surprise to the attacker who uses it: new concepts may bubble up from middle-level planners and the leadership may opt for them only at the last minute, after a long history of suppressing or arguing over them. Doctrinal revolutions in practice usually follow long and hesitant evolutions in theory. If a future victim fails to perceive the new doctrine during its peacetime gestation, before it has crystallized and really *becomes* the new doctrine, it is harder to fault its judgment. Should the victim be blamed for blindness to change when the attacker who later adopts it is still blind to it? Doctrinal factions contend within the military establishments of both attacker and defender. If the innovative faction barely wins in the former and barely loses in the latter, the defender's failure to be ready is disastrous but hardly egregious.

Perhaps achievement of doctrinal warning can only be tentative, by paying close attention to the progress of dissident strategists or 'oddballs' writing in enemy military journals, or by extrapolating from apparently anomalous aspects of enemy exercises, or by anticipating circumstances that would allow the enemy to shift its doctrine easily.[82] But a defender cannot plan against a *tabula rasa*, cannot have a totally flexible strategy of his own – that would be no strategy at all. A military establishment must organize and train according to some assumptions about enemy strategy, the best educated guess possible. Perhaps the western allies in 1940 did blunder because inertia or inattentiveness. But the Wehrmacht was incompletely committed to the blitzkrieg concept, not only until the May attack, but even beyond. Resistance to Guderian's tactics, and second thoughts in the direction of slowing the advance to secure flanks, continued as the attack progressed. Guderian was told to halt on more than one occasion and had to protest furiously to gain permission to press on.[83]

Some critics of U.S. defense policy charge that U.S. planners have endangered security by failing to understand Soviet doctrine, particularly on nuclear warfare. Richard Pipes believes the Soviets have a serious and ambitious nuclear strategy inconsistent with the dominant American conceptions of rationality and deterrence, and that Americans 'are as oblivious to these staggering innovations in the art of war as the French and British in their time had been to German strategy of the armored Blitzkrieg. There is a striking parallel between their faith in passive defenses anchored on the Maginot Line and ours in a "sufficient" deterrent.'[84] Raymond Garthoff mined Soviet military writings too, but came up with very different conclusions, more reassuring ones that minimize the salient differences between dominant American and Soviet views.[85]

Pipes and Garthoff are both experts on the Soviet Union, yet disagree radically. How should military experts and policymakers, who do not read Russian and who are unfamiliar with the intricacies of Soviet politics and culture, decide to hedge against Soviet doctrine? There is no solution free of subjectivity or ideological inhibition. This limp answer, matched with the earlier analysis, suggests two unhappy conclusions for the future. First, the technical revolution in intelligence collection of recent decades reduces vulnerability to surprise only at the margins, because miscalculation and sluggishness in political decisions are more the sources of surprise than lack of information. Second, since history provides few grounds for believing surprise can be avoided, the best defense posture is one that *assumes* surprise and provides a cushion for survival in the face of it. Surprise succeeds despite warning, so defense must succeed despite surprise.[*]

Notes

* For helpful criticisms of an earlier draft I thank Major General Shlomo Gazit, Michael Handel, John Mearsheimer, and Janet Stein.

1 For eight case studies on which this article is based see, Richard K. Betts, *Surprise and Defense* (Washington, D.C.: Brookings Institution, forthcoming), chaps. 2 and 3.

2 Graham T. Allison, *Essence of Decision: Explaining the Cuban Missile Crisis* (Boston, Mass.: Little, Brown and Co., 1971), pp. 120–22.

3 See Roberta Wohlstetter, 'Cuba and Pearl Harbor: Hindsight and Foresight,' *Foreign Affairs* 43 (July 1965): 696, 698.

4 Amnon Sella, ' "Barbarossa": Surprise Attack and Communication,' *Journal of Contemporary History* 13 (July 1978): 557.

5 Ibid., p. 563; Adam B. Ulam, *Stalin: The Man and His Era* (New York: Viking Press, 1973), p. 537.

6 Guy Chapman, *Why France Fell* (New York: Holt, Rinehart and Winston, 1968), p. 94.

7 William L. Shirer, *The Collapse of the Third Republic* (New York: Simon and Schuster, 1969), p. 607.

8 Major-General Sir Kenneth Strong, *Men of Intelligence* (New York: St. Martin's Press, 1971), p. 93; John Erickson, *The Road to Stalingrad* (New York: Harper & Row, 1975), pp. 96, 107, 110–12; Harrison Salisbury, *The 900 Days: The Siege of Leningrad* (New York: Harper & Row, 1969), pp. 30–32.

9 Barton Whaley, *Codeword Barbarossa* (Cambridge, Mass.: MIT Press, 1973), p. 7.

10 Sella, 'Surprise Attack and Communication,' pp. 558, 564, 566–68, 578–79; and Georgi Zhukov, *The Memoirs of Marshal Zhukov* (New York: Delacorte Press, 1971), p. 236. Earlier, in the Battle of France, similar but self-inflicted problems occurred. Processing blockages, staff shortages, and transmission times between allied headquarters and formations in the field prevented intelligence from catching up with the pace of German operations. See F. H. Hinsley et al., *British Intelligence in the Second World War* (Cambridge: Cambridge University Press, 1979), vol. 1, pp. 131, 137–38, 144, 147.

11 Roberta Wohlstetter, *Pearl Harbor: Warning and Decision* (Stanford, Calif.: Stanford University Press, 1962), pp. 83, 361–62, 366–67.

12 H.A. DeWeerd, 'Strategic Surprise in the Korean War,' *Orbis* 6 (Fall 1962): 441.

13 'Intelligence Warning of the Tet Offensive in South Vietnam (Interim Report),' 11 April 1968, declassified 3 December 1975, p. 5, reprinted in U.S., Congress, House, Select Committee on Intelligence, *Hearings, U.S. Intelligence Agencies and Activities, Part 5: Risks and Control of Foreign Intelligence*, 94th Cong., 1st sess., 1975, p. 1997.

14 Steve Chan, 'The Intelligence of Stupidity: Understanding Failures in Strategic Warning,' *American Political Science Review* 73 (March 1979): 175.

15 Wohlstetter, *Pearl Harbor*, p. 385.

16 Donald T. Campbell, 'Systematic Error on the Part of Human Links in Communication Systems,' *Information and Control* 1 (1958): 341–47, 349–51.

17 Confidential source.

18 Quoted in Julian Critchley, *Warning and Response* (New York: Crane, Russak and Co., Inc., 1978), p. 50.

19 Hinsley et al., *British Intelligence in the Second World War*, vol. 1, pp. 138, 145.

20 U.S., Congress, Senate, Select Committee on Intelligence, *Staff Report, U.S. Intelligence and the Oil Issue, 1973–1974*, 95th Cong., 1st sess., 1977, pp. 3–4.

21 See Avi Shlaim, 'Failures in National Intelligence Estimates: The Case of the Yom Kippur War,' *World Politics* 28 (April 1976): 378.

22 Chan, 'Intelligence of Stupidity,' p. 173.

23 James F. Schnabel, *Policy and Direction: The First Year* (Washington, D.C.: Department of the Army, Office of the Chief of Military History, 1972), p. 64.

24 Ezer Weizman, *On Eagles' Wings* (New York: Macmillan Co., 1976), p. 209.

25 Chan, 'Intelligence of Stupidity,' p. 172.

26 Robert Axelrod, 'The Rational Timing of Surprise,' *World Politics* 31 (January 1979): 244–45.

27 See Michael I. Handel, *Perception, Deception, and Surprise: The Case of the Yom Kippur War*, Jerusalem Paper No. 19 (Jerusalem: Leonard Davis Institute for International Relations, Hebrew University, 1976), p. 11.

28 R. T. Paget, *Manstein: His Campaigns and His Trial* (London: Collins, 1951), p. 19.

29 Barton Whaley, *Stratagem: Deception and Surprise in War* (Cambridge, Mass.: MIT Center of International Studies, 1969), pp. 176–79, 187, 188.

30 Roberta Wohlstetter, 'The Pleasures of Self Deception,' *Washington Quarterly* 2 (Autumn 1979): 54.

31 George Burns Williams, 'Blitzkrieg and Conquest: Policy Analysis of Military and Political Decisions Preparatory to the German Attack upon Norway, April 9, 1940' (Ph.D. diss., Yale University, 1966), p. 465; Johan Jørgen Holst, 'Surprise, Signals and Reaction: The Attack on Norway, April 9th, 1940 – Some Observations,' *Cooperation and Conflict* 1 (1966): 39.

32 Quoted in Shirer, *Collapse of the Third Republic*, pp. 606–7.

33 Henry L. Mason, 'War Comes to the Netherlands: September 1939-May 1940,' *Political Science Quarterly* 78 (December 1963): 557, 562–64. Hinsley et al., *British Intelligence in the Second World War*, vol. 1, p. 135.

34 Major L.F. Ellis, *The War in France and Flanders: 1939–1940* (London: Her Majesty's Stationery Office, 1953), pp. 344–46.

35 Sella, 'Surprise Attack and Communication,' p. 256.

36 Wohlstetter, *Pearl Harbor*, pp. 137, 151.

37 Ibid., p. 397.

38 Zeev Schiff, *October Earthquake: Yom Kippur 1973*, trans. Louis Williams (Tel Aviv: University Publishing Projects, 1974), pp. 17–18.

39 Handel, *Perception, Deception, and Surprise*, p. 32.

40 Holst, 'Surprise, Signals, and Reaction,' p. 36.

41 E. L. Woodward and Rohan Butler, eds., assisted by Margaret Lambert, *Documents on British Foreign Policy 1919–1939*, Third Series, vol. II: *1938* (London: His Majesty's Stationery Office, 1949), Document 553, p. 14.

42 Wohlstetter, *Pearl Harbor*, p. 269.

43 John Despres, Lilita I. Dzirkals, and Barton Whaley, *Timely Lessons of History: The Manchurian Model for Soviet Strategy*, R-1825-NA (Santa Monica, Calif.: Rand Corporation, July 1976), p. 17. Stalin had terminated the nonaggression treaty before the attack, but the terms of the treaty required a full year's notice for abrogation.

44 U.S., Congress, Senate, Committees on Armed Services and Foreign Relations, *Hearings, Military Situation in the Far East*, 82d Cong., 1st sess., 1951, Part 3, p. 1991.

45 Quoted in Ibid.

46 Lt. Gen. E.L.M. Burns, *Between Arab and Israeli* (New York: Obolensky, 1963), p. 179.

47 Moshe Dayan, *Story of My Life* (New York: William Morrow, 1976), p. 341.

48 'Japan was not a country that could give an ultimatum to Russia. . . . The Russians in Port Arthur scarcely considered the Japanese to be people' (Denis Warner and Peggy Warner, *The Tide at Sunrise: A History of the Russo-Japanese War, 1904–1905* [New York: Charterhouse, 1974], p. 11).

49 Hinsley et al., *British Intelligence in the Second World War*, pp. 120–22.

50 Alexander L. George, 'Warning and Response: Theory and Practice,' in *International Violence: Terrorism, Surprise and Control*, ed. Yair Evron (Jerusalem: Leonard Davis Institute for International Relations, Hebrew University, 1979), pp. 17, 19.

51 'We also refused to believe our intelligence [in 1950] because it would have been very inconvenient if we had: we would have had to do something about it. In the end, of course, it was much more inconvenient not to have believed our intelligence, but those acquainted with statecraft and politics know how much easier it is to rectify an error of omission, even at tremendous cost, than to make an embarrassing decision in advance' (DeWeerd, 'Strategic Surprise in the Korean War,' pp. 451–52).

52 Alexander L. George and Richard Smoke, *Deterrence in American Foreign Policy* (New York: Columbia University Press, 1974), p. 574.

53 Axelrod, 'Rational Timing of Surprise,' p. 246.

54 Whaley, *Stratagem*, p. 232.

55 General Waldemar Erfurth, *Surprise*, trans. Stefan T. Possony and Daniel Vilfroy (Harrisburg, Pa.: Military Service Publishing Company, 1943), pp. 39, 6.

56 Whaley, *Stratagem*, p. 146.

57 Richards J. Heuer, Jr., 'Strategic Deception: A Psychological Perspective' (Paper delivered at the Twenty-first International Studies Association convention, Los Angeles, Calif., March 1980), pp. 16, 47.

58 F. W. Winterbotham, *The Ultra Secret* (New York: Harper & Row, 1974), p. 32.

59 Guenther Blumentritt, *Von Runstedt: The Soldier and the Man*, trans. Cuthbert Reavely (London: Odham's Press, 1952), pp. 65–66.

60 Lieutenant Colonel A. L. Elliott, 'The Calculus of Surprise Attack,' *Air University Review* 30 (March–April 1979): 62.

61 Whaley, *Stratagem*, p. 18.

62 Jon McLin, 'NATO and the Czechoslovakian Crisis, Part II: Invasion, Reaction, and Stock-taking,' *American Universities Field Staff Reports*, West Europe Series, vol. 4, no. 4 (Hanover, N.H.: American Universities Field Staff, February 1969), p. 6.

63 Critchley, *Warning and Response*, pp. 21–22.

64 See George and Smoke, *Deterrence in American Foreign Policy*, pp. 520–21.

65 Lilita I. Dzirkals, *'Lightning War' in Manchuria: Soviet Military Analysis of the 1945 Far East Campaign*, P-5589 (Santa Monica, Calif.: Rand Corporation, January 1976), p. 28.

66 Hinsley et al., *British Intelligence in the Second World War*, vol. 1, pp. 117–118.

67 General Heinz Guderian, *Panzer Leader*, trans. Constantine Fitzgibbon (London: Futura Publications Limited, 1974), p. 42.

68 Wohlstetter, *Pearl Harbor*, pp. 358–361, 365.

69 Ibid., p. 369; John Deane Potter, *Yamamoto: The Man Who Menaced America* (New York: Viking Press, 1965), pp. 53–54; Alvin D. Coox, 'Pearl Harbor,' in *Decisive Battles of the Twentieth Century: Land-Sea-Air*, eds. Noble Frankland and Christopher Dowling (New York: David McKay Co., Inc., 1976), p. 145.

70 Handel, *Perception, Deception, and Surprise*, pp. 46–47.

71 Holst, 'Surprise, Signals and Reaction,' p. 35.

72 Mason, 'War Comes to the Netherlands,' p. 566.

73 Ellis, *War in France and Flanders*, p. 346.

74 Wohlstetter, 'Cuba and Pearl Harbor,' p. 698.

75 Avigdor Haselkorn, 'Israeli Intelligence Performance in the Yom Kippur War,' Hudson Institute Discussion Paper 2033 (Croton-on-Hudson, N.Y., July 1974), pp. 1, 15n.

76 R.H.S. Stolfi, 'Equipment for Victory in France,' *History* 52 (February 1970): 1–20.

77 Guderian, *Panzer Leader*, p. 41.

78 Robert Jervis, 'Cooperation Under the Security Dilemma,' *World Politics* 30 (January 1978): 189.

79 Barbara Tuchman, *The Guns of August* (New York: Dell Publishing Co., Inc., 1963), p. 61.

80 Marshal S. S. Biriuzov, 'The Lesson Learned Too Well,' in *Stalin and His Generals: Soviet Military Memoirs of World War II*, ed. Scweryn Bialer (New York: Pegasus Publishers, 1969), p. 137.

81 See John Mearsheimer, 'Precision-guided Munitions and Conventional Deterrence,' *Survival* 21 (March–April 1979): 68–76, and sources cited in his notes 2 and 3, for arguments and counterarguments.

82 See Net Assessment Task Force, 'The Critical Properties of Sudden Attack: A Study Proposal,' mimeographed (Washington, D.C.: U.S. Air Force, Headquarters, November 1976), p. 75.

83 Ulrich Liss, *Westfront 1939/40: Errinerungen des Feindarbeiters im O.K.H.* [Western Front 1939–40: memoirs of an alienated worker in the Army High Command] (Neckargemund, Germany: Kurt Vowinckel Verlag, 1959), pp. 106–7, 143–44; Guderian, *Panzer Leader*, pp. 89–92, 99, 101, 107, 109–10, 117–19. Hitler also prevented the complete exploitation of the advance by stopping Guderian's forces short of Dunkirk, where the British Expeditionary Force was subsequently evacuated.

84 Richard Pipes, 'Rethinking Our Nuclear Strategy,' *Wall Street Journal*, 12 October 1978. See also, idem., 'Why the Soviet Union Thinks It Could Fight and Win a Nuclear War,' *Commentary* 64 (July 1977): 21–34.

85 Raymond L. Garthoff, 'Mutual Deterrence and Strategic Arms Limitation in Soviet Policy,' *International Security* 3 (Summer 1978): 112–47.

Reprinted with permission from R.K. Betts, 'Surprise Despite Warning: Why Sudden Attacks Succeed', *Political Science Quarterly* 95/4 (1980) 551–72.

7 What to do when traditional models fail

Carmen Medina

This article makes the case for radical change in how analysts are managed and argues that the way ahead is in offering insight alongside policy-makers. Intelligence officers still believe that the trade-craft of intelligence analysis adds value for the hard-pressed policymaker. However, Medina asks whether the traditional model of an 'analytical shop' which focuses on synthesis and keeps the analysts separate from decision-makers and indeed collectors, remains effective. Medina proposes a more forward leaning and realist approach tailored to the demands of policy-makers. Over the last five years, analysts have increasingly been spread through the intelligence process, but the trend remains controversial.

The great challenge facing analysts and managers in the Directorate of Intelligence (DI) is providing real insight to smart policymakers. Meeting this challenge is hard, but intelligence officers have long believed that careful attention to the tradecraft of intelligence analysis would lead to work that added value to the information available to policymakers. During its 50-plus years, the CIA, we believed, evolved a model that needed only successful execution to produce quality intelligence analysis. When we faltered, we blamed the analysts (or the collectors), but not the model.

What if the failing, however, lies not with the analysts but with the model they are asked to follow? Customer needs and preferences are changing rapidly, as is the environment in which intelligence analysis operates. Yet the DI's approach to analysis has hardly changed over the years. A DI analyst from decades ago would recognize most of what a typical analyst does today, from reading traffic to preparing finished intelligence. Stability is often comforting, but in the DI's case change may be what is most needed.

The current model

On the CIA's public internet website, the DI defines its mission as the provision of timely, accurate, and objective intelligence analysis on the full range of national security threats and foreign policy issues facing the United States. The website outlines the different types of analytic support that might be useful to a customer at any given time. DI officers provide analysis that helps officials work through their policy agendas by: addressing day-to-day events; apprising consumers of developments and providing related background information; assessing the significance of developments and warning of near-term consequences; and signaling potentially dangerous situations in the future.

A key aspect of this model is that it focuses first on developments. In fact, the analysts' work process is structured around developments. They spend the first quarter or more of their workday reading through the 'overnight traffic' to determine what is new. They report what is new to their colleagues and superiors and then often to the policymaking community. The 'new thing' may be an event – the death of a world leader or the precipitous decline of an Asian currency. Or it may be an item of intelligence reporting on a situation of interest – from signals, imagery, human-source, open-source, or other type of collection. This basic model has guided the DI's work for decades.

More recently, DI managers have realized that the specific interests of customers must have greater weight in determining what to do on any given day. As a result, the model has acquired an additional step – understanding customer feedback to determine policymaker interests. This new step, however, merely supplements the pivot around which the analytic work turns – identification of the new development.

Critical, sometimes unstated, assumptions underpin this tradecraft model:

Assumption 1: Policymakers need a service that tells them what is going on in the world or in their particular area of concern.

Assumption 2: Policymakers need help in determining what an event means.

Assumption 3: The CIA and specifically the DI have unique information about what is happening.

Assumption 4: DI analysts are particularly insightful about what these developments may mean.

When models fail

Models work only as long as they suit the environment in which they operate. If reality changes, then it is a good bet that the model needs to evolve as well. The DI's tradecraft model was developed during the 1960s and 1970s and optimized against the characteristics of that period. It was an era of information scarcity – truth about the world's many closed societies was a rare commodity. Communicating across borders and with other governments was hard – government leaders rarely talked to each other on the phone and summits among world leaders were unusual events. Ideology was a key driver in international relations – it was always important to know how far left or right a government would tack. These traits do not describe today's environment.

Analysts today have to add value in an era of information abundance. The policymaker, an intelligence consumer, has many more ways of staying informed about recent developments, intelligence-related or not. The responses to a survey of customers of the Senior Executive Intelligence Bulletin (SEIB) conducted in late 2000 are illustrative. When asked to identify the unclassified information sources they relied on, 85 percent of the respondents picked all four of the following sources: foreign newspapers and weekly periodicals; US newspapers and weekly periodicals; their professional networks; and official, informal communications, such as e-mail.

Policymakers today also read raw intelligence reports on a regular basis. Twenty to thirty years ago, analysts in the DI had the fastest access to incoming intelligence information and could count on seeing particularly criticalcables before policymakers. Today, thanks to information technology, policymakers often read the raw traffic at the same time as, if not before, analysts. In a 1998–1999 survey, SEIB customers were asked, 'What other sources of daily intelligence do you read?' Almost one-half of the respondents volunteered that they often read raw traffic. Given that 'raw traffic' was not offered as a specific choice, the real percentage was almost certainly higher than the write-in responses indicated.

Analysts today have to dig deep to surpass the analytic abilities of their customers. Modern communication technologies and evolving diplomatic practices now allow government leaders to communicate with each other freely and often. US officials even talk to opposition party leaders. This makes it much easier for policymakers to be their own analysts – to gain insights into the intentions of other governments and decipher what developments may mean. The DI has probably always underestimated the extent to which policymakers serve as their own analysts. Arguably, policymakers have never needed the DI to tell them that riots undermine governments or that currency crises shake investor confidence. Today, however, they no longer even need much help deconflicting signals from other governments.

Analysts today have to reach beyond political analysis, an area in which it is particularly hard to provide value to policymakers. The ideological orientation of governments is no longer the important issue in international relations; it has been replaced by a growing list of non-traditional issues that tend to defy ideological definition. In the DI, however, political analysis is still king. We want to follow the ins and outs of political activity in any number of countries even though the audience for this type of analysis is not as broad as it once was. A recent study of articles in the SEIB, for example, revealed that 70 percent dealt mostly with analysis of political developments. In contrast, a much wider variety of issues was covered in memos written directly in response to questions from senior customers. Only about one-third of those memos – whose topics presumably matched what was most on the policymakers' minds – covered political matters, and many of those discussed the behavior and attitudes of foreign leaders, a sub-category of political analysis that remains of high interest to senior policymakers.

The move toward non-traditional issues is already underway, evidenced by the creation of specialized Centers to deal with terrorism, weapons proliferation, and narcotics and crime. Nonetheless, too many of our flagship products still reflect a political analysis bias. We need to do a better job aligning our publishing strategies with emerging realities.

Analysis in some other conventional areas can still provide value-added, but, like political analysis, the challenge is greater than before. Economic analysis faces daunting competition from the open-source world and those analysts need either to serve consumers who are not economic specialists or to identify niche substantive areas where the Agency can still provide unique support. Scientific and military analyses are borderline issues that defy easy solutions. A number of our senior customers, particularly in civilian agencies, cannot serve as their own experts on technical topics, so there is more room for the intelligence analyst to provide value-added. The issue for military analysis, however, is which agency should be primarily responsible. This is now a crowded field, occupied not only by the DI and the Defense Intelligence Agency, but, increasingly more to the point, by the strong intelligence centers at the unified military commands. The DI is still in the process of defining its comparative advantage in military analysis.

Analysis that fits the new environment

So, how does the DI, or anyone, do intelligence analysis in an era of information abundance, wellconnected policymakers, and non-traditional issues? First, we need new assumptions:

New Assumption 1: Most of the time, policymakers have a good sense of what is going on in their areas of concern.

New Assumption 2: Policymakers frequently understand the direct consequences of events and their immediate significance.

New Assumption 3: The CIA – and particularly the DI – often lacks unique information about developments, especially in the political and economic spheres. Raw intelligence is ubiquitous and can get to policymakers before it reaches the analysts.

New Assumption 4: Policymakers need the greatest help understanding non-traditional intelligence issues. There is still a market for political analysis and certainly for related leadership analysis, but to be successful in traditional areas the DI must generate unique insights into relatively well-understood problems.

A DI optimized against these assumptions would understand current developments, but only as the necessary foundation for its real contribution to policymakers. Analysts would specialize in complex analysis of the most difficult problems. They would focus on the policymakers' hardest questions. Their goals would include identifying new opportunities for policymaking and warning first of discontinuities that could spell danger.

What does this mean in practical terms? How would the practice of intelligence analysis change?

Analysts must focus on the customer. For many analysts, particularly those involved in political work, the focus would shift from tracking developments in their particular accounts to addressing the specific, hard questions of policymakers. An analyst, for example, would often start her day by reviewing feedback and tasking from customers, instead of first reading the morning traffic. We need to use technology and a network of high-caliber representatives at policy agencies to create stronger links between analysts and customers.

Analysts must concentrate on ideas, not intelligence. Because the DI has no monopoly over the dissemination of intelligence reporting, synthesizing it for others is a poor investment of its time and talent. This particularly applies to political and economic analysis; policymakers do in fact often need help deciphering technical reports on such issues as proliferation and information warfare. In many substantive fields, the DI can best serve the policymaker by tackling the hard questions and trying to develop more reliable ways of identifying and understanding emerging issues. To do this kind of work well, the DI will need keen critical thinkers open to unconventional ideas, perhaps even more than it will need regional experts. Customers are actually pretty good at letting us know what issues keep them up at night; we have to stop dismissing these questions as either too hard or not intelligence-related.

To free analysts to do this work, we will need to de-emphasize products that largely describe what has just happened. This will be hard because there are customers who want such products, which are seen as convenient, free goods. But if our relatively painless experience last year with the elimination of the *Economic Intelligence Weekly*, a decades-old publication that reviewed economic developments, is any guide, policymaker demand for such products is shallow at best.

Analysts must think beyond finished intelligence. Analysts are schooled in the need to produce validated, finished intelligence – 'finished' meaning that it has been carefully considered, officially reviewed, coordinated with colleagues, and sent out under official cover. The main problem is that such products often cannot keep pace with events or even with information sources. DI officers who deal frequently with customers – including those who carry the *President's Daily Brief* to the most senior officials – report that many products short of finished intelligence often satisfy the needs of policymakers. These include annotated raw intelligence, quick answers to specific questions, informal trip reports, and memoranda of conversation. Too many intelligence analysts and managers remain fixated on formal products even as policymakers move further away from them in their own work. As anyone who has done a recent tour at a US Embassy knows, most of the real scoop on world events is now exchanged in informal e-mails and telephone calls. Our adherence to the increasingly outdated concept of finished intelligence is what makes the DI wary of such informal intelligence practices as electronic 'chat rooms' and other collaborative venues.[1]

Analysts must look to the Centers as models. If you sit long enough on a DI career service panel, you will still hear some managers say that certain analysts in the Counter-terrorism Center or the Crime and Narcotics Center are not doing real DI work. They are producing little in the way of finished intelligence, and they are spending a lot of time doing individual tasks that meet very specific customer needs. Instead of being perceived as outside the DI mainstream, the Centers should be recognized as early adapters of the new model. Their focus on customer requirements, collaborative work, and less formal products speaks to the future.

The Old Analysis	21st Century Analysis
Cautious/Careful	Aggressive/Bold/Courageous
Fact-based	Intuitive
Concrete/Reality-based	Metaphor-rich
Linear/Trend-based	Complex
Expert-based	Humble, Inclusive, Diverse
Hierarchical	Collaborative
Precedent-based	Precedent-shattering
Worst-case/Warning-focused	Opportunistic/Optimistic
Text-based	Image-rich
Detached/Neutral	Customer-driven/Policy-relevant

Now for something completely heretical

As policymakers continue to raise the standards for intelligence analysis, we may need to change more than just our assumptions and work habits. The fundamental characteristics of intelligence analysis, carefully developed during the last half of the twentieth century, may in fact need to be completely rewritten. The transition might look something like the box at the right.

The qualities of 'old analysis' are familiar to any intelligence professional. We pride ourselves on carefully basing our judgments on fact, on our expertise, on our ability to warn, and on our neutrality. Some might argue that these are clearly the analytic qualities that must persist under any scenario, regardless of whether we have addressed the needs of our customers.

Perhaps not. To really help smart policymakers, we may need to adopt new practices, new habits of thinking, and new ways of communicating our analysis.

To tell a policymaker something he does not already know, we have to be prepared to take risks in our thinking, to 'go to print' with new, adventurous analytic lines before anyone else. This is not always our current style. Almost everything an analyst learns teaches her to be conservative: do not jump to conclusions, consider all sources, coordinate your views with colleagues. At best, an analyst will occasionally lean forward, when in fact she must strive to be several steps ahead of the policymaker on a regular basis.

It is difficult to generate new ideas when you have to stay close to the facts. New ideas are often intuitive, based on one or two stray bits of information that coalesce into new insight. Analysts in the 21st century will not only have to develop their intuition, they – and their managers – will also have to trust it.

Analysts today spend considerable time identifying patterns in recent events and then projecting them onto the future. This is trend analysis. Unfortunately, policymakers who are smart – and most are – can easily do this for themselves. The analysts' real value increasingly will lie in identifying discontinuities that shatter precedents and trends.

Analysts are often good at identifying what is not likely to work in a given situation; however, policymakers are usually more interested in figuring out what can work. While courses in the Intelligence Community teach analysts how to warn, there are no handbooks on how to identify new opportunities for policymakers.

The most controversial contention may be that 21st century analysts will need to become less independent and neutral in favor of greater tailoring to customer needs. Some critics have already noted that our customer focus in recent years is eroding our detachment from policymaking. The usual answer is to assert that customer focus and neutrality are compatible; but in truth they are not completely. The more we care, as we should, that we have an impact on the policymaking community, the less neutral we become, in the sense that we select our topics based on customer interests and we analyze those aspects that are most relevant to policymakers. Analysts understandably are confused by this new direction. They were taught, they say, to produce intelligence analysis that focuses on events and developments, not customers. It is not their job to worry about whether or not it has impact.

This is the most significant and difficult consequence of working in an information-rich era lacking in significant ideological conflict. Analytic detachment and neutrality are values bred of the Cold War, when foreign policy observers often compensated for lack of information with ideologically based assertions. Intelligence analysts correctly tried not to do that – they were reliably objective.

Being completely neutral and independent in the future, however, may only gain us irrelevance. We need, of course, integrity in our analysis – we must be willing to say things that are uncomfortable for the Pentagon or the State Department and that are not compatible with the goals of policymakers. But we should not pretend that integrity and neutrality are the same thing or that they are dependent on each other. Neutrality implies distance from the customer and some near mystical ability to parse the truth completely free from bias or prejudice. Integrity, on the other hand, rests on professional standards and the willingness to provide the most complete answer to a customer's question, even if it is not the answer he wants to hear. Neutrality cannot be used to justify analytic celibacy and disengagement from the customer. If forced to choose between analytic detachment and impact on policymaking, the 21st century analyst must choose the latter.

Note

1 The need to escape the constraints of finished intelligence was highlighted more than five years ago by Carol Dumaine, a DI officer currently leading the Directorate's Global Futures Partnership, who has written extensively on new models for intelligence analysis. In 1996, for example, in a submission to an in-house electronic discussion database, she noted that the future intelligence officer would 'produce unfinished intelligence – all of it on line, interactive, iterative, multidimensional, an interdisciplinary fabric of specialist contributions, and available 24 hours a day to trusted consumers.'

Reprinted with permission from Carmen Medina, 'What To Do When Traditional Models Fail', *Studies in Intelligence* 46/3 (2002) pp.23–9. (It is also worthwhile looking at the response – S.R. Ward, 'Evolution Beats Revolution in Analysis', *Studies in Intelligence* 46/3 (2002) pp.29–36).

THE ANALYSIS OF INTELLIGENCE

Further reading: Books and reports

R.K. Betts, *Surprise Attack: Lessons for Defense Planning* (Washington D.C.: Brookings Institution 1982).

Richard K. Betts and Thomas G. Mahnken, (eds.) *Paradoxes of Strategic Intelligence: Essays in Honor of Michael I. Handel* (London: Frank Cass 2003).

Hal Ford, *Estimative Intelligence* (McLean VA: AFIO 1993).

Peter Gill and Mark Pythian, *Intelligence in an Insecure World* (Cambridge: Polity 2006) chapter 5.

Michael Herman, *Intelligence Power in Peace and War* (Cambridge: Cambridge University Press 1996) chapters 6–7.

Richard Heuer, Psychology of Intelligence Analysis (Washington FDC: CIA Center for the Study of Intelligence 1999).

Emphraim. Kam, *Surprise Attack: The Victim's Perspective* (Cambridge MA: Harvard University Press 1988)

Roger Z. George and Robert D. Kline (eds.), *Intelligence and National Security Strategist: Enduring Issues and Challenges* (Washington DC: National Defense University Press, CSI, 2004), part VII, pp.295–359.

Sherman Kent, *Strategic Intelligence for American Foreign Policy* (Princeton: Princeton University Press 1949).

I Janis, *Victims of Groupthink*. (Boston: Houghton Mifflin 1972)

Loch K. Johnson & James J. Wirtz, *Intelligence and National Security: The Secret World of Spies* (NY: Oxford University Press, 2nd ed. 2007).

Walter Laqueur, *World of Secrets: The Uses and Limits of Intelligence*, (NY: Basic Books 1985).

A. Levite, *Intelligence and Strategic Surprises* (NY: Columbia University Press 1987)

Mark Lowenthal, *Intelligence: From Secrets to Policy* (Washington DC: CQ Press, 3rd Ed 2006), chapter 6.

W. Matthias, *America's Strategic Blunders: Intelligence Analysis and National Security Policy, 1936–1991* (University Park PA: The Pennsylvania University Press 2001).

Abram N. Shulsky and Gary J. Schmitt, *Silent Warfare: Understanding the World of Intelligence* (Dulles, VA: Brassey's Inc., 2002) chapter 3.

Jennifer E. Sims, and Burton L. Gerber (eds.), *Transforming U.S. Intelligence* (Washington, DC: Georgetown University Press 2005).

J. J. Wirtz, *The Tet Offensive: Intelligence Failure in War* (Ithaca NY: Colombia University Press 1991)

R. Wohlstetter, *Pearl Harbor: Warning and Decision* (Stanford: Stanford University Press 1962).

Further reading: Essays and articles

Willis Armstrong et al, 'The Hazards of Single Outcome Forecasting' in Bradford Westerfield (ed.) *Inside the CIA's Private World* (New Haven: Yale University Press 1995) pp.238–54.

B. Berkovitz, 'Intelligence in the Organisational Context: Co-ordination and Error in National Estimates,' *Orbis* 29/3 (1985) pp.571–96.

B. Berkowitz, 'Failing to Keep Up With the Information Revolution', *Studies in Intelligence* 47/1 (2003) pp.67–75

R K Betts, 'Analysis, War, Decision: Why Intelligence Failures are Inevitable' *World Politics* 31/2 (1978) pp.61–89.

Shlomo Gazit, 'Intelligence Estimates and the Decision maker', *Intelligence and National Security* 3,/3 (1988) pp.261–67

Steve Chan, 'The Intelligence of Stupidity: Understanding Failures in Strategic Warning', in: *The American Political Science Review* 73/1 (1979), 171–180.

Shlomo Gazit, 'Estimates and Fortune-Telling in Intelligence Work,' *International Security* 4/4 (1980) pp.36–56.

Shlomo Gazit, 'Intelligence Estimates and the Decision-Maker,' *Intelligence and National Security* 3/3 (1988) pp.261–287.

Roger Z George, 'Fixing the Problem of Analytical Mind-Sets: Alternative Analyses', *International Journal of Intelligence and Counterintelligence* 17/3 (2004) pp.385–404.

Malcolm Gladwell, 'Connecting the Dots. The Paradoxes of Intelligence Reform,' *The New Yorker* 10 March 2003, pp.83–88.

Douglas Hart and Steven Simon, 'Thinking straight and talking straight: Problems of intelligence analysis', *Survival* 48/1 (2006) pp.35–60.

Michael Herman, 'Intelligence and the Assessment of Military Capabilities: Reasonable Sufficiency or Worst Case?', *Intelligence and National Security* 4/4 (1989) pp.800–812.

G.W. Hopple, 'Intelligence and warning: implications and lessons of the Falkland Islands War,' *World Politics* 36/3 (1984) pp.339–61

Loch Johnson, 'Analysis for a New Age,' *Intelligence and National Security* 11/4 (1996) pp.657–671.

Sherman Kent, 'Estimates and Influence,' in Donald P. Steury, (ed.), *Sherman Kent and the Board of National Estimates: Collected Essays* (Washington DC: CIA/Center for the Study of Intelligence, 1994), pp.33–42.

Woodrow Kuhns, 'Intelligence Failures: Forecasting and the Lessons of Epistemology', in R.K. Betts and T. Mahnken (eds.), *Paradoxes of Strategic Intelligence* (London: Frank Cass 2003) pp.80–100.

David Vital, 'Images of Other Peoples in the Making of Intelligence and Foreign Policy.' *International Journal of Intelligence and Counterintelligence* 16/1 (2003) pp.16–33.

Frank Watanabe, 'Fifteen Axioms for Intelligence Analysts,' *Studies in Intelligence* 1/1 (1997).

Bradford Westerfield, *Inside the CIA's Private World*, (New Haven: Yale University Press 1995) Section V, pp.207–31.

S.R. Ward, 'Evolution Beats Revolution in Analysis', *Studies in Intelligence* 46/3 (2002) pp.29–36

J.J. Wirtz, 'Intelligence to Please: The Order of Battle Controversy During the Victnam War', *Political Science Quarterly* 106/2 (1991) pp.239–63.

Essay questions

- How far do you accept R.K. Betts's hypothesis that 'intelligence failures are inevitable'?
- Can the organizational reform of intelligence have an impact on the main pathologies of intelligence analysis and interpretation?
- 'Attempts at resolving failures in the realm of analysis have focused on the organizational, but the roots of the problem are psychological'. Discuss.
- Just how close should analysts be to the policy-makers?

8 American Presidents and their intelligence communities

C.M. Andrew

This article examines American leaders and their relationship with their intelligence community. It argues that, until 1945, few of George Washington's successors matched his ability to make use of intelligence. Moreover amongst the post war presidents, only three – Eisenhower, Kennedy and Bush – have shown a flair for intelligence. The relations between U.S. presidents and their intelligence communities have gone through three phases: The 'Age of Innocence,' which lasted until World War II; America's 'Age of Transformation' began with the country's entry into World War II; and the 'Age of Uncertainty,' which in Andrew's judgement continues, and began after Kennedy's assassination. Overall, during the twentieth century, America's Presidents often underestimated the value of the intelligence they received during the Cold War, and frequently overestimated the potential of covert action.

During the Revolutionary War (1775–83), thanks chiefly to General George Washington, American intelligence and covert action outclassed those of Britain. Washington's early experience in the French and Indian Wars had convinced him that 'There is nothing more necessary than good Intelligence to frustrate a designing enemy, & nothing that requires greater pains to obtain.' His correspondence with the officers of the Continental Army contained frequent requests for 'the earliest Advises of every piece of Intelligence, which you shall judge of Importance'. Washington's passion for intelligence, however, sometimes made him reluctant to delegate. He wrote absent-mindedly to one of his agents: 'It runs in my head that I was to corrispond with you by a fictitious name, if so I have forgotten the name and must be reminded of it again.' Two centuries later, the head of the intelligence community, William Casey, told a Senate committee, 'I claim that my first predecessor as Director of Central Intelligence was . . . George Washington, who appointed himself.' The next 30 presidents, however, rarely showed much enthusiasm for intelligence operations. Not until the Cold War did any of Washington's successors rival his flair for intelligence.

Age of innocence

During the nineteenth and twentieth centuries relations between presidents and their intelligence communities have gone through three distinct phases. The first and longest was the *Age of Innocence*, which endured, with few interruptions, until the Second World War. Despite the experience of the Revolutionary War, the United States was the last major power to acquire a professional foreign intelligence service and a codebreaking agency. Because of its relative isolation and self-sufficiency, it had less need of foreign intelligence than the great powers of Europe. During the First World War, the United States was thus ill-equipped to compete with the intelligence agencies of the main combatants. President Woodrow Wilson seemed proud of his own ignorance. After the War, he publicly poked fun at his own prewar innocence: 'Let me testify to this my fellow citizens, I not only did not know it until we got into this war, but I did not believe it when I was told that it was true, that Germany was not the only country that maintained a secret service.' The success of British intelligence in exploiting the naïveté of Wilson during the First World War and of Franklin Roosevelt at the start of the Second laid the foundations for an unprecedented Anglo-American intelligence alliance which still remains the most special part of the Special Relationship.

During the 1914–18 War both German and British intelligence agencies found it much easier to operate in the United States than in wartorn Europe. Immediately after the outbreak of war in Europe, Germany took the offensive in a secret war within the United States. 'The German government', writes Wilson's biographer, Arthur S. Link, '. . . mounted a massive campaign on American soil of intrigue, espionage, and sabotage unprecedented in modern times by one allegedly friendly power against another.' The most spectacular exploit of the German agents was the huge explosion at the freight yard on Black Tom Island in New York harbour in July 1916, which destroyed two million pounds of explosives awaiting shipment to Russia. Almost every window in Jersey City is said to have been shattered by the blast. This and other covert operations proved a public relations disaster for the German cause.

The disaster was skilfully exploited by British intelligence. Profiting from American innocence and German bungling, it gradually succeeded in winning the confidence not merely of the fragmented American intelligence community but also of President Wilson himself. The youthful British station chief in the United States, Sir William Wiseman, became the confidant of Wilson's confidant and chief adviser, Colonel Edward House, and through House succeeded in gaining access to the president. Wiseman found Wilson 'ready to discuss everything on the frankest terms'. He was probably the only intelligence officer ever to be informed (by House) that the president of the United States found his reports 'a perfect joy'. Lord Northcliffe concluded during his official missions to the United States in 1917 that Wiseman was 'the only person, English or American, who had access at any time to the President or Colonel House'. Though Northcliffe was guilty of some exaggeration, there is no doubt that Wilson had greater confidence in Wiseman than in his own Secretary of State; he spent much of his 1918 summer vacation in Wiseman's company.

Like Wilson, Franklin Roosevelt was initially more impressed by the British intelligence services than by those of the United States. Roosevelt's experience as Wilson's Assistant Secretary of the Navy goes far to explain his later willingness as president to begin intelligence collaboration with Britain even before Pearl Harbor. During a visit to London in 1918, FDR had listened spellbound as Rear-Admiral Sir Reginald 'Blinker' Hall, Director of Naval Intelligence and the most powerful of Britain's First World War intelligence chiefs, explained how British spies crossed the German-Danish border each night, went by boat to the North Sea island of Sylt and thence by flying boat to Harwich. When Hall's Second World War successor, Rear-Admiral John Godfrey, visited Washington in the summer of 1941, he was amazed to be regaled by FDR's recollections of these and other amazing operations of Britain's 'wonderful intelligence service' in 1914–18. Godfrey thought it prudent not to tell the president that the exploits which had so impressed him a quarter of a century earlier were in fact wholly fictitious. Hall had invented them to conceal from the young Assistant Secretary of the Navy that his best intelligence came from the Admiralty's codebreakers rather than from spies. Had Roosevelt realised how much signals intelligence (Sigint) the Admiralty produced, he might well have deduced – correctly – that Britain was tapping the American transatlantic cable, which for part of the winter of 1916–17 also carried German diplomatic traffic. And had he deduced that, he might have suspected – also correctly – that the British had broken American as well as German codes. The celebrated revelation of the Zimmermann telegram, which smoothed the United States' entry into the First World War in April 1917 by disclosing an absurd German plot to lure Mexico into the war, was at one level a successful British deception. To conceal the fact that the German telegram had been intercepted on an American cable, Hall pretended that he had first obtained it by espionage in Mexico City.

At the beginning of the Second World War, British intelligence once again took advantage of Roosevelt's naïveté. In October 1940 FDR approved Sigint collaboration with the British, unaware that the British were simultaneously breaking American ciphers. Sir William Stephenson, the wartime station chief of the British Secret Intelligence Service(SIS) and head of British Security Coordination (BSC) in New York, set out to emulate the earlier triumphs of Wiseman and Hall. Convinced that brilliantly stage-managed revelation of German intrigues in Mexico early in 1917 had played a critical role in bringing the United States into the First World War, Stephenson planned to use similar intelligence on Nazi conspiracies in Latin America to persuade Roosevelt to enter the Second. Since, however, there were no real Nazi conspiracies of sufficient importance, Stephenson decided to invent them. Among the BSC forgeries with which he deceived Roosevelt was a forged map which, he claimed, had been obtained by British agents from a German diplomatic courier in Argentina. Roosevelt made this shocking document the centrepiece of his 'Navy and Total Defense Day Address' on 27 October 1941:

> . . . I have in my possession a secret map, made in Germany by Hitler's government – by planners of the New World Order . . . The geographical experts of Berlin have ruth-lessly obliterated all the existing boundary lines; they have divided South America into five vassal states, bringing the whole continent under their domination. . . . This map, my friends, makes clear the Nazi design not only against South America but against the United States as well.

Roosevelt's most outspoken attack on Nazi Germany before Hitler's declaration of war on the United States thus relied on bogus intelligence foisted on him by Sir William Stephenson.

By far the best genuine intelligence available to Roosevelt before Pearl Harbor was 'Magic' (decrypted Japanese diplomatic traffic). FDR, however, failed to grasp its import-ance. Though he took a personal, if ill-informed, interest in spies and secret agents, and personally appointed Colonel William J. 'Wild Bill' Donovan to the new post of Coordinator of Information in July 1941 (and, a year later, as head of the Office of Strategic Services, OSS), he tolerated an astonishing level of confusion in the production of Sigint. To resolve interservice rivalry after the breaking of the Japanese 'Purple' cipher in September 1940, Roosevelt approved an absurd arrangement by which Japanese intercepts on odd dates were decrypted by military cryptanalysts and on even dates by their naval rivals. Early in 1941 he sanctioned another eccentric interservice compromise which gave his naval aide the right to supply him with 'Magic' during odd months and accorded the same privilege to his military aide in even months. But there was no provision for supplying the President with Sigint either on Sundays or on weekday evenings. It is impossible to imagine Churchill tolerating such a system for a single day. The compromise began to break down in the summer after the president's military aide, General Edwin 'Pa' Watson absentmindedly filed a 'Magic' folder in his wastepaper basket. The bizarre odd/even date cryptanalytic compromise continued to cause confusion until Pearl Harbor. In the early hours of Saturday 6 December 1941, a naval listening station near Seattle picked up the first 13 parts of the now celebrated 'fourteen-part message' containing the Japanese rejection of the final American terms for settling the crisis. The intercepts were forwarded by teleprinter to the Navy Office in Washington. As 6 December was an even date, the Navy, to its dismay, had to pass the intercepts on to the Army. Since the civilian staff of the Military Signal Intelligence Service stopped work for the weekend at midday on Saturdays, the Army, to its even greater chagrin, had to enlist naval assistance on an Army Day while it tried desperately to salvage military honour by arranging a civilian night shift until the next Navy day began at midnight. While the bureaucratic black comedy continued in Washington, the Japanese fleet crept up, unnoticed, on Hawaii.

After Pearl Harbor FDR mostly left the management of wartime intelligence to his commanders and chief advisers. With little interference from the president (unlike Churchill), the American and British high commands made better use of intelligence than ever before in the history of warfare. Roosevelt's lack of understanding of intelligence meant, however, that the American intelligence community never approached the level of coordination achieved by its British ally. Even after the reforms which followed Pearl Harbor, for example, the American military and naval Sigint agencies collaborated more successfully with the British than they did with each other. The gifted intelligence analysts of OSS were hamstrung by being denied access to Sigint.

Age of transformation

American entry into the Second World War none the less began a second phase in the relationship between the presidency and the intelligence community: the *Age of Transformation*, which saw the emergence of the United States as an intelligence superpower during the 1940s and 1950s. The president who did most to shape today's US intelligence community was, ironically, the postwar president who understood least about intelligence. During his three months as Roosevelt's last vice-president, Harry Truman had been kept in ignorance of intelligence as of many other affairs of state. On becoming president in April 1945, he was initially hostile to the idea of peacetime espionage. But both his briefings on 'Ultra' (of which he had previously known nothing) and his own experience of 'Magic' during the final stages of the war against Japan persuaded him of the importance of Sigint. Truman's biographers fail to mention that a week before he closed down OSS in September 1945, he signed a secret order authorising the Secretaries of War and the Navy 'to continue collaboration in the field of communications intelligence between the United States Army and Navy and the British, and to extend, modify or discontinue this collaboration, as determined to be in the best interests of the United States'. That collaboration was to lead in June 1948 to the signing of the UKUSA Sigint agreement by Britain, the United States, Canada, Australia and New Zealand. Though it ranks as the first global peacetime intelligence alliance, the UKUSA agreement is still as conspicuously absent from most histories of the Cold War as ULTRA was from histories of the Second World War published before the mid-1970s.[2]

The almost total absence of Sigint from histories of the Cold War reflects, first and foremost the lack of source material. Not a single decrypt produced by the National Security Agency, the largest and most expensive intelligence agency in the history of Western civilisation, has yet been declassified. More than 40 years after the Korean War, we know far less about American Sigint during that conflict (though its role, according to a CIA assessment, was 'critical') than we knew about 'Ultra' 30 years after the Second World War. When NSA files for the Cold War period finally become available some time during the twenty-first century, they are certain to generate thousands of doctoral dissertations and some interesting reassessments of American foreign policy. These reassessments will no doubt include George Bush's policy during the abortive Russian coup of August 1991. NSA had remarkable success in monitoring the communications of two of the coup leaders, KGB chief Vladimir Kryuchkov and Marshal Dmitri Yazov, with regional military commands. Small wonder that Bush described Sigint as 'a prime factor' in the making of his foreign policy.

The sources for presidents' involvement with Humint are vastly more numerous than for Sigint. The gaps in the available archives are nonetheless considerable. Hardly any of the President's Daily Briefs, for example, have yet been declassified. Despite the problems of sources, however, it is clear that Truman took longer to come to terms with Humint than with Sigint. Early in 1946 he approved the creation of the Central Intelligence Group (CIG), a small analytical agency intended to collate and process intelligence collected by the rest of the intelligence community. Truman celebrated the occasion with a notably eccentric White House lunch. The President solemnly presented his guests with black cloaks, black hats and wooden daggers, then called forward his chief of staff, Fleet Admiral William D. Leahy, and stuck a large black moustache on his upper lip. As this comic ritual indicates, Truman still did not take the idea of American peacetime espionage entirely seriously. What he hoped for from the CIG was help in coping with the daily deluge of sometimes contradictory cables, despatches and reports on the complex problems of the outside world. He told the first DCI (Director of the CIA) Rear Admiral Sidney W. Souers, whom he dubbed 'Director of Centralized Snooping', that what he needed was a 'digest every day, a summary of the despatches flowing from the various departments, either from State to our ambassadors or from the Navy and War departments to their forces abroad, wherever such messages might have some influence on our foreign policy'. Thus was born what later became the President's Daily Brief. According to one of its early assistant editors, R. Jack Smith (later CIA Deputy Director for Intelligence), 'It seemed almost that the only CIG activity President Truman deemed important was the daily summary.'

By the summer of 1946, according to his special counsel, Clark Clifford, Truman 'felt he had given the CIG concept a fair test and that it had failed'. He accepted, in principle, the case for the creation of the Central Intelligence Agency, but insisted that it be postponed until after the establishment of a single Department of Defense, which he regarded as a greater priority. 'I never had any thought when I set up the CIA', claimed Truman in retirement, 'that it would be injected into peacetime cloak and dagger operations.' It is hard to imagine Truman authorising the 1961 landing in the Bay of Pigs or the other operations to dispose of Fidel Castro approved by his successors. But it is equally difficult to take at face value his later attempts to disclaim all responsibility for covert action. In 1964 Allen Dulles (DCI from 1953 to 1961) privately reminded Truman of his own 'very important part' in the origins of covert action. Dulles wrote to the Agency General Counsel, Lawrence Houston:

> I . . . reviewed with Mr Truman the part he had had in supplementing the overt Truman Doctrine affecting Greece and Turkey with the procedures largely imple-
> mented by CIA to meet the creeping subversion of communism, which could not be
> met by open intervention, [or] military aid, under the Truman plan. I reviewed the
> various covert steps which had been taken under his authority in suppressing the Huk
> rebellion in the Philippines, of the problems we had faced during the Italian elections in
> 1948, and outlined in some detail the various points raised in the memorandum

furnished me [on other covert operations] . . . At no time did Mr Truman express other than complete agreement with the viewpoint I expressed . . .

Contrary to the maxim prominently displayed on Truman's desk, the buck – so far as covert action was concerned – was intended to stop well short of the Oval Office. In June 1948 Truman signed NSC (National Security Council) 10/2, formally establishing the principle of 'plausible deniability'. Covert operations, Truman ordered, were to be 'so planned and executed that any US Government responsibility for them is not evident to unauthorised persons and that if uncovered the US Government can plausibly disclaim any responsibility for them.' So far from being, as he later claimed, entirely opposed to 'peacetime cloak and dagger operations', Truman was the first president to found a peacetime covert action agency, and to take steps to distance the president from responsibility for its actions.

General Dwight D. Eisenhower was the first President since Washington already well informed about intelligence when he took the oath of office. Ike had been convinced of its importance both by the shock of Pearl Harbor and by his own experience as a wartime supreme commander. His administration was second only to Truman's in shaping the post-war intelligence community. Ike learned at first hand during the Second World War the value of Sigint. Soon after his arrival in Britain in June 1942 as commander of American military forces, he was briefed personally on Ultra by Churchill, one of its greatest enthusiasts, after dinner at Chequers, the country home of British prime ministers. At the end of the war, Eisenhower sent his 'heartfelt' congratulations to the the the staff of the British Sigint agency at Bletchley; he told Churchill's intelligence chief, Major-General Sir Stewart Menzies, that Ultra had been 'of priceless value to me': 'It has simplified my task as commander enormously. It has saved thousands of British and American lives and, in no small way, contributed to the speed with which the enemy was routed and eventually forced to surrender.' During Ike's two terms as president unprecedented peacetime resources were poured into Sigint. By 1956 NSA had almost 9,000 employees, with as many more again working under NSA direction in the service cryptologic agencies. Though Eisenhower understood little of computer science, he was determined that NSA – like Bletchley – should have the most advanced Sigint technology. In 1957 he authorised Project Lightning, the world's largest government-supported computer research programme. NSA headquarters at Fort Meade, Maryland, contained the biggest and most sophisticated computer complex in the world.

During the Second World War Eisenhower also acquired a passion for imagery intelligence (Imint) which lasted for the rest of his life. His curiosity for what could be observed from the air was so great that on Independence Day 1944, to the alarm of his staff, he asked the Ninth Air Force commander, 37 year old Major-General Elwood R. 'Pete' Qesada, to fly him over German-occupied France jammed in the rear seat of a Mustang P-51 single-engine fighter. The main gap in US intelligence when Eisenhower became president was, he believed, Imint from the Soviet Union. He made frequent references to the postwar findings of the US Strategic Bombing Surveys, which emphasised the accuracy and importance of aerial photography in both the European and Pacific theatres. The surprise caused by the Soviet test of a thermonuclear device in 1953 added urgency to Eisenhower's demand for the Imint gap to be rectified. So did the 'bomber-gap' controversy inaugurated in 1954 by the problems of estimating the numbers of Soviet 'Bison' bombers.

The Imint revolution of the 1950s, begun by the U-2 spyplane and continued by the spy satellite, owed much to Eisenhower's own enthusiasm for it. From the moment the U-2 flew its first mission over the Soviet Union on 4 July 1956, Eisenhower personally reviewed and approved every flight. The main priority of U-2 missions over the Soviet Union until they were abruptly halted in May 1960 was to seek out and monitor intercontinental ballistic millies (ICBM) production and deployment sites as well as atomic energy facilities. Besides the one launch pad at the main test centre at Tyura Tam, ICBMs were discovered at only one other site at Plesetsk. Imagery intelligence reassured Eisenhower that the United States was ahead of the Soviet Union in both weapons development and the deployment of strategic weapons. 'It is no exaggeration to say', he wrote in his memoirs, 'that . . . there was rarely a day when I failed to give earnest study to reports of our progress and to estimates of Soviet capabilities.' The U-2, he claimed, 'provided proof that the horrors of the alleged "bomber gap" and the later "missile gap" were nothing more than imaginative creations of irresponsibility.'

Soon after Kennedy's election victory in 1960, Eisenhower sat in on a series of secret meetings during which Richard Bissell, the CIA Director of Plans [operations], and Art Lundahl, Director of the National Photographic Interpretation Center (NPIC), two of the most gifted and persuasive briefers in American history, described in detail the remarkable progress made by imagery intelligence since the mid-1950s. Ike triumphantly told the president-elect, 'The enemy has no aerial photographic systems like ours!' The sudden revelation of the extraordinary intelligence on the Soviet Union provided by overhead reconnaissance made an indelible impression on Kennedy. During the election campaign, he had attacked the Eisenhower administration for allowing 'a missile gap' to develop between the United States and the Soviet Union. Imint showed that the gap did not exist. According to one of the Imint experts involved in these and later briefings, 'Eisenhower and Kennedy shared an insatiable craving for knowledge of their Soviet adversary, and photo inter-pretation became a prime source of satisfying that craving.' Lundahl's relationship with Kennedy became as close and confident as it had been with Eisenhower. He later became the only photographic analyst ever to be awarded, among his many honours, both the National Security Medal and an honorary British knighthood.

The Imint which revealed the presence of Soviet missile sites on Cuba in the autumn of 1962 justified the high hopes placed in it by Kennedy. But NPIC analysts were able to interpret the U-2 photographs so successfully only because of the detailed intelligence on missile site construction provided by Colonel Oleg Penkovsky, an Anglo-American mole in Soviet military intelligence. The early warning provided by the intelligence community gave EXCOM (the President's crisis committee) a week in which to consider its response to the most dangerous crisis of the Cold War. 'Intelligence', said the future DCI, Richard Helms, 'bought [Kennedy] the time he needed.'

To a much greater degree than is usually recognised, the Imint revolution stabilised the Cold War. Had the United States remained as ignorant about the Soviet nuclear strike force as it had been up to the mid-1950s, there would have been more and worse 'missile gap' controversies and missile crises. At the very least, the Cold War would have become dis-tinctly colder. Had the Soviet missile sites in Cuba been discovered, as Soviet leader Nikita Khrushchev had intended, only when they became operational, a peaceful resolution of the crisis would have been much more difficult.

Age of uncertainty

In less than a quarter of a century, thanks to the Second World War and the Cold War, the United States had become an intelligence superpower. Roosevelt, Truman, Eisenhower and

Kennedy were all, in different ways, personally involved in that transformation. The *Age of Transformation*, however, was succeeded by an *Age of Uncertainty* which still continues. Since Kennedy's assassination in 1963 presidents have tended, more often than not, to take for granted their daily diet of all-source global intelligence. Indeed, they have frequently seemed disappointed by it. All remember international crises which took them by surprise, and most are inclined to treat the surprises as intelligence failures. 'What the hell do those clowns do out there in Langley?', President Nixon demanded after the unexpected overthrow of the Cambodian leader, Prince Sihanouk, in 1970. Eight years later, Jimmy Carter asked much the same question, more politely phrased, when he was suddenly informed that the Shah was in danger of losing his throne.

The intelligence community has had its fair share of failures. Presidents' recurrent disappointment with the intelligence they have received since the Cuban Missile Crisis, however, has also derived from the exaggerated expectations created by the emergence of the United States as an intelligence superpower. The more sophisticated intelligence has become, the higher presidential expectations have risen. According to Robert Gates (DCI, 1991–3): '. . . Presidents expect that, for what they spend on intelligence, the product should be able to predict coups, upheavals, riots, intentions, military moves, and the like with accuracy.' Though good intelligence diminishes surprise, however, even the best cannot always prevent it. Some intelligence analysts during the Cold War, argues Gates, showed 'a confidence in their judgments they [could] not reasonably justify'. Anxious to impress each incoming president with the sophistication of its product, the intelligence community was understandably reluctant to emphasise its own limitations. It was thus partly responsible for raising unrealistic expectations in the White House.

As former presidents and their advisers look back on the Cold War, they tend to forget the truth of Eisenhower's dictum that intelligence on what the Soviets *did not* have' was often as important as information on what they did. If subsequent presidents had possessed as little intelligence on the Soviet Union as Truman, the conclusion of the Strategic Arms Limitation Treaty 1 agreements with the Soviet Union in 1972 would have been impossible. The secret 'national technical means' developed by the intelligence community made it possible first to limit, and then to control, the nuclear arms race.

The key to the major successes and failures of American intelligence lie as much in the Oval Office as at Langley. Among postwar presidents, only three – Eisenhower, Kennedy (briefly) and Bush – have shown a flair for intelligence. Kennedy's assassination was a disaster for the CIA. His immediate successors, Lyndon Johnson and Richard Nixon, rank among the ablest of all American presidents in the spheres of, respectively, domestic and foreign policy. Neither, however, was emotionally equipped to manage the intelligence community. Johnson absurdly suspected the Agency of having plotted to make sure he lost the Democratic nomination to Kennedy in 1960. John McCone, a remarkably able DCI, eventually resigned because of his inability to gain the president's ear. Johnson replaced him with his devoted Texan supporter, retired Vice Admiral William F. 'Red' Raborn Jr., the least successful of all DCIs. Not till the Tet offensive of early 1968 did Johnson prove temperamentally capable of coming to terms with gloomy CIA estimates on the Vietnam War. Richard Helms, Raborn's deputy (and, later, his successor), recalled LBJ complaining at a private dinner in the White House family quarters:

> Let me tell you about these intelligence guys. When I was growing up in Texas, we had a cow named Bessie. I'd go out early and milk her. I'd get her in the stanchion, seat myself and squeeze out a pail of fresh milk. One day I'd worked hard and gotten a full pail of

milk, but I wasn't paying attention, and old Bessie swung her shit-smeared tail through that bucket of milk. Now, you know, that's what these intelligence guys do. You work hard and get a good program or policy going, and they swing a shit-smeared tail through it.[3]

There was no danger that Raborn, like McCone, would be tempted to play the role of Bessie.

Despite Richard Nixon's flair for international relations, his election as President was another blow for the CIA. At Nixon's first meeting after his election victory with his future National Security Adviser, Henry Kissinger, he denounced the CIA as a group of – 'Ivy League liberals' who 'had always opposed him politically'. Besides his generalised suspicions of Langley 'liberals', Nixon clung – like Johnson – to the absurd conspiracy theory that the Agency had conspired to lose him the 1960 election to Kennedy. He was convinced that the CIA had secretly given information intended to undermine the Republican programme to Senator Stuart Symington, whom Kennedy had made head of a special committee on the Defense Establishment during the election campaign. According to Richard Helms, 'He believed Allen Dulles had fed Stuart Symington with information on the missile gap – why I never understood, but I want to tell you it lingered.' Nixon, wrote the CIA deputy leader, Jack Smith, 'never forgot or forgave' the CIA for his defeat by Kennedy.

Though presidents often underestimated the value of the intelligence they received during the Cold War, they frequently overestimated the secret power which covert action put at their command. Even Truman, after at first opposing covert action, approved a series of secret operations in the Soviet Bloc which were doomed to failure. Eisenhower's misjudgments in the field of covert action were on a much larger scale. Though the Second World War taught Ike the value of Sigint and Imint, it left him with a distorted understanding of Humint. He saw the role of human intelligence agencies less in terms of intelligence collection than as a means of continuing in peacetime the wartime covert operations carried out behind enemy lines by OSS, the British Special Operations Executve, partisans and resistance movements. Covert action was a central part of Eisenhower's Cold War strategy. He changed the motto on the massive rosewood desk in the Oval Office from Truman's 'The Buck Stops Here' to *Suaviter in modo, fortiter in re* (Gently in manner, strong in deed'). Eisenhower was a master of what Fred Greenstein has called 'hidden-hand leadership'. Behind the ready smile and the relaxed manner lay iron resolution. He left the public role of the uncompromising Cold War warrior to the Secretary of State, John Foster Dulles, while he himself tried to radiate goodwill as well as firmness. It was Eisenhower, not Dulles, however, who made foreign policy. Covert action was an essential part of that policy, offering an apparently effective alternative to the unacceptable risks and costs of open military intervention. He believed there was no other way of fighting the Cold War effectively against a ruthless enemy. 'I have come to the conclusion', he wrote privately, 'that some of our traditional ideas of international sportsmanship are scarcely applicable in the morass in which the world now founders.'

Eisenhower's DCI, Allen Dulles, said later that 1953 and 1954 were his best years in the CIA. As one Agency official put it, he had 'the American flag flying at his back and the President behind him.' The apparent ease with which Prime Minister Mossadeq was overthrown in Iran and Arbenz was forced from power in Guatemala reinforced Eisenhower's exaggerated expectations of what covert action could achieve. Truman's last DCI, Walter Bedell Smith (Ike's former wartime chief of staff), privately predicted on handing over to Allen Dulles that covert action in the Eisenhower presidency would get out of hand. 'In short', according to a CIA in-house history, 'Bedell Smith anticipated a fiasco like the Bay of Pigs, although that did not happen until eight years later.' In December 1959, J.C. King, head of the CIA's Western Hemisphere Division, recommended to Allen Dulles that 'thorough consideration be given to the elimination of Fidel Castro'. The DCI showed no immediate enthusiasm for killing Castro. The President, however, demanded 'drastic' action. Eisenhower loyalists have found it difficult to accept that the President could have authorised the farcically unsuccessful plots to assassinate Castro subsequently devised by the CIA. It is, however, barely conceivable that the decision to kill Castro was made without the President's knowledge and against his wishes. Nor was Castro the only foreign leader Ike was prepared to have assassinated. Just as Eisenhower had regarded the initial proposals of the 5412 [Covert Action] Committee for dealing with Castro as too feeble, so he expressed 'extremely strong feelings' on the inadequacy of its initial plans for covert action against the pro-Soviet Prime Minister of the former Belgian Congo, Patrice Lumumba. Thus admonished by the president, the Committee 'finally agreed that planning for the Congo would not necessarily rule out "consideration" of any particular kind of activity which might contribute to getting rid of Lumumba.'

Kennedy inherited from Eisenhower a disastrously exaggerated notion of the proper limits of covert action. It seems likely that the impression made on Kennedy soon after his election victory by Bissell's dramatic exposition of the wonders of Imint may have helped to blind him to the limitations of the covert operations being run by Bissell's directorate in Cuba. A new administration with the fresh and critical minds assembled in the Kennedy Camelot might have been expected to see through the wishful thinking behind the Cuban operation. That they did not do so was due in part to their ignorance of peacetime intelligence. But though Kennedy blamed himself after the Bay of Pigs for having been 'so stupid', the fiasco did nothing to deter him from continuing covert attempts to topple Castro. The main pressure for Operation 'Mongoose', which was intended to 'overthrow the Communist regime', came not from the CIA but from the White House. And though Kennedy's supporters, like Eisenhower's, find it difficult to accept, the strong probability is that the continued attempts to assassinate Castro had the blessing of the president.

Until the 1970s, the failures of covert action had few domestic consequences for the presidency. Remarkably, Kennedy's personal popularity actually rose in the wake of the Bay of Pigs. With the Watergate scandal, however, the national mood began to change. The most powerful government ever to fall as a result of American covert action was that of the United States itself in 1974. Secret operations had an irresistible, and ultimately fatal, attraction for the conspiratorial side of Nixon's complex personality. He became the first president to set up a White House covert action unit to operate against his political enemies. The bungling of the Watergate burglars outdid even that at the Bay of Pigs. Nixon's attempted coverup cost him the presidency. The fate of his successors in the White House during the 1970s and 1980s was also, though in different ways, powerfully affected by covert action. By pardoning Nixon, and thus appearing to condone his attempted cover-up of Watergate, Ford probably sacrificed the 1976 presidential election. The failure of the covert operation to rescue the Tehran hostages may have cost Carter the next election in 1980. Iran-Contra, which revived both the bungling and the illegality of White House covert action in the Nixon era (albeit against very different targets), reduced Reagan's administration to its lowest ebb and for a few months put his survival as president in doubt.

'Of all the Presidents I worked for [from 1968 to 1993]', says Robert Gates, 'only Bush did not have exaggerated expectations of intelligence.' Bush was the first DCI to be elected president. His experience at Langley gave him a clearer grasp than perhaps any previous president of what it was reasonable to expect from an intelligence estimate. 'Measuring intentions', he rightly emphasised, '. . . is an extraordinarily difficult task.' Bush's own electoral defeat in November 1992, forecast by almost no political pundit after his triumph in the Gulf War 18 months earlier, aptly illustrated the difficulties of political prediction. Some of the columnists who failed to foresee Bush's electoral demise nonetheless castigated the CIA for failing to predict political change in the Soviet Union with far greater accuracy than they themselves had shown in forecasting the outcome of a presidential election in the United States.

Victory in the Cold War and the disintegration of the Soviet Bloc during the Bush administration served to prolong the *Age of Uncertainty*. To a greater extent than most other modern intelligence communities, that of the United States was a product of the Cold War. In its main intelligence ally, Britain, both the major collection agencies, the Secret Intelligence Service and Government Communication Headquarters, and the main assessment system, the Joint Intelligence Committee, were already in place during the Second World War. The United States's principal postwar intelligence adversaries, the KGB and the GRU, went back, despite changes in their names, almost to the foundation of the Soviet state. By contrast, the main American agencies, CIA, National Security Agency, National Reconnasiance Office and the Defence Intelligence Agency, as well as the National Security Council, though drawing on some earlier precedents, were all founded during the Cold War. The end of the Cold War thus produced greater uncertainty in the United States about the function of foreign intelligence than in most other Western states. To paraphrase Dean Acheson's famous remark about post-imperial Britain, the US intelligence community at the beginning of the Clinton administration seemed to many observers, probably including the new president, to have lost an old enemy and not yet found a new role.

Bush's view of the post-Cold War role of the American intelligence community was probably clearer than Clinton's. 'In sum', Bush told an audience at Langley in November 1991, 'intelligence remains our basic national instrument for anticipating danger, military, political and economic.' For all the talk of peace dividends and new intelligence horizons, the main future intelligence priority remains the traditional need to monitor threats to American security. In the euphoria generated by the end of the Cold War, there was a tendency to forget that the nuclear age had not also ended. Though the prospect of an Armageddon between nuclear super-powers has – at least temporarily – receded, other dangers remain.

In the spring of 1990 both the intelligence community and the Bush administration were gravely concerned by the apparent danger of nuclear confrontation between Pakistan and India. Though almost unnoticed by the media at the time, that episode undoubtedly foreshadows some of the international crises which will preoccupy the presidents of the next century. It also illustrates the crucial role that intelligence will continue to play in alerting presidents to potential Third World conflicts involving the use of weapons of mass destruction.

In May 1990 India massed 200,000 troops, including five brigades of its main attack force, in the disputed territory of Kashmir, close to the Pakistan border. In a conventional war, it was clear that Pakistan would risk a repetition of the disastrous two-week defeat of December 1971, which had led to the loss of Bangladesh (then East Pakistan). Intelligence reports to Bush concluded that, by mid-May, Pakistan had assembled at least six, perhaps ten, nuclear weapons, and might already have deployed them on her American-built F-16 jet fighters. Nuclear planning, analysts suspected, was in the hands not of the Pakistani Prime Minister, Benazir Bhutto, but of President Ghulam Ishaq Khan, and the Army chief of staff,

General Mirza Aslam Beg. Both, the CIA believed, were capable to ordering a nuclear strike against New Delhi rather than run the risk of another humiliation at the hands of the Indian Army. India, with a larger nuclear arsenal than Pakistan, would certainly respond in kind. 'The intelligence community', recalls Robert Gates, 'was not predicting an immediate nuclear war. But they *were* predicting a series of clashes that would lead to a conventional war that they believed would then inevitably go nuclear.' The Deputy DCI, Richard J. Kerr, who coordinated the intelligence assessment in May 1990, was convinced that, 'We were right on the edge. . . . The intelligence community believed that without some intervention the two parties could miscalculate – and miscalculation could lead to a nuclear exchange.'

At the height of the crisis Bush ordered Gates to fly as his personal representative on an urgent mission first to President Khan and General Beg in Islamabad, and then to the Indian Prime Minister, Vishwanath Pratap Singh, in New Delhi. Gates took with him personal letters from Bush appealing for restraint from both sides. 'The card that I played heavily', he recalls, 'was that I was not a diplomat but an intelligence officer by training, and that the reason I was there was that the American government, watching the two sides, had become convinced that they were blundering toward a war and that they [might] not even know it.' To demonstrate the accuracy of American intelligence, Gates 'told the Pakistanis and the Indians in excruciating detail what their own forces were doing – right down to the deploy-ment of individual aircraft and units down to the company level, distances between artillery units, and numbers of tanks in various places'. President Khan told Gates that he could give the Indians a secret assurance that Pakistani training camps for Kashmiri 'freedom fighters' would be closed down. At a meeting with Indian leaders in New Delhi on 21 May, Gates gained permission for American military attachés to visit the frontier region in Kashmir and neighbouring Rajasthan. They were able to report that Indian forces were ending their exercises and that no invasion was imminent. About two weeks after Gates left New Delhi, intelligence reports revealed that the leading officials in the Indian and Pakistani foreign ministries had begun regular meetings and that the two governments had agreed to other confidence-building measures. For a brief period, however, the intelligence reaching Bush had suggested perhaps the most serious threat of nuclear conflict since the Cuban missile crisis.

Like all previous inventions in human history, chemical, biological and nuclear weapons will – sooner or later – inevitably proliferate. DCI James Woolsey told the House Select Intelligence Committee in 1993 that by the year 2000 twenty states are likely to possess intermediate-range ballistic missiles. Without a combination of traditional human spies and advanced technical intelligence, the United States will find it impossible either to monitor or to slow down the proliferation of weapons of mass destruction.

Conclusion

The fortunes of the intelligence community in the twenty-first century will continue to be heavily influenced by the personalities, as well as the policies, of the presidents they have served. In a high-tech world, the human factor remains crucially important. The character and experience of the President help to determine not merely how much interest, but also what sort of interest, he takes in intelligence. Franklin Roosevelt's temperament led him to take a much keener interest in spies and covert operations than in cryptanalysis – despite the fact that codebreakers provided by far the best intelligence available to him. Truman's personality, by contrast, made him initially far less suspicious of codebreakers than of spies. The attitudes to the intelligence community of every incoming president since Truman have been significantly, sometimes strikingly, different from those of his predecessor. Even the new president's choice of DCI – as witness, for example, Carter's nomination of former Vice Admiral Stansfield Turner and Reagan's of William J. Casey – can have a major impact on the intelligence community. The influence of the DCI varies – sometimes greatly – from one administration to the next. Bush's relations with Robert Gates were closer than those between any president and DCI since the days of Eisenhower and Allen Dulles. Clinton, by contrast, had only a distant relationship with Woolsey. Whereas Bush, himself a former DCI, was a committed supporter of the CIA, Clinton's dissatisfaction with the Agency's performance helped to prompt Woolsey's resignation in December 1994.

Many of the future threats to American security in the twenty-first century are still unpredictable at the end of the twentieth. But, as the world becomes increasingly compressed into a global village, these threats will surely become both more numerous and more varied than during the Cold War. Changing threats will doubtless prompt further changes in the American intelligence community. Bush may well have been right, however, to argue during his valedictory address to the CIA in January 1993 that, 'We need more intelligence, not less.' The presidents of the next century, like their Cold War predecessors, will continue to find an enormously expensive global intelligence system both fallible and indispensable.

Notes

1 The sources on which this article are based are discussed in detail in my book, *For the President's Eyes Only: Secret Intelligence and the American Presidency from Washington to Bush*, published by Harper Collins in New York in Feb. 1995; and in London in June 1995.
2 The few books which mention the UKUSA agreement usually give the date as 1947. Dr Louis Tordella, Deputy Director of NSA from 1958 to 1974, who was present at the signing, confirms that the date was 1948. See: Christopher Andrew, 'The Making of the Anglo-American Sigint Alliance', in Hayden B. Peake and Samuel Halpern (eds.), *In the Name of Intelligence: Essays in Honor of Walter Pforzheimer* (Washington, DC: NIBC Press, 1994).
3 I owe this quotation to Dr Robert Gates.

Reprinted with permission from C.M. Andrew, 'American Presidents and their Intelligence Communities', *Intelligence and National Security* 1/4 (1995) pp.95–113.

9   Squaring the circle

Dealing with intelligence-policy breakdowns

K.L. Gardiner

Here Keith Gardiner, a long-serving CIA analyst, offers some explanations for breakdowns between the intelligence community and the policy-maker. They turn in part upon attempts to develop typologies of how analysts and policy makers think. The result is an interesting behaviourist view of the intelligence-policy dichotomy.

While serving as Deputy Director of Central Intelligence, Robert Gates wrote that '. . . intelligence collection and assessment are black arts for most presidents and their key advisers, neither adequately understood nor adequately exploited. For intelligence officers, presidential and senior level views of the intelligence they receive and how they use it (or not) are just as unfamiliar . . .'.[1]

There are many possible reasons why this kind of intelligence-policy breakdown occurs. Among the most important are 'behavioral' explanations, particularly those that look at questions of personality and temperament. One of the problems that has to be faced when attempting to find behavioral reasons why analysts and policy-makers sometimes work at cross-purposes is the lack of real data on how individuals in each community function. We are left primarily with our own anecdotal accounts and those of a few writers whose statements seem to have the ring of truth. We simply do not have broad-based evidence of such common assertions as 'policy-makers don't like the unknown and the uncertain', even though such statements do make deductive sense and often tally with our personal observations.

Our knowledge of analysts is somewhat better, because some testing data exist, and we benefit from organized introspection. None the less, we do not have much 'scientific' evidence about how analysts' minds work that can be used to show differences from or similarities with policy-makers. Despite these uncertainties, it is impressive how uniform, or at least compatible, the beliefs are of a number of writers who come from widely varied backgrounds about how policy-makers tend to function, how they differ from analysts, and how these differences lead to tension and imperfect working relations.[2]

Some crucial distinctions

On balance, policy-makers enjoy possessing and using power. They tend to be decisive and confident. They also are fundamentally at ease with themselves, and not particularly self-critical or willing to accept criticisms. Analysts tend to distrust power and those who enjoy exercising it. They are usually more comfortable with criticism, especially in giving it. Basically, they have questioning personalities.

Whenever possible, policy-makers make hard decisions quickly. Though they often are 'too busy' to do everything they need to do, this frequently occurs because they are more comfortable being active rather than inactive (that is, more contemplative). Analysts, however, are given to extensive examination of an issue, in part because they would prefer to avoid making decisions that call for action.

Policy-makers dislike ambiguity and complexity because these qualities impede decision-making. Analysts, however, believe that the real world *is* ambiguous and uncertain, and they see their primary role as reflecting it as faithfully as possible. Over-simplification is to be avoided.

To policy-makers, the world is a highly personalized place. They seek allies to move their ideas forward and, particularly, they personalize conflict. Anything that impedes acting out their vision of how things should be amounts to a personal attack, and they do not like to be reminded of the limits of their influence. Analysts are ostensibly more objective and are rewarded for identifying problems and obstacles.

Policy-makers feel quite vulnerable. Although they like their accomplishments to be recognized, they also believe that they run the risk of ridicule, personal attack or some other negative feedback (such as losing their jobs) if they are perceived too often as wrong or as standing unsuccessfully in the way of some other policy-maker's vision of what needs to be done. Analysts have much greater latitude to be perceived as wrong or ineffective without risking their self-esteem or jobs.

A personalized process

From a behavioral viewpoint, the policy-maker tends to see himself as a person with power who arrived at and remains in his position because of personal relationships with other powerful people. His main occupation within the bureaucracy and in the outside world is to use his power to achieve personal goals. Because he has to compete with other policy-makers of roughly equal power in trying to win acceptance for his ideas, he spends much of his time negotiating, bargaining and maneuvering as he attempts to construct or become part of a winning coalition. For him, individuals opposed to his policy views have to be vanquished or co-opted.

In this setting, intelligence analysis is simply one more resource that the policy-maker can use either to help decide how to advance toward his goal or to help fend off the attacks of those who would seek to thwart him. Given the action/goal focus inherent in his institutional environment and job function, his attitude toward the intelligence he receives is going to be shaped primarily by how useful it is in describing situations, commenting on options and forecasting obstacles. Above all, however, he will be searching for information and analysis that helps him increase his influence over other individuals, especially those in his own government.

Failed solutions

Most works on intelligence and policy-making seem not to venture beyond discussions of institutional settings, job functions and general behavior. While often enlightening about the kinds of problems that can inhibit policy-makers' use of intelligence, they do not offer much in the way of solutions. The three most widely suggested remedies that these analyses seem to lead to are:

–   The analyst has to strive to be policy-relevant without sacrificing professional integrity.

– Policy-makers should provide more guidance to intelligence officials concerning what they need and more feedback on the usefulness of what they receive.
– Policy-makers have to learn to trust and listen to reputable analysts, usually through extended personal contact, even when they are delivering 'bad' news.

These 'solutions' do not provide much help. The first prescription does not deal with the central question of what constitutes 'policy relevance'. There are many cases, such as the intelligence community consensus in 1983 that US policy in Lebanon was not working, where the community believed that its work was highly relevant and well presented but where it still did not achieve cognitive acceptance. This latter term is used by former Israeli intelligence chief Major General Shlomo Gazit to mean that the analysis was assimilated and understood in the way the analyst meant for it to be understood.[3] The rub is that, despite what the intelligence community believes, the policy-maker might argue that the analysis was not relevant because it did not deal adequately with the policy he had already decided upon and was trying to implement.

Regarding the second solution, there have been efforts since the dawn of organized intelligence to persuade decision-makers to be more forth-coming with guidance and feedback. As others have noted, however, the successes in this area are always temporary. Backsliding inevitably occurs, particularly at moments of rising foreign policy conflict or when policy-makers change. As for the third remedy, there are at least two problems with saying that intelligence-policy-making problems can largely be solved by creating a bond of trust between policy-maker and analyst through personal contact. One is that in a government the size of ours no policy-maker can have a regular personal relationship with all the analysts who write on subjects of interest and concern to him. The second is that more needs to be known about what exactly blocks the development of that trust and what could stimulate it.

Cognitive structures

This line of reasoning suggests a need to move to another level of analysis, one that gets at whether good working relations are being impeded by predictable differences or dissimilarities in how analysts and policy-makers take in and use information. The differences are predictable because they derive from contrasting personality characteristics that each camp brings to the work-place. In this context 'personality' refers to what can be called the *structure* of personalities and how that affects communication between two individuals. The critical dimension seems to be the cognitive structures: how their minds tend to 'see' the world about them and, most important, how they process that information and come to conclusions about what to do with it.

I have discovered two good examples of approaches that do examine cognitive structures and that cast additional light on the intelligence-policy breakdown problem. The first is contained in a lecture delivered by Professor Richard Neustadt in 1986, in which the focus is on how the thinking of US presidents seems to differ from that of various expert policy analysts who contribute to presidential decisions.[4] Neustadt is especially interested in understanding how presidents make choices, particularly among what appear to be incompatible objectives, and how their approach to making choices differs from that of the experts who supply information and analysis relevant to these decisions. Much of what Neustadt says also appears to apply more broadly to policy-makers and to their relationships to analysts.

One of Neustadt's most interesting arguments involves the difference in the purposes for which policy-makers and analysts 'think' and the time-frames they implicitly adopt as they decide when they must make final judgements. In one sense, the policy-maker's timeframe is the here-and-now, because he is constantly thinking about or taking action. In another sense, however, he tends to leave his timeframe almost open-ended. He seldom will completely give up a goal, preferring instead to take whatever time is necessary to achieve it, even if faced with what he will interpret as temporary setbacks.

One outcome of this way of thinking is that the policy-maker can live much more comfortably and for a much longer time than the analyst with what appear to be incompatible objectives. Particularly when he cannot obtain his goal with a quick decision, the policy-maker is motivated to keep as many options open as he can for arriving at his vision and for seeing the world in a fashion that supports his belief that his goals are still attainable. Thus, the policy-maker avoids as long as possible the notion that he has to trade off one goal for another. If other people are the problem, the policy-maker will depend on the belief that he eventually will be able to bend them to his purposes. If inanimate events are the complication, the policy-maker often holds to a trust in luck or the unknowability of the future to retain his belief that his objectives are not really inherently incompatible or that one must be sacrificed to attain the other. For Neustadt, the classic case of this was the former President Reagan's refusal from 1981 to 1984 to give up cutting taxes, increasing defense spending, and seeking a balanced budget, even though experts kept telling him that these goals were absolutely incompatible.

The analyst's view of the world and how he thinks about it is much different. Rather than trying to take action, his task is to order the world mentally so that he can understand it. To support decision-making, this involves breaking apart the policy-maker's goals into ostensibly achievable parts, assigning mental priorities to what needs to be achieved and in what order, surveying the world to see what actual and potential barriers there are to achievement, and reaching judgements on an action's chances of success. This can be an enormously complicated mental task, particularly if many goals and linkages are involved. To simplify this analytical task the analyst is strongly motivated to identify incompatibilities as soon as possible and to suggest that some goals be sacrificed for others sooner rather than later.

The MBTI method

Neustadt's approach is based essentially upon an intuitive grasp of the differences between the ways policy-makers and analysts think. The Myers-Briggs Type Indicator (MBTI) is another method for defining personality differences. One of its main values is that it provides detailed categories for predicting how such differences will influence behavior. The MBTI characterizes human personality in terms of the ways individuals prefer to think and act, thereby creating a useful structure for assessing recurring patterns of behaviour and relationships. The MBTI approach helps to distinguish between clusters of personality preferences that tend to characterize analysts and policy-makers, respectively. An MBTI technique that converts personality characteristics into temperaments can be used, for example, to demonstrate that policy-makers and analysts have significantly different temperaments that may cause them to conflict.

How, then, do action-oriented, operational-minded policy-makers behave? In MBTI terms policy-makers are intensely duty-oriented, and they see their primary duty as deciding on and then implementing policy actions that move toward the achievement of fairly specific goals. They are predisposed to making incremental improvements rather than sweeping changes. Quite authority-conscious, they understand how to use bureaucratic procedures to accomplish their plans. Policy-makers also like to decide about an issue as soon as possible so that they can move on to other issues and other decisions. They are impatient with or do not understand abstract ideas about the future or about other issues that have no immediate importance. Because of their 'realistic' focus, they put highest value on 'solid facts', and they can absorb a large amount of detail on any subject that they believe at the moment is important. They dislike complications – in the form, for example, of inconvenient facts, unhelpful analysis or uncooperative people – which might force them to reconsider decisions they have already made.

In MBTI terms, the contrast with the analytic style that dominates the culture of the intelligence community is stark. The latter is dominated by visionaries who prefer to focus on the big picture, future possibilities, and the abstract patterns and principles that underlie and explain facts. Analysts are fundamentally critics, and their products often disclose flaws in current policy solutions that the policy-makers have worked so hard to achieve.[5]

There is another factor that almost certainly helps establish what appear to be a dominant 'operational' personality style in action agencies and a controlling 'analytical' personality style on the production side of intelligence agencies. The institutional norms and needs of the two kinds of organizations probably tend to bring out and reward contrasting clusters of personality and cognitive traits in their personnel. In an action agency, for example, even those policy-makers whose preferences are non-operational will tend to behave like operators, because otherwise they are not competitive. In essence, institutions attract and are defined by people who prefer to behave in certain ways because of the structure of their personality, and the power of this institutional culture tends to force everyone in it to adapt to the dominant style.

Issue evolution

There probably are times when policy-makers are more open to information and analysis, even if conveyed in a theoretically non-preferred style, than they are at other times. This type of categorization could take many forms. One recent effort focuses on the various stages through which issues often seem to evolve as they are dealt with by a policy-maker.[6]

In the first stage the issue may exist, at least as part of the portfolio of an analyst, but it does not immediately affect the duties, job performance or power position of the policy-maker. Thus, he is indifferent to the issue and largely uninterested in any analysis of it.

In the second stage, the issue – probably because of some action-forcing event – has become very relevant to the policy-maker, but he has not yet had time to decide what to do about it. At this stage, the policy-maker is likely to be most open to factual intelligence and to analysis that stimulates ideas about how to respond. He also is motivated to reach out and include in his effort to build a winning coalition anyone, including analysts, who he believes can contribute to his ability to perform effectively in his bureaucratic struggle. Because he is eager to make a decision, this stage often does not last long.

In the third stage, the policy-maker has developed a strong sense of what should be done. He has decided the issue, even if his decision has not yet been fully accepted by others. At this point, his interest in information and, especially, analysis has sharply narrowed. He wants only that which immediately informs him about the implications of his proposed course of action and the prospects for implementing it. He probably tends to resist analysis which might force him to rethink his decision.

The fourth phase involves implementing a policy designed to resolve an issue. At this juncture, the policy-maker, having committed himself to a course of action, generally is only interested in analysis that directly carries forward and supports his plan. The analyst whose product casts any doubt on the probable success of the policy becomes part of the enemy camp.

This situation is understandably painful to analysts. In a sense, the policy-maker has moved in an opposite direction to the expert who wants to support him; whatever personality differences exist have become increasingly aggravated. After the initial moment when the policy-maker discovers the importance of the issue and is open to contributions from all sources, he becomes more and more closed to the 'objective' presentations of the analyst, who is trained and predisposed to offer increasingly nuanced, detailed, and critically expressed assessments as his understanding of the policy issue grows.

Other categorizations that differentiate among various situations in which the possibility of dissonance is likely to vary between analyst and policy-maker are also possible. We might, for example, distinguish between the policy-maker (or administration) who is newly arrived in his job and who has not yet formed hard conclusions about what needs to be done from one who has come to closure on goals and strategy. Moreover, the level of ideological fervor invested in a goal may make a difference, as may the degree to which any issue 'reminds' a policy-maker of a historical precedent to which he reacts strongly.

If the personality and cognitive structures of analysts and policy-makers and their respective cultures generally are more different than similar, it is no wonder communication can be so difficult. It is not lack of goodwill or the desire to co-operate on either side that tends to undermine the utility of the intelligence-policy relationship. Rather, it is that intelligence is often presented in a style that is inherently difficult for policy-makers to digest. Moreover, policy-makers appear temperamentally incapable of giving the kind of clear, definitive signals the analyst seeks regarding the action goals the policy-maker is pursuing, his objective judgement about his situation as it unfolds, and what kind of intelligence support would be most helpful. He simply tends not to think for himself in those terms about the world and what he is trying to do, so why should he do that for the analyst?

Bridging the gap

In searching for ways to overcome these barriers, monitoring interchanges between policy-makers and analysts is probably a good place to begin. If credible ways can be found to demonstrate to both sides that significant structural differences exist in how each views the world and copes with it, the first step toward reducing those differences will have been taken.

Most of the other initiatives that might help probably have to begin with the analyst and his managers. The policy-maker has too much information, analysis and advice available from other, more compatible sources to make a major effort to reorient himself toward intelligence. Even so, the co-operation of policy-makers is essential if the barriers are to be removed.

The analytical community could do at least four things that might reduce the impact of personality differences between policy-makers and analysts. The first and second depend upon creating new or strengthened personal links with policy-makers. The third involves making intelligence analysis all but indispensable to policy-makers in their bureaucratic battles. And the fourth turns on developing new means and forms to convey analysis to policy-makers in a way that fits in with their preferred methods of perceiving and thinking.

Role of leadership

Success or failure in improving the utility of intelligence analysis will be determined largely by the types of people chosen to lead intelligence agencies. More than ever, the analyst and the policy-maker depend on intelligence chiefs to understand the different worlds they both live in and to bridge the gap between them. Perhaps more conscious attention needs to be given to selecting people at the top of the intelligence pyramid who can function comfortably in both worlds. In *Real World Intelligence*, Herb Meyer describes that kind of person:

> An intelligence chief must be able to walk comfortably on both sides of the street. To lead the outfit itself, the chief must have those qualities that mark an intelligence officer: a passion for facts, a taste for delving deeply into issues, an insatiable curiosity about what is really going on in far-off places and about arcane subjects. Yet to work effectively with the chief executive – to understand what the chief executive needs from his intelligence outfit (and) to deliver finished intelligence products in a form the executive can absorb – the intelligence chief must also have the qualities that make a successful policymaker: a taste for action, the capacity to make decisions when they need to be made, regardless of whether or not all the facts are available, the ruthlessness to accept small losses in pursuit of larger gains.[7]

There are problems associated with placing in charge of analysis those who are as comfortable with the world of power as they are with the world of thought. The first is that, while we all know individuals in the intelligence community who are or probably could be 'switch-hitters', there are not many who meet the requirement. More important, however, is the danger that, once in close touch with policy-makers and already sharing some of their proclivities for enjoying power, this kind of intelligence chief may move too far from his analytical roots. If that occurs, the gap that earlier separated analysts from policy-makers begins to move inside the intelligence community to everyone's detriment. In particular, analysts lose faith that their boss can understand and defend their interests and needs, and he loses the ability to motivate them.

Liaison links

A second change the intelligence community could make – probably the most effective one – would be to find ways to put analysts in closer contact with policy-makers. Robert Gates describes certain improvements that have been made in this regard over the last eight years. The President's Daily Brief (PDB), for example, is delivered in person by a senior analytical officer of the CIA each day to the President's top foreign policy advisers. In addition, the Director of Central Intelligence for several years now has met routinely each week with these same individuals to determine their priority intelligence needs. Gates sees this progress as fragile and highly perishable, however, and calls for something more institutionalized.[8]

In my view, what is probably required is the creation of a cadre of intelligence liaison officers who would sit in the policy agencies rather than visit them periodically from Langley. Under this concept, which is not new, these intelligence 'brokers' would act as middlemen between the analysts and the policy people. They would simultaneously interpret the policy-maker's needs, guide the analyst in the most effective ways to respond, deliver the product directly, and provide feedback from one to the other. Moreover, these officers also could be provided with the most modern communications capabilities to enable them to query analytical offices directly and to receive analytical contributions immediately.

The key task of an intelligence broker probably would be to decipher what are the real analytical needs of the policy-maker. As Sherman Kent noted in 1949: 'Intelligence cannot serve if it does not know the doers' minds; it cannot serve if it has not their confidence; it cannot serve unless it can have the kind of guidance any professional man must have from his client'.[9] Gates echoed the same sentiment 40 years later: 'Contrary to the view of those who are apprehensive over a close relationship between policymakers and intelligence, it is not close enough. More interaction, feedback, and direction as to strategies, priorities, and requirements are critical to better performance'.[10]

Perhaps one reason for this impasse is that too much emphasis has been placed on persuading policy-makers that they must do better in this area. Instead of decrying the policy-maker's incapacity to provide direction, perhaps it is time to place a surrogate for the analyst – the intelligence broker – in close enough contact with the policy-maker that the broker can try to distill appropriate feedback and guidance from what he hears and observes.

Another important task for intelligence brokers would be to persuade policy-makers that intelligence analysis is *useful* and then to find or stimulate analysis that fits the need. Most policy-makers probably would welcome analysis that helps them to develop a sound picture of the world, to list the possible ways to achieve their action goals, and to influence others to accept their visions. The last point may be the key one. Intelligence analysis will adhere, will be accepted, when policy-makers believe that they will be at a competitive disadvantage within the bureaucracy and with foreign challengers if they do not have and understand it. It may be that if just a few more policy-makers than now came to be perceived by others as better equipped to negotiate and to get their viewpoint accepted because they have intelligence aides and analytical support, it would not be long before others sought the same resources.

There are risks. Placing analysts in closer contact with policy-makers, even if indirectly through liaison officers, increases the danger that analysis will become politicized. Policy-makers will become even more intent on finding or generating assessments that prove they are right in their interagency struggles. And the temptation to 'join the team', especially for an intelligence officer who sits daily in the action agency, would be great.

Much of what will be necessary to defend objectivity when policy-making and analysis are in closer proximity will become clear only when that situation actually develops. One part of the solution probably will take the form of more education for analysts as to what constitutes professional integrity and how to maintain it. Another part might involve slowly expanding the consciousness of policy-makers about the risks to their ability to make wise decisions if they routinely try to distort what intelligence analysis has to offer. Most likely, some kinds of institutional measures also will be necessary, both to ensure that the primary loyalty of those in touch with policy-makers remains attached to their intelligence home base and to provide an independent 'court of appeal' to those analysts – or even policy-makers – who believe that crucial analysis is being corrupted. Any such moves would be a welcome sign that intelligence analysis is seriously beginning to count.

Presenting the product

The fourth element in increasing the utility of intelligence analysis might be the most wrenching for the analytical community. There probably is a need to change the style of writing and what is produced for top-level policy-makers, seeing them as a distinctly different kind of consumer. There is something on which to build. Typescripts, which are usually written for specific individuals, are often better received than most hardcover publications. Intelligence assessments and research papers are crucial for developing a knowledge base, for reaching analytical conclusions, and for communicating with other experts. But, as one analyst knowledgable of the MBTI approach has pointed out, they are written in the big-picture, dry, analytical style, about as far removed as can be imagined from the way policy operators prefer to take aboard information.

Another analyst makes a similar point. He believes that analysts strongly prefer to transmit knowledge through writing, because only writing can capture the full complexity of what they want to convey. Policy consumers, however, tend to seek what can be called 'news' rather than knowledge; they are more comfortable with a mode of communication that more closely resembles speech.[11]

I believe that many of the 'improvements' made in presentation and analytical approaches in the last few years have not helped this problem. For example, more 'Key Judgement' sections are written because we understand high-level readers have little time to digest long papers. But these sections, although concise, are often more abstract and dry than the main discussion from which they are drawn. Similarly, the move toward more sophistication in making prediction by use of such devices as alternative scenarios and indicators may be more satisfying and 'honest' intellectually, but there is a good chance they do not even marginally help the policy-maker to use intelligence analysis more effectively. Finally, the extended, hierarchical review process that most intelligence analysis undergoes before dissemination probably removes any vestige of the personal, conversational style that might appeal to a policy-maker.

If these observations are valid, the following improvements could be made:

- Circulate *no* hardcover publications to the highest-level policy-makers. Instead, recast the intelligence judgements reached in these vehicles into punchy typescripts tailored for them individually. Because much of what we write is of little use to them, we would probably make a net gain by cutting back on the quantity of analysis sent to them.
- Communicate analysis in a more aphoristic, conversational manner. If colorful, anecdotal language gets a better reception, it should be used to help convey analytical information and judgements.
- Use briefing to impart analysis, whenever possible. Human contact is what works best, and it gives analysts their best opportunity to develop trust, obtain feedback, and become sensitive to the needs of particular consumers.
- Overhaul the review process. Although today's disseminated analysis has a corporate imprint, that is of little value if it has minimal impact.

One final thought on the utility to policy-makers of national estimates: it may be useful for the intelligence community to go through the extraordinary labor involved in the national estimates process on a given issue, but it is about the least likely way that can be devised to influence the policy process. With a few exceptions, estimates are not issued until all significant negotiations and compromises have taken place among the relevant policy-makers. A more useful process can almost certainly be found if the intelligence community really believes its collective judgements should influence policy decisions.

Notes

1 Robert M. Gates, 'An Opportunity Unfulfilled: The Use and Perceptions of Intelligence at the White House' in *The Washington Quarterly*, Washington, DC, Winter 1989, p. 36.
2 These writers include Professors Richard K. Betts, Robert Jervis, and Richard E. Neustadt, former DIA official G. Murphy Donovan, former State Department official Thomas L. Hughes, and former CIA official Herbert E. Meyer.
3 Shlomo Gazit, 'Intelligence Estimates and the Decision Maker' in *Studies in Intelligence*, Central Intelligence Agency, Washington, DC, Fall 1988.
4 Richard E. Neustadt, 'Presidents, Politics and Analysis', paper presented at the University of Washington, Seattle, Washington, May 1986.
5 The MBTI material is interpreted from research by Otto Kroeger and Janet M. Thuesen, *Type Talk* (New York: Delacorte Press, 1988), and by David Keirsey and Marilyn Bates, *Please Understand Me* (Del Mar, CA: Prometheus Nemesis Books, 1978). These books provide an excellent introduction to understanding the MBTI approach.
6 This model is being developed by the CIA and Harvard participants in the John F. Kennedy School project on Intelligence and Policy.
7 Herbert E. Meyer, *Real World Intelligence* (New York: Weidenfeld & Nicolson, 1987), p. 88.
8 Gates, op. cit., p. 42.
9 Sherman Kent, *Strategic Intelligence* (Hamden, CT: Archon Books, 1965), p. 182.
10 Gates, op. cit., p. 40.
11 Robert S. Sinclair, *Thinking and Writing: Cognitive Science and the Directorate of Intelligence*, unclassified monograph published by the Center for the Study of Intelligence, Central Intelligence Agency, Washington, DC, January 1984, pp. 24–5.

Reprinted with permission from K.L. Gardiner, 'Squaring the Circle: Dealing with Intelligence-Policy Breakdowns', *Intelligence and National Security* 6/1 (1991) pp. 141–152.

INTELLIGENCE AT THE TOP: PRODUCER–CONSUMER LINKAGE

Further reading: Books and reports

Richard K. Betts and Thomas G. Mahnken, (eds.) *Paradoxes of Strategic Intelligence: Essays in Honor of Michael I. Handel* (London: Frank Cass 2003).
Richard K. Betts, *Enemies of Intelligence: Knowledge and Power in American National Security* (NY: Columbia University Press 2007).
Harold P. Ford, *CIA and the Vietnam Policy Makers* (Washington DC: Center for the Study of Intelligence 1998).
Harold P. Ford, *Estimative Intelligence: The Purposes and Problems of National Intelligence Estimates* (Lanham, MD: University Press of America 1993)
Peter Gill and Mark Pythian, *Intelligence in an Insecure World* (Cambridge: Polity 2006) chapter 6.
Michael Handel (ed.), *Leaders and Intelligence* (London: Frank Cass, 1989)
Michael Herman, *Intelligence Power in Peace and War* (Cambridge: Cambridge University Press 1996) chapter 15.
Ephraim Kam, *Surprise Attack: The Victim's Perspective* (Cambridge, MA: Harvard University Press 1988).
Sherman Kent, *Strategic Intelligence for American Foreign Policy* (Princeton: Princeton University Press 1949).
Roger Z. George and Robert D. Kline (eds.), *Intelligence and National Security Strategist: Enduring Issues and Challenges* (Washington, DC: National Defense University Press 2004), part IX, pp. 417–459.
R. Jeffreys-Jones, *Cloak and Dollar: A History of American Secret Intelligence* (New Haven CT: Yale University Press, 2nd Ed 2002).

Loch K. Johnson & James J. Wirtz, *Intelligence and National Security: The Secret World of Spies* (NY: Oxford University Press, 2nd ed 2007).

Sherman Kent, *Strategic Intelligence for American Foreign Policy* (Princeton: Princeton University Press 1949).

Walter Laqueur, *World of Secrets: The Uses and Limits of Intelligence*, (NY: Basic Books, 1985).

Ariel Levite, *Intelligence and Strategic Surprise* (NY: Columbia University Press, 1987).

Mark Lowenthal, *Intelligence: From Secrets to Policy* (Washington D.C.: CQ Press, 3rd Ed 2006), chapter 9.

Abram N. Shulsky & Gary J. Schmitt, *Silent Warfare: Understanding the World of Intelligence* (Dulles, VA: Brassey's Inc. 2002). ch 3 & 8.

Jennifer E. Sims, & Burton L. Gerber, (eds.) *Transforming U.S. Intelligence* (Washington, DC: Georgetown University Press 2005).

Bradford Westerfield, *Inside the CIA's Private World* (New Haven: Yale University Press 1995) Section VI, pp.333–66.

Roberta Wohlstetter, *Pearl Harbor: Warning and Decision* (Stanford: Stanford University Press 1962).

Further reading: Essays and articles

R.K. Betts, 'Policymakers and Intelligence Analysts: Love, Hate or Indifference?,' *Intelligence and National Security* 3/1 (1988) pp. 184–189.

R.K. Betts, 'Surprise, Scholasticism and Strategy,' *International Studies Quarterly*, 33/3 (September 1989) 329–43. [and rejoinder by Levite, *International Studies Quarterly* 33/3 (September 1989) 345–349.]

Richard K. Betts, 'Intelligence Warning: Old Problems, New Agendas', *Parameters* 28/1 (Spring 1998) pp.26–35.

S. Chan, 'The Intelligence of Stupidity: Understanding Failures in Strategic Warning' *American Political Science Review* 73/1 (1979) pp. 171–180.

Michael Handel, 'The Politics of Intelligence', *Intelligence and National Security* 2/4 (1987) pp. 5–46.

A.S. Hulnick, 'The Intelligence Producer-Policy Consumer Linkage', *Intelligence and National Security* 1/2 (1986) pp.212–33.

Robert Jervis, 'The Politics and Psychology of Intelligence and Intelligence Reform', *Forum* 4/1 (2006) pp. 1–9.

Robert Jervis, 'Intelligence and Foreign Policy', *International Security* 11/3 (1986–7) pp. 141–161.

Robert Jervis, 'Strategic Intelligence and Effective Policy' in A. Farson, D. Stafford and W. Wark (eds) *Security and Intelligence in a Changing World: new Perspectives for the 1990s* (London: Frank Cass 1991), pp.165–81.

R.V. Jones, 'Intelligence and Command' *Intelligence and National Security* 3/3 (1988) pp.288–298.

Martin Petersen, 'The Challenge of the Political Analyst', *Studies in Intelligence* 47/1 (2003) pp. 51–6.

Essay and seminar questions

- If we accept Betts's hypothesis that 'intelligence failures are inevitable', how should the leaders of states approach the problem of surprise?
- Which political leader of the last hundred years proved to be the most sophisticated user of intelligence? Does your example suggest that good performance reflects personal temperament, or else past experience in the world of intelligence?
- Why are the leaders of democratic states typically poor consumers of intelligence? Can anything be done to change this state of affairs?
- Does intelligence-gathering produce a safer and more stable world? Or does it provoke neighbours, increase risk, and encourage policy-makers in the belief that they are omniscient?

---

10 International intelligence co-operation

An inside perspective[1]

Stephen Lander

In this essay, Stephen Lander argues that the threats faced by the West are such that a step change in multilateral co-operation is necessary, at least on those issues of collective security where all are affected by the same threats. The nature of the current situation, it is suggested, requires a new UKUSA Treaty involving not just signals intelligence, nor just the traditional Five Eyes allies (USA, UK, Canada, Australia, New Zealand) but also the key European players. Notwithstanding this, the hazards of wider sharing with smaller partners are also explored in this article, which explains why the panacea of sharing everything is not necessarily productive.

International Intelligence cooperation is something of an oxymoron. Intelligence services and intelligence collection are at heart manifestations of individual state power and of national self-interest. The very language used about the work makes the point. British legislation talks about 'national security' and the UK's 'defence and foreign policies'. The role of the UK agencies is, thus, essentially to support and supplement other government activities where adversaries' secrets are involved. In terms of international relations, the role is, therefore, necessarily competitive if not aggressive. Intelligence is able, to pull out a few examples, to (a) maximise the effectiveness of your own armed forces by illuminating others' capabilities and dispositions; (b) to secure comparative political or strategic advantage internationally by disclosing others' intentions; or (c) to protect the safety and well-being first and foremost of your own citizens, if necessary at the potential expense of someone else's (e.g. action against people smuggling and the deportation of terrorists). The competitive nature of intelligence work is from time to time reflected in international political debate and in press speculation.

Harry Hinsley was involved in the negotiations with the United States which led in 1946 to the signals intelligence (sigint) treaty known as the UKUSA Agreement. Though largely unappreciated outside the two intelligence communities, that agreement has been central not only to sigint exchanges, but more generally to Anglo-Saxon transatlantic intelligence cooperation ever since. International intelligence cooperation more generally is the subject for discussion here. The sections that follow will lay out some observations on the role of intelligence in government, the nature of intelligence work, and how those features impact on international relationships. Additionally, it will take stock of that long-running UK-US relationship, reflect on the development of European cooperation and wider contacts, and then look briefly at one aspect of future needs. Two words of warning are in order. First, since there is a poverty of accurate public comment about intelligence sharing (or the alleged lack of it) it is necessary to provide some factual material about what does happen which may be familiar to those already knowledgeable about the area. Second, as a Security Service employee for 27 years my perspective is dominated by the need to address threats to UK security. That has led me to look for examples to illuminate my points from intelligence about threats, rather than from intelligence as opportunity.

The role of intelligence and government

So far as the essentially competitive nature of intelligence work is concerned, developments since the end of the Cold War have pulled in different directions. On the one hand, the collapse of the Warsaw Pact and the demise of the strategic threat to the West posed by the Soviet Union have led to greater competitiveness and divisions between the former Western allies, and thus between their intelligence services. When there was NATO on our side and the Warsaw Pact on theirs, there was clarity about friend and foe. Since then, that clarity has departed and states can now much more easily be allies on one issue and adversaries on another. Differences of European perspective on the Balkans in the 1990s or more recently on the war in Iraq make the point.

For the intelligence community in the UK, this has led to some schizophrenia about international relationships, with close collaboration possible with allies on some issues (such as terrorism and drugs), but no-go areas on others where there are foreign policy tensions. The UK has clearly not been alone in finding these relationship issues more complex than they used to be, with policy differences in particular about the Middle East complicating the intelligence exchanges in Europe and beyond.

Pulling in the opposite direction in respect of international cooperation since the end of the Cold War has, of course, been the emergence of a new strategic threat, that of terrorism, not this time from nationalist or separatist groups with an essentially one-country focus, such as, to cite two of many, the Provisional IRA (PIRA) or the Popular Front for the Liberation of Palestine (PFLP), but from al-Qaeda (AQ) and its like with their internationalist and wide-ranging aspirations. I might make the point here that a threat that operates virtually irrespective of nationality and national borders poses particular challenges for intelligence services and for international collaboration between states.

There is a third post-Cold-War phenomenon that requires reference: the emergence of what may best be described as intelligence diplomacy. Whether it is intelligence chiefs at Camp David with the prime minister and the president, or visiting India and Pakistan to carry government messages about Kashmir, or travelling to Moscow to raise concerns about proliferation of Russian weapons technologies, this has been a feature of agency life that is new. It reflects not some general invasion of diplomatic space by spies, but the recognition by governments that there are relationships and understanding in their intelligence communities which can be used diplomatically. That recognition has arisen in the UK, I suggest, because of the far greater relevance of agency work post-Cold-War to the day-to-day concerns of government and the greater familiarity of ministers and senior officials with the agencies' business which has resulted.

A comparison of the Joint Intelligence Committee (JIC) first-order requirements for intelligence (what might best be described as Her Majesty's Government's (HMG's) wish list for other people's secrets) for today and, say, 1980 would, I imagine, make the point. In 1980 those requirements presumably included something like

- the organisation and capabilities of Warsaw Pact forces;
- the staff identities, modus operandi and operations of the Soviet intelligence services;
- the same for the East European intelligence services;

- Soviet relations with Cuba and Angola;
- etc.

These are all important subjects given the strategic context, but hardly the day-to-day concern of ministers and Parliament. Now, I imagine that today's JIC first-order list probably includes something like:

- international terrorism, and the whereabouts, capabilities
- and intentions of AQ members in particular;
- heroin and cocaine smuggling, people, routes and methods;
- weapons of mass destruction (WMD) programmes and plans;
- terrorism associated with Northern Ireland;
- the Middle East peace process;
- the security situation in Iraq and Afghanistan;
- etc.

These were all subjects about which government is exercised at many levels. They matter to government on a daily basis and also importantly to the media. The two, of course, go together.

It is worth pointing out that this greater government and media familiarity with the agencies, and legislation to govern their activities have not, unfortunately, killed off all the myths. Indeed the more divorced from reality the myths the more persistent they appear to be. They range from the trivial, such as the universal media habit of describing my former agency (the Security Service) by the name (MI5) it formally gave up in 1931, via the irritating (the bizarre accusation that someone in the agencies was responsible for the 1980s murder of a UK peace campaigner named Hilda Murrell), to the serious (Peter Wright's alleged Wilson Plot, which he recanted after his book[2] was published and he had made his money). On this last I noted with some amusement the then Labour Party chairman's reported claim during the summer of 2003 in the Iraq dossier context that 'elements in the Intelligence Services' were trying to undermine the Prime Minister (the very words, of course, mirrored those that emerged in the furore around the Peter Wright story). This was, as everyone now knows, without foundation and as the government made clear in the House of Commons. The criticism of the dossier did not come from the agencies. But the allegation, if accurately reported, represented brilliant party management. What better way to secure back bench support for the Prime Minister at a difficult time than to assert a threat to him from the spooks, and in terms that would ring bells from the past?

But I digress. To sum up so far: Changes since the end of the Cold War have made the world of intelligence more competitive and complex. At the same time there has developed an increased need for collaboration between states on issues such as terrorism, drugs, people smuggling and WMD proliferation, and those global issues are just the ones on which good intelligence is vital to real understanding and effective action. But the changes I have described have not altered the underlying position that intelligence services are national instruments that are required to be, if not selfish of their national interest, then self-centred about it. Against that background, I suggest, the key test for international intelligence collaboration is not a desire for closer political relations, or sentiment, let alone inaccurate media assertions that it does not exist at all or is ineffective, but utility. Collaboration is not an end in itself. It is utility that drives collaboration.

The United States

I come now to look at the UK's different international intelligence relationships. The grand-father of them all, of course, is the relationship with the United States. The multi-volume *Official History of British Intelligence in the Second World War*, of which Harry Hinsley was the editor-in-chief, charts its origins. That magisterial work, published between 1979 and 1990, remains the only official history of secret agency activity published by any of the warring powers.

So much is on the public record. What may be less well known is Hinsley's contribution behind the scenes to two developments that have shaped significantly the UK's intelligence agencies of today. One was direct and the other indirect. They were: (a) his part in the negotiation in the 1946 UKUSA Agreement to which I have already referred; and (b) his help in securing a very reluctant Mrs Thatcher's agreement in 1985 to the publication of the last two volumes of the *Official History*, both largely about the Security Service's work (on strategic deception and on security and counter-intelligence). She had opposed publication of the earlier volumes while in opposition and remained reluctant to have anything said in public about 'my' Security Service. The prime minister's files[3] record her 1984 view that 'too much has been said and written about intelligence and less should be in future'.

That 1985 agreement (the volumes appeared in 1990) was the first chink in that formid-able Thatcher armour on the subject of agency avowal. It seems bizarre now that govern-ment persevered with the fiction for so long that government organisations did not exist which had office blocks in central London, hundreds of staff, and names that featured in the press with monotonous, and usually sensationalist, regularity. It was another great man, Tony Duff, by then recalled from retirement to be the director general (DG) of the Security Service who was able in 1987, very largely because of his own personal standing with Mrs Thatcher following his role in the war cabinet during the Falklands War, to build on that chink to secure acceptance of the need for legislation for the Security Service. That became the Security Service Act 1989. The Intelligence Services Act 1994, with its element of parliamentary oversight, naturally followed and there has been further legislation regulating agency activity since, most notably the Regulation of Investigatory Powers Act 2000.

It is difficult to overstate the impact on the agencies of this body of legislation. In my view it has been wholly beneficial (though that is not to say that scrutiny by MPs has always been entirely comfortable or that the need for additional due process has not been costly). We moved from a position that was based on the rather dubious assumption that if something was not expressly illegal then it was okay. We now had the assurance of statute law as opposed to the insecurity of the royal prerogative, under which much agency activity hith-erto notionally took place. That change played a key part in the 1990s and beyond in making the agencies more self-confident and thus more effective. I was myself party to preparation of the legislation and drafted instructions for clauses (for concessions in the House that were never used) on retention of records. It is worth noting that had the opposition pressed the point and those clauses been enacted, much of the history (at least of the Security Service's Cold War casework) would probably have disappeared. As it is, with guidance from the Lord Chancellor's Advisory Council on Public Records, a policy for the Service's long-term retention of records has been agreed with a view to deposit at the National Archive. Deposit, moreover, that is now well underway.

To return to the US relationship, the *Official History* shows that it is now more than sixty years old. Its origins were in exchanges of naval intelligence which went back to the late 1930s, but they deepened and extended after American entry into the war, and again at the end of the war as the Soviet threat and the treachery of the atom spies[4] became apparent. The immediate post-war period saw the creation of agency architecture on both sides of the Atlantic which has remained to this day: in the US, the CIA and National Security Agency (NSA) were set up and the FBI's intelligence divisions were strengthened, while in Britain the Government Code and Cypher School at Bletchley was turned into a new civil service organisation, the Government Communications Headquarters (GCHQ), with headquarters initially in London.

In those early years the relationship was a more equal one than it has since become. The UK agencies had had a good war, retained worldwide knowledge and capabilities and in the Security Service and Secret Intelligence Service (SIS) had a length of experience and records and international connections unmatched across the Atlantic. But the UK side was not in good shape. Some of their best talent, like Harry Hinsley himself, returned to academic life or left for other careers at the end of the war, and the UK economy was unable to sustain the agencies (as much else) on a wartime footing despite the emerging Soviet threat. Moreover, the UK agencies were to face, not only the shock of the discovery of the atom spies (which, of course, affected both sides of the Atlantic), but also the emerging evidence of Soviet penetration of the UK intelligence community itself. Sorting out the consequences of those two blows was to take two decades and, in my view[5], to leave the UK community with a defensiveness, introspection and damagingly strict need-to-know culture that it only finally shook off during the 1980s and 1990s under the pressures of responding to terrorism and with new generations of staff.

If the UK and US communities started as equals at the end of the war, they soon ceased to be so. Indeed, so much has changed for both countries in the intervening years as to raise the question of why the special intelligence relationship has survived at all. To rehearse the obvious, for the US there has been an enormous growth in political, military and economic power, and a consequent growth in the resources and capabilities available to the US agencies, and in the expectations of them. The Director of Central Intelligence alone, I understand, now commands more resources than the UK Ministry of Defence, armed forces, aid budget, Foreign Office and intelligence agencies combined. By comparison, for the UK there has been economic and geographical retrenchment: the end of empire, the withdrawal from east of Suez, the departure from Hong Kong, the shrinking of the armed forces, membership of the EU with its domestic European horizons etc., and for much of the period an economic growth rate slower than that of most developed countries. For the UK agencies themselves there was for a time some financial safety in invisibility with Treasury cost cutting really only biting at the end of the Cold War (and interestingly just, it now transpires, when government was wanting more not less intelligence). However, there were years when the UK government spent more on subsidising Concorde than on the secret vote, and the end of empire meant withdrawal from overseas intelligence and security commitments and relationships. Those had remained a significant part of the Security Service's work, for example, until well into the 1960s.

Whatever the relationship now is, it is, therefore, most certainly not one of equals. Looking today at the transatlantic relationship following the wars in Afghanistan and Iraq and the continuing close relationship between Prime Minister and President, it is easy to forget that there have been periods of antagonism and difficulty. These have not always been as visible as Suez, but there were, for example, sharp disagreements over the Balkans in the 1990s, and a history of differences of perspective over Israel/Palestine going back many years, not to mention cashmere sweaters and bananas or genetically modified food. Closer to the intelligence home there was the famous row (about access to UK information about its spy investigations) with J. Edgar Hoover's FBI and, more recently, there have been difference of assessment over a range of important issues.

To all appearances, however, the special intelligence relationship is in as good shape today as at any time in the last sixty years. There are, I suggest, some obvious and some rather less obvious reasons for this. To start with the obvious. First, the intelligence relationship is part of a wider political relationship and depends in good measure on that wider context. The US and UK governments share many preconceptions about international issues and naturally pull together in international fora such as NATO and the UN. The special relationship thus continues to be special first and foremost in the political arena and that drives behaviours elsewhere. It drives it most importantly in the military context. Military operations of the kind the US and UK have shared over the last decade plus (Iraq twice, Kosovo and Afghanistan, to mention the main ones) are great generators of requirements for intelligence that can be shared about what is going on before, during (when good sigint remains as vital today as it was in the Second World War) and after the conflict. In a very real sense, therefore, recent UK/US military deployments have strengthened the intelligence relationship.

Second, the relationship also pretty obviously prospers because of long-standing institutional arrangements and the habits that flow from them. Thus, to pick out two examples at random, both sides are used to the sharing of analytical judgements in both capitals. Even more importantly for the sigint agencies (NSA and GCHQ), the institutional integration that has flowed from the 1946 UKUSA Agreement is so widespread that sigint customers in both capitals seldom know which country generated either the access or the product itself. Why should these happy habits change when they seem so familiar and there do not seem to be any obvious downsides?

Turning now to what are perhaps some of the less obvious reasons why the special intelligence relationship continues to prosper, one might mention, first, the issue of competence. The US agencies are seen as such valuable partners to their UK counterparts because of their scale, reach, resources and capabilities, but in some respects the reverse also remains true. This is first and foremost because the UK agencies, unlike any other potential intelligence ally, retain worldwide and subject-wide capabilities. That is partly because the UK still has worldwide Dependent Territories providing sigint and other intelligence collection opportunities (what I heard one US intelligence chief define as 'islands with aerials' and he included the UK in the list), but it goes beyond that and involves, for example, languages, expertise on Africa and parts of Asia (including critically in recent years on Afghanistan) as well as the Middle East, and, nearer home, unrivalled experience of dealing (in Northern Ireland) with a major and long-running terrorist threat.

Second, there is the place of intelligence in government. At heart the place of the US and UK intelligence communities in government is the same. The differences between the US and UK constitutional arrangements are many and well known, but behind them in both countries intelligence is routinely and regularly used across government. It is seen as a collective asset, not as in many countries the property of an individual minister or an individual department, or, as in some, occupying a space almost divorced from government entirely. Assessment is more decentralised in the US than the UK (where the JIC provides one view for ministers), it is true, but decision-makers on both sides of the Atlantic expect to use intelligence routinely. Since so much intelligence is shared, the UK Weekly Survey of Intelligence and the Presidential Intelligence Brief probably look very similar most weeks and that tends to reinforce the closeness of the world view of the two governments. And that in turn, of course, reinforces the intelligence relationship.

Third comes a list of softer issues about personalities, shared experiences, friends in adversity, etc. which may not carry political or public weight but matter in institutional relationships, particularly those which have an operational element. Thus it matters that in George Tenet as the Director of Central Intelligence, the CIA had, in my view, its most internationalist chief for a generation, that it was UK intelligence chiefs who flew to Washington on 12 September 2001 to offer support to a shell-shocked US intelligence community, and that there is a long institutional history of joint operational activity against the Soviet services in particular, but more recently on the ground in Afghanistan and Iraq. Those joint activities generate friendships, trust with sensitive material, mutual respect and confidence, as well as understanding about constraints and difficulties. They matter.

But the main reason why the intelligence relationship remains in such good shape is, of course, because both sides perceive that it is needed. In short, my utility point applies. Both sides need help in a dangerous world. Despite US military, political and economic power, it remains vulnerable to terrorism, the proliferation of weapons of mass destruction and drugs, especially cocaine. The UK agencies are able to add significant value on those and other subjects, and remain, in consequence, most trusted and valued allies. For the UK's part, US assets and capabilities give HMG a breadth and depth of intelligence coverage worldwide that its own resources could never command.

Europe

I turn now to relationships in Europe. In one sphere, that of military intelligence, these are also of long standing, since they go back to the early days of NATO in the 1950s. But routine exchanges of intelligence on a bilateral basis did not really get going until the 1960s, and then only with a selection of partners, such as the Scandinavian services. This was because the KGB First Chief Directorate handled the UK and Scandinavia with the same people in its Third Department and thus there were in consequence benefits to the UK and Scandinavian colleagues in working together on the KGB target. But it was not really until the terrorism of the 1970s and 1980s that some relationships in Europe moved onto the kind of easy operational footing that had so long been familiar with the US agencies.

For the Security Service, the main, though not the only, driver for this increased and deepened collaboration was the struggle with PIRA. Not only did PIRA seek to mount attacks on British targets in Europe in three periods in the 1970s and 1980s, but it also saw Europe as one route by which to secure the arms and munitions it needed to sustain its struggle against the UK. A look at the map will tell you which countries were important to the UK in responding to these efforts: France, the Netherlands, Belgium and, because of the presence of UK troops who became a PIRA target, Germany.

When the history of the Troubles[6] comes to be written, I imagine that the French seizure of the ship the *Eksund* in 1987 with its enormous supply of Libyan weapons destined for PIRA, and the failure of PIRA's 1987–91 campaign of terrorism against British targets in continental Europe (with more terrorists arrested than British subjects killed) will be seen as one of the turning points. The PIRA had aspired to 'drive the Brits out of Ireland' with its Libyan-supplied weaponry. It failed to achieve that aim first in Europe, second in Northern Ireland and finally in England in the period up to its second ceasefire in 1997. There were other drivers towards peace, of course, notably the political aspirations of Sinn Fein politicians, which were adeptly handled by successive British (and other) governments. What is not well known is the part played by European services in that success. Throughout the period

1987–91, a number of those services played a very full part in intelligence work on PIRA. In a real sense, therefore, the UK's defences did not begin at Dover, but across the continent of Europe.

A similar phenomenon was apparent more recently in relation to North African and in particular Algerian terrorism, but in this case with France being the principal protagonist. France, you will recall, was from the mid 1990s the target of Algerian terrorists because of its support for the military-backed regime in Algeria. It looked for support and assistance from its neighbours. If all, including the UK, were somewhat slow to get going against this new target, much has been achieved since, with Italy, Spain and the Benelux countries as well as the UK and France achieving considerable intelligence-based success against this new terrorist phenomenon.

There was another development during the period of perhaps greater long-term signifi cance; the development of multilateral European intelligence structures and collaboration. Multilateral European exchanges of intelligence started in the 1960s when the Club of Berne, involving security services from nine West European countries including the UK, was set up. That Club now has 17 members and is growing as the EU expands. Its member services are involved variously in EU policy- and decision making fora. It remains, however, a manifestation of inter-governmental cooperation, not of the European Union. Heads of service meet twice a year and working groups cover various aspects of security business. Most years exercises test surveillance handover arrangements across borders and young agency staff attend training courses managed country by country on a rotating basis. Intelligence is routinely shared through a secure network managed by the UK.

The value of these institutional arrangements lies, not critically in the information exchanged at meetings, though that has been valuable on some practical issues, but in the mutual confidence and understanding and the personal friendships that they bring. Without that institutional history much of the cross-border operational collaboration in Europe of the last twenty years would have been inconceivable, given the differences of approach, powers and competence of the various services. Language, once a barrier, is one no longer with English, and sometimes French, the operational languages of choice.

The rest of the World

I should say something briefly about the UK's intelligence relationships elsewhere. These are many and varied. The Security Service alone has contacts with intelligence agencies in over a hundred countries and SIS even more than that. But taking them all together, they divide broadly into three rather different categories.

First, the old Commonwealth (Australia, Canada and New Zealand), with whom relationships remain close although for reasons of geography the exchanges have limits. All three, however, contribute to the shared sigint pool, and each has valued expertise on which the UK has from time to time relied.

Second, services and countries that are playing an important part in the war on terrorism in general and on AQ in particular, such as Jordan, Egypt, Singapore, India and some of the Gulf states (and Pakistan and Saudi Arabia, which are effectively the frontline states of the struggle).

Third, those who are able and willing to provide the UK with access to intelligence or raw reporting relevant to JIC requirements. There are a large number of countries involved. The arrangements are often reciprocal.

Taken together, these relationships add to UK knowledge and understanding in areas, like the Pacific, where its own reach is limited and contribute to the shared international understanding of global threats such as terrorism and drugs.

The future

You may remember a BBC news exclusive in 2003 about a British national of Indian origin arrested by the FBI who had allegedly been trying to sell surface-to-air missiles to AQ. There were lurid stories about what he was alleged to have said to undercover FBI officers about killing the US President. The commentary on the report ran something like this: 'At last the intelligence agencies of the UK, US and others including the Russians are working together properly.'

I hope I have said enough to demonstrate that cooperation is not new, i.e. that agencies have been 'working together properly' for some time. Indeed, I could argue that there has been a history of successful collaboration on a scale and with a geographical spread that the media little appreciate. In fact, not a day now goes by without each of the UK agencies contacting an international partner. The volume of exchanges is large. Contact is routine. The right question, therefore I suggest, is not whether cooperation is going on, nor whether it produces results (which it certainly does) but whether there is enough cooperation or whether it could deliver more. Is the level and intensity of cooperation sufficient for the UK's needs in a post-Cold-War world? A world in which, as I have said, there is ambiguity about friend and foe and growing threats posed by non-state actors.

'Enough' is, of course, a subjective term and no two commentators would be likely to agree on what constituted sufficiency in this context. At one extreme there is the simplistic approach adopted by much of the UK media at least and by some politicians (usually those who have not been in government) which assumes, for example, that if there is a terrorist attack or some other visible negative in international relations then there must have been an intelligence failure, i.e. in this context there had not been enough international cooperation. As an example, you could read the UK press in the weeks after the 11 September attacks as they strained to blame the British government for what had happened. (A two-hour transit at Gatwick in April 2001 by some of the terrorists, for example, became a press accusation that the attacks had been planned in London.) At the other extreme, long-running relationships can continue to be justified by their occasionally delivering intelligence that meets JIC requirements even if quite low down the food chain.

The 'intelligence failure' accusation, of course, raises questions about how you do measure success and failure in the intelligence business. This is not straightforward and it may be useful to comment on it briefly. Intelligence agencies seek to find out adversaries' secrets. Those adversaries, states or groups or individuals, go to great lengths to protect their secrets. A success rate of 100% is self-evidently unachievable against pretty well any target of any seriousness. Let me take terrorism as an example. A terrorist organisation that is unable to keep its secrets is pretty soon going to cease to operate. What then is it realistic to expect of intelligence? Contexts vary, but it has been claimed that intelligence was preventing four out of every five planned PIRA attacks in the late 1980s and early 1990s. That was a very high success rate indeed born of long experience of a cohesive target and considerable multi-agency effort, but the terrorists still got through on a number of occasions, most notably with three big bombs in London in 1992, 1993 and 1996 and, of course, in the atrocity at Omagh. When one looks at AQ the context is different. The target is much less easily identifiable, and when identified often less accessible to the intelligence-gathering techniques that proved successful against PIRA. A lower success rate in preventing AQ attacks could, in any realistic judgement, therefore still represent a good performance. In fact there has in recent years been quite a measure of success in breaking up AQ or linked groups before they were able to mount attacks, much of it out of sight of the media, and deriving largely from international exchanges of leads to individuals. But no one can feel comfortable that the risk is reducing as a result. If success is to be measured in removal of this threat altogether then there is still a very long way to go.

What about failure? Failure in the intelligence business comes, in my view, not when pre-emptive intelligence about a terrorist attack cannot always be secured, but (a) when there is insufficient intelligence to warn in general terms about a threat or about the risk of adverse political developments—it is reasonable for governments to expect early warning of problems coming so that preparations can be made—(b) where intelligence is available and it has not been assessed correctly or used effectively—that failure, of course, may lie outside the intelligence community—or (c) where the intelligence is just plain wrong. This does happen, but it is rather less common than commentators would suggest. It is far more often merely incomplete.

To return to my analysis, so far as the UK's international cooperation is concerned, how much is enough? The UK's most pressing intelligence needs today, at least on the defensive side, might be listed as (a) better understanding of WMD programmes world-wide leading to opportunities for disruption; (b) pre-emptive intelligence on terrorism threatening the UK or UK interests and allies overseas; (c) intelligence on the production, distribution, financing and sale of hard drugs; (d) intelligence about identity fraud and misuse; and (e) intelligence on migration patterns and illegal immigration facilitation (people smuggling).

Now these are, I suggest, all subjects on which it is unlikely that one country will enjoy a monopoly of intelligence and understanding. If cooperation internationally can add value in any of these areas then it has obvious utility. In fact, some of these problems are so pressing and so difficult to address that almost any help is worth having. An easy answer to the question of whether there is enough cooperation, therefore, is that there can never be enough. But some collaboration is more useful than others. Let me explain more precisely what intelligence cooperation actually involves. There are, I suggest, four distinct aspects.

First comes the sharing of intelligence-based assessments.[7] This has long been a currency in the Five Eyes community in which UK (the JIC), US, Canadian, Australian and New Zealand assessments are shared routinely. This works well and gives wider perspectives to all parties. There are some subjects on which national sensitivities preclude sharing, but the volume of exchanges remains high.

So far as the sharing of assessments (as opposed to other forms of collaboration) in Europe is concerned, it is early days and there is much room for further development. However, it is unrealistic to think that any shared appreciation here will supersede the views taken in the various capitals. Also there are dangers that come from unfulfilled expectations. Some continental European politicians are on record as seeing such exchanges of assessments as helping to interdict terrorists at home. They will be disappointed. Assessments, even intelligence-based ones, are not the vehicle for tasking enforcement or other operational activity. That requires pre-emptive intelligence, such as precise reporting about plans or intentions, sometimes backed up with operational collaboration, as happened in the work against PIRA and Algerian terrorists to which I have already referred.

Second comes the sharing of assessed but single-source reporting. This is the currency with which Whitehall is most familiar from the UK agencies. In the UK it provides the building blocks for policy-making, for assessment by the JIC and, on occasion, for the deployment of operational resources, including by law enforcement. It is a product not universally available internationally. Some services elsewhere, for example, only circulate assessments not single-source reporting to their governments.

Third comes raw product. This is seldom exchanged routinely, but is particularly valuable because it enables recipients to visit and revisit the material in the light of developing understanding of the target.

Finally comes operational collaboration. This involves agency personnel from different countries working together against a common target and may involve surveillance, joint agent handling, sharing of linguists, exchanges of technical know-how and equipment, common training, sharing of analytical staff, etc. It happens where there is a pressing shared need that goes beyond the capacity or capability of one country to address.

There are opportunities for the UK for enhanced collaboration with others in each of these four areas, but, in my view, only two really matter: good quality single-source reporting and raw product exchange. Assessments are basically a marketing tool for intelligence, and operational collaboration will always follow need and shared objectives. How then to maximise the sharing of intelligence and product for the future? I suspect that many services can in principle see the possibility that routine sharing of building-block intelligence might add up to more than the sum of the parts. Indeed I am aware that there has even been discussion of that facility much ridiculed in intelligence circles (because of its inherent improbability), the international database.

Such sharing is in my view an idea whose time has probably come. Threats from non-state actors are difficult to address because they are informal, mobile, variably organised and unpredictable (i.e. all the things that states usually are not). Intelligence agencies in the West, however large and competent, will only ever be able to collect successfully against a part of the target. Accidents of coverage will then constrain thinking. That argues for putting a number of countries' perceptions and intelligence together to understand a larger part of the picture and to generate more leads for counteraction. If that sounds like an obvious proposition, then you have probably misunderstood the difficulties and the novelty of such an arrangement. Just to mention a few of the problems:

(a)   Different countries have different collection philosophies. Some collect haystacks and store them, while others collect hay and store needles, while others again only ever collect needles and not very many of them. The risk of sharing haystacks with needle keepers is that they would not be able to use the material effectively or would be swamped.

(b)   Shared intelligence can create competition over who acts and where/when, and there is a danger of blue on blue conflicts as a result.

(c)   For countries to share reporting there has to be a presumption that in-country coordination arrangements, including with law enforcement, are effective. This is self-evidently not the case almost everywhere. The UK has probably as good a story to tell as anyone with various coordination mechanisms (the JIC, with the police, the multi-agency Joint Terrorism Assessment Centre, etc.), but it has to be worked at hard.

(d)   Legislation in Western countries often precludes the sharing of product outside national borders or to other than specified organisations (UK interception legislation, for example, operates on the basis of continued agency control of and responsibility for the product that it has obtained under warrant).

(e)   The problem of other allies. How could some EU countries, for example, be party to new arrangements and not others, but if all are in, will anyone contribute any sensitive reporting?

I could go on. In short, multilateral sharing is counter-cultural, since it cuts across what I said earlier about agencies needing to be self-centred about their own national interests, and because of the inherent unevenness of international relationships.

Nevertheless, whatever the practical difficulties, I believe that the threats faced by the West are such that a step change in multilateral cooperation is necessary, at least on those issues of collective security where all are affected by the same threats. My utility test would be met because the risks and costs of sharing your own national material would be more than outweighed by the benefits of access to others'. It argues, I suggest, for a new UKUSA Treaty involving not just sigint, nor just the Five Eyes allies, but also the key European players. The foresight of those nearly sixty years ago, including Harry Hinsley, who negoti- ated the UKUSA Agreement has served the UK well. Perhaps the time has come for a new treaty for a new century.

References

Wright, P. (1987) *Spycatcher* (London, Heinemann)

Notes

1 This essay has been adapted from a speech presented in October 2003 as the fifth annual Harry Hinsley Lecture at St John's College, University of Cambridge.
2 The allegation that Wright himself and Security Service colleagues attempted to undermine the then prime minister, Harold Wilson, is set out in his book (Wright 1987).
3 Files not yet released to the National Archive.
4 The post-war discovery that a number of those working on both sides of the Atlantic on the programmes that led to the creation of the UK and US atom bombs had passed substantial details of their work to Soviet intelligence.
5 This is a personal reflection; as the archives become available it will be open to historians to form a more considered judgement.
6 The term used to describe both the sectarian divide between Protestant and Catholic in Northern Ireland and the terrorism perpetrated by those on both sides of that divide.
7 Assessments are judgements, usually based on reporting from a variety of sources without direct attribution.

Reprinted with permission from S. Lander, 'International Intelligence Co-operation: An Inside Perspective', *Cambridge Review of International Affairs* 17/3 (2004) pp.481–93.

LIAISON: INTELLIGENCE CO-OPERATION

Further reading: Books and reports

Wolf Blitzer, *Territory of Lies, the Exclusive Story of Jonathan Jay Pollard: The American Who Spied on His Country for Israel and How He Was Betrayed* (NY: Harper & Row 1989). [a US-Israeli case]
Michael Herman, *Intelligence Power in Peace and War* (Cambridge: Cambridge University Press, 1996) chapter 12.

Jay Jakub, *Spies and Saboteurs: Anglo-American Collaboration and Rivalry in Human Intelligence Collection and Special Operations, 1940–45* (London: Macmillan 1998), pp.185–96.

Walter Lacer, *World of Secrets: The Uses and Limits of Intelligence*, (NY: Basic Books 1985).

Y. Melman, & D. Raviv. *Friends in Deed: Inside the U.S.-Israel Alliance*, (NY: Hyperion 1994) see especially chapters 4, 7, 15.

Jeffrey T. Richelson & Des Ball, *The Ties That Bind: Intelligence Co-operation Between the UKUSA Countries* (London: Unwin Hyman 1990).

Jeffrey T. Richelson, *The US Intelligence Community* (Boulder: Westview 5th ed 2007) chapter 12.

Peter Schweitzer, *Friendly Spies: How America's Allies Are Using Economic Espionage to Steal Our Secrets* (New York: Atlantic Monthly Press 1993).

Jennifer E. Sims, and Burton L. Gerber, (eds.). *Transforming U.S. Intelligence* (Washington DC: Georgetown University Press 2005).

M. Yossi and D. Raviv, *The Imperfect Spies: A History of Israeli Intelligence* [published in the US as: every spy a prince] (London: Sidgwick & Jackson 1989).

Further reading: Essays and articles

Richard J. Aldrich, 'Dangerous Liaisons: Post September 11 Intelligence Alliances', *Harvard International Review* 24/3 (2002) pp.50–54.

Richard J. Aldrich, 'Transatlantic Intelligence and Security Cooperation,' *International Affairs* 80/4 (2004) pp.731–54.

A.S. Hulnick, 'Intelligence Cooperation in the Post-Cold War Era: A New Game Plan?' *International Journal of Intelligence and Counterintelligence* 5/4 (1991–1992) pp.455–465.

Sir Stephen Lander,. 'International Intelligence Cooperation: An Inside Perspective.' *Cambridge Review of International Affairs* 17/3 (2004) pp.481–493.

Stephen Lefebvre, 'The Difficulties and Dilemmas of International Intelligence Cooperation', *International Journal of Intelligence and Counterintelligence* 16/4 (2003) pp.527–542.

Bjorn Müller-Wille, 'EU intelligence cooperation: A Critical Analysis', *Contemporary Security Policy* 23/2 (2002) pp.61–86.

Björn Müller-Wille, 'The Effect of International Terrorism on EU Intelligence Co-operation', Journal of Common Market Studies, 46/1 (2008) pp.49–73.

Derek S. Reveron, 'Old Allies, New Friends: Intelligence-Sharing in the War on Terror', *Orbis* 50/3 (2006), pp.453–68.

J.T. Richelson, 'The Calculus of Intelligence Cooperation.' *International Journal of Intelligence and Counterintelligence* 4/3 (1990) pp.307–323.

William Rosenau, 'Liaisons Dangereuses? Transatlantic Intelligence Co-operation and the Global War on Terrorism', in *Co-operating Against Terrorism: EU-US Relations Post September 11--Conference Proceedings* (Stockholm, Sweden: Swedish National Defence College, 2007) pp.31–40.

M. Rudner, 'Britain Betwixt and Between: UK SIGINT Alliance Strategy's Transatlantic and European Connections', *Intelligence and National Security* 19/4 (2004) pp.571–609.

Martin Rudner, 'Hunters and Gatherers: The Intelligence Coalition Against Islamic Terrorism,' *International Journal of Intelligence and Counterintelligence*, 17/2 (2004) pp.193–230.

Jennifer E. Sims, 'Foreign Intelligence Liaison: Devils, Deals, and Details, *International Journal of Intelligence and Counterintelligence* 19/2 (2006) pp.195/217.

A. Svendsen, 'The globalization of intelligence since 9/11: frameworks and operational parameters', *Cambridge Review of International Affairs* 21/1 (2008) pp.131–146.

J.I. Walsh, 'Intelligence-Sharing in the European Union: Institutions Are Not Enough', *Journal of Common Market Studies* 44/3 (2006) pp.625–43.

Michael Warner, Michael. 'Intelligence Transformation and Intelligence Liaison,' *SAIS Review* 24/1 (2004) pp.77–89.

Bradford Westerfield, 'America and the World of Liaison', *Intelligence and National Security* 11/3 (1996) pp.523–60.

T. Wetzling, 'European Couterterrorism Intelligence Liaison', in S. Farson et al (eds.) *PSI Handbook of Global Security and Intelligence*, Vol 2 (Westport CT: Praeger, 2008) pp.498–532.

Essay questions

- 'There are no "friendly" liaison services . . . they are not on our side, they are on their own side' (Garrett Jones, CIA) Discuss.
- Identify the main problems and benefits that are involved in close intelligence co-operation between states.
- How far do you agree with Stephen Lander's assertion that the old formal intelligence alliances – such as UKUSA – will need to be made more inclusive for the Twenty-first century?
- Why has European Union intelligence co-operation proved to be controversial and difficult?

Part 2

Intelligence, counter-terrorism and security

The problem for intelligence is as much to discover the values of a shadowy adversary as to learn locations and plans.

Martha Crenshaw[1]

SUMMARY

Intelligence and 9/11

We still have more to learn about the intelligence dimension of the 9/11 attacks. A number of classified inquiries that were conducted into the role of the various intelligence services remained closed to us. Typically in August 2007, Congress decided to release a short and redacted summary of an investigation by the Central Intelligence Agency completed in 2005 by the CIA's Inspector General, John Helgerson. His inquiry had discovered that more than fifty people saw a message that focused on two of the members of the team of hijackers who participated in the 9/11 attacks, well before the event. The reluctance to share this information more widely inside and outside the CIA was condemned as a systemic problem. In this respect, the report confirmed the findings of the 9/11 report, which had criticised the lack of sharing between the CIA and FBI. Intriguingly it also added that there was also considerable infighting between the CIA and NSA, which is responsible for US signals intelligence.[2]

The classified CIA's internal report also accused the senior leadership of the Agency of failing to take pre-emptive action against Osama bin Laden in advance of the attacks. Although Helgerson focused his criticism on the then DCI, George Tenet, the fact that Al Qaeda had been active against the United States for at least a decade before 9/11 has rendered this game of organised hindsight rather problematic. It has allowed many individuals to make partisan comments about the failure of either the George W. Bush presidency, or the previous Clinton administration, to unleash a covert war against Al Qaeda. American covert action against terrorism under any previous president had been notably modest. The most interesting element of the many 9/11 inquiries was perhaps the historical survey of counter-terrorism by Timothy Naftali.[3] This makes fascinating reading and offers the counterintuitive observation that, far from the United States being trigger-happy in its response to international terrorism, it has tended to agonise before taking any physical action. Restraint was the common theme for all administrations – including that of Ronald Reagan.

The application of history has been far from absent. Commentators have rushed to observe that 9/11 enjoys some parallels with Pearl Harbor, a Japanese plan for a surprise attack which began to gestate in the mid-1930s. The 9/11 attacks were also planned over a long time period, with the training of operatives beginning as early as September 1999. Arguably, this underlines the nature 9/11 as a 'normal' intelligence failure which illustrates many of classical observations about warning and surprise made by leading scholars such as Michael Handel and Richard K. Betts. Although there were some failures of collection, a lack of raw information was not the main problem. Instead, the frequency of warnings about Al Qaeda in preceding years had tended to dull the senses of policy-makers. Bureaucratic dysfunction prevented a full sharing of information, but more importantly, psychological dissonance prevented intelligence officers from anticipating an innovative attack using aircraft. The warnings that did make their way to a higher level were met by inaction. There was no single 'moment of failure' and instead it constituted a chain of events.

Finally, 9/11 alerts us to the chronic lack of public understanding about intelligence, and especially the lack of proper historical context. Surprise attacks are difficult to avoid and therefore, as phenomena, they are both normal and natural. Instead of recognising this, the American public have tended to ask 'how could this happen?' Limited leads, which were hard to distinguish at the time against a background of considerable noise, now appear with hindsight to be highly significant. The unspoken question underlying many of the inquiries was a search for the cause of an improbable event that should not have happened. In fact, what was surprising was that there had not been more major attacks on American soil since 1989. In common with many surprise attacks, including Pearl Harbor, this presumption has had an unfortunate tendency given rise to conspiracy theory. Disturbingly wide circulation has been given to theories about pre-knowledge of 9/11. Even retired CIA officers have engaged in ludicrous speculation about a controlled detonation in the twin towers.[4]

Intelligence and Iraqi WMD

If 9/11 had placed intelligence under increased public scrutiny, few could have anticipated the extent to which it would be under the spotlight by the summer of 2003. In Washington, Ottawa, Canberra, and indeed all the major European capitals, politicians and policy-makers argued over strategies of prevention and pre-emption. This debate was driven by intelligence appreciations that fused anxiety about the proliferation of WMD with the idea of a 'new terrorism' that was more likely to resort to the use of these weapons. Many argued that terrorists were now less inclined to use terrorism as a tactic to enhance political bargaining, as nationalist separatist groups had done in the 1970s. Instead, they were simply intent on destroying their enemies. This, in turn, seemed to point towards early action to forestall or 'pre-empt' this possibility. However, as Robert Jervis has argued, the problem with pre-emption is that it is predicated on accurate and unambiguous intelligence, meanwhile mistakes in this area are costly and counter-productive.[5]

Iraq was a painful lesson. American policy-makers confidently asserted that Iraq had usable weapons. In London, the Cabinet Office released two dossiers on Iraq, which it claimed provided the public with unprecedented intelligence material. However, one of these proved to have been part-plagiarised from a student's thesis, while the other proved to have been constructed from a small number of sources. Once the invasion of Iraq produced no weapons there were media-led accusations of the political manipulation of intelligence, and of an unhealthy proximity between pubic relations and the intelligence process. Most spectacularly, in December 2003, the Chief of the Iraq Survey Group, David Kay, who was initially confident of finding weapons, conceded that intelligence community had failed utterly on the issue of Iraqi WMD. The game was up.

In early 2004, President Bush announced the creation of a Commission on the Intelligence

Capabilities of the United States Regarding Weapons of Mass Destruction led by Laurence Silberman and Charles Robb. The Silberman – Robb Commission reported a year later in March 2005. It asserted that the US intelligence community had been badly wrong in almost all aspects of its analysis of Iraqi WMD. The strongest criticism was levelled at credulous handling of human sources, including Iraqi defectors. Particular attention was directed at an individual codenamed 'Curveball', an Iraqi defector controlled by the German foreign intelligence service, the BND. Relations between the BND and the CIA were notably poor. Allegations persist that this agent exaggerated what he knew because he was close to the Iraqi National Congress who earnestly wished to see an American invasion of Iraq.[6]

Days before the announcement of the American commission, Tony Blair initiated a similar panel to investigate UK intelligence, headed by the former Cabinet Secretary, Lord Butler of Brockwell. Parallel intelligence inquires were soon underway in countries as diverse as Australia, Denmark and Israel. Both the UK and US inquiries found their remits were tightly drawn to prevent them from examining how policy-makers employed the intelligence that they received on Iraq's weapons programmes. As Philip Davies and Anthony Glees have observed, one of the effects of the many intelligence inquiries has been to drive account-ability downwards. In the UK, constitutional tradition has emphasised ministerial responsi-bility to a sovereign parliament. However, the inquiries into intelligence have tended to direct public attention away from the decision-makers towards intelligence producers and analysts, often at quite a low level.[7] Both reports gave new details of intelligence activities related to Pakistan's AQ Khan network, arguably a proliferation story that was more important than Iraq.[8]

The issue of Iraqi WMD was complex because it combined chemical, biological and nuclear issues. It was also confusing because the policy-makers advocating war had advanced at least three different types of proposition. First, they had argued that Iraq seemed to have retained weapon stocks from before 1991, hiding them from UN inspectors. Second, that Iraq was seeking precursor materials abroad to expand its current programmes or to create new ones. Third, that Iraq was continuing to manufacture WMD and that this was a live and 'ongoing' process. Prime Minister Tony Blair underlined this latter point in his personal forward to the UK dossier on Iraqi WMD in 2002. In reality most of the evidence related to the first two contentions was already known and was of little importance. Biological and chemical materials from 1991 would have had a limited shelf-life and were likely to be non-viable. Efforts to acquire precursor materials from around the world merely placed Iraq among a group of many other countries that were engaged in similar activities. They only important contention was that of ongoing manufacture. In retrospect, it is now clear that London and Washington had almost no evidence for this.

Numerous apologists have offered explanations for the Iraqi WMD intelligence failure. Some have argued that the secret stockpiles remain hidden and nurtured a Macawberish hope that eventually something might turn up. Even the Butler report observed wistfully 'Iraq is a very big place, there is a lot of sand'.[9] Others have argued that the weapons were secretly moved to countries such as Syria or Pakistan. Little evidence for any of these theories has surfaced. More plausibly, strategic commentators have suggested that Iraq's own miscalculations were a contributory factor. In long conversations with his minders and interrogators, Saddam has explained that he was more worried about continuing to deter Iran than the United States and felt obligated to maintain some uncertainty in the minds of Teheran as deterrent to invasion. He was therefore reluctant to make a categorical statement that the cupboard was bare. However, by 2001 it seems that Saddam was privately in no doubt that Iraq lacked a WMD capability.[10]

Western intelligence also misread Iraq's overall strategy. Saddam's priorities were not to manufacture WMD, but instead to see sanctions lifted. His thinking seems to have been that the UN inspections were not really important so long as he kept enough technical personnel to reconstitute WMD activities far in the future. In 2003, the Americans captured Dr. Mahdi Obeidi, who had run Saddam's nuclear centrifuge programme in the 1990s. He revealed that he still had minimal plans and components for a nuclear centrifuge – the core of any nuclear programme – buried in his front garden. However, these were mere fragments and it would have required more than decade of work to reconstruct a viable programme.[11]

The case of intelligence and Iraqi WMD will be studied for years to come, since secret intelligence has rarely been tied to policy in such a public way. Undoubtedly, policy-makers sought to exaggerate the picture of the threat posed by Iraqi WMD. However, there were also profound problems with the collection and analysis of intelligence. Even countries like Germany, which did not support the invasion of Iraq, found that their intelligence communities had firmly asserted the existence of weapons. Ironically, Western intelligence, through their commendably close co-operation, had generated a form of 'Groupthink'. Only the Canadians and the Dutch voiced serious scepticism. The effects of the Iraq episode will be long-term, since in the eyes of the Arab world, the fallacious nature of the claims serve to undermine the legitimacy of all subsequent activities. More importantly, it has become harder to deal with the real danger posed by WMD through pre-emption because of the low state of public confidence in intelligence.

Intelligence and counter-terrorism

Many of the problems that became apparent after 2001 had their origins in the previous decade. Following the end of the Cold War, both the policy-makers and the intelligence agencies scanned the horizon for new enemies and failed to spot the emergent threats. Many had accepted the predictions of Francis Fukuyama that the future international system would be populated by peaceful democratic states competing economically. In turn, this contributed to a downsizing of human intelligence activities, precisely the kind of capability that is most important in the context of counter-terrorism. We also witnessed the growth of a risk-averse culture that made the recruitment of agents with a criminal past more difficult. By 1999, the United States had only limited independent human intelligence on terrorism and was largely dependent on liaison. Downsizing also had its impact on signals intelligence, since the NSA took on virtually no new employees for several years before 9/11.[12]

Accordingly, the main characteristic of the current cohort of counter-terrorism intelligence officers is youth. Less than half the personnel now working for the CIA or MI5 have been in the service more than three years. Yet it takes perhaps ten years for an agent-runner to achieve their full potential. Recruiting additional staff has been facilitated by increased funds, but a more serious challenge is posed by diversity. Many of those who would be most suitable fail to obtain clearances because of nationality issues, meanwhile foreign language training remains weak. For example, in 2005, the UK's airborne signals intelligence component was 50% short on its complement of speakers in key languages such as farsi and pashtun.

The world's leading intelligence agencies have displayed divergent approaches to counter-terrorist intelligence. The United States has taken a 'Fortress America' approach, attempting to keep the threat as far away from the homeland of the United States as possible. In part this reflects and anxiety about the shortcomings of the FBI that have failed to modernize or to build a serious domestic intelligence capability. Instead, the tendency has been to operate a vigorous 'seize and strike' campaign against known opponents overseas, often working closely with local allies. Rendition and interrogation has been a strong feature of this. By contrast, the UK initially operated a more passive 'watch and wait' approach derived from Northern Ireland, believing that terrorists that are in play, rather than in prison, were a valuable source of intelligence. It also reflected a belief that many groups within the UK would not target their host country. The short-comings of this policy were revealed in July 2005 when London suffered multiple bomb attacks.[13] Since 2005, the main impediment for the UK security services has been the large number of potential targets who are now thought to be worthy of surveillance. Estimates by successive head of MI5 have put this number at approximately 2,000 people. With the recognition of a home-grown security problem, UK approaches have also become more risk-averse.[14]

The scale of this task has certainly led to the rapid expansion of the dedicated security agencies. However, a less noted, but equally important phenomena is the way in which all government departments in Europe and the United States have become security elements charged with resilience and even to some extent intelligence gathering. The need to join up all aspects of government has placed a higher premium on intelligence fusion centres such as the UK's Joint Terrorism Analysis Centre (JTAC) which connects not only the lead agencies but elements from all over Whitehall and beyond. A good example of this is the role of economics and financial intelligence. This arcane area was relatively under-developed in the 1990s and has required close international co-operation to track the movement of funds through a deregulated financial system.[15]

Counter-intelligence

Since 9/11, the fashionable business of counter-terrorism has tended to crowd out the time-honoured tradition of counter-intelligence and also the work that intelligence agencies once conducted against organised crime. Historically, security intelligence agencies such as the American FBI, the UK's MI5 and the French DST have carried out a wide range of tasks, including security vetting and counter-subversion. One of their most traditional activities is counter-intelligence, which focuses on protecting government secrets from the espionage activities of foreign powers. Counter-intelligence increasingly extends to the protection of private organisations, such as large companies and research centres. Since 1990, commercial espionage has become a major issue because of the accelerating global economy, raising concerns about 'friendly spies'. It can also include the protection of private citizens who are émigrés from other countries and who are at risk from people in the countries from which they originate. On 1 November 2006, a fatal attack with radioactive poison on Alexander Litvinenko, a former Colonel in the Russian Federal Security Service living in exile in London, re-focused attention on this troubling issue.

Thwarting the espionage activities of foreign powers can encompass a wide range of activities. The lead element is usually the domestic security service who often watches known foreign agents, collects and analyses information on their activities and, if necessary, takes action against the hostile intelligence services. In some cases this results in diplomatic expulsion. Overseas intelligence services also have security sections designed to prevent hostile penetration and also to seek to counter-penetrate their adversaries at home and abroad. Moreover, most sensitive government departments also boast a security section. The world of 'spy versus spy', which is characterised by double agents and dubious defectors, is often viewed as an anachronistic Cold War landscape. However, this 'the wilderness of mirrors' remains a persistent feature of current situation because of the growing number of recent espionage cases involving China and Russia.

Efforts against hostile espionage often overlap with other categories of security work. Some overseas intelligence and security services are thought to sponsor guerrilla and terrorist groups as proxies. During the Cold War, the CIA assisted the Joseph Svimbi in Angola and the Mujahadeen in Afghanistan. The KGB cultivated the PLFP and PLO for a long time. A 1974 photograph shows Yasar Arafat with Vasili Fyodorovich Samoilenko, his KGB contact. The KGB trained Arab guerrillas at its Balashikha special-operations training school on the outskirts of Moscow and supplied a range of weapons used in its attacks in the Middle East. It is thought that PLO intelligence officers also attended one-year courses at the KGB's Andropov Institute, as a result a number of them ended up being recruited by the KGB. The PLO also developed a relationship with East European intelligence services, including the Roumanian DIE.[16] However, in the 1980s, the services of countries like Libya, Syria and Iran quickly eclipsed the KGB as sponsors. Terrorist organisations themselves often boast elaborate intelligence collection networks and undertake thorough target reconnaissance before launching an attack. In some parts of the world, such as the Balkans, the intelligence services have enjoyed a symbiotic relationship with both political factions and organised crime.

Nevertheless, counter-intelligence remains a narrower term than security intelligence or counter-subversion. Peter Gill defines the wider compass of security intelligence as the efforts of the state to gather information about any perceived threat deriving, not only from espionage but also from economic sabotage, foreign propaganda and political violence. The extent to which domestic security agencies in democratic states have spent their time monitoring fringe political groups, as opposed to legitimate threats, remains a highly contested subject. However, on balance, democratic states tend to allocate more resources to foreign intelligence agencies that look outwards, rather than to domestic surveillance agencies looking inwards. By contrast, totalitarian and authoritarian regimes are often described as 'security intelligence states', denoting their obsession with regime protection that pervades their approach to both domestic security and foreign intelligence. Even their overseas activities tend to prioritise the surveillance of exiles and dissidents abroad.

Notes

1 Martha Crenshaw, 'Theories of terrorism: Instrumental and Organizational Approaches', *Journal of Strategic Studies* 10/4 (1987) p.18.
2 Joby Warrick and Walter Pincus, 'CIA Finds Holes in Pre-9/11 Work Agency Reluctantly Releases 2-Year-Old Document Critical of Tenet', *Washington Post*, 22 August 2007.
3 This has now been published as Timothy Naftali, *Blind Spot: A Secret History of US Counter-terrorism* (NY: Basic, 2005).
4 R.A. Goldberg, 'Who Profited From the Crime? Intelligence Failure, Conspiracy Theories and the Case of September 11', in LV Scott and PD Jackson (eds.) *Understanding Intelligence in the 21st Century Journeys in Shadows* (London: Routledge, 2004) pp.249–61.
5 Robert Jervis, 'Why the Bush Doctrine Cannot be Sustained', *Political Science Quarterly*, 120/3, (2005), especially pp. 358–65.
6 Bob Drogin, *Curveball: Spies, Lies, and the Con Man Who Caused a War* (NY: Random House, 2007).
7 Anthony Glees & Philip H.J. Davies, *Spinning the Spies: Intelligence Open Government and the Hutton Inquiry* (London: The Social Affairs Unit, 2004).
8 For a detailed analysis see Gordon Corera, *Shopping for Bombs: Nuclear Proliferation, Global Insecurity, and the Rise and Fall of the A.Q. Khan Network* (Oxford: Oxford University Press, 2006).
9 'Report holds out the possibility that WMD may still be found . . . one day', *Telegraph*, 14 July 2004.

10 Scott Pelley, 'Interrogator Shares Saddam's Confessions', CBS News, 27 January 2008, http://www.cbsnews.com/stories/2008/01/24/60minutes/main3749494_page2.shtml

11 Mahdi Obeidi, *The Bomb in My Garden: The Secrets of Saddam's Nuclear Mastermind* (NY: Wiley, 2005).

12 Richard H. Shultz, Jr. and Andrea J. Drew, *Insurgents, Terrorists, and Militias: The Warriors of Contemporary Combat*, (NY: Columbia University Press, 2006).

13 Wyn Rees & Richard J Aldrich, 'Contending cultures of counterterrorism: transatlantic divergence or convergence?', *International Affairs* 81/5, (2005) pp.905–923.

14 Eliza Mannigham-Buller, 'The International Terrorist Threat to the United Kingdom', in Peter Hennessy (ed.), *The New Protective State* (London: Continuum 2007) p.67.

15 Martin Rudner, 'Financial Intelligence, Terrorism Finance, and Terrorist Adaptation,' *International Journal of Intelligence and CounterIntelligence* 19/1 (2006) pp.32–58.

16 Christopher Andrew and Vasili Mitrokhin, *The Mitrokhin Archive II: The KGB and the World*, (London: Allen Lane, 2005), pp.246–59.

11 Strategic surprise and the September 11 attacks

Daniel Byman

This essay examines the failure to anticipate the terrorist attacks of September 11 from four perspectives: cognitive biases of government analysts and policy makers concerned with terrorism, organizational pathologies of key bureaucracies such as the CIA and the FBI, political and strategic errors of senior government officials, and the unusual nature of al Qaeda. Drawing on past studies of strategic surprise, it argues that agencies such as the CIA at times did impressive work against the terrorist organization, but that in general the U.S. government, and the U.S. intelligence community in particular, lacked a coherent approach for triumphing over the skilled terrorists it faced. In hindsight, it is clear that numerous mistakes at all levels of the U.S. government and the broader U.S. analytic community made strategic surprise more likely.

Introduction

The quest to understand, and to lay blame for, the terrorist attacks on September 11, 2001 began even before the fires stopped burning. Pundits, policy makers, and analysts alike have cast the net of responsibility widely. Presidents Clinton and Bush are excoriated for letting bin Laden slip through their fingers. The Central Intelligence Agency and Federal Bureau of Investigation are lambasted for dithering in the face of a looming threat. Other analysts look outside the United States, painting a picture of al Qaeda as a formidable adversary against which even the most robust counterterrorism program would fail.

Of the many troubling features of the attacks, their sheer surprise was most disturbing to many Americans. The attacks shattered U.S. complacency and replaced it with fears of a new and menacing organization that seemed to threaten our very survival (Byman 2003). As journalist Peter Bergen notes, 'Suddenly, the blithe days of dot-com billionaires, Puff Daddy's legal problems, and Gary Condit's evasions about the missing Chandra Levy had disappeared like a delightful mirage' (Bergen 2002, p. 226).

This essay focuses on understanding the September 11 attacks and, more broadly, the U.S. response to the emergence of al Qaeda, within the context of strategic surprise. Strategic surprise encompasses both warnings of a threat and the response to it (Betts 1982, p. 87).[1] This focus on surprise is essential not only for understanding what allowed the September 11 attacks to happen, but also for prevailing against terrorism. Terrorists depend on secrecy and surprise to conduct successful operations (and indeed to survive) against a far stronger state (Bell 1994; Hoffman 1998, pp. 170–71; McCormick & Owen 2000; Crenshaw 2002, p. 57).

Although September 11 has few parallels, the problem of strategic surprise is not new. This essay first probes the scholarship on strategic surprise and organizational learning for insights into the question of warning. This probe offers four frames for understanding difficulties in providing warning: cognitive failures by analysts and policy makers; bureaucratic pathologies that inhibit an effective response; the tradeoffs and limits policy makers face; and the nature of the adversary. The remainder of the essay uses these four analytic frames in a detailed look at September 11 and the U.S. government response to the rise of al Qaeda.

Are surprise attacks really surprising?

Warning failures, including catastrophic ones, are not new for those concerned with national security. Betts (1978, 1982) has even argued that intelligence failures are natural, as well as inevitable. Pearl Harbor is perhaps the most notorious of surprises for Americans, but other notable surprise attacks include the Egyptian crossing of the Suez Canal at the onset of the Yom Kippur War in 1973, the German attack on France through the Ardennes forest in 1940, and the German invasion of Russia in 1941, all of which caught the victims flat-footed (Wohlstetter 1962; Chan 1979; Betts 1982; Stein 1982; May 1986, 2001; Levite 1987; Cohen & Gooch 1991).[2]

Scholars have turned to the study of individual psychology, small group behavior, organizational theory, and bureaucratic politics, among other disciplines, to understand why seemingly competent intelligence organizations and sensible policy makers are surprised by events that, in hindsight, seem obvious (Allison 1971, Janis 1972, Halperin 1974, Jervis 1976). Perhaps more troubling, some policy makers heard the warning but nevertheless did little to stave off disaster. In the case of September 11, it is essential to know the particular characteristics of al Qaeda that made surprise more attainable for the organization.

Cognitive problems for analysts and policy makers

Discerning a looming danger can be exceptionally difficult. Analysts and policy makers must transform fragmented and weak data into a coherent vision of the future – a task that challenges even the best minds. Their imaginations must leap, discerning a future threat where none existed in the past.

Analysts' and policy makers' biases and preconceptions shape how information is received and analyzed. Such a framework is necessary; information cannot be interpreted in an analytic void (Betts 1978, p. 63). At times, however, the framework indiscriminately filters out contradictory information, leading to disaster. Cohen & Gooch (1991), for example, contend that Israeli intelligence (and policy makers) clung to 'the Concept' – the belief that the militarily inferior Egypt would not start a war unless it had the means of striking Israel proper and neutralizing the Israeli Air Force – despite evidence of Egyptian preparations to attack (Cohen & Gooch 1991, pp. 114–15; Jervis 2002). Similarly, Snook (2000) contends that one of the reasons for the tragic friendly-fire incident that led to the downing of two U.S. Black Hawk helicopters over Iraq in 1994 was that the F-15 pilots expected, and wanted, to engage the enemy and incorrectly 'saw' the Black Hawks as Iraqi Hind helicopters. Thus 'they created the two Hinds; then they shot them down' (p. 98).

Analysts may seek consensus rather than appraising alternative explanations. This problem, often particularly acute in small groups, has been labeled 'groupthink' (Janis 1972), and it often inhibits effective analysis by discouraging reappraisal or any other challenge to the existing wisdom. In 2004, members of the Senate Select Committee on Intelligence blamed 'groupthink' as one reason why the intelligence community did not properly assess Iraq's weapons of mass destruction program (U.S. Senate Select Committee on Intelligence 2004).

One of the most common problems when trying to tease out a new pattern of behavior and thus prevent surprise is the 'signal to noise ratio.' Wohlstetter's *Pearl Harbor: Warning and Decision*, one of the first and best looks at the question of surprise attack, famously found that the 'noise' of irrelevant information drowned out the 'signal' of a looming threat for analysts looking at the question of where Japan might attack (Wohlstetter 1962, pp. 1–2, 111–12; Chan 1979). Only in hindsight was the true signal clear.[3] Wohlstetter contends, 'In short, we failed to anticipate Pearl Harbor not for want of relevant materials, but because of a plethora of irrelevant ones' (p. 387).

Even when the signal can be discerned with some certainty, it is often presented in a way that inhibits effective warning. At times, intelligence is politicized and presented to policy makers in a way that justifies their preconceptions and preferred policies. Overwarning is another problem. Intelligence assessments often overreact to previous errors that under-estimated a threat but do not correct sufficiently when a threat is overestimated (*Report of a Committee of Privy Counsellors* 2004, p. 112, para. 456). The intelligence community may cry wolf so often that policy makers become inured to the danger and dismiss reports of a looming crisis (Betts 1978).

Intelligence analysts and policy makers at times do not understand all the dimensions of the threat they face, and this lack can cause a 'failure to anticipate' (Cohen & Gooch 1991, pp. 95–131). For example, in 1973, Israel analysts assumed that Israel's tactical superiority made an attack from its neighbors inconceivable; they ignored the strategic and political logic of such an attack. As a result, Israel suffered a near-disastrous surprise (Levite 1987; Cohen & Gooch 1991, pp. 95–131). Often, this inability to anticipate occurs because of changes in the adversary's capabilities and procedures. The French, for example, were caught off-guard in 1940 partly because they did not recognize that new German tactics and organizational concepts would enable an armored breakthrough.

At times, intelligence analysts may correctly identify a problem but policy makers' own biases do not change sufficiently for them to address the new problem. In his classic book on strategic surprise, Betts (1982) declares that '*the primary problem in major strategic surprises is not intelligence warning but political disbelief*' (p. 18, author's italics). Like intelligence analysts, policy makers have biases and see only part of the overall picture. This limited view leads to many mistakes.[4]

Bureaucratic pathologies

Even if individuals can overcome data weaknesses and their own cognitive limits to sound an alarm, the institution as a whole may not fully recognize the problem and shift its procedures and resources accordingly. Once some members of an organization know about a threat, why would the organization as a whole not incorporate this knowledge into its procedures? Organization theory offers insights into this knotty question.

Different organizations have different cultures, a generalization as true for intelligence and national security agencies as it is for businesses. Knowledge is transmitted and the task at hand approached in highly different ways, with profound implications for overall perform-ance. The 'rules' in an organizational handbook or a doctrine manual may be far from the practice on the ground (Snook 2000, pp. 190–92). A particular concern of many organiza-tional cultures facing a new situation is whether change is in keeping with the institution's current identity (Cook & Yanow 1996, p. 451). Submarine warfare, for example, was a clear possibility before both world wars. However, no major navy prepared for antisubmarine warfare, because they saw their mission and identity as linked to large surface-unit action. As a result, they were unprepared for what in hindsight was an obvious development (Herwig 1998).

Organizations and their procedures often remain constant despite mounting problems with the task at hand. Cohen & Gooch (1991) depict the British Gallipoli campaign in this light, arguing that the failure of British commanders to correct the disastrous actions (and, most important, inactions) of their subordinates led to an overall failure at Suvla Bay (Cohen & Gooch 1991, pp. 156–63). More broadly, institutions often do not change their approaches to problem solving – their 'organizational frames' (Eden 2004, p. 50) – despite the inadequacy of their current approach. At times, responsibility may be too diffuse; everyone has some share of the overall problem, so no particular person considers it his or her job to act (Snook 2000, pp. 135–36).

Political limits on effective policy

Warning occurs in a policy context, which depends on politics. Information provided by intelligence agencies is an important factor in shaping policy, but it is only one of many (Herman 2004). The presidency is only one element of government, and it must accommodate as well as attempt to shape such diverse actors as the Congress, the media, the bureaucracies, and public opinion (Neustadt 1991, Howell 2003, Pfiffner 2004). Important decisions such as going to war or making a major shift in foreign policy can be particularly problematic (Lian & Oneal 1993).

In addition to the need to work with many actors with different agendas, another common problem is competing priorities that divert attention and resources. Policy makers must choose their battles, and they often have limited resources. They cannot solve every problem or mitigate every risk. Moreover, policy makers' attention often gyrates wildly from crisis to crisis, giving them little time to study long-term trends (Blackwill & Davis 2004).

Policy makers also have limited abilities to redirect bureaucracies. In the United States, intelligence agencies are often criticized for not respecting civil liberties. These concerns led Congress and the executive branch to monitor and limit the agencies' power, and several scholars contend these restrictions have limited the agencies' effectiveness (Hitz 2004, Johnson 2004).

The nature of the adversary

Some intelligence challenges are more demanding than others, and this difficulty affects the collection and use of intelligence. For example, Lord Butler's investigation into the British government's use of intelligence on Iraq's weapons of mass destruction program found that many problems arose in the handling and interpretation of intelligence owing to 'the difficulty of achieving reliable human intelligence on Iraq' (*Report of a Committee of Privy Counsellors* 2004, p. 109, para. 443).

The warning problem of terrorism is exceptionally difficult, compounding the challenges that individual analysts, bureaucracies, and policy makers face with regard to strategic surprise. As Pillar argues,

> The basic problem that terrorism poses for intelligence is as simple as it is chilling. A group of conspirators conceives a plot. Only the few conspirators know of their intentions, although they might get help from others. They mention nothing about their plot to anyone they cannot absolutely trust. They communicate nothing about their

plans in a form that can be intercepted. . . . They live and move normally and inconspicuously, and any preparations that cannot be done behind closed doors they do as part of those movements. The problem: How do we learn of the plot?

(Pillar 2004b, p. 115)

Moreover, as Pillar contends, 'The target for intelligence is not just proven terrorists; it is anyone who *might* commit terrorism in the future' (p. 115, author's italics).

The problem of tactical warning is particularly vexing. Investigations of attacks before September 11 emphasized that tactical warning may be lacking even though strategic warning was sound. In 1985, the 'Report of the Secretary of State's Advisory Panel on Overseas Security' (the 'Inman Report') examined the bombings of the U.S. Embassy and Marine barracks in Lebanon and concluded, 'If determined, well-trained and funded teams are seeking to do damage, they will eventually succeed.' The inquiry into the 1996 Khobar Towers attack and the investigation of the 1998 embassy bombings both found strategic warning was sound even though tactical warning was lacking (Pillar 2004b, p. 125). In January 1999, the 'Report of the Accountability Review Boards on the Embassy Bombings in Nairobi and Dar es Salaam' (better known as the 'Crowe Commission') contended that 'we cannot count on having such intelligence to warn us of such attacks.'

Deception and denial compound the problem of surprise. Skilled adversaries do their best to counter intelligence gathering. Encryption, limits on the dissemination of sensitive information, and other means are used to inhibit standard means of intelligence collection. Adversaries also scheme to mislead each other (Shulsky 2002, pp. 116–25). Famously, British intelligence during World War II successfully fed false information to German agents on British shores to mislead them as to the location of Allied landings on the French coast, a deception operation vital to the success of the Normandy landings. Ironically, fear of deception can also lead to failures, as suspicions of deception may lead intelligence agencies to discount true information (Betts 1982, p. 109). Fear of deception also reinforces the importance of existing analytic biases. Contrary information may be suspected of being 'disinformation' whereas confirming information may wrongly be treated as accurate.

The above four perspectives are analytically distinct, but in practice interact. It is best to view the components of surprise and warning as a system, as it is often characteristics of the system rather than any particular component of it that lead to mistakes and disaster (Perrow 1999, p. 66).

A closer look at September 11

September 11 represents a failure, but the nature of the failure is unclear. Many things went wrong in many places and at many levels, making the exact problems hard to pinpoint, diffusing responsibility, and obscuring the path ahead. This section discusses whether an alarm was sounded and then notes various opportunities that analysts and policy makers missed.

Was the alarm sounded?

The intelligence community, particularly the CIA, did well in providing strategic warning of an al Qaeda threat. The identity of the foe, the scale of its ambitions, and its lethality were known and communicated in a timely manner. The CIA had begun its warning about al

Qaeda even before the simultaneous attacks on two U.S. embassies on August 7, 1998 made the danger clearer to many observers (Coll 2004, p. 383). After the embassy bombings, warning with regard to al Qaeda became a top priority, and even weak pieces of intelligence led to the sounding of the alarm. In journalist Steve Coll's description, 'It was a vast, pulsing, self-perpetuating, highly sensitive network on continuous alert' (Coll 2004, p. 417).

By 2001, the system was on high alert, and any policy maker (or member of the general public) who cared to look could see the CIA's concern. In February 2001, Director of Central Intelligence (DCI) George Tenet testified publicly that bin Laden and his organization posed 'the most immediate and serious threat' to the United States (Tenet 2001) – a clarion example of strategic warning. Senior policy makers from both the Clinton and Bush administrations have testified that Tenet and other CIA officials warned that al Qaeda was planning lethal 'spectaculars' against Americans (Woodward 2002, p. 34). The FBI also added its voice to the warning. Louis Freeh, then FBI Director, testified on May 10, 2001 that a primary objective of al Qaeda 'is the planning and carrying out of large-scale, high-profile, high-casualty terrorist attacks against U.S. interests and citizens and those of our allies, worldwide' (Freeh 2001).

This strong strategic warning, however, was accompanied by a failure to learn clues about the specifics of the attack on the U.S. homeland, which led to a devastating failure of tactical warning. If policy makers listened to intelligence, they would know al Qaeda was coming, but they would not know when, where, or how.

Missed opportunities for intelligence

Even though the plotters made several mistakes and 'the system was blinking red,' in the words of the 9/11 Commission's report, much of the plotters' activity went on undetected (National Commission 2004, pp. 254–77). The missed opportunities include the following:

- Working with Malaysian internal security forces, the CIA covered a meeting of key operatives, several of whom were involved in the September 11 plot, but lost track of them when the meeting ended.
- The CIA did not 'watchlist' two key plotters, Khalid al-Midhar and Nawaf al-Hazmi, to prevent them from entering the United States, despite learning that they had U.S. visas and were traveling to the United States. Nor did the CIA pass this or related information to the FBI promptly.
- Several suggestive leads were not pursued. For example, in July an alert FBI agent in the Phoenix, Arizona office noted in an electronic communication that an 'inordinate number of persons of investigative interest' (*Report of the Joint Inquiry* 2002, pp. 2–3) were seeking flight training in the area and called for a more comprehensive investigation into the matter – a warning ignored by FBI headquarters.
- The jihadist Zacarias Moussaoui fell into the hands of the FBI in Minnesota because of suspicions that he might be trying to hijack a plane. Moussaoui had links to several of the plotters, including Ramzi Binalshibh, one of the masterminds. This information was not briefed up the chain of command at the FBI (though DCI Tenet was briefed!), despite the high level of threat being communicated in general.
- During their time in the United States, the hijackers had contacts with several Islamist radicals whom the FBI already was monitoring.
- The CIA scrapped a plan to kidnap bin Laden that some experts believe had a reasonable chance of success. Several military strikes against bin Laden were also called off

because of concerns about intelligence of uncertain reliability (Coll 2004, pp. 484–85, 564; National Commission 2004, pp. 181–82, 267–75).

Policy mistakes

In hindsight, U.S. policy toward al Qaeda also had several fatal flaws that allowed the organization to flourish. Perhaps most important, U.S. policy left the issue of terrorist sanctuary unresolved. In Afghanistan, al Qaeda was allowed to build an army of like-minded radicals outside the reach of the United States and its allies. Richard Clarke, the senior counterterrorism official for the Clinton administration and for the Bush administration through September 11, notes to his dismay that the United States allowed 'the existence of large scale al Qida bases where we know people are trained to kill Americans' (National Commission 2004, p. 213). Even more troubling, al Qaeda enjoyed a permissive environment in the West, where it could recruit, raise money, and otherwise sustain its cause.

Before September 11, the United States had no coherent counterterrorism policy with regard to Pakistan and a vague policy with regard to Saudi Arabia, although both were central to the effort against al Qaeda. Pakistan was the Taliban's primary sponsor, and it also backed jihadist groups as part of its campaign against India in Kashmir. The Saudi regime did not directly back al Qaeda itself, but it often turned a blind eye as its citizens bankrolled and swelled the ranks of affiliated jihadist groups. The result was stagnation in policy even as the threat metastasized (Coll 2004, p. 571).

The United States also relied too heavily on law enforcement tools such as trials and arrests to fight al Qaeda before September 11. Law enforcement has several weaknesses as a counterterrorism instrument. Even successful law-enforcement measures often fail to nab the terrorist masterminds. In addition, trials place considerable demands on the resources of the intelligence community, which might otherwise be spent disrupting future attacks (Pillar 2001, pp. 80–89). Arrests and trials did little against the army being built in the haven in Afghanistan, which was perhaps the biggest challenge for fighting al Qaeda.

Why were the opportunities missed?

The four frames derived from various social science literatures offer insights into why analysts and policy makers missed these potential opportunities to disrupt the plot and to tailor U.S. policy to counter al Qaeda.

Cognitive failures

Even those most concerned with al Qaeda failed to grasp the dimensions of the threat. Former New Jersey Governor Thomas Kean, the Chairman of the 9/11 Commission, reports a vast 'failure of imagination' (http://www.cnn.com/2004/ALLPO LITICS/07/22/911.report/).[5] Policy makers often failed to recognize that, unlike past terrorist groups, al Qaeda had both the capability and intention of inflicting mass casualties on America (Benjamin & Simon 2002). President Bush at first thought the first plane strike on the North Tower of the World Trade Center may have been due to a pilot's heart attack (Woodward 2002, p. 15). Even Clarke, one of the most perspicacious observers of al Qaeda, underestimated the threat; he had gloomily predicted an attack in which 'hundreds' of Americans would die (National Commission 2004, p. 344).

But the 'failure of imagination' was in practice more complex. The problem for officials such as Tenet, Berger, and Clarke was not in failing to imagine that al Qaeda could and would kill thousands. Indeed, they devoted considerable attention to the possibility that al Qaeda would acquire and use a chemical, biological, or nuclear weapon or agent to this end. However, their imaginations did not transform their day-to-day actions. As Deputy Secretary of State Richard Armitage noted after the attacks, 'I don't think we really had made the leap in our mind that we are no longer safe behind these two great oceans' (Coll 2004, p. 542). Their minds often soared, but their guts did not clench.

For analysts looking at al Qaeda, the signal-to-noise problem was immense. In 2001, CIA analysts tracked possible al Qaeda plots in Europe, Africa, and the Middle East. The U.S. homeland was also of concern, but it was lost in the data swamp of information related to overseas attacks. These overseas threats, moreover, were not always pure noise but rather were often signals of other attacks. Al Qaeda was indeed plotting attacks in Europe and the Middle East, as later events would show.

The FBI suffered from a bias in assuming that the threat would focus outside the United States. The Bureau's analysts did not challenge their own preconceptions, even though by 1998 it was clear that bin Laden was seeking recruits to attack the United States and developing an infrastructure here (Coll 2004, p. 420). In part, this bias existed because of how the FBI viewed Islamist terrorist groups. The Bureau correctly recognized that Hizballah, Hamas, and other religio-nationalist groups primarily operate in the United States to raise money. Conducting an attack here would be illogical, killing the golden goose. Al Qaeda, however, had in the past proved willing to jeopardize its logistics and fundraising bases in pursuit of a successful attack.

The CIA also had its set of blinders to the danger at home, in part because of its successful collection of the wrong information. The CIA collected considerable intelligence on the danger of al Qaeda attacks overseas, which led to warnings in Italy, the Persian Gulf, and elsewhere in 2001. More general indications of a major attack were interpreted in the light of this information that pointed to an attack overseas.

Another problem for warning was the shift in adversary tactics. Using airplanes as weapons was innovative, and there was relatively little intelligence suggesting al Qaeda would do this. Its use of different types of attack platforms (truck bombs in Africa, a boat bomb in Yemen, and so on) did not lead analysts to anticipate that the organization would innovate yet again.

The tremendous sensitivity to any potential threat led to overwarning. Any mention of al Qaeda activity was conveyed to senior policy makers, and indeed often to the President himself. The result was a 'warning fatigue' with regard to al Qaeda – a problem that only grew after September 11 (Posner 2003; Anonymous 2004, p. 84).

The cognitive failures were perhaps even worse among policy makers than among intelligence analysts. Despite the repeated warnings of Tenet and others, it is not clear where terrorism was on the overall U.S. priority list. Many former and current U.S. officials claim that terrorism was 'a top priority' well before September 11, but for both the Clinton and Bush administrations, so too were Iraq, China, the Balkans, missile defense, military reform, and other foreign policy issues (Coll 2004, p. 541). Policy makers 'knew' al Qaeda was a growing danger, but they were not able to shift their attention sufficiently to reflect this.

As a result of this lack of prioritization, each agency focused on the issues of greatest importance to them. The CIA was responsible for supporting war-fighting in Iraq and the Balkans, monitoring China and other potential rivals, providing economic analyses, and so on. For the FBI, deadbeat dads, drug running, and infrastructure protection demanded resources. There was no single plan everyone followed, and counterterrorism was at times neglected or not given enough money or manpower.[6]

Neglect and confused priorities characterized U.S. policy toward Afghanistan for many years. Before the embassy bombings in 1998, Afghanistan was neglected (Coll 2004, pp. 5–6, 15). In its regional policy, the State Department focused on issues ranging from a possible nuclear exchange between India and Pakistan to the disruption of democracy in Nepal. When Afghanistan came on the radar screen, it was usually with regard to narcotics or human rights violations, not terrorism (Coll 2004, p. 383; Albright 2003, p. 363). Although the United States focused far more on terrorism as the decade went on, these other concerns did not go away and greatly complicated efforts to press the Taliban on terrorism issues. As Clarke notes, the Taliban knew that it would not escape U.S. pressure by surrendering bin Laden; the United States would still harp on women's rights, narcotics, and other issues (Clarke 2004, p. 208).

Another indicator of a cognitive disjuncture between the knowledge of individuals and the logical actions that should flow from that knowledge is the limited attention given to defensive measures against terrorism, particularly in the United States itself. Despite the finding of various commissions that specific tactical intelligence is *likely* to be lacking when we face a skilled adversary – and the intelligence community's warning that al Qaeda was planning lethal attacks – policy makers initiated few defensive measures in the United States. They relied on intelligence for defense even though they knew intelligence (particularly at home) was flawed.

Bureaucratic pathologies

Part of the reason for the lack of tactical warning was that the intelligence community and other institutions did not respond to the strategic warning and sufficiently strengthen their ability to collect, analyze, and disseminate information or act on what they did know. In addition, some institutions, including the U.S. military, did not embrace counterterrorism as a mission despite the high level of strategic warning.

Continued CIA weaknesses

On December 4, 1998, George Tenet declared:

> 'We are at war. I want no resources or people spared in this effort' (Coll 2004, p. 435). Yet despite this rhetoric and Tenet's strenuous effort to warn policy makers of the danger, the CIA did not significantly shift resources from other priorities to counterterrorism or change its culture and focus. As one intelligence officer long involved in assessing al Qaeda lamented, lower-level intelligence officers 'knew a runaway train was coming at the United States, documented that fact, and then watched helplessly – or were banished for speaking out – as their senior leaders delayed action, downplayed intelligence, ignored repeated warnings . . .'
>
> (Anonymous 2004, p. ix).

Resource allocation is one primary area where action did not match the level of threat (Coll 2004, p. 435). How much can Tenet be faulted? The DCI's lack of budget authority contributes to this problem (Scowcroft 1996, p. 143; Johnson 1996, p. 35). Because the DCI controlled only perhaps 15% of the pre-September 11 intelligence budget, much of the intelligence community felt no compulsion to observe the DCI's directives if they ran counter to their own bureaucratic imperatives. Consequently, even though the DCI 'declared war' on al Qaeda, no agency dramatically changed its priorities.

If the DCI had controlled more of the intelligence community's budget and people, it is plausible that far more money could have been devoted to counter-terrorism. The evidence from Tenet's track record at the CIA, however, suggests that changes would have been limited. Before the attacks, when pressed by policy makers to transfer more money to the al Qaeda effort, the CIA claimed that none of its other programs could be ended or curtailed to free up resources (Clarke 2004, p. 210). Nevertheless, under Tenet the CIA expanded counterterrorism efforts even as intelligence budgets for other programs declined (*Report of the Joint Inquiry* 2002, pp. 250–69). This indicates that other agencies, too, might have increased spending on counterterrorism. Conceivably, much of the money that went to support military programs through technical means, which dwarfs the amount spent on human intelligence, could have been transferred to beef up the CIA's human intelligence programs.

Operational weaknesses compounded the budget problems. The CIA also did not penetrate al Qaeda's upper echelons. As discussed below, this failure was partly due to the nature of the adversary, and it is clear that by the late 1990s such a penetration was a priority target for the CIA [*Report of the Joint Inquiry* (2002), pp. 387–88; for an incorrect contrary claim, see Bamford (2004), p. 156]. However, some critics maintain that the Agency did not have the proper approach for targeting jihadists – a fault of institutional response, not just of intelligence collection in general. In part, this was because the Agency continued to operate its personnel out of U.S. government buildings, and even its 'nonofficial cover' (NOC) officers tended to be fake businessmen. None of these could operate in a mosque without giving themselves away. One former CIA officer claimed, 'The CIA probably doesn't have a single truly qualified Arabic-speaking officer of Middle Eastern background who can play a believable Muslim fundamentalist who would volunteer to spend years of his life with shitty food and no women in the mountains of Afghanistan' (Gerecht 2001).[7]

Analysis on al Qaeda was also often weak. Despite the CIA's awareness of the danger, it often lacked detailed knowledge of the enemy. Clarke, for example, criticized the CIA for not recognizing the importance of Khalid Shaykh Mohammad, the mastermind of September 11, claiming that he could have been snatched in Qatar had this been known (Clarke 2004, p. 153). This problem was not simply due to the difficulty of gaining information on al Qaeda. Rather, the CIA's emphasis was on operations against al Qaeda, and efforts to build a full picture of the organization did not receive sufficient support. Indeed, no comprehensive intelligence assessment of al Qaeda was drafted until after September 11. This lack of an estimate appears to go against the traditional CIA emphasis on detailed analysis, one of its core missions. However, in the CIA most of the detailed, long-term analysis was done by the area divisions of the Directorate of Intelligence, whereas the primary emphasis of the CIA's Counterterrorist Center (CTC) was on operations (it reports to the DCI through the Deputy Director of Operations), which made it less likely to focus on analysis. Most of the CTC's 'analysis' focused on collection issues linked to operations rather than on broader estimates and strategic assessments (National Commission 2004, pp. 118, 342).

Risk aversion was another problem for the CIA. As the 9/11 Commission contended, the CIA was 'an organization capable of attracting extraordinarily motivated people but institutionally averse to risk' (National Commission 2004, p. 93.) Director of Operations James Pavitt, for example, questioned whether the effort to work with the Northern Alliance against the Taliban was worth the high possibility that a case officer might die in an accident in a rickety helicopter en route – an instance of what other critics have called a general risk aversion to physical danger (Coll 2004, pp. 519, 524; Gerecht 2001).

This risk aversion, however, was sensible from an institutional perspective. As Coll notes, the CIA was 'conditioned by history to recoil from gung-ho "allies" at the National Security Council.' The institution had learned that these allies often turned to covert action in lieu of making tough policy decisions and – when things went poorly – hung the CIA out to dry (Coll 2004, p. 395).

Culturally and procedurally, the CIA was focused on the threat overseas. The CIA, of course, is prohibited from running operations on U.S. soil, and in the wake of several scandals revealed in the 1970s, the Agency is exceptionally sensitive to the charge that it might be spying on Americans. As a result, its resources, collection capabilities, and analysis are focused on the overseas threat. Not surprisingly, even when it identified the possible 'signal' of an attack on U.S. soil, its activities were focused on gathering 'noise' (or, more accurately, other signals) related to al Qaeda activities overseas.

The above problems reflect how the broader institutional mission interfered with successful counterterrorism. The CIA's reluctance to divert resources from other concerns, change collection platforms to emphasize NOCs, focus on dangers at home rather than overseas, and engage in politically risky covert action reflected the institution's history and identity rather than the threat of al Qaeda.

Was the FBI asleep at the switch?

The list of FBI shortcomings revealed after September 11 is long. The FBI not only failed to intercept the plotters, but more generally did not appreciate the danger the country faced – in sharp contrast to the CIA. Before September 11, the FBI was not properly structured or oriented for counterterrorism or, more broadly, for intelligence work. This failure occurred in part because of the FBI's culture, but also because the organization did not learn and respond properly as information about al Qaeda grew.

Prior to September 11, the Bureau often failed to collect information relevant to counterterrorism. For example, when Abdul Hakim Murad was interviewed in connection with his participation in a plot to bomb as many as 12 airplanes over the Pacific in 1995, the FBI did not devote attention to his possible plans to crash an airplane into CIA headquarters – a harbinger of the September 11 plot. Nor did the FBI place opportunities for collection in context; for example, it failed to link suspicious flight-training activity in Arizona or the arrest of an Islamic extremist (Moussaoui) in Minnesota to the heightened national threat level. In general, the FBI did not train its operatives sufficiently in intelligence collection or provide collectors with sufficient resources, particularly with regard to surveillance and translation (National Commission 2004, p. 77).

Often what information the FBI did collect was not disseminated, even internally. The FBI's antediluvian computer system and case-file approach to holding information meant that information was not regularly passed from the field to headquarters, nor to other FBI agents and analysts who might be working on similar problems. The FBI did not see itself as part of the national security apparatus and did not share information with the national security community (Benjamin & Simon 2002, p. 298; National Commission 2004, p. 358).

As a result, the FBI did not inform policy makers of the jihadist threat at home. Two former White House officials working on counterterrorism in the National Security Council wrote about learning FBI information from trial transcripts of al Qaeda suspects, noting, 'In many instances, we discovered information so critical that we were amazed that the relevant agencies did not inform us of it while we were at the NSC' (Benjamin & Simon 2002, pp. xii–xiii). It is not surprising that policy makers, agencies, and analysts outside the FBI never learned of this information – most of the FBI did not know of it either.

Nor did the FBI conduct strategic analysis. Clarke (2004) depicts the FBI as plodding and hidebound, comfortable in its ignorance of al Qaeda (p. 192). The office created to do strategic analysis atrophied. The FBI had only two analysts looking at information on the bin Laden threat, and it did not prepare a document like the National Intelligence Estimate to assess the al Qaeda threat to the United States or the radical Islamic presence in this country (National Commission 2004, pp. 93, 265).

The Bureau's culture and organization fostered these problems. Before September 11, the FBI was primarily a law enforcement agency, and it was probably the world's best. But law enforcement focuses on prosecuting a case, not on understanding a broader network. Law enforcement emphasizes gathering specific evidence, not collecting and sharing possibly relevant information. Given this organizational ethos, it is not surprising that terrorism was viewed as a criminal matter and treated accordingly. In addition, FBI leaders emphasized finding the perpetrators of the last attack rather than stopping the next one (Watson 2002).

The FBI's organizational structure both reflected this culture and worsened it. The decentralized field-office structure allowed offices to set their own priorities, few of which focused on terrorism or al Qaeda. The 56 FBI field offices in the United States were all independent fiefdoms in which local priorities took precedence (Clarke 2004, p. 219; Kessler 2002, p. 432).

The FBI also faced many restrictions – and tremendous political scrutiny – on its functions related to counterterrorism. For example, in 1996, right-wing conservatives joined liberal civil libertarians to block legislation that would allow multipoint wiretaps, which are useful for tracking terrorists who change phones or use multiple phones. In addition to restricting the tools the FBI could use, this odd alliance made the FBI exceptionally sensitive to investigating religious-based terrorism in the United States (Benjamin & Simon 2002). Congressional investigations into deaths at Ruby Ridge and Waco further increased FBI sensitivity. In general, the FBI preferred to err on the side of respect for civil liberties, setting a high bar for surveillance.

FBI procedures separating intelligence from law enforcement cases – the so-called 'Wall' – reflected the Bureau's problems on this issue. The rules were confusing and were often interpreted in the most restrictive way, which hindered efforts to track al Qaeda activities in the United States (National Commission 2004, pp. 78–80, 271). However, given the FBI's law enforcement culture, the inherent problems of the Wall were not as troubling as they would be for an intelligence organization. Moreover, because the Bureau did not appreciate the growing danger, it felt little need to change course. Thus, despite grumbling among the ranks, FBI leaders did not press hard to lower the Wall.

The problems of the Wall stemmed from leadership. Former FBI Director Louis Freeh reportedly disdained technology and thus did not invest in systems to improve data storage, retrieval, and sharing (Kessler 2002, p. 422). Much of Freeh's attention on counterterrorism was related to investigating attacks that had happened overseas, such as the Khobar Towers bombing (Walsh 2001). Freeh also worsened the problem of local fiefdoms, cutting staff at headquarters and placing the lead in the field for operations (National Commission 2004, p. 76).

The missing military

The CIA, the FBI, and other members of the intelligence community are not the only institutions in the line of fire. The military is also often criticized for not having embraced the counterterrorism mission (Coll 2004, p. 572; Benjamin & Simon 2002, pp. 292–96). Policy makers turned to the military for help against al Qaeda but went away empty-handed. In addition to not preparing an outright invasion plan, the military opposed using special operations forces to snatch al Qaeda operatives in countries such as Afghanistan, Sudan, and Qatar (Clarke 2004, pp. 143, 152–53). The military also rebuffed President Clinton's suggested use of a special operations force raid as one way to intimidate al Qaeda. More generally, the military resisted NSC requests for military options. Clark contends, 'The White House wanted action. The senior military did not and made it almost impossible for the President to overcome their objections' (p. 145). Clinton himself notes, 'It was clear to me that the senior military didn't want to do this . . .' (Clinton 2004, p. 804).

A particular military concern appears to have been the inappropriate use of limited force against al Qaeda (National Commission 2004, pp. 120–21). General Henry Shelton, then the Chairman of the Joint Chiefs of Staff, believed that the deployment of special operations forces or other 'boots on the ground' missions would probably fail, since intelligence was poor and they lacked a secure base of operations. In his view, any military mission should involve thousands of soldiers or else it risked turning into a humiliating operational disaster (Coll 2004, p. 497) like the ill-fated 'Desert One' hostage rescue mission in 1980.

Shelton's view has a point. The military has a role to play in counterterrorism, but barring outright invasion, that role is quite different from the military's normal function, which is to literally interpose itself between the American people and their enemy. Limited uses of military force make a poor deterrent, seldom inflict meaningful damage that reduces terrorists' capabilities, anger allies, and may rally supporters for the terrorists (Pillar 2001, pp. 102–9; Jervis 2002, p. 39).

The military, like the CIA, sought to minimize risk with regard to counterterrorism. Using special operations forces or even launching cruise missiles had a high risk of failure given the hostile operating environment and the lack of precise intelligence. But these risks would have been more acceptable if military leaders had considered the problem a grave one. They did not. Moreover, the military did not take steps to improve its capabilities significantly, either by gathering its own intelligence to improve the likely success of a special operations force mission or by arranging bases in nearby staging areas. Even while threat warnings grew, the military did not adapt.

No domestic response

There is little to report on the responses of other agencies linked to homeland security with regard to al Qaeda. Only those in the corridors of power in Washington heard the steady drumbeat of strategic warning that al Qaeda was coming. Nor did the day-to-day threat reporting or even the public testimony make a strong impression, as state and local officials and noncore national security agencies such as the Immigration and Naturalization Service did not see terrorism as their concern. The 9/11 Commission reported, 'In sum, the domestic agencies never mobilized in response to the threat. They did not have direction, and they did not have a plan to institute. The borders were not hardened. Transportation systems were not fortified. Electronic surveillance was not targeted against a domestic threat.

State and local law enforcement were not marshaled to augment the FBI's efforts. The public was not warned' (National Commission 2004, p. 265).

Limited institutional management

Many of the problems of the CIA, the FBI, the military, and other institutions involved in counterterrorism can be laid, at least in part, at the feet of policy makers. It is the duty of elected officials to impose their will on unelected elements of the government, and they have the authority to do so. Policy makers, however, did a poor job imposing their will on various bureaucracies that were not aggressive in counterterrorism. The FBI's investigation of President Clinton for various scandals gave it effective immunity from White House over-sight (Benjamin & Simon 2002, pp. 298–306). Nor did the President impose his will on the military, perhaps because of widespread distrust of his credentials on security in the military and among the public.

Despite its often frantic engagement on counterterrorism issues, the Clinton administra tion suffered from an unwillingness to place counterterrorism in the context of overall U.S. foreign policy. As Pillar (2001) has argued, 'Terrorism is primarily a foreign policy issue, as well as a national security issue' (p. 9). Key decision makers, including the President, Vice President, National Security Advisor, and Attorney General, paid little attention to integrat-ing counterterrorism into relations with such countries as Afghanistan, Pakistan, or Saudi Arabia, or to broader issues such as terrorism fundraising, popular hostility to the United States in the Middle East, or other long-term counterterrorism concerns. The activities of Clarke's Counterterrorism Support Group were often independent of the regular policy and agency meetings related to foreign relations (Coll 2004, p. 407; National Commission 2004). The result was repeated surges in action, but only limited sustained institutional change.

Resources were another issue. Neither administration provided a massive resource boost to key counterterrorism agencies; nor did they ensure that the existing budgets of those agencies were devoted appropriately to counterterrorism. The FBI budget grew consider-ably in the mid-1990s, and so did the CIA's resources for counterterrorism. The FBI, however, spent much of its money on concerns unrelated to al Qaeda (National Commission 2004, pp. 76–77). The CIA also tried to use spending increases to preserve many of its other programs rather than diverting resources to counter al Qaeda.

The White House did not provide clear authorities, particularly with regard to the assas-sination of bin Laden. Directing the CIA to kill him through covert action would have required a significant change in the CIA's rules for covert action, which in general prohibited assassination (Fredman 1997). Not surprisingly for a bureaucracy burned by accusations of 'rogue' behavior in the past, the CIA sought to have its authorities made crystal clear. The White House, on the other hand, preferred to give more general guidance, retaining deni-ability, and the Justice Department wanted to avoid giving the CIA unfettered authority to kill (Coll 2004, pp. 423–24; National Commission 2004). Each institution followed its own political and bureaucratic imperatives, and the result was the worst of all worlds – a dis-juncture between senior policy makers and the operators on the ground. Senior aides to Clinton recall that the President's desire to kill bin Laden and his associates 'was very clear to us early on' (Coll 2004, p. 426). In the absence of clear authority, however, the CIA told its Afghan clients, 'You are to capture him [bin Laden] alive' (Coll 2004, p. 378).[8]

Limits on policy makers

Policy problems often stemmed from legitimate political limits or tradeoffs that made it difficult for senior leaders to focus on al Qaeda. Moreover, even those policy makers most concerned with al Qaeda had to contend with the ignorance, indifference, or conflicting preferences of other political actors. Many of the 'obvious' responses to the rise of al Qaeda only became politically feasible after the carnage of the attacks generated the political will.[9]

Policy makers often had priorities other than counterterrorism. President Clinton, for example, met with Pakistan's Prime Minister Sharif several times in the years before September 11; Pakistan's nuclear program often headed the list of topics to discuss, as did the related problem of an Indo-Pak war over Kargil (Reidel 2002). The problem of Saudi Arabia also proved difficult for policy makers to address. When counterterrorism specialists criticized the kingdom, its defenders in the State Department and the Pentagon responded that other, more vital interests were at stake. As a result, the massive Saudi financial support to radical causes did not receive sufficient attention (Coll 2004, p. 512).[10]

The problems were interrelated, but a clear solution (even in hindsight) was evasive (Posner 2004). Bush administration policy makers saw the al Qaeda problem as tied to the Afghanistan problem, which was in turn tied to Pakistan. Developing a policy toward one required developing a policy toward all – a logical point, but one that slowed down efforts to confront al Qaeda even as threat reporting was increasing (Coll 2004, pp. 559–60; Clarke 2004, p. 232). When pressing both countries, moreover, the United States had few levers. Sanctions already in place because of Pakistan's nuclear programs meant that commercial incentives or threats were not available, as there were no real economic ties. Military-to-military relations had deteriorated as well (Kux 2001, Benjamin & Simon 2002, Griffin 2003). Saudi Arabia, of course, was a key ally on whom the United States depended for many of its vital interests, particularly with regard to Iraq, the Middle East peace process, and oil price stability. Standard forms of military or economic pressure thus were not available and almost certainly would have backfired (Lippman 1994; Gause 1995, 2002).

Dramatic change with regard to homeland defense or going to war against the Taliban was also politically difficult. As the 9/11 Commission contends, 'It is hardest to mount a major effort while a problem still seems minor. Once the danger has fully materialized, evident to all, mobilizing action is easier – but it then may be too late' (National Commission 2004, p. 350). It is striking that no political leaders of either party were calling for a dramatic change with regard to homeland defense, U.S. policy toward Afghanistan or Pakistan, or other tectonic shifts that seem obvious only in hindsight.

Policy makers keenly felt the limits of the possible and thus turned to law enforcement measures because they were feasible and would demonstrate responsiveness to the various attacks. They knew covert action had at best a limited chance of success, even under favorable conditions. Clinton's National Security Advisor Sandy Berger and Secretary of State Madeleine Albright have contended that Congress, the American people, and U.S. allies would have opposed the use of ground forces in Afghanistan against al Qaeda before the September 11 attacks (Albright 2003, p. 375; Coll 2004, p. 408; National Commission 2004, p. 349). Because the military option was apparently off the table, law enforcement remained one of the most important means of fighting terrorism, along with using the CIA and allied intelligence agencies to disrupt activities abroad. The Congressional 9/11 Inquiry found that this reliance was really a default decision rather than a strategic one, with many law enforcement officials themselves seeing their role as an adjunct to other measures such as military action (Hill 2002).

Policy makers also had to balance risk, particularly when using the military. There were several instances when the CIA may have had information on bin Laden's location (or, more meaningfully, his future location), which made him vulnerable to cruise missile strikes. This information, however, usually came from one source whose accuracy was dubious at best. Failure could prove disastrous. The 1998 missile strikes on Afghanistan had lionized bin Laden, and a subsequent miss would further enhance his stature. In addition, if the strike killed any of the women and children at the target site it would further damage America's reputation. Other officials feared that the United States was already being painted as a 'Mad Bomber' because of its attacks in Iraq and Serbia and that the strikes might destabilize Pakistan. One strike was called off in part because it might kill members of the United Arab Emirates royal family who may have been hunting with bin Laden. Even in hindsight, it is hard to judge the right course here. The CIA later found that bin Laden was present at only one of the three supposed sightings (Clarke 2004, pp. 20, 201–2, 422, 448). Had policy makers been risk acceptant, the errant strikes might have elevated bin Laden's status, jeopardized relations with a key ally in the Gulf, and made the United States look foolish and brutal in attacking noncombatants.

The nature of the adversary

Too often, assessments of failure focus on the mistakes of the victim rather than on the skill of the adversary. Most terrorist groups fall into the intelligence category of 'hard targets.' Their members are difficult to identify, their actions difficult to anticipate, and their organizations difficult to infiltrate. Only 50% of terrorist groups survive a year, and only 5% survive a decade; those that endure generally are skilled at minimizing their exposure to government law enforcement and intelligence agencies (Hoffman 2002b, p. 84). Typically, terrorist groups are composed of small cells, where ties of kinship and neighborhood often cement a strong ideological commitment. Frequently, they blend into sympathetic, or often intimidated, local communities that are not willing to cooperate with security services. Much of the stock in trade of standard intelligence analysis, such as imagery analysis, is of little help in counterterrorism.

Even within the rarified world of terrorism, al Qaeda is an exceptionally difficult target to counter. Al Qaeda is also large by the standards of terrorist organizations, and its ties to other radical groups make it even larger. The hard core of terrorists who have sworn loyalty to bin Laden probably numbers in the hundreds, and the organization has helped train and support tens of thousands of insurgents who passed through its camps in Afghanistan. Al Qaeda is also tied to radical groups as far afield as South Africa, the Philippines, Mauritania, Uzbekistan, and dozens of other countries. Globalization has increased the organization's potency, both by helping it unite its operatives and preach its message from the remote confines of Afghanistan and by increasing resentment of the United States (Anonymous 2002, p. 179; Bergen 2002, p. 35; Cronin 2002/2003; Gunaratna 2002, pp. 8, 95; Hoffman 2002a, p. 307).

The survival or collapse of a terrorist group depends on its ability to maintain operational security. Al Qaeda's inner core is extremely sensitive to this issue. For example, the instructions of the 'jihad manual' that al Qaeda has circulated focus on blending in and ensuring that the overall organization is not disrupted. bin Laden himself employed only trusted Arabs as bodyguards and avoided using cell phones (Coll 2004, p. 492). The September 11 plotters also tried, at times unsuccessfully, to preserve operational secrecy.

Al Qaeda has demonstrated an ability to revise its methods and structure in response to setbacks or failures. Its operatives regularly review lessons learned in order to improve the chances of success for future attacks (Hoffman 2002a, p. 307). This gives the organization the ability to recuperate quickly from disaster or successful countermeasures.

Before September 11, al Qaeda had also forged an unprecedented relationship with a state. The organization had an exceptionally close relationship with the Taliban regime, bound by a shared ideology, close friendships, and al Qaeda's provision of manpower and financial support to the regime. The United States' failures to persuade and coerce the Taliban into giving up al Qaeda gave the organization a secure base (Anonymous 2002, Bergen 2002, Burke 2003, Griffin 2003).

For U.S. intelligence and policy makers, the nature of the adversary had tremendous consequences for the resulting failures to stop the attacks. The safe haven in Afghanistan made collection far more difficult and required that the United States remove a regime from power in order to disrupt al Qaeda's activities there. Al Qaeda was also hard to disrupt because of its transnational nature and large size, both of which enabled it to lose a cell or skilled operatives yet continue operations elsewhere. Finally, the organization's professionalism made collection and disruption difficult because, unlike many terrorist groups, it made relatively few mistakes.

Responding to the next failure

When we examine the failures of counterterrorism before September 11, it is clear that no single measure, by itself, would have made America safe. Although this essay breaks down the weaknesses that contributed to al Qaeda's successful attacks on September 11 into several categories, these problems are highly interdependent. A simple change at one level or another would have had profound repercussions, but more comprehensive changes were necessary to tackle the broader danger of al Qaeda.

After September 11, policy makers tried to solve many of these problems. Terrorism, of course, became a top priority for the Bush administration, with the full support of the Congress and the American people. On an institutional level, the military, the CIA, the FBI, and the various agencies involved in homeland security made numerous changes designed to help them better fight al Qaeda. U.S. foreign policy also changed dramatically, with the United States overthrowing the Taliban and making al Qaeda a priority in many of its bilateral relations.

Although these steps have led to considerable progress, new problems have emerged. Support for jihadism has risen, even as al Qaeda as a discrete organization appears under siege. Anti-Americanism in particular is rife (Anonymous 2004, Pillar 2004a). Stopping 'the next 9/11' will require not only avoiding the mistakes that allowed the first attack but also adapting to the changing strategic environment.

Yet we must recognize that when dealing with terrorist organizations in general, and when confronting such a skilled organization as al Qaeda in particular, some attacks will inevitably succeed. Indeed, more than three years after the attacks, warnings that another catastrophic strike is imminent remain constant. Policy makers thus must focus not only on preventing the next attack but on ensuring the proper response should an attack nevertheless occur. This effort includes consequence management, making sure that hospitals, fire fighters, and other emergency personnel have the proper procedures, training, and resources. Just as important, however, is expectations management. Terrorists 'win' through the psychological damage they spread, not through the physical carnage they inflict (Hoffman 1998). Leaders who dampen rather than feed this panic will do far more to defeat terrorists than would any particular covert-action measure or military strike.

Acknowledgments

I thank Andrew Amunsen, David Edelstein, Lynn Eden, and Robert Jervis for their help and comments on earlier versions of this essay.

The *Annual Review of Political Science* is online at http://polisci.annualreviews.org

Notes

1 Levite (1987) defines strategic surprise at length with a different emphasis on the response to warning. In contrast to Betts, he contends that if the policy maker recognizes the problem but does not prepare properly, the resulting crisis is not strategic surprise but unpreparedness (pp. 1–3).

2 Most assessments of strategic surprise, however, focus on surprise in war – traditionally the most important national security concern. Pearl Harbor, the Yom Kippur War, intelligence weaknesses before the two world wars, and the potential of the Soviet Union to conduct a surprise nuclear attack during the Cold War have received particular scrutiny.

3 At times, intelligence agencies may 'successfully' collect the wrong information. In Vietnam, the CIA made methodologically sound estimates of the Viet Cong's order of battle based on information captured from the enemy – information that enemy commanders had distorted in order to deceive their own superiors about how well they were doing. Similarly, Israel's interpretation of 'the Concept' came in part from excellent intelligence on senior Egyptian officials who believed it. Israel, however, failed to recognize that the dismissal of these individuals meant the Concept might not hold (Cohen & Gooch 1991, p. 116; Wirtz 1991).

4 It is always easiest, and most politically rewarding, to blame disaster on the men (and, more rarely, women) at the top. After September 11, a cottage industry of finger-pointing sprang up, with book after book blaming one leader or another. President Clinton, for example, is blamed for obstructing the FBI and the CIA, ignoring opportunities to seize bin Laden from the Sudan, refusing to authorize military force against al Qaeda after numerous attacks, and in general fiddling while al Qaeda plotted to burn down America (Miniter 2003, Bossie 2004). President Bush, of course, did not escape unscathed. Making much of the Bush family's business and personal ties to the Saudi royal family, journalist Craig Unger contends that the September 11 disaster began in the 1970s, when the Saudis began their successful courtship of the Bush family – a courtship that, according to Unger, led the Bush administration to ignore Saudi complicity in the rise of al Qaeda (Unger 2004). However, studies of strategic surprise have shown that almost never is a single leader the real problem (Cohen & Gooch 1991).

5 Ironically, with regard to Iraq, intelligence analysts and policy makers are accused of having their imaginations run away with them. Analysts and policy makers did not sufficiently scrutinize many facts about Iraq's programs, and they even extrapolated on them with little reason, all to support the idea that Iraq had a massive but concealed weapons of mass destruction program. I thank Robert Jervis for pointing out this contrast.

6 Even today, prioritizing terrorism is exceptionally difficult because its lethality is quite low although its psychological impact is high. The number of deaths from terrorism is minuscule compared to other sources of death, such as traffic accidents, heart disease, and cancer. As John Mueller (unpublished manuscript) notes, 'Even with the September 11 attacks included in the count, the number of Americans killed by international terrorism since the late 1960s . . . is about the same as the number killed over the same period by lightning – or by accident-causing deer or by severe allergic reaction to peanuts' (p. 1).

7 The emphasis on the 'super spy,' however, may be misguided. Although many critics of the CIA grouse that it lacks individuals who can directly penetrate an organization like al Qaeda, such an expectation ignores how the terrorist organization itself vets candidates, preserves operational security, and otherwise screens for penetration. Indeed, as Pillar (2004b) contends, 'Terrorist operations that are funded on one continent, planned on another continent, and carried out on a third by perpetrators of multiple nationalities (as was true of the attacks of September 11) are unlikely to reveal their entire shape to even the most skilled local collection effort. Living where the water is bad, by itself, is apt to yield more stomach ailments than insights about terrorism – insights that are just as likely to be gleaned in the papers being pushed at Langley' (pp. 128–29).

8 This debate took on an aspect of unreality, as both policy makers and CIA operatives knew that their Afghan agents would probably disregard any instructions to exercise restraint. Afghans were not used to 'any culture of nitpicking lawyers' (Coll 2004, p. 378), and both the White House and the CIA believed they would just shoot everyone in an attempt to 'capture' bin Laden. Moreover, the CIA lacked the information on bin Laden's location that was necessary to make an assassination probable.

9 This essay does not address the important issue of whether U.S. foreign policy contributed to the rise of al Qaeda by fomenting anger around the world. Chomsky, for example, contends that U.S. support for the *mujahedin* in Afghanistan, U.S. support for Israeli atrocities, and U.S. involvement in oppression in general led to the September 11 attacks (Chomsky 2001). Nor does the essay address policy toward the 'root causes' of terrorism. Policy makers of all stripes are often chided for not attacking the root causes of terrorism and the grievances that make terrorists sympathetic – a seemingly obvious recommendation (Hitz 2004, p. 160). Unfortunately, neither policy makers nor academics know what the root causes are. Poverty, oppression, and other ills are often mentioned, but there seems little indication that such problems are motivating al Qaeda. Indeed, when radical jihadist organizations affiliated with al Qaeda are included, the number of motivations becomes staggering (Jervis 2002, pp. 41–42; Kepel 2002; Pillar 2004a, p. 31). In my judgment, the effort to find root causes ignores much of the logic of terrorism – that it is a tactic used by people who feel they have few other means for achieving their ends.

10 An ignorance of events in Pakistan and Saudi Arabia made it even more difficult to craft an effective policy. Because shaping internal politics in these countries was not a policy priority, little intelligence was collected. For many years, the United States did not see Islamic extremism in Pakistan as an independent policy problem. The CIA in the 1980s focused on gathering information about the Afghan insurgency and the nuclear program, not on Pakistani politics (Coll 2004, p. 57). Similarly, U.S. intelligence on developments in Saudi Arabia was always limited.

Literature cited

Albright M. 2003. *Madam Secretary*. New York: Miramax Books

Allison G. 1971. *Essence of Decision*. Boston: Little Brown

Anonymous. 2002. *Through Our Enemies' Eyes: Osama bin Laden, Radical Islam, and the Future of America*. Washington, DC: Brassey's

Anonymous. 2004. *Imperial Hubris: Why the West is Losing the War on Terror*. Washington, DC: Brassey's

Bamford J. 2004. *A Pretext for War: 9/11, Iraq, and the Abuse of America's Intelligence Agencies*. New York: Doubleday

Bell JB. 1994. The armed struggle and underground intelligence: an overview. *Stud. Confl. Terrorism* 17:115–50

Benjamin D, Simon S. 2002. *The Age of Sacred Terror*. New York: Random House

Bergen PL. 2002. *Holy War, Inc.: Inside the Secret World of Osama bin Laden*. New York: Simon & Schuster

Betts R. 1978. Analysis, war, and decision: why intelligence failures are inevitable. *World Polit.* 21:61–89

Betts R. 1982. *Surprise Attack: Lessons for Defense Planning*. Washington, DC: Brookings Inst.

Blackwill RD, Davis J. 2004. A policymaker's perspective on intelligence analysis. See Johnson & Wirtz 2004, pp. 112–19

Bossie DN. 2004. *Intelligence Failure: How Clinton's National Security Policy Set the Stage for 9/11*. Nashville, TN: WND Books

Burke J. 2003. *Al-Qaeda: Casting a Shadow of Terror*. New York: I.B. Tauris

Byman D. 2003. Al Qaeda as an adversary: Do we understand the enemy? *World Polit.* 56(1):139–63

Chan S. 1979. The intelligence of stupidity: understanding failures in strategic warning. *Am. Polit. Sci. Rev.* 73(1):171–80

Chomsky N. 2001. *9–11*. New York: Seven Stories

Clarke R. 2004. *Against All Enemies*. New York: Free

Clinton WJ. 2004. *My Life*. New York: Knopf

Cohen EA, Gooch J. 1991. *Military Misfortunes: The Anatomy of Failure in War*. New York: Vintage

Coll S. 2004. *Ghost Wars: The Secret History of the CIA, Afghanistan, and bin Laden, from the Soviet Invasion to September 10, 2001*. New York: Penguin

Cook SDN, Yanow D. 1996. Culture and organizational learning. In *Organizational Learning*, ed. MD Cohen, LS Sproull, pp. 430–59. London: Sage

Crenshaw M. 2002. The logic of terrorism: terrorist behavior as a product of strategic choice. In *Terrorism and Counterterrorism: Understanding the New Security Environment*, ed. RD Howard, RL Sawyer, pp. 55–67. Guilford, CT: McGraw Hill

Cronin AK. 2002/2003. Behind the curve: globalization and international terrorism. *Int. Sec.* 27(3):30–58

Eden L. 2004. *Whole World on Fire: Organizations, Knowledge, & Nuclear Weapons Devastation*. Ithaca, NY: Cornell Univ. Press

Findings of the Final Report of the Senate Select Committee on Intelligence and the House Permanent Select Committee on Intelligence Joint Inquiry into the Terrorist Attacks of September 11, 2001. December 10, 2002. U.S. Senate Select Committee on Intelligence and U.S. House Permanent Select Committee on Intelligence. http://intelligence.senate.gov/findings.pdf

Fredman J. 1997. Covert action, loss of life, and the prohibition on assassination. *Stud. Intel.* 15–25

Freeh LJ. 2001. *Statement for the Record on the Threat of Terrorism to the United States*. U.S. Senate Committees on Appropriations, Armed Services, and Select Committee on Intelligence (May 10)

Gause FG III. 1995. *Oil Monarchies*. New York: Counc. For. Relat. Press

Gause FG III. 2002. Be careful what you wish for: the future of U.S.-Saudi relations. *World Polit. J.* Spring:37–50

Gerecht RM. 2001. The counterterrorist myth. *Atlantic Monthly* July/August. http://www.theatlantic.com/cgi-bin/send.cgi?page=http%A//www.theatlnatic.com/issues/. Downloaded July 19, 2004

Gertz B. 2003. *Breakdown: How America's Intelligence Failures Led to September 11*. New York: Plume

Goodson LP. 2001. *Afghanistan's Endless War: State Failure, Regional Politics, and the Rise of the Taliban*. Seattle, WA: Univ. Washington Press

Griffin M. 2003. *Reaping the Whirlwind: Afghanistan, Al Qa'ida and the Holy War*. Sterling, VA: Pluto

Gunaratna R. 2002. *Inside Al Qaeda*. New York: Columbia Univ. Press

Halperin M. 1974. *Bureaucratic Politics and Foreign Policy*. Washington, DC: Brookings Inst.

Herman M. 2004. Intelligence and national action. See Johnson & Wirtz 2004, pp. 224–33

Herwig HH. 1998. Innovation ignored: the submarine problem – Germany, Britain, and the United States, 1919–1939. In *Military Innovation in the Interwar Period*, ed. W Murray, AR Millet, pp. 227–64. New York: Cambridge Univ. Press

Hill E. 2002. *Joint Inquiry Staff Statement. Hearing on the Intelligence Community's Response to Past Terrorist Attacks Against the United States from February 1993 to September 2001*. http://intelligence.senate. gov

Hitz FP. 2004. Unleashing the rogue elephant: September 11 and letting the CIA be the CIA. See Johnson & Wirtz 2004, pp. 390–96

Hoffman B. 1998. *Inside Terrorism*. New York: Columbia Univ. Press

Hoffman B. 2002a. Rethinking terrorism and counterterrorism since 9/11. *Stud. Confl. Terrorism* 25:303–16

Hoffman B. 2002b. The modern terrorist mindset. In *Terrorism and Counterterrorism: Understanding the New Security Environment*, ed. RD Howard, RL Sawyer, pp. 75–95. Guilford, CT: McGraw Hill

Hopple GW. 1984. Intelligence and warning: implications and lessons of the Falkland Islands War. *World Polit.* 36(3):339–61

Howell WG. 2003. *Power without Persuasion: The Politics of Direct Presidential Action*. Princeton, NJ: Princeton Univ. Press

Janis I. 1972. *Victims of Groupthink*. Boston: Houghton Mifflin

Jervis R. 1976. *Perception and Misperception in International Politics*. Princeton, NJ: Princeton Univ. Press

Jervis R. 2002. An interim assessment of September 11: What has changed and what has not? *Polit. Sci. Q.* 117(1): 37–54

Johnson L. 1996. *Secret Agencies: U.S. Intelligence in a Hostile World*. New Haven, CT: Yale Univ. Press

Johnson L. 2004. Covert action and accountability: decision-making for America's secret foreign policy. See Johnson & Wirtz 2004, pp. 370–89

Johnson LK, Wirtz JJ. 2004. *Strategic Intelligence: Windows Into a Secret World.* Los Angeles: Roxbury

Kepel G. 2002. *Jihad: The Trail of Political Islam,* transl. AF Roberts (from French). Cambridge, MA: Harvard Univ. Press

Kessler R. 2002. *Bureau: The Secret History of the FBI.* New York: St. Martin's

Kux D. 2001. *The United States and Pakistan, 1947–2000: Disenchanted Allies.* Baltimore, MD: Johns Hopkins Univ. Press

Levite A. 1987. *Intelligence and Strategic Surprises.* New York: Columbia Univ. Press

Lian B, Oneal J. 1993. Presidents, the use of military force, and public opinion. *J. Confl. Resolut.* 37(2):277–300

Lippman TW. 1994. *Inside the Mirage: America's Fragile Partnership with Saudi Arabia.* Boulder, CO: Westview

May E. 2001. *Strange Victory: Hitler's Conquest of France.* New York: Hill & Wang

May ER, ed. 1986. *Knowing One's Enemies: Intelligence Assessment before the Two World Wars.* Princeton, NJ: Princeton Univ. Press

McCormick GH, Owen G. 2000. Security and coordination in a clandestine organization. *Math. Comput. Model.* 31:175–92

Miller J. 2002. *The Cell: Inside the 9/11 Plot and Why the FBI and the CIA Failed to Stop It.* New York: Hyperion

Miniter R. 2003. *Losing Bin Laden: How Bill Clinton's Failures Unleashed Global Terror.* Washington, DC: Regnery

National Commission on Terrorist Attacks Upon the United States. 2004. *The 9/11 Commission Report: Final Report of the National Commission on Terrorist Attacks Upon the United States.* New York: W.W. Norton

Neustadt RE. 1991. *Presidential Power and Modern Presidents: The Politics of Leadership from Roosevelt to Reagan.* New York: Free

Perrow C. 1999. *Normal Accidents: Living with High-Risk Technologies.* Princeton, NJ: Princeton Univ. Press

Pfiffner JP. 2004. *The Modern Presidency.* Lexington, KY: Wadsworth

Pillar P. 2001. *Terrorism and U.S. Foreign Policy.* Washington, DC: Brookings Inst.

Pillar P. 2004a. Counterterrorism after Al-Qaeda. *Washington Q.* 27(3):101–13

Pillar P. 2004b. Intelligence. In *Attacking Terrorism: Elements of a Grand Strategy,* ed. AK Croning, JM Ludes, pp. 115–39. Washington, DC: Georgetown Univ. Press

Posner GL. 2003. *Why America Slept: The Failure to Prevent 9/11.* New Home: Random House

Posner R. 2004. The 9/11 report: a dissent. *N.Y. Times Book Rev.* Aug. 29. http://www.nytimes.com/2004/08/29/books/review/29postnerl.html?

Reidel B. 2002. *American diplomacy and the 1999 Kargil summit at Blair House.* Cent. Advanced Study of India. http://www.sas/upenn.edu/casi/reprots/RiedelPaper051302.htm

Report of a Committee of Privy Counsellors. 2004. *Review of Intelligence on Weapons of Mass Destruction.* London: Stationery Off.

Report of the Joint Inquiry Into Intelligence Community Activities before and after the Terrorist Attacks of September 11, 2001. 2002. Washington, DC: U.S. Gov. Printing Off.

Scowcroft B. 1996. *Statement before the Permanent Select Committee on Intelligence, House of Representatives.* Reprinted in *IC21: The Intelligence Community in the 21st Century.* Washington, DC: U.S. Gov. Printing Off.

Shulsky A. 2002. *Silent Warfare: Understanding the World of Intelligence.* Washington, DC: Brassey's

Snook SA. 2000. *Friendly Fire: The Accidental Shootdown of U.S. Black Hawks Over Northern Iraq.* Princeton, NJ: Princeton Univ. Press

Stein JG. 1982. Military deception, strategic surprise, and conventional deterrence: a political analysis of Egypt and Israel, 1971–73. *J. Strat. Stud.* 5(1):94–121

Tenet G. 2001. *Worldwide Threat 2001: National Security in a Changing World. Statement before the U.S. Senate Select Committee on Intelligence.* http://www.cia.gov/cia/ public affairs/speeches/2001/UNCLASWW T 02072001.html

Unger C. 2004. *House of Bush, House of Saud: The Secret Relationship between the World's Two Most Powerful Dynasties*. New York: Scribner

U.S. Senate Select Committee on Intelligence. 2004. *Report of the Senate Select Committee on Intelligence on the U.S. Intelligence Community's Prewar Intelligence Assessments on Iraq*. Washington, DC: U.S. Gov. Printing Off.

Walsh E. 2001. Louis Freeh's last case. *New Yorker* May 14. http://newyorker.com/archive/content/?010924fr archive06

Watson D. 2002. *Testimony before the House and Senate Intelligence Committees*. http://intelligence.senate.gov/0209hrg/020926/watson.pdf

Wirtz J. 1991. Intelligence to please? The order of battle controversy during the Vietnam War. *Polit. Sci. Q.* 106(2):239–63

Wohlstetter R. 1962. *Pearl Harbor: Warning and Decision*. Stanford, CA: Stanford Univ. Press

Woodward B. 2002. *Bush at War*. New York: Simon & Schuster

Reprinted with permission from Daniel Byman, 'Strategic Surprise And The September 11 Attacks', *Annual Review of Political Science* 8 (2005) pp.145–170.

12 Deja Vu?

Comparing Pearl Harbor and September 11

James J. Wirtz

This essay argues that it is hardly surprising that parallels exist between the attack on Pearl Harbor and the terrorist attacks of September 11 because both events are examples of a more common strategic phenomenon – the surprise attack. Although they occurred half a century apart and evolved from different contexts, common pattern can be discerned in the events leading up to surprise and its consequences. Exploring these similarities can help cast the tragedy of September 11 in a broader context, an important initial step in reducing the likelihood of mass-casualty terrorism.

During my first trip to Hawaii, I made my way to a place considered sacred by most US citizens, the USS Arizona memorial at Pearl Harbor. Survivors often greet visitors to the memorial, answering questions and retelling their memories of the day that the Japanese attacked the US Pacific Fleet. When it came my turn, I asked what the weather was like that fateful morning. The answer was 'like today.' A few puffy clouds dotted the blue Hawaiian skies, a light breeze pushed ripples across the turquoise water of the harbor, stirring the warm tropical air to create one of the most idyllic anchorages on earth. September 11 also dawned clear and blue over New York City, the kind of late summer day that highlights perfectly the United States' front door, the spectacular edifice of promise and prosperity that is lower Manhattan. Given the setting, it is no wonder that the events of both Pearl Harbor and September 11 came as a complete shock to eyewitnesses. Neither could have happened on a more pleasant morning. We now know, however, that initial eyewitness interpretations of both of these surprise attacks, as bolts out of the blue, were incorrect. Indications of what was about to happen were available before the Japanese attack on Pearl Harbor. In fact, one of the accepted tenets of the literature on surprise attacks is that in all cases of so-called intelligence failure, accurate information concerning what is about to transpire can be found in the intelligence system after the fact. It is thus to be expected that revelations will continue about the signals that were in the intelligence pipeline prior to the terrorist attacks of September 11. And as in the aftermath of Pearl Harbor, the US government will hold a series of investigations to discover how organizational shortcomings or mistakes made by specific officials were responsible for the intelligence failure that paved the way for the destruction of the World Trade Center and the attack on the Pentagon.

It is not surprising that similarities exist between the attack on Pearl Harbor and the terrorist attacks of September 11 because both events are examples of a more general international phenomenon – the surprise attack. Despite the fact that they occurred over 50 years apart and involve different kinds of international actors with highly different motivations, a pattern exists in the events leading up to surprise and its consequences. Exploring these similarities can help cast the tragedy of September 11 in a broader context, an important initial step in reducing the likelihood of mass-casualty terrorism in the future.

Warning signs

Although Pearl Harbor and the September 11 attacks are sometimes depicted as totally unanticipated events, both incidents were preceded by clear indications that the United States faced an imminent threat. Prior to Pearl Harbor, US-Japanese relations had reached a nadir. By the summer of 1941, the administration of US President Franklin Roosevelt had placed economic sanctions on the Japanese to force them to end their war against China. These sanctions were the proximate cause of the Japanese attack. Japanese officials believed that the US embargo against them would ruin their economy, while destruction of the US fleet would provide them with some maneuvering room. They intended to quickly seize resource-rich lands in the Far East, fortify their newly conquered lands, and then reach some sort of negotiated settlement with the United States.

The Roosevelt administration recognized that it faced a crisis with Japan, although senior officials in Washington did not realize that Oahu was in danger until it was too late. In their minds, it made no sense for the Japanese to attack the United States because they simply lacked the economic resources or military capability to defeat the US military in a long war. In an ironic twist, the Roosevelt administration was ultimately proven correct in this estimate. The Japanese attack on Pearl Harbor eliminated the possibility of US acquiescence to the creation of a Japanese empire in the Pacific as well as the eventual peace arrangement Japan hoped to achieve.

The situation that faced the United States was even more clear cut, if not quite as grave, prior to September 11. Various studies and commissions (such as the government's Gilmore commission) described the ongoing struggle against terrorism and predicted that a significant terrorist attack on the continental United States was a virtual certainty. The United States was actually engaged in a war with Al Qaeda, an international network of terrorist groups, throughout the 1990s. Al Qaeda may have been loosely linked to the militias that battled US Ranger units in Somalia in 1993. Al Qaeda also was involved in the bombing of the office of the program manager for the Saudi Arabian National Guard in Riyadh in November 1995 and in the attack on the Khobar Towers complex in Dahran in July 1996.

These attacks on US interests in 1995 and 1996 changed the way forward deployed US forces operated within the Arabian Peninsula. New 'force protection' regulations were promulgated to protect US military personnel, requiring commanders to observe stringent requirements to ensure their safety. In Saudi Arabia, US operational units were consolidated at Prince Sultan Air Base and advisory components were moved to Eskan Village, a housing complex south of Riyadh. Intelligence collection efforts also concentrated on the new threat, providing forces throughout the region with improved tactical and operational warning. At times, US forces were placed at 'Threatcon Delta' in expectation of an immediate attack. The hardening of the 'target' on the Arabian Peninsula forced Al Qaeda to look for vulnerabilities elsewhere.

Any lingering doubts about the ongoing threat were dispelled by Al Qaeda's bombing of the US embassies in Kenya and Tanzania in August 1998 and the attack against the USS Cole in October 2000. The United States even returned fire following the 1998 embassy attacks by launching cruise missile strikes against suspected terrorist training camps in Afghanistan and a pharmaceutical plant in Sudan that was believed to have links to

Al Qaeda. US government agencies had a clear idea that Osama bin Laden was committed to attacking US interests globally. Bin Laden's 1998 *fatwa* represented a declaration of war on the United States and called upon supporters to kill US officials, soldiers, and civilians everywhere around the world. This assessment of bin Laden's intentions was reflected in a variety of publicly available sources. The US Congressional Research Service published a compelling warning about bin Laden's campaign of terror entitled 'Terrorism: Near Eastern Groups and State Sponsors' on September 10, 2001. A compelling description of bin Laden's alliance with the Taliban and his political agenda was even published in *Foreign Affairs* in 1999.

Pearl Harbor and the terrorist attacks on September 11 were not bolts out of the blue. But because they were generally perceived to have occurred without warning, they both have changed attitudes and produced policies that have reduced the likelihood and consequences of surprise attack. Pearl Harbor focused strategists' attention on the need to avoid the consequences of surprise attack, especially when it came to US nuclear deterrent threats. The fear of a surprise attack made the nuclear balance of terror appear delicate. As a result, enormous efforts were undertaken to guarantee that US strategic forces could survive a Soviet nuclear attack and still be able to assure destruction of the Soviet Union. Today, the administration of US President George Bush is trying to minimize the effects of a potential terrorist incident by improving homeland defenses and consequence management, spending US$35 billion on homeland defense programs. US military forces also are pre-empting attacks by taking the battle to the terrorists and by training foreign militaries to deal with the threat.

Structural vulnerabilities

Despite common misperceptions, it was the US Army, and not the US Navy, that was responsible for the defense of Pearl Harbor in December 1941. This division of responsibilities helped to create the conditions for surprise. When Washington issued a war warning to its forces in Hawaii, Army officers took steps to safeguard against sabotage, locking up ammunition and concentrating aircraft on the center of runways so they could be more easily guarded. In contrast, Navy officers thought that the war warning would prompt a vigorous effort on the part of the Army to use long-range aircraft to patrol the waters around Oahu. Army officers thought that Naval intelligence had been keeping tabs on the whereabouts of the Japanese fleet; they did not realize that Navy analysts had lost track of Japanese aircraft carriers in the weeks leading up to Pearl Harbor. Further, the Army and Navy staffs on Oahu never confirmed their expectations about what each other was doing to safeguard the islands from attack. Even perfect liaison between the services, however, might not have been enough to prevent disaster because no mechanism existed to collect and disseminate all-source intelligence to the operational commanders who could put it to good use. There is little evidence to suggest that the Japanese knew about these organizational weaknesses in Hawaii's defenses, but organizational shortcomings facilitated their effort to catch the US fleet unprepared.

Al Qaeda might have understood the organizational weakness that reduced the likelihood that its operatives would be detected before they struck. While there was a unified command structure in the Persian Gulf to address the local terrorist threat, organizational responsibilities in the US government largely diverged at the water's edge. The Department of Defense and the Central Intelligence Agency (CIA) focus on foreign threats and intelligence collection, while the Federal Bureau of Investigation focuses on internal security and investigating crime. Local and State police forces operate in their own jurisdictions and US airport security, until recently, was largely the responsibility of private firms. Additionally, the defin-ition of terrorism was not without organizational consequences. Was it a form of war or a type of natural disaster that would fall under the jurisdiction of the Federal Emergency Management Agency? Was it a homegrown threat involving high explosives (e.g. the destruc-tion of the Alfred P. Murrah Federal Building in April 1995) or a new type of threat involving weapons of mass destruction (e.g. the Aum Shinrikyo attack on the Tokyo subway in March 1995)? And as this debate about the likelihood and form of mass-casualty terrorism unfolded in the years leading up to September 11, front-line government agencies in the war against domestic terrorism were allowed to atrophy. US Customs and Immi-gration agents now find themselves unprepared for their new role in combating domestic terrorism.

US citizens tend to focus on technological solutions to problems, often forgetting that organization shapes the ability to respond to emerging challenges. Strong organization – the ability to orchestrate the efforts of a vast array of individuals and bureaucratic actors – is imperative if the United States is to effectively spend its resources in the war on terrorism. Despite inter-service rivalry and bureaucratic preferences, the organizational shortcomings that existed prior to Pearl Harbor were relatively easy to minimize compared to the bureau-cratic and legal challenge created by today's war. After Pearl Harbor, clearer lines of responsibility were drawn between the services. By contrast, legal questions and scores of jurisdictional issues presently complicate official efforts to create the governmental structures and relationships needed to generate a comprehensive response to terrorism.

Technological surprise

The ability to utilize technology creatively played an important role in both the Japanese attack on Pearl Harbor and the terrorist attacks of September 11. When historians write about technical surprise, they focus on the unexpected introduction of hardware or weapons that cannot be quickly countered by an opponent. The attack on Pearl Harbor, for example, was made possible when the Japanese developed an aerial torpedo that could function in the shallow waters of Pearl Harbor. But the Japanese success at Pearl Harbor was made possible by a broader integration of technology with a new concept of operations that brought the full capability of carrier aviation to bear in a decisive way. This demonstration of professional military prowess combined new technology, tactics, and strategy in a surprisingly devastating way. Carrier aviation itself was not a secret, but the Japanese exploited this new technology with so much daring and skill that it was impossible even for those who understood the threat posed by Japan to recognize that they faced such grave and immediate danger.

Al Qaeda also achieved a technological surprise on September 11. Again, there was nothing particularly novel about the use of aircraft to conduct a suicide mission – ironically it was the Japanese who introduced the kamikaze during the October 1944 US invasion of the Philippines. But by using a host of modern technologies produced by the information revolu-tion and globalization, Al Qaeda operatives were able to plan, orchestrate, and execute a major 'special operations' attack without the hardware, training, or infrastructure generally associated with conducting a precision strike at intercontinental ranges. Al Qaeda used the Internet, satellite telephones, and cell phones to coordinate their international operations, especially to communicate with operatives in the United States. They also used the inter-national banking system to fund cells in the United States without drawing undue attention. Al Qaeda operatives rode the rails of the information revolution, harnessing international communication and financial networks to carry out their nefarious scheme.

In both instances of surprise, the opponent used technology in an innovative way to launch a devastating over-the-horizon attack. And prior to both attacks, the technology employed was actually well known to US officials and officers. Indeed, in the case of the September 11 attacks, US citizens, as the major beneficiaries and supporters of globalization, were probably the world's leading experts when it came to harnessing new instruments of communication and commerce. However, they lacked a keen awareness of the desperation and creativity of their enemies, leading them to underestimate opponents' willingness to find ways to circumvent defenses to gain the element of surprise.

The interest-threat mismatch

During the 1990s, the debate about the United States' role in world affairs revolved around concerns about the interest-threat mismatch. In the aftermath of the Cold War, low-level, nagging threats – ethnic violence, terrorism, or just instability and unrest – permeated parts of the world. Some observers suggested that these threats had little effect on US national interests. People who suggested that the United States become involved in places like Rwanda or even Kosovo, for instance, were really thinking with their hearts and not their heads. The issue was not whether the United States should work to stop genocide. Instead, the concern was that intervention meant an open-ended US commitment to social engineering that realistically had little prospect of success. Intervention was an option available to the United States, but it was not without opportunity costs and significant risks. Intervening in far away places like Afghanistan to stop Taliban human rights abuses or to deny Al Qaeda a secure base of operations was never even considered. Bush ran his 2000 presidential campaign on reducing the United States' international 'over-commitments' abroad. The United States' 'casualty aversion' seemed to be a major factor in limiting US intervention to stop ethnic violence and other forms of carnage. Anti-democratic and anti-market forces, specifically a fundamentalist backlash against the way globalization spreads Western culture, was not deemed of sufficient strength to pose a significant security threat.

In the late 1930s, the US intelligence community also perceived a mismatch between US interests and the desirability of responding to the threats that were emerging across the globe. This perception is difficult to explain in hindsight, given the genocidal and aggressive policies of the Nazi regime and Japan's imperial ambitions. On the eve of Pearl Harbor, the Nazis had overrun virtually all of Europe and Japan had been engaged in a war in China for nearly a decade. Still, the United States seemed to believe that they could somehow escape the wave of fascism and violence that was sweeping the globe.

Both Al Qaeda and Imperial Japan attacked the United States in an effort to limit US influence and to stop the spread of free markets, democracy, and liberal ideas into the Middle East and East Asia. Japan believed that US officials would not have the will to challenge their initiatives in Asia; Japanese leaders felt US 'casualty aversion' would lead to a negotiated settlement in Asia. Bin Laden apparently expected a relatively ineffectual US military response (again driven by US concerns about casualties) that would in the end spark a revolution in moderate Arab regimes, if not a full blown clash of civilizations between Islam and the West. Bin Laden and the Japanese, however, underestimated how surprise attacks would alter the political balance within the United States and the way US citizens perceived foreign threats. Both also failed to recognize how quickly US military power could be brought to bear against them.

Aftershock

Many more points of comparison are possible between Pearl Harbor and September 11. At Pearl Harbor, the US military stopped about 8 percent of the attacking force from either reaching its target or returning home. On September 11, airline passengers actually stopped 25 percent of the attacking force from reaching its target, saving a US landmark from severe damage or total destruction. US intelligence analysts issued a war warning before the Pearl Harbor attack, and the US military managed to engage the enemy. On September 11, intelligence reports of possible terrorist threats had not yet been translated into a compelling warning, and the US military failed to interfere with Al Qaeda's suicide mission.

It also is too early to make a full comparison between the two events. Japan's experience after Pearl Harbor was so unpleasant that the war inoculated Japan's leaders and public alike against aggression and armed conflict. By contrast, Al Qaeda faces extermination. Pearl Harbor had a generation effect on young people in the United States, serving as a warning that the possibility of aggression and surprise can never be eliminated in international relations. However, it remains unclear what lessons the young will draw from witnessing the destruction of the World Trade Center on live television.

Pearl Harbor and September 11 are similar in at least one more important respect. Both surprise attacks renewed US interest in world affairs, creating a popular conviction that suffering and oppression in distant places can only be ignored at the expense of US security. Both attacks halted a creeping isolationism and both prompted changes in US government and a renewed commitment to the defense of democracy and economic liberty. The origins of the Department of Defense, the CIA, and a host of intelligence agencies and programs can be tied to that fateful morning over 60 years ago. One can only wonder how the United States will change as the effects of September 11 begin to ripple across governmental institutions and popular culture. We can hope that these changes will not only reduce US vulnerability to mass-casualty terrorist attacks but also eliminate the incentives for others to carry out terrorist acts in the future.

Reprinted with permission from James J. Wirtz, 'Deja Vu? Comparing Pearl Harbor and September 11', *Harvard International Review* 24/3 (2002) pp.73–77.

INTELLIGENCE AND 9/11

Further reading: Books and reports

Richard A. Clarke, *Against All Enemies: inside America's War on Terror* (NY: Free Press 2004), pp.205–47.

Der Spiegel, *Inside 9–11: What Really Happened* (NY: St Martin's 2002).

Y. Fouda and N. Fielding, *Masterminds of Terror: The Truth Behind the Most Devastating Attack the World Has Ever Seen* (NY: Arcade Publishing 2004).

Bill Gertz, *Breakdown: How America's Intelligence Failures Led to September 11.* (NY: Plume 2003).

Seymour Hersh, *Chain of Command: The Road from 9/11 to Abu Ghraib* (NY: HarperCollins 2003).

Loch Johnson & James Wirtz (eds.), *Intelligence and National Security: The Secret World of Spies* (NY: Oxford University Press, 2nd ed 2007).

Mark Lowenthal, *Intelligence: From Secrets to Policy* (Washington DC: CQ Press, 3rd ed 2006).

J. Miller, *The Cell: Inside the 9/11 Plot and Why the FBI and the CIA Failed to Stop It* (NY: Hyperion 2002).

G.L. Posner, *Why America Slept: The Failure to Prevent 9/11*, (NY: Random House, 2003).

Richard Posner, *Preventing Surprise Attacks: Intelligence Reform in the Wake of 9/11*, (NY: Rowan and Littlefield 2005).

Jennifer E. Sims, and Burton L. Gerber, (eds.) *Transforming U.S. Intelligence* (Washington, DC: Georgetown University Press 2005).

S. Strasser (ed.), *The 9/11 Investigations: Staff Reports of the 9/11 Commission* (NY: Public Affairs Press 2004).

A. Zegart, *Spying Blind: The CIA, the FBI, and the Origins of 9/11* (Princeton: Princeton University Press 2007)

Further reading: Essays and articles

Frederic L. Borch, 'Comparing Pearl Harbor and "9/11": Intelligence Failure? American Unpreparedness? Military Responsibility?' *The Journal of Military History* 67/3 (2003) pp.845–860.

Hans DE Bruijn, 'One fight, one team: The 9/11 Commission Report on Intelligence, Fragmentation and Information', *Public Administration* 84/2 (2006) pp.267–87.

Ted Galen Carpenter, 'Missed Opportunities: The 9/11 Commission Report and US Foreign Policy', *Mediterranean Quarterly* 16/1 (2005) pp.52–61.

Steve Clarke, 'Conspiracy Theories and the Internet: Controlled Demolition and Arrested Development', *Episteme: A Journal of Social Epistemology* 4/2 (2007) pp.167–180.

Erik J. Dahl, 'Warning of Terror: Explaining the Failure of Intelligence Against Terrorism', *Journal of Strategic Studies* 28/1 (2005) pp.31–55.

Richard A. Falkenrath, 'The 9/11 Commission Report', *International Security* 29/3, (2004–5) pp.170–190 (see also the animated correspondence that followed).

Helen Fessenden 'The Limits of Intelligence Reform', *Foreign Affairs* 84/6 (2005) pp.106–120.

R.A. Goldberg, 'Who Profited From the Crime? Intelligence Failure, Conspiracy Theories and the Case of September 11', Ch.6. in LV Scott and PD Jackson (eds.) *Understanding Intelligence in the 21ˢᵗ Century Journeys in Shadows* (London: Routledge, 2004) pp.249–61.

MA Goodman, '9/11: The Failure of Strategic Intelligence', *Intelligence and National Security* 18/4 (2003) pp.59–71.

Stéphane Lefebvre,. 'A Look at Intelligence Analysis.' *International Journal of Intelligence and Counter-intelligence* 17/2 (2004) pp.231–264.

Charles F. Parker & Eric K. Stern 'Blindsided? September 11 and the Origins of Strategic Surprise', *Political Psychology* 23/3 (2002) pp.601–630.

J Wirtz, 'Responding To Surprise', [compares responses to Pearl Habor and 9/11] *Annual Review of Political Science* 9 (2006) pp.45–65.

James J. Wirtz, 'Deja Vu? Comparing Pearl Harbor and September 11', *Harvard International Review* (Fall 2002) pp.73–77.

Amy B Zegart, 'September 11 and the Adaption Failure of US Intelligence Agencies,' *International Security* 29/4 (2005) pp.78–111.

Amy B. Zegart, 'An Empirical Analysis of Failed: Intelligence Reforms Before September 11,' *Political Science Quarterly* 121/1 (2006) pp.33–60.

Essay and seminar questions

- Was 9/11 intelligence failure one of the collection, analysis or response to intelligence?
- What were the lessons of 9/11 for American intelligence?
- 'The intelligence failures that led to 9/11 were long-term and lay in the decade following the end of the Cold War.' Discuss.
- How far do you agree with Amy Zegart's assertion that the intelligence failures that resulted in 9/11 are about the failure of organizations to adapt?
- A second Pearl Harbor? Consider the similarities and differences between 11 September 2001 and 7 December 1941.

13 Reports, politics, and intelligence failures

The case of Iraq

Robert Jervis[1]

The intelligence failure concerning Iraqi weapons of mass destruction (WMD) has been the center of political controversy and official investigations in three countries. This article reviews the Report on the U.S. Intelligence Community's Prewar Intelligence Assessments on Iraq, Senate Select Committee on Intelligence, 7 July 2004, Review of Intelligence on Weapons of Mass Destruction, a Report of a Committee of Privy Councillors to the House of Commons, 14 July 2004 (the Butler Report), Report to the President of the United States, The Commission on the Intelligence Capabilities of the United States Regarding Weapons of Mass Destruction, 31 March 2005. It explores the reasons for their deficiencies and the failure itself. This case and the investigations of it are similar to many previous ones. The investigations are marred by political bias and excessive hindsight. Neither the investigations nor contemporary intelligence on Iraqi WMD followed good social science practices. The comparative method was not utilized, confirmation bias was rampant, alternative hypotheses were not tested, and negative evidence was ignored. Although the opportunities to do better are many, the prospects for adequate reform are dim.

'The trouble with this world is not that people know too little, but that they know so many things that ain't so', Mark Twain.

'If it were a fact, it wouldn't be intelligence,' General Michael Hayden, then head of the National Security Agency, now Deputy Director of National Intelligence, quoted in Bob Woodward, *Plan of Attack* (2004) 132.

'We missed the Soviet decision to put missiles into Cuba because we could not believe that Khrushchev could make such a mistake', Sherman Kent, 'A Crucial Estimate Relived', *Studies in Intelligence*, Spring 1964.

Failures, investigations, organizations, and politics

Failure may be an orphan, but often it is a closely observed one. This is true for the misjudgment of Iraq's programs weapons of mass destruction (WMD), featuring British, Australian, and American post-mortems, with the American intelligence community (IC) going furthest, formally retracting its estimate and conducting public as well as secret analyses of what went so wrong.[2] As interesting as all these studies are, the very failure that occasioned them provides a context that we need to take account of. One review of some of the British reports put it well: 'Inquiries are a continuation of politics by other means, as Clausewitz might have said. In the nature of the case, these inquiries were more political than most. They were steeped in high politics and played for high stakes.'[3] If history is a guide, we should not expect too much. There were four official investigations in the years following Pearl Harbor and while they made public much valuable information, they could not explain what had happened or settle the political debate.[4]

None of this is unique to intelligence organizations. The official commission to investigate the *Challenger* space shuttle disaster (1986) was superficial, with the best work being the independent analysis of its maverick member, Richard Feynman. But it took a decade of research by an outside sociologist, Diane Vaughan, to understand the organizational routines that both made it possible for NASA to operate smoothly and laid the foundations for accident.[5] Furthermore, NASA ignored this analysis, with the result that the same organizational flaws led to the disintegration of *Columbia* years later.

The reaction of the Catholic Church to sexual abuse followed a similar pattern: to protect the organization, wrong-doing was first ignored and then covered up, with short-run benefit to the clergy but at great cost to some parishioners and, eventually, to the institution itself. Universities are no better: they argue that their mission requires that outsiders fund but not police them, and then do little self-examination and self-correction.

Did intelligence matter?

If intelligence services do not stand out in having a hard time reforming themselves, they are unusual in that their major errors are believed to be so consequential. In fact, the relationships between policy and intelligence in Iraq and elsewhere are complex and often unclear. One argument (analyzed in the reports and discussed below) is that the intelligence was politicized – i.e., illegitimately influenced by the IC's knowledge of the answers the policymakers wanted to hear. More obviously, causation is believed to run the other way, as intelligence informs policy. The fact that only those countries that supported the war held investigations is consistent with this view (although another possible reason is that intelligence is not seen as important in France and Germany), and most of the investigations imply a link between intelligence and policy. They almost have to: if there were none, why bother with the investigation?

Many parties have an incentive to agree. Anyone who favored the war but grew uneasy after WMD were not found was happy to point a finger at intelligence. This was bipartisan in that many people from both parties fell into this category. But there were partisan differences as well, and in the US members of both parties felt different cross-pressures. Democrats could shield themselves from the unfortunate consequences of supporting the war by blaming intelligence, but doing so would also shield the Bush administration by treating it as the innocent victim of intelligence incompetence. It would also force Democrats to face the uncomfortable question that presidential candidate John Kerry alternately dodged and mishandled: 'Would you have supported the war if you had known that Saddam did not have active WMD programs?' For Democrats, then, the best way out was not, or not only, to blame faulty intelligence, but to argue that the errors stemmed from politicization. They had been misled; the administration had done the misleading.

For Republicans in general and the administration in particular, the first line of defense was that intelligence had not been badly in error, that WMD would be found or had been spirited across the border to Syria. Once this became untenable, the claim of politicization had to be refuted in the face of common sense. The Republicans also had to deflect attention from the ways in which the administration distorted intelligence to bolster its policy, and they resisted allowing the investigations to even look at this question. In the end, the Senate Select Committee on Intelligence (SSCI) was able to proceed only on the basis of an agreement that this question would be put off to the second phase of the inquiry. At this writing, it is unclear whether it will ever take place.

The Republicans still could be asked whether intelligence mattered in the sense of whether they would have favored the war if they had known the truth about Saddam's programs. Most Republicans in Congress have been able to avoid the question, but President George W. Bush has been forthright in his affirmation that he would have proceeded anyway, arguing that Saddam wanted WMD, especially nuclear weapons, and that sanctions and inspections could at best have slowed him down. Furthermore, Saddam was a tyrant and so there was a great danger that he would make enormous trouble once he had them. Previously acceptable risks were too great to run in the post-9/11 world. Prime Minister Tony Blair has taken a similar position. This argument is not without merit, but it implies a much reduced role for intelligence. If the fundamental danger is the existence of tyrannical regimes, neither spies nor satellites are needed to tell us who fits into this category. This turns on its head the familiar cautious claim that one must judge capabilities rather than intentions. Here the former were relatively benign yet drastic action was necessary because the malign nature of the regime would eventually lead it to do evil.

The fact that Bush and Blair say that they would have gone to war even if they had known of Saddam's reduced capabilities does not mean that this is correct and that the intelligence was irrelevant, however. In fact, these two points are somewhat different. Intelligence might have strongly contributed to the policy even if Bush and Blair are accurately describing their own preferences because the reluctance of many members of the Labour Party, Democrats, and perhaps Secretary of State Colin L. Powell was overcome only by the belief that the Iraqi dictator had growing WMD capability.

It is less clear whether the intelligence directly affected Bush and Blair. Their statements that they would have proceeded had they known the truth are not definitive, even though they do not seem to have been affected by the increased uncertainty that has characterized post-Iraq WMD intelligence on other countries and the revision of the Iranian estimate to say that it is unlikely that Iran could develop nuclear weapons in less than ten years.[6]

First and most obviously, although saying that they would have followed a different policy had they been better informed would have shifted the blame to intelligence, it would also have made them seem credulous and admitted that the war was unnecessary.

Second, the fact that they responded to the revelations about the true state of Saddam's programs by redoubling their commitment to spreading democracy may be a marker of the political and psychological need to find adequate justification for a policy that otherwise would lack one. Cognitive dissonance indicates that when a person acts in a way that later seems to have been foolish, he will place greater weight on any factors that can be used to justify the policy. Thus had WMD been found, subsequent policy might not have so fervently favored democracy and, symmetrically, the adoption of this policy may indicate that the belief that Saddam had WMD indeed was a necessary component of the decision for war.

Third and most importantly, it is unlikely that Bush and Blair can know what they would have done had they understood the truth. People are not aware of the reasons that move them; even an introspective person with incentives to estimate how he or she would have behaved with different information cannot do this.[7] My sense is that once Bush moved towards war in the late winter and spring of 2002, he would not have been deflected by accurate estimates (which, in any case, could not have definitively said that Saddam lacked vigorous programs). But if the judgment of the IC when Bush assumed office had been accurate, then perhaps he would have developed a different position.

Investigations, secrecy, and very political science

That the reports are highly partisan does not render them valueless or impossible to judge. Political scientists and historians work with political documents all the time, trying to understand them in their political context and assessing how the authors' goals and interests effect what they are saying. One of our standard ways to do this is to look at the underlying data, for example examining a state paper in light of the field reports and discussions that fed into it. But this is just what we *cannot* do with these reports. Most of the massive documentation on which they rest remains classified, and so we cannot tell whether the reports accurately summarize and characterize it. Although we can be at least somewhat reassured by the fact that the reports are generally consistent with each other, to a significant degree we must take what they say on trust. This is never a good way to proceed, and it is especially dubious when the studies are highly political. Ironically, the reports note that intelligence analysts lacked sufficient access to their sources and so should have exercised greater caution, but they do not seem to realize that the same stricture must be applied to the documents they have produced.

Secrecy similarly inhibits another mechanism that usually aids us in judging works of contemporary history. In most cases, those who feel wronged will come forth with their own accounts. We welcome memoirs in part because they call up competing versions. In this case, the people who are best positioned to write rebuttals are the intelligence professionals, and their positions prevent them from doing so.

Some evidence for the role of partisan politics in the reports is provided by their tone and the extent to which they point to a simple conclusions. Here the SSCI report stands out in its weaknesses, and the obvious (but perhaps not only) explanation is the partisan context in which it was written. As I noted earlier, the report itself was a product of a political compromise, and of all the reports it is the only one with dissenting appendices. I suspect that it is not an accident that the SSCI report is most dismissive of the claims that the intelligence was politicized, is starkest in the blame it attributes to the IC in general and to the CIA in particular, and judges intelligence by naïve standards. Although it gives us the largest volume of raw intelligence reports, its tone and the extent to which it deflects blame from the administration most sharply raise the question of trustworthiness.

An additional complication with the SSCI report is that significant portions of it are 'redacted' (i.e. blacked out by CIA for security reasons) because the report was written in a highly classified form and only submitted for clearance once it was completed. Indeed, the summary sections were never submitted, perhaps because SSCI did not want to give CIA advance notice of what was in them, and so had to be withheld from the public even if they contained no classified material. The WMD Commission and Butler Report were conceived from the start as chronicles that could be publicly released except for a few sections, with the result that they are much easier to read.

Meanings of intelligence failure

These reports set out to document and explain the intelligence failures concerning Iraq's WMD programs, but the notion of intelligence failure is more ambiguous than they acknowledge. On this and several other scores the Butler Report is most sophisticated, SSCI is least, and the WMD Commission is in between, although closer to the former.

Being wrong

The most obvious sense of intelligence failure is a mismatch between the estimates and what later information reveals to have been true. This is simultaneously the most important and least interesting sense of the term. It is most important because this is what policy-makers and the public care about. To the extent that policy depends on accurate assessments, almost the only thing that matters is accuracy.[8]

In two ways the brute fact of the intelligence failure is uninteresting, however. First, it does not take intensive probes to decide that there was a failure here; all that is required is the knowledge that what was found in Iraq did not match the assessments. Second, the fact that intelligence often is in error does not surprise scholars and should not surprise policy-makers. Much of the history of international politics can be written in terms of intelligence failures, starting with the report in the Bible that the spies that Moses sent to the Land of Israel overestimated the strength of the enemies to be found there.[9] Although most attention has been paid to surprise attacks because the failures here are so traumatic, broadening the focus reveals many more cases.[10]

Any specific instance of intelligence failure will, by definition, seem unusual, but the fact of the failure is itself quite ordinary.[11] This may be unfortunate, but is not mysterious. Intelligence is a game between hiders and finders, and the former usually have the easier job. Intentions, furthermore, often exist only in a few heads and are subject to rapid change. Deception is fairly easy and the knowledge that it is possible degrades the value of accurate information (Stalin was very skeptical about what he was being told by his spies at Los Alamos and within the British government on the grounds that his adversaries could not be so incompetent to allow this kind of penetration). In summary, the only fault with Clausewitz's view is that he restricts it to wartime: 'Many intelligence reports in war are contradictory; even more are false, and most are uncertain.'[12]

Although hints of this realization appear in the Butler and WMD Commission reports, its disturbing implications are shunted aside. If intelligence is often erroneous, there may be little to be gained by going back over any particular case of failure. The details are interesting and may constitute an explanation in the sense of spelling out the intervening links of cause and effect, but the meticulous focus on them misses the larger truth. One might think that the IC might point this out, but to do so would be to imply that its contribution to policy must remain limited because of the high probability of error.

The second and related implication is more disturbing: reforms are not likely to bring great improvement. Of course, any improvement is to be welcomed and may be worth great effort, but the very fact that intelligence failures have occurred in all countries and all eras indicates that while there may be better or worse systems in terms of accuracy (and we do not even know whether this is the case[13]), errors are likely to be frequent even if we do better. I believe that few intelligence professionals would disagree with this statement; it is worth making only because political entrepreneurs imply that their remedies, such as the establishment of a Director of National Intelligence (DNI), will cure the disease, and responsible members of the political elite seem to believe that once the system is fixed we will never be fooled again.[14]

The third implication follows from this: by failing to understand the essential problem, leaders will indulge in policies that are premised on a high degree of accuracy from intelligence. Of course action requires assumptions about what the world is like, but great confidence in the judgments rendered may lead to insufficient attention being given to policy that is less sensitive to intelligence inputs and surprises.

Reasonable expectations

If the first sense of failure as intelligence being inaccurate is straightforward, this is less true of the second sense, which is a falling short of what we could expect a good intelligence service to have done. Judgments here must be much more subjective, and so it is perhaps not surprising that the reports are content to criticize without developing clear standards. To proceed, we need to separate collection from assessment because what can be expected from the latter depends in part on what information is available. All the reports remark on the paucity of good information produced by technical means because overhead photography and signals intelligence could not reveal what was being said and done under the rooftops. The sort of intercepts that Secretary of State Powell quoted in his UN speech were ambiguous, and some seemingly impressive evidence from overhead photography proved to be misleading. While perhaps better efforts could have yielded a bit more from technical intelligence, no one has suggested more than a marginal difference in usable output was likely.

Human intelligence (Humint) was also in short supply and its problems will be discussed later. Part of the reason was that the US and UK relied heavily on UN inspections in the years when they were in place and never developed substitutes when they were withdrawn. How much could have been reasonably expected is a difficult question, however, and depends in part on knowing how good Humint is on several similar targets. The WMD Commission indicates that it is not better for North Korea and Iran, and I do not see any reasons to believe that it was below what is apparently quite a low average, a conclusion reinforced by the fact that no country was able to get adequate Humint about Iraq. The US and the UK erred in allowing their covert collection services to wither, but it is far from clear what greater effort would have yielded. According to Bob Woodward, the full-court press instituted to support the invasion produced a great deal of information, but much of it appears to have been wrong.[15] The best information would come from scientists and technicians who were actually working on WMD, and this circle is small and difficult to penetrate.

It is clear that Iraq was a case of collection failure in that the evidence collected was scattered, ambiguous, and often misleading. But this is just what Clausewitz would lead us to expect, and so it is harder to say whether it was a failure in terms of what is usual and whether reforms are likely to produce marked improvement.

The second part of the question is whether the ICs made good use of the information at hand. The pre-report consensus was that the errors were egregious. SSCI agrees. The WMD Commission does as well, but with many more qualifications. The Butler Report points to problems but does not render an overall judgment. (In general the Butler Report is not as overtly critical as are the American reports, which may reflect British understatement and the belief that blaming intelligence would inappropriately excuse the political leadership.) My review circles around this question, and, in summary I think that while the analysis could have been significantly better, the result would have been to make the judgments less certain rather than to reach a fundamentally different conclusion. We like to think that bad outcomes are to be explained by bad processes, but this needs to be demonstrated rather than assumed, something the reports do only occasionally. If history had been different and Secretary of State Powell had not spent several days closely querying intelligence officials about the information that would go into his UN speech, I am sure that critics would have said that many of the mistakes would have been avoided if the Secretary had exercised this kind of due diligence. If I am right that although some serious (and correctable) errors were made, the processes were not as flawed as the reports claim, this is good news in that the system was not horribly broken, but bad news in that there are few fixes that will produce more than marginal (but still significant) improvements.

To analyze the performance of the ICs we need to avoid equating being wrong with having made avoidable and blameworthy errors. SSCI in particular falls into this trap, as is shown by the fact that it almost always equates reasonable, well-grounded inferences with those that proved to be correct. We can see the problem by asking the obvious counterfactual: would the same report have been written if the estimates had turned out to be correct? This is implausible, yet it is what SSCI implies. After all, its argument is not that the conclusions were wrong – we knew that already – but that the analytical processes were badly flawed. Often, this was indeed the case. But SSCI reasons backwards: incorrect answers must have been the product of flawed procedures. Politically, this way of proceeding makes a good deal of sense; intellectually it does not.

Description of the intelligence failure

Before turning to the explanations the reports offer for the failure, we should present their descriptions of it, realizing that the line between the two is blurred.

Too much certainty

The reports are clearly correct to note that many of the ICs' judgments were stated with excessive certainty: while the preponderance of evidence indicated that Iraq had WMD, it was not sufficient to prove it beyond reasonable doubt. In effect, the IC should have said that the evidence was good enough to convict Saddam in a civil suit, but not in a criminal prosecution.[16]

The public version of the assessments were especially culpable in this regard, but even the classified ones gave an unjustified impression of certainty.[17] Part of the reason for this is that the infamous October 2002 National Intelligence Estimate (NIE) was produced with great haste. The Presidential Daily Briefs (PDBs) were even more stark, in part because they reflected first impressions derived from[18] recent information and had to be brief.[19] Other reasons for the excess certainty were that analysts overestimated the number of independent sources reporting to them, and they failed to carefully consider the significance of negative reports and the absence of evidence, as we will discuss below.

A related problem was that finished intelligence did not do a good job of conveying levels of certainty to consumers. Post-mortems reveal that there are no accepted standards for how to do this. The Butler report notes that while consumers thought that terms such as 'likely' and 'probable' were conveying subtle differences of meaning, intelligence actually used the terms interchangeably, choosing among them for stylistic reasons.[20] In any event, it is doubtful whether consumers were looking for subtle differences in degrees of certainty. Furthermore, although the problem of conveying degrees of confidence is real and reforms are underway, solutions may be beyond reach. ICs have grappled with this problem for years and the fact that several alternatives have been tried and abandoned indicates the depth of the difficulties.

No alternatives considered

A second facet of the failure was the lack of consideration given to alternative explanations. This is not to say there were no disagreements. The American reports document the sharp splits over whether the aluminum tubes that Iraq was surreptitiously importing indicated that Iraq was reconstituting its nuclear program and whether the fact that the software that Iraq procured for its Unmanned Aerial Vehicles (UAVs) included maps of the US implied a threat to the American homeland. Some people also had doubts about the reliability of the testimony of the now notorious informant 'Curveball' that Iraq had mobile facilities for producing biological weapons. But no general alternative explanations for Saddam's behavior were offered. There were no 'Red Teams' to attack the prevailing views; no analyses commissioned from Devil's Advocates; no papers that weighed competing possibilities.[21]

Relatedly, the ICs failed to realize that some evidence that was consistent with their interpretations was consistent with other views as well. Indeed, analysts often seemed to think that the latter was not the case, which meant that they saw the evidence as not only fitting with their explanation, but as giving independent support to it and therefore as justifying greater confidence in the overall judgment. In general, Iraq's use of fronts and other surreptitious means to obtain dual-use material was taken as evidence that it was pursuing forbidden programs. While this inference was consistent with the behavior, it neglected 'the fact that Iraq typically used front companies and evaded UN sanctions for imports of purely legitimate goods.' More specifically, the majority of the ICs believed that the fact that Iraq used intermediaries to procure the aluminum tubes meant that they were intended for uranium enrichment. But, as the Department of Energy (DOE) noted at the time, Security Council resolutions prohibited Iraq from importing such material for conventional military uses, which means that the behavior did not discriminate between the two main hypotheses.[22]

Most strikingly, no one proposed a view close to that we now believe to be true. This was a serious failure, but one that needs to be placed in context. No observers outside the government, including opponents of the war, proposed serious alternatives, and no one, including analysts in the Arab world, provided a description of Saddam's motives and behavior that was close to what we now think is correct. There is no reason to think that any alternative would have been seen as highly credible had it been proposed, and indeed it is hard to argue that any alternative fit the available evidence better than the prevailing one. The reports do not explicitly argue to the contrary, but neither do they explicitly consider the question, which is essential to their task.

Insufficient imagination

Related to the fact that alternatives were not considered is the argument, made more by the WMD Commission and the Butler Report than by SSCI, that the ICs should have been more imaginative. This claim is familiar: it is a conclusion of a recent re-analysis of the failure to understand the revolt that unseated the Shah of Iran[23] and is the standard view of intelligence before 9/11, where intelligence 'failed to connect the dots'. This phrase, which the reports on Iraq WMD shrewdly avoid, betrays a fundamental misunderstanding of the problem. In 9/11, Iraq, and most other cases there were countless dots – all of them, not only those whose significance is apparent in retrospect – and they could have been connected in a great many ways. To take the 9/11 case, I am sure that if we look back at all the information that was received rather than only the bits that we now know could have led us to the plot, we will find a huge number of possible alarms that looked as troubling as the danger that turned out to be the real. In retrospect the presence of a handful of Arabs in flying schools without obvious employment prospects called for immediate investigation, but if the attacks had been delivered by chemical trucks, we would now be bemoaning the failure to see the significance of the scattered warnings – which I am sure we could find – about Arabs who were enrolled in truck-driving schools.

A lack of imagination may have been shown by the ICs' unwillingness to think about puzzling aspects of Iraq's behavior. Had the ICs asked why Saddam was refusing to do all he could to avoid war, they might have been led in an interesting and highly policy-relevant direction. After the war, there were scattered reports that France and Russia had told Saddam that they would restrain the US, and this may have played a role in his decision (and if these countries did believe that Washington would back down, this probably was the most consequential of all the intelligence failures). Working backwards from his recalcitrance, and combining it with any intelligence on what French and Russian diplomats were saying, could have led the ICs to flag this possibility. The obvious policy would have been for the US and UK to tell France and Russia in the strongest possible terms that their opposition would not deter the coalition, and that those countries could best contribute to peace by making this clear to Saddam. Of course they might not have been willing to comply, and it might not have made a difference, but imagination does seem to have been absent here.

More centrally, few in the ICs felt the need to go beyond the obvious proposition that Saddam was developing active WMD programs. Similarly, in the case of Iran in 1978, intelligence thought it was clear that the Shah would live up to his reputation for ruthlessness and crack down if the disturbances grew serious. Before 9/11 most of the concern about terrorism focused on the kinds that had occurred previously. This pattern makes sense. Intelligence analysts are selected and trained to be careful, to stay close to the information, and to resist speculation. Indeed, there are good reasons why the IC resists being highly imaginative. There are few limits on what can be imagined, and those who urge the community to be more imaginative have said little about how this should be done in a sensible way and how the IC should test the alternatives.

Furthermore, in one sense, the ICs were too imaginative about Iraq in putting together scattered and ambiguous information to form a stark and dramatic picture. They ended up speculating without realizing that they were doing so. While one can legitimately reply that this kind of outrunning the evidence was not imaginative because the picture painted was a familiar one, the analysts were seeing a world beyond the incoming reports.

Explanations for the failure

Although the reports are heavier on detail than generalization, they do provide some broad explanations for the failure. These are marred by a glaring methodological defect, however. This is the lack of comparative analysis to probe the arguments being made. This leads to their missing an obvious puzzle: apparently all intelligence services in all countries and most private analysts came to roughly the same conclusions about the Iraqi programs.[24] Part of the reason may be that each gained confidence from knowing the others' conclusions, but the uniformity of the failure indicates either that analytical and methodological flaws were universal or that somehow each service made its own errors that led to the same faulty conclusions. The latter is unlikely and the former casts doubt on the explanations offered and indicates that no simple reorganization or changes in analytic tradecraft are likely to solve the problems.

An understanding of the need for comparisons also reminds us that reports like these are exercises in searching on the dependent variable. That is, we have post-mortems only after failure, not after successes.[25] Even if we did them well, and even if we found that certain factors were present in all the cases, we would not be on firm ground in making causal inferences – namely, in providing an explanation – unless we could also establish that those factors were absent in cases of intelligence success. Oxygen is not a cause of intelligence failure despite its being present in all such cases.

When we turn to the accounts offered below, it is far from clear that the factors highlighted distinguish cases of failure from those of success. Although the reports, especially the WMD Commission and the Butler Report, do look at other WMD cases in which intelligence did better, as far as we can tell (some of these sections remain classified) they make no use of these comparisons to develop their explanations. Neither do they note that all intelligence services seem to have reached the same conclusions despite their different national cultures, biases, and ways of proceeding. Also ignored is the apparent fact that most senior Iraqi officials believed that their country had WMD. (This illustrates a potential danger of good intelligence: had the US or UK tapped into what these people were saying, any lingering doubts would have been dispelled as the ICs ignored the possibility of what is known as Red-on-Red deception.[26])

It is also unfortunate that the reports leave underdeveloped comparisons between what different agencies said or between what the IC said on one issue as opposed to another on Iraq. SSCI uses the correct conclusions of some parts of the IC (Air Force intelligence in the case of UAVs, DOE in the case of the aluminum tubes) as a way of castigating the Central Intelligence Agency (CIA), but the comparisons remain of limited use because SSCI does not explore whether the factors that they think generated the wrong judgments were present in the correct ones as well, as I will discuss below often was the case.

The need for comparisons sheds disturbing light on the argument for the failure of imagination. Intelligence failure may be associated with lack of imagination, but I suspect that similar patterns are present in successes as well. The reason for this is explained by Richard Betts, who notes that we bring to cases our general beliefs and implicit theories of the world.[27] These usually are correct, which means that most of the time we are better off being guided by them rather than exercising great imagination, and that surprises occur when the other's behavior is in fact extraordinary. If we were more imaginative in the latter cases we might have gotten them right; but if we were generally more imaginative we would have been wrong in many standard cases. Of course what we want is a way of determining when the normal patterns will hold and when they will not, and perhaps this is the main task of intelligence. But without some magic key, we must live with the conundrum that the same ways of thinking that produce an accurate picture of normal adversary behavior will fail when the country or situation is odd.

Groupthink

In one of its main conclusions, SSCI argues that a 'groupthink' dynamic led intelligence community analysts, collectors and managers to both interpret ambiguous information as conclusively indicative of a WMD program as well as ignore or minimize evidence that Iraq did not have active and expanding weapons of mass destruction programs.'[28] Taken literally, this is simply incorrect. Groupthink is, as its name implies, a small group phenomenon, as is made clear in Irving Janis' book that is the founding text, one of the few pieces of academic research that is cited by SSCI.[29] The driving motor is the posited tendency for tightly-knit groups to seek the comfort and confidence that comes from mutual agreement and approval. Such an atmosphere not only leads people to refrain from disturbing the group consensus, but to not even entertain disturbing thoughts. Intelligence on Iraq was not developed by small groups, however. A great deal of work was done by individuals, and the groups were large and of a shifting composition.

Excessive consensus

In fairness to SSCI, it is using the term groupthink in a colloquial rather than a technical sense. What is claimed to be at work are general pressures of conformity and mutual reinforcement. Once the view that Iraq was developing WMD was established there not only were few incentives to challenge it, but each person who held this view undoubtedly drew greater confidence from the fact that it was universally shared.

There is much to this, but again it needs more careful scrutiny than the reports gave it. First, the general consensus did not prevent vigorous disagreements on specific issues, espe cially over UAVs and the aluminum tubes. But excessive conformity may have come up in one odd aspect of the latter discussion. Although DOE thought that the tubes were not designed to enrich uranium, it did not dissent from the judgment that Iraq was reconstituting its nuclear program. Presumably DOE's analysts believed that Iraq was developing weapons through some other, unspecified, route, but their reasoning was not queried by the other agencies because for their purposes what was crucial was the conclusion that Iraq was reconstituting.[30] It was this after all, that was of most concern to the policy-makers, and there seemed to be no point in figuring out why DOE disagreed on the tubes yet agreed with the conclusion. In fact, it would have been worth learning whether the rest of the IC felt that the DOE's analysis of how Iraq could develop weapons without the tubes had merit because, if it did not, there would have been more reason to question the conclusion.

More centrally, the reports would have served us better had they probed the notions of conformity and consensus. Conformity is often warranted; the fact that several conscientious and intelligent people believe something is a valid reason for me to believe it. In many cases, everyone believes the same thing because there are good reasons to do so, which is one reason why cases of success are likely to be characterized by as high levels of agreement and mutual reinforcement as are cases of failure. What needs to be avoided is unthinking con- formity in which everyone quickly accepts conventional wisdom, thereby reinforcing and perpetuating it without further examination. In practice, however, it is not easy to separate justified from unjustified conformity, and while the latter may have been the case in Iraq, this needs to be demonstrated.[31]

Failure to challenge assumptions

In parallel with the diagnosis of excessive conformity is the argument that assumptions were insufficiently examined. Thus SSCI said the NIE 'suffers from a "layering" effect whereby assessments were based on previous judgments without carrying forward the uncertainties'.[32] The other reports reach similar judgments, and I think it is clear that much of the reason why each new bit of information that *could* be interpreted as showing that Iraq had active programs *was* interpreted in this way was the hold of the belief that Saddam was doing all that he could to get WMD. Ambiguities were missed or downplayed, alternative interpret- ations rarely were fully considered (for example concerning Iraq's failure to account for all the missing chemical and biological weapons), and when they were, as with the tubes and UAVs, the more damning implications won support in part because they fitted with the prevailing view.

Important also were beliefs that extended beyond Iraq. According to a biological weapons specialist in the State Department's Bureau of Intelligence and Research (INR), one reason why the IC was quick to accept the evidence that Iraq was developing mobile labs was that 'the U.S. BW analysts generally think that BW programs historically have shifted [away] from large-scale fixed facilities. . . . So it's very appealing to the analysts to learn about a mobile BW program. It fits with what we think the state of BW programs worldwide are heading toward.'[33]

Perhaps the most general assumption was that Saddam's policy was consistent, coherent, and unchanging. He had sought WMD before the 1991 Gulf War and afterwards had tried to continue them in the face of sanctions. The elements of his behavior, although distressing, fit together and embodied a comprehensible plan. Since Saddam was a dictator, there was every reason to expect the regime to be a unitary actor as well. In fact it now appears that Saddam did *not* have a coherent plan, his control was less than complete, and the regime was less than fully competent.[34] Thus SSCI notes that, contrary to what CIA assumed, the reason why the aluminum tubes had specifications unnecessarily precise for rocket motors was that the Iraqi engineers were inexperienced and erred on the side of caution.[35] More importantly, almost everyone assumed that Saddam's behavior and plans remained relatively stable, whereas it now appears that in the late 1990s he realized that he would not be able to develop robust WMD programs in the face of sanctions and bombings like those the US and UK carried out in 1998. As David Kay, first head of the post-war Iraq Survey Group, says: 'One of the hardest things to do in the world of intelligence is to discern change. . . . When people's behavior has been consistent, you tend to predict the future based upon the past.'[36] It appears that the ICs never asked whether Saddam's approach had changed.

The impact of assumptions and beliefs needs to be understood rather than merely criticized, however. Many correct inferences about Iraq WMD were based on strong assumptions, as I will note later, and it is impractical to reexamine all assumptions all the time, which means that knowing that many faulty estimates rest on mistaken and unexamined assumptions does not provide practical guidance. There is no such thing as 'letting the facts speak for themselves' or drawing inferences without using beliefs about the world; it is inevitable that the perception and interpretation of new information will be influenced by established ideas.[37]

This means that there is not likely to be a completely satisfactory way to proceed. But the reports are correct that crucial assumptions should be made explicit in order to make the analysts conscious of them and to alert consumers to those they might want to dispute. The exercise is much easier in hindsight, of course, and carrying it out in the Iraq case might not have changed the estimate. It now appears that intelligence needed to question whether the regime's refusal to provide full cooperation with inspectors could have been explained by anything other than hiding forbidden programs and whether its past use of chemicals and history of WMD programs were highly diagnostic of what it was doing in 2002. Although it is not quite correct to say that these assumptions were so deep that the analysts were not aware of them, they were never explicitly defended because they seemed obvious and were widely shared. (It is worth noting that outside observers also failed to question these beliefs, which did not rest on classified information.)

It is even more difficult to specify ahead of time which assumptions should be reexamined. In principle, it might be useful to make all assumptions explicit. But is it really necessary to start a paper by explaining that the other country is populated by human beings? One wants to concentrate on assumptions that are not subject to dispute in the ordinary course of analysis, are central to the conclusions (what some in the American IC call 'linchpins'), and are amenable to sensible analysis.

Confirmation bias and negative evidence

Although the reports do not use the term 'confirmation bias,' they see this phenomenon at work. Cognitive psychologists have documented the propensity for people to seek information that confirms their beliefs and to gloss over what could contradict them.[38] This occurred at every stage, from requests to the field for information, to what was reported (and not reported), to what the analysts paid attention to. Thus as focus shifted to Iraq in the wake of the successful war in Afghanistan, CIA agents around the world were told to seek information about Iraq's progress toward obtaining WMD. This made sense, but the obvious danger in asking people to be on the look-out for certain kinds of information is that they and their sources will find it.

During World War II, British intelligence saw this as a trap, and when it received preliminary reports about a new German weapon it was careful to phrase inquiries to other agents in neutral terms that did not disclose what it believed the Germans might be developing. It appears that CIA did not take this precaution, and by making it clear what it was seeking may have led its agents and sources to bring in any information, even if insubstantial, and – most importantly – to ignore reports of lack of activity. 'None of the guidance given to human intelligence collectors suggested that collection be focused on determining *whether* Iraq had WMD. Instead, the requirements assumed that Iraq had WMD and focused on uncovering those activities . . .'[39]

Even without this specific bias, I suspect that it was rare for negative information to be solicited or reported. Agents were not likely to press for what their sources did *not* see; I doubt if the field reported that various sources did *not* have any information that Saddam was actively pursuing WMD even if these people were well-placed; had such reports came in to the Reports Officers at the Directorate of Operations (DO), I doubt if they were passed on to the analysts in the Directorate of Intelligence (DI). Finished intelligence apparently never sought to evaluate the number and significance of reports by knowledgeable informants who did not see traces of WMD programs.

Negative reports rarely if ever led to requests for follow-up by headquarters whereas positive ones did. The fact, glaringly significant in retrospect, that the increased collection efforts yielded little was not considered worthy of note.[40] By its nature, positive evidence is much more striking and vivid than is its absence, and psychologists know that vivid information has impact out of proportion to its diagnostic content. It stands out, will be noted, and sticks in the memory. Negative evidence and things that do not happen tend to be overlooked. Often they should not be, and it is disturbing but not surprising that the IC found it hard to comply with SSCI's request that it turn over this kind evidence because there is no simple way to retrieve it from memory or files.[41]

'Absence of evidence is not evidence of absence', as Secretary of Defense Donald Rumsfeld famously said. Like many mantras, there is quite a bit to this, but it conceals quite a bit as well. There are indeed numerous cases in which an adversary's action or capabilities were not preceded by any detected signs. But presumably even Rumsfeld would acknowledge that absence of evidence can be significant. If it were not, one would be in the absurd position of arguing that lacking positive evidence that a country is not pursuing WMD (and it is not clear what this could be), we should assume that it is.[42] (But it is chastening to note that the Western ICs were unaware that the Soviet – and Russian – governments continued robust biological weapons programs after signing the treaty banning it and that Albania had developed chemical weapons.[43])

Cases in which specified behavior does not occur or in which evidence is absent are highly significant if an important proposition or argument implies the contrary. Political scientists refer to this kind of evidence as 'dogs that do not bark', borrowing from the Sherlock Holmes short story in which Holmes, but not Watson, realizes that the fact that the murder victim's dogs did not bark the night he was killed shows that the murderer was an acquaintance: had he been a stranger, the dogs would have barked. As this example shows, negative evidence and events that do not occur are not automatically or uniformly important, but matter when a significant argument or proposition implies that they *should* be present.

A heightened awareness of this logic and the attendant research design of focusing on relevant negative cases have greatly improved social science over the past several years. Intelligence (and these post-mortems as well) has not come to fully appreciate this. This is not surprising, because it requires thinking in a counter-intuitive way that comes from an explicit consideration of the hypothetico-deductive method. We move naturally from evidence to inference, but it takes greater self-consciousness to see that to test our propositions we need to ask what events should occur and what evidence should be observable if this argument or explanation is correct.

In the Iraq case, doing so would have helped in three related ways.

First, it could have corrected for the propensity to note only corroborating facts. Thus although intelligence considered Iraq's use of 'code words to compartmentalize BW program elements' as diagnostic, apparently it missed the fact that code words were not used to 'conceal acquisition of BW related equipment, and impair Western measures to monitor Iraqi technology acquisition'.[44]

Second, asking 'If Iraq has reconstituted its nuclear program, what would it have to do?' might have pointed intelligence to areas that should have been probed more deeply, such as the lack of evidence that Iraq was seeking the components other than tubes that it would have needed if it were building centrifuges.[45]

Third, an explicit focus on the potential importance of negative information could have restrained the confirmation bias in collection. More specifically, headquarters in both the US and the UK could have instructed their agents to look for and report not only WMD activities, but also cases in which people who might have known about them in fact saw nothing.

Denial and deception

Intelligence analysts knew that some reports were negative and that there were great gaps in what they saw of Iraq's WMD programs. But, as the reports note, this was easy to explain – and explain away – by Iraq's denial and deception campaign. The experience with the UN inspectors was especially clear and vivid. Iraqi officials would own up to activities only when confronted by direct evidence. They did what they could to thwart the inspectors, including moving materials and records out the back door when the inspectors arrived at the front. Machinery would be hidden, even buried, and any information was hard to come by. So it is not surprising that intelligence concluded that it was seeing only a fraction of the Iraqi program.

This made sense, being consistent with previous Iraqi behavior and explaining why there was not more direct evidence. The inference also was consistent with the behavior of other states, especially the USSR, which had trained many of the Iraqis. The problem was that the ICs treated deception and denial as a given rather than as a hypothesis to be tested and never asked what information might lead to the conclusion that activities were missing rather than being hidden. Unfortunately, this is a very difficult hypothesis to disprove. Here more than elsewhere, Rumsfeld's mantra applies.

Even if the ICs had been more careful and explicit, it is not clear how they could have gone about deciding whether their faith in Iraq's denial and deception was justified. But it is disturbing that the ICs did not seem to realize that the proposition that many of Iraq's activities were hidden was both central to their conclusions and was just that – a proposition, and one that did not rest on direct evidence such as a series of recent deceptions that they had unmasked. Neither did they appear to realize that their belief was essentially impossible to disconfirm. The failure to detect concealment merely testified to its success, and any evidence of deception and denial could – and probably would – have been taken as proof that many activities remained undiscovered.[46]

There are no easy solutions here, but what the ICs should have done was to note the central and hard-to-'confirm role of beliefs about Iraqi denial and deception, increase their efforts to penetrate it, and alert the policy-makers to the fact that the projected activities could not be directly seen. The ICs could at least have asked themselves what should be concluded if what they were seeing was not the tip of the iceberg, but the bulk of it. In other words, did the observed activities support the conclusion that Iraq had robust WMD programs? Goethe famously said, 'We are never deceived, we deceive ourselves.' The irony here is that the US and the UK deceived themselves into believing that Iraq's deception campaign was central. The final embarrassment was that when Secretary Powell raised the subject in his speech to the UN, he called his 'colleagues' attention to the fine paper that the United Kingdom distributed yesterday which describes in exquisite detail Iraqi deception activities': it soon was discovered that this paper had been plagiarized.

Overlearning

It is well known that people not only learn from the past, but overlearn from it.[47] A recent and important event is likely to leave a deep imprint on people, especially when they were in error. People will be sure not to make the same mistake again – and are more likely to commit the opposite error. This helps explain both the ICs' certainty that Iraq was engaging in deception and denial and the main conclusion that it had active WMD programs. After the 1991 Gulf War the ICs found to their dismay that they had greatly underestimated Saddam's WMD activities, partly because Iraq had deployed an undetected deception program. They therefore became especially vigilant, which meant they were unlikely to miss activities that were taking place, but the inevitable cost was to increase the risk of making more out of the information than they should have.

Human intelligence

The reports attribute some of the intelligence error to three basic shortfalls of Humint.[48] Most obviously, the amount of Humint was slight. It is not clear how many sources the Americans drew on; the British had five, none of whom claimed firsthand knowledge of the programs. The ICs had relied heavily on information from the UN inspectors, and when they were forced out in 1998 adequate sources were not developed to fill the gaps. It seems clear that insufficient attention was given to the problem throughout the 1990s, but, as I noted earlier, it is hard to say what reasonable expectations should be in this area. Unfortunately but typically, the reports do not raise this question, but merely indicate that we must do better. The reports do make clear, however, that they were surprised by how few sources were available, that conclusions were often drawn from what only one or two people had said, and that the analysts did not focus on and indeed sometimes did not know how few sources they had.

A second problem was that most of the Humint was misleading. These two points combine to reproduce Woody Allen's famous line: 'Such bad food, and small portions too.' The best known and perhaps most important source was 'Curveball', whose testimony convinced analysts that Iraq was using mobile laboratories to produce biological agents. It turns out that although some of the sources may have been accurate in relaying what they heard others say, little if any of the information was true. The most obvious explanation was that the sources had come through the Iraqi National Congress (INC), an organization that had an interest in leading people to believe that Saddam was vigorously pursuing WMD. But it now appears that this was rarely the case and the reasons for the misinformation remain a mystery, probably varying from one source to another. It is also worth noting that apparently no national service did much better than the others in producing Humint or separating truth from fiction.

Third, all of the reports stress that the analysts did not know enough about the sources they were relying on. Sources are loathe to disclose all of the details about the sub-sources who report to them; agents in the field rarely give a complete picture of their sources; Reports Officers at CIA Headquarters remove significant identifiers before passing the material to the analysts, as well as deciding what material is valuable enough to send on at all. The results are that analysts are given only a generic description of the source, and indeed one that can vary from one report to another, which in this case led the analysts to overestimate the number of different sources who were reporting. In other cases, the descriptions omitted important details about the source's specific expertise and access that would have helped the analysts judge the information.

The problems were even greater when the source was under the control of a foreign service, as was the case with 'Curveball'. German intelligence kept him to themselves, arguing incorrectly that he did not speak English and was anti-American, and the only direct contact was a single meeting with an American who was highly skeptical about 'Curveball's' reliability. Furthermore, his information flowed not through DO, but through Defense Humint Services (DHS) which was unwilling or unable to push the Germans for information about him. Even when DHS has direct access, it does not appear to do as thorough a job of vetting and passing on information about sources as does DO.

There are real limits to DO's role as well. Some Reports Officers apparently believe that the analysts are in the best position to validate the source by determining whether the information fits with other evidence at their disposal. Not only did many DI analysts fail to understand this, but the danger of circularity and confirmation bias is heightened by this approach – the fact that information fits with prevailing views will validate the source, and the reliability of the source will lend credence to the information. While the problem is often described as DO not providing enough information to DI, part of the difficulty is that DO did not scrutinize the sources with sufficient care.[49]

The reports generally reinforce the widespread view that the paucity of Humint was a major cause of the Iraq debacle. But while of course more information from well-placed sources would improve intelligence, this is a good deal more difficult than simply increasing the amount of Humint. When dealing with WMD capabilities, let alone the country's intentions, the number of well informed people will be small. Furthermore, even if vetting were done much better, it will remain more an art than a science and will produce both false positives and false negatives. Indeed for this reason Humint is generally suspect, and it seems to have been given unusual credence in this case, probably because little else was available. While Humint then contributed greatly to the failure, it is ironic, although not necessarily foolish, that the prescription is to get more Humint.

Information sharing

Another prescription is for much greater information sharing within the IC.[50] In what seems like common sense, Senator Pat Roberts, chair of SSCI, argues that 'Key terrorism analysts . . . must be given access to every single piece of relevant intelligence data concerning threats to the homeland.'[51] Clearly it was not helpful when DO described Ambassador Joseph Wilson, who was sent to Niger to ascertain whether Saddam was seeking uranium, as 'a contact with excellent access who does not have an established reporting record'.[52] This is not only a matter of DO saying more to DI, however. The vetting of sources probably would be best done by both branches pooling their impressions. Furthermore, information collectors are often in a good position to see when analysts have made insufficient use of available information or conversely have overestimated the extent to which their judgments are rooted in hard evidence or specific reports.

The freer flow of information should not be limited to human sources. One reason why analysts believed that Iraq had stepped up production of its chemical weapons was that they saw increased activity at the suspected production sites. But the WMD Commission says that what the analysts did not know was that the satellites had been re-programmed to provide more frequent coverage and so what they were seeing reflected a change in American surveillance, not Iraqi behavior.[53] A footnote in the report undercuts this claim, but even if it is not true, the point remains that discussion of who needs what information within the IC should not be restricted to Humint. For example, in some instances analysts may need to know a great deal about the technical details of a collection system in order to think about what sorts of information could and could not have been gathered.

The WMD Commission correctly remarks that the terminology we use may implicitly accept undesirable boundaries within the IC: 'To say that we must encourage agencies to "share" information implies that they have some ownership stake in it.'[54] Anyone who has worked in or around CIA knows the proprietary attitude of the directorates, especially DO. But, as usual, there are problems with the prescription. Not only will it meet a great deal of resistance, but fully sharing information reduces the value of the division of labor. For DO to pass on all information to DI would be to swamp it.

Furthermore, the withholding of information at all levels reflects not only the fact that the information is power, but legitimate security concerns. Spies like Aldridge Ames and Robert Hanssen would have done even greater damage had there been less compartmentalization. While some barriers have to be broken down, I doubt that there is a perfect way to balance the competing needs involved, and I suspect that some years from now a distinguished panel will attribute a security debacle to the excessively free flow of information within the IC.

The reports point to other problems of information filtering within CIA, especially the screening out of doubts about 'Curveball'.[55] Much remains unclear, including the extent and depth of the doubts and whether they were conveyed to Deputy Director McLaughlin.[56] Ironically, if McLaughlin was informed (which he denies), then information flowed more appropriately and fewer corrections are within reach. But even under the best interpretation, the IC in general and CIA in particular failed to develop mechanisms and forums for scrutinizing 'Curveball's' reliability and conveying judgments up the hierarchy.

Politicization

To the surprise of many, the reports rejected the most widely held explanation for the failure, which is that policy-makers exerted illegitimate influence on the IC to give the answers they wanted to hear.[57] Contrary to my initial impressions, I think the reports are largely correct, although definitive judgments are impossible because of the multiple and subtle effects that can be at work.

The reports skip over some practices that could be included under the rubric of politicization, most obviously that leaders in the US and UK gave inaccurate accounts about intelligence in order to garner political support. Most famously, the President said that the British reported that Saddam had sought uranium from Africa (true, but the implication that American intelligence agreed was not), the Vice President and the Secretary of Defense said that there was solid evidence for connections between Iraq and Al Qaeda, and many policy-makers insisted that the WMD threat was 'imminent'. The intelligence community disagreed, and Director of Central Intelligence (DCI) George Tenet testified that he privately corrected officials for claims like these.[58]

In some cases, the line between distortion and legitimate if questionable emphasis is hard to draw. The most striking case is Tony Blair's use of intelligence that Saddam could use chemical weapons within 45 minutes of deciding to do so.[59] He not only implied that the information was more solid than it was (blame on this point must be shared with the IC), but left the impression that these weapons could reach the entire region and so showed the Saddam was a great menace with evil intent. Blair omitted the crucial point that these were short-range battlefield weapons, which actually pointed to Saddam's *defensive* orientation because such readiness would have had value only as a safeguard against a swift attack on him.

Here and in many instances, officials in the US and the UK engaged in 'cherry-picking' and 'stove-piping.' The former is highlighting reports that support the policy to the exclusion of contradictory ones that may be more numerous and better-established; the latter here refers to the delivery of selected raw intelligence to policy-makers, bypassing intelligence analysts who could critically evaluate it. These practices can be defended as within the prerogatives and even the duties of top officials to reach their own conclusions, but when used to justify policies to the public they incorrectly imply the backing of the intelligence community.

Most attention has been focused on politicization in the more insidious form of pressure on the IC to provide analyses that support decisions. The head of MI6 came back from a trip to Washington in July 2002 convinced that 'Bush wanted to remove Saddam, through military action, justified by the conjunction of terrorism and WMD. But the intelligence and the facts were being fixed around the policy.'[60] On the other hand, the crudest form of politicization in which superiors changed the papers coming up to make them conform to policy did not occur, and few analysts have leaked reports that they were unduly pressured on WMD, something that might have been expected if they had been.[61] Perhaps Rumsfeld's mantra applies, as is implied by the following exchange between a member of SSCI's staff and Richard Kerr, who headed CIA's internal review:

Mr Kerr: 'There's always people who are going to feel pressure in these situations and feel they were pushed upon.'

Committee Interviewer: 'That's what we've heard. We can't find any of them, though.'

Mr Kerr: 'Maybe they are wiser than to come talk to you.'[62]

I doubt whether this is the bulk of the story, however. My confidential interviews with CIA officials at several levels of the hierarchy did not find anyone excusing his or her errors as resulting from political pressure. Of course they might have felt that admitting to having given in to pressure was worse than admitting to have been honestly mistaken, and, as I noted earlier, people are often unable to understand how they reached their judgments. As an analyst put it at the confirmation hearings for Robert Gates as DCI, which provided the most extensive discussion of this issue: 'politicization is like fog. Though you cannot hold it in your hands, or nail it to a wall, it does exist, it is real, and it does affect people.'[63] Perhaps only those who were there can tell whether they felt such influence, but unanimity is not likely, as depending on personality and political views what one person interprets as probing questions another will feel as pressure.

So better evidence may be provided by relevant comparisons. *All* intelligence services believed that Iraq had active WMD programs, even those of countries that opposed the war.[64] At minimum, this shows that political pressure was not necessary to reach the conclusions that the American and British ICs did. Furthermore, on other aspects of Iraq CIA resisted strong administration pressure. Three months before the war the National Intelligence Council warned that the aftermath of the invasion was not likely to be easy and that invading might increase support for terrorists in the Islamic world.[65] Even more strikingly, intelligence consistently denied that there was significant evidence for Saddam's role in 9/11 or that he might turn over WMD to Al Qaeda, holding to this position in the face of frequent administration statements to the contrary, repeated inquiries and challenges that can only be interpreted as pressure, and the formation of a unit in the Defense Department dedicated to finding such connections.[66] The administration's pressure was illegitimate, but the lack of success not only speaks to the integrity of the intelligence officials, but also cuts against the claim that the reports on WMD were biased by the desire to please.

Comparing the differences within the American IC also casts doubt on the politicization thesis, although this is not without ambiguity. The State Department's INR was the most skeptical member of the community and Air Force intelligence dissented on the UAVs, yet State and Defense were the two most policy-oriented agencies. DOE dissented on the aluminum tubes, and there is no evidence that political pressure was exerted; if it was, it does not seem to have had any effect. But Secretary of State Powell's standing may have permitted him to shield his intelligence officials, and the fact that for much of the country intelligence is equated with the CIA may have meant that the latter bore the brunt of the pressure, perhaps because it was ostensibly removed from politics.

A final comparison is with the Clinton-era estimates. There were significant differences, especially in the claim that Saddam had reconstituted his nuclear program, was increasing his stockpiles of chemical weapons, and that he had mobile biological laboratories. But the latter possibility was beginning to be reflected in assessments in 2000 as 'Curveball's' reports started coming in, and the changes in the nuclear and chemical assessments also corresponded to new information. Thus much of the gap between the Bush and Clinton estimates can be explained in terms of reports from the field, and the gap between the two sets of estimates is a good deal less than that which separated them both from what we now believe to have been true.

This does not mean that political pressure had no role at all. At the very least, it created (and probably was designed to create) an atmosphere that was not conducive to critical analysis and that encouraged judgments of excessive certainty and eroded subtleties and nuances. Analysts and intelligence managers knew that any suggestion that Saddam's capabilities were limited would immediately draw hostile fire from their superiors. In this political climate it would have been hard for anyone to ask if the conventional wisdom about Saddam's WMD programs should be reexamined. Thus when at the last minute an agent questioned the use of information from 'Curveball' in Secretary of State Powell's speech, his boss replied: 'Let's keep in mind that this war's going to happen regardless of what Curveball said or didn't say, and that the Powers That Be probably aren't very interested in whether Curveball knows what he's talking about.'[67] It is also possible that the desire to avoid the painful value trade-off between pleasing policy-makers and following professional standards created what psychologists call 'motivated bias' in favor of producing estimates that would support, or at least not undermine, policy. This is not unusual. In Britain in the 1930s even without explicit pressure the estimates of the balance of power with Germany changed in the wake of policy shifts.[68]

Perhaps the best evidence of politicization has not been noted by the reports or other critical commentary, probably because it was something that did not happen: it appears that the ICs did not make any reassessments once UN Monitoring and Verification Commission (UNMOVIC) inspections resumed and found no traces of WMD.[69] This was a significant failing, and I suspect that the reason is that by this point it was clear to the ICs that the US and UK were committed to overthrowing Saddam and that any re-evaluations would be unacceptable.

Politicization represents the tribute that vice plays to virtue and may be a modern phenomenon. That is, leaders at least in the US and UK now need to justify their foreign policies as being based on the findings of intelligence professionals, as was illustrated by the fact that Secretary of State Powell demanded that DCI Tenet sit right behind him when he made his Security Council speech spelling out the evidence against Iraq. This is a touching faith in the concept of professionalism and how much can be known about other states. It is not the only way things could be. A leader could say 'I think Saddam is a terrible menace. This is a political judgment and I have been elected to make difficult calls like this. Information rarely can be definitive and while I have listened to our intelligence services and other experts, this is my decision, not theirs.' Perhaps unfortunately, this is politically very difficult to do, however, and a policy-maker who wants to proceed in the face of ambiguous or discrepant information will be hard pressed to avoid at least some politicization of intelligence.[70]

Specific analytical errors

Thanks to their great detail, the reports turned up interesting specific analytical failings. The bitter, prolonged, and indecisive battle over the aluminum tubes revealed several things that the IC did wrong. Because the tubes were seen as the least ambiguous indicator of Iraq's nuclear program, the issue was the focus of intense IC concern and resources. But the discussion was muddled. Although puzzles remain, it appears that there was a history of strong and unresolved disagreements between CIA and DOE dating back a decade or more. Relatedly, the inter-agency group (the Joint Atomic Energy Intelligence Committee) designed to rule on such matters never did so. Partly because the discussion was not well structured, people sometimes talked past each other. In particular, the questions of whether the tubes *could* have been used for uranium enrichment and the much stronger argument that Iraq had procured them for this *purpose* often were blurred.[71] The evidence for the former claim was fairly convincing, but what correctly made the most impact on analysts and consumers was the less substantiated inference that Iraq had sought the tubes in order to further the nuclear program. Another major blunder entered in here. Throughout most of the discussion, the Army's National Ground Intelligence Center (NGIC) argued that 'the tubes were, technically speaking, poor choices for rocket bodies', which we now know was in fact their true use.[72] NGIC, which presumably had great expertise in this area, apparently missed the Italian rockets that served as the model for the Iraqis.

Throughout, the reports note that each bit of evidence the ICs used was ambiguous or impeachable, and yet formed the basis for far-reaching conclusions. Each account lent credence to the others. This is indeed what happened, but it is not clear that this was as unwarranted as the reports imply. If Saddam was in fact producing one kind of WMD, it was likely that he was producing others as well. Of course, evidence of nuclear activities did not prove that 'Curveball' was correct, for example, but it did paint a picture in which his reports made a great deal of sense. If each report were worthless, the sum total of even a large number of them would still be zero, although the listing them together would give them an air of credibility. But if there was a reasonable probability that any one of them were correct, the fact that there were several did indeed make the positive finding more reasonable. The 'mosaic effect' may be such that pieces of information, each ambiguous in itself, together provide quite convincing evidence.

It is not clear how we are to determine this is the case, however. The reports are correct to fault the IC for not being explicit, and perhaps not even aware, about the inference processes involved, but they were not necessarily inappropriate.[73] A study of how scientists came to accept the argument for global warming explains that 'each story [about an aspect of the phenomenon], bizarre in itself, was made plausible by the others'.[74]

More broadly, it is often not clear what inferences should be drawn from certain information. To take a current example, should the discovery of A. Q. Khan's nuclear network increase our estimate of the probability that North Korea might sell nuclear materials to terrorists? On the one hand, most of us were surprised that Khan, with or without the knowledge of the Pakistani government or intelligence service, would have undertaken these activities. It therefore both reminds us that things we consider unlikely if not unimaginable can indeed happen and that nuclear information and material can spread in unorthodox ways. On the other hand, we could say that the fact that Khan, despite his nefarious activities, refrained from selling to terrorists means that the probability of North Korea or any other country doing so is quite low, perhaps even lower than we had thought before. I do not think there is any rule for telling which inference is most likely to be correct.

One point the reports miss is that whereas Saddam's refusal to fully cooperate with the inspectors did seem to imply that he was conducting forbidden activities, his behavior in the 18 months preceding the war was hard to understand even if he did have things to hide. His actions made it almost certain that the US would overthrow him and his behavior therefore was figuratively and perhaps literally suicidal. Since national leaders seek to avoid this fate, there was a puzzle whether or not Saddam had WMD. I do not think it would have been reasonable to expect the ICs to have unraveled it, but noting that Saddam's behavior was inexplicable might have sparked doubts and productive thought. The ICs displayed an unfortunate but perhaps typical lack of curiosity.

Another puzzle is given insufficient attention by the reports. This is that Saddam's son-in-law, Hussein Kamel, who defected from Iraq in 1995 and brought a great deal of valuable information about Iraq's forbidden programs, told interviewers that the old material had been destroyed and that the programs were moribund. But the version that reached the public was that he testified that the programs were continuing. Indeed, for many outside observers, this was a major reason for believing that Saddam was continuing to vigorously pursue WMD.

There are two mysteries here. First, who spread the false reports and why were they not corrected? The Bush administration had an interest in maintaining the myth, but it is hard to see how Clinton's did. Second, why did the ICs not pay more attention to Kamel's testimony? In retrospect his reports were very revealing and one would think that they might have led the ICs to believe that Saddam no longer had active programs. The failure of the post-mortems to raise the question may reflect their falling victim to one of the analytical problems that bedeviled intelligence: because Kamel did not loom large in the assessments, the reports did not think to explain the absence.[75]

Empathy and context

The reports echo other studies of intelligence in attributing part of the failure to a lack of area knowledge and empathy. As with many of their criticisms, there is much to this. Few members of the IC spoke Arabic, had lived in Iraq, or were familiar with the country's culture, history and political system, and it is hard to deny that a priority must be recruiting and training people with these skills.

But we need to inject some cautionary notes, starting with the fact that the countries in the region reached basically the same conclusions that the West did. Furthermore, even though local knowledge was limited in the US and UK, their ICs were not without empathy. They did try to see the world as Saddam did, and partly for this reason believed that he had great incentives to get WMD (which in fact was correct). They also understood that he saw himself under siege by the US, which is not always the case when the perceiving state believes that its intentions are benign. Indeed, the attempt to empathize may have made it more difficult to understand how little information reached Saddam from the outside world, how isolated he was from even his inner circle, and how corrupt his regime had become. Nevertheless, three aspects of the limits on empathy are relevant, including an especially troubling one that brings us to the heart of the failure.

First, intelligence failed to integrate technical and political analysis sufficiently. Most estimates of Iraq's WMD programs were supervised by the National Intelligence Officers (NIOs) for the relevant weapons and drew most heavily on the Weapons Intelligence, Nonproliferation, and Arms Control division of CIA. Regional analysts and the NIO for Near East and South Asia were involved, but usually less than centrally. Thus questions of Iraqi WMD capabilities were not treated in the context of Saddam's political system, fears, and intentions.[76] I doubt if this was an exceptional case. The specialization, division of labor, and caution that characterize a large intelligence organization like CIA is more conducive to studying trees than the forest. But, to return to one of my dismal themes, it is unlikely that greater integration would have produced the correct answer. Indeed, in some ways the analysts not only implicitly took account of the political context, but also overweighted it. It was less the specific signs of WMD activity that led them to conclude that Saddam had robust programs than it was their sense of his political objectives and outlook.

Second, analysis usually assumes foreign actors are rational as Americans understand rationality, and often as unitary as well. Empathizing with confusion, improvisation, and corruption is very difficult. As Douglas Ford explains, during World War II the UK never was able to understand Japanese 'long-term plans and the [strength of the military] opposition to be encountered [in Burma] owing to the Japanese high command's failure to devise a coherent strategy'.[77] Saddam's Iraq lacked a coherent strategy as well, and it is not surprising the ICs had great trouble discerning it.

Third, and central to the Iraq case, empathy is difficult when the other's beliefs and behavior are strange and self-defeating. It was hard for the US to guess that Japan might attack Pearl Harbor because it made no sense for a country to attack another with an economy more than five times larger. Although the US did not entirely discount the possibility that Khrushchev would put missiles in Cuba, it was surprised that he did so because it correctly believed that such a move could not be sustained. American analysts and decision-makers similarly failed to anticipate the Soviet deployment of troops to Afghanistan because they knew that this would be foolish.[78] Three days before Hitler attacked the Soviet Union, the British ambassador told a Soviet diplomat the German military build-up was 'one of Hitler's moves in the "war of nerves". . . . But a war? . . . An attack? I find it difficult to believe. It would be crazy!' The Soviet diplomat agreed: 'An invasion [of Russia] always ends badly for the initiators.'[79]

Many intelligence failures are then bilateral in that one state is taken by surprise because it is unable to anticipate the other's intelligence failure. I believe this is the central reason for the American and British failures in Iraq. It is not surprising that intelligence failed to grasp Saddam's strange and self-defeating outlook; it is particularly difficult for analysts to get it right when the truth is implausible, and the role of plausibility is central in this and many other cases.

The importance of plausibility

The fundamental reason for the intelligence failures in Iraq was that the assumptions and inferences were reasonable, much more so than the alternatives. This is recognized by the WMD Commission and the Butler Report, although they shy away from the full implications. Saddam had vigorously pursued WMD in the past (and had used chemical weapons to good effect), had major incentives to rebuild his programs, had funds, skilled technicians, and a good procurement network at his disposal, and had no other apparent reason to deceive and hinder the inspectors. In fact, even if there had been no errors in analytic tradecraft I believe that the best-supported conclusion was that Saddam was actively pursuing all kinds of WMD, and probably had some on hand. The judgment should have been expressed with much less certainty, the limitations on direct evidence should have been stressed, and the grounds for reaching the assessments should have been explicated. But while it would be nice to believe that better analysis would have led to a fundamentally different conclusion, I do not think this is the case.

If before the war someone had produced the post-war Duelfer Report, I am sure that she would have been praised for her imagination, but would not have come close to persuading. Even now, the report is hard to believe. To take one example, who would have believed that the reason why Saddam's scientists would not account for much of the missing anthrax was that they feared his anger if he learned that they had dumped it near one of his palaces? Did it make any sense that 'by late 2002 Saddam had persuaded himself . . . that the United States would not attack Iraq because it already had achieved its objectives of establishing a military presence in the region'?[80]

More generally, Duelfer tells us that Saddam was particularly concerned about maintaining the appearance of WMD in order to deter Iran, that he feared that unlimited inspections would allow the US to pinpoint his location and assassinate him, that private meetings between the inspectors and scientists were resisted because 'any such meeting with foreigners was seen as a threat to the security of the Regime', and that 'Iraq did not want to declare anything that documented use of chemical weapons [in the war with Iran] for fear the documentation could be used against Iraq in lawsuits'.[81] Saddam's central motivation apparently was first to end sanctions and inspections and then to reconstitute his programs, all the while keeping his real and perceived adversaries at bay. 'This led to a difficult balancing act between the need to disarm to achieve sanctions relief while at the same time retaining a strategic deterrent. The Regime never resolved the contradiction inherent in this approach.'[82]

This is putting it mildly. Full compliance with the inspectors was the only way that sanctions were going to be fully lifted, especially after 9/11. It is true that revealing that Saddam had no WMD would have reduced his deterrence, but the fear of such weapons could not and did not prevent an American attack, and Iran was hardly spoiling for a fight and could not have assumed that the West would stand aside while it greatly increased its influence by moving against Iraq. Saddam's policy was foolish and self-defeating, and this goes a long way to explaining the intelligence failure. When the situation is this bizarre, it is not likely to be understood.[83]

The central analytical error was not that inferences were driven by their plausibility in light of previous Iraqi behavior and the sense they made of Saddam's goals and general capabilities, but that the analysts did not make this clear and probably did not even understand it. The ICs should have tried to separate the role of plausibility from the impact of the specific reports and done more to understand and communicate not only their final judgments, but how they reached them.[84] This also helps explain what SSCI means when it says that many IC conclusions were 'not supported by the intelligence' and instead were the products of 'analytical judgments'.[85] This is correct, but misguided in implying that the latter are somehow illegitimate – in fact, they are the bread-and-butter of intelligence analysis. Direct reports that are valid and unambiguous are extremely rare. To tell the IC to shy away from analytical judgments would be to condemn it to silence on almost all important questions, just as a similar prescription for science would stymie any comprehension of our world. Deductions and indirect inference are central to the enterprise of understanding. The real problem in Iraq and many other cases was that the ICs and policy-makers were unaware of the extent to which the conclusions did rest on these kinds of judgments.

Being strongly influenced by plausibility can be criticized as being closed-minded or assumption-driven. But this is a powerful and legitimate habit of the mind, necessary for making sense of a complex and contradictory world, and it is responsible for many correct as well as incorrect inferences. At least some of the reason why CIA analysts were (rightly) unconvinced that there was a close and collaborative relationship between Al Qaeda and Iraq was that such ties did not fit with how they believed the regime operated and saw its self-interest. Although information pointing to such a connection was not reliable or abundant, there were enough scattered reports so that someone who had a different reading of the regime could have placed more faith in them, as the ad hoc Defense Department intelligence unit and administration leaders did. Similarly, although INR is to be praised for rejecting the reports that Iraq was making a serious effort to buy uranium from Niger, if SSCI's summary is correct the explanation is less that these analysts read the evidence more carefully than that they found the whole idea implausible because Iraq would not 'risk such a transaction when they were "bound to be caught." '

In the same way, those in Air Force intelligence who dissented from the judgment that the procurement of mapping software covering the US meant that Iraq might be planning to use UAVs against the American homeland did so 'because they did not believe that the UAVs were intended for CBW delivery use and, therefore, Iraq would have no need to use the UAVs in the U.S.'[86]

For the ICs to have explained more carefully why judgments were reached would have had multiple benefits. It would have alerted consumers to trains of reasoning that they could question; it would have told consumers and analysts what evidence, direct and indirect, was being relied on; it would have sensitized analysts to their assumptions and instances in which they were engaged in illegitimate 'bootstrapping.' After first seeing evidence as consistent with established views because of the latter's plausibility, in some instances in the Iraq case (and I am sure in many others) this evidence was then used as a reason to be even more certain that these views were correct. This is a form of circular thinking that leads to excessive confidence.

Conclusions

Underlying several of the weaknesses of the American IC may be the pressure to produce current intelligence, which apparently has increased since Bush assumed office.[87] Although the IC did not lack in-depth knowledge of the technical questions of WMD, it may have lacked the time as well as incentives to step back, re-examine central assumptions, explore alternatives, and be more self-conscious about how it was drawing its conclusions. With a projected increase in the size of DI and the responsibility for the PDB moving to the DNI, it is possible that there will be room for more time-consuming kinds of analysis, but this will only happen with improved middle-level management and leadership from the top of IC, which is not likely to be forthcoming.

Despite the many errors, most of the ICs' general conclusions, although wrong, were reasonable. Indeed the Flood Report 'acknowledges that it is doubtful that better process would have changed the fundamental judgments about the existence of WMD'.[88] In places, the WMD Commission comes close to seeing this, and the Butler Report can be read in this way as well. SSCI strongly implies the opposite. But even the former two leave the impression that some (unspecified) alternative fits the evidence better than the ICs' assessments. I suspect that the reports shied away from this question because of excessive hindsight and a failure of political nerve. To have admitted that although errors were made and the process could be improved, no conceivable fix would have led to the correct judgment would have been met with incredulity and undercut the recommendations.

The reports are right to find fault; better analysis would have highlighted the central role of assumptions, pre-existing beliefs, and views of what was plausible. By doing so, it would have facilitated their reexamination, although it probably would not have changed them. Carl Sagan reminds us that 'extraordinary claims require extraordinary evidence', and by the mid-1990s the claim that Saddam was actively developing WMD programs was ordinary and therefore did not require extraordinary evidence to be confirmed. This makes sense of the exchange in which Bush reacted to CIA's presentation of recent evidence for Saddam's programs by asking whether 'this is the best we've got?' and received Tenet's now-infamous reply: 'Why, it's a slam-dunk!'[89] Bush was focusing on the specific evidence he had just heard; Tenet was moved by the plausibility of the entire picture.

Similarly, the UNMOVIC and IAEA inspectors may have been more skeptical that Iraq had WMD programs not only because they lacked some information that intelligence had and were strongly influenced by their firsthand exposure to the absence of evidence of a program, but because their job was only to inspect, not to reach judgments, and they therefore were less influenced by their general beliefs about how Iraq's behavior fitted together. If the ICs had been aware of the extent to which their interpretations of specific reports were influenced by what they already believed, they would have been more sensitive to the paucity of direct evidence, and would have been less certain in what they believed and conveyed to policy-makers.[90]

While many of the recommendations of the reports and of the CIA's internal studies are designed to keep assessments closer to available evidence and so decrease the likelihood of their being confidently wrong, as they were on Iraq, they do less to increase the chance that the judgments will be right. Many are useful, such as the call for more and better post-mortems covering successes as well as failures and the greater use of 'Red Teams' and Devil's advocates. These recommendations, however, are not new and the reports might have tried to find out why they had never been implemented on a sustained basis (as well as noting that they would not have led to a different outcome in the Iraq case.)[91]

Of course the most far-reaching reform was the establishment of a DNI that grew out of the 9/11 Commission.[92] Much of the WMD Commission report discusses how to organize the DNI's office. Whatever one thinks about the call for a large number of new high-level positions, it is chastening to realize that there is no reason to expect that such arrangements would have prevented the terrorist attacks or the Iraq failure.

So while these reports convey a great deal of useful information and will be mined by scholars for years to come, they are not satisfactory either intellectually or for improving intelligence. I think we can be certain that the future will see serious intelligence failures, some of which will be followed by reports like these. Reforms can only reduce and not eliminate intelligence errors, and in any event there is no reason to expect that the appropriate reforms will be put in place.[93] Perhaps a later scholar will write a review like this one as well.

Acknowledgement

I would like to thank Richard Betts, Peter Gourevitch, Deborah Larson, Melvyn Leffler, Rose McDermott, Paul Pillar, Marc Trachtenberg, James Wirtz, and several members of the intelligence community for ideas and comments.

Notes

1 Truth in reviewing requires me to say that I chair the CIA's Historical Review Panel which advises the Director on declassification policies and priorities, wrote a post-mortem for the CIA on why it was slow to see that the Shah of Iran might fall that located a number of errors which recurred in the Iraq case ('Analysis of NFAC's Performance on Iran's Domestic Crisis, Mid-1977–November 1978', declassified as CIA-RDP86B00269R001100110003-4), and led a small team that analyzed the lessons of the Iraq WMD failure. This essay has been cleared by the CIA's Publications Review Board, but nothing was deleted and there is nothing of substance I would have added if I had not had to submit it.

2 The *Report of the Inquiry into Australian Agencies*, Canberra, July 2004 (the Flood Report) is not as detailed as the US and UK reports and I will say little about it. The UK House of Commons Foreign Affairs Committee and the Intelligence and Security Committee had investigations and reports, although what is of value in them for our purposes is subsumed by the Butler Report. The UK also held a special investigation into the suicide of David Kelly and the related question of whether the British government had 'sexed up' its public dossier on WMD (the Hutton Report). The Butler Report covers some issues of policy as well as intelligence, in part because in the UK the line between the two is not as sharply drawn as in the US. Indeed, 'assessment is really viewed in the UK as a *government* function and not specifically an *intelligence* function': (Philip Davies, 'A Critical Look at Britain's Spy Machinery', *Studies in Intelligence*, 49/4 (2005), 41–54). For other analyses of the Butler Report, see Philip Davies, 'Intelligence Culture and Intelligence Failure in Britain and the United States', *Cambridge Review of International Affairs* 17 (Oct. 2004), 495–520;

Nigel West, 'UK's Not Quite So Secret Services', *International Journal of Intelligence and Counter-Intelligence* 18/2 (Spring 2005), 23–30; Mark Phythian, 'Still a Matter of Trust: Post-9/11 British Intelligence and Political Culture', ibid. 18 (Winter 2005–2006), 653–81; Alex Danchev, 'The Reckoning: Official Inquiries and The Iraq War', *Intelligence and National Security* 19/3 (Autumn 2004), 436–66 Prime Minister Blair gave his response to the Butler Report in a speech to the House of Commons on 13 July 2004. For Central Intelligence Agency (CIA) responses, see Associated Press, 'CIA Revising Pre-Invasion Iraq Arms Intel', *New York Times*, 2 Feb. 2005; CIA Directorate of Intelligence, 'Continuous Learning in the DI: May 2004 Review of Analytic Tradecraft Fundamentals', Sherman Kent School, CIA, *Tradecraft Review* 1 (Aug. 2004); Richard Kerr *et al.*, 'Issues for the US Intelligence Community', *Studies in Intelligence* 49/3 (2005), 47–54. For earlier discussions of the intelligence failures, see Peter Bamford, *Pretext for War: 9/11, Iraq, and the Abuse of America's Intelligence Agencies* (New York: Doubleday 2004) and, especially, John Prados, *Hoodwinked: The Documents that Reveal How Bush Sold Us a War* (New York: New Press 2004). These accounts do little to explain the failures, however. It also appears that intelligence made errors in other areas, especially in underestimating the deterioration of Iraq's infrastructure. But little attention has been focused here, or on areas of intelligence success, especially in anticipating the obstacles to political reconstruction.

3 Danchev, 'Reckoning', 437.

4 The four investigations of Pearl Harbor conducted in the five years after it failed to settle the basic questions, as shown by Martin Melosi, *In the Shadow of Pearl Harbor: Political Controversy over the Surprise Attack, 1941–46* (College Station: Texas A&M Press 1977), and it took an unofficial (but government sponsored) study much later to shed real light on the problems in an analysis that remains central our understanding not only of this case, but to surprise attacks in general (Roberta Wohlstetter, *Pearl Harbor: Warning and Decision* [Stanford UP 1962]).

5 Diane Vaughan, *The Challenger Launch Decision: Risky Technology, Culture, and Deviance at NASA* (Univ. of Chicago Press 1996); Vaughan draws in part on Charles Perrow, *Normal Accidents with High Risk Technologies* (New York: Basic Books 1984); for another superb analysis of this type see Scott Snook, *Friendly Fire: The Accidental Shootdown of U.S. Black Hawks Over Northern Iraq* (Princeton UP 2000).

6 Steven Weisman and Douglas Jehl, 'Estimate Revised on When Iran Could Make Nuclear Bomb', *New York Times*, 2 Aug. 2005.

7 Much of this literature is summarized in Timothy Wilson, *Strangers to Ourselves: Discovering the Adaptive Unconscious* (Cambridge, MA: Harvard UP 2002). For a further discussion of this and related issues see Robert Jervis, 'Understanding Beliefs', *Political Psychology*, forthcoming).

8 For a good argument that intelligence mattered less in the Cold War than is generally believed, see John Lewis Gaddis, 'Intelligence, Espionage, and Cold War History', *Diplomatic History* 13/2 (Spring 1989), 191–212; for the general (and overstated) claim that intelligence matters little in warfare, see John Keegan, *Intelligence in War* (London: Hutchinson 2003). For a small but important case in which good intelligence derived from intercepted cables guided policy, see Ken Kotani, 'Could Japan Read Allied Signal Traffic? Japanese Codebreaking and the Advance into French Indo-China, September 1940', *Intelligence and National Security* 20 (June 2005), 304–20. Not only may policy be independent of intelligence, which may not have been the case in Iraq, but good policy may rest on bad intelligence. In the most important case of this kind, in prevailing on his colleagues to continue fighting Nazi Germany in June 1940, Winston Churchill utilized estimates of German strength that were even more faulty than the WMD estimates: David Reynolds, 'Churchill and the British 'Decision' to Fight on in 1940: Right Policy, Wrong Reasons', in Richard Langhorne (ed.), *Diplomacy and Intelligence During the Second World War*, Cambridge, UK: Cambridge 147–67.

9 Numbers 13: 1–2, 31–32; for the most recent report of an intelligence failure, see Bill Gertz, 'Analysts Missed Chinese Buildup', *Washington Times*, 9 June 2005.

10 The literature is enormous: the best discussion is Richard Betts, *Surprise Attack* (Washington DC: Brookings Institution 1982); the classic study is Wohlstetter, *Pearl Harbor*, see also Emphrain Kam, *Surprise Attack: The Victim's Perspective* (Cambridge, MA: Harvard UP 1988). Good historical studies are Ernest May, ed., *Knowing One's Enemies: Intelligence Assessment Before the Two World Wars* (Princeton UP 1984) and the special issue of *Intelligence and National Security* 13/1 (Spring 1998) edited by Martin S. Alexander on 'Knowing Your Friends: Intelligence Inside Alliances and Coalitions from 1914 to the Cold War', also in book form that year, now available from Routledge. For a detailed study of the failure of American, Dutch, and UN intelligence to anticipate the capture of Srebrenica and the massacre of the men captured there, see Cees Wiebes, *Intelligence and the War in*

Bosnia, 1992–1995 (Munster: Lit 2003). Much of this work rests on analysis of how individuals process information and see the world, as I have discussed in *Perception and Misperception in International Politics* (Princeton UP 1976). For an application of this approach to improving intelligence, see Richards Heuer, *Psychology of Intelligence Analysis* (Washington DC: CIA Center for the Study of Intelligence 1999). For a superb study of individual differences in accuracy of predictions and willingness of change one's mind, see Philip Tetlock, *Expert Political Judgment* (Princeton UP 2005). In my post-mortem on why CIA was slow to see that the Shah of Iran might fall (note 1), I came to the conclusion that many of the problems centered on organizational habits, culture, and incentives, however. For all their weaknesses in this area, democracies probably do a better job of assessing their adversaries than do non-democracies: Ralph White, 'Why Aggressors Lose' *Political Psychology* 11/2 (June 1990), 227–42; Dan Reiter and Allan Stam, *Democracies at War* (Princeton UP 2002).

11 Of course, it would be difficult to determine the percentage of cases in which intelligence was right or wrong, even leaving aside the questionable nature of such a dichotomy. Indeed, probably the more interesting metric would be a comparison of the success rate of the IC with that of informed observers who lack access to classified information.

12 Carl von Clausewitz, *On War*, ed. and translated by Michael Howard and Peter Paret (Princeton UP 1976), 117. The Butler Report uses this quotation as its headnote.

13 The Israeli service is often help up as a model, but for a review of its errors, see Ephraim Kahana, 'Analyzing Israel's Intelligence Failures', *International Journal of Intelligence and CounterIntelligence* 18/2 (Summer 2005), 262–79.

14 For the cogent but politically unacceptable argument that 'if the September 11 and Iraq failures teach us anything, it is that we need to lower our expectations of what intelligence analysis can . . . do', see Thomas Mahnken, 'Spies and Bureaucrats: Getting Intelligence Right', *Public Interest* No.81 (Spring 2005), 41. This would mean trying to design policies that are not likely to fail disastrously if the supporting intelligence is incorrect.

15 Bob Woodward, *Plan of Attack* (New York: Simon & Schuster 2004).

16 I am grateful to Richard Betts for this formulation.

17 For comparisons between the classified and public American reports, see SSCI, 286–97; Jessica Mathews and Jeff Miller, 'A Tale of Two Intelligence Estimates', Carnegie Endowment for International Peace, 31 March 2004; Donald Kennedy, 'Intelligence Science: Reverse Peer Review?' *Science* 303, 26 March 2004; Center for American Progress, 'Neglecting Intelligence, Ignoring Warnings', 28 Jan. 2004, <www.americanprogress.org/site/pp.asp?c=biJRJ8OVF&b=24889>. One of the main recommendations of the Butler Report was that the Joint Intelligence Committee (JIC) not issue public estimates which, contrary to precedent, it did in this case.

18 WMD Commission, 50.

19 WMD Commission, 50.

20 Butler Report, 13.

21 Israeli intelligence did employ a Red Team, but its arguments were found to be unpersuasive: Kahana, 'Analyzing Israel's Intelligence Failures', 273–4. This serves as a good reminder that many of the prescriptions offered in the report would not have changed the outcome. In fact, academic research casts doubt on the efficacy of this approach: Charlan Nemeth, Keith Brown and John Rogers, 'Devil's Advocate Versus Authentic Dissent: Stimulating Quality and Control', *European Journal of Social Psychology* 31 (Nov./Dec. 2001), 707–20. Within CIA, the best work on the related approach of Alternative Analysis: see especially his exposition of how this method could have been used before the Soviet missiles were discovered in Cuba: 'Alternative Analysis and the Perils of Estimating: Analyst-Friendly Approaches', unpublished MS, 6 Oct. 2003.

22 SSCI, 20–21, 106.

23 'Iran: Intelligence Failure or Policy Stalemate?' Working Group Report No.1.

24 Only a few scattered individuals dissented. According to Hans Blix, France's President Jacques Chirac was one of them, remarking on the propensity of intelligence services to 'intoxicate each other': Hans Blix, *Disarming Iraq* (New York: Pantheon 2004) 129.

25 For a brief discussion of an intelligence success, see David Robarge, 'Getting It Right: CIA Analysis of the 1967 Arab-Israeli War', *Studies in Intelligence* 49/1 (2005), 1–8. For a discussion of some of the earlier CIA post-mortems, see Douglas Shyrock, 'The Intelligence Community Post-Mortem Program, 1973–1975', *Studies in Intelligence* 21 (Fall 1997), 15–22; also see Woodrow Kuhns, 'Intelligence Failures: Forecasting and the Lessons of Epistemology', in Richard Betts and

Thomas Mahnken, eds. *Paradoxes of Strategic Intelligence* (London: Frank Cass 2003), 80–100; John Hedley, 'Learning from Intelligence Failures', *International Journal of Intelligence and CounterIntelligence* 18 (Fall 2005), 435–50. Douglas MacEachin, a former career CIA official, has done a series of excellent post-mortems: *The Final Months of War With Japan: Signals Intelligence, U.S. Invasion Planning, and the A-Bomb Decision* (Washington DC: CIA Center for the Study of Intelligence 1998); *Predicting the Soviet Invasion of Afghanistan: The Intelligence Community's Record* (Washington DC: CIA Center for the Study of Intelligence 2002); *U.S. Intelligence and the Confrontation in Poland, 1980–1981* (University Park: Pennsylvania State UP 2002).

26 In fact, as the NIE was being written, confirming reports were received from a very well placed source. This was so sensitive that it was not shared with the analysts and so did not effect the estimate, but it reinforced the confidence of those in charge of the exercise and of the top policy-makers: WMD Commission, 117.

27 Richard Betts, 'Warning Dilemmas: Normal Theory vs. Exceptional Theory', *Orbis* 26 (Winter 1983), 828–33.

28 SSCI, 18.

29 Irving Janis, *Groupthink: Psychological Studies of Policy Decisions and Fiascoes*, 2nd ed. (Boston: Houghton Mifflin 1983); for later research in this area see Paul 't Hart, Eric Stern and Bengt Sundelius, eds., *Beyond Groupthink: Political Group Dynamics and Foreign Policy-Making* (Ann Arbor: Univ. of Michigan Press 1997).

30 WMD Commission, 183.

31 For reports of pressures to conform within CIA, see WMD Commission, 191–94; for the argument that the State Department's Bureau of Intelligence and Research (INR) has developed a culture that encourages dissent and the CIA has not, see Justin Rood, 'Analyze This', *Washington Monthly* (Jan./Feb. 2005), 18–21.

32 SSCI, 22. In the mid-1980s a similar conclusion was reached by CIA's Senior Review Panel based on examining a number of cases from 1945 to 1978: Willis Armstrong *et al.*, 'The Hazards of Single-Outcome Forecasting', originally in Studies in Intelligence 28 (Fall 1984) and declassified in H. Bradford Westerfield, Inside CIA's Private World: Declassified Articles from the Agency's Internal Journal, 1955–1992 (New Haven, CT: Yale UP 1995), 238–54. Political psychologists have similarly argued that much information is ordinarily processed 'online', i.e., that as new information is received it is melded with the person's standing judgment on the subject, with the person not being aware of how the latter was formed. See, for example, Kathleen McGraw and Milton Lodge, 'Review Essay: Political Information Processing', *Political Communication* 13 (Jan.–March 1996), 131–38; Charles Taber, 'Information Processing and Public Opinion,' in David Sears, Leonie Huddy, and Robert Jervis, eds., *Oxford Handboook of Political Psychology* (New York: Oxford UP 2003), 433–76. An interesting possible case is the CIA's over-estimate of the time it would take the USSR to produce an atomic bomb. It was so sure that the USSR suffered from a great shortage of uranium that it missed the signs that large-scale enrichment was underway: Donald Steury, 'Dissecting Soviet Analysis, 1946–50: How the CIA Missed Stalin's Bomb', *Studies in Intelligence* 49/1 (2005), 24–25.

33 SSCI, 161–62.

34 In addition to the Duelfer Report, see James Risen, 'The Struggle for Iraq: Intelligence; Ex-Inspector Says CIA Missed Disarray in Iraqi Arms Program', *New York Times*, 26 Jan. 2004.

35 SSCI, 102–3. Of course the general problem is that there are an infinite number of non-rational, non-unitary explanations that can account for any bit of data.

36 David Kay, 'Iraq's Weapons of Mass Destruction', *Miller Center Report* 20 (Spring/Summer 2004), 8. It also does not help when a CIA analyst is newly assigned to a case, he or she starts by 'reading into', not the field reports, but the finished intelligence that gives the office's established views.

37 Jervis, *Perception and Misperception in International Politics*, Chapter 4.

38 For a summary, see Ziva Kunda, *Social Cognition: Making Sense of People* (Cambridge, MA: MIT Press 1999), 112–20.

39 SSCI, 21, also see 268.

40 WMD Commission, 93; James Rissen, 'C.I.A. Held Back Iraqi Arms Data, U.S. Officials Say', *New York Times*, 6 July 2004. For the dismissal of negative evidence that was received in another case, see Gabriel Gorodetsky, *Grand Delusion: Stalin and the German Invasion of Russia* (New Haven, CT: Yale UP 1999), 282.

41 SSCI, 3.

42 Iran's president reacted to the fact that lack of hard evidence that Iran was seeking nuclear weapons had not dispelled Western suspicions (justified, in my view) by declaring: 'Usually, you cannot prove that sort of thing [i.e., that a country is not seeking weapons]. How can you prove that you are not a bad person?' (Quoted in Steven Weisman and Warren Hoge, 'Iranian Leader Promises New Proposals to End Nuclear Impasse', *New York Times*, 16 Sept. 2005). As I will discuss in the next section, the paucity of evidence can be explained by the other's deception and denial activities, an argument made by the US in this case as well as about Iraq: Bill Gertz, 'U.S. Report Says Iran Seeks to Acquire Nuclear Weapons', *Washington Times*, 16 Sept. 2005.

43 Mahnken, 'Spies and Bureaucrats', 37.

44 SSCI, 184.

45 SSCI, 107. For a fascinating discussion of the ignoring of negative evidence from signals intelligence in the 1964 Gulf of Tonkin incident, see Robert Hanyok, 'Skunks, Bogies, Silent Hounds, and Flying Fish: The Gulf of Tonkin Mystery, 2–4 August 1964', *Cryptologic Quarterly* 19/4–20/1 (Winter 2000–Spring 2001) esp. 31–2, 41, 43–4, available at <www.gwu.edu~nsaarchiv/NSAEBB/NSAEBB132/relea00012.pdf>

46 Many estimates are built on beliefs that cannot be disconfirmed, and in most of these cases analysts and consumers fail to realize this. For example, as unrest grew in Iran in 1978 intelligence believed that if it were really serious the Shah would crack down, and the fact that he did not do so was taken as evidence that the situation remained in control. In 1941 both Stalin and most British officials believed that Hitler would not attack without making demands first and that some of the alarming signs emanated from the bellicose German military rather than Hitler, beliefs that only the attack itself could dispel: Gorodetsky, *Grand Delusion*, esp. 180–86.

47 Jervis, *Perception*, Chapter 6.

48 See, for example, WMD Commission, 22–178, 285–6, 320–21, 367, 437.

49 For a discussion of similar weaknesses in the British system, see Butler Report, 102–4, and Davies (note 2). Late in the process (Dec. 2002) DO apparently did express skepticism about 'Curveball's' reliability: WMD Commission, 95–98. The most detailed discussion of Curveball is Bob Drogin and John Goetz, 'How U.S. Fell Under the Spell of "Curveball," ', *Los Angeles Times*, 20 Nov. 2005.

50 WMD Commission, 285–86, 320–21, 437. This complaint is usually focused on Humint, but SSCI (p.27) reports that CIA refused too share other information as well, and other agencies are not likely to be more forthcoming – information, after all, is power.

51 Pat Roberts, 'Comments & Responses: Intelligence Reform', *National Interest*, No.81 (Fall 2005), 8.

52 SSCI, 43, also see, 46.

53 WMD Commission, 125–26; SSCI, 267–68. For some of the dangers of close contact between analysts and collectors, see Garrett Jones, 'It's A Cultural Thing: Thoughts on a Troubled CIA,' Part 1, 28 June 2005, Foreign Policy Research Institute, <www.fpri.org/endnotes/20050628.americawar.jones.ciaculture.html>.

54 WMD Commission, 321. For the (plausible) claim that when the Reagan White House was trading arms for hostages, political consideration led to the withholding of information on Iran and the status of political 'moderates', see the memo from an Iran analyst to the Deputy Director of Intelligence, 2 Dec. 1986, printed in John Gentry, *Lost Promise: How CIA Analysis Misserves the Nation* (Lantham, MD: UP of America 1993), 276–81.

55 SSCI, 247–51; WMD Commission, 87, 105, 195. Also see discussion of familiar problems on other issues in SSCI, 94, 239–46.

56 Bob Drogin and Greg Miller, 'Curveball and the Source of Fresh CIA Rancor,' *Los Angeles Times*, 2 Apr., 2005; Statement of John E. McLaughlin, former Director of Central Intelligence, April 1, 2005 (http://www.fas.org/irp/offdocs/wmd_mclaugh-lin.html).

57 On politicization in general, see H. Bradford Westerfield, 'Inside Ivory Bunkers: CIA Analysts Resist Managers' "Pandering" – Part I,' *International Journal of Intelligence and CounterIntelligence* 9 (Winter 1996/97) 407–24; Westerfield, 'Inside Ivory Bunkers: CIA Analysts Resist Managers' 'Pandering' – Part II,' ibid 10 (Spring 1997), 19–56; Richard Betts, 'Politicization of Intelligence: Costs and Benefits,' in Betts and Mahnken (note 24) 59–79; a personal account of some bitterness but also persuasiveness is Gentry (note 53). My analysis assumes that the administration believed that Saddam had WMD. Although this seems obvious, one significant bit of behavior raises doubts: the failure of US forces to launch a careful search for WMD as they moved through Iraq. Had there been stockpiles of WMD materials, there would have been a grave danger that these would

have fallen into the hands of America's enemies, perhaps including terrorists. I cannot explain this failure, but the rest of the US occupation points to incompetence.

58 Douglas Jehl, 'C.I.A. Chief Says He's Corrected Cheney Privately', *New York Times*, 10 March 2004.

59 Butler Report, 125–27, which concludes that the Joint Intelligence Committee (JIC) 'should not have included the '45 minute' report in its assessment and in the Government's [public] dossier without stating what it was believed to refer to'; for related US intelligence, see SSCI, 251–52.

60 Memo of 23 July 2002 from Matthew Rycroft to David Manning, which is printed in many places, for example *New York Review of Books*, 9 June 2005, 71.

61 For a summary of the leaks about such pressure see Joseph Cirincione, 'You Can't Handle the Truth', *Carnegie Non-Proliferation*, 2 April 2005.

62 SSCI, 484–85.

63 Quoted in Gentry, *Lost Promise*, 243.

64 The comparison between the views of different services can shed light on various causal propositions. Thus the common claim that Stalin was taken by surprise by Hitler's attack because of the particular infirmities of his intelligence system, although partly correct, needs to be reconsidered in light of the fact that Soviet and British estimates were closely parallel until the last weeks. Gorodetsky, *Grand Delusion*, esp. 264–65, 281.

65 Douglas Jehl and David Sanger, 'Prewar Assessment on Iraq Saw Chance of Strong Divisions,' *New York Times*, 28 Sept. 2004.

66 For some evidence, but a muddy interpretation, see SSCI, 357–65.

67 SSCI, 249; also see WMD Commission, 189–91.

68 Wesley K. Wark, *The Ultimate Enemy: British Intelligence and Nazi Germany, 1933–1939* (Ithaca, NY: Cornell UP 1985). The literature on motivated bias is discussed and applied to international politics in Robert Jervis, Richard Ned Lebow, and Janice Gross Stein, *Psychology and Deterrence* (Baltimore, MD: Johns Hopkins UP 1985). Lord Hutton's report clearing the Blair government of the BBC's charges that it distorted intelligence notes the possibility that analysts were 'subconsciously influenced' by their knowledge of what the government wanted to hear: quoted in Brian Urquhart, 'Hidden Truths,' *New York Review of Books*, 25 March 2004, 44. For a fascinating case of motivated bias in science, see Frank Close, *Too Hot to Handle: The Race for Cold Fusion* (Princeton UP 1991).

69 SSCI, 404–22 analyzes the extent to which the US provided intelligence to UNMOVIC, and the Butler Report, 87 briefly mentions the lack of assessments.

70 John Bolton, often accused of putting illegitimate pressure on intelligence, apparently believed that the problem instead was that members of the IC was over-reaching and trying to censor his 'political judgment as to how to interpret this data', in the words of one of his top aides (Douglas Jehl, 'Released E-Mail Exchanges Reveal More Bolton Battles', *New York Times*, 24 April 2005, and Jehl, 'Bolton Asserts Independence On Intelligence,' ibid. 12 May 2005). Unfortunately, it is much harder for anyone below the level of the president or perhaps the cabinet to make clear that what he or she is giving is a judgment different from that of the IC, because it would invites the obvious question of whether the president agrees.

71 WMD Commission, 49, 56; SSCI, 85–119; the same problem appeared in the UK: Butler Report, 130–34. Some of the discussions of chemical weapons and UAVs also displayed this ambiguity: SSCI, 204, 221–30.

72 WMD Commission, 55, also see 67–68 and SSCI, 93–4, 100–2.

73 For a brief but trenchant discussion, see the Butler Report, 11; for discussion of a similar issue in judging the evidence of the existence of a bird long believed to be extinct, see James Gorman, 'Ivory-Bill or Not? Proof Flits Tantalizingly Out of Sight,' *New York Times*, 30 Aug. 30, 2005, Section F.

74 Spencer Weart, *The Discovery of Global Warming* (Cambridge, MA: Harvard UP 2003), 89.

75 For brief mentions of Kamel's testimony, see SSCI, 218; Butler Report, 47–48, 51.

76 WMD Commission, 173; apparently this was also true in Australian intelligence: Flood Report, 26.

77 Douglas Ford, 'Planning for an Unpredictable War: British Intelligence Assessments and the War Against Japan, 1937–1945,' *Journal of Strategic Studies* 27/1 (March 2004) 148; for other examples, see Gorodetsky, *Grand Delusion*, 233; Stephen Budiansky, *Her Majesty's Spymaster* (New York: Viking 2005), 203.

78　MacEachin, *Predicting the Soviet Invasion of Afghanistan*, 46.

79　Quoted in Gorodetsky, *Grand Illusion*, 305, 308. Shortly before he was overthrown in 1974, Archbishop Makarios of Cyprus dismissed the possibility because a coup would lead to an invasion by Turkey and so 'would not make sense, it would not be reasonable': quoted in Lawrence Stern, *The Wrong Horse* (New York: New York Times Books 1977), 106.

80　*Comprehensive Report of the Special Advisor to the DCI on Iraq's WMD*, 30 Sept. 2004 (hereafter Duelfer Report) Vol.3, Section on Biological Warfare, 56; Vol.1, Regime Strategic Intent, 32. In parallel, the American chief of intelligence in Vietnam looked back at the Tet offensive and declared: 'Even had I known exactly what was to take place, it was so preposterous that I probably would have been unable to sell it to anybody. Why would the enemy give away his major advantage, which was his ability to be elusive and avoid heavy casualties?' (quoted in William Westmoreland, *A Soldier Reports* (Garden City, NY: Doubleday 1976), 321.

81　Duelfer Report, 29, 55, 62, 64 (this and subsequent references are to Vol.1). John Mueller had earlier speculated that Saddam's limitations on the inspectors were motivated by his fear of assassination: 'Letters to the Editor: Understanding Saddam', *Foreign Affairs* 83 (July/Aug. 2004), 151.

82　Duelfer Report, 34, also see, 57. The Duelfer Report itself should not be considered definitive. In many places it reads like a collection of note-cards, much information remains unexploited, and there is some tension between this report and Kay's views (note 37). Ending economic sanctions and ending inspections would not necessarily have coincided and it is not clear which of them was viewed as most troublesome, and why. The UN resolutions provided for the latter to continue even after the former ended, and Saddam had terminated inspections in 1998. This presents a puzzle because if inspections had been the main barrier, Saddam should have resumed his programs at that point, as most observers expected. But it is hard to see how the sanctions were inhibiting him because after the institution of the Oil for Food program and extensive oil smuggling, the regime had sufficient cash to procure what it needed.

83　Several other cases in which the behavior seems puzzling made sense once one understood the situation the other was in and the strategy it was following. Thus the US and Israel were taken by surprise by President Sadat's Egyptian and Syrian attack in 1973 because they failed to appreciate Sadat's desperation, the military improvements he had instituted, and his idea that what was needed was not a massive military victory, but enough of an effort to convince Israel that the status quo was untenable and to bring the US in as a broker. Here empathy would have been difficult, but not out of the question. It was even harder with Saddam because his behavior does not seem to have been the product of any reasonable calculation.

84　For a related argument, see WMD Commission, 10, 12, 173, 175.

85　SSCI, 187, 192, 194, 204, 213. The Butler Report makes a similar point about some instances of British intelligence, but without implying that this was illegitimate: 73, 75.

86　SSCI, 38, 228.

87　The Flood Report sees a similar trend in Australia: 69. But here as in many places it is difficult to make the crucial comparisons to the way things were in the past. A history of the Directorate of Intelligence reports that in the 1960s its leaders believed that long-term research had been sacrificed to the pressures of current intelligence: Anne Karalekas, 'History of the Central Intelligence Agency', in William Leary, ed., *The Central Intelligence Agency: History and Documents* (Tuscaloosa: Univ. of Alabama Press 1984), p.100. When I did the post-mortem on why the CIA was slow to see that the Shah might fall (note 1) I concluded that some of the reason was the pressures for current intelligence, which left analysts with not only little time but also little inclination or ability to look beyond the recent cables.

88　Flood Report, 27.

89　Woodward, *Plan of Attack*, 249. By this point Tenet may have also been biased by his knowledge that CIA had a string of sources in Iraq whose lives (and those of their families) would be sacrificed if the US did not invade: Jake Blood, *The Tet Effect: Intelligence and the Public Perception of War* (London: Routledge 2005), 176.

90　WMD Commission, 47, 408.

91　For a discussion of the failure of previous CIA attempts to institutionalize competing views, see Gentry, *Lost Promise*, 53, 58, 63, and 94.

92　For justly critical reviews of the 9/11 Commission report, see Richard Posner, 'The 9/11 Report: A Dissent,' *New York Times Books Review*, 29 Aug. 2004; Richard Falkenrath, 'The 9/11 Commission Report: A Review Essay,' *International Security* 29 (Winter 2004–2005) 170–90; Joshua Rovner and

Austin Long, 'The Perils of Shallow Theory: Intelligence Reform and the 9/11 Commission,' *Journal of Intelligence and CounterIntelligence* 18 (Winter 2005–2006), 609–37. For more of an explanation than a defense, see Ernest May and Philip Zelikow, 'Sins of Commission?' *International Security* 29 (Spring 2005), 208–9. For a good discussion of the 9/11 case, see Charles Parker and Eric Stern, 'Bolt From the Blue or Avoidable Failure? Revisiting September 11 and the Origins of Strategic Surprise', *Foreign Policy Analysis* 1 (Nov. 2005), 301–31.

93 Recent signs are not encouraging: see the testimony of Michael Hayden, Deputy Director of National Intelligence: <http://intelligence.house.gov/Reports.aspx?Section=122>. More on the right track is 'A Tradecraft Primer: Structured Analytic Techniques for Improving Intelligence Analysis', Sherman Kent School, CIA, *Tradecraft Review* 2 (June 2005). For discussions of some of the barriers to reform, see Richard Russell, 'A Weak Pillar for American National Security: The CIA's Dismal Performance Against WMD Threats', *Intelligence and National Security* 20/3 (Sept. 2005), 466–85; Gentry, *Lost Promise*, esp. 93–107, 184; Rood, 'Analze This'; Mahnken, 'Spies and Bureaucrafts'; Jones, 'It's A Cultural Thing: Thoughts on a Troubled CIA,' Part 2, 19 Aug. 2005, Foreign Policy Research Institute, <www.fpri.org/endnotes/20050819. americawar.jones.culturetroubledcia.html>.

Bibliography

Armstrong, Willis, *et al.* 'The Hazards of Single-Outcome Forecasting,' originally in Studies in Intelligence 28 (Fall 1984), 57–70 and declassified in H. Bradford Westerfield, ed., Inside CIA's Private World: Declassified Articles from the Agency's Internal Journal, 1955–1992 (New Haven, CT: Yale UP 1995), 238–54.

Bamford, James. *A Pretext for War: 9/11, Iraq, and the Abuse of America's Intelligence Agencies* (New York: Doubleday 2004).

Betts, Richard. 'Politicization of Intelligence: Costs and Benefits', in Betts and Mahnken, eds., *Paradoxes of Strategic Intelligence* (London: Frank Cass 2003), 59–79.

Betts, Richard. 'Warning Dilemmas: Normal Theory vs. Exceptional Theory', *Orbis* 26/4 (Winter 1983), 828–33.

Betts, Richard. *Surprise Attack* (Washington DC: Brookings Institution 1982).

Blix, Hans. *Disarming Iraq* (New York: Pantheon 2004).

Blood, Jake. *The Tet Effect: Intelligence and the Public Perception of War* (London: Routledge 2005).

Budiansky, Stephen. *Her Majesty's Spymaster* (New York: Viking 2005), 203.

CIA Directorate of Intelligence, 'Continuous Learning in the DI: May 2004 Review of Analytic Tradecraft Fundamentals', Sherman Kent School, CIA, *Tradecraft Review* 1 (Aug. 2004).

CIA Directorate of Intelligence, 'A Tradecraft Primer: Structured Analytic Techniques for Improving Intelligence Analysis,' Sherman Kent School, CIA, *Tradecraft Review* 2 (June 2005).

Cirincione, Joseph. 'You Can't Handle the Truth', *Carnegie Non-Proliferation*, 2 April 2005.

Clausewitz, Carl von. *On War*, ed. and translated by Michael Howard and Peter Paret (Princeton UP 1976), 117.

Close, Frank. *Too Hot to Handle: The Race for Cold Fusion* (Princeton UP 1991).

Danchev, Alex. 'The Reckoning: Official Inquiries and The Iraq War', *Intelligence and National Security* 19/3 (Autumn 2004), 436–66.

Davies, Philip. 'A Critical Look at Britain's Spy Machinery', *Studies in Intelligence* 49/4 (2005), 41–54.

Davies, Philip. 'Intelligence Culture and Intelligence Failure in Britain and the United States,' *Cambridge Review of International Affairs* 17/3 (Oct. 2004), 495–520.

Davis, Jack. 'Alternative Analysis and the Perils of Estimating: Analyst-Friendly Approaches,' unpublished MS, 6 Oct. 2003.

Drogin, Bob and Greg Miller. 'Curveball and the Source of Fresh CIA Rancor', *Los Angeles Times*, 2 April 2005.

Falkenrath, Richard. 'The 9/11 Commission Report: A Review Essay', *International Security* 29/3 (Winter 2004/2005), 170–90.

Ford, Douglas. 'Planning for an Unpredictable War: British Intelligence Assessments and the War Against Japan, 1937–1945', *Journal of Strategic Studies* 27/1 (March 2004).

Gaddis, John. 'Intelligence, Espionage, and Cold War History,' *Diplomatic History* 13/2 (Spring 1989), 191–212.

Gentry, John. *Lost Promise: How CIA Analysis Misserves the Nation* (Lantham, MD: UP of America 1993).

Gorodetsky, Gabriel. *Grand Delusion: Stalin and the German Invasion of Russia* (New Haven, CT: Yale UP 1999).

Hanyok, Robert. 'Skunks, Bogies, Silent Hounds, and Flying Fish: The Gulf of Tonkin Mystery, 2–4 August 1964', *Cryptologic Quarterly* 19/4–20/1 (Winter 2000–Spring 2001).

Hart, Paul 't, Eric Stern and Bengt Sundelius, eds. *Beyond Groupthink: Political Group Dynamics and Foreign Policy-Making* (Ann Arbor: Univ. of Michigan Press 1997).

Hedley, John. 'Learning from Intelligence Failures,' *International Journal of Intelligence and Counter-Intelligence* 18/3 (Fall 2005), 435–50.

Heuer, Richards. *Psychology of Intelligence Analysis* (Washington DC: CIA Center for the Study of Intelligence 1999). <www.americanprogress.org/site/pp.asp?c=biJRJ8OVF&b=24889>.

Janis, Irving. *Groupthink: Psychological Studies of Policy Decisions and Fiascoes*, 2nd ed (Boston: Houghton Mifflin 1983).

Jervis, Robert, Richard Ned Lebow, and Janice Gross Stein. *Psychology and Deterrence* (Baltimore, MD: Johns Hopkins UP 1985).

Jervis, Robert. 'Analysis of NFAC's Performance on Iran's Domestic Crisis, Mid-1977–7 November 1978', declassified as CIA-RDP86B00269R001100110003–4.

Jervis, Robert. 'Understanding Beliefs', *Political Psychology*, forthcoming.

Jervis, Robert. *Perception and Misperception in International Politics* (Princeton UP 1976).

Jones, Garrett. 'It's A Cultural Thing: Thoughts on a Troubled CIA', Part 1 and Part 2, 28 June 2005 and 19 Aug. 2005, Foreign Policy Research Institute, <www.fpri.org/endnotes/20050819.americawar.jones.culturetroubledcia.html>.

July 23, 2002 Memo from Matthew Rycroft to David Manning, *New York Review of Books*, June 9, 2005, 71.

Kahana, Ephraim. 'Analyzing Israel's Intelligence Failures', *International Journal of Intelligence and CounterIntelligence* 18/2 (Summer 2005), 262–79.

Kam, Emphraim. *Surprise Attack: The Victim's Perspective* (Cambridge, MA: Harvard UP 1988).

Karalekas, Anne. 'History of the Central Intelligence Agency', in William Leary, ed., *The Central Intelligence Agency: History and Documents* (Tuscaloosa: Univ. of Alabama Press 1984).

Kay, David. 'Iraq's Weapons of Mass Destruction,' *Miller Center Report* 20 (Spring/Summer 2004), 8.

Keegan, John. *Intelligence in War* (London: Hutchinson 2003).

Kennedy, Donald. 'Intelligence Science: Reverse Peer Review?' *Science* 303, 26 March 2004; Center for American Progress, 'Neglecting Intelligence, Ignoring Warnings', 28 Jan. 2004, <www.americanprogress.org/site/pp.asp?c=biJRJ8OVF&b=24889>.

Kerr, Richard *et al.* 'Issues for the US Intelligence Community,' *Studies in Intelligence* 49/3 (2005), 47–54.

Kotani, Ken. 'Could Japan Read Allied Signal Traffic? Japanese Codebreaking and the Advance into French Indo-China, September 1940', *Intelligence and National Security* 20 (June 2005), 304–20.

Kuhns, Woodrow. 'Intelligence Failures: Forecasting and the Lessons of Epistemology', in Richard Betts and Thomas Mahnken, eds., *Paradoxes of Strategic Intelligence* (London: Frank Cass 2003), 80–100.

Kunda, Ziva. *Social Cognition: Making Sense of People* (Cambridge, MA: MIT Press 1999), 112–20.

MacEachin, Douglas. *U.S. Intelligence and the Confrontation in Poland, 1980–1981* (University Park: Pennsylvania State UP 2002).

——. *Predicting the Soviet Invasion of Afghanistan: The Intelligence Community's Record* (Washington, D.C.: CIA Center for the Study of Intelligence 2002).

——. *The Final Months of War With Japan: Signals Intelligence, U.S. Invasion Planning, and the A-Bomb Decision* (Washington DC: CIA Center for the Study of Intelligence 1998).

Mahnken, Thomas. 'Spies and Bureaucrats: Getting Intelligence Right', *Public Interest* No.81 (Spring 2005).

Mathews, Jessica and Jeff Miller. 'A Tale of Two Intelligence Estimates', Carnegie Endowment for International Peace, 31 March 2004.

May, Ernest and Philip Zelikow. 'Sins of Commission?' *International Security* 29/4 (Spring 2005), 208–9.

May, Ernest, ed., *Knowing One's Enemies: Intelligence Assessment Before the Two World Wars* (Princeton UP 1984).

McGraw, Kathleen and Milton Lodge. 'Review Essay: Political Information Processing', *Political Communication* 13/1 (Jan.–March 1996), 131–38.

Melosi, Martin. *In the Shadow of Pearl Harbor: Political Controversy over the Surprise Attack, 1941–46* (College Station: Texas A&M Press 1977).

Mueller, John. 'Letters to the Editor: Understanding Saddam', *Foreign Affairs* 83/4 (July/Aug. 2004), 151.

Nemeth, Charlan, Keith Brown, and John Rogers. 'Devil's Advocate Versus Authentic Dissent: Stimulating Quantity and Quality', *European Journal of Social Psychology* 31/6 (Nov./Dec. 2001) 707–20.

Parker, Charles and Eric Stern. 'Bolt From the Blue or Avoidable Failure? Revisiting September 11 and the Origins of Strategic Surprise', *Foreign Policy Analysis* 1/4 (Nov. 2005), 301–31.

Perrow, Charles. *Normal Accidents: Living with High Risk Technologies* (New York: Basic Books 1984).

Phythian, Mark. 'Still a Matter of Trust: Post-9/11 British Intelligence and Political Culture', *International Journal of Intelligence and CounterIntelligence* 18/4 (Winter 2005–2006), 653–81.

Posner, Richard. 'The 9/11 Report: A Dissent', *New York Times Books Review*, 29 Aug. 2004.

Prados, John. *Hoodwinked: The Documents that Reveal How Bush Sold Us a War* (New York: New Press 2004).

Reiter, Dan and Allan Stam. *Democracies at War* (Princeton UP 2002).

Report of the Inquiry into Australian Agencies, Canberra, July 2004 (the Flood Report).

Reynolds, David. 'Churchill and the British 'Decision' to Fight on in 1940: Right Policy, Wrong Reasons,' in Richard Langhorne (ed.), *Diplomacy and Intelligence during the Second World War* (Cambridge, UK: Cambridge UP 1985), 147–67.

Robarge, David. 'Getting It Right: CIA Analysis of the 1967 Arab-Israeli War', *Studies in Intelligence* 49/1 (2005), 1–8.

Roberts, Pat. 'Comments & Responses: Intelligence Reform', *National Interest*, No.81 (Fall 2005).

Rood, Justin. 'Analyze This', *Washington Monthly* (Jan./Feb. 2005), 18–21.

Rovner, Joshua and Austin Long. 'The Perils of Shallow Theory: Intelligence Reform and the 9/11 Commission,' *Journal of Intelligence and CounterIntelligence* 18/4 (Winter 2005–2006), 609–37.

Russell, Richard. 'A Weak Pillar for American National Security: The CIA's Dismal Performance against WMD Threats', *Intelligence and National Security* 20/3 (Sept. 2005), 466–85.

Shyrock, Richard. 'The Intelligence Community Post-Mortem Program, 1973–1975', *Studies in Intelligence* 21/3 (Fall 1997), 15–22.

Snook, Scott. *Friendly Fire: The Accidental Shootdown of U.S. Black Hawks Over Northern Iraq* (Princeton UP 2000).

Special Issue of *Intelligence and National Security* 13/1 (Spring 1998), edited by Martin Alexander on 'Knowing Your Friends: Intelligence Inside Alliances and Coalitions from 1914 to the Cold War.'

Statement of John E. McLaughlin, former Director of Central Intelligence, 1 April 2005 <www.fas.org/irp/offdocs/wmd_mclaughlin.html>.

Stern, Lawrence. *The Wrong Horse* (New York Times Books 1977).

Steury, Donald. 'Dissecting Soviet Analysis, 1946–50: How the CIA Missed Stalin's Bomb', *Studies in Intelligence* 49/1 (2005), 24–25.

Taber, Charles. 'Information Processing and Public Opinion', in David Sears, Leonie Huddy, and Robert Jervis, eds., *Oxford Handboook of Political Psychology* (New York: Oxford UP 2003), 433–76.

Testimony of Michael Hayden, Deputy Director of National Intelligence <http://intelligence.house.gov/Reports.aspx?Section=122>.

Tetlock, Philip. *Expert Political Judgment* (Princeton UP 2005).

Urquhart, Brian. 'Hidden Truths', *New York Review of Books*, 25 March 2004, 44.

Vaughan, Diane. *The Challenger Launch Decision: Risky Technology, Culture, and Deviance at NASA* (Univ. of Chicago Press 1996).

Wark, Wesley K. *The Ultimate Enemy: British Intelligence and Nazi Germany, 1933–1939* (Ithaca, NY: Cornell UP 1985).

Weart, Spencer. *The Discovery of Global Warming* (Cambridge, MA: Harvard UP 2003).

West, Nigel. 'The UK's Not Quite So Secret Services', *International Journal of Intelligence and Counter-Intelligence* 18/2 (Spring 2005), 23–30.

Westerfield, H. Bradford. 'Inside Ivory Bunkers: CIA Analysts Resist Managers' "Pandering" – Part I', *International Journal of Intelligence and CounterIntelligence* 9/4 (Winter 1996/97), 407–24.

Westerfield, 'Inside Ivory Bunkers: CIA Analysts Resist Managers' "Pandering" – Part II,' *International Journal of Intelligence and CounterIntelligence* 10/1 (Spring 1997), 19–56.

Westmoreland, William. *A Soldier Reports* (Garden City, NY: Doubleday 1976).

White, Ralph. 'Why Aggressors Lose', *Political Psychology* 11/2 (June 1990), 227–42.

Wiebes, Cees. *Intelligence and the War in Bosnia, 1992–1995* (Munster: Lit 2003).

Wilson, Timothy. *Strangers to Ourselves: Discovering the Adaptive Unconscious* (Cambridge, MA: Harvard UP 2002).

Wohlstetter, Roberta. *Pearl Harbor: Warning and Decision* (Stanford UP 1962).

Woodward, Bob. *Plan of Attack* (New York: Simon & Schuster 2004).

Working Group, 'Iran: Intelligence Failure or Policy Stalemate?' Working Group Report No.1, 23 Nov. 2004 (Georgetown University: Institute for the Study of Diplomacy, Edmond A. Walsh School of Foreign Service).

Reprinted with permission from Robert Jervis, 'Reports, Politics, and Intelligence Failures: The Case of Iraq', *Journal of Strategic Studies* 29/1 (2006) pp.3–52.

14 Intelligence and Iraq

The UK's four enquiries

Richard J. Aldrich

During 2003 and 2004 the UK intelligence community underwent a 'season of enquiry' relating to intelligence, the Iraq War and the 'War on Terrorism'. This essay discusses each of the four enquiries in turn and argues that while the debate has been intense, much has been missed. The enquiries have largely focused on specific administrative issues, while the media have focused on blame-casting. Although the enquiries have been useful in underlining the extent of genuine 'intelligence failure', wider reflections about the nature and direction of UK intelligence have been conspicuously absent. None of the enquiries has dealt with the difficult issue of how intelligence analysis might interface with modern styles of policy-making. More broadly, it is argued that there is a growing mismatch between what intelligence can reasonably achieve and the improbable expectations of politicians and policy-makers.

Introduction

During a period of twelve months, between July 2003 and July 2004, Whitehall and Westminster produced no less than four different intelligence enquiries. Each examined matters related to the Iraq War and the 'War on Terrorism'. Although the term 'unprecedented' is perhaps over-used, we can safely say that such an intensive period of enquiry has not occurred before in the history of the UK intelligence community. The immediate parallels seemed to be in other countries, since similar investigations into 'intelligence failure' have been in train in the United States, Israel, Australia and even Denmark. These various national enquiries have proceeded locally and largely unconscious of each other's existence. However, the number of different enquiries in the UK and the extent of the media interest in them recall the 'season of enquiry' that descended upon the American intelligence community in 1975 and 1976.[1]

Although the intensity of the debate about connections between Britain's intelligence community and members of the core executive was considerable, the overall results were less than impressive. The remits of all four UK enquiries were narrowly drawn. Initially, the focus was 'the dossiers' published by No.10 Downing St: one in September 2002 on Iraq's weapons of mass destruction (WMD), the other in February 2003 on Iraq and its security services. Later, the focus shifted to the death of the unfortunate Dr David Kelly, a WMD expert working for the Ministry of Defence, and then finally to the performance of the intelligence services themselves. Public attention was concentrated upon the extent to which these enquiries might produce 'incriminating facts' about the distortion of intelligence. Meanwhile, wider observations and reflections about intelligence were not much in evidence.[2]

By mid-2003, the UK political class had convinced itself that in some sense intelligence had been 'fixed' or heavily distorted by political pressures. While there can be no doubt that intelligence was artfully selected to present what officials have called 'the best possible case for war', these were largely matters of over-simplification and exaggeration. While the cautious qualifications of intelligence analysts were stripped away, the basic story was not changed significantly by the government publicity teams. This was more a case of 'intelligence failure'.[3] We now know that most Western intelligence agencies got it wrong, believing that Saddam Hussein had some existing WMD capability and thinking that he was seeking to enhance it. Those holding such views included not only the intelligence communities of the United States and Israel, who had long voiced anxieties about these matters, but also the intelligence communities of countries like Germany, who enjoyed significant intelligence capability in the Middle East. Some waverers were convinced by the extent to which the German foreign intelligence service – the BND – agreed about the existence of Iraqi WMD, despite the fact that Berlin opposed military intervention. In retrospect the BND has not chosen to probe its own record publicly.[4]

Journalists and politicians were therefore barking up the wrong tree with regard to intelligence and Iraq. Although omissions and misrepresentations regarding Iraqi WMD certainly occurred along the UK's path to war, any real sleight of hand probably lay in other areas. There was misrepresentation about the ambiguous and hesitant nature of the Attorney-General's advice on the legality of war, advice that was initially described to the public as unproblematic. More importantly, there was an attempt to disguise the point at which Washington decided on war with Iraq and the early moment at which the UK decided on support for Washington's policy.[5] There were also issues about military operations that were conducted by the allies before the expiry of President Bush's 48 hour ultimatum, delivered on the evening of Monday, 17 March 2003.[6]

In all these matters, UK observers were hampered by a shortage of whistleblowers. The only exception was the decision of Katherine Gunn, a translator at Government Communications Headquarters (GCHQ), the UK's signals intelligence agency, to reveal an e-mail from the US National Security Agency, concerning the issue of eavesdropping on the United Nations. Although Gunn was arrested, the government case against her was quickly dropped when her defence team appeared likely to probe the issue of the British attorney-general's advice on going to war in Iraq, and this inadvertently steered blundering journalists back towards more promising lines of enquiry. The ambivalent text of the attorney-general's full advice was eventually leaked in February 2005. No-one else squealed. Some half a dozen intelligence officers decide to depart from the Secret Intelligence Service (SIS) because of unhappiness over the handling of Iraq and other issues related to the public exposure of intelligence, at a time when that service has been re-engaging staff aged over 65. However, these individuals did not speak publicly. Some went to jobs in the private sector and others were allowed to move sideways into alternative roles around Whitehall. Every effort was made to accommodate them.[7]

The obsession with the idea of political interference in intelligence, rather than the issue of intelligence performance, is certainly one reason why the more nuanced aspects of this remarkable year of enquiries have been overlooked. However, matters were also made difficult by the nature of the four enquiries themselves, which were all problematic in different respects. The first enquiry by the Parliamentary Select Committee on Foreign Affairs, reporting in July 2003, was remarkably politicised. The second enquiry by the Intelligence and Security Committee, reporting in September 2003, placed a narrow interpretation on a narrow remit. In January 2004, a third enquiry, chaired by Lord Hutton, into the death of Dr David Kelly reported. Although this enquiry delivered much classified material into the public domain it was not formally focused on intelligence. A final enquiry into intelligence and WMD, chaired by Lord Butler, reported in July 2004. Although this was seemingly the most important of the four, it was carefully steered away from issues of how intelligence connected with high-level decisions. Moreover, the chairs of the various enquiries were open to ingenious argument about the need for secrecy to override accountability.

Notwithstanding this, these enquiries generated fascinating material. Imperfect as they are, they tell us much about the current UK intelligence system. This short essay attempts to review these four enquiries in turn, ignoring the vexed matters of probity and propriety. Instead it asks what insights into UK intelligence we might divine from each one of the enquiries.

The Parliamentary Select Committee on Foreign Affairs (FAC)

The first enquiry was launched in June 2003 by the House of Commons Select Committee on Foreign Affairs, chaired by the stalwart Labour MP, Donald Anderson.[8] It is often referred to as the FAC enquiry, and its members were no strangers to issues of WMD, counter-terrorism and even perhaps intelligence, having considered these matters in several previous reports.[9] The FAC's purpose in this enquiry was to establish whether the Foreign and Commonwealth Office (FCO), within the framework of government as a whole, presented 'accurate and complete information' to Parliament in the run up to Iraq war, especially with regard to WMD.[10]

The FAC enquiry showed that the decision to release intelligence material to the public in the form of dossiers that had been honed by the No.10 publicity machine was an important factor, perhaps the key factor, in determining how this material was received. Pre-existing relations between Fleet Street and the No.10 press machine were already unhappy. After examining the first dossier produced on Iraqi WMD in September 2002, many Whitehall journalists leapt to the conclusion that the Joint Intelligence Committee (JIC) had been under strong political pressure to change its line.[11] One of the most interesting aspects of the FAC enquiry was the manner in which it revealed the phenomenon of 'Groupthink' in several places. The term 'Groupthink' has been widely used with regard to the approach to intelligence on Iraq and other intelligence failures, but it applied no less to the gentlemen of the press. On rather limited evidence they 'assessed' that there had been political meddling with regard to how intelligence information was presented. The furore generated by public accusation and counter-accusation eventually resulted in the resignation of BBC Director-General Greg Dyke.[12]

The FAC enquiry came to right conclusion. It asserted that on the evidence, Alastair Campbell, Prime Minister Tony Blair's director of communications, 'did not exert or seek to exert improper influence' on the drafting of the September 2002 dossier on WMD. It also concluded that the claims made in the September dossier were probably 'well founded' on the basis of the intelligence then available, albeit the emphasis given to some particular facts was peculiar. In short 'allegations of politically inspired meddling' could not be established.[13] The enquiry correctly observed that the International Institute for Strategic Studies (IISS) in London had produced a report on Iraqi WMD shortly before the government dossier of September 2002 and had come to much the same conclusions.[14]

Journalists were not the only professionals vulnerable to 'Groupthink'. In reality, almost all intelligence analysts, including those who had been associated with the United Nations Special Commission on Iraq (UNSCOM) and the United Nations Monitoring and Verification Commission (UNMOVIC), believed that Iraq still had some WMD capability.[15] In fairness, not all analysts believed that the programme had been much enhanced and many were of the view that Iraq's activities did not constitute a threat to the UK, or warrant military intervention. However, the spectrum of opinion was delimited by a reluctance to question conventional wisdom. There was a systemic belief – almost an ideological conviction – that all militarist dictators wish to acquire WMD and that they are all working busily to do so. This belief was so entrenched among intelligence analysts that the possibilty that Iraq had no WMD was not really considered. In other words, a lack of current evidence of WMD could not simply mean that there were no WMD. All of the analysts were wrong to a greater or a lesser degree.

What the FAC enquiry also showed was that the tendency to believe that Saddam had 'something' was reinforced by other factors. First, Iraq's deliberate obstruction of the UN's weapons inspectors throughout the 1990s, and second, the fact that the Western intelligence agencies got things in Iraq wrong in the past. In 1991 the intelligence agencies not only failed to spot the Kuwait invasion, they also underestimated Saddam's strategic weapons programme. Although more than a decade had passed between 1991 and the release of the dossier of September 2002, it is important to remember that analysts (such as Dr David Kelly) often spend their entire career in this highly specialist field. Those who had underestimated Iraq's WMD in 1991 were the same people who were doing the over-estimating in 2002. Understandably perhaps, they did to wish to have egg on their face a second time.[16]

Although the FAC enquiry found it hard to uncover specific details on WMD intelligence – it was relying on off-the-record briefings – it scored some success in examining a later 'dossier', produced in February 2003, concerning Saddam's mendacious security apparatus.[17] This second dossier revealed little about its origins other than the fact that it was informed by a variety of sources, including 'intelligence material'. In reality it turned out that the dossier had been largely plagiarised by the government's Coalition Information Centre (CIC) from three articles by Ibrahim al-Marashi, a research associate at the Center for Nonproliferation Studies of the Monterey Institute of International Studies who was also a D.Phil student at St Antony's College, Oxford.[18] The government had committed several blunders here. The schoolboy-style plagiarism cast a veil of dishonesty over all the material issued in 'dossier' form. The co-option of the work of the research student without his permission was not only unethical but also potentially exposed members of his family, who still lived in Iraq, to real risk. Moreover, the ability of academics to map the way in which key words in al-Marashi's dissertation had been changed offered the FAC a precise guide to how the CIC was seeking to sell its story.[19] One of the plagiarised articles comments that the Iraqi security service had a role in 'aiding opposition groups in hostile regimes', but the CIC changed this in its dossier to read 'supporting terrorist organisations in hostile regimes'.[20] Some of the anonymous drafters from the CIC were tracked down and 'dossier-ology' emerged as a new science.[21]

However, wider issues were missed. Arguably, the saga of the dossiers revealed remarkable incompetence in the matter of how to put intelligence into the public domain in order to inform policy debate. The appearance of the dossiers had brought forth the comment that this had never happened before. Strictly speaking this was not the case. Although civil servants behaved as if they had never done this before, government, in fact, had long experience of putting intelligence material into the public domain in order to justify policy. During the Cold War, a department existed within Britain's Foreign Office, the Information Research Department, that did little else except place intelligence material into the public domain with the cooperation of journalists. A similar unit, the Information Policy unit, in Northern Ireland in the early 1970s made intelligence material available to journalists.[22] In addition, the SIS has made extensive material available to writers for several books on Soviet espionage. More broadly, over the last twenty years, much reportage on matters relating to subjects such as terrorism in the Middle East was in fact provided to journalists through a well-developed system of Whitehall contacts.[23]

The issue of how to place intelligence material in the public domain became more important during the wars in the former Yugoslavia. This related in part to material derived from overhead imagery assets that revealed the scale of the humanitarian disaster being experienced by the populations in the region and pointed to the conduct of war crimes, thus underpinning UK assertions that intervention in Yugoslavia was necessary. At a later point, similar issues occurred relating to the extent to which material gathered by GCHQ might be used to inform the activities of the International Criminal Tribunal for the former Yugoslavia (ICTY).[24] Overall, a great deal of experience was gained during these difficult episodes. At the end of the 1990s a classified review was conducted that sought to learn some of the intelligence lessons offered by the Kosovo experience. One of the major recommendations was that more thought had to be given to the issue of how intelligence material was put into the public domain to inform policy and public debate. However, during 2002 and 2003 there was no evidence that this long and extensive experience had been remembered, still less applied.[25]

All these years of experience pointed to one thing: journalists are more inclined to trust spies than spin doctors. Had the British government chosen to release sanitised JIC papers rather than to craft dossiers containing selected JIC material, many misunderstandings would have been avoided. Ultimately, government was forced to release this material anyway. The members of the FAC enquiry had sections of a JIC report read out to them by the then foreign secretary, Robin Cook. Later, the Butler report reproduced large sections of JIC reports in order to show the public what it should have seen a year before. Moreover, the witnesses who were eventually paraded before the Hutton enquiry could have been made available to a parliamentary select committee at an earlier stage. Allowing the chair of the JIC, or members of the Defence Intelligence Staff, to take a limited range of questions would have carried weight. This is not to suggest that the policy outcomes would have been different, but the public understanding of the difficulties involved in assessing WMDs would have been stronger.[26]

The FAC enquiry was part of a wider programme of work undertaken by the select committees of the House of Commons. Since their reform and re-invigoration in the 1980s, these committees have provided one of the UK's main systems of scrutiny and accountability. They are one of the main portals for interchange between Whitehall and Westminster.[27] Accordingly, the most striking aspect of the FAC report is the section dealing with cooperation – or lack of it – from the intelligence services. In Whitehall-speak, the intelligence chiefs 'blanked' the FAC enquiry. The committee addressed this issue forthrightly:

> We are strongly of the view that we were entitled to a greater degree of cooperation from the Government on access to witnesses and to intelligence material. Our Chairman wrote to . . . the Cabinet Office Intelligence Co-ordinator; the Chairman of the Joint Intelligence Committee; the Chief of Defence Intelligence; the Head of the Secret Intelligence Service; and the Director of GCHQ. None of them replied. It was the Foreign Secretary who informed us that they would not appear . . . We asked for direct

access to Joint Intelligence Committee (JIC) assessments and to relevant FCO papers. That was refused, although some extracts were read to us in private session.[28]

The frustrations experienced by the FAC enquiry in attempting to interrogate the UK intelligence process are interesting from the point of view of accountability. In the past, many have argued that the UK's main intelligence oversight mechanism, the Intelligence and Security Committee (ISC), created in 1994, should have been set up as an additional Parliamentary Select Committee. Advocates of the select committee model for intelligence accountability have asserted that it would be more appropriate for such a committee to report to parliament. Instead, the current ISC reports to the prime minster, and a sanitized version of its report, which replaces sensitive material with asterisks, is later released to parliament and the public. In short, the ISC is a committee of parliamentarians, but is owned by the prime minister.[29]

Significantly, the FAC used its report to recommend that the ISC be reconstituted as a parliamentary select committee.[30] It argued that ministers were using the existence of the ISC to block their own access to intelligence related matters that fell legitimately within the ambit of foreign affairs. However, the FAC's experience contradicts its own recommendation. Although critics of the current ISC have long argued that formal select committee powers would allow the ISC to sequester documents and to compel witnesses to appear before it (the ISC currently cannot do this), the FAC's experience with intelligence matters suggests that these formidable select committee powers exist largely in name only. In practice, as we know from parallel American episodes, the factor that determines the effectiveness of such committees of enquiry is the number of supporting staff. Neither the ISC nor any of the parliamentary select committees has adequate support staff. However, as we shall see, the ISC, armed with its single intrepid investigator, was at least inside the ring of secrecy. Comparing the efforts of the FAC and ISC suggests that the configuration of the current ISC is more effective for its current purpose, albeit the ISC experience was not without its problems.[31]

The Intelligence and Security Committee (ISC)

The ISC was set the task of enquiring into whether intelligence on Iraqi WMD was properly assessed and whether it was accurately reflected in government publications. In common with the FAC, it came to the conclusion that journalists had been wrong in their more specific allegations regarding the government's interpretation of the intelligence provided on the WMD issue. The ISC noted that the September 2002 dossier on Iraqi WMD had been endorsed by the JIC and that it drew on the intelligence assessments then available. The committee also agreed that this dossier was not 'sexed up' by Alastair Campbell or any other member of the No.10 public relations team.[32]

Just like the FAC, the need for the ISC to slay the pervasive myth of gross political interference prevented it from reflecting more widely. Admittedly, poring over the minute issues of language and tracking what Campbell did and did not do was what the ISC was tasked with. However, it also has to be said that these detailed tasks came naturally to the ISC, given that its historical tendency has been to examine work-a-day issues of costs and efficiency rather than to think about more strategic questions. Major issues are sometimes identified by the ISC, but they are rarely addressed or explored in any depth. For example, the ISC noted that it needed to report on how intelligence was placed in the public domain and on relations between the intelligence services and the media. It promised to investigate this area once the Hutton enquiry had reported in January 2004. However, in the event its 'findings' on this matter were weak, being limited to a couple of pages in its report of 2004–5. The report's comments on this important subject consisted of a statement of known facts and some platitudinous observations. The issue of how government might put intelligence material into the public domain still awaits serious investigation.[33]

When looking specifically at the issue of Iraqi WMD, the ISC found significant data but did seem to know what to do with it. The ISC noted that the foreword of the WMD dossier of September 2002, penned by the prime minister, had talked about the Iraqis' 'continued' production of chemical and biological weapons. However, the ISC also identified that in reality, the UK had no information to show 'continued' production or any intelligence about the amounts of agents produced. The JIC 'did not know what had been produced and in what quantities'. In other words this was not an estimate – it was a guestimate. The JIC had 'assessed' that production had continued to take place, but this assessing was little more than a hunch. The ISC for its part merely observed that this 'uncertainty should have been highlighted' to give a balanced view.[34]

This issue was significant because it shed light on the general nature of the process of 'estimating' biological and chemical weapons stocks. The JIC was merely doing what it had done for half a century. The evidence of several decades, and especially the evidence on the issue of chemical and biological weapons, suggests that it is almost impossible for the JIC to get it right. Whatever decade we pick we can find assertions by the JIC that such weapons are a very hard target to estimate and the only thing it was sure about was that it was unlikely to get the estimate right.[35] This problem is not about to change. It follows logically from this that any policy of pre-emption based on unqualified assertions about WMD stocks was heading for trouble. Given that the UK and the US spent much of 2002 emphasising their shift towards new strategies of pre-emption, this surely deserved further comment, perhaps even extensive comment. It is in the nature of things that intelligence-led policies in this area are going to be wrong much of the time. This was the sort of strategic issue that the ISC should have addressed, but in practice was inclined to avoid.

In retrospect, we can also chart some odd discrepancies between the committees. Indeed, the committees themselves found comparison hard to resist. The FAC had chosen in its report to comment on the ISC, while the ISC responded to the FAC in a special annex. On the main issue, namely whether the unclassified dossier largely reflected the classified intelligence assessments, the FAC and ISC were in step. However, the ISC took issue with the FAC's statement that the UK was 'heavily reliant' on US intelligence, including on material obtained from defectors or exiles. The ISC asserted confidently that the UK intelligence community had 'a number of their own reliable sources, including sources in Iraq'.[36] The ISC's implication that UK intelligence sources concerning Iraq were in any sense 'reliable' were roundly contradicted by the later Butler Report, which revealed SIS reporting on Iraq as notably weak. One is inclined follow Butler and not the ISC on this matter.[37]

Both Butler and the ISC disagree with the FAC on the vexed issue of information provided by exiles and defectors, insisting that in contrast to the sources of intelligence used in Washington they played no part in the Whitehall picture. Defectors are notorious in the world of intelligence for 'gilding the lily', or exaggerating the value of the information that they carry. However, the former FCO minister Ben Bradshaw told the FAC in April 2003 that, 'the bulk of the evidence that we have since the weapons inspectors left . . . is based on intelligence, is based on defections and is based on what we know the Iraqi regime has tried to import'. Bradshaw's assertions about Britain drawing on defector material are confirmed by the September 2002 dossier, which explicitly cites 'evidence from defectors' on mobile biological facilities. Who were these defectors that Bradshaw refers to? Are these references to CIA material provided to Whitehall by Washington?[38] A comparison of the FAC, ISC and Butler reports reveals odd disparities and perhaps indicates the limits of the ability of the ISC to probe some of these matters. Ultimately, the ISC is only just inside the ring of secrecy and to an extent has to believe what it is told.

The Hutton report on Dr David Kelly (HUTTON)

Lord Hutton's report was specifically an investigation into the circumstances surrounding the death of David Kelly. Nevertheless, intelligence was woven into the fabric of its deliberations and much time was spent exploring the issue of the September 2002 dossier on WMD. Hutton re-affirmed the view taken by both the FAC and ISC that the dossier broadly reflected the JIC material and did not contain deliberate distortions. Not unlike the Scott enquiry of 1996, the Hutton investigation was run by a judge, with the result that the gathering of evidence was meticulous. However, like Scott, Hutton did not know very much about intelligence. Accordingly, the report written by Lord Hutton was dry and seemed to move past some of the most interesting evidence that he had gathered. Nevertheless, for those who took time to peruse the raw material there were fascinating things to read. Two short examples will serve here.

First, the Hutton enquiry unearthed e-mails that suggested that the more important figures around Prime Minster Tony Blair were aware that the evidence concerning Iraqi WMD was rather thin. The missing figure here is Cabinet Secretary Sir Andrew Turnbull, who remains a cypher in the whole affair. However, Hutton did secure an e-mail written by Jonathan Powell, Blair's chief of staff, to the chair of the JIC, John Scarlett. On the eve of publication of the September 2002 dossier, Powell observed:

> The document does nothing to demonstrate a threat, let alone an imminent threat, from Saddam . . . We will need to make it clear in launching the document that we do not claim that we have evidence that he is an imminent threat . . . if I was Saddam I would take a party of western journalists to the Ibn Sina factory or one of the others pictured in the document to demonstrate there is nothing there. How do we close off that avenue to him in advance?

Perhaps more than any other document, this e-mail captures the proactive nature of No.10 Downing Street in the autumn of 2002.[39]

This proactivism was revealed by the Hutton enquiry in a second piece of evidence. Taking evidence from a UN weapons inspector, Scott Ritter, Hutton uncovered an SIS propaganda operation. Whitehall later confirmed that the SIS had developed an operation to gain public support for sanctions and the use of military force in Iraq. This was called 'Operation Mass Appeal' and was designed to place stories in the media about Saddam Hussein's nerve gas stocks.[40] This revelation was especially interesting, given that some observers have long maintained that while the SIS's capability for paramilitary activities is small, much effort is put into information operations. In 2005, Lord Butler also expressed interest in this operation.[41]

More broadly, the Hutton enquiry underlines the manner in which one revelation leads to another. Although, as this essay makes clear, over time much intelligence had been placed in the public domain through 'private channels' and off-the-record briefings, the dossiers did this more ostentatiously. Once this line had been crossed, the argument could always be made for revealing a little more. Doubtless, those working on the JIC reports and dossiers of 2002 and 2003 had no inkling of just how much would be revealed about UK intelligence by the time the various enquiries had completed their business. Hutton shows us that the placing of intelligence material in the public domain usually leads to the release of further material, perhaps more than one would wish. Individual civil servants were inclined to draw similar, but perhaps more personal conclusions. Intelligence officers and policy advisers alike learned that in the twenty-first century everything is disclosable. Hutton underlined this point by discussing remarkable e-mails that revealed the casual style of new government in No.10. In 2003 no-one would have dreamed that such material would make its way onto an enquiry website. Perhaps this was 'e-Gov' of a kind that Whitehall had not really envisaged.

It is hard to resist the notion that the Hutton Enquiry has reinforced the new culture of destruction unleashed by the UK Freedom of Information Act, which was implemented in January 2005. The authorities announced a new era of public transparency; however, this was accompanied by a new private phenomenon called 'shredding day'. Up and down the country, civil servants in even the smallest local government offices were urged to trawl their filing cabinets for compromising material and to dispose of it. The Freedom of Information Act is probably a good thing for journalists who want an easy way of chasing issues such as the expense accounts of ministers. It is probably a bad thing for political historians who hope that even sensitive records will eventually be available to us.[42]

The Butler report on intelligence and IRAQ (BUTLER)

Lord Butler's report stated that its remit was to focus on the performance of UK intelligence regarding Iraqi WMD. In reality it focused on some parts of UK intelligence and not others. It cleared the Defence Intelligence Staff at the Ministry of Defence. It let the JIC off lightly and said nothing about GCHQ or about the interface between intelligence and high policy. It saved most of its fire for the SIS, its internal structures and its weak product. Butler, in common with many academic commentators, liked the explanation of 'Groupthink'. The report went a long way to offering a genuine explanation of what had happened, but Lord Butler also perhaps allowed his committee to escape pointing the finger at single individuals.

Butler confessed himself to be shocked at the thinness of SIS reporting on Iraq. He could not square the lack of reliable human agent reporting with Blair's confident assertions before parliament with regard to Iraqi WMD. Butler stated quite simply that 'SIS did not have agents with first-hand knowledge of Iraq's nuclear, chemical, biological or ballistic missile programmes'. Several of the sources used by the SIS in 2003 were dismissed as indirect and poor. Some of their reports had to be 'withdrawn' after the war had been launched, but this information was not circulated to all the original recipients of the reports.[43]

For almost half a century most personnel within the SIS had been divided between two different types of sections. The first were operational collection or 'production' elements, often organised by region, whose staff recruited spies and gathered intelligence. The second type were the 'requirements' sections, which fielded enquires from Whitehall and collated the material for despatch to consumer departments. They were also tasked with evaluating and 'validating' the reliability of the reports received from the operational elements. In other words the operational elements produced the goods and the requirements sections provided quality control.[44]

In 1994 this time-honoured system was changed. The UK government was looking for a post-Cold War peace dividend. In reality there was not a lot of peace about and the scale of the SIS's tasks were not much diminished. Tracking the diverse conflicts of the new world disorder was, if anything, a harder job. However, modest cuts were called for and so in 1994, the SIS underwent a reorganisation in which the requirements sections were combined with the operational or collection elements. This change also reflected the introduction of an intranet distribution system into Whitehall, called the UK Intelligence Messaging System. Arguably, the new architecture involved a possible conflict of interest, for the producers were effectively doing more of their own quality control. This should not happen in any well-managed intelligence system. One of Butler's recommendations was to improve quality control, and a senior member of the SIS has been tasked with implementing changes that flow from the report.[45]

The state of the JIC was also addressed by Butler. He recommended that in future the chair of the JIC should not be combined with other roles. (In recent times it has sometimes been combined with the role of UK Intelligence Co-ordinator). Moreover, he urged that the incumbent be someone used to dealing with, and presumably fending off, ministers and other very senior government figures. He suggested this might well be a senior Whitehall official in his last post. In the past, the ISC called for chairs of the JIC to be drawn from the intelligence community. Butler's recommendation now reverses that advice.[46]

Even in 2005, the press continued to ask the wrong questions with regard to the British intelligence community. While Butler was still taking evidence, journalists focused on the selection of John Scarlett, the chairman of the JIC, as the next chief of the SIS, replacing Sir Richard Dearlove. Many argued that the selection of Scarlett was somehow inappropriate. In fact, as an excellent field officer and a succesful former station chief in Moscow, he was the right man for the job. Butler, at least implicitly, was asking a different question. Should John Scarlett, who was a rising SIS officer, have been made chair of the JIC in 2001? In that position he had been outranked by much of his own committee, including the chiefs of the three secret services and the two permanent under-secretaries. Scarlett's career had not made him an expert in the realm of analysis, since no part of SIS does much analysis. In the 1990s, Scarlett had been the SIS's director of Security and Public Affairs. Butler clearly thought that Scarlett was a good intelligence officer but that this particular appointment in 2001 had been an odd decision.

Butler also advanced a long-overdue argument for the expansion of the UK Assessments Staff, who reside in the Cabinet Office and who constitute the 'engine room' of the JIC. It also called for the professionalisation of analysis within the UK intelligence system. This is not a new point, indeed it was made by Lord Franks in his review of the circumstances leading up to the Falklands War in the 1980s, but Lord Franks' wise suggestion was ignored.[47] Given that the ISC has been in existence for almost a decade, it is somewhat embarrassing that we have had to wait for an ad hoc enquiry to initiate a re-think about the nature and resourcing of assessment. This issue is so important that it is hard to see how the ISC has managed to miss it. The UK spends some £1.5 billion on intelligence, but this material that is so expensively gathered is processed through a machine on which rather little is spent.[48]

Although the JIC is often said to 'produce' JIC reports, this is misleading. In fact the Assessments Staff produce drafts of JIC reports, which the committee members then approve, or adjust or send back for redrafting. What is remarkable is that the Assessments Staff is no bigger than it was at its creation in the late 1960s.[49] This compares with the growth of the Cabinet Office staff as a whole (of which the JIC is part) from approximately

700 to over 2,500.[50] The UK government has always been proud of the JIC and the attendant assessment staff, so much so that it was presented as the flagship of open government in the 1990s, being described as 'The central intelligence machinery'.[51] It is all the more surprising then that little has been spent on the supporting staff, perhaps for decades. The culture of the UK intelligence system has always been known for being 'assessment-lite'. So much material is fed relatively raw from the collecting agencies into operational departments, sometimes through narrow channels. Since 11 September 2001, we have heard – ad nauseam – that the CIA has too many analysts and not enough human agents; perhaps the UK intelligence system did not have enough of either.[52]

Butler also expressed the hope that the Assessments Staff would be developed in such a way that it would be able to think 'radically'. However, Butler offered no radical prescriptions. Indeed, he stopped short of adopting calls from previous JIC luminaries for the Assessments Staff to include secondees from outside government.[53] One former JIC chairman, Roderic Braithwaite, had even called for the JIC to be chaired by an outsider, possibly an academic with an international relations background. This is not such a radical idea. In the United States, the most senior intelligence review group, the National Intelligence Committee, has been chaired by Professor Joseph Nye, who was most recently dean of the Kennedy School of Government at Harvard University. However, these sorts of ideas were given no quarter by Butler, and it is safe to assume that 'Groupthink' will continue.[54]

Butler's report is also fascinating for its omissions. Although it claims to be a report into UK intelligence, it mentions Britain's largest and most expensive overseas intelligence gathering agency, GCHQ, only once. The single reference is not an especially revealing one, for it occurs in the glossary and explains that GCHQ stands for 'Government Communications Headquarters'. Phrases such as 'signals intelligence' and 'comint' are nowhere to be seen. It is thought that earlier drafts of the Butler report did contain some discussion of signals intelligence but that these were removed. What these passages contained is anyone's guess. Some insist that the excellent assistance that the US and the Germans had given to the Iraqis with regard to communications security during the 1980s, especially help with the installation of fibre-optic cables, rendered much of Iraqi communications inaccessible. Others have argued that in a typically authoritarian state, Saddam's underlings were exaggerating what they had achieved in the WMD field and it was this that GCHQ and NSA were picking up. We will wait some time before we know what the signals intelligence story was. However, with this extraordinary omission, the published report (and there is no classified version) cannot really be said to have fulfilled its remit.

Butler passes over some of the most serious issues remarkably lightly. These issues are all about how intelligence connects to the higher echelons of government. Butler notes that the Ministerial Committee on the Intelligence Services is the most senior Whitehall committee dealing with intelligence matters. Butler discovered that this committee had never met in the seven years during which Tony Blair's government had been in office, and he recommended that it should meet. However, perhaps what Butler should have said was that in 2001 the ISC had recommended that this committee should meet and that Blair ignored the ISC's recommendation. In 2002 a vexed ISC noted this and 'strongly recommended' that the committee should meet, but again nothing happened in the following year. Blair's remarkable reluctance to join with his ministerial colleagues to discuss intelligence matters tells us a great deal about the way in which intelligence interfaces with No.10 Downing Street.[55]

The No.10 system is addressed in Butler's concluding paragraphs. This section of the report is perhaps the most interesting, but it is also the most arcanely worded. Here Butler addresses the problem of national security policy made on the sofa. There is an unmistakable dismay – although it is expressed in the opaque language of a mandarin – at an administration that has abandoned many formal committees and subcommittees, the traditional engine room of British government. Butler's main point was that this lack of process means that much of the wealth of experience and judgement available in the system is not brought to bear on difficult decisions. Moreover, when things go wrong and the accountability machine moves in, the paucity of records prevents enquirers from examining how decisions were made.[56]

Butler might have added that this new and informal style at the top was part of the problem for the modern JIC. As we have seen, journalists were quick to suggest that the JIC had somehow been suborned or corrupted. Even the FAC enquiry suggested (wrongly) that Alastair Campbell might have 'chaired' intelligence meetings. Instead, the problem was how a rather traditional piece of intelligence machinery, one that prided itself on procedure and on the delivery of objective facts, was going to adjust to a new style of informal government that preferred subjective policy advice. As early as 1998, some seasoned Whitehall observers had identified that adjusting to the new-style Blair machine was an ongoing problem for the JIC.[57]

Michael Herman, a former secretary of the JIC and also the UK's leading theorist of intelligence, recently reflected on the intelligence lessons that might be drawn from the Cold War. His comments also have a contemporary resonance that may not be entirely unintentional. He observed that one of these lessons was the virtue of keeping a certain distance between intelligence and policy, and even maintaining a certain 'intelligence puritanism' over the precise use made of the JIC's conclusions. He adds, intelligence works for government but its role should really be one of an objective assessor, 'not that of the lawyer whose client wants all the help he can get in pursuing his chosen case'. In making this argument he follows in the tradition of Sherman Kent, who believed that a key role of intelligence was to speak truth to power.[58]

How close, or how distant should the relationship between collectors, analysts and policy-makers be? In the world of the professional intelligence officer this debate has been rumbling on for decades. Although history suggests that mixing up analysts and policy-makers eventually results in problems, this has nevertheless been the long-term trend.[59] In peacetime, the increasing sophistication of secure online communication systems has meant that policy-makers themselves can access more and more raw material and have tended to become their own analysts. In wartime, the appetite for old-fashioned analytical reporting remains immense.[60] What is clear is that the cultural context of intelligence has changed rapidly in the last few years. Since 11 September 2001, policy-makers have used convenient arguments about new situations and 'new threats' to sweep away old conventions that they found irksome or restrictive, but which nevertheless reflected lessons hard-learned over decades.[61] Press advisers and publicity people from No. 10 may not have chaired intelligence meetings, but they certainly attended meetings of the JIC. Had anyone ever suggested this possibility to Percy Cradock, one-time chairman and stalwart of the JIC system in the 1980s, there would have been an audible explosion.[62]

Notes

The author would like to acknowledge the support of a Leverhulme Fellowship, which facilitated the research for this paper.

1 Loch K. Johnson, *A season of inquiry: the Senate intelligence investigation* (Lexington, KY, 1985).

2 Much has already been written about the four enquiries. See in particular, Alex Danchev, 'The reckoning: official inquiries and the Iraq War', *Intelligence and National Security* 19 (3) (Autumn 2004), 436–66; Michael Herman, 'Intelligence and the Iraqi threat: British joint intelligence after Butler', *Journal of the Royal United Services Institute* 149 (4) (August 2004), 18–24. The Hutton enquiry has been subjected to detailed analysis in Anthony Glees and Philip H.J. Davies, *Spinning the spies: intelligence, open government and the Hutton enquiry* (London, 2004). Butler has been analysed by Ian Davis and Andreas Persbo in 'After the Butler report: time to take on the Group Think in Washington and London', *BASIC papers: occasional papers in international security*, no. 46 (July 2004). Peter Gill, 'Intelligence oversight since 9/11: information control and the invasion of Iraq', a paper delivered at the 'Making Intelligence Accountable' workshop in Oslo, 19 September 2003, is available at http://www.dcaf.ch/news/Intel%20Acct_Oslo%200903/Gill.pdf (12 May 2005).

3 Herman, 'Intelligence and the Iraqi threat', 18.

4 The French Direction Générale de la Sécurité Extérieure took a contrary view and as early as 2002 declared the Iraqi WMD threat to be a myth, see 'French intelligence service assesses Iraqi war potential', *Foreign Broadcast Information Service*, 25 September 2002. The Dutch are also thought to have been somewhat sceptical.

5 Leaked documents suggest that the date at which war seemed certain now appears to have been 23 July 2002, see Michael Smith, 'Blair planned Iraq war from start', *Sunday Times*, 1 May 2005.

6 The issue of the date at which the allies knew that the United States had decided on war is emphasised in Andrew Wilkie, *Axis of deceit* (Melbourne, 2004). A number of special forces operations seem to have been launched into Iraq before the deadline expired.

7 The only SIS officer to have departed and to have been named is Mark Allen, see Richard Norton-Taylor, 'Another top MI6 officer quits', *Guardian*, 6 December 2004. Private information.

8 House of Commons Select Committee on Foreign Affairs, 'The decision to go to war with Iraq', ninth report of the session 2002–3, HC 813-I, vol. 1, 3 July 2003 (hereafter cited as HC 813-I, 'The decision to go to war with Iraq').

9 For example, House of Commons Select Committee on Foreign Affairs, 'Foreign policy aspects of the War against Terrorism', seventh report of the session 2001–2, HC 384, 20 June 2002, paragraphs 11–22.

10 HC 813-I, 'The decision to go to war with Iraq', 7, paragraph 3.

11 The September 2002 dossier, 'Iraq's weapons of mass destruction: the assessment of the British government', can be viewed at http://www.number-10.gov.uk/output/Page284.asp (24 July 2005).

12 'Groupthink' is most fully discussed in Davis and Persbo, 'After the Butler report'. The concept was invented by Janis Irving, *Victims of Groupthink* (Boston, 1972). See also Janis Irving, *Groupthink: psychological studies of policy decisions and fiascos* (2nd edn, Boston, 1982).

13 HC 813-I, 'The decision to go to war with Iraq', 29, paragraphs 84–6.

14 HC 813-I, 'The decision to go to war with Iraq', 9, paragraph 8. However, opinion varies as to the extent to which the IISS has drawn on informal assistance from Whitehall in preparing some of its estimates.

15 HC 813-I, 'The decision to go to war with Iraq', 9, paragraph 10.

16 The ISC concluded that by 1995 UNMOVIC inspections had revealed Iraq's pre-1991 nuclear programme to have been more advanced than the UK JIC had thought, see Intelligence and Security Committee, 'Iraq weapons of mass destruction – intelligence and assessments', Cm. 5972, 14, paragraph 35, 9 September 2003, (hereafter Cm 5972, ISC, 'Iraq weapons').

17 CIC dossier, 'Iraq – Its infrastructure of concealment, deception and intimidation', February 2003.

18 Other material was taken from articles in *Jane's Intelligence Review*. For a full analysis see the evidence submitted to the FAC by Dr Glen Rengwala of Cambridge University, available at http://middle eastreference.org.uk/fac030616.html (15 May 2005).

19 HC 813-I, 'The decision to go to war with Iraq', 5, conclusion 8.

20 HC 813-I, 'The decision to go to war with Iraq', 39, paragraph 125. Although the ISC has since made public the SIS contribution to this dossier, the material on supporting terrorist organisations does not seem to have come from the SIS either.

21 Perhaps the worst tactical blunder committed by No.10 Downing Street was to lay itself open to

some freelance intelligence work by academics. The February 2003 dossier was placed on the No.10 website as a Word file. Officials had failed to remove the metadata from the file, which included a log of the last 10 changes that had been made to the data. The UK government, and indeed other governments, have at least learned this lesson and have since moved to making documents available as PDF files, which do not retain such data. See 'The key backroom players', *Evening Standard*, 25 June 2003.

22 On the IRD see Paul Lashmar and James Oliver, *Britain's secret propaganda war* (London, 1998). On the Information Policy unit see Paul Foot, *Who framed Colin Wallace* (London, 1989).

23 The SIS reportedly made material available to Gordon Brooke-Shepherd for *The storm petrels: the first Soviet defectors, 1928–1938* (New York, 1978), and more recently for *The iron maze: the Western secret services and the Bolsheviks* (London, 1998).

24 Regarding ICTY, the then foreign secretary, Robin Cook, stated that he had given assurances to the tribunal 'that we will provide them with all our intelligence', adding that it was 'quite a remarkable and unique step' for a government to show its intelligence to an international court. Exactly what sort of material was eventually provided remains a matter of debate. House of Commons, Foreign Affairs Committee, minutes of evidence, 28 April 1999, question 186, available at http://www.publications.parliament.uk/pa/cm199899/cmselect/cmfaff/188/9042804.htm (22 July 2005).

25 Ministry of Defence, *Kosovo: lessons from the crisis*, Cm 4724, June 2000, paragraph 6.33, available at http://www.kosovo.mod.uk/lessons/ (22 July 2005). Also private information.

26 For JIC excerpts see, for example, the report of Lord Butler's enquiry, 'Review of intelligence on weapons of mass destruction', HC 898, 14 July 2004, (hereafter HC 898 Butler); see in particular Annex B, 'Intelligence assessments and presentation: from March to September 2002', 163.

27 Gavin Drewry (ed.), *The new select committees* (Oxford, 1989).

28 HC 813-I, 'The decision to go to war with Iraq', 8, paragraph 6.

29 Members of parliament in the UK have frequently called for accountability to be focused on the select committee model. Typically, in June 1999 the chairman of the Home Affairs select committee, Labour MP Chris Mullin, called for reform of the ISC, arguing that its reconstitution as a new select committee on intelligence would have the power to 'summon witnesses and to obtain papers'. It would also be appointed by parliament and not the prime minister. BBC News, 22 June 1999, 'Spies need scrutiny', available at http://news.bbc.co.uk/1/low/uk_politics/374764.stm (20 May 2005).

30 HC 813-I, 'The decision to go to war with Iraq', 49, para.165. See also Danchev, 'The reckoning', 436–7.

31 On the ISC generally, see: P. Gill, 'Reasserting control: recent changes in the oversight of the UK intelligence community,' *Intelligence and National Security* 11 (2) (1996), 313–31.

32 Cm. 5972, ISC, 'Iraq weapons', paragraphs 106–8.

33 The committee concluded that this area involved striking a 'difficult balance' and required 'further thought', Intelligence and Security Committee, 'Annual report 2004–5', Cm. 6510, April 2005, 31, paragraph 88 (hereafter Cm. 6510, ISC 'Annual report 2004–5').

34 Cm. 5972, ISC, 'Iraq weapons', 48, conclusion N.

35 See, for example, Joint Intelligence Committee, 'Russian interests, intentions and capabilities', JIC (48) 9 (0), 23 July 1948, L/WS/1/1173, India Office war staff records, British Library. In this document, under both biological and chemical weapons, the JIC noted 'we have no knowledge' but 'must assume'.

36 Cm 5972, ISC, 'Iraq weapons', see Annex B, 'ISC comments on Foreign Affairs committee report', 56.

37 It is now clear that there was extensive pooling of allied intelligence in this area, not least at an annual WMD intelligence conference lasting a week that was attended by about 50 specialists from the UK, USA and Australia; see Wilkie, *Axis*, 91–2.

38 Foreign Affairs Committee, 'Foreign policy aspects of the War against Terrorism', seventh report, Session 2001–02, HC 384, Q 292. See also the September 2002 dossier, 'Iraq's weapons of mass destruction: the assessment of the British government', 22, paragraph 13, available at http://www.number-10.gov.uk/output/Page284.asp (22 July 2005).

39 E-mail from Jonathan Powell to John Scarlett, 17 September 2002; Hutton enquiry evidence, CAB/11/69.

40 Nicholas Rufford, 'Revealed: how MI6 sold the Iraq war', *Sunday Times*, 28 December 2003.
41 HC 898, Butler, 120, paragraph 485.
42 Richard Allen, 'Whitehall shredding files before they have to be disclosed', *The Times*, 23 December 2004; Sandra Laville, 'Livingstone faces shredding enquiry, *Guardian*, 22 March 2005.
43 HC 898, Butler, 105, paragraph 436.
44 The most detailed analysis is offered in Philip Davies, 'MI6's requirements directorate: integrating intelligence into the machinery of British central government', *Public Administration* 78 (1) (Spring 2000), 29–49. See also Philip Davies, *MI6 and the machinery of spying* (London, 2004).
45 HC 898, Butler, 99–103, paragraphs 398–423. I am also indebted to Philip Davies for his comments on this matter.
46 HC 898, Butler, 143–4, paragraphs 591–7.
47 A. Danchev (ed.), *The Franks report* (London, 1992).
48 HC 898, Butler, 144, paragraphs 598–601.
49 Herman, 'Intelligence and the Iraqi threat', 18.
50 Her Majesty's Stationery Office, *Civil Service statistics* (London, 1970), 20, Table 5; Department for Environment, Food and Rural Affairs, 'Sustainable development the government's approach – delivering UK sustainable development together', 7 March 2005, available at http://www.sustainable-development.gov.uk/publications/uk-strategy/uk-strategy-2005.htm (20 May 2005).
51 Cabinet Office, *Central intelligence machinery* (London, 1996).
52 David Omand, the Security and Intelligence coordinator, set up the Butler implementations group (BIG) to oversee the required changes. See Cm. 6510, ISC, 'Annual report 2004–5', 31. paragraph 66.
53 Herman, 'Intelligence and the Iraqi threat', 22.
54 Glees and Davies, *Spinning the spies*, 96.
55 Intelligence and Security Committee, 'Annual report 2001–2', Cm. 5542, 8 May 2002, 7, paragraph 10. Elements of this situation are reminiscent of the manner in which Nixon and Kissinger re-arranged the US NSC architecture in 1970.
56 HC 898, Butler, 148, paragraph 611
57 Peter Hennessy, *British prime ministers since 1945* (London, 1999), 501–2.
58 Michael Herman, 'Threat assessment and the legitimation of policy?', *Intelligence and National Security* 18 (3) (Autumn 2003), 178.
59 James Wirtz, 'Intelligence to please? The order of battle controversy during the Vietnam War', *Political Science Quarterly* 106 (2) (Summer 1991), 239–63.
60 Carmen Medina, 'The coming revolution in intelligence analysis: what to do when traditional models fail', *Studies in Intelligence* 46 (3) (2000), 23–8; S.R. Ward, 'Evolution beats revolution in analysis', *Studies in Intelligence* 46 (3) (2000), 29–36.
61 On the forgetting of history, see Christopher Andrew, 'Intelligence analysis needs to look backwards before looking forward: why lessons of the past can help fight terror of the future', June 2004, available at http://ctstudies.com/index.html (22 July 2005).
62 Cradock's classic account of the JIC is *Know your enemy: how the Joint Intelligence Committee saw the world* (London, 2002).

Reprinted with permission from Richard J. Aldrich, 'Whitehall and the Iraq War: The UK's Four Intelligence Enquiries', *Irish Studies in International Affairs* 16 (2005) pp.73–88.

INTELLIGENCE AND WMD

Further reading: Books and reports

James Bamford, *A Pretext for War: 9/11, Iraq, and the Abuse of America's Intelligence Agencies* (NY: Doubleday 2004).
Geoffrey Barker, *Sexing it Up: Iraq, Intelligence and Australia* (Sydney: UNSW Press, 2003).
Hans Blix, *Disarming Iraq* (NY: Pantheon NY, 2004).

Y. Bodansky, *The secret history of the Iraq War* (NY: Harper 2004).

The Butler Report, *Review of Intelligence on Weapons of Mass Destruction* HC 898 (London: HMSO, 2004)
   http://www.fas.org/irp/world/uk/butler071404.pdf

Bob Drogin, *Curveball: Spies, Lies, and the Con Man Who Caused a War* (NY: Random House 2007).

Tyler Drumheller, *On the Brink: An Insider's Account of How the White House Compromised American Intelligence* (NY: Carroll & Graf 2006).

Jason D Ellis & Geoffrey D. Kiefer, *Combating Proliferation: Strategic Intelligence and Security Policy* (Baltimore: Johns Hopkins University Press 2004).

Peter Gill and Mark Pythian, *Intelligence in an Insecure World* (Cambridge: Polity 2006) chapter 7.

Anthony Glees & Philip H.J. Davies, *Spinning the Spies. Intelligence, Open Government and the Hutton Enquiry* (London: Social Affairs Unit 2004).

J.P. Pfiffner and M. Pythian (eds.) *Intelligence and national security policymaking on Iraq* (Manchester: Manchester University Press, 2008).

George Tenet, *At the Center of the Storm* (NY: HarperCollins Publishers Inc 2006)

Craig R. Whitney, *The WMD Mirage: Iraq's Decade of Deception and America's False Premise for War* (NY: Public Affairs Reports 2005)

Andrew Wilkie, *Axis of Deceit, The Story of the intelligence Officer who risked All to Tell the Truth about WMD and Iraq* (Melbourne: Black Inc 2004).

Further reading: Essays and articles

A. Danchev, 'Story Development, or, Walter Mitty the Undefeated', in A. Danchev & J. Macmillan (eds.), *The Iraq War and Democratic Politics* (London: Routledge 2004) pp.238–60.

Ian Davis and Andreas Persbo, 'After the Butler report: time to take on the Group Think in Washington and London', *BASIC papers: occasional papers in international security*, 46 (July 2004) available at http://www.basicint.org/pubs/Papers/BP46.htm

Philip Davies, 'Intelligence Culture and Intelligence Failure in Britain and the United States', *Cambridge Review of International Affairs* 12/3 (October 2004) pp.495–520.

Lawrence Freedman, 'War in Iraq: Selling the Threat', *Survival* 46/2, (2004) pp.7–49.

Peter Gill, 'Keeping "Earthly Awkwardness": Failures of Intelligence in the United Kingdom', in T.C. Bruneau & Steven C. Boraz (eds.), *Reforming Intelligence: Obstacles to Democratic Control and Effectiveness* (Texas University Press, 2007) chapter 4.

Malcolm Gladwell, 'Connecting the Dots', *The New Yorker*, 10 March 2003.

Chaim Kaufmann, 'Threat Inflation and the Failure of the Marketplace of Ideas: The Selling of the Iraq War', *International Security* 29/1 (2004) pp.5–48.

Eunan O'Halpin, 'British Intelligence and the Case for Confronting Iraq: Evidence from the Butler and Hutton Reports,' *Irish Studies in International Affairs* 16 (2005) pp.89–102. [http://www.ria.ie/cgi-bin/ria/papers/100537.pdf]'

Kevin Russell, 'The Subjectivity of Intelligence Analysis and Implications for U.S. National Security Strategy.' *SAIS Review*, 24/1 (2004) pp.147–163.

Essay questions

- To what extent was the Iraqi WMD fiasco in the USA a product of intelligence failure and to what extent the result of inappropriate interference by policy-makers and politicians?
- What problems and weaknesses in the UK intelligence system have been illuminated by the Iraqi WMD saga and the 4 subsequent inquiries held in 2003 and 2004?
- Looking at Iraq and the issue of WMD since 1990, on balance, do intelligence services help to stabilise the international system – or do they present a source of risk?
- What does the Iraqi WMD episode tell us about national intelligence culture and about 'Groupthink'?

15 Intelligence and strategy in the war on Islamist terrorism

John R. Schindler

For the first time since the late 1940s, Washington is attempting a comprehensive analysis of the role and performance of the American intelligence system. In rethinking intelligence, it needs to address that the sixth column – Islamist terrorists residing in states that knowingly or unknowingly give them sanctuary – is the weak underbelly in the war on terror. To defeat this sixth column, important personnel, doctrinal, and cultural issues need to be addressed. The experience of other countries that have had success in fighting terrorism suggests that the United States must focus on offensive counterintelligence, penetrating terrorist groups, and creating mistrust amongst them.

The American public has engaged in an unprecedented level of debate about the role and performance of the country's intelligence services since 9/11. Never has the nation undertaken to examine the missions and organization of intelligence in the remarkably open manner witnessed since then. Not since the late 1940s, at the dawn of the Cold War, has the U.S. government attempted to critique and reorganize its secret services in such a comprehensive fashion, and that earlier reorganization occurred without any real public scrutiny. Although the media has delivered myriad revelations about the inner workings of the intelligence community, the plethora of detail now in the public domain has done little to clarify what is wrong with intelligence, American style.

This debate has laid bare the organizational dysfunctions of the 15-agency intelligence apparatus, but insufficient attention has been paid to important personnel, doctrinal, and cultural issues. Instead, we have seen multiple schemes of reorganization, all of them pledging to set right various wrongs. What should the role of American intelligence be in the war on terror? What do we mean by intelligence, and what do we want it to do? From what foreign models can we profitably learn, and which should we avoid? Above all, how can we transform the doctrine and culture of the intelligence community to defeat terrorism?

Current problems

Anyone surveying the mountain of recent literature about America's secret services might be forgiven for concluding that the intelligence community is a hopeless, bumbling bureaucracy resembling nothing so much as a highly secretive and expensive Department of Health and Human Services. Although the Cold War ended fifteen years ago, America's intelligence agencies have yet to fundamentally alter their modes of operation and thinking to reflect new realities.

In fairness, it was not apparent before 9/11 that America needed, or even wanted, radically reinvented intelligence agencies; certainly Congress was content to keep Cold War laws on the books that restricted espionage to the norms of those times. But then the Iraq War offered an abundance of lessons learned in the how-not-to's of intelligence.

Human intelligence. The battlefield-technical intelligence in which America excels seems to have made little difference in the lightning overthrow of Saddam's regime. Despite massive investment in signals and imagery intelligence and the ability to push highly classified products to the warfighter, the quality of the intelligence reaching tactical ground units was hardly better than that available to American soldiers in Normandy in 1944.[1]

The saga of how the intelligence community was fooled on the issue of Iraqi WMD is still incomplete, but evidently things went very wrong indeed, for many reasons. The depressing tale of questionable human sources, most notoriously the Defense Intelligence Agency (DIA)'s mishandling of the untrustworthy Iraqi defector it codenamed "Curveball," raises serious questions about the sources and methods of intelligence collection and analysis.[2]

Finished Analysis. Whatever the failures of U.S. human intelligence on Saddam's ramshackle regime—failures that are difficult to comprehend given that Iraq had been a high-priority target for the intelligence community since August 1990—no element of the intelligence system emerges from the war with less credit than "finished analysis." The CIA's spies, residing in its Directorate of Operations, have long been accustomed to political storms; the analysts who comprise the Agency's Directorate of Intelligence (DI), on the other hand, have seldom gotten negative press. The DI, heirs of the Office of Strategic Services' ivory tower–like analysis effort during World War II, has been well regarded in academia and the press, who have always preferred deskbound analysts to actual spies. The Iraq saga demonstrates, however, the perils of the venerable analysis model bequeathed to the DI by Sherman Kent at the beginning of the Cold War. The image of the DI that emerges from the administration-sponsored Silberman-Robb WMD Report of March 2005 is that of a congenitally risk-averse organization mired in outmoded social-science models and lacking in deep knowledge. The CIA recruits many competent analysts, but the Directorate's modus operandi forces them to become generalists of little utility, discouraged from developing in-depth knowledge of any particular region or problem.[3]

Mediocrity. Although the 9/11 and WMD Commissions highlighted many serious problems with American intelligence, their own analyses have been highly selective. Those commissions largely skirted the issue of how the intelligence community loses the truly talented in alarming numbers. It is difficult to see how American intelligence can be bettered without addressing head-on what David Ignatius, espionage commentator for the *Washington Post*, has termed "the dreadful mediocrity of the intelligence community."[4]

Critiques. No less ominous is the specter of what one observer has labeled "intelligence critique fatigue."[5] Although the 9/11 and WMD commissions offer many suggestions on how to improve intelligence, their whole is less than the sum of their parts in this regard. Reshaping the intelligence community cannot be achieved in an atmosphere of endless studies and critiques. Moreover, these commissions represent a new model of evaluating intelligence through standing bodies, beyond the House and Senate intelligence committees, that subjects these secret agencies to a level of scrutiny to which no other federal agencies are held.

Chronology. The commissions seemingly adhere to an unreasonable faith in the perfectibility of intelligence. Just as troubling is their lack of discussion of *when* things went wrong. Unless they believe that American intelligence was ineffective from the start, when did things begin to go bad? This is important to determine, so that the intelligence community can set its wrongs right. Yet despite CIA veterans' claims that America's spies need to rediscover their "golden age," those who seek to reform the intelligence community are silent on how this dysfunctional intelligence apparatus got that way.

Declassification. Any honest historical retrospective of the intelligence community's development for forensic purposes quickly runs aground on the shoals of declassification. Washington has declassified and released virtually everything about U.S. intelligence activities before 1946, but little thereafter. Almost all operational information from the early Cold War on (and essentially all signals intelligence, the most important source) remains off-limits to researchers. How, then, can anyone outside the intelligence community make any assessment about what worked before and where things started to go wrong?

Domestic intelligence. America's sprawling intelligence system is the culmination of sixty years of post–World War II practice, and a corporate mindset wholly immersed in *foreign* intelligence. America's lead counter-intelligence agency, the only component with a substantial internal mission, is the FBI, which until recently has been a marginal player in the intelligence community. Despite the present-day imperative to protect the homeland from internal as well as external threats, our intelligence system is wholly unequipped to do this. It is far from clear that the recent changes to FBI structure announced by President Bush will improve the situation.

It was until recently an American point of pride that the nation was the only modern Western state without a bona fide domestic intelligence agency; this now appears to be a distinct liability, particularly in light of the FBI's persistent inability to accomplish its domestic security missions. Seldom noted is how the intelligence community's exclusively foreign focus throughout its existence has shaped current realities. During the early Cold War, FBI Director J. Edgar Hoover eschewed too-close cooperation with the intelligence community, while after his departure in 1972 Congress pushed the FBI out of real collaboration with other intelligence agencies.

This had both operational and psychological effects. For many states, and most undemocratic ones, foreign intelligence is simply an extension of domestic concerns. During the last century, the most, as well as the least, effective espionage services were secret police agencies with a mandate to operate abroad. The most effective included the Soviet KGB, East Germany's Stasi, and Fidel Castro's *Dirección de Inteligencia*. The Soviet intelligence system, which it bequeathed to its satellites, owed its success in large part to its well-honed conspiratorial mindset (the Russian term for espionage tradecraft is *konspiratsiya*), which was the product of a secret police culture devoted foremost to defeating internal enemies. Although developing a secret police culture is the last thing America now needs, the recent failures of our secret agencies may be less the result of people or structures than of its intelligence model.

The fifth column—and sixth

It is difficult to question the verdict of one leading intelligence thinker who concluded that as we face the new Islamic terrorist threat, "We face an utterly different threat that we're almost perfectly unsuited to deal with."[6]

First, to understand the threat. The main politico-theological movement behind the upsurge of radicalism in the modern Muslim world is Salafism. A neo-orthodox variant of Islam that appeared in North Africa in the late nineteenth century, the Salafi movement's aim has been to reform Islam in line with the teaching of early Muslims, particularly the "pious forefathers"; it has an anti-Western bias and dislikes "official" Islam, which it considers decadent and compromised. Nevertheless, Washington has been reluctant to move beyond platitudes about "terrorism" to call the foe what it is. The reasons for this are political, and it is likely that this rhetorical reticence will diminish as the war against radical Islamism drags on.[7]

The Islamist movement consists of two groups: those advocating a *dua* (calling), and the jihadists, who advocate a violent approach. The former proselytizes, while the latter favors war. But the division between these tendencies is not firm. Many advocates of *dua* are at best conditional in their condemnations of violence and terror, and many move into more aggressive forms of Islamism. For Westerners, conditioned to see preachers and warriors as opposite social types, this is often difficult to understand. Hence efforts to present the powerful and pervasive Muslim Brotherhood—the representative *dua* movement—as a nonviolent, even progressive organization are misguided and betray a miscomprehension of the essentials of radical Islam. The Muslim Brotherhood has begotten numerous terrorists who have perpetrated terrorist crimes around the world, killing thousands.[8] Among them was Ayman al-Zawahiri, Al Qaeda's number-two man.

A similar willingness to overlook inconvenient facts can be detected in judgments about Al Qaeda itself. Bin Laden's "base" was transformed on 9/11 in the eyes of most terrorism experts and intelligence analysts from a loose, essentially criminal network into a tightly controlled, global hydra with linked cells embedded in dozens of countries. The truth is somewhere in the middle. Bin Laden's organization certainly made the most of modern telecommunications, forming an efficient, distributed, global *jihadi* network. But if subsequent U.S. and allied counterterrorism measures reduced the organization's ability to conduct "big weddings" such as 9/11, the London attacks of July 7 show that groups inspired by Al Qaeda are nonetheless able to conduct lethal, albeit smaller scale, attacks.[9]

From the outset, Al Qaeda was misunderstood both inside and outside the intelligence community. It was never the wholly self-sufficient entity it proclaimed itself to be. In truth, from its outset in the mid-1980s, at the height of the Afghan jihad, it had important relations with several foreign intelligence agencies: Saudi Arabia's and Pakistan's during the Afghan campaign, Sudan's in the early 1990s, followed by intermittent ties with the intelligence services of both Iraq and Iran beginning in the mid-1990s.[10] Although Washington overstated Saddam's links with Al Qaeda before the war, bin Laden did have a relationship with Iran's secret services, the Revolutionary Guards Corps (Pasdaran). Former CIA case officer Robert Baer has confirmed tactical cooperation between Al Qaeda and Pasdaran since 1996, as well as an actual alliance between bin Laden and Pasdaran-controlled terrorist groups such as Hezbollah.[11] Al Qaeda would not likely allow itself to become a fulltime surrogate for any intelligence service, but its history demonstrates a pattern of partnering with secret agencies in a manner that has bolstered its resilience and lethality.

Moreover, the preeminent threat to the United States is less a bin Laden-driven terror network than a global Islamist insurgency. The extended U.S. war in Iraq has increased the ideological fervor of Salafi preachers and fighters worldwide. Al Qaeda still offers local terrorist groups inspiration and sometimes training and logistical support, but bin Laden himself no longer exercises his pre-9/11 style of command and control over the movement.

These changes, which promise to transform the Salafi threat into an even more dangerous foe, become evident in profiles of mujahideen and their motivations. The old-style recruits before 9/11 were well-educated, of an upper middle-class background, and typically came from the wealthier Arab countries. Most joined the movement in their mid-twenties. Today, as expert Marc Sageman has observed, "the trajectory is changing," and the new generation of Salafi recruits is younger, less educated, and more alienated.[12]

In many European countries, police and secret services have noted a disturbing movement of youths to Iraq and other *jihadi* fronts, eager to gain martyrdom in attacks on American interests. The emergence of European Muslims as a key participant in the global Salafi insurgency is an ominous portent of the new threat. What such volunteers lack in skills and sophistication they can more than compensate for with fiery fanaticism and unprecedented numbers, as the London bombings of July 7 demonstrated.

The presence of an Islamist fifth column in America needs to be acknowledged. Thanks to Saudi money and years of benign (or not) neglect by the authorities, American Islam on a per-capita basis is considerably more infected with Salafi radicalism than most Muslim countries in Africa or Asia. That said, there are healthy signs of moderation in at least some corners of American Islam since 9/11, and more important, domestic counterterrorism seems to be working passably well.

There is no room for complacency—America's glaring lack of any real border security remains the great imponderable. But it is certainly not coincidental that Al Qaeda has failed to execute a major operation in the United States in four years. This can be attributed to effective police and intelligence work on the home front, but also to the seeming lack of wherewithal of the enemy. Mohammed Atta's operation may have been the last of its kind. Al Qaeda apparently lacks the ability to manage large-scale, complex operations employing sleeper terrorists in the United States.

The next major Salafi attack on America, however, will likely be launched by terrorists infiltrated from abroad, perhaps through porous borders, not by home-based operatives. The leading threat comes from terrorists living abroad in countries that provide them sanctuary—the sixth column. If pro-Western states on the fringes of the Mediterranean and the former Soviet Union fail to stem the Islamist tide, our predicament will grow dire indeed. However, such countries have a much better track record of keeping armed Islamism in check—though we may not approve of their methods—than any Western state.

Some of armed Salafism's sanctuaries are the semi-failed states that surround the periphery of the Muslim world, lawless zones of banditry without real borders. But many of its most attractive bases are Western countries we consider allies in the war on terrorism. In this unsecured front, safe haven is usually offered by accident, through liberal asylum laws, poor domestic security, and anti-American political climates. Jamie Campbell, a leading expert on European Islamism, has pronounced the United Kingdom as home to "the most sought-after terrorists in the world," and Sir John Stevens, former chief of the Metropolitan Police, estimates that Britain now houses "at least 100 Osama bin Laden-trained terrorists [and] probably nearer 200."[13] There is no reason to believe that the situation in Canada, another close U.S. ally and intelligence partner with many immigrants linked to the Islamist International, is any better.

However, the situation in European countries with large populations of alienated Muslims is worse still.[14] In France, crime-infested ghettos of second-generation Algerians have become breeding grounds for Al Qaeda's next wave. Although Islamists generally refrain from attacks on France on grounds of expediency—it would be poor planning to force French security services to act decisively against them—their desire to bring the jihad to America and Israel cannot be doubted. Jean-Louis Bruguière, France's leading terrorism expert, has described the situation concisely: "It's not the result of a command structure giving direct orders, but of people talking: scattered networks in which operatives talk and a strategy develops."[15]

French journalist Mohamed Sifaoui has provided a chilling portrait of these lethal informal networks of grassroots activists.[16] Of Algerian origin, Sifaoui penetrated a Paris-based cell of Algerian Islamists in late 2002 almost by accident. For three months, he observed the quotidian behavior of the "brothers": angry and alienated yet in many ways Westernized, the young men spent their days raising funds, propagandizing, and hanging out. They may have been deeply enamored of bin Laden, but they were not part of any formal Al Qaeda network, nor were *les moujahidine* strong on Salafist theory; for them, the jihad was about style and symbol. Some of the "brothers" were sufficiently motivated to take part in the war directly, in Chechnya, Iraq, or elsewhere.

America's counterinsurgency campaign in Iraq constitutes a "jihad Super Bowl" of sorts. However, it would be unwise to overestimate the numbers of imported mujahideen in Iraq, as the U.S. military has frequently done; the pipeline of recruits has not kept pace with the outrage our occupation of Iraq has inspired across the Muslim world. Many Salafi activists of the sixth column are standing on the sidelines, biding their time in safe sanctuaries, waiting to see how the war develops.

Counterterrorism successes and failures

Failing to learn from foreign examples is a perennial pitfall for America's intelligence services. Most of our spies are monolingual and believe deep down that we can do things better than foreigners. In fact, in counterterrorism, the recent experiences of others offer many valuable lessons. In particular, we and our allies in the war on terror have much to learn from the cases of Yugoslavia, Israel, and Algeria.

Yugoslavia

Throughout its existence, Tito's Yugoslavia waged a bitter struggle with terrorists resident abroad bent on destroying the country. Beginning in the mid-1960s this transformed into a full-fledged war against terrorism that would last to the fall of communist Yugoslavia. Tito's secret services bore the hallmarks of their Soviet parents: cunning operations, an emphasis on covert political warfare, a willingness to use lethal force, and the effective employment of provocations and conspiracy. That Yugoslavia's intelligence apparatus defeated Stalin's in the five-year espionage war that followed the 1948 Tito-Stalin split says something about the effectiveness of Belgrade's state security organs.[17]

From the end of World War II, the Titoist regime fought anticommunist émigrés residing in the West who planned acts of terrorism against it, conducted by remnants of the wartime Ustasha dictatorship in Croatia and by anticommunist Serbs. Yugoslavia's record of blunting attacks for fifteen years after 1945 was close to total, thanks to extensive penetration of émigrér organizations by the Yugoslav secret police. Beginning in the early 1960s, however, the situation grew more ominous for Belgrade as the ranks of Yugoslavs abroad swelled and anti-Tito groups were rejuvenated. Thus began a twenty-year campaign of terrorism, which included armed raids into Yugoslavia, the murder of Yugoslav representatives in the West, bombings of diplomatic facilities, assassination attempts against top Yugoslav officials, several international airplane hijackings, and the bombing of a Yugoslav airliner over Czechoslovakia in 1972. Radical érmigrés who had found safe haven in the West to plot their terrorism— what Belgrade termed the "sixth column"—became Yugoslavia's number-one enemy.[18]

In the mid-1960s, the Titoist regime commenced a comprehensive covert action campaign to destabilize and discredit this "enemy emigration" resident in the West. Its concept was a modified version of Soviet operations against the USSR's own émigrés, which had their origin in the anti-emigration activities of the tsarist Okhrana beginning in the 1880s. Belgrade's strategy included assassination as an integral component, which business the KGB had largely gotten out of, at least in the West, by 1960, after several embarrassing incidents.[19] Belgrade, with its good relations with Western capitals, had less to fear politically from "wetwork" (a term derived from Russian intelligence, for "getting blood on your hands") gone bad than Moscow did. Furthermore, Tito's secret police, which had employed assassination against the émigrés on a highly selective basis (including a 1957 operation against Ante Pavelic, the wartime Ustasha dictator, in Buenos Aires), concluded that there was no risk of "blowback." That is, it would be impossible to make the radical émigrés more extremist than they already were; hence all methods could be employed.

The 25-year counterterrorism campaign that followed was one of the great open secrets of the Cold War. Both the East and West knew about it, but it was in neither of their interests to publicize it. The "special program" of the Yugoslav secret police killed more than a hundred émigrés in the West, crippling every terrorist group agitating against Belgrade, with minimal repercussions for the Titoist regime. By the early 1980s, terror attacks virtually ceased. Despite some particularly obvious assassinations (including the gunning down of Enver Hadri, a Kosovar Albanian activist, in Brussels in 1990, the last confirmed assassination), few suspects were ever arrested in the murders, which most Western police and intelligence services attributed to internecine struggles among violent Balkan émigrés— precisely as Belgrade wished. Besides, the secret police took care to ensure that all wetwork was done by agents without traceable ties to the Yugoslav government; many were underworld criminals. Hardly any of the assassinations that resulted, and none of them perpetrated in the United States, were ever solved.[20]

This antiterrorism strategy worked because Belgrade eventually was able to penetrate every significant terrorist group arrayed against it. The intelligence it gathered allowed the secret police to identify leaders and plot destabilization operations. Surviving leaders of the Croatian Revolutionary Brotherhood—the largest of the anti-Belgrade groups, established in Australia in 1961 and responsible for dozens of acts of terrorism—have said that some sixty of their members were killed by the Yugoslav secret police abroad (almost twenty others died in raids into Yugoslavia).[21] It is now known that the Brotherhood was heavily penetrated by the Yugoslav secret police from its beginnings.

Unsolved murders among émigrés fostered a climate of constant suspicion, indeed paranoia, that rendered collaboration among terror factions functionally impossible. Every radical émigré group believed that it alone had escaped penetration by Tito's secret police, and that the other groups had been penetrated by *agents provocateurs* or were actually under Belgrade's control (as indeed some were). Under such conditions, no united émigré front against Belgrade ever emerged.

Abduction was another successful tactic. Émigré terrorists were sometimes kidnapped in the West and either disappeared or later showed up in Yugoslavia; in either case, onetime partners could not know whether the missing man had gone willingly or was a penetration agent. The classic case was Krunoslav Draganovic, a senior Croatian cleric in Rome and a wanted war criminal who was responsible for arranging the escape of much of the Ustasha leadership to South America in 1945. For two decades he was a key figure in radical Croatian émigré networks in Europe, planning and financing terror and sabotage missions against Yugoslavia from inside the Vatican. He disappeared mysteriously in 1967 and then reappeared at a press conference in Belgrade three months later, where he extolled the virtues of Titoism. Many believed Draganovic had been kidnapped, but Croatian radicals abroad had to consider the shocking prospect that one of their top officials had been a communist agent all along.[22]

Yugoslavia's cunning war on terrorism could do nothing to solve the grave problems of the Titoist state, which succumbed to political and economic crises after the Cold War. Nonetheless, the Belgrade secret police's counterterrorism strategy stands as a model of how to wage a vigorous covert war against terrorists living abroad in de facto safe havens. Yugoslavia defeated its sixth column in perhaps the most successful counterterrorism campaign ever devised, one that has been entirely overlooked by terrorism specialists and analysts.

Israel

In contrast, Israel's endless war against terrorism has been widely studied. Though Israel's tough measures are often praised by the U.S. military, the intelligence community has been more circumspect, with ample cause. Muscular methods for challenging raiders and saboteurs date to Israel's first years (one of the founders of the trade was the young army officer Ariel Sharon). However, Israel's modern counterterrorism policies trace their origins to the early 1970s, in reaction to the rise of radical Palestinian terrorism. After the 1972 Munich Olympics disaster, the Israeli military commenced direct action against the PLO and related groups, including a daring August 1973 raid on Beirut—led by future prime minister Ehud Barak—that killed several senior PLO members. More controversial were assassinations conducted in Europe and the Middle East by Israeli intelligence, operations Mossad sometimes bungled and failed to keep particularly secret. The murder in 1973 of an innocent waiter, mistaken for a PLO higher-up, in Norway was a particular low point. The 1970s assassination campaign against Palestinian radicals damaged, but did not cripple, the PLO; moreover, Israeli intelligence seems to have discounted the idea that a more radical and tenacious adversary than the PLO could emerge, a process that the assassination policy might encourage.

Mossad officers and agents still persisted in performing occasional assassinations abroad. Sloppy tradecraft resulted in such incidents as the September 1997 arrest of two Mossad officers in Amman after they attempted to poison a senior Hamas official. In the 1990s, Israel also experimented with the novel tactic of overt assassinations of terrorists, such as the February 1992 killing of several top Hezbollah officials in southern Lebanon. This became standard procedure with the onset of the al-Aksa intifada in September 2000, beginning a wave of what the Israel Defense Forces tactfully refer to as "targeted killings" of Palestinian extremists in Gaza and the West Bank. Israel has demonstrated the potential, and limits, of using airpower against terrorism, beginning with an IDF helicopter attack near Bethlehem in early November 2000 that killed one wanted terrorist and wounded another. Airborne targeted killings offer Israel a militarily safe and cost-effective tactic against high-priority terrorists that has put several wanted Palestinians out of action, in most cases permanently. Their influence on U.S. tactics is clear. But despite assertions by some IDF officials that the policy was a success, there is room for doubt.

Not all of the attacks have been against top terrorists. Some were aimed at small fish whose involvement in the intifada is questionable, some targeted killings have resulted in significant collateral damage, and there has been some blowback—for instance, the fall 2001 murder of Rehavan Zeevi, Israel's tourism minister, in retaliation for the targeted killing of PFLP General Secretary Abu-Ali Mustafa two months before.

Israeli abductions of terrorists have been a more effective policy in recent years than airborne assassination. Within months of the outbreak of the al-Aksa intifada, Israeli secur-ity forces were kidnapping wanted Palestinians rather than killing them, a better policy on several levels: the abducted terrorists frequently provide valuable intelligence under interro-gation, there is no "martyr" to inspire revenge killings, and fellow terrorists are left to wonder what really happened. The effectiveness of targeted killings can be deduced from the IDF's late January 2005 announcement that it was suspending the practice.[23]

American counterterrorists have a great deal to learn from Israeli counterparts, with their long experience with violent Islamism. The operational methods of the IDF, Mossad, and par-ticularly the General Security Service (popularly known as Shin Bet) in most cases are more mature and effective than American methods. Shin Bet interrogators, for example, receive three years of instruction in Arabic and psychology before they deal with terrorist suspects. Yet the Israeli experience also demonstrates that toughness is no substitute for coherent strategy, and that governments are best served when necessarily covert activities stay secret.

Algeria

A further cautionary tale is provided by Algeria, a country that has been wracked by a bitter Islamist insurgency for nearly fifteen years. Algiers seems to have largely defeated the mujahideen, but the cost has been enormous. The civil war has claimed well over 100,000 lives, plus some 7,000 missing, to say nothing of the widespread economic destruction. When the Algerian military preemptively refused to let the Islamic Salvation Front (FIS) take power in early 1992 through elections that FIS was likely to win, *jihadi* Islamists—the Armed Islamic Group (GIA), which appeared suddenly in 1993 and quickly carved out a reputation as the blood-thirstiest band of holy warriors anywhere—replaced *dua* Islamists. Its atrocities discredited the Islamists at home and abroad, and by the end of the 1990s GIA was a spent force, thanks to its own excesses and vigorous counterinsurgency tech-niques.[24] GIA bitter-enders have formed a successor group, the Salafist Group for Preach-ing and Combat, which remains a threat in Algeria and France, but it lacks GIA's numbers and fanaticism.

The details of Algeria's seemingly successful counterterrorism campaign remain murky. Algiers relied on techniques that no Western government would countenance, including widespread repression and police-state methods, and the conspiratorial methods of Algerian intelligence produced grave blowback. The first open sign that things in Algeria were more mysterious than initially believed came in 2001 with the publication in France of an insider's account by Habib Souaida, a former junior officer in Algerian special forces, who revealed his participation in atrocities against civilians in which Algerian troops, camouflaged as GIA fighters, would commit murder and mayhem to discredit the Islamists. Souaida's allega-tions created a sensation in France and Algeria, and Algiers attempted to undermine him. However, Souaida's success in a 2002 libel trial against him—among its revelations was the testimony of top Algerian intelligence officials that GIA was "the creation of the security services"—proved that his depiction of what he called *la stratégie de la tension* was substantially accurate. Algeria's dirty war, despite its successes, demonstrates that conspiracy and provoca-tion can create problems worse than those they seek to solve.[25]

The counterintelligence imperative

There is no danger that America's sprawling, bureaucratized, legalistic, and unimaginative intelligence community can craft a counterterrorism strategy *à l'algérienne*. Organizational obstacles to creating any coherent counterterrorism strategy are high, particularly our lack of a genuine domestic intelligence agency. All the same, it can be noted that U.S. counterintelligence circa 1941–45, despite a deeply divided system and ferocious bureaucratic turf wars, performed generally effectively at home and abroad. The community's cultural shortcomings are more significant problems than organizational ones today, and they are more difficult to address: its seemingly unalterable business-as-usual mentality, its aversion to contrary viewpoints, its cancerous careerism, and its difficulties translating rhetoric into programs and policies.[26] Repairing these defects, which in most cases are a by-product of policies that appeared in the 1970s, will take time and vigorous leadership.

No part of the intelligence community is weaker than counterintelligence. Throughout its history, American intelligence has generally given short shrift to counterintelligence, viewing it as an arcane art of only modest relevance to "real" espionage or analytical work, an unpleasant subdiscipline best left to the police. The dominance in American counterintelligence of the FBI, with its legalistic orientation, has not helped matters. The mid–Cold War excesses of Hoover's FBI and James Angleton's Counterintelligence Staff at CIA, both of which spent time looking for mostly imaginary Red agents to the detriment of enhancing operations and public trust, only worsened the problem. And the intelligence community's post–Cold War counterintelligence debacles, including some of the most damaging security lapses in U.S. history—the Ames and Nicholson cases at CIA, Hanssen at FBI, Montes at the DIA—indicate that American counterintelligence may now be worse than it has ever been.

American counterintelligence doctrine views its task in entirely defensive terms, as a security function aimed at keeping bad sorts out of the intelligence community. It prefers dubious technical fixes such as the polygraph over common-sense security procedures. In recent decades, it has failed to manage even its defensive functions properly, leading to its "miserable record" cited by former National Security Agency director William Odom in his clarion call for intelligence reform.[27]

The spy threat is clearly rising, aided by well-intentioned intelligence community initiatives to disseminate as much intelligence as possible as far as technology can take it. even though this will provide highly sensitive information to moles with a few clicks of a mouse. Since 9/11, some forty Americans have been turned away from intelligence community jobs due to possible affiliations with terrorist groups, and counterintelligence veterans speak of the actuarial certainty that foreign spies have penetrated our intelligence agencies. The threat is now so serious that Washington has announced that it will begin a strategic counterintelligence program to "preempt threats." The Chinese have emerged as the leading problem, with as many as 3,000 front companies in the United States; Russia, Israel, France, and North Korea are other ranking concerns.

However, current initiatives remain defensive in focus, aiming to neutralize penetrations. Skeptics note that a previous effort was made in the 1980s to get serious about counterintelligence, yet our activities remain as uncoordinated and ineffectual as ever. Counterintelligence must get its house in order to protect secrets, and this is only the first step required.

The narrow focus of American counterintelligence clouds judgments about what counterspies are supposed to be doing. The Curveball story, demonstrating DIA's basic inability to vet sources, is a classic example. That counterintelligence is used sparingly as a quality-control method was demonstrated painfully by the 1987 revelation by a high-placed defector that every Cuban source run by U.S. intelligence since the mid-1960s had actually been a Havana-controlled double agent. The intelligence community has done too little to prevent such debacles from happening again.

Our spies are too narrowly focused to be able to see counterintelligence for what it is: potentially one of the most effective weapons in the war on terrorism. The strategic purpose of counterintelligence is not preventing moles, but using offensive counterespionage to gain control of the enemy's intelligence apparatus. This fact is clearly understood by others—above all the Russians, who perfected the art.

Counterintelligence experts are not always likeable: they tend towards the obsessive—a byproduct of their obscure craft—and they rarely bring good news. America grooms few serious counterintelligence professionals, who must be unorthodox thinkers with a flair for the conspiratorial, buttressed by deep knowledge of the language, history, and culture of their target. We need many more such unconventional people, along with a strategic concept of how intelligence can be used to defeat Islamist terrorism, if we wish to protect our secrets and take the covert war to the enemy.

The way ahead

The limits of purely military methods to defeat armed Salafism are painfully evident in Iraq, and diplomatic and economic efforts against the global Islamist insurgency will take years to bear fruit. But how exactly can intelligence defeat terrorism? Beyond the obvious fact that foreknowledge, acted on, can stop bad guys, there are few answers to this question. Intelligence professionals rightly fear being asked to play the predictive game, connecting the proverbial dots right and fast 100 percent of the time. The military certainly wants more intelligence, though Pentagon pleas for "more HUMINT" are less for spies than for situational awareness, given its lack of linguistic and cultural skills relevant to the Muslim world.

It seems indisputable that the global Salafi insurgency we face today is larger, less controlled, and potentially more dangerous than the pre-9/11 Al Qaeda. Operationally, the jihad-oriented Islamist International resembles a loose multinational mafia more than a coherent, hierarchical organization. Where are its critical nodes and key vulnerabilities?

Disrupting *jihadi* finances is an attractive idea, but impractical due to the small amounts of money involved and the difficulty of differentiating good funds from bad; going after the money is a partial solution at best. Removing the leadership through assassination or capture presumes that Al Qaeda continues to exert operational control over anything outside of the mountainous Afghan-Pakistani frontier, which is unlikely. Moreover, for every top terrorist we put out of action, there are many mid-grade mujahideen waiting to fill bigger shoes, just as in the mafia. Putting bin Laden and Zawahiri out of action is desirable, but its impact on the worldwide Islamist movement will inevitably be small. Similarly, public diplomacy to burnish America's image in the *umma* will do little to blunt the appeal of Salafi propaganda in the Islamic world; any Muslim who is willing to listen to pleasingly packaged U.S. arguments is not the sort who pines for martyrdom.

The only real vulnerability of the emerging decentralized Salafi insurgency is its distributed nature. There is a consistent pattern of small groups of like-minded angry young men gathering at a particular place, usually a radical mosque. Each "bunch of guys," usually with only a handful of members, can only do so much damage on its own; it must join forces with other bunches of guys to undertake major attacks, or to gain funding and training from veteran holy warriors. That such cells are able to metastasize through joining other cells demonstrates the mutual trust of Islamist circles. Simply put, Atta and his "brothers," and many others like them, were able to grow in the deadly fashion they did because they trusted fellow fighters; they did not presume that people they had never met, and did not know, might be enemies in disguise.

In this implicit trust lies the main vulnerability of the global Salafi insurgency. To exploit this, American intelligence must foment fear, mistrust, and paranoia in the ranks of terrorists. The goal must be preventing cooperation among cells of mujahideen resident in safe havens by making them believe, or at least plausibly fear, that other cells are penetrated by American intelligence. Accomplishing this will require a sound strategy crafted and executed by a "covert political warfare operations directorate within the government" like that advocated by George Kennan in 1948 as a method of countering the Soviet Union.[28]

Espionage as practiced by the CIA throughout its history has minimal relevance to the needs of the war on terrorism, and hardly any place at all in the aggressive strategy proposed here. Traditional CIA methods, which emphasize officers serving under official cover in U.S. diplomatic facilities, with heavy reliance on intelligence provided by foreign governments (what CIA terms "liaison"), may still be effective against other targets, but their utility against the Salafi insurgency is minimal. Defeating terrorism requires operatives serving in hotspots under non-official covers. Unfortunately, as Directorate of Operations veteran Reuel Marc Gerecht has noted, the Agency has never taken non-official cover operations very seriously, and it is difficult to see how it can generate enough of them to accomplish what needs to be done, given that careerism has limited the talent pool.

The Pentagon's small espionage staff is even less capable. Recent announcements that the Defense Department is "dramatically expanding" its clandestine activities across the world should raise concerns, given the Pentagon's past problems in this arena. Controlled by DIA, Defense's tiny spying arm, known as the Defense HUMINT Service, has made more than its share of missteps. Since its 1996 birth, its primary mission has been running the defense attaché program. Today's dramatic expansion of DIA HUMINT in personnel and mission, bringing it into the front lines of the covert war against the mujahideen, is a matter of concern, given its limited experience. DIA may be able to provide battlefield intelligence to the warfighter, but its ability to conduct espionage in the big leagues is doubtful. Increasingly close integration between operational and intelligence elements in the Defense Department, amounting to a merger of special operations and espionage functions, ought to be welcomed for its audacity but watched closely.

The executive agent for any new intelligence strategy of the sort proposed here may have to be a new organization, apart from existing CIA and Defense Department entities, to avoid learning bad practices; the sort of person required for such work, and the career path involved, will be radically different from current norms. Fortunately, going after the Islamist terrorist through a strategy of penetration and destabilization, though it will take years to pay the desired dividends, will be inexpensive. The first steps, such as creating front organizations—our own Islamic charities and foundations—can be run largely from the United States. Large numbers of personnel are not required. Indeed, the current move to dramatically increase intelligence community numbers—President Bush mandated a 50-percent increase in ciaoperations officers and analysts and equivalent growth at other agencies in late 2004—may only make matters worse. Mere numbers cannot compensate for missing expertise or ability, nor will it fix a broken tradecraft model.

Advocating a program that requires only modest funding and small numbers of personnel runs contrary to Washington's bureaucratic imperative. But it is just what we need to do in order to build a cohesive, dedicated, and well trained intelligence organization to defeat violent Islamism. We need a small group of audacious thinkers and risk-takers, whose mentality is as non-bureaucratic as feasible in a federal program. The new counterterrorism worldview must be strategic and immersed in offensive counterintelligence, aimed at taking the war to the enemy by penetrating terrorist groups and destroying them by setting them against each other. Defeating the new global Islamist insurgency, our sixth column, can be achieved by building the intelligence system America needs. Doing so is only a matter of will.

Notes

1 William Nolte, "Keeping Pace with the Revolution in Military Affairs," *Studies in Intelligence*, vol. 48, no. 1, 2004; John Ferris, "A New American Way of War? C4ISR, Intelligence and Information Operations in Operation 'Iraqi Freedom': A Provisional Assessment," *Intelligence and National Security*, Winter 2003.
2 The Curveball debacle is explained concisely in Bob Drogin and Greg Miller " 'Curveball' Debacle Reignites CIA Feud," *Los Angeles Times*, Apr. 2, 2005.
3 See Richards Heuer, "Limits of Intelligence Analysis," and Peter R. Neumann and M. L. R. Smith, "Missing the Plot? Intelligence and Discourse Failure," *Orbis*, Winter 2005.
4 David Ignatius, "Can the Spy Agencies Dig Out?" *Washington Post*, Apr. 15, 2005.
5 Richard A. Posner, "Intelligence Critique Fatigue," *Washington Post*, Apr. 6, 2005.
6 Greg Treverton, quoted in Siobhan Gorman, "Fewer, Better Spies Key to Intelligence Reform, Former Official Says," *GovExec.com*, Mar. 18, 2005.
7 For more on this, see John Calvert, "The Mythic Foundations of Radical Islam," *Orbis*, Winter 2004.
8 Youssef H. Aboul-Enein, "Al-Ikhwan Al-Muslimeen: The Muslim Brotherhood," *Military Review*, July-Aug. 2003.
9 See Bruce Hoffman, "The Changing Face of Al Qaeda and the Global War on Terrorism," *Studies in Conflict and Terrorism*, Nov.–Dec. 2004.
10 Malise Ruthven, *A Fury for God: The Islamist Attack on America* (London: Granta, 2002), pp. 236–39.
11 *Christian Science Monitor*, July 15, 2002.
12 Marc Sageman, "Understanding Terror Networks," FPRI e-note, Nov. 1, 2004, at www.fpri.org.
13 Jamie Campbell, "Why Terrorists Love Britain," *New Statesman* (London), Aug. 9, 2004; *The Telegraph* (London), Mar. 6, 2005.
14 See Zachary Shore, "Can the West Win Muslim Hearts and Minds?" *Orbis*, Summer 2004.
15 *Le Figaro*, Mar. 29, 2003; Sebastien Rotella, "Terrorists at the Table," *Los Angeles Times*, Mar. 6, 2005.
16 Mohamed Sifaoui, *Mes "frères" assassins: Comment j'ai infiltré une cellule d'Al-Qaida* (Paris: Cherchemidi, 2003).
17 On Titoist intelligence, see Marko Milivojevic, "The Role of the Yugoslav Intelligence and Security Community" in J. Allcock, J. Horton, and M. Milivojevic, eds., *Yugoslavia in Transition: Choices and Restraints* (London: Allen Unwin, 1992).
18 Ljiljana Bulatovic and Bozidar Spasic, *Smrt je njihov zanat: Dokumenti ustaskog terorizma* (Belgrade. Politika, 1993), pp. 71–106; Dragan Ganovic, *Teroristi iz seste kolone: Dokumentarna hronika o teroristickoj aktivnosti protiv Jugoslavije* (Belgrade: Borba, 1979).
19 KGB support to Bulgaria's reputed role in the May 1981 assassination attempt against John Paul II, seemingly supported by recent revelations from Stasi files (see *Corriere della Sera* (Milan), Mar. 30, 2005) would be an exception, as was the KGB's logistical support to the assassination of Georgi Markov by the Bulgarian secret police in London in 1978.
20 See Bozidar Spasic, *Lasica koja govori: Osnovne pretpostavke borbe protiv terorizma* (Belgrade: Knjiga-Komerc, 2001).
21 *Slobodna Dalmacija* (Split), Oct. 12, 2000.
22 See Norman J. W. Goda, "The Ustasa: Murder and Espionage," in R. Breitman, et al., eds., *U.S. Intelligence and the Nazis* (Washington, D.C.: National Archives, 2004).
23 *Yedot Aharonot* (Tel Aviv), Nov. 22, 2001; *Haaretz* (Tel Aviv), Jan. 30, 2005.
24 Stephen Ulph, "Algeria's GIA: down and out," *Jane's Islamic Affairs Analyst*, Feb. 2005.
25 Habib Souaida, *La sale guerre: La témoignage d'un ancien officier des forces spéciales de l'armee algérienne* (Paris: Découverte, 2001); *Libération* (Paris), Dec. 23, 2002; *NRC Handelsblad* (Rotterdam), Mar. 29, 2004; Adam Shatz, "One Big Murder Mystery," *London Review of Books*, Oct. 7, 2004.
26 See the recent memoir of Arabic-speaking former CIA DO officer Melissa Boyle Mahle, *Denial and Deception: An Insider's View of the CIA from Iran-Contrato 9/11* (New York: Nation, 2004).

27 William E. Odom, *Fixing Intelligence: For a More Secure America* (New Haven: Yale University Press, 2002), p. 167.
28 George Kennan, Policy Planning Staff Memorandum, May 4, 1948, National Archives and Records Administration, RG 273, Records of the National Security Council, NSC-10/2, available at http://academic.brooklyn.cuny.edu.

Reprinted with permission from John R Schindler, 'Defeating the Sixth Column: Intelligence and Strategy in the War on Islamist Terrorism', *Orbis* 49/4 (2005) pp.695–712.

16 Intelligence in Northern Ireland

B. Bamford

This article examines the role and effectiveness of counter-terrorist intelligence operations in Northern Ireland. Specifically, it examines the methods of gathering intelligence as well as how the information was used, while also addressing some of the wider moral and legal implications of intelligence activities for a liberal democratic society. It argues that British intelligence was ultimately very effective but at the price of employing some highly dubious methods.

> 'Today we were unlucky, but remember we only have to be lucky once'.[1]
>
> Statement by the Provisional Irish Republican Army

Introduction

In October 1984 the Provisional IRA detonated a bomb in Brighton, England, narrowly missing then British Prime Minister Margaret Thatcher.[2] Their near success represented an intelligence failure for the British. But in that regard it was a relatively rare exception. British intelligence was ultimately very effective in the Northern Ireland conflict, but at the price of employing some highly dubious methods. Although the intelligence apparatus initially experienced some major setbacks during the early years of the conflict, by the late 1970s the security forces achieved a considerable amount of success in identifying terrorists and containing the violence in Northern Ireland. Indeed, to a very large extent they had penetrated a number of terrorist groups at some of their most senior levels and were able to 'tap' into the thinking of the groups' senior commands that, in turn, enabled them to thwart terrorist attacks. Although this article does not offer a comprehensive examination of intelligence-gathering and covert operations; it does seek to identify some of the difficulties of gathering and using intelligence. In so doing, the difficult and often complex issues raised are such that they may never be satisfactorily resolved. Before turning to those issues however, some background on the conflict is essential.

Background to the conflict

Northern Ireland's latest 'troubles' began in August 1969, after a series of civil rights demonstrations led by the Northern Ireland Civil Rights Association (NICRA) had demanded the Protestant regime at Stormont to address some legitimate grievances on the part of the Catholic community. The situation quickly deteriorated however, as Protestant fears of a general Catholic 'emancipation' resulted in a wave of sectarian violence. As the scale of violence and civil disorder increased in its intensity, Northern Ireland's largely Protestant police force, the Royal Ulster Constabulary (RUC), became overwhelmed and incapable of coping with the civil unrest. It was in that context that British troops were introduced in a peacekeeping capacity to maintain law and order and to stave off a civil war by keeping the two warring communities apart. During the early phase of the conflict, the overall security effort was under the control of the military.[3]

During that time, a number of terrorist or paramilitary organizations emerged from both sides of the sectarian divide. From the Protestant/Unionist community these groups included the Ulster Defence Association (UDA), the Ulster Volunteer Force (UVF) and the Ulster Freedom Fighters (UFF). Those groups wanted to remain part of the United Kingdom and made no secret of their intention to violently resist any attempt to unite Northern Ireland with the Republic of Ireland.[4]

The Catholic/Republican community saw a resurgence of the Irish Republican Army (IRA) activity. Not only did this group violently oppose British rule in Northern Ireland, but it sought to unify the North with the Republic. As the situation in Northern Ireland deteriorated, some IRA members exploited the situation in the hopes that an escalation of violence would eventually result in political concessions. Within the IRA itself, disagreement over its policy led to a split in December 1969 between those who believed in a political solution and the more extreme militant Republicans. The Official IRA was an outgrowth of the former while the Provisional IRA (PIRA) represented the latter. The activities of the PIRA only exacerbated the already unstable situation in Northern Ireland. Throughout the period 1970 to 1971 the group was organizing and acquiring weapons and money for a wider campaign against the British. They set up 'no-go' areas in the Catholic areas of Belfast and Londonderry where the PIRA established itself as a de facto authority that challenged the Stormont regime and, later, British rule by denying the security forces access to those areas. The PIRA conducted its first operation in February 1971 when a sniper shot and killed a British soldier; and in April 1971 the group began its bombing campaign. The PIRA quickly emerged as the principal threat to Britain. Indeed, the PIRA terrorist campaign was one of the longest and most vicious in history. Not only had the PIRA conducted attacks in Northern Ireland, but the group operated against the mainland and, later, against UK interests in Europe. For those reasons, the PIRA became a major preoccupation for British intelligence.[5]

Although initially welcomed by the Catholics, the army's use of counter-insurgency tactics, such as internment without trial in August 1971, the use of controversial interrogation techniques on prisoners, enforcing curfews and conducting house searches alienated the Catholic community. During the counter-insurgency phase of the conflict, based on their largely 'out-of-date' intelligence information, the military rounded up and imprisoned a number of suspected terrorists. By all accounts internment without trial was a disaster as it succeeded in further alienating the Catholic population, since most of those interned were Catholics who espoused Republican ideals.[6]

In January 1972 a series of demonstrations increased tensions between the security forces and Catholics that eventually culminated in 'Bloody Sunday'. The events of that day effectively destroyed the credibility of the British Army in the eyes of the Catholic population. Although there is a debate as to whether it was the IRA or the army that fired first, what is clear is that at some point soldiers from Britain's Parachute Regiment shot and killed 13 unarmed civilians and wounded several others. 'Bloody Sunday' became a rallying cry for the PIRA and galvanized the Catholic population against the army and the Protestant regime. By March the Unionist regime at Stormont had been suspended and direct rule imposed by London. On 21 July 1972, in what became known as 'Bloody Friday', the PIRA detonated 40 bombs in the span of 45 minutes, killing seven people and wounding several others. Ten days later, on 1 August, the British Army launched operation MOTORMAN to regain control of the Catholic areas in Belfast and Londonderry.[7]

In the ensuing years, the British attempted to work out some kind of political settlement that would be acceptable to Protestants and Catholics alike. The failed 1973 Sunningdale initiative that proposed a power-sharing Northern Ireland Government was an example of one such attempt. Although the British Government had succeeded in preventing another full-blown civil war on the island, it found itself in the unenviable position of having to find a political solution while simultaneously combating an insurgency. In the interim the government instituted a range of policies that were designed to combat the terrorist threat while restoring some sense of normalcy to Northern Ireland.[8]

Although a distinction had always been drawn between Great Britain and Northern Ireland with regard to the introduction of repressive laws, together they formed the United Kingdom, a liberal democratic state. Despite having deployed a range of counter-insurgency tactics from 1970 to 1975, the British did not introduce some of the more repressive measures, such as forced resettlement, not only because of the constraints imposed by having to operate in a liberal democratic state, but also because it was simply not a practical option. The major dilemma facing the British Government was whether to allow a united Ireland with a Protestant minority or to resettle one million Protestants somewhere in Britain – both of which were politically impossible and would have created an even greater injustice.[9]

In recognition of the political inadequacy of the measures adopted to counter the terrorist threat, the government sought more acceptable ways to maintain stability in Northern Ireland. To that end it commissioned Lord Diplock to investigate the matter and make recommendations. Diplock proposed dealing with the terrorist problem through special legal measures. His report advised modifying the legal and judicial systems by introducing special jury-less courts, the so-called 'Diplock courts', to better handle the difficulties, such as the intimidation of jury members, involved in trying terrorists. The government's acceptance of Diplock's recommendations eventually led to a new policy initiative. Significantly, it led to the passing of the 'draconian' Northern Ireland (Emergency Provisions) Act in 1973. The legislation was designed to provide security forces with the necessary powers to prevent and disrupt terrorist activity. As internment without trial was in the process of being phased out, greater powers of arrest and detention were introduced in an effort to cope with the difficulties of gathering evidence to convict terrorists as well as to gather intelligence. At the time, convicted terrorists were designated as a 'special category' prisoner and were not placed among the general population in prison. But that was to change as the British Government adopted a new policy for dealing with terrorists.[10]

In January 1977, the new policy outlined in 'The Way Ahead' sought to demilitarize the conflict through a policy that emphasized 'criminalization'. Although the army continued its 'low profile' patrolling it was no longer in control of the overall security effort. Under a policy of 'police primacy', the RUC was given control of Northern Ireland's security. Criminalization ended the 'special category' status of those convicted of terrorist offences. That eventually led to the Hunger Strikes, led by Bobby Sands, in 1980–81, in an effort to restore the 'special category' status for terrorist prisoners. Besides severely straining Anglo-Irish relations, the Hunger Strikes resulted in a groundswell of popular support for the PIRA's political wing, Provisional Sinn Fein (PSF). The following year, in 1982, PSF entered electoral politics just as the PIRA initiated a renewed wave of violence. Despite the tenuous political situation, in 1985, the British Government was able to secure the Anglo-Irish Agreement that established a consultative role for the Irish Government on matters relating to Northern Ireland. Furthermore, it introduced an all-Ireland framework for any potential political settlement that may arise. In an effort to grant assurances to the Protestants, the British required any proposed unity with the Irish Republic to be based on majority consent in the North.[11]

By the late 1980s and early 1990s, it was apparent to many, including the PIRA, that their dual strategy (the Armalite and the ballot box) was a failure. In 1987, the *Eksund*, a ship carrying 120 tons of arms from Libya, was intercepted off the coast of France. This essentially robbed the PIRA of an ability to further escalate the violence. That, along with a number of unsuccessful high-profile bombing attempts to be discussed later, spelled failure for the military wing of the PIRA. On the political front the situation was no better. PSF failed to achieve a strong political support base among the citizens of the Irish Republic. According to Henry Patterson, PSF received 'less than 2% of the vote and had no-one elected' in the 1987 election.[12] By 1989, Gerry Adams, the president of PSF, announced that the two-pronged strategy had failed. At the time, some secret discussions began between Adams and a British MI6 officer, Michael Oatley, through a backchannel. Those discussions eventually resulted in the beginnings of the Northern Irish Peace Process.[13]

The 1993 Downing Street Declaration was an important move towards a political settlement. Essentially, the Irish and British prime ministers told PSF and the PIRA that if they renounced violence they could participate in the future of Northern Ireland. Also, it explicitly stated that Britain had no strategic interest in Northern Ireland. Although the resulting peace-process degenerated into a resumption of the PIRA's campaign between 1994 and 1997, they eventually returned to the peace talks. The Irish Peace Process and the 1998 Belfast Agreement has significantly reduced the level of violence, both in Northern Ireland and in Great Britain. Although the PIRA has held to its cease-fire other elements remain committed to violence. These groups include the Real IRA and the Continuity IRA. Those splinter groups have attempted to perpetuate the level of violence as happened in 1998 when a large bomb exploded in Omagh, killing 29 people. Although the threat from Irish terrorism has receded considerably, it nonetheless remains very real as most of the terrorist groups, Republican and Loyalist alike, have not given up their weapons. The continuing presence of those organizations presents a serious challenge to Britain's security forces.[14]

Counter-terrorist intelligence in Northern Ireland

A defining feature of counter-terrorism is that the security forces are combating groups that go to great lengths to conceal their whereabouts and their activities. In an often quoted phrase Frank Kitson identified a major dilemma for the security forces. According to him, in these types of operations 'the problem of defeating the enemy consists very largely of finding him'.[15] The clandestine nature of terrorist organizations requires the security forces to intensify the efforts to gather intelligence so that the threat posed by these groups can be countered. Although much of the initial information sought on a particular group is very basic (e.g. membership, structure etc.), it can be very difficult to acquire when the security forces are operating in a hostile environment and when they do not enjoy the support of the population. This was the situation that prevailed in Northern Ireland at the outset of the conflict.[16]

Initially, the two major problems were a lack of up-to-date intelligence on the one hand and the absence of a central organization to direct and coordinate the intelligence-gathering effort. According to David Charters, 'the RUC's files were out of date, and their intelligence network in the Catholic areas badly neglected'.[17] Keith Jeffery observed that such a state of affairs was not uncommon for the British in their colonial counter-insurgency campaigns. According to him, 'a common characteristic of British counter-insurgency practice – at least in the early stages of a campaign – is confusion of aims, of command, of organization and of intelligence'.[18] The consequence of that confusion from the outset meant that the various intelligence agencies went about gathering intelligence on their own. Part of the problem, however, was the different types of intelligence required by the security forces. The three types of intelligence sought were background (political), operational (military) and criminal – all of which were used for very different purposes: to aid policy decisions, to locate and engage the 'enemy' and for criminal prosecutions.[19]

Because the RUC had lost public confidence they were unable to obtain and develop background intelligence that is critical for counter-terrorist operations. That was a crucial disadvantage because, according to one army manual, 'intelligence takes time, and much depends on building up mutual confidence between the security forces and the local populations'.[20] Paul Wilkinson asserted that

> the development of a reliable high quality intelligence service is not easily accomplished . . . the police may lose confidence and cooperation of certain key sections of the population. This is especially probable where the police has been controlled, administered and staffed predominantly by one ethnic or religious group, and hence is regarded as partisan by rival groups. In such conditions, it often becomes impossible for the police to carry out normal law enforcement functions, let alone develop high standards of criminal investigation and intelligence work.[21]

That was precisely what had happened in the early stages of the conflict in Northern Ireland.

With the RUC completely discredited in the eyes of the Catholic population, the army quickly assumed responsibility for gathering intelligence. That was an on-going task as the PIRA was continuously recruiting new members. Indeed, from the outset of intelligence-gathering operations the major problem was that the PIRA was growing faster than the intelligence network.[22] In Northern Ireland intelligence was obtained by employing three gathering techniques: surveillance, interrogation and the use of agents and informers.

Surveillance

The army's *Land Operations Volume III – Counter-Revolutionary Operations* stated that in urban counter-terrorist operations, 'it is probable that the police and Special Branch [intelligence-gathering apparatus] will be ineffective'. Since the bulk of intelligence information can be readily obtained through overt sources, the manual identified 'good observation, constant patrolling and the quick passage of information' as relatively simple ways to acquire background information.[23] According to Keith Maguire, those activities enabled the army to build 'a street-by-street and family-by-family analysis of the no-go areas'.[24] Gathering that kind of information made it possible to build up a knowledge base of the Catholic community that, in turn, enabled the army to identify people in order to build up a profile of allegiances and familial and political associations, as well as to identify who the 'visitors' were and who was out of place. Normally that information would have been readily available were it not for the RUC having been discredited. Further complicating matters was the widespread suspicion and mistrust coupled with fear of terrorist reprisals among the Catholic community that precluded the possibility of anyone coming forward to volunteer any kind of information to help the army.[25] The acquisition of overt background information through routine activities such as patrolling and establishing observation posts provided the army with a foundation from which it could develop the background information into contact information.

To obtain contact information from surveillance activities, the army began using special 'plain clothes' units such as the Mobile Reconnaissance Force (MRF) to gather covert intelligence.[26] The army manual quoted above also highlighted the importance of covert surveillance noting that 'it is also essential that less overt methods are employed' to gather intelligence.[27] Established by Brigadier General Frank Kitson, based on his experience with 'counter-gangs' during the Mau Mau insurgency in Kenya, the MRF units conducted a variety of covert surveillance operations in Catholic neighbor-hoods.[28] Those operations included the infamous 'Four Square Laundry' company, the operation of a massage parlor, and the use of mobile surveillance units that worked with PIRA informers, known as 'freds', whose task it was to identify and observe the activities and associations of PIRA members. According to former IRA chief of staff Sean MacStiofain, the unit was 'after "contact" intelligence; that is a name, an address, a photograph or word of a planned operation that would lead them to men, equipment or explosives'.[29] According to Martin Dillon, in their efforts to obtain the required information, the MRF used some imaginative if not 'amateurish' intelligence-gathering methods.[30]

The Four Square Laundry operation was particularly sophisticated as it was a legitimate business that provided laundry services at a reasonable price! The laundry van used in the operation was outfitted with cameras and other surveillance equipment that gathered detailed information on households and people in the neighborhood. A female member of the unit went door-to-door collecting the laundry while her male counterpart remained in the van observing the neighborhood. According to MacStiofain,

> the intelligence was gathered in two ways, by direct observation and conversation in the target areas and by scientific examination of the washing itself . . . If men's shirts of two different sizes came from a household where there was only supposed to be a young family, intelligence officers could conclude that somebody besides the man of the house was staying there. If that house was on their watch list, they now had a contact lead. The scientific tests would show traces of lead, powder or explosives on clothing, or a spot of gun oil on bed linen, an indicator that a weapon had been under a pillow at a certain address.[31]

Upon its return from the testing lab, the laundry was cleaned and returned to the customer without them becoming aware of the real purpose of the laundry service.[32]

For a period of time those operations undoubtedly yielded a significant amount of background intelligence, yet virtually nothing is known about whether any 'contact' intelligence was obtained. After a few months the MRF operations were exposed when a 'fred', suspected by the PIRA as being an informant, 'spilled' the entire operation to his interrogators. The PIRA immediately ambushed the laundry van, killing the driver (the woman got away), but bungled the operation against the massage parlor because one of the terrorists accidentally discharged his weapon after having dropped it. Despite the operation having been 'blown', the army and the RUC Special Branch were still able to gather covert intelligence from the interrogation of prisoners and by using informers and agents within the PIRA.[33]

Interrogation

A second method that was used to gather intelligence was interrogation. Interrogation was a direct method of obtaining current background information from prisoners. According to the Camberley Paper, that was produced by the army in 1979, interrogation's 'chief function is to provide detailed and up to date background information for commanders to develop rather than immediate contact information to be acted on in the raw state'.[34] That view of interrogation resulted from Britain's use of highly controversial interrogation techniques on 14 PIRA prisoners in 1971. Keith Jeffery described the process of interrogation in-depth that 'involved the so-called "five techniques" of sensory deprivation: suspects were forced to stand leaning towards a wall, taking their weight on outstretched fingers, their heads were hooded, they were subject to continuous and monotonous noise, and deprived of both food and sleep'.[35] The use of those highly dubious methods were successfully exploited by PIRA propaganda and caused damage to Britain's international reputation as they clearly impinged on human rights.[36] For example, the European Court of Human Rights ruled that the 'five techniques' constituted torture and criticized them as 'inhuman and degrading treatment'.[37]

The political problems that arose from the use of in-depth interrogation were a result of the army's attempts to acquire instant 'contact information'. According to Jeffery, 'since interrogation is such a valuable source and since information is frequently only of oper-ational use if it is produced quickly, there are temptations sometimes to use excessively rough methods'.[38] Tony Geraghty similarly noted that 'most military interrogation is apolitical and tactical. That is, the job is designed to extract from the prisoner-of-war instant information about his formation: its location, its arms, its leaders and morale. It cannot be a subtle process, since time is of the essence'.[39] That manner of interrogation was clearly permitted in the army's training manuals. For instance, the army's *Keeping the Peace (Duties in Aid of the Civil Power) 1957* stated that interrogation of 'a captured or surrendered person for immedi-ate exploitation . . . is legitimate'.[40] Likewise the army's *Land Operations Volume III – Counter-Revolutionary Operations* noted that 'immediate tactical questioning in the field, before the initial shock of capture has worn off, may yield good results'.[41]

Due to the controversy surrounding in-depth interrogation techniques, the army and the RUC were forced to refine their methods. Whereas the above manuals stressed the need to obtain instant information immediately following the capture of a prisoner, the 1979 Camberley Paper stressed the need for a trained interrogator who was familiar with the prisoner to question him/her. It also stressed that

> interrogation can only be carried out successfully once full scale records are held at a low enough level, since the essentials of good interrogation consist of detailed local knowledge on the part of the interrogator and efficient records, which enable him to know 90% of what the prisoner knows before he starts, so that he can use this to trick the remaining 10% out of the prisoner.

Significantly, it stated that interrogation 'only pays off when the intelligence organization is fully reinforced and decentralized and after legal action has been taken to provide the right basis for it'.[42]

According to former British Army officer Robin Evelegh, the primary purpose of interro-gation should be to persuade the prisoner to defect and work for the security forces as an informer. Based on his experience as a unit commander in Northern Ireland, he suggested that 'what in fact is required for successful interrogation, ending in useful information and possibly a defection, is an intimate knowledge of the milieu in which the suspect moves'.[43] He observed that

> it is almost impossible for a questioner to interrogate successfully unless he can build a psychological link, a sort of empathy, between himself and the suspect. Indeed, it is agreed by all experienced and successful detectives that the first requirement for obtaining information is to win the suspect's confidence, not to frighten him. A frightened man will often admit anything, even to crimes he cannot possibly have committed.[44]

Thus, successful interrogation depends upon a combination of accurate and up-to-date intelligence records, as well as the ability for an interrogator to relate to the prisoner.

Agents and informers

It is widely accepted that the best source of intelligence is obtained through human sources. As Jeffery noted, 'the most rewarding source of information about insurgents and terrorists is human intelligence from within the target organization itself'.[45] With regard to the conflict in Northern Ireland, Mark Urban left little doubt as to the value of informers. According to him, 'the effects of the informer war are profound: the level of violence is reduced; the republican community is rendered increasingly paranoid and must eliminate a proportion of its own membership in an attempt to retain its integrity'.[46]

There were two ways to obtain human intelligence. The first consisted of the use of informers – persons from within the target organization. The second required the use of agents who were fed into and maneuvered into a certain position within the target organization. Depending upon their position within the terrorist organization, agents and informers can provide two types of information of use to intelligence services. The first is background information that includes the membership of the organization and its structure. The second and most important type of information pertains to operations. Such information may include 'occasional tactical information such as the precise details of some projected operation or the whereabouts of a wanted person or weapons cache'.[47]

Recruiting informers involved exploiting a person's weaknesses. For example, *The Green Book*, the PIRA's official handbook, cautioned its members that 'dependency on alcohol is also a major weakness which the Special Branch will be quick to exploit'.[48] 'Turning' someone was most often achieved through financial incentives, threat of imprisonment, or other, morally questionable, methods such as threatening to expose marital infidelity, deviant lifestyles or exposing or threatening one's loved ones.[49]

Initially, the PIRA was structured on the model of a British Army brigade. That structure clearly had its weaknesses, since a possible agent or informer could have a steady access to information as it was a relatively open and insecure structure. Also, because the brigade was based in the community its members were well known. In recognition of the group's vulnerable structure to penetration from informers and agents, in the late 1970s, the PIRA reorganized. This considerably reduced the possibility of infiltration by the security forces. Writing in 1997, John Horgan and Max Taylor noted that 'the structures as they stand today strongly mitigate against the damaging losses incurred through the informant procedures while also guarding against suffering heavy losses through infiltration'.[50] Despite the seemingly more secure structure, there was one serious weakness. Certain positions in the upper echelons of the group became permanent. Therefore, as Moloney remarked, the cellular reorganization was also a weakness because an agent or informer in central command could do more damage then under the previous brigade structure.[51]

Although the security forces were successful in penetrating the PIRA after its reorganization, the information obtained was more difficult to use as they were compelled to protect the identity of their source. Whereas under the previous brigade structure, the security forces could act on the intelligence supplied by informants with the understanding that it would be difficult for the PIRA to trace the information back to any one informant, by the late 1970s, this was no longer the case. After 1977, the use of any information provided would have to be considered carefully as any blatant exploitation of such information might result in the agent or informer being exposed. To protect informers, the Camberley Paper suggested that the army (or the police) make it appear as though 'the information came from a different quarter e.g. from interrogation of a prisoner'.[52] As will be seen in a later section of this article, the security forces on two notable occasions credited surveillance as the source of information for their success in countering two major PIRA bombing operations, when evidence suggests that the information was provided by an army agent code-named 'Steak Knife' who had infiltrated the upper echelons of the PIRA.[53]

Throughout the conflict the security forces ran a number of terrorists-turned-informers at a number of different levels within the PIRA's organizational structure. In some cases, the security forces managed to recruit young Catholic males in their early teens and persuade them to join the PIRA. Urban estimated that between 1976 and 1987, the security forces received information from approximately 50 informers. Penetrating the group at a number of levels had several benefits, the most important being that if one agent was compromised, others (unknown to him or her) would remain in place. It also provided the security forces with the utilitarian option of sacrificing one agent in an attempt to protect the rest, should the PIRA suspect an informant at work. Yet such methods of operating began to venture into a grey area in terms of legality and moral acceptability, as will be discussed later with regard to the 'Steak Knife' affair.[54]

Running agents and using informers to infiltrate the PIRA was an extremely dangerous job. The PIRA adhered to strict rules when dealing with traitors. The *Green Book* clearly stated that 'no volunteer should succumb to approaches or overtures, blackmail or bribery attempts, made by the enemy and should report such approaches as soon as possible. Volunteers who engage in loose talk shall be dismissed. Volunteers found guilty of treason face the death penalty'.[55] If caught, the traitor faced lengthy interrogation and torture before receiving his/her death sentence. After killing the traitor, the PIRA would dump the body along a road or in an alley to send a strong message to its members about the consequences of treason.

One of the advantages of agent-running activities was its psychological impact on the terrorist organization. Agent-running had the potential to weaken the PIRA's cohesion from within by having it focused on an internal 'molehunt'. Agent-running has an adverse effect on the group's morale, operational readiness and effectiveness. It can throw the group off-balance by removing the group's initiative – they do not know what information has been compromised and who is working as an informer. Robin Evelegh asserted that 'the development of informers within a terrorist organization has the effect of accelerating and multiplying damage as trust breaks down and energies are turned to collective introspections'.[56] Peter Taylor similarly noted that 'more than anything else, the informant or agent is the instrument by which the enemy can be demoralized or destroyed'.[57] As will be seen, the security forces, to a large extent, achieved those results when informers were used as witnesses in the supergrass trials of the 1980s.

Organization of the intelligence apparatus in Northern Ireland

Success in an 'intelligence war' is often determined by the level of organization of the intelligence-gathering apparatus. For example, priorities must be set and agreed upon by a committee with representatives from a variety of agencies. Coordination of the intelligence-gathering effort is critical to reduce the possibility of duplication of work as well as to avoid compromising agents and informers unnecessarily. A centralized analysis structure staffed by a cross-section of members of the respective agencies is also important for achieving the best possible intelligence product. Although the above principles were widely known throughout the security apparatus in Northern Ireland, they were largely disregarded by the different agencies that were operating there because of the confusion at the outbreak of the conflict. It was not until the late 1970s that the security forces reorganized their intelligence apparatus.[58]

By the late 1970s the British had developed a rather extensive intelligence-gathering network in Northern Ireland that involved the military, the RUC and the Security Service (MI5). This system was not without its problems however. Agency rivalries and coordination problems, themselves reflections of the larger problem of the lack of centralized direction and coordination, had on occasion impeded successful intelligence-gathering. In fact some have maintained that the lack of coordination had led to a number of agents being exposed and murdered.[59]

Urban noted that 'the advent of police primacy in 1976 . . . coincided with a pronounced shift towards the improvement of intelligence-gathering and the establishment of more effective methods for its exploitation'.[60] An important development in the coordination of the intelligence-gathering effort was the pooling of raw intelligence in one central location, the Castlereagh RUC station, 'where [the] army and police decide jointly how to exploit it'.[61] Although it did not remedy all of the organizational problems, the appointment in 1979 of retired MI6 chief Sir Maurice Oldfield as Security Coordinator was certainly a major step in the right direction. According to Taylor, 'what Oldfield did was straighten out the lines of communication and ensure that intelligence was properly co-ordinated so it could be used to maximum effect'.[62]

By the time the policy initiative 'The Way Ahead' was instituted the security forces had in place a very sophisticated and extensive surveillance system. The system included: the use of helicopters for border surveillance; the introduction of the Special Air Service Regiment (SAS) to patrol and to man covert observation posts in South Armagh; the use of 'Listeners' and 'Watchers' along with 'bugging' devices in most public places; as well as the capability of more intrusive methods, such as planting 'bugging' devices in specified targets' homes and vehicles. Tony Geraghty described 'the "new village" in Ulster [as] an invisible cage of electronic and human surveillance thrown around selected homes and neighborhoods, Orwellian in its implications for a liberal society'.[63]

The 'criminalization' policy required the British to rely on a combination of intelligence and policing techniques that ultimately proved relatively successful in containing the violence. As a result of this policy, a greater emphasis was placed on obtaining criminal intelligence, whereas prior to this, it was the acquisition of 'contact' information for purely military purposes that was sought. What the security forces now needed was hard evidence that would secure a conviction in a court of law. That meant that new investigative techniques had to be developed for terrorist investigations. According to Geraghty, the new approach 'slow and painful in its evolution, finally combined painstaking, forensic police investigation – with massive surveillance of suspects'.[64] At the time, forensic science was in its infancy and had not yet achieved the level of sophistication that it later would in the 1990s. Furthermore, terrorist groups developed countermeasures that made gathering forensic evidence at the crime scene far more difficult. In response to the difficulties involved in obtaining evidence, the security forces staged a daring move to secure convictions for hundreds of known terrorists by using informers as witnesses in what became known as the 'supergrass' trials.[65]

Using intelligence

The supergrass trials

The 'criminalization' policy eventually resulted in the so-called 'supergrass' trials in the early 1980s. The trials decimated the ranks of both Loyalist and Republican terrorist groups. A 'supergrass' was an informer who testified against his/her former comrades in exchange for a lighter sentence and witness protection. That kind of testimony was problematic for obvious reasons, not the least of which was the character of the informant, him/herself a terrorist. In the end, the trials were unsuccessful as many of the convictions were later overturned when witnesses retracted their evidence or simply because judges had serious doubts about the quality of the informant's testimony. Despite the doubts of the judiciary there was little doubt among many of the terrorist organizations involved in the trials as to the credibility of the testimony. According to Maguire, 'the terrorist groups found the trials a gold mine for intelligence-gathering on their rivals and opposite numbers'. Immediately following the trials the groups engaged in assassination campaigns designed to destroy each other's organization as well as to 'snuff out' any remaining informers within their own ranks. The assassinations and mistrust engendered by the 'supergrass' trials effectively destroyed the Irish National Liberation Army (INLA) and caused serious problems for the PIRA.[66]

Although one cannot discount the chaos the 'supergrass' trials caused within terrorist groups, they were also an example of valuable operational intelligence wasted on attempted criminal prosecutions.[67] Robertson maintained that 'information gathered about domestic threats may be used to support or initiate prosecutions and trials but, in intelligence work, a trial is often a symptom of failure – failure to turn the uncovering of an agent against the enemy or to manipulate the information going to a hostile group'.[68] In light of the more stringent evidential requirements to satisfy the courts, the security forces developed new operational methods that had grave implications for a liberal democratic society.

It has been argued that a 'shoot-to-kill' policy was sanctioned at the highest levels of the British Government.[69] Although never officially admitted, the large number of terrorists killed during this period, in circumstances where many believe that an arrest could have been made, is seen as evidence that such a policy existed. For seemingly inexplicable reasons it appears as though the security forces, having known in advance about an attack, waited until the last possible moment to apprehend or kill the terrorists. That method of operating went against the British Government's entire counter-terrorism policy that emphasized prevention and police intervention at the preparatory stages of a terrorist plot. Furthermore, it reflected a weakness in the policy of 'criminalization', owing to the judiciary's reluctance to convict based on intelligence and informer testimony that did not meet the high threshold of evidence required in a court of law. To satisfy the evidential requirements, Maguire asserted that the security forces changed their approach and set 'ambushes [that] had to be carefully organized because security forces could obtain convictions only if the terrorists were caught in the act – a smoking gun scenario'.[70] Yet attempting to catch terrorists as they were conducting an operation dramatically increased the chances of a violent, often deadly, confrontation.

Special operations

Jeffery offered an important insight when he stated that 'in circumstances where security forces may be acquiring fairly good operational intelligence, but which is not of sufficient quality to use for criminal prosecutions, the authorities may be tempted to use the information to inform "special operations" against the terrorists'.[71] Yet special operations were inherently risky because they involved highly trained soldiers intercepting or preempting terrorists during or just before the commission of their violent acts. Furthermore, as Charters noted, special forces have a tendency to operate 'in a "grey" legal, moral and political environment, without clear guide-lines as to their mission, powers and constraints'.[72] In the 1980s the security forces in Northern Ireland made effective use of the operational intelligence received and mounted covert operations that often resulted in deadly ambushes. In that respect, it appeared that in certain situations the security forces had abandoned the route to prosecution that was the desired outcome under the policy of 'police primacy' in favor of a more militaristic response.

One of the most spectacular ambushes occurred in May 1987 when the SAS killed eight PIRA members as they attempted to bomb the Loughgall police station. An article in *The Times* on 7 May 1987 reported that 'the SAS presence in Northern Ireland is to be augmented as part of the Government's plans to tackle the new wave of terrorist violence unleashed by the IRA'.[73] Two days later, on 9 May, a headline stated 'Eight IRA men die in battle'. On the night of 8 May, in what became known as 'the worst single loss of terrorist life since 1972', the security forces had successfully thwarted a PIRA attack on the Loughgall RUC station. The operation was the direct result of 'good' intelligence and excellent coordination of security forces. According to the article, 'it appeared that the security forces had operated on a tip-off and were waiting for the attack'.[74] The attack involved 'driving a digger with a bomb on board [to] completely destroy' the police station. The security forces, having known in advance of the impending attack, evacuated the police station and brought in RUC sharpshooters and the SAS. They waited until the terrorists had arrived and were moving in on the police station before the security forces opened fire, killing all eight terrorists and one civilian that was passing by, but not before the bomb exploded, seriously damaging the empty police station.[75]

The Loughgall ambush demonstrates that by the late 1980s the security forces had achieved a considerable measure of success in obtaining high quality intelligence that was both accurate and extremely reliable. Although the security forces suggested that the information came from surveillance of the suspects, a number of authors have pointed to an informer, possibly 'Steak Knife', as the source of the information.[76] Whether it was due to a change in strategy or simply because it was too difficult to operate in Britain, the PIRA became increasingly active on the European Continent. This led to one of the most impressive intelligence successes in Britain's counterterrorist campaign when a bomb plot on Gibraltar was thwarted. Like the Loughgall ambush, the Gibraltar incident bore all the hallmarks of a successful counter-terrorism intelligence operation: the early detection of a terrorist plot, good inter-agency and international cooperation, the timely maneuvering of security forces into position and effective surveillance. But there was one problem. At the last minute events quickly got out of control and the three members of the 'active service unit' (ASU) were killed. Indeed, *The Guardian* described the operation as 'a brilliant bit of intelligence-cooperation and shadowing which turned to human chaos at its denoue-ment'.[77]

In late November 1987 British intelligence was informed that three members of the PIRA, Danny McCann, Mairead Farrell and Sean Savage, had left Belfast bound for Spain.

The British quickly alerted Spanish authorities who placed the three under surveillance. A fourth person, identified by Spanish authorities as Mary Parkin (an alias), was detected after having made a number of visits to Gibraltar to reconnoiter a military parade ground. It soon became apparent to British intelligence that the ASU intended to bomb a ceremonial changing of the guard parade to be held on 8 March. The soldiers participating in the parade belonged to the 1st Battalion of the Royal Anglian Regiment and had recently completed a two-year tour of duty in Northern Ireland. The British Governor of Gibraltar, who had been alerted to the presence of the ASU, specifically requested Britain's elite counterterrorist unit, the SAS.[78]

Leaving Spain in mid-November, McCann, Farrell and Savage traveled separately to a number of Western European countries before returning to Spain near the beginning of March 1988. Upon their return the Spanish authorities resumed their surveillance of the trio. Having each rented a car, on 6 March, the trio began the final stage of their operation. One car, a Ford Fiesta, was parked near Gibraltar on the Spanish side of the border, while the other, a Renault 5, was parked near the parade ground in Gibraltar. Although the security forces had been alerted to the presence of the unit on 4 March, Savage, the driver of the Renault 5, managed to cross the border into Gibraltar undetected. However, McCann and Farrell, who had crossed the border into Gibraltar on foot to meet up with Savage, had been detected. The trio stayed in Gibraltar for nearly three hours before they attempted to return to the Spanish side of the border. Unbeknownst to them, their every move was being closely monitored by undercover surveillance teams. In fact, most of the people on the street that afternoon were 'plain clothes' members of the security forces including police, the SAS and MI5 officers.[79]

It was at that point that the operation 'went drastically wrong when a police car inadvertently sounded its siren and alerted the three suspects'.[80] At the coroner's inquest the SAS men claimed that they had shouted a warning to 'stop' and then opened fire on the terrorists. Members of the security forces later stated that the terrorists made sudden moves that prompted the SAS to engage them. Whatever the version of events, the fact remained that the three were engaged and killed by the SAS.[81]

Meanwhile, the Spanish authorities searched for the third vehicle, its whereabouts was unknown. A search of the Renault 5 yielded very little, however, in the Ford Fiesta, the getaway car, police found wires, detonators, tools and false passports. Despite the evidence of bomb components, the authorities could not find a bomb. All that changed on Tuesday evening, 8 March, when the Spanish authorities located the third car in an underground parking lot in Marbela, an approximate hour and a half drive from Gibraltar. Inside the car, the authorities discovered a bomb that contained 144 lbs of a Czech-made explosive called Semtex surrounded by nearly 200 AK-47 rounds and a timer set for 11:20 am. The authorities later determined that the car parked inside Gibraltar was used to reserve a parking spot for the third car that contained the bomb set to detonate 'at the height of the parade'.[82]

Although the operation resulted in the death of the trio, it was still successful in preventing an act of terrorism and clearly demonstrated the effectiveness of Britain's intelligence-gathering techniques. As Maguire noted, 'operational intelligence is crucial in preventing terrorist attacks'.[83] One news article commented that 'the Provisionals must be alarmed that their ranks have been penetrated by the security forces or that surveillance within Northern Ireland is now so comprehensive that it is difficult for them to mount spectacular operations'.[84]

In its aftermath, the Gibraltar incident showed the moral ambivalence of a liberal democratic society toward the use of lethal force in counter-terrorism operations. One article commented that 'the deaths of terrorists give little cause for regret. Yet the manner of these deaths matters. It is of paramount importance that the rule of law is seen to prevail and that we should continue to hold the moral high ground in the struggle against terrorism'.[85] Given that the security forces had tracked the terrorists so closely it is at least doubtful that lethal force was used only as a last resort. For example, as Leslie Macfarlane noted,

> the situation is significantly altered where the security forces, on the basis of information received, lay a trap for terrorists planning a raid and where in the ensuing shoot-out a number of terrorists are killed. The question here is whether the terrorists could have been stopped and arrested without 'shooting to kill'.[86]

Macfarlane identified the central question that surrounded the entire Gibraltar operation. Yet no one can say for certain that an arrest was possible. Not only did critics charge that there had been no attempt to arrest the terrorists, they also denounced the actions of the SAS as an act of terrorism. At the inquest, the government suggested that there was a 'foul up' at the last minute that resulted in the death of the three as opposed to their arrest. The research into the shootings by Ian Jack provided some particularly compelling evidence that a 'shoot-to-kill' operation may have been planned from the outset. For instance, the coroner's examination of the bodies of McCann, Farrell and Savage revealed wounds that indicated they were shot in the back and were still being shot as they fell face down on the ground. Secondly, the chief of police granted permission to the SAS to arrest three times and rescinded it twice within an hour on the grounds that he wanted to be absolutely sure of the identity of the trio. Jack found that rather odd if the three were only going to be arrested. Beyond these, there were also questions surrounding whether or not the Spanish police lost the trio. This issue in particular has spawned claims and counterclaims from both the Spanish and British Governments.[87]

Despite the above criticisms of the operation, the Gibraltar incident provides a convenient example that underscores the fundamental unpredictability of counter-terrorism special operations. It is important to remember that the security forces were dealing with extremely dangerous individuals who were believed to be armed. Also, the security forces had not located the bomb and believed that the trio had remote detonators. In the end, the jury ruled the killings lawful, yet questions remain unanswered regarding the operation.[88]

Despite the uncertainties surrounding special operations, in situations where 'good' operational intelligence is received they can be very effective. According to Neil Livingstone,

> covert action must be viewed as a tool that falls someplace between diplomacy and war in the range of options available to the nation's policymakers. In the absence of an effective covert capability, a nation is left with the wholly unsatisfactory choices of doing nothing in those situations where diplomacy has failed and in resorting to the other extreme of using conventional military force.[89]

Furthermore, they can demoralize the terrorist group by essentially beating them at their own game.

Control, accountability and collusion

The activities of intelligence agencies are by necessity highly secretive. As discussed earlier in the agent-running section of this article, any breach of security resulting in the identity of an agent being exposed is a death sentence. Yet having to operate behind a 'veil of secrecy' raises very serious concerns about democratic accountability and whether or not the security forces are operating within the rule of law. As the two previous examples of special operations demonstrated, although the security forces had killed the terrorists, their actions were deemed lawful; but what if it is necessary to misdirect a hit-squad to kill an innocent person in place of a prized agent? Agent-handlers adhere to the principle that the agent must be protected at *all* costs. As will be seen, that sometimes involved agent-handlers, albeit indirectly, in the murder of innocent people because of a need to maintain an irreplaceable source of intelligence within the upper echelons of the PIRA. That practice raised an important question: to what extent is it acceptable in a democratic society to allow the activities of agents and, in some cases, their handlers to break the law to the point that they become involved in serious criminal offences? Writing in 1977, Paul Wilkinson observed that a 'dangerous consequence of a large and ill-controlled secret intelligence and subversion apparatus is that it may end up recruiting assassins and 'dirty tricks' operators for special assignments'. He noted that the danger was that the organization could get 'out of control'.[90]

The partial publication of the *Stevens Inquiry* in 2003 offered a rare glimpse into the activities of the agent-running units in Northern Ireland. The inquiry, headed by the Metropolitan Police Commissioner, John Stevens, addressed issues of control and accountability and stressed the need for the security forces to operate within the law. It revealed that allegations of collusion between the security forces and Loyalist paramilitaries were in fact true. His report was similar to one conducted by the Deputy Chief Constable of the Greater Manchester Police, John Stalker, in 1984. Stalker investigated after-action reports filed by the police after six people were killed in three separate incidents from 11 November to 12 December 1982. He was later removed from the case in 1986 on account of a 'misconduct' charge, but many believed that he was discredited by the RUC Special Branch because he was too close to uncovering the truth about those killings. Like Stalker before him, Stevens also met with considerable resistance from the RUC and the army, who attempted to obstruct his investigations.[91] The major findings of the report included 'collusion, the willful failure to keep records, the absence of accountability, the withholding of intelligence and evidence, and the extreme of agents being involved in murder'. The report continued, noting that 'these serious acts and omissions have meant that people have been killed or seriously injured'.[92]

The inquiry focused on two murders: Patrick Finucane and Brian Adam Lambert. Significantly, it examined the roles of two British intelligence agents in those murders. William Alfred Stobie was a quartermaster for the UDA; he supplied the murder weapons in both murders. According to the report, 'Stobie was recruited as an agent by the RUC Special Branch in November 1987 following his arrest for the murder of Brian Adam Lambert for which he was released without charge'.[93] Although Stobie provided his handlers with information about the planned murder of Patrick Finucane, a Republican lawyer, they failed to provide any warning about the imminent threat to his life. He was arrested by the third inquiry team and the case went to court in November 2001, however, the principal witness failed to testify and Stobie was released. The report states that 'two weeks later Stobie was shot dead. His murder was claimed by the loyalist terrorist group the "Red Hand Defenders" '.[94]

Brian Nelson, an army agent and UFF member, was arrested by the inquiry team in January 1990 for contributing to the murder of Finucane. According to the report, 'Nelson was aware and contributed materially to the intended attack on Finucane. It is not clear whether his role in the murder extended beyond passing a photograph, which showed

Finucane and another person, to one of the other suspects'.[95] The report noted that when he was arrested in 1990, Nelson 'had been in possession of an "intelligence dump". This had been seized by his FRU [Force Research Unit] handlers when my first Inquiry had begun, in September 1989. This crucial evidence had been concealed from my Inquiry team'.[96] Significantly, it stated that 'Brian Nelson's role also raised a number of issues arising from the work of the Force Research Unit (FRU), the army's agent-handling unit in Northern Ireland'.[97] The report suggested that the army would stop at nothing to protect its agents and obstruct Stevens' investigation:

> there was a clear breach of security before the planned arrest of Nelson and other senior loyalists. Information was leaked to the loyalist paramilitaries and the press. This resulted in the operation being aborted. Nelson was advised by his FRU handlers to leave home the night before. A new date was set for the operation on account of this leak. The night before the new operation my Incident room was destroyed by fire. This incident, in my opinion, has never been adequately investigated and I believe it was a deliberate act of arson.[98]

The report also mentioned that classified intelligence documents had been passed to Loyalist paramilitary groups. It stated that 'the advance in forensic technology has resulted in identi-fication of eighty-one people who had left their fingerprints on classified documents that they had no lawful reason to possess'.[99]

In concluding his report, Stevens asserted that 'the unlawful involvement of agents in murder implies that the security forces sanction killings'. He charged that 'the coordination, dissemination and sharing of intelligence were poor. Informants and agents were allowed to operate without effective control and to participate in terrorist crimes. Nationalists were known to be targeted but were not properly warned or protected'.[100] The *Stevens Inquiry* is still ongoing, yet already it has provided damaging information about agent-running operations in Northern Ireland.

In May 2003 news broke about Stevens' decision to interview an army agent code-named 'Steak Knife' about 'his role in murders and abductions in Northern Ireland'. 'Steak Knife' was an extremely important army agent, as he was a senior member of the PIRA's internal security unit, known as the 'Headhunters'. As Henry McDonald noted, 'the "Headhunters" task is to track down, interrogate, torture and kill suspected informers inside the IRA's ranks'. The article revealed that 'Steak Knife is known to have personally overseen the murder of at least a dozen informers during the Troubles. This means that the security forces were prepared to let men die, sometimes even those who were not informers, in order to protect their prize asset inside the IRA organization'.[101]

In an interesting twist of the story, 'Steak Knife' had been marked for assassination by a UFF hit squad, however Nelson, the army's agent inside the UFF's intelligence unit, warned his handlers about the planned assassination. In turn, the army handlers directed Nelson to divert the hit squad to another target, Francisco Notarantonio.[102] That was especially important as the *Stevens Inquiry* made mention that Nelson's involvement in the murder of Finucane involved passing off a photograph of him to the UFF hit squad. This implies that he was in a position to redirect Loyalist hit squads from targets within the PIRA who were operating as British agents.

Both the *Stevens Inquiry* and the 'Steak Knife' affair raised serious and troubling questions about how those involved in agent-running controlled their agents. However, the British Government has established regulations under the Regulation of Investigatory Powers Act

2000 (RIPA) that require oversight and accountability, as well as current and up-to-date record-keeping for these kinds of operations precisely to avoid these situations from arising. Yet is it practical or realistic to expect that agents not partake in any criminal activities? One must remember that the sole purpose of agent-running is to cultivate the source of information. That requires the handlers to attempt to maneuver the agent into the most advantageous position from where s/he can provide the best possible information. That, in turn, means that the agent – to prove his/her commitment to the group – must be involved in criminal activities. After all, doing so was the only way to rise through the ranks of the PIRA. As the Loughgall and Gibraltar operations demonstrate, the information obtained through human sources is often very accurate and can save a lot of innocent lives. It is surely an area shrouded in ethical and legal ambiguity, but it begs the question to what extent do the ends justify the means?

Whether it was 'shoot-to-kill' or collusion between the security forces and Loyalist paramilitaries, the activities of the security forces raised many questions concerning the legality of their operations as well as democratic accountability. If they were operating with the consent of the government, its implications for a democratic state are obvious. However, if the security forces were essentially operating on their own, as Mark Urban and the *Stevens Inquiry* has suggested, then the situation was even worse because it showed a complete lack of control on behalf of the government for its security forces.[103] Some have suggested that those practices subtly transform the nature of a liberal democratic state. According to Ronald D. Crelinsten and Alex P. Schmid, 'when agents of the state begin consistently to shoot suspects without bothering to arrest them, or to mistreat them during interrogation in order to force confessions, then the state has moved far along the road to a regime of terror'.[104] Furthermore, it also went against the 'criminalization' policy by resorting to 'wartime' measures.

Conclusion

Although the intelligence and security forces experienced a number of failures during the Northern Ireland conflict, they were ultimately very effective in containing the violence. No intelligence service is capable of providing 100 per cent accurate intelligence, however, judging by the major successes of the security forces throughout most of the 1980s, it is probably fair to say that they came relatively close. That said, it is important to note that there are limits to an intelligence service's ability to predict surprise attacks. Implicit in the PIRA statement quoted at the beginning of the article was the notion that Britain's intelligence agencies had to be lucky always. As subsequent PIRA attacks have clearly shown, even one successful attack can have devastating consequences. [105] The laws of probability suggest that terrorist organizations which make a concerted and determined effort to attack their enemies will eventually succeed. Yet the existence of competent intelligence agencies greatly reduces that possibility.

This article has also raised a number of issues concerning the functioning of the intelligence community. An important principle for a successful intelligence-gathering apparatus is the central direction of the overall effort, as well as the central 'pooling' of raw intelligence to provide the most effective and efficient analysis of the material. Governments must also ensure that in situations where many agencies are operating, the intelligence-gathering activities are coordinated. Intelligence can provide good information, but it is up to the government to decide how best to use it to their advantage. It is also essential that governments engaged in protracted counter-terrorism campaigns understand both, the uses and limitations of intelligence material. More important, however, is the need for governments to ensure the full accountability of their intelligence services and that their actions are clearly within the law, particularly in the area of agent-running.

Notes

 1 Quoted in Stewart Tendler and Richard Ford, 'Seaside Blast May Signal Mainland Bombing Campaign', *The Times*, 13 October 1984, p.2.
 2 Ibid.
 3 John Newsinger, 'From Counter-Insurgency to Internal Security: Northern Ireland 1969–1992', *Small Wars and Insurgencies* 6/1 (Spring 1995) p.91.
 4 See for example Steve Bruce, *The Red Hand: Protestant Paramilitaries in Northern Ireland* (Oxford: Oxford University Press 1992).
 5 A fairly accurate first hand account of this period is presented in Sean MacStiofain, *Revolutionary In Ireland* (Great Britain: Saxon House 1974) pp.123–43. See also Ed Moloney, *A Secret History of the IRA* (London: Penguin Books 2002) pp.71–7; J. Bowyer Bell, *A Time of Terror: How Democratic Societies Respond to Revolutionary Violence* (New York: Basic Books 1978) pp.215–16; Tim Pat Coogan, *The I.R.A.* (London: Harper Collins Publishers 2000) p.375.
 6 Newsinger (note 3) pp.93–8.
 7 See Tony Geraghty, *The Irish War: The Hidden Conflict Between the IRA and British Intelligence* (Baltimore: The Johns Hopkins University Press 2000) pp.54–66; Coogan (note 5) p.344. See also 'Ulster's Bloody Sunday', *Newsweek*, 14 February 1972, pp.30–32, 36.
 8 Keith Jeffery, 'Security Policy in Northern Ireland Some Reflections on the Management of Violent Conflict', *Terrorism and Political Violence* 2/1 (Spring 1990) pp.21–34.
 9 Laura Donohue, *Counter-Terrorist Law and Emergency Powers in the United Kingdom 1922–2000* (Dublin: Irish Academic Press 2001) pp.307–8; Newsinger (note 3) pp.93–4.
10 See Lord Diplock, *Report of the Commission to Consider Legal Procedures to Deal With Terrorist Activities in Northern Ireland* Cmnd. 5185 (London: HMSO 1972); Geraghty (note 7) pp.91–102.
11 See 'RUC/Army Joint Public Relations Policy – The Way Ahead', GOC/CC Joint Directive 12 January 1977; Coogan (note 5) p.498; Newsinger (note 3) pp.99–108. For a discussion on the Anglo-Irish Agreement 1985 see Michael J. Cunningham, *British Government Policy In Northern Ireland 1969–1989: Its Nature and Execution* (Manchester: Manchester University Press 1991) pp.172–80.
12 Henry Patterson, 'Gerry Adams and the Modernization of Republicanism', *Conflict Quarterly* 10/3 (Summer 1990) p.16.
13 See Moloney (note 5) pp.392–427; Coogan (note 5) pp.620–96.
14 Paul Wilkinson, *Terrorism Versus Democracy: The Liberal State Response* (London: Frank Cass 2000) p.85; See also Coogan (note 5) pp.639–99. For a 'behind the scenes' examination of this period see Moloney (note 5) pp.375–492.
15 Frank Kitson, *Low Intensity Operations: Subversion Insurgency & Peacekeeping* (London: Faber and Faber 1971) p.95.
16 Grant Wardlaw, *Political Terrorism: Theory, Tactics, and Counter-Measures* (Cambridge: Cambridge University Press 1982) pp.131–6; David Charters, 'Counterterrorism Intelligence: Sources, Methods, Process, and Problems', in idem (ed.), *Democratic Responses to International Terrorism* (New York: Transnational Publishers 1991) pp.227–34.
17 David Charters, 'Intelligence and Psychological Warfare Operations in Northern Ireland', *RUSI Journal* 122/3 (September 1977) p.23.
18 Jeffery, 'Security Policy in Northern Ireland' (note 8) p.118.
19 Jeffery, 'Intelligence and Counter-Insurgency Operations: Some Reflections on the British Experience', *Intelligence and National Security* 2/1 (January 1987) p.139.
20 Ministry of Defence, Defence Council, *Land Operations Volume III – Counter-Revolutionary Operations* (London: Ministry of Defence 29 August 1969) Part I 'Principles and General Aspects', para. 261.
21 Paul Wilkinson, *Terrorism and the Liberal State* (London: Macmillan 1977) p.136.
22 Charters, 'Intelligence and Psychological Warfare Operations in Northern Ireland' (note 17) p.23.
23 MOD (note 20) Part 2 'Internal Security', para. 128.
24 Keith Maguire, 'The Intelligence War in Northern Ireland', *International Journal of Intelligence and Counterintelligence* 4/2 (1988) p.154.

25 David Charters, Dominick Graham and Maurice Tugwell, *Trends In Low Intensity Conflict* (Ottawa: Department of National Defence 1981) pp.5–40–5–41.

26 Mark Urban, *Big Boys' Rules: The SAS and the Secret Struggle Against the IRA* (London: Faber and Faber 1993). Urban asserted that this unit has changed its name many times over the course of the 'troubles' but its task of gathering intelligence has remained the same. Other names included 4 Field Survey Company, 14 Intelligence Company and the currently operating Force Research Unit (FRU).

27 MOD (note 20) Part 2 'Internal Security', para. 128.

28 Urban (note 26) pp.35–6.

29 MacStiofain (note 5) p.318.

30 Martin Dillon, *The Dirty War* (London: Hutchinson 1988) p.56.

31 MacStiofain (note 5) p.319.

32 See Gillian Linscott, 'Army "Laundryman" Shot Dead', *The Guardian*, 3 October 1972, p.1; Christopher Sweeney, 'Soldier in Disguise is Shot Dead in Ulster', *The Times*, 3 October 1972, p.1; Simon Hoggart and Derek Brown, 'Army Admits Spy Base but Denies Deaths', *The Guardian*, 6 October 1972, p.1.

33 Probably the best account of this unit appears in Urban (note 26) pp.35–46; see also Dillon (note 30) pp.25–57; Roger Faligot, *Britain's Military Strategy in Ireland: The Kitson Experiment* (London: Zed Press 1983) pp.30–39.

34 *Counter Revolutionary Warfare* (Staff College Camberley 1979) précis 2–3 (hereafter Camberley Paper).

35 Jeffery, 'Intelligence and Counter-Insurgency Operations' (note 19) p.135.

36 Camberley Paper (note 34) précis 3 DS A 1; Colonel M.A.J. Tugwell, 'Revolutionary Propaganda and the Role of the Information Services in Counter-Insurgency Operations', *Canadian Defence Quarterly* 3/2 (Autumn 1973) p.29.

37 Judge Bennett, *Report of The Committee of Inquiry into Police Interrogation Procedures In Northern Ireland* Cmnd. 7497 (London: HMSO 1979) para. 153.

38 Jeffery, 'Intelligence and Counter Insurgency Operations' (note 19) p.134.

39 Geraghty (note 7) p.46.

40 War Office, Army Council, *Keeping the Peace (Duties in Support of the Civil Power) 1957* (London: War Office 10 April 1957) para. 212.

41 MOD (note 20) Part 1 'Principles and General Aspects', para. 311.

42 Camberley Paper (note 34) précis 2, para. 10.

43 Robin Evelegh, *Peace-Keeping in a Democratic Society: The Lessons of Northern Ireland* (Montreal: McGill-Queen's University Press 1978) p.133.

44 Ibid., p.134.

45 Jeffery, 'Intelligence and Counter-Insurgency Operations' (note 19) p.139.

46 Urban (note 26) p.245.

47 Camberley Paper (note 34) précis 2–2.

48 *The Green Book* quoted in Dillon (note 30) p.495.

49 Evelegh (note 43) p.136.

50 John Horgan and Max Taylor, 'The Provisional Irish Republican Army: Command and Functional Structure', *Terrorism and Political Violence* 9/3 (Autumn 1997) p.21; see also C.J.M. Drake, 'The Provisional IRA: A Case Study', *Terrorism and Political Violence* 3/2 (Summer 1991) p.47.

51 Moloney (note 5) p.332.

52 Camberley Paper (note 34) précis 2–2.

53 See British Irish Rights Watch, 'Stakeknife' at http://www.birw.org/Stakeknife.html (last accessed 17 July 2004).

54 See Raymond Gilmour, *Dead Ground: Infiltrating the IRA* (London: Warner Books 1999) p.115; Urban (note 26) p.244.

55 Dillon (note 30) p.487.

56 Evelegh (note 43) p.72.

57 Peter Taylor, *Stalker: The Search for the Truth* (London: Faber & Faber 1987) p.59.

58 See WO (note 40) para 207; MOD (note 20) Part 1 'Principles and General Aspects', para. 268; Lt.-Col. T. Smith, 'Counter Terrorism: Administrative Response in the United Kingdom', *Public Policy and Administration* 2/1 (Spring 1987) p.55.

59 See Geraghty (note 7) p.136.

60 Urban (note 26) p.238.
61 Charters *et al.* (note 25) p.5–35.
62 Taylor (note 57) p.59.
63 Geraghty (note 7) p.74.
64 Ibid., p.74.
65 Ibid., pp.81–90.
66 See S.C. Greer, 'The Supergrass System in Northern Ireland', in Paul Wilkinson and A.M. Stewart (eds), *Contemporary Research on Terrorism* (Aberdeen: Aberdeen University Press 1987) pp.510–35; David Bonner, 'Combating Terrorism: Supergrass Trials In Northern Ireland', *The Modern Law Review* 51/1 (January 1988) pp.23–53; Maguire (note 24) p.157.
67 Jeffery, 'Intelligence and Counter-Insurgency Operations' (note 19) p.143.
68 K.G. Robertson, 'Intelligence Terrorism and Civil Liberties', in Wilkinson and Stewart (note 66) p.557.
69 See for example Geraghty (note 7) pp.74–5, 102; Coogan (note 5) pp.575–80.
70 Maguire (note 24) p.159.
71 Jeffery, 'Security Policy in Northern Ireland' (note 8) p.31.
72 David Charters, 'From Palestine to Northern Ireland: British Adaptation to Low-Intensity Operations', in David Charters and Maurice Tugwell (eds), *Armies in Low-Intensity Conflict: A Comparative Analysis* (London: Brassey's Defence Publishers 1989) p.209.
73 Robin Oakley, 'Bigger Role for SAS in N. Ireland', *The Times*, 7 May 1987, p.1.
74 Richard Ford, 'Eight IRA Men Die in Battle', *The Times*, 9 May 1987, pp.1–2.
75 Ibid. p.1.
76 See for example Coogan (note 5) pp.576–77.
77 'Verdict is Muddle not Murder', *The Guardian*, 19 October 1988, p.1.
78 See Tony Dawe *et al.*, 'How the Spanish Police and SAS Kept Track of Suspects', *The Times*, 8 March 1988, pp.1, 20.
79 Ibid. pp.1, 20. See also 'Spanish Security Officer to Testify', *The Guardian*, 25 September 1988, p.3.
80 'SAS Explains Why IRA Team Were Shot in Gibraltar', *The Guardian*, 11 September 1988, p.1.
81 See 'SAS Killings in Gibraltar Ruled Lawful', *The Guardian*, 19 October 1988, p.4; see also Raymond Murray, *The SAS In Ireland* (Dublin: The Mercier Press 1990) pp.434–7.
82 'Explosives in Third IRA Car Found in Spain', *The Times*, 9 March 1988, p.1.
83 Maguire (note 24) p.161.
84 'How Police and SAS Kept Track of Suspects' (note 78) p.20.
85 'Gibraltar Verdict', *The Daily Telegraph*, 1 October 1988, p.10.
86 Leslie Macfarlane, 'Human Rights and the Fight Against Terrorism in Northern Ireland', *Terrorism and Political Violence* 4/1 (Spring 1992) p.94.
87 See Ian Jack, 'Gibraltar', *Granta* 25 (Autumn 1988) pp.13–86; Robin Oakley, 'MPs Accuse SAS of Terrorist Act', *The Times*, 11 March 1988, p.1; 'Spanish Security Officer to Testify' (note 79).
88 Urban (note 26) pp.204–5; 'SAS Killings in Gibraltar Ruled Lawful' (note 81).
89 Neil C. Livingstone, *The War Against Terrorism* (Lexington: D.C. Heath and Company 1982) p.162.
90 Wilkinson, *Terrorism and the Liberal State* (note 21) p.126.
91 A good account of the Stalker affair is Taylor (note 57). For his own account see John Stalker, *Stalker* (London: Harrap 1988).
92 Sir John Stevens, *Stevens Inquiry: Overview & Recommendations* (17 April 2003) para. 1.3 at http://news.bbc.co.uk/2/shared/spl/hi/northern_ireland/03/stephens_inquiry/pdf/stephens_ inquiry.pdf (last accessed 17 July 2004).
93 Ibid. para. 2.5.
94 Ibid. para. 2.8.
95 Ibid. para. 2.12.
96 Ibid. para. 3.3.
97 Ibid. para. 2.13.
98 Ibid. para. 3.4.
99 Ibid. para. 2.14.
100 Ibid. para. 4.7–4.9.
101 Henry McDonald, 'Army's Top IRA Agent Slips Out of Ulster', *The Observer*, 11 May 2003.
102 Ibid.
103 Urban (note 26) p.241.

104 Ronald D. Crelinsten and Alex P. Schmid, 'Western Responses to Terrorism: A Twenty-Five Year Balance Sheet', *Terrorism and Political Violence* 4/4 (Winter 1992) p.335.

105 The 1994 Bishopsgate bomb that wrecked London's financial district as well as the 1996 bombing of Canary Wharf development offices were among the most costly, in financial terms, and damaging terrorist attacks in Britain to date. Coogan (note 5) pp.587–8 estimated the damage from the Bishopsgate bomb at £2 billion. The BBC estimated the damage as at least £350 million. See BBC News, 'The IRA campaigns in England' at http://news.bbc.co.uk/2/hi/uk_news/1201738.stm (last accessed 17 July 2004).

Reprinted with permission from B. Bamford, 'The Role and Effectiveness of Intelligence in Northern Ireland', *Intelligence & National Security*, 20/4 (2005) pp.581–607.

SECRET INTELLIGENCE AND COUNTER-TERRORISM

Further reading: Books and reports

J. Adams et al, *Ambush The War Between the SAS and the IRA* (London: Pan, 1988).

Anonymous, [Michael Scheuer], *Imperial Hubris: Why the West Is Losing the War on Terror* (NY: Brassey's, 2004).

Robert Baer, *See No Evil: The True Story of a Ground Soldier in the CIA's War on Terrorism* (NY: Three Rivers Press, 2003).

J Boyer Bell, *Dynamics of the Armed Struggle* (London: Frank Cass 1998) chapter on intelligence.

Richard A. Clarke, *Against All Enemies: inside America's War on Terror* (NY: Free Press 2004).

Duane D. Clarridge, *A Spy for All Seasons: My Life in the CIA* (NY: Scribner's, 1997). [creation of the CT centre]

R.D. Crelinsten, *Intelligence and Counter-Terrorism in a Multi-Centric World* (Stockholm: Swedish National Defence College, War Studies Research Reports No.13, 2006)

Peter Chalk & W. Rosenau, *Confronting 'the Enemy Within': Security Intelligence, the Police, and Counterterrorism in Four Democracies* (Santa Monica, CA: Rand 2003).

A. Cronin & J. Ludes (eds.), *Attacking Terrorism: Elements of a Grand Strategy* (Washington DC: Georgetown University Press 2004) pp.115–40.

T. Geraghty, *The Irish War: The Hidden Conflict Between the IRA and British Intelligence* (London: Harper Collins, 1998).

Peter Hennessy (ed.), *The New Protective State: Government, Intelligence and Terrorism* (London: Continuum 2007)

J. Holland, *Phoenix: Policing in the Shadows* (London: Hodder, 1997).

Loch K. Johnson & James J. Wirtz, *Intelligence and National Security: The Secret World of Spies* (NY: Oxford University Press, 2nd ed 2007).

Walter Laqueur, *No End to War: Terrorism in the Twenty-First* (NY: Continuum 2004) pp.119–46.

M. McGartland, *50 Dead Men Walking* (London: Blake, 1997)

Richard A. Posner, *Countering Terrorism: Blurred Focus, Halting Steps* (NY: Rowman & Littlefield 2007).

John R. Schindler, *Agents Provocateurs: How Intelligence Can Defeat Al Qa'ida* (NY: Zenith, 2009).

Jennifer E. Sims, and Burton L. Gerber, (eds.) *Transforming U.S. Intelligence* (Washington, DC: Georgetown University Press, 2005).

M.L.R. Smith, *Fighting for Ireland: The Military Strategy of the Irish Republican Movement* (London: Routledge, 1997).

M. Smith, *The Spying Game* (London: Politico, 2000).

P. Taylor, *Brits: The War Against the IRA* (London: Bloomsbury, 2001).

Gregory F. Treverton, *State and Local Intelligence in the War on Terrorism* (Washington DC: RAND, 2006).

Further reading: Essays and articles

Charles Cogan, 'Hunters not gatherers: Intelligence in the twenty-first century', *Intelligence. and National Security*, 19/2 (2004) pp.304–321.

D.A. Charters, 'Counter-Terrorism Intelligence: Sources, Methods, Processes and Problems' in D.A. Charters (ed.), *Democratic Responses to International Terrorism* (NY: Transnational Publishers 1990) pp.227–267.

Charles Cogan, 'Hunters not gatherers: Intelligence in the twenty-first century', *Intelligence. and National Security* 19/2 (2004) pp.304–321.

S.A. Farson, 'Criminal Intelligence vs. Security Intelligence: Re-evaluation of the Police Role in the Response to Terrorism' in D.A. Charters (ed.), *Democratic Responses to International Terrorism* (NY: Transnational Publishers 1990) pp.191–227.

L. Freedman, 'The Politics of Warning: Terrorism and Risk Communication', *Intelligence and National Security* 20/3 (2005) pp.379–418.

Peter Gill, 'Securing the Globe: Intelligence and the Post-9/11 Shift from "Liddism" to "Drainism", *Intelligence and National Security* 19/3 (2004) pp.467–489.

Michael Herman, 'Counter-Terrorism, Information Technology and Intelligence Change', *Intelligence and National Security* 18/4 (December 2003) pp.40–58.

Bruce Hoffman, 'Intelligence and Terrorism: Emerging Threats and New Security Challenges in the Post-Cold War Era,' *Intelligence and National Security* 11/2 (1996) pp.207–223.

Paul R Pillar, 'Counterterrorism after Al Qaeda,' *The Washington Quarterly* 27/3 (2004) pp.101–113.

Martin Rudner, 'Financial Intelligence, Terrorism Finance, and Terrorist Adaptation,' *International Journal of Intelligence and CounterIntelligence* 19/1 (2006) pp.32–58.

Jennifer E. Sims, Intelligence to Counter Terror: The Importance of All Source Fusion, *Intelligence and National Security* 22/1 (2007) pp.38–56.

Gregory Treverton, 'Terrorism, Intelligence and Law Enforcement: Learning the Right Lessons.' *Intelligence and National Security* 18/4 (2003) pp.121–40.

Wesley Wark, 'Learning Lessons (and how) in the War on Terror: The Canadian Experience,' *International Journal* 60/1 (2004–2005) pp.71–90.

Essay questions

- To what extent may terrorist organizations be considered to be simply malignant forms of non-state secret service ?
- Why does intelligence in the counter-terrorist context present the liberal state with special problems?
- Was there a particular UK doctrine of counter terrorist intelligence that emerged from Northern Ireland? Does it remain valid?
- How far do you accept that a successful counter-terrorist intelligence strategy should be dominated by aggressive clandestine collection using human agents?
- How do the intelligence requirements of the police, the military and the civilian agencies differ in a counter-terrorism campaign? How can the tensions best be resolved?

17 Counterintelligence

The broken triad

Frederick L. Wettering

This essay offers a comprehensive review of the functions of counterintelligence and discusses how they overlap with cognate areas such as physical security and communications security. It argues that United States counterintelligence confronts difficulties in this area because of longstanding problems in three areas. The first obstacle is presented by a range of legal impediments. The second reflects American political culture that renders it averse to intelligence general and counterintelligence in particular. The third reflects bureaucratic rivalry. The latter has worsened with the dramatic shift of the FBI into overseas operations and the appearance of many FBI legal attaches or 'legats' alongside their CIA counterparts in overseas embassies.

> "There is one evil I dread and that is their spies . . . I think it a matter of some importance to prevent them from obtaining intelligence about our situation."
>
> George Washington, 24 March 1776

United States counterintelligence is alive but not well. Its triad of three essential functions is: protecting secrets, frustrating attempts by foreign intelligence services to acquire those secrets, and catching Americans who spy for those foreign intelligence services. The first of these functions is in effect broken, that is, not being performed. The second and third operate haphazardly at best, so that counterintelligence is not being effectively conducted by U.S. counterintelligence agencies today. In fact, it has never been effectively conducted.

The reasons for this conclusion go to the nature of American society, which, from its inception, has been suspicious of a too-powerful federal government. In addition, the anti-government reaction of the American public (and the U.S. Congress) in the 1960s and 1970s to the Vietnam War, Watergate, COINTELPRO abuses of the FBI, and revelations about apparent CIA abuses of American norms and laws revealed in the Pike and Church Committee Reports had catastrophic effects on counterintelligence. Other causes include the generally uncooperative nature of bureaucracies, and their special dislike of security and counterintelligence, the litigious nature of contemporary Americans, and the national cultural bias against informing and informers.

Counterintelligence officers, especially at the Central Intelligence Agency (CIA), tend to dismiss the protection of secrets as "merely" security. Indeed, in the counterintelligence profession "security" officers are looked down on as poor cousins who have to deal with safe closings and employee thefts rather than the exciting business of catching spies. This hubris has resulted in a split throughout both the federal government and the private sector which has resulted in two bureaucracies: "security" and "counterintelligence." Yet, physical and personnel security are actually major components of counterintelligence.

CIA officers tend to put other activities under the rubric of counterintelligence. One is protection of intelligence collection operations by tightening up tradecraft and vetting sources carefully. This is, in reality sui generis, so much a part of the intelligence collection operations that it is excluded here. In this journal a few years back, a former colleague, George Kalaris, also mentioned recruitment of foreign intelligence officers as a major function of offensive counterintelligence.[1] (CIA operations officers like to split counterintelligence into "offensive" measures, primarily recruitment and double agent operations, which they see as fun to do and really important; and "defensive" measures, such as surveillance, personnel and physical security, investigations, and police work, which they see as drudge work done by the FBI and security personnel. But this definition is too dismissive of much of what counterintelligence is all about. Kalaris also mentioned counterterrorism and denial and deception efforts as part of counterintelligence. These latter two functions have developed into separate intelligence disciplines, and thus, they too will not be discussed here.

The functions of counterintelligence

I. Protecting secrets

The obvious first responsibility of counterintelligence is to protect information, usually classified and hereafter referred to as secrets considered important to national security. Two aspects to this function are: physical security, which involves keeping secrets away from all except those who need to be aware of them, and personnel security, which involves making sure that the people who are made aware of secrets protect those secrets responsibly. Other security measures include ethnic recruiting, technical security issues, and encryption.

Physical security

Much of physical security is obvious, and involves mechanical measures—safes, passwords, identification badges, security guards, alarms, and related measures. But the very latest in all physical security measures is now available for sale to foreign buyers, thus giving them the opportunity to study these systems and devise countermeasures. Indeed, the United States government has given modern security technology away to such intelligence adversaries as Russia, under the rubric of facilitating the safeguarding of Russian nuclear materials.[2]

The most obvious physical security measures are the keeping of potential foreign spies away from secret information by denying them access or proximity, and preventing American and other spies from walking off with them. There is a long, rich history of foreign spies collecting information while working as foreign employees of the U.S. Government or contractor firms, using building construction as a point of attack, and using visitors to facilities that house secrets. Exit control, that is, preventing spies from walking off with secret papers, film, and diskettes, is yet another problem area in security.

Foreign employees

In 1938, J. Edgar Hoover, the Director of the Federal Bureau of Investigation (FBI), sent a Special Agent Beck to the U.S. Embassy in Moscow to examine security there. He reported that secrets, including code books and sensitive correspondence, were left unguarded. Local

Russian employees, all in the pay of the NKVD (the Soviet security service, predecessor of the KGB) had access everywhere and to everything, including the code room.[3] Tyler Kent, a young American code clerk at the time, had an NKVD-supplied bimbo (the NKVD/KGB calls them "swallows") in his bed in the embassy, as did many other American officials.[4] He subsequently was recruited by the NKVD. Five decades later, in 1987, FBI counterintelligence expert David Majors visited the U.S. Embassy in Moscow and found the physical situation little improved.[5] Despite several embarrassments and subsequent tightening of security, in March 1997, a naked Russian soldier was found in the shower of the U.S. chargé d'affaires' residence within the guarded compound. He was apparently an army deserter who had no trouble scaling the wall and entering the residence.[6] Even now, while a handful of super-secure "Inman" embassies (named after former National Security Agency [NSA] Director Admiral Bobby Inman) have been constructed, the vast majority of U.S. diplomatic missions remain sadly vulnerable in terms of physical security.

Construction or renovation of offices abroad has its own physical security perils, best exemplified by the U.S. embassy in Moscow. In 1953, the embassy was moved to an apartment building, which was reconstructed using local workers. It was also unguarded at night. In 1964, forty secret microphones were discovered built into its walls, as well as a secret tunnel leading out of the basement.[7] In constructing the new U.S. embassy chancery building in Moscow in 1979, State Department bureaucrats incredibly allowed all materials to be provided locally, from Russian suppliers. Unsurprisingly, the building was riddled with hundreds of listening devices. This embarrassment to the State Department is still standing in Moscow inside the U.S. compound.[8] Building construction remains a problem for U.S. government and contractor offices overseas.

For decades, U.S. counterintelligence officials from the FBI, CIA, and State Department pleaded with State Department diplomats to eliminate or curtail the access of hundreds of local employees at the U.S. embassies and consulates inside the former Warsaw Pact nations of Eastern and Central Europe. Everyone involved was fully aware that all these local employees were reporting to the KGB (or its equivalent services). Yet, the "professionals" at the State Department refused to fire them or restrict their access.[9] The problem was not confined to the Warsaw Pact. For example, in 1979 a foreign employee of the American embassy in Paris was caught stealing classified documents and fired.[10]

The hiring of foreign nationals in the United States poses its own security problems. French intelligence, for example, regularly sought to place employees within targeted U.S. firms with high-tech secrets.[11] Chinese intelligence regularly uses its scientists in U.S. firms as intelligence sources and collectors.[12]

In fact, foreign employees can expect to be targeted by their home intelligence services if they occupy positions with access to secrets either abroad or in the United States. The U.S. counterintelligence community needs to be better prepared to deal with this fact.

Visitors

When the Cold War was declared over in 1993, shortly after the demise of the Soviet Union, physical security safeguards at installations housing secrets, such as they were, were greatly relaxed. Even before that, in 1985, the Director of Central Intelligence raised concerns about the U.S. Department of Energy's (DOE) foreign visitors program, as did the General Accounting Office in its reports in 1988 and 1997.[13] The 1999 President's Foreign Intelligence Advisory Board's (PFIAB) Special Report cited numerous instances of sloppy or nonexistent safeguarding of classified material at the Department of Energy (DOE) nuclear weapons laboratories.[14] Paul Redmond, a former head of CIA counterintelligence, noted on television on 12 December 1999, that after 1993 the State Department issued non-escort badges to several foreign officials, including those from Russia. Redmond also noted that the director of the Defense Intelligence Agency did the same thing with foreign military attachés, including Russians, giving them free run of the Pentagon.[15] Surprisingly, they, in fact, had similar access in the 1970s, and used it to steal anything they could lay hands on, according to a KGB officer.[16] Redmond also reminded viewers of a 1998 incident when an entire day's worth of top secret intelligence reports was taken from Secretary of State Madeleine Albright's office by an unidentified man and has never been recovered, nor has the man been identified.[17]

According to information in the 1999 Defense Authorization Bill, 6,398 foreigners visited the three DOE "weapons labs" (Los Alamos, Sandia, and Lawrence Livermore, where nuclear and other weapons research and development is conducted and weapons information is archived) in 1998. Of these, 1,824 were from countries involved in arms proliferation or espionage, such as China, Russia, and India.[18] Once the matter became a national sensation in early 1999, DOE Secretary Bill Richardson, under pressure from Congress, mandated a temporary ban on all foreign visitors to these labs. The 1999 Report of the House Select Committee (Cox Committee) which investigated Communist Chinese espionage, stated authoritatively that "The PRC (Peoples' Republic of China) also relies heavily on the use of professional scientific visits, delegations, and exchanges to gather sensitive technology."[19] But less than six months later Secretary Richardson (incredibly) announced that visits—including long-term visits—of foreign nationals to DOE labs would resume.[20]

Dr. Bruce Alberts, president of the National Academy of Sciences and a leading critic of the DOE ban, stated that it was "unfair to foreign scientists," would cause other countries to impose bans on American scientists, would affect U.S. ability to implement and verify nuclear arms agreements, and would affect the ability of the labs to attract first-rate scientific talent.[21] Dr. Rodney Nichols, president of the New York Academy of Sciences, while giving lip service to zero tolerance for lax security and espionage, seemed to miss the connection with foreign visitors when he stated that "an overzealous security bureaucracy, shutting down thousands of productive exchanges every year, must not be tolerated."[22] This mindset that science is more important than secrets or counterintelligence is pervasive at the DOE.

Exit control

Other government agencies are equally negligent regarding physical security. Fawn Hall (the former secretary to Oliver North at the National Security Council during the Ronald Reagan Administration) admitted to Congress that she removed secret papers from the Old Executive Office White House complex by concealing them in her clothing. Aldrich (Rick) Ames, a CIA officer, downloaded secrets onto a floppy diskette on his Agency computer and left the premises with them in his pocket. Jonathan Pollard regularly walked out of the U.S. Naval Intelligence Support Center with his briefcase full of secret papers destined for the Israelis.[23] Other western democracies suffer from the same problems. Recently, a senior officer of Canadian intelligence reportedly left a computer diskette containing the names of confidential informants and contacts in a phone booth, while a Royal Canadian Mountie had a list of informants (and his revolver) stolen from the trunk of his car.[24]

As the 1999 special investigative report of the President's Foreign Intelligence Advisory Broad (Rudman Report) noted, "Every administration set up a panel to review the national labs. The problem is that nothing is done. . . . Security and counterintelligence responsibilities have been "punted" from one office to the next."[25] This, unfortunately, is indicative of government in general. Even the most elementary of precautions—keeping potential intelligence agents away from facilities and personnel with secrets—appears beyond the capabilities of the U.S. counterintelligence and security communities, as does stopping employees from exiting offices with secrets.

Personnel security

The essence of personnel security is to determine that those who have access to secrets as a result of their jobs are people of sufficient probity and responsibility who will safeguard that data. Here, the counterintelligence community has traditionally failed badly, and continues to do so. Key elements of personnel security counterintelligence are background investigations and reinvestigations, polygraph examinations, and the "need to know" principle. Numerous other programs involve the detection of employees with problems such as alcohol and substance abuse, financial problems, and marital problems that might affect their performance as custodians of classified information, and mechanisms to assist separated employees find new jobs. These important elements also address some major causes of why an American might spy, but being widespread and generally noncontroversial matters, they will not be discussed further here.[26]

Background investigations

A basic step in the personnel security process is the background investigation, required when someone is proposed for a security clearance which gives access to secrets. Historically, this counterintelligence tool has been very poorly used, thereby allowing several hundred members of the U.S. Communist Party and supporters of the Soviet Union, who had been recruited by Soviet intelligence in the 1930s and 1940s, into sensitive and senior positions in such agencies as the State, Treasury, Agriculture, and Justice Departments, and the Office of Secret Services (OSS), to spy for the USSR. These inroads were documented in detail by John Earl Haynes, Harvey Klehr, and Fridrikh Firsov in the groundbreaking book *The Secret World of American Communism* (Yale University Press, New Haven, CT, 1995). Their information was confirmed by the release of the NSA's "Venona" communications intercepts.

In 1995, 50,000 firms were working as United States government contractors, conducting classified research or production, and 3.2 million secret or above security clearances had been issued.[27] The Defense Department recently admitted that it currently has a huge backlog of new clearance investigations and reinvestigations. The Pentagon also disclosed that over 2.4 million military, civilian, and contractor employees hold defense security clearances (the government-wide figure is over 3 million). Of that total, about 524,000 hold "top secret" clearances and 1.8 million hold "secret" clearances.[28] Many of these employees have been given "temporary" access, pending the completion of the background investigation.

People who do background investigations are not usually well-paid, and the job has no career prospects. Civil liberties concerns have blocked investigators from access to employees' bank accounts and investments, as well as lifestyles. The sheer number of employees with sensitive access precludes any double check of employee-volunteered information unless the subject comes under suspicion from other investigative leads. As a result, background investigations tend to be cursory, usually involving an interview of the references the applicant listed, as well as verification of employment, academic records, and checking the person's name with various law enforcement agencies for criminal records.

Classic examples of poor background investigations include the case of Sergeant Jack Dunlap, who worked at the NSA and spied for the KGB for at least three years (1960–1963). Paid a modest military salary of $100 per week, Dunlap had a pleasure boat, a Jaguar, and two Cadillacs in his driveway. Counterintelligence officers became fully aware of Dunlap's espionage only after his suicide in 1963, when secret materials were found in his garage.[29] Larry Wu-Tai Chin had over $700,000 in real estate holdings, dropped $96,000 while gambling in Las Vegas, and was repeatedly audited by the Internal Revenue Service (IRS), all of which went unnoticed by the CIA.[30] NSA defectors William Martin and Bernon Mitchell, homosexuals who had serious lifestyle problems, went undetected by NSA.[31] Thirty years later, Rick Ames drove a Jaguar, lived in a $500,000 home fully paid for, and had an extravagant lifestyle, yet he passed a CIA reinvestigation, which included a new background check.[32]

Recent reforms as a result of the Ames case give U.S. law enforcement investigators greater access to financial and investment data, and provide for greater FBI control over personnel security at the CIA, but this is useful only in the investigation of people who have already come under counterintelligence scrutiny. The sheer volume of information cannot be routinely checked, and is thus of little value to basic counterintelligence. Private contractors are not exempt from poor personnel security practices: the cases of Christopher Boyce, James Harper, William Bell, and Thomas Cavanagh, all contractor spies, stand testament to this.[33] The number of people to be screened is beyond the capabilities of the U.S. counterintelligence establishment (including contractors), and there is little prospect of change.

Reinvestigations

To the best of my knowledge, only the CIA, FBI, and NSA routinely reinvestigate employees after a certain number of years. Other agencies do it on a random basis. And some never reinvestigate. When an employee acquires a top secret or special access clearance to highly compartmented information, a reinvestigation is supposed to take place every five years (for example: the Department of Energy "Q" clearance giving its holder access to nuclear secrets). The Pentagon recently admitted to being more than 905,000 reinvestigations behind.[34] A DOE study showed that from 1947 to 1972 over one million Q clearances were applied for, with only 0.2 percent turned down.[35] Many investigators have indicated that this reinvestigation is often a mere review of an individual's file, without any new field investigation. Again, the numbers defeat the counterintelligence investigators. Even special clearances are widely handed out. Because of a lack of personnel and budget, as well as civil liberties concerns, reinvestigations are not a serious counterintelligence check.

Polygraph examinations

Polygraph examinations serve three separate counterintelligence purposes. First, they intimidate would-be disclosers of secrets from doing so for fear of being caught. Second, when used on a routine basis they can reveal deceptions which can lead to confessions, or at least more intensive scrutiny. Third, they can be used as a follow-up investigative tool should a person come under suspicion from other means. Examples of all three are available: Chinese spy Larry Wu-Tai Chin retired from the CIA rather than face a periodic reinvestigation and polygraph examination. Sergeant Jeffrey Carney, a spy for East Germany's Stasi, changed jobs to avoid having to undergo a polygraph test. The CIA maintains that Harold

Nicholson, a spy for the KGB and SVR (the latest incarnation of the KGB's foreign intelligence component), came to the attention of counterintelligence officers when he failed a routine re-polygraph exam.[36] CIA secretary Sharon Scranage, when confronted with a failed re-polygraph, confessed to giving information to her Ghanaian lover.[37] NSA's Jack Dunlap, mentioned earlier, committed suicide following an unsatisfactory polygraph which had aroused counterintelligence suspicions of him.[38] Los Alamos scientist Wen Ho Lee reportedly failed a polygraph on what are known as counterintelligence (CI) questions (for example, unreported contact with foreign officials and passage of information) which (belatedly) played a part in his investigation.[39]

The polygraph is a vital tool of counterintelligence, yet it is opposed by most Americans, including legislators and the courts. Only a handful of government agencies use it. During my years on the National Security Council staff (1981–1984), I and others argued vociferously for polygraph examinations for all who read the most sensitive intelligence, primarily to find out who was leaking very sensitive information to the press. This suggestion actually made it into a draft Presidential order, but Secretary of State George Shultz threatened to resign if it were to be applied to the State Department. Certain senior White House aides also expressed opposition, for easily imaginable reasons. The idea was quietly dropped.

In the wake of a massive leak of U.S. nuclear weapons secrets, Energy Secretary Richardson announced in June 1999 that 12,000 DOE weapons laboratory scientists would henceforth be polygraphed.[40] An ensuing loud outcry from scientists and legislators resulted in that order being gutted.[41] In December 1999, Richardson reversed himself, stating that only a few hundred scientists would eventually (over a five-year period) face a polygraph exam.[42] New Mexico Senators Pete V. Domenici and Jeff Bingaman supported the protesting scientists, and publicly questioned the polygraph's reliability.[43] U.S. Supreme Court Justice Clarence Thomas, speaking on an 8 to 1 Court ruling disallowing polygraph results as evidence in military courts martial (*U.S. v. Scheffer*), stated "There is simply no consensus that polygraph information is reliable." Justice John Paul Stevens, in dissent, noted studies indicating that Defense Department studies show that polygraphs have an accuracy rating of about 90%, which is comparable to fingerprint identification.[44] But American attitudes concerning civil liberties, distrust of government, and disrespect for secrets of any kind make mandatory routine polygraph examinations only a pipedream of counterintelligence officers, not a reality.

Need to know principle

"Need to know" is an axiom of counterintelligence, requiring that employees be given access only to those secrets that they need to know and no others. A variation is known as "compartmentation," that is, restricting access to secret information to only those with a need to know. It has never worked in practice, despite periodic reforms demanding that it be rigorously enforced. The 1986 U.S. Senate Select Committee Report, "Meeting the Espionage Challenge: A Review of Counterintelligence and Security Programs," was one such futile effort insisting on a new effort to implement the need to know principle.

From time to time, certain categories of information are restricted, but inevitably the readership list grows and grows. A classic example is the CIA's *National Intelligence Daily*, a daily summary of overnight intelligence items designed for the members of the National Security Council. Readership eventually grew to the thousands. In 1998 its publication was suspended because a number of entries regularly found their way into the daily newspapers, especially Bill Gertz's column in the *Washington Times*. Doubtless, within a short time, a similar publication will develop a wide readership.

The proliferation of special access clearances is another example of the laxity of compartmentation. The 1999 PFIAB Special Report noted that one weapons lab in 1990 and 1991 had granted "Q" clearances to more than 2,000 employees who did not need access to the information.[45] The CIA, burned by Rick Ames's access to vast areas of intelligence outside his "need to know," has made a major effort to tighten up computer access, but at the same time is promoting functional "centers" covering areas such as counterintelligence, counterterrorism, and nonproliferation, thereby merging operations and intelligence personnel in one functional office and widely expanding the circle of knowledge of sensitive intelligence and operations. Counterintelligence reforms at CIA after the Ames scandal resulted in, among other things, a wider dissemination of CIA secrets to the FBI and to the National Counterintelligence Center (NACIC), a multi-agency organization.

Defense against ethnic recruiting

Counterintelligence defense against the targeting of ethnic Americans needs a separate assessment. Most of the more than 50 foreign intelligence services which operate in the United States (and numerous others which operate against Americans when they are abroad), practice ethnic recruiting, that is, seek to recruit persons of the same ethnic background as the foreign intelligence officer. A classic example is the Robert Kim case. Kim, a Korean-American working as a Navy intelligence analyst, was persuaded by the South Korean military attaché to give him Pentagon secrets.[46] Russia, China, India, and Israel are avid practitioners of this tactic, with the Chinese taking it to the extreme of recruiting only ethnic Chinese.[47]

Yet attempts to warn hyphenated Americans of this danger have been met with outcries of discrimination. Despite the fact that in 1998 Peter Lee, a Los Alamos laser scientist, confessed to passing secrets to China, the investigation of Wen Ho Lee produced an immediate outcry of discrimination from various Chinese-American organizations (as well as the PRC).[48] The same thing happened to television reporter Connie Chung when, in 1995, she broadcast a report that many PRC visitors were performing intelligence missions. After vociferous protests from Sino-American groups, she was forced to apologize on air, and subsequently lost her anchor job on the CBS Evening News.[49]

Even stating the fact that foreign intelligence organizations practice ethnic recruiting has come under attack. In 1993, a Hughes Company security briefer was forced to publicly apologize when his warning about the PRC's targeting of Chinese Americans resulted in protests from Chinese-American groups.[50] When a Defense Department security officer wrote in a 1995 study that the Israeli services targeted American Jews, Jewish organizations, led by B'nai B'rith, demanded that heads roll.[51] The analysis was quite correct, and was repeated in a General Accounting Office (GAO) study of economic espionage in 1996.[52] Fearing political incorrectness if not persecution, the GAO identified Israel only as "Country A" in the study. The targeting of ethnic Americans by foreign intelligence services is a reality, but the discomfort of Americans in discussing, thinking about, or dealing with it will continue to inhibit counterintelligence measures.

Infosec

Computer security is often termed "infosec" in governmentese. Any number of senior counterintelligence officials, including FBI Director Louis Freeh, have warned that the computers which house U.S. secrets are very vulnerable. The Cox Committee Report noted that at DOE "classified information had been placed on unclassified networks, with no system for either detection or reliable protection".[53] The 1999 PFIAB Special Report added a long list of computer security shortcomings.[54] Simple yet effective measures, such as removing the disk drives so as to prevent copying of data to disks, done by the CIA after Ames's espionage became confirmed, is not widespread in government. Russian intelligence hackers penetrated Defense Department establishments and DOE laboratories. An early penetration effort at DOE, done by hackers in the pay of the KGB, was chronicled by Cliff Stoll in his book *The Cuckoo's Egg*.[55] In 1998, a hacker group calling themselves "Masters of Downloading" bragged publicly that they had stolen the means to cripple U.S. military communications, a claim denied by the Pentagon.[56]

More serious threats recently came from Russia and China. An FBI investigation, called "MOONLIGHT MAZE," noted in 1999 that Russian hackers had penetrated Defense Department and other government agency computers, as well as those of contractors.[57] After the United States inadvertently bombed the PRC embassy in Belgrade, Yugoslavia, in early 1999, Chinese hackers reportedly attacked U.S. Defense computer sites, allegedly revealing an astonishing 3,000–4,000 "back doors" into U.S. computer systems that had apparently been created by Chinese agents.[58] The FBI subsequently admitted that its new infosec unit, the National Infrastructure Protection Center (NIPC), is badly under strength.[59] The NIPC was created as a result of President Bill Clinton's 1998 Presidential Decision Directive (PDD-63) to protect the national infrastructure.

In addition to professional intelligence hackers, an increasing number of dangerous semi-professional hacker groups are targeting research sites. One such group, Milw0rm, boasted in 1997 of penetrating the Indian government's classified nuclear research site, a feat repeated by three teenage hackers in 1998, while Global Hell members attacked the White House and FBI websites. Many hacker groups, such as LOpht, Phrack, Masters of Downloading, Cult of the Dead Cow, Global Hell, the Chaos Computer Club, Milw0rm, and others maintain websites where they openly share hacking tips, while others provide free of charge the latest state-of-the-art software hacking tools, such as "SATAN" and "Back Orifice." Hacker magazines, both online and over the counter, such as *2600* and *Phrack*, also offer hacking tips.

In sum, the offense, represented by both intelligence service hackers and semi-professional private groups, is well ahead of counterintelligence defense in terms of protecting computer information security, and is likely to stay ahead in the foreseeable future.

TSCM

Technical security countermeasures (TSCM) are a collection of technical efforts to detect the technical penetrations of facilities by foreign intelligence services to collect intelligence. The best-known are the electronic audio listening devices, or bugs. TSCM is a standby collection technique for all major intelligence and security services. The United States has proven particularly vulnerable to this technical espionage. Widely known is the story of the reproduction of the great seal of the United States hanging in U.S. Ambassador George Kennan's office in the Moscow embassy which, in 1952, was discovered to have a listening device concealed therein.[60]

TSCM measures usually involve trained technicians who, using both sophisticated electronic and x-ray devices, as well as painstaking physical examination, "sweep" an area to discover any such devices. In 1944, the very first TSCM sweep uncovered 120 microphones in the Moscow embassy. In 1962, another 40-odd were uncovered in another sweep. Before the new U.S. chancery was occupied in the late 1970s, sweepers found a very large number of listening devices built into walls, girders, and other parts of the building.[61] In a late 1960s case called "Gunman," CIA technicians discovered that IBM electric typewriters in the Moscow embassy had been bugged by the Soviets so that the electronic radiations could and were being detected by Soviet receivers which could convert the signals into keystrokes.[62]

A solid defense measure was introduced in the 1970s, both at home and abroad, with special acoustically-shielded rooms, often called "bubbles," being installed. These counter-audio and other techniques and hardware are excellent counterintelligence measures. But they are expensive, still too few in number, and unwieldy to use on a daily basis, and thus fall victim to the American character trait of not doing anything that makes demands on resources which might be "better" used elsewhere, and which calls for sacrificing certain "freedoms." The problem is compounded by the huge number of U.S. facilities under attack, not just by the Russians but by most world services.

TSCM simply has far too few resources dedicated to it compared to the breadth of the attacks. Sweeps, even of highly-threatened facilities, are made too infrequently. The problem continues: as recently as December 1999, Department of State security officials discovered a Russian listening device planted in a seventh floor (executive level) conference room at the State Department.[63] The number of facilities to be swept is far too huge for the very limited number of "sweepers," who burn out quickly, and other measures such as bubbles. As a result, this form of counterintelligence is a recurring failure.

Encryption

Encryption of communications is a wonderful counterintelligence tool, but like sweep teams and bubbles is not used nearly enough to secure U.S. secrets. Despite the fact that the National Security Agency supplies effective and widespread encrypted communications instruments and methods, U.S. communications are under massive intercept attack by Russian (and other) signals intelligence (sigint) units. KGB defector Vasily Mitrokhin devotes several pages of his book, *The Sword and The Shield*, to the great intelligence gains of these (sigint) efforts against U.S. communications.[64] He notes that the Russians maintained signals intelligence sites located in Soviet diplomatic installations to listen in on telephone calls, telexes, faxes, cellular phone calls, radio communications (via radio, microwave, and satellite signal intercept capabilities). Other Soviet (sigint) listening sites were located in Mexico City and Lourdes, Cuba, where both the SVR (successor to the KGB's foreign intelligence arm) and GRU have maintained a massive collection of antennas and personnel even subsequent to the fall of the USSR. To expect that Russia has closed any of these installations since Mitrokhin's defection is unrealistic. Other defectors have confirmed Mitrokhin's disclosure that Americans are very open in discussing secrets on unprotected communications channels, despite the wide availability of encrypted, secure communications.[65] In the 1999 Kosovo fighting, Serbian forces were able to evade much NATO bombing damage because they were reportedly listening in on U.S. pilots' radio chat which gave away targets in advance.[66]

Part of the problem is the sheer volume of communications involved in, for example, a military deployment. But another part of the problem is the American cultural trait of avoiding any counterintelligence procedure that is too intrusive or value-conflicting. The end result is continuing failure to protect American secrets, despite yeoman efforts by counter-intelligence agencies and the NSA.

Other measures

Many corporations now routinely monitor employee e-mail. But several government agencies and contractors refuse to do so, even though many of their personnel openly correspond electronically with colleagues overseas, including Russia and China. Similarly, regular scrutiny of telephone and fax records is rare. The security, rather than counterintelligence, officers generally charged with conducting these measures are often both untrained and legitimately concerned about possible violations of employees' rights and their own personal liability. Photocopy machines in areas where classified information is developed and stored are uncontrolled throughout the federal government. Routine "trash trawling," the examination of employees' trash, is considered anathema unless done by a law enforcement agency. Firewalls on computers are weak or nonexistent. (Some government offices inexplicably use a firewall made in Israel.)

Attempts to rectify these situations are usually met by passive resistance and noncompliance. Overworked and undertrained security officers cannot enforce such other measures. Foreign nationals on most staffs are generally untouchable. And in private industry and at American universities, they often come either free or inexpensively from foreign firms and governments.

II. Frustrating foreign intelligence operatives

The second major function of counterintelligence is to frustrate the efforts of foreign intelligence operatives to steal U.S. secrets. This can be accomplished in numerous ways: expelling them or denying them entry; controlling their movements and access; surveilling them by physical and/or electronic observation; and using "double agents" to preoccupy and mislead them. A key precondition to these efforts is knowing who the operatives are.

Knowing who they are

Essential parts of any counterintelligence effort are good record-keeping and the sharing of information among agencies. This aspect of counterintelligence has been improved as a result of reforms in the aftermath of the Ames case. A widespread knowledge exists in the overall counterintelligence community about the known and suspected foreign intelligence officers, and the modus operandi of the foreign intelligence services. But information concerning visitors who may be known or suspect intelligence collectors is not well-circulated. Until 1998 foreign visitors to U.S. weapons laboratories went largely unreported to DOE counterintelligence, especially after 1993 and the perceived ending of the Cold War.

Record-keeping is the heart of any counterintelligence program. The U.S. counterintelligence community has had excellent records, built up mostly from painstaking debriefings of intelligence defectors and assets, as well as examination of the results of double-agent cases and the surveillance of intelligence officers. During the Cold War there was also widespread sharing among NATO allies of information on Warsaw Pact intelligence personnel. Identification and record-keeping are made difficult by the use of non-official cover by foreign spies, and by the use of nonprofessionals to collect intelligence—a major modus operandi of the Chinese services.

Recently, cooperation among Western services has cooled somewhat, as allies now also consider themselves competitors engaging in economic espionage against each other. The expulsions of alleged CIA officers from France in 1995 and Germany in 1997 are indicative of this new wariness.[67]

Expelling or denying entry to intelligence officers

The single most effective counterintelligence technique the United States or any other state used to suppress foreign spying is the expulsion or denial of entry to others' intelligence officers, but the positive results are generally short-term. Most intelligence personnel operate with the protection of diplomatic status, or "official cover," as it is known in the business. But even as "diplomats," their visa requests always receive extra scrutiny by counterintelligence services. During the Cold War, NATO counterintelligence officials cooperated in exchanging information on hostile intelligence officers, and in denying visas to known or heavily-suspect intelligence operatives. This seriously handicapped the Warsaw Pact services.

Mass expulsion of intelligence officers is also effective in seriously damaging espionage operations, at least for a time. For example, KGB operations were crippled in Britain in 1971 when Prime Minister Edward Heath authorized the expulsion, with publicity, of 105 KGB and GRU personnel. In 1986, President Ronald Reagan authorized the FBI to mount a similar effort in which 80 KGB and GRU officers under diplomatic cover were expelled from the United States. In his book on the KGB, written in collaboration with British scholar Christopher Andrew, KGB defector Oleg Gordievsky, a former head of the KGB office in Britain, states that in 1971 "the golden age of KGB operations came to an end. The London residency never recovered from the 1971 expulsions."[68] Yet, according to former CIA counterintelligence chief Paul Redmond, despite heavy expulsions, the Russian intelligence presence in the United States today is as large or larger than at the height of the Cold War.[69]

If expulsions with publicity and visa denials are so successful, why are they not done more often? The answer is twofold: first, the foreign governments always retaliate, although not always proportionately. More important, such expulsions seriously damage relations with the state whose suspect diplomats have just been expelled. Important bilateral and multi-lateral agreements, and trade relations—the basic elements of diplomacy and state-to-state relations—are put at risk. Mutual hostilities increase, and diplomatic "hawks" are encouraged. As a result, presidents, prime ministers, and especially foreign ministries and the State Department, almost always oppose such expulsions. The CIA also opposed the 1986 expulsions, fearing retaliation. The customary method is to ask, without fanfare, that detected intelligence officers quietly leave the country. Occasionally, an intelligence officer involved in an operation deemed particularly damaging may be expelled with publicity. For example, Stanislav Borisovich Gusev, a Russian diplomat caught remotely operating a listening device in the State Department, was expelled for espionage on 8 December 1999.[70] But earlier that year, three Russian diplomats had been quietly expelled without publicity. The bottom line is that mass expulsions with fanfare can cripple a foreign state's espionage effort for a time, but the diplomatic cost is almost always too high for leaders to accept such recommendations.

Using physical surveillance

Physical surveillance, the most common technique of counterintelligence agencies worldwide, is very labor intensive and boring, and positive results are few and far between. It can be divided into three parts: static surveillance, mobile surveillance, and electronic and other surveillance.

A. STATIC SURVEILLANCE

Static or fixed-point surveillance is observation of a place, perhaps a suspect's residence, or a "choke-point," where suspects regularly have to pass, or, more commonly, the chancery building of a foreign embassy whose personnel include intelligence officers. These surveillances have three purposes: to alert a mobile surveillance team when a subject exits or passes by so that the team might pick the suspect up; to chronicle a suspect's movements and/or visitors; and to attempt to identify would-be spies walking into a foreign embassy to volunteer their services. The results admirably serve the first two purposes of counterintelligence; that is why surveillance exists on most major embassies (including American embassies) around the world.

The third purpose, catching prospective spies, is, frankly, not well-served. For example, in the United States, the most important volunteer spies have walked through the front door of the Russian chancery on 16th Street in Washington, D.C. to offer their services without being identified by the FBI. Martin and Mitchell, Dunlap, Ronald Pelton, Edward Lee Howard, and Robert Lipka are perfect examples. The FBI has, however, caught some "bottom-feeder," or low-level (and dumb), would-be spies who made the mistake of calling or writing to the Soviet embassy to volunteer their services, or somehow drew attention to themselves while visiting that embassy. Charles Anzalone, Kurt Lessenthien, Randy Jeffries, and Thomas Cavanagh made the mistake of phoning and writing to the Soviet embassy, not realizing that the FBI has means of detecting call-ins and write-ins.[71] Edwin Moore tossed a package of secrets over the wall of the embassy compound with a note offering his services. Thinking it might be a bomb, KGB security officers turned the package over to the police unopened.[72]

In the main, static surveillance has a very narrow window of usefulness to counterintelligence, and is better suited to watching suspects and catching low-level would-be spies than to catching heretofore undiscovered real spies coming in off the street.

B. MOBILE SURVEILLANCE

Mobile surveillance can be done in many ways: on foot, cycle, vehicle, and aircraft. The classic Hollywood-style "tail" is on foot, exemplified in the old spy movie *Walk East on Beacon*. This type of surveillance, very common worldwide, is designed for two purposes: to intimidate and discourage a suspect from undertaking an illegal act relating to espionage, and catching the suspect in the act of undertaking some aspect of espionage.

Mobile surveillance is extremely labor intensive, and therefore prevalent in Third World countries where manpower is not a problem. It is often combined with fixed-point surveillance and/or electronic surveillance. Following a well-trained intelligence operative without revealing the surveillance is extremely difficult. This is not a problem if the purpose is to intimidate. Both the KGB and FBI have long practiced close and obvious surveillance of foreign diplomats suspected of being intelligence officers. But officers of major intelligence services are given extensive training in surveillance detection and evasion techniques, and are rarely intimidated. The autobiographies of a Polish and a Soviet intelligence officer assigned to spy in the United States reveal that, while each had great respect for FBI surveillance, both were confident they could beat it when necessary.[73] The FBI's surveillance record is mixed. A large number of Soviet and Russian intelligence officers have been caught by the Bureau while committing an intelligence act (most often involving putting things in or taking some out of a "dead drop"—a place to conceal money, documents, film, etc.)

Similarly, some real spies have been caught this way. But rarely will a spy be caught without having first come under suspicion by some other means.

FBI surveillance, unfortunately, has missed some big ones. In 1947, Hoover's most wanted man, Gerhard Eisler (an East German Comintern agent working with the U.S. Communist Party), eluded FBI surveillance while on trial and fled by ship.[74] In 1985, Ed Howard (CIA-trained in surveillance detection and evasion) evaded FBI surveillance and fled to Mexico.[75] Even the FBI's elite surveillance team, called the "Super-Gs," was beaten by Rick Ames (also CIA-trained and FBI-trained as well) who managed to elude surveillance, load a dead drop with a devastating package of stolen secrets, and then signal (often with a chalk mark) his KGB handler that the drop was loaded.[76]

The Hollywood idea that both the spy and handler will be caught *in flagrante delicto* by counterintelligence surveillants is, frankly, no longer a reality when it concerns important spies and major intelligence services. In 1959, it was still possible; FBI surveillance of the USSR's Washington embassy GRU officers caught them in a meeting with U.S. Army Lt. Colonel William Whalen, who was later convicted as a Soviet spy.[77] But today, foreign intelligence services respect current FBI surveillance capabilities and avoid face-to-face meetings with their spies within the United States. Important spies are no longer met in-country but rather abroad, in a safer environment, usually by a highly-trained officer of an elite, highly-compartmented part of the foreign intelligence service. Only when intelligence officers get sloppy (as does happen, surprisingly, but usually with spies of lesser importance) do counterintelligence forces have a real chance to catch them in the act with their spy. In summary, mobile surveillance has serious limitations in terms of catching important spies or frustrating foreign intelligence officers. It does have some deterrent effect which results in foreign intelligence services moving the spy business quickly offshore.

C. ELECTRONIC AND OTHER SURVEILLANCES

Electronic surveillance by means of telephone taps (teltaps) or electronic listening devices (bugs), and other forms of surveillance, such as "mail covers" (intercepts), serve to frustrate foreign intelligence officers by identifying their contacts, and either subsequently blocking their communications or enabling them to be converted to "double agents." Electronic devices also assist mobile surveillance with such tools as "beacons" which broadcast the location of a vehicle or item. Cell phone taps can also pinpoint a location. The famous O. J. Simpson low-speed motor vehicle chase is an example. The California police initially located him through his cell-phone, which constantly broadcast its location when turned on.

These special surveillance tools are very useful to counterintelligence. Teltaps and bugs can serve other purposes besides discovering contacts or tracing the movements of suspects. They are a primary means of collecting evidence of espionage when a suspect is identified as a spy or a foreign diplomat as an intelligence officer. They can also tell much about the character of an intelligence officer, perhaps enabling counterintelligence personnel to target him/her for recruitment.

In terms of frustrating espionage efforts, the utility of electronic and other devices is limited, and presupposes that foreign intelligence officers will meet a real or would-be spy in the United States. Intelligent would-be spies (the most dangerous) know the dangers of meeting a foreign intelligence officer in the United States (a testimony to the FBI's overall effectiveness and intimidatory effect). Instead, as Harold Nicholson and others did, they will meet in another country, where surveillance may be less likely or effective.

III. Catching American spies

The overall record of United States counterintelligence at catching spies is not good. Approximately 100 Americans have been caught and convicted of espionage since World War II. A number of others were caught but not convicted, or even not prosecuted, given the very rigorous American legal requirements to prove espionage. The FBI noted in 1997 that it had over 200 active espionage cases under investigation and 800 economic espionage cases.[78] Anecdotal reports suggest that the large quantity of information given U.S. counterintelligence from just two sources, KGB defector Vitaly Mitrokhin and the CIA-captured East German "Stasi" (State Security Agency) files, puts the number of still not uncovered American spies at several hundred.

Author Ronald Kessler, citing unidentified FBI sources, earlier claimed the number is "more than 1,000."[79] The Stasi files alone held data on 13,000 spies, including some nine Americans, according to *Der Spiegel* magazine.[80] The then-CIA Director James Woolsey stated on the NBC television program "The Today Show" in 1994 (probably reflecting on Mitrokhin's information, which had been smuggled to Britain in 1992) that there were large numbers of leads to people who undertook espionage in the Cold War, in the United States and elsewhere, and in several parts of the U.S. government.[81] Woolsey attributed these leads to information obtained after the collapse of Communist governments in Eastern Europe, particularly East Germany (a clear reference to the Stasi files), and probably information from Hungary and Czechoslovakia which led to the wrap-up of the five sergeants of the Clyde Lee Conrad spy ring in the 1980s. The famous "Venona" decryptions of Soviet intelligence messages during World War II leave yet unidentified 178 Russian code names of American spies.[82]

The most effective sources of identification of U.S. spies are defecting foreign intelligence officers and the spies themselves. The second most effective is the decryption of coded messages, primarily electronic. The third most effective are CIA and other intelligence efforts to acquire this information, including attempts to recruit foreign agents who have such knowledge. A fourth is through double agents. Last are the methods described earlier.

Gifts of information

The United States and Russia have both benefitted from unwarranted bonanzas when extraordinarily well-informed intelligence officers, spies, and informants have volunteered their services and/or information. Aldrich Ames just about wiped out the stable of U.S. spies in Russia (estimated at around 20) when he gave their names to a Russian contact and asked for $50,000 in return.[83] CIA acquisition of the East German State Security (Stasi) files has resulted in the arrest and trial of four Americans who had worked for Stasi during the Cold War, as well as hundreds of Germans.[84] Most of the information on the Conrad spy ring of five army sergeants was probably from CIA acquisition of foreign intelligence files. In fact, a majority of the great "successes" of counterintelligence have been gifts from volunteers. KGB defector Reino Hayhanen gave up Soviet illegal "Colonel Rudolf Abel" (true name Willie Fischer).[85] Polish defector Michal Goleniewski gave up MI6 spy George Blake, Harry Houghton, and West German BND spies Hans Felfe and Hans Clemens.[86] Vitaly Yurchenko gave the FBI and CIA Edward Howard and Ronald Pelton.[87] Chinese defector Yu Shensan gave up Larry Wu-Tai Chin to the CIA.[88] A Polish CIA spy revealed the spying of contractors William Bell and James Harper.[89] FBI spy Earl Pitts was identified by a defector, Russian diplomat Rollan Dzheikiya.[90] NSA spy Sergeant David Boone was almost certainly identified by Mitrokhin. NSA spy Ronald Lipka was uncovered when his former KGB case officer, Oleg Kalugin, identified him too closely in his memoirs.[91] KGB senior officer Oleg Gordievsky gave up Norwegian diplomat Arne Treholt and the entire British stable of KGB agents when he defected. The "red diaper" spies (so named because of their affiliation with Communism at a young age), Marie Squillicote, Kurt Stand, and James Clark, were uncovered by the Stasi files.[92]

In fact, the history of U.S. counterintelligence is replete with deus ex machina gifts. In 1938, a naturalized American, William Sebold, born in Germany, reported his recruitment by German Abwehr, and through his efforts the FBI identified over 60 German agents in the United States. The eight German spies who were landed on Long Island from a submarine during World War II were not caught by the FBI's clever efforts, as Director Hoover announced at the time, but because one of the eight phoned the FBI and gave himself up and betrayed his comrades.[93] In 1938, Whittaker Chambers gave State Department Assistant Secretary Adolph Berle a list of GRU spies in the State Department, including Alger Hiss, Lawrence Duggan, and Noel Field. Berle wrote a memo for his diary, incredibly warned Duggan, and then dropped the matter.[94] Hoover refused to even speak to Chambers, who was not believed credible until interviewed by Congress in 1948 (and when his information became confirmed by the Venona intercepts). Similarly, Elizabeth Bentley gave the FBI the names of over 70 NKVD (KGB) agents, but she was not fully believed until the Venona information began verifying her statements in 1948. In 1943, a disgruntled KGB officer sent the FBI an anonymous letter completely identifying every Soviet intelligence officer in Washington D.C.[95] In 1945, the defecting GRU code clerk Igor Gouzenko gave U.S. and Canadian authorities the names of several important GRU spies, including its entire Canadian stable of agents. Vasily Mitrokhin, a KGB archivist, may have presented the greatest gift of all when he defected in 1992—thousands of pages of KGB archives, with clues to hundreds of Soviet spies.[96]

The careers of many spies could have been far shorter and much less damaging had the American counterintelligence community only listened to disgruntled spouses and ex-spouses. The most damaging spy to the United States has been, beyond a shadow of a doubt, John Walker—a judgment shared by former KBG officers Gordievsky and Mitrokhin. Walker spied for the USSR from 1967 to 1985. Yet the damage he did could have been lessened had the FBI paid better attention to two telephone calls: from his ex-wife Barbara and daughter Laura reporting his espionage.[97] In 1982, Patrizia di Palma, the Italian ex-wife of Glenn Souther, a major KGB spy with access to U.S. Navy strategic secrets, reported his espionage to the Naval Investigative Service. Her claim went uninvestigated and Souther spied for three more years before fleeing to the Soviet Union.[98] The wife of Douglas Groat, a CIA official charged in 1998 with passing secrets to a foreign power, stated that she notified the FBI in 1985 that he had passed secrets to two foreign operatives. She claimed she was interviewed by two FBI agents, but her allegations were dismissed because Groat had left her a few months before.[99] These incidents reflect a serious lack of counterintelligence training, and perhaps some male sexist behavior in discounting allegations from a credible source.

The U.S. counterintelligence record on reception of defectors and other volunteers is not strong. Defectors have come to the United States and not been debriefed on a timely basis, if at all, starting with Georgi Agabekov in 1930, an OGPU (an early version of the KGB) *rezident* who was murdered by the OGPU in 1939. A top GRU officer, "Walter Krivitsky" (true name Samuel Ginsberg), fled to the United States in 1937 to avoid Stalin's death purges. He had no serious reception from the FBI or any other government agency, and had to tell some of his story through a book, *Stalin's Agent*, and articles sold to the now defunct

Saturday Evening Post magazine. His death in 1941 was almost certainly an NKVD or GRU "hit" to silence him.[100] At the same time, a top NKVD intelligence general, "Alexander Orlov"(true name Leiba Felbin), fled to the United States, also to avoid Stalin's death purges. Orlov was not interviewed by the FBI until 1953, when he sold a denunciation of Stalin to *Life* magazine. An outraged Hoover belatedly ordered an interview, but Orlov successfully concealed his extensive knowledge of Soviet spies from both FBI and CIA interrogations.[101]

More recently, key volunteers have been turned away. Oleg Penkovsky, "the spy who saved the world," was turned away from America's Moscow embassy in 1960.[102] Worse still, spies seeking asylum have been returned to certain execution. Igor Gouzenko was almost given back to the Russians by the Canadians in 1945. To America's national shame, KGB defector Yuri Nosenko was badly and illegally mistreated for three years in the United States, and defector Yuri Loginov, a KGB illegal, was returned from South Africa in 1969 to the Soviets (and was immediately executed) because James Angleton and the CIA were mesmerized by the paranoid ravings of a previous defector, Anatoly Golitsyn.[103] Lastly, in 1991, the CIA's Soviet Operations Chief, Milton Bearden, ordered his field personnel not to accept KGB volunteers, which probably explains why Mitrokhin finally went to the British for asylum.[104]

A strong case can be made that the large majority of the most important spy cases went undetected until someone told the United States about them. This reflects little credit to the entire American counterintelligence community.

Decoding breakthroughs

The biggest bonanza of all came in 1948 when the Army Security Agency, later to become the National Security Agency (NSA), began to solve Soviet wartime intelligence messages that had been intercepted but not previously decoded. These Venona messages ultimately identified by code name some 350 spies. Nearly half of them were identified, including the famous nuclear spies Klaus Fuchs and Ted Hall. The British spy ring known as the "Cambridge Five": Kim Philby, Guy Burgess, Donald Maclean, Anthony Blunt, and John Cairncross were also identified from Venona.

Earlier, in 1940, the British had decoded German military intelligence (Abwehr) messages encoded on the "Enigma" machine, and were able to identify and neutralize or turn every German spy in Britain. Such decoded messages rarely give the name of the spy, but provide clues to his identity, thereby making the counterintelligence community's job much easier. While these breakthroughs are few and far between, when they occur, the counterintelligence forces are given a tremendous leg up in neutralizing the espionage efforts of the target country.

CIA and other agency collection efforts

In 1991, the CIA reportedly purchased the East German Stasi's files, which provided clues to the identification of 13,000 East German spies, from a Russian transport officer in charge of shipping them out of East Germany.[105] Various CIA and FBI recruitments of foreign intelligence officers have identified other officers and their spies. These operations are major sources of counterintelligence leads, but further discussion of this properly belongs in a discussion of intelligence collection, not counterintelligence.

Double agents

Double agents are spies who fall into either of two categories: (a) foreign spies who have been discovered and subsequently agree to work for their counterintelligence captors to avoid penalties; (b) or "dangles," controlled sources who are dangled in front of a foreign intelligence officer, often by directly volunteering to spy, in hopes that the officer will bite and attempt to recruit the dangle. From such agents a counterintelligence officer hopes to learn the identity, method of operation, and spy equipment provided by the intelligence service to "their" spy. The effort also offers an opportunity to preoccupy the other side's officers, keeping them occupied and without time to chase valid targets. Lastly, it offers opportunities for disinformation. The British used their best double agent, codenamed GARBO, to effectively confound the German leadership about the Normandy landings in 1944.[106]

Disinformation has become a separate, "hot" new discipline in the U.S. intelligence community. But information obtained from such double agents is often minimal. Intelligence officers have learned not to expose their best techniques to new, volunteer sources, and to be suspicious of their information. Dangles and double agents must produce good intelligence information or they will be dropped. And making real secrets available to give away in such fashion is often difficult. Only double agents from current or previously denied areas, such as Cuba, East Germany, or the former Soviet Union, have proven really effective because so little is or was known about their countries and governments, and almost any information has been welcomed by intelligence analysts.

Double agents are time-consuming, and the payoff generally so slight, that as a rule the CIA avoids them, leaving them to the military intelligence and the FBI.

IV. Why U.S. counterintelligence does not work

There are three reasons why United States counterintelligence methods do not work. The first is a problem with U.S. law. The second deals with two American cultural traits which have assumed the importance of fixed and binding customs, or "mores." The third has to do with traditional bureaucratic behavior.

A. U.S. LAW PROBLEMS

Since the 1950s Supreme Court under Chief Justice Earl Warren and even earlier, United States espionage law has posed major burdens on the counterintelligence community. Prevailing law is based primarily on the 1917 Espionage Act (now 18 US Code 794) which requires that four elements be proven before an espionage conviction can occur: The accused person must (1) knowingly communicate or deliver to (2) a foreign entity (3) material related to national security (third requirement) with (4) intent to injure the United States, for the advantage of the foreign entity, or for personal gain. For a counterintelligence service to develop and prove all four parts, absent a confession or catching the suspect "in the act," is extraordinarily difficult. For example, a State Department official, Felix Bloch, was observed secretly meeting a known Soviet intelligence officer and passing him papers.[107] But, the U.S. government was unable to prove that the papers contained national security information, and thus Bloch was not even tried. Months and even years of observing a suspect are often required in order to build up a case which would stand up in court. Yet, during this period the spies continue to spy, and, as Ames did, cause even further damage.

Of the many leads to spies provided to U.S. counterintelligence by the Stasi files and

Mitrokhin papers, only a handful have yet been brought to trial, largely because meeting the four conditions of proof is difficult when counterintelligence receives information of espionage in years gone by. That explains, for example, why Ted Hall was not prosecuted for his nuclear spying for the KGB in the 1940s.[108] It also explains why FBI agents had to pose as foreign intelligence officers to nail Earl Pitts, Daniel King, Robert Lipka, Robert Boone, and the "red diaper babies."[109]

Even when all four elements appear to have been developed, the government faces the additional problem of the right of "discovery." This first arose at the Judith Coplon trial in 1948. Coplon had been caught passing notes containing classified information to her KGB lover. Her lawyers successfully demanded, under the right of discovery, all FBI files remotely related to the case. J. Edgar Hoover reluctantly agreed, but was so outraged by the negative public reaction to material in the FBI files revealed by the defense that he ordained that the FBI no longer would risk arresting a suspect unless all vital information was protected, and would result in a "slam-dunk" prosecution. One reason why Coplon's conviction was later overturned was that the U.S. government refused to make public the Venona material which identified her as a spy.[110]

This threat of exposure of secret information obtained by the defense under discovery motions is called "greymail." In 1980, Congress, at the urging of the counterintelligence community, provided some relief from greymail by passing the Classified Information Procedures Act (CIPA), which allows the government to present the material ex parte and in camera to the judge, that is, secretly, without the defense present. But this does not relieve the government from giving the defense classified information that is directly relevant, and fear of exposure of this information still constrains counterintelligence agencies and government prosecutors. This fear reportedly inhibited the government from trying both Oliver North and CIA Costa Rica station chief Joseph Fernandez during the Iran-Contra investigations, and to a downgrading of the charges against Douglas Groat.[111]

B. AMERICAN MORES

Alexis de Tocqueville in his treatise on the American people, *Democracy In America*, noted in 1830 that democracies are not good at secrecy or perseverance in foreign affairs. Tocqueville had it right: the sad truth is that Americans do not like or respect secrets. Newspapers are full of leaks of classified information, even from the highest levels of government.

Revelations of secrets are often inadvertent: Ronald Reagan, when denouncing the 1986 terrorist bombing of the "La Belle" discotheque in Berlin, blamed Libya and inadvertently revealed that the NSA had intercepted Libyan communications, a secret of the highest magnitude. Scientist George Keyworth admitted that he had perhaps talked too much about the neutron bomb to Chinese scientists during a visit to China in 1980 but felt no remorse, claiming the information was "just physics."[112] Congressman Robert G. Torricelli (D., New Jersey) made public classified information about Central America, and was shortly thereafter elected to the U.S. Senate. Senator Daniel Patrick Moynihan (D., New York) has attacked government secrecy as undermining the accountability of government to the people, a serious point which has great validity.

Taken together, these are indications of a profound cultural trait which has become one of America's mores, which Webster's Dictionary defines as "the fixed customs or folkways of a particular group that are morally binding upon all members and necessary to its welfare and preservation."

A second U.S. cultural trait is the dislike of informers. Most children are taught that it is bad to "tattle" on others. During the controversy over President Bill Clinton's affairs ABC anchorman Jack Ford, a former practicing attorney, explained on a television show why everyone loathed Linda Tripp, stating that in his experience no jury member likes an informer, and that jurors tend to disregard informer-supplied information.[113] This trait, also a "mor," has serious counterintelligence implications. Defectors are often not well received, and their information is not considered strong evidence in an espionage trial. People are also disinclined to report on others. Sergeant Jeffrey Carney noted that a colleague walked in on him photographing secret documents, but never reported it.[114]

A third "mor" is American distrust of government. This goes back to the beginning of U.S. history as a nation. The federal government was hopelessly weak under the Articles of Confederation because Americans feared a strong central government. Only after the tacking on of a Bill of Rights was the Constitution ratified by the crucial states of New York and Virginia. The writings and statements of Thomas Jefferson and James Madison warn consistently against a strong central government. In modern history, civil libertarians have allied themselves with civil rights advocates and political conservatives in attempting to limit the powers of federal government, as is very well documented by Gary Wills in *A Necessary Evil: A History of American Distrust of Government* (New York: Simon & Schuster, 1999).

The misbehavior and malfeasance of recent Presidents certainly has fed this distrust, as have the exposed transgressions of the FBI and the CIA. The very fact that the United States had neither an intelligence nor a counterintelligence agency for most of its history stands testament to this view. Since the 1960s Hollywood has fed the American fear of government, and especially the FBI, CIA, and NSA, in a plethora of feature films.

C. BUREAUCRATIC BEHAVIOR

Students of organizational behavior affirm that bureaucracies never give up "turf" or authority. The common bureaucratic response to a shortcoming is to ask for more money and create new bureaucratic entities. That behavior has occurred in the counterintelligence community, most recently in 1994 after the Ames case surfaced. President Clinton, in Presidential Decision Document 24, reshuffled and renamed several counterintelligence coordinating committees. Congress voted lots more money for the FBI and CIA counterintelligence bureaucracies. An FBI officer was put in charge of a new bureaucracy, the National Counterintelligence Center (separate from the CIA's counterintelligence center and the new FBI counterintelligence center), and other FBI officers were inserted at the top level in the CIA's counterintelligence and security offices. This has somewhat improved bureaucratic and organizational communications, albeit largely one way, from CIA to the FBI. The FBI is legendary for not sharing its information with any other agency.

In addition, the FBI has been moving aggressively in the last decade in bureaucratically usurping the authority of its rivals. The FBI attempted a takeover, partly successful, of the Drug Enforcement Administration. In the counterintelligence field, the FBI has upset the intent of the 1947 National Security Act, as well as several Presidential executive orders which mandated that the Bureau would be in charge of counterintelligence at home, with CIA in charge abroad. The FBI has obtained a congressional mandate to investigate terrorist crimes against Americans abroad, and has leveraged this and other congressional grants of authority to challenge the CIA in foreign countries.

In the last two years the FBI has opened many new overseas offices, seriously contesting traditional CIA turf in dealing with foreign intelligence and security organizations.[115] This has created further bureaucratic muddle and moved the FBI into operations where it has little expertise nor a necessary freedom of action. Sam Papich, a senior FBI officer, stated in response to Senate legislation (the Boren-Cohen Bill) which would have given all counter-intelligence authority to the FBI, that the FBI was incapable of doing CIA duties abroad, which necessarily involve breaking the laws of foreign countries.[116] The author and journalist Mark Riebling noted that three "solutions" have been proposed for U.S. counterintelligence problems: give all counterintelligence to the FBI (supported by then Senators Dennis DeConcini, [D., Arizona], William Cohen [R., Maine], and David Boren [D., Oklahoma]); give all counterintelligence to the CIA (supported by Congressman Larry Combest [R., Texas]; or create a third, "super" organization which would command both the FBI and CIA in counterintelligence (variations attributed to Kenneth de Graffenried, former CIA counterintelligence officer Newton "Scotty" Miler, and former National Security Adviser Anthony Lake).[117] My thesis is that none of these will work bureaucratically or politically. The best that can be reasonably expected is some improvement in coordination between the CIA's overseas collection and counterintelligence roles and the FBI's domestic counterintel-ligence role. And the swing toward throwing more authority at the FBI to a large degree adds to the bureaucratic muddle and will not improve counterintelligence, merely competition.[118]

Notably, after each major spy scandal, counterintelligence coordination improves between agencies. Some of the reforms have also improved interagency communication. But basic bureaucratic behavior consistently precludes developing an efficient counterintelligence system. This was best evidenced when, in 1981, de Graffenried became the Intelligence Director on the National Security Council Staff. He was committed to creating a single effective counterintelligence czar or oversight staff to mandate coordination between the FBI and CIA, and otherwise improve coordination and training in those agencies. But in his seven years on the White House Staff, de Graffenried, even with his incredible talent, and despite his best efforts and the authority of his office was able to achieve only minor, piecemeal reforms.[119] Bureaucratic inertia and self-defense was too strong.

V. Sea change needed

"When you're catching spies, you have a bad counterintelligence service. When you're not catching spies, you have a bad counterintelligence service. You can't have it both ways!"

Judge William Webster, former Director of Central Intelligence.

An examination of its component parts shows United States counterintelligence to be indeed broken. Bureaucratic rivalries, American ethics and mores, and operational realities show that a truly effective U.S. counterintelligence program cannot be effected without a sea change in American political attitudes.

References

1 George Kalaris and Leonard McCoy, "Counterintelligence for the 1990s." *International Journal of Intelligence and Counterintelligence*, Vol. 2, No. 2, Summer 1987, pp. 179–187.
2 Energy Secretary Bill Richardson's Address to the National Press Club, 3 March 1999.
3 Letter from J. Edgar Hoover to Major General Edwin M. Watson, Secretary to the President, dated 13 December 1940, which forwarded the attached Beck memorandum to President Roosevelt. See also Ambassador Charles "Chip" Bohlen's recollections of lax security in his memoirs, *Witness To History* (New York: W. W. Norton, 1973), especially p. 15.
4 Ray Bearse and Anthony Read, *Conspirator: The Untold Story of Tyler Kent* (New York: Doubleday,

1991), p. 36. See also the Beck Report (footnote 1) for discussion of Embassy employees Donald Nichols, John Morgan, Sylvester Huntkowski, and James Lewis and their Soviet paramours.

5 Mark Riebling, *Wedge: The Secret War Between the FBI and CIA* (New York, Alfred A. Knopf, 1994), p. 351.

6 Reuters, cited in *Toronto Globe and Mail*, 21 March 1997.

7 Ronald Kessler, *Moscow Station: How the KGB Penetrated the American Embassy* (New York: Pocket Books, 1989), pp. 29–30.

8 Ibid, pp. 107–109.

9 Ibid., pp. 12–16.

10 Frank Greve, "In the World of Espionage, France Emerges as U.S. Adversary," *Philadelphia Inquirer*, 24 October 1992. Also, same author and paper, 18 April 1993.

11 Peter Schweitzer, *Friendly Spies: How America's Allies Are Using Economic Espionage to Steal Our Secrets* (New York: Atlantic Monthly Press, 1993), pp. 96–126.

12 Nicholas Eftimiades, *Chinese Intelligence Operations* (Annapolis, Md: Naval Institute Press, 1994), pp. 28–29. See also Vernon Loeb, "Chinese Spy Methods Limit Bid to Find Truth, Officials Say," *The Washington Post*, 21 March 1999, and Bill Gertz, "Big Rise in Chinese Visitors Poses an Intelligence Threat," *Washington Times*, 18 January 1992.

13 See General Accounting Office, GAO/RCED-87-72, *DOE Reinvestigation of Employees Has Not Been Timely*, 1987, and GAO/RCED 89-31, *Major Weaknesses in Foreign Visitor Controls At Weapons Laboratories*, 1989.

14 President's Foreign Intelligence Advisory Board Report (Rudman Commission), *Science at Its Best, Security at Its Worst: A Report on Security Problems at the U.S. Department of Energy*, June 1999 (henceforth PFIAB Report). My copy was obtained from the Federation of American Scientists (FAS) website, www.fas.org., making page citation problematical. See p. 11 of the chapter "Recurring Vulnerabilities" in the FAS download.

15 Paul Redmond interview, "NBC Meet the Press," 12 December 1999. See also Bill Gertz, "Pentagon Lets in Russians," *Washington Times*, 22 June 1993.

16 Yuri Shvets, *Washington Station: My Life as a KGB Spy in America* (New York: Simon & Schuster, 1994), p. 35.

17 Redmond interview, NBC's "Meet the Press." See also, "State Department Tightens Security After Loss of Secret Documents," *The Washington Post*, 20 March 1998.

18 William Broad and Judith Miller, "Scientists Criticize Limits on Foreign Visitors to Laboratories," *The New York Times*, 3 December 1999.

19 *U. S. National Security and Military/Commercial Concerns With the Peoples' Republic of China*. Select Committee, United States House of Representatives, (Washington, D.C.: U.S. Government Printing Office, 1999) Vol. 1, p. 39 (hereafter, Cox Report).

20 Broad and Miller, op cit.

21 Ibid.

22 Ibid.

23 Ruth Sinai, "It's Not So Hard to Walk Out with Secret Documents," Associated Press, 5 August 1993.

24 John Grey, "Gaffes Damage Intelligence Agency's Image," *South China Morning Post*, 6 December 1999.

25 PFIAB Report. The citation is found at the section entitled "Root Causes," p. 5.

26 Lynn Fischer, "Espionage: Why Does It Happen?," *Security Awareness Bulletin*, Department of Defense Security Institute (DoDSI), Number 1–94, pp. 1–8.

27 Christopher Andrew and Oleg Gordievsky, *KGB: The Inside Story of Its Foreign Operations from Lenin to Gorbachev* (London: Hodder and Stoughton, 1990), p. 381.

28 Walter Pincus, "Huge Backlog for Security Checks Tied to Pentagon Computer Woes," *The Washington Post*, 30 November 1999. See also, Walter Pincus "900,000 People Awaiting Pentagon Security Clearances," *The Washington Post*, 20 April 2000.

29 Norman Polmar and Thomas B. Allen, *Spy Book: The Encyclopedia of Espionage* (New York: Random House, 1997), p. 179.

30 The Maldon Institute, "America's Espionage Epidemic," Washington D.C., 1996, pp. 22–23.

31 On Martin and Mitchell, see Polmar and Allen, op. cit., pp. 356, 372.

32 On Ames, see Ibid, p. 22.

33 See Ibid., pp. 56 (Bell), 83 (Boyce), 104 (Cavanagh), 254 (Harper).

34 Pincus, "Huge backlog. . . ."

35 U.S. Department of Energy, *Counterintelligence Newsletter*, 1997, p. 4.

36 David Wise, "The Spy Who Sold the Farm," *GQ Magazine*, March 1998, p. 294.

37 Maldon Institute, op. cit. pp. 30–33.

38 Andrew and Gordievsky, op. cit., p. 381.

39 Bob Drogin, "Secrets, Science Are Volatile Mixture at Los Alamos," *Los Angeles Times*, 1 April 1999.

40 Vernon Loeb, "Polygraphs Start for 5,000 at Energy," *The Washington Post*, 21 June 1999.

41 Walter Pincus and Vernon Loeb, "Lie Tests Anger Lab Scientists," *The Washington Post*, 23 September 1999.

42 Walter Pincus and Vernon Loeb, "Energy Chief to Allow Foreign Scientists to Visit Labs," *The Washington Post*, 3 December 1999.

43 Vernon Loeb, "Senators Challenge Energy Polygraph Plan," *The Washington Post*, 26 September 1999.

44 David G. Savage, "High Court Bars Use of Polygraph Test as Defense," *Los Angeles Times*, 1 April 1998. See also Aaron Epstein, "Ruling Rejects Lie Detector Evidence," *Philadelphia Inquirer*, 1 April 1998.

45 PFIAB Report, p. 8 of the section, "Recurring Vulnerabilities."

46 Brooke Masters, "Va. Man Sentenced to 9 Years in Spy Case," *The Washington Post*, 12 July 1997.

47 Former FBI China analyst Paul Moore, quoted in Vernon Loeb, "Inside Information," *The Washington Post*, 18 October 1999. Also see Paul Moore, "Spies of a Different Stripe," *The Washington Post*, 31 May 1999.

48 Erik Eckholm, "China Detects Racism in U.S. Report on Spying," *The New York Times*, 1 June 1999. Also, Fox Butterfield and Joseph Kahn, "Chinese in U.S. Say Spying Casts Doubt on Their Loyalties," *The New York Times*, 16 May 1999, and David Stout, "Lee's Defenders Say Scientist Is Victim of Witch Hunt Against China," *The New York Times*, 11 December 1999.

49 *The New York Times*, 23 October 1994, p. 36.

50 Ralph Vartabedian, "Asian-American Workers View Hughes Memo as Ethnic Insult," *Los Angeles Times*, 27 July 1993.

51 Kevin Galvin, "Jewish Group Protests . . .," Associated Press, 29 January 1996.

52 General Accounting Office, GAO/T-NSIAD-96-114, *Economic Espionage: Information on Threat from U.S. Allies*, 28 February 1996.

53 Cox Report, Vol. 1, p. 94.

54 PFIAB Report, p. 9 of section "Recurring Vulnerabilities."

55 Cliff Stoll, *The Cuckoo's Egg* (New York: Simon & Schuster, 1989).

56 Chris Albritton, Associated Press, 28 April 1998.

57 Roberto Suro, "FBI Cyber Squad Termed Too Small," *The Washington Post*, 7 October 1999.

58 Lisa Hoffman, *Washington Times*, 24 October 1999.

59 Roberto Suro, op. cit.

60 Kessler, *Moscow Station*, p. 25.

61 Christopher Andrew and Vasily Mitrokhin, *The Sword and The Shield: The Mitrokhin Archive and the Secret History of the KGB* (New York: Basic Books, 1999), pp. 338, 312.

62 Mark Reibling, *Wedge*, p. 361.

63 David A. Vise & Steve Mufson, "State Dept. Bug Seen as Major Security Breach," *The Washington Post*, 9 December 1999.

64 Andrew and Mitrokhin, op. cit, pp. 337–354.

65 Juan Tamayo, "Soviets Spied on Gulf War Plans from Cuba, Defector Says," *Miami Herald*, 3 April 1998.

66 Dana Priest, "Serbs Listening in on NATO," *The Washington Post*, 1 May 1999.

67 Terry Atlas, "French Spy Charges Highlight Trade Wars," *Chicago Tribune*, 23 February 1995, and Alan Cowell, "Bonn Said to Expel U.S. Envoy Accused of Economic Spying," *The New York Times*, 10 March 1997.

68 Andrew and Gordievsky, pp. 523–524.

69 Redmond, "Meet the Press."

70 David A. Vise and Vernon Loeb, "State Department Bugged: Russian Accused of Spying," *The Washington Post*, 9 December 1999.

71 "Rendezvous at the Cockatoo: The Cavanagh case," *Security Awareness Bulletin*, No. 1–186, December 1985, Department of Defense Security Institute (DoDSI), Richmond, Va., p. 2.

72 *Recent Espionage Cases: Summaries and Sources*, July, 1997, DoDSI, Richmond.

73 Shvets, *Washington Station*, pp. 40–41, 53–56; Pawel Monat and John Dille, *Spy in the U.S.* (New York: Berkeley, 1961), pp. 22–28, 46–53; Ronald Kessler, *Spy vs. Spy* (New York: Scribner's, 1988), pp. 36–37, 124–125.

74 Robert Lamphere and Tom Schachtman, *The FBI-KGB War: A Special Agent's Story* (New York: Random House, 1986), p. 64. Also, Max Lowenthal, *The Federal Bureau of Investigation* (New York: William Sloane, 1950), p. 433.

75 David Wise, *The Spy Who Got Away* (New York: Random House, 1988), pp. 198–205.

76 Excerpt from *The Enemy Within*, by Tim Weiner, David Johnson, and Neil Lewis, published in *Rolling Stone*, 29 June 1995, p. 34. See also *Betrayal: The Story of Aldrich Ames, American Spy*, same authors (New York: Random House, 1995) pp. 228–229.

77 William Corson and Robert Crowley, *The New KGB: Engine of Soviet Power*, (New York: William Morrow, 1985), p. 461.

78 Michael Sniffen, "FBI Is Conducting 200 Spy Investigations," Associated Press, 2 February 1997. See also Frank Swoboda, "Economic Espionage Rising, FBI Director Tells Congress," *The Washington Post*, 29 February 1996.

79 James Rowley, "FBI Seeking Scores of Once-KGB Spies, Book Says," *Associated Press*, 3 August 1993. The author is quoting from Ronald Kessler's book, *The FBI*.

80 *The Washington Post*, 22 November 1998.

81 Bill Gertz, "Woolsey Expects Exposure of More Spies," *Washington Times*, 20 April 1994.

82 John Earl Haynes and Harvey Klehr, *VENONA: Decoding Soviet Espionage in America* (New Haven, CT: Yale University Press, 1999), p. 339.

83 Weiner, Johnson and Lewis, *Betrayal*, p. 37.

84 The four Americans who worked for Stasi and have been tried are the three "Red Diaper" spies, Kurt Stand, Marie Squillicote, and James Michael Clark, and an American nuclear researcher in Germany (tried by the Germans), Jeffrey Schevitz. Stand, Squillicote, and Clark confessed; while Schevitz admitted spying, he also unsuccessfully claimed that he was a double agent for the CIA. See the public indictment of Squillicote et al. See also Tim Weiner, "Spies Just Wouldn't Come in from The Cold," *The New York Times*, 15 October 1997; Jamie Dettmer "Stasi Lured Americans to Spy for E. Germany," *Washington Times*, 14 November 1994; and Terence Petty, "American Arrested as Suspect Spy for Former East Germany," Associated Press, 5 May 1994.

85 Lamphere and Schachtman, p. 273.

86 Jeffrey Richelson, *A Century of Spies:Intelligence in the Twentieth Century* (New York: Oxford University Press, 1995), pp. 272–274. Also, Andrew and Mitrokhin, p. 438.

87 Richelson, pp. 390–391 .

88 Ibid., pp. 395–396.

89 Ibid., p. 375.

90 Walter Pincus, "Paper Cites ex-Soviet Envoy in Spy Hunt," *The Washington Post*, 27 December 1996.

91 Andrey Streletsky, "Another Russian Spy Arrested," *Moscow Nezavisimaya Gazeta*, 27 February 1996. See also Oleg Kalugin and Fen Montaigne, *The First Directorate: My 32 Years in Intelligence and Espionage Against the West* (New York: St. Martin's Press), pp. 82–83.

92 Walter Pincus, "FBI Finds Leads in Files of Former East German Spy Service," *The Washington Post*, 11 October 1997.

93 The German cases have been well-documented in a Columbia House television history series titled "Spies" that has run on several channels. The History Channel has also done documentaries on the ill-fated German spies.

94 Sam Tanenhaus, *Whittaker Chambers: A Biography* (New York: Random House, 1997), pp. 162–163.

95 Jim Wolf, "Anonymous 1943 Letter to FBI Unmasked Soviet Spies," Reuters, 3 October 1996.

96 See Andrew and Mitrokhin, op. cit.

97 John Barron, *Breaking The Ring* (Boston: Houghton Mifflin, 1987), pp. 42–44.

98 Ronald Kessler, *The Spy in the Russian Club* (New York: Scribner's, 1990), pp. 49–51.

99 James Risen, "Warning on Spy Ignored, ex-Wife Says," *Los Angeles Times*, 8 April 1998.

100 For a discussion of Krivitsky's death, see Eugene Lyons, *The Red Decade* (Arlington House, 1941), pp. 378–379.

101 John Costello and Oleg Tsarev, *Deadly Illusions* (New York: Crown, 1993), pp. 340–341. The book discusses Orlov's career and how he evaded revealing any NKVD secrets.

102 Jerrold L. Schecter and Peter Deriabin, *The Spy Who Saved the World* (New York: Scribners, 1992), pp. 5–6.
103 Chris Steyn, "Ex-KGB General Meets Former State Security Chief," *Johannesburg Star*, 23 September 1995. See also Corson and Crowley, *The New KGB*, pp. 350–351.
104 James Risen, "An Extraordinary Link for Archenemies in Spying," *Los Angeles Times*, 31 December 1997.
105 Jamie Dettmer, "Stasi Lured Americans to Spy in E. Germany," *Washington Times*, 14 November 1994.
106 J. C. Masterman, *The Double-Cross System in the War of 1939–1945* (New Haven, CT: Yale University Press, 1972), pp. 156–157.
107 David Wise, "Was Oswalda Spy, and Other Cold War Mysteries," *New York Times Magazine*, 6 December 1992, p. 36.
108 See Joseph Albright and Marcia Kunstel, *Bombshell: The Secret Story of America's Unknown Atomic Spy Conspiracy* (New York: Random House, 1997), for a semi-confession from Hall to his spying.
109 On Pitts, see Charles W. Hall and Ann O'Hanlon, "Espionage Suspect Depicted as Eager to Sell His Loyalty," *The Washington Post*, 19 December 1996; "Navy Petty Officer Charged with Giving Secrets to Russia," *Reuters/Orlando Sentinel*, 30 November 1999 (King); William Carlen, "How the FBI Broke Spy Case That Baffled Agency for 30 Years," *Wall Street Journal*, 21 November 1996 (Lipka); James Risen, "Spy Agency's ex-Analyst Arrested," *The New York Times*, 14 October 1998 (Boone); Brooke Masters, "DC Couples' Spymaster Testifies," *The Washington Post*, 9 October 1998.
110 Lamphere and Schachtman, *The FBI-KGB War*, pp. 100–104; 107–123.
111 Raymond Bonner, "Prosecution Will Mean Tug of War Over Secrets," *The New York Times*, 11 December 1999.
112 James Risen, "In China, Physicist Learns, He Tripped Between Useful Exchange and Security Breach," *The New York Times*, 1 August 1999.
113 Jack Fordon MSNBC's "Imus in the Morning," 17 December 1999.
114 Jeff Stein, "The Mole's Manual," *The New York Times*, 5 July 1994. See also "Turning a Blind Eye to Spies," *Harper's Magazine*, September 1994, p. 16.
115 R. Jeffrey Smith and Thomas Lippman, "FBI Plans to Expand Overseas," *The Washington Post*, 20 September 1996.
116 Riebling, *Wedge*, p. 458.
117 Ibid., p. 459.
118 Jim McGee, "The Rise of the FBI," *The Washington Post Magazine*, 20 July 1997, pp. 10–15, 25–26.
119 See Kenneth de Graffenried, "Building for a New Counterintelligence Capability: Recruitment and Training," in Roy Godson, *Intelligence Requirements for the 1980s: Counterintelligence* (Washington, D.C.: National Strategy Information Center, 1980), pp. 261–272. Also, see Mark Riebling, *Wedge*, pp. 349, 364, 393, 395, 399, 455–456, 459.

Reprinted with permission from Frederick L. Wettering, 'Counterintelligence: The Broken Triad,' *International Journal of Intelligence and Counterintelligence* 13/3 (2000) pp.265–300.

COUNTER-INTELLIGENCE

Further reading: Books and reports

Eric M. Breindel & Herbert Romerstein, The Venona Secrets: The Soviet Union's World War II Espionage Campaign against the United States and How America Fought Back (NY: Basic Books, 1999).

Robert J. Lamphere & Tom Shachtman. *The FBI-KGB War: A Special Agent's Story* (NY: Random House, 1986).

John J. Fialka, *War by Other Means: Economic Espionage in America* (NY: Norton 1997).

Loch K. Johnson & James J. Wirtz, *Intelligence and National Security: The Secret World of Spies* (NY: Oxford University Press, 2nd ed 2007).

Roger Z. George and Robert D. Kline (eds.), *Intelligence and National Security Strategist: Enduring Issues and Challenges* (Washington DC: National Defense University Press, CSI 2004), Chapters 18 & 19, pp.251–72.

Bill Gertz, Bill. *Enemies: How America's Foes Steal Our Vital Secrets – and How We Let It Happen* (NY: Crown 2006).

R. Godson, *Dirty Tricks or Trump Cards: US Covert Action and Counterintelligence* (New Brunswick, NJ: Transaction, 2003).

J.E. Haynes & H. Klehr, *Venona: Decoding Soviet Espionage in America* (New Haven: Yale University Press, 1999).

Michael Herman, *Intelligence Power in Peace and War* (Cambridge: Cambridge University Press 1996) chapter 10.

R. Jeffreys-Jones, *The FBI: A History* (New Haven CT: Yale University Press, 2007).

Mark Lowenthal, *Intelligence: From Secrets to Policy* (Washington D.C.: CQ Press, 3rd Ed 2006), chapter 7.

Jeffrey Richelson, *The US Intelligence Community* (Boulder: 5th edition Westview 2007) chapter 14.

Abram N. Shulsky & Gary J. Schmitt, *Silent Warfare: Understanding the World of Intelligence* (Dulles, VA: Brassey's Inc. 2002) pp.99–127.

Office of the Director of National Intelligence. *The National Counterintelligence Strategy of the United States of America, 2007.* (Washington, DC: GPO 2007). [*http://www.ncix.gov/publications/policy/CIStrategy.pdf*]

Peter Schweizer, *Friendly Spies: How America's Allies Are Using Economic Espionage to Steal Our Secrets* (NY: Atlantic Monthly Press 1993).

A.G. Theoharis, *Chasing Spies: How the FBI Failed in Counterintelligence But Promoted the Politics of McCarthyism* (NY: Ivan R. Dee, 2002).

Michelle K. Van Cleave, *Counterintelligence and National Strategy* (Washington, DC: School for National Security Executive Education, National Defense University Press 2007).

Nigel West, *Venona: The Greatest Secret of the Cold War* (London: HarperCollins, 1999).

Bradford Westerfield (ed.), *Inside the CIA's Private World* (New Haven: Yale University Press 1995) Section VII and especially Chapter 29.

David Wise, *Cassidy's Run: The Secret Spy War over Nerve Gas* (NY: Random House 2000).

Further reading: Essays and articles

Christopher Andrew. 'The VENONA Secret', in *War, Resistance and Intelligence: Essays in Honour of M.R.D. Foot*, ed. Kenneth G. Robertson (Barnsley, UK: Leo Cooper, 1999).

James B. Bruce, 'Laws and Leak of Classified Intelligence: The Consequences of Permissive neglect', *Studies in Intelligence* 47/1 (2003) pp.39–49.

B. Champion, 'A Review of Selected cases of Industrial Espionage', *Intelligence and National Security* 13/2 (1998) pp.123–44.

David A. Hatch, 'VENONA: An Overview', *American Intelligence Journal* 17/1–2 (1996) pp. 71–77.

George F. Jelen, 'The Defensive Disciplines of Intelligence.' *International Journal of Intelligence and Counterintelligence* 5/4 (1991–1992) pp.381–399.

Lisa A Kramer & Richards J. Heuer, 'America's Increased Vulnerability to Insider Espionage.' *International Journal of Intelligence and Counterintelligence* 20/1 (2007) pp.50–64.

James M. Olson, 'The Ten Commandments of Counterintelligence,' *Studies in Intelligence* 11 (2001) pp.81–87.

S.D. Porteous, 'Economic Espionage', *Intelligence and National Security* 9/4 (1994) pp.735–52.

Peter Schweizer, 'The Growth of Economic Espionage: America Is Target Number One.' *Foreign Affairs* 75/1 (1996) pp.9–14.

Michelle K. Van Cleave, 'Strategic Counterintelligence: What Is It and What Should We Do About It?' *Studies in Intelligence* 51/2 (2007) pp.1–13.

Raymond W. Wannall, 'Undermining Counterintelligence Capability,' *International Journal of Intelligence and Counterintelligence* 15/3 (2002) pp.321–329.

Michael Warner & Robert Louis Benson. 'Venona and Beyond: Thoughts on Work Undone.' *Intelligence and National Security* 12/3 (1997) pp.1–13.

Essay questions

- What has been the main cause of security failures inside intelligence agencies since 1989?
- Why has the history of 'Venona' proved so controversial and what does it tell us about counter-intelligence in general?
- The French intelligence chief, the Count de Marenches, has asserted that two states can simultaneously be close partners on matters such as counter-terrorism but also economic espionage adversaries. Do you agree?
- Why have relations between foreign intelligence and domestic security agencies on counter-intelligence traditionally been poor? How might they be improved?

Part 3

Ethics, accountability and control

I might prefer democracy to communism, communism to death, and death to prolonged torture by the secret agents of a democratic society

William Connolly[1]

SUMMARY

Accountability and oversight

Accountability and oversight are widely regarded as fundamental to the development of effective intelligence communities. Not only are there strong legal and moral arguments as to why these systems should be in place, there is also evidence that they can lead to more effective intelligence agencies. Proper accountability and regulation encourages public co-operation with the intelligence and security services. It also prompts the services to review their own activities and to avoid some of the many pitfalls that await them. Intelligence agencies have historically presented a challenge to the components of government that conduct routine administrative and financial audit. Measuring the effectiveness of a road-building programme is not to hard, but how does the Treasury measure success in the realm of signals intelligence? The budgetary process for intelligence is important but often neglected by scholars of intelligence and the sums are large, with the United States now spending close to $50 billion per year in this realm.

Widely accepted models of civil-military relations imply that the strategic direction to a nation's intelligence community should emerge from politicians in a democratically elected government. This includes not only an over-arching national security strategy but also regular feedback on operational performance. At the same time those involved in political processes are properly kept at arms length from field activities. Democratic control normally manifests itself through ministerial responsibility. Civilian policy-makers define the role of intelligence and seek to ensure it serves the core executive. Senior policy-makers and their officials are the key consumers and also engage in routine tasking through variants of the intelligence cycle. While in theory ministers and secretaries of state have responsibility for these matters and can be called to account in assemblies and parliaments, in reality these matters tend to lie in the hands of senior professional bureaucrats.

Democratic states have developed an elaborate system of oversight, accountability and regulation for intelligence. The most obvious manifestation is the passing of laws that govern intelligence and security and associated areas such as official secrecy. Detailed review by legislative assemblies is increasingly carried out through specialist committees that examine intelligence and security matters or else financial issues. This reflects the tradition that legislatures are often tasked with the auditing of expenditures and encouraging good management. In the United States, financial control remains the most powerful democratic check upon the agencies, albeit it can be something of a blunt instrument. The United States pioneered specialist oversight committees in the 1970s, Australia and Canada developed their mechanisms in the 1980s, but most European countries did not adopt them until the 1990s. Accountability committees are often the highest profile political mechanisms but are of variable effectiveness. One symptom of this is the way in which they are rarely tasked with examining major intelligence failures. Instead, 'fiascos' are often the subject of independent public inquiries. Judges are frequently selected to conduct independent inquiries into intelligence abuses that affect civil rights.

An independent judiciary is central in administering the regulatory framework within which intelligence operations are conducted. The judiciary can play an important role in monitoring intelligence activity, based on its authority within a particular democratic system. Traditionally they have examined complaints against intelligence services by both citizens and disgruntled employees. However, the executive has increasingly tended to divert areas of national security away from direct judicial review by setting up quasi-judicial commissioners and tribunals, or else special courts. These are often chaired by judges but have less independence than a court. Specialist courts may be created to oversee invasive intelligence activities and to grant warrants for particular operations, such as the US Foreign Intelligence Surveillance Court. In Europe, judicial oversight is complicated by the operation of supra-national courts and legislation. This reflects the direct incorporation of the European Convention on Human Rights into national intelligence legislation and regulation passed in member states of the European Union since 1989.

Many intelligence services also boast internal legal mechanisms in the form of Legal Counsels and Inspector Generals. The role of the legal counsel is a time-honoured one in the American intelligence system, perhaps reflecting the fact that the founding father of the CIA, William Donovan was a Washington lawyer. By contrast, in Europe, while intelligence services have always taken legal advice, the advent of a substantial legal echelon awaited the 1990s. The test of legality, rather than clandestinely, is an increasingly important one for most services. Countries as diverse as the United States, Australia and South Africa have made use of Inspectors General, providing the equivalent to an internal affairs unit within a police force. In the United States the role of the Inspector General was strengthened in the wake of the Iran Contra affair in the 1980s and has the advantage of being inside the ring of secrecy.

Since 1989, the twin process of democratisation and globalisation have meant that informal controls generated by civil society have become increasingly important. By definition, nature of informal control is unclear, but investigative journalists often working in conjunction with whistleblowers, professional bodies of retirees, think-tanks, non governmental organizations (NGOs) and lobby groups focused on civil rights take an increasing interest in monitoring secret services. These informal methods can work either independently or in combination with formal mechanisms. Journalists and campaigners have often been instrumental in triggering inquiries. Reports concerning rendition in the American press in November 2005 set in train three significant European inquiries into rendition during 2006.

Oversight and accountability has been transformed by democratic transition. This is most visible in Eastern Europe and South America. In Eastern Europe, communist regimes relied on a vast apparatus of propaganda and security to maintain domestic control. The emphasis was upon regime security while the foreign intelligence services enjoyed an important role in neutralising subversion from abroad. Reforming these states has been an important part of democratic consolidation. The UK and the Netherlands were instrumental in persuading these countries to undertake a process of renewal that incorporated parliamentary regulation and democratic oversight. Ironically, the subsequent admission of the eastern states into NATO has meant that some of the more liberal legislation on freedom of information passed after 1989 has had to be curtailed.[2]

Western Europe has also witnessed a revolution, albeit of a quieter sort. In 1989, following an important case before the European Court of Human Rights, most European states chose to avow their secret services and place them on the stature books. Although some states had some form of accountability committee, this became more widespread. More fundamentally, there was a greater emphasis upon law and regulation. Intelligence agencies have moved from doing what they could get away with to what doing what is permitted. The intelligence and security services were pleasantly surprised in the 1990s, finding that the law was a permissive facilitator. However, since 2005, the efforts of European institutions to extend ECHR to their overseas liaisons has proved more problematic. A profound mismatch between the new style of intelligence operations, which is increasingly multinational, and national accountability, is becoming apparent.

Accountability has loomed large in recent years, partly against the background of anxiety about abuses. We have heard less about oversight. Bodies that provide a repository of wisdom and experience have been in decline. One of the questions that we need to pose is how well we will learn from our recent history in the realm of intelligence and security? An obvious weakness over the last decade has been a failure to base new policy on any systematic effort to learn lessons from past deficiencies. Good review and accountability mechanisms allow us to learn from our own mistakes and those of our allies and partners. The empirical material is there. One need only think of the wealth of documentation that now surrounds the September 11 attacks and the failures of intelligence on Iraqi weapons and mass destruction. Yet one wonders whether there yet exists effective review mechanisms for learning lessons. Most external review bodies attached to legislatures have proved unsuited to the task. They are often focussed on auditing, financial probity and work-a-day management. They are not engineered to promote sustained reflection or to look five years ahead.[3]

Civil rights

Accountability and oversight mostly pertains to specific political and legal mechanisms that are designed to 'guard the guardians'. However, the subject of intelligence and security services are inextricably linked to wider issues of surveillance in society and the general monitoring of behaviour, something that is often regarded as a ubiquitous aspect of modernity. The rise of systematic surveillance seems to have moved hand in hand with technology and urbanisation, symptomised by the arrival of police forces and passports by the nineteenth century. Much of this reflected concerns about public order, but other significant developments that entailed 'watching' included medical surveillance and epidemiology. Partly because of the connections between surveillance and modernity, the debates over this subject connect with wider notions of governance and society. Together with surprise attack, surveillance is perhaps one the most heavily conceptualised and theorised areas and has given rise to a parallel field often referred to as 'surveillance studies'. This reflects an interest in the social consequences of modern electronic and computer technology, which have raised surveillance to a new level. Most people now leave an electronic trail as part of their everyday lives, with the result that surveillance can be conducted on a far larger scale and the product can be 'warehoused' for decades. The writings of Jeremy Bentham outlining his concept of a 'Pantopticon' prison where order was kept through watching, together with the ideas of Michael Foucault in his study *Discipline and Punish*, are the most frequent textual reference points. Recent theorists, including Anthony Giddens, have devoted sustained attention to the connections between surveillance and modernity.[4]

In modern literature, surveillance has often formed the basis for utopian and dystopian visions, including Huxley's *Brave New World* and Orwell's *1984*. However, over the last twenty years we have witnessed new and unexpected trends in surveillance. First, we have seen the rise, not so much of one big brother, but of many little brothers. The majority of surveillance is now privatised and consists of commercial information collected by retailers. This trend has been reinforced by the privatisation and fragmentation of the communications industry. The way in which Amazon remembers its customers and offers them new books that they might like, based on previous purchase patterns is an example of this commercial 'dataveillance'. However, the state increasingly demands access to these private databases. Second, the miniaturisation of cameras and other electronic equipment has given rise to counter-surveillance. Abuses by agents of the state are increasingly likely to be captured by members of the public on camera. While the state and security services boast powerful surveillance systems they are increasingly watched, as well as watching.[5]

Surveillance is a matter of growing public debate. This reflects not only the growth in surveillance, but also new developments such as biometrics and the tendency to aggregate data. Biometrics are held out by some to be a panacea that will offer reliable identifiers that cannot be forged or stolen. Others view biometrics as a further invasion of the ultimate private realm – the human body – by the state. Perhaps more important is data aggregation. In the past there were practical barriers to the amount of data that could be gathered on an individual. Digital record keeping has eroded this impediment. Neural network computing and data-mining can be used to combine a range of different datastreams to create a virtual person. Google, for example, warehouses previous Google searches by each individual. An aggregation of all past Google searches by an individual provides a remarkably detailed profile of that person's thoughts and interests.

Oversight and accountability arguably offers protection against the most invasive form of surveillance, for example the use of secret operatives to watch or enter the domestic realm. However, historically, the main protection for the citizen against excessive surveillance was cost, since watching with human beings is very expensive. Technology is eroding this protection. This is alarming, since states have historically tended to use information they gather on their citizens for purposes other than those permitted. Surveillance also tends to 'chill out' fringe political activity that is legal. Ultimately, privacy is a deeply existential concept. It is difficult to demonstrate its material worth or how invasion of privacy results in physical damage. However all human societies have placed a high value on privacy, especially in the domestic context.

Ethics

Ethical debates over intelligence tend to draw an implicit distinction between the international and the domestic. Debates about intelligence in the context of international relations have connected with obvious realist sources of legitimisation, including ideas of 'Just War'. In addition, intelligence professionals have frequently argued that intelligence activity, taken collectively, might even represents a public good. While each state might pursue its intelligence objectives in isolation, collectively the result is a more transparent and reassured international system. Governments frequently point to arms control verification as an area where intelligence is self-evidently ethical and has hoped to stabilise the international system. However, there are clear examples of operations that have proved destabilising and have constituted a source of risk. The cancellation of the Eisenhower-Khrushchev summit of 1960 following the shootdown of the Gary Powers U-2 aircraft is an obvious example.[6]

Domestically, different ethical standards are often applied. Ethical justifications normally take the form of necessity and least harm. Managers are prevailed upon to ask whether surveillance is genuinely necessary in order to prevent some greater harm occurring. They are also asked to consider whether the information required can be obtained by techniques that are not invasive. Although surveillance in European and the United States enjoys a complex framework of legal regulations, sometimes what is legal is confused with what is ethical. Paper-trails are created but it is often just so much paper, vexing to the operatives and not very meaningful in terms of regulation or restraint. Moreover, the boundaries between domestic and international surveillance are eroding. A hotmail message sent between two friends in the same town may pass through another country enroute. Should this message be regarded as domestic or international?

Current ethical dilemmas are often related to the desire for pre-emptive intelligence. On the one hand, it can be argued that foreknowledge can allow the state to address threats such as terrorism in a surgical manner and without alienating the ethnic communities from whom militants seek to gain support. Others argue that the shift towards pre-emptive intelligence has resulted in more invasive practices and the more widespread use of agents. Moreover, the globalized nature of many current threats, most obviously jihadist terrorism, has accelerated the pace of intelligence liaison and has resulted in close relationship with many states whose ethical standards are low. In part this has been addressed by physical separation. However, many have asked how ethical is the use of intelligence that typically has been obtained by torture. Some countries, such as the UK, have ruled it as inadmissible in courts.

Covert action or special operations are different again and tend to draw their ethical underpinnings from the literature on intervention. In many cases, the actions undertaken do not necessarily change their ethical or legal status because they are carried out covertly. However, for those who argue a connection between democracy, transparency and ethical behaviour in the international system, covert action presents a major problem. The ability of Prime Ministers and Presidents to conduct 'secret wars' arguably permits policy-makers to escape the liberal democratic institutional norms that might guarantee a more stable international system.

Torture and assassination

Torture and assassination are two questionable activities that have given rise to a considerable specialist literature. Their salience since 9/11 warrants detailed discussion. Typically, in December 2007 the US House of Representatives approved legislation to bar CIA operatives from using waterboarding during the questioning of suspected terrorists, drawing a veto threat from President George W. Bush. Most intelligence professionals would argue that suspects should always be persuaded to talk voluntarily. This is not only for reasons of law and morality, but also because information given freely is more likely to be true. Under pressure from torture, even of a mild kind, suspects may say anything in order to seek relief. A professional interrogator, with perhaps ten years of experience, will normally take pride in being able to get a suspect to talk without physical pressure.

The most famous British example was Colonel Robin 'Tin Eye' Stephens, an MI5 officer who wore a monocle and presided over Camp 020, where MI5 detained hundreds of foreign spies during the Second World War. He was willing to use threats – but not force – because he claimed it did not work. Very few spies held out against him. However, the British have not always been so gentle. As Richard Popplewell has discovered, in the First World War, British intelligence officers working in the Middle East would sit their own agents on an 'electric carpet' when questioning them. If they suspected them of lying they would subject them to two or three electric shocks through the legs and pelvis.[7]

In many different countries, the most common sort of torture is sensory deprivation. This can involve using hoods on prisoners for long periods before interrogation. It often includes a sound machine which produces 'white noise', a disturbing high pitched sound. Stress positions might also be employed. Often little food or drink is given. Most commonly detainees are deprived of sleep. Although this leaves few physical signs of mistreatment, it can be very damaging psychologically. The European Court has declared these practices to be illegal.

Torture, including sensory deprivation, has become widespread around the world for two reasons. First, the 'War on Terror' has produced many thousands of suspects and yet there are few skilled interrogators. Therefore, suspects end up being handled by the sort of personnel who worked at Abu Ghraib, part-time soldiers with limited training and less intelligence. Second, soldiers in all modern armies are themselves subjected to mock interrogations during training, so that they know what they might have to endure if captured. This counter-interrogation training is often all they know about interrogation. It was never expected that they would draw on these experiences in this way and use the techniques themselves.

Proponents of torture in academia and elsewhere tend to make two arguments. Firstly, they present the 'ticking bomb' scenario in which a greater evil can only be prevented though the use of torture. This was often held to be a hypothetical situation, but the intelligence that allowed the frustration of planned attacks on airliners in the UK in August 2006 may well have been secured through torture of a suspect in Pakistan. It looks less hypothetical now. Second, some have argued that torture is such a widespread reality that we need to deal with this by regulating it through torture warrants in order to minimise the level of abuse. This latter argument has been made by the Harvard lawyer, Alan Dershowitz.

However, for every person tortured, we lose other voluntary informants who do not come forward because they are frightened or disgusted. Trust, not fear, is the most valuable weapon for an intelligence officer. Torture is not only immoral and illegal, it is also ineffective. Proponents also ignore the wider point made by Sir Richard Dearlove, former Chief of MI6, that this has cost America the moral high ground. The strategic battle is essentially an informational one in which competing truths advance claims to offer a superior way of life. Here torture represents a spectacular own goal.

In contrast to torture, assassination plans tend to emanate from the highest political level and are often somewhat personal. In 1986, Ronald Reagan, who had himself been injured in an assassination attempt, ordered an air raid on Libya which attacked the home residence of President Gaddafi. Although he escaped, his adopted daughter Hanna was killed. Israel has been one of the active employers of assassination in order to degrade the effectiveness of its opponents. The messy boundary between terrorism and insurgency has blurred the ethical line between assassination and 'targeted killing' on the battlefield.

Opponents of assassination argue that, over and above the ethical arguments, democratic states should if possible avoid assassination for practical reasons. First, the leaders of democratic states are intrinsically vulnerable and likely to be repaid with the same coin.

Second, the person who is removed through assassination may be replaced with someone more effective. This argument helped to stymie as planned operation to assassinate Adolf Hitler during the Second World War. Hitler's erratic leadership was ultimately judged to be an aid to the Allied cause.[8]

Notes

1 William Connolly, *The Terms of Political Discourse* (Lexington Mass: Heath, 1973) p.51
2 Alasdair Roberts, *Blacked Out* (Oxford: Oxford University Press, 2007), pp.129–31.
3 Wesley Wark, 'Learning Lessons (and how) in the War on Terror: The Canadian Experience,' *International Journal*, 60/1 (2004–2005) pp.71–90.
4 Frank Webster, *Theories of the Information Society* (Routledge, London 1995).
5 Louise Amoore & Marieke Goede, 'Governance, risk and dataveillance in the war on terror', *Crime, Law and Social Change*, 43/2 (2005) pp.149–173.
6 Michael R. Beschloss, *Mayday: Eisenhower, Khrushchev, and the U-2 Affair* (NY: Harper & Row, 1986).
7 Oliver Hoare (ed.) *Camp 020: MI5 and the Nazi Spies*, (London: Public Record Office, 2000); Richard Popplewell, 'British intelligence in Mesopotamia 1914–16', *Intelligence & National Security* 5/2 (1990) pp.139–172.
8 Roger Moorhouse, *Killing Hitler* (London: Jonathan Cape, 2006).

18 Partisanship and the decline of intelligence oversight

M.C. Ott

This essay advances the proposition that the U.S. system of intelligence oversight by Congress has a long and venerable history, and has offered a workable solution to the difficult problem of oversight. However, oversight bodies that belong to legislatures requires favourable conditions if they are to operate effectively and are vulnerable to changes in political climate. In recent years, and especially since 9/11, Senate-conducted intelligence oversight has encountered a range of problems and is less and less effective.

The 11 September 2001 terrorist assault on the United States highlighted the absolute centrality of intelligence in the nation's defense. National security specialists have been in general agreement for several years that the greatest postwar security threat would come from terrorist networks utilizing powerful conventional explosives and 'weapons of mass destruction' (chemical, biological, and nuclear). General agreement has developed that the first line of defense against such threats lies in the formation of effective relationships with foreign intelligence and domestic counterintelligence agencies.

From this vantage point the airliner assaults on New York City and the Pentagon, and the subsequent postal anthrax attacks, constituted dramatic and costly failures of intelligence. Those failures are highlighted by the fact that the Central Intelligence Agency (CIA) and the broader intelligence community had been focused for nearly three years on Osama bin Laden's al-Qaeda network as their prime terrorist target. As late as March 2001, the Director of Central Intelligence (DCI) George J. Tenet gave the U.S. Senate Intelligence Oversight Committee the following upbeat assessment of the counterterrorism effort:

> Here in open session, let me assure you that the Intelligence Community has designed a robust counter terrorism program that has preempted, disrupted, and defeated international terrorists and their activities. In most instances, we have kept terrorists off-balance, forcing them to worry about their own security and degrading their ability to plan and conduct operations.

With the mass casualty and biological warfare thresholds already crossed, chemical and nuclear terrorist attacks must now be seen as well within the realm of possibility. Under these circumstances, a highly effective intelligence community is not merely desirable, it is vital.

Strengthening United States intelligence capabilities will involve a panoply of initiatives and upgrades across the whole range of intelligence collection (technical and human), analysis, and operations. This much is widely understood. What is not appreciated is that congressional oversight of intelligence is a key element in the effective functioning of the Intelligence

Community (IC). When oversight has been capable and constructive, it has been a major asset to the IC. When degraded or misused, it has been an albatross around the neck of the intelligence agencies.

In May 2001, a Senate hearing room was the scene of a gala reception commemorating the 25th anniversary of the Senate Select Committee on Intelligence (SSCI). Creation of the SSCI was an event worth remembering because the American system for legislative oversight of intelligence is unique in the world. The quarter-century experience with that system has been eventful, with both impressive achievements and discouraging reversals. But at present, a once robust mechanism is in disarray; 'Humpty Dumpty' is badly broken. But lessons can be learned. The obvious question is: Can the pieces be put back together? The answer is not at all obvious. Only through a thorough understanding of the regulatory mechanism can improvements be made.

Intel's historical high stakes

Although intelligence may or may not be the world's second oldest profession, it has long been a key instrument of national statecraft and even survival. Americans have tended to view the intelligence profession with some ambivalence – with attitudes ranging from romantic idealization to moral condemnation. For all that, intelligence has played a major role in U.S. security and foreign policy over the last half century. Currently, the United States spends in excess of $30 billion annually supporting an elaborate and far-flung intelligence capability, and that expenditure is on the rise. Throughout the Cold War, both the U.S. and the Soviet Union regarded intelligence as a key element in determining the outcome of that global struggle. At critical junctures, such as the Cuban Missile Crisis and support of the Afghan mujahidin against the Soviet occupation, the Intelligence Community was a key element in success. On the negative side, the roll call of presidential administrations that have been burned, sometimes badly, by covert intelligence operations gone awry, is long. Presidents Dwight D. Eisenhower and the U-2; John F. Kennedy and the Bay of Pigs; and Ronald Reagan and Iran-Contra are simply three examples. Every President since Harry S Truman has faced some major controversy as a direct outgrowth of intelligence activities. In the Bill Clinton administration the epicenter was China, with a succession of high profile brawls involving satellite sales, political campaign contributions, and alleged nuclear espionage.

In short, for good or ill, intelligence is a high stakes enterprise. This will be increasingly true in the years ahead. For the foreseeable future, the most likely threat to U.S. security will come from international terrorist networks – possibly tied to a 'rogue' state like Iraq, or, as President George W. Bush has termed them, the 'Axis of Evil,' which includes Iran and North Korea. Those threats will, in turn, be imbedded in, and arise from, toxic social, economic, and political circumstances – particularly in parts of the Muslim world – producing a kind of free-floating rage that can be exploited and channeled by terrorist organizers. The burden of defense against such threats falls heavily upon various intelligence agencies working with the Federal Bureau of Investigation (FBI). As the threats become more diversified and sophisticated, the demands on intelligence collection, analysis, and operations grow apace.

The needs of democratic governance

While the assertion that intelligence is important to national security is not novel, how the United States has attempted to reconcile the imperatives of an effective intelligence capability with the quite different and, in some respects, opposite, imperatives of democracy, is very much so. Modern authoritarian regimes from Josef Stalin's Soviet Union to General Augusto Pinochet's Chile to contemporary China and Cuba consider a robust (and generally brutal) intelligence establishment the key instrument of regime survival. The structure, processes, and values that animate a dictatorship, of whatever political coloration, are symbiotically compatible with a strong, intrusive intelligence apparatus.

For political democracies, however, the picture is very different. Democratic government rests on five working requirements: openness and participation, disaggregation of power, rule of law, privacy, and mutual trust. To consider each in turn:

(a) Democracy assumes an informed electorate capable of rational choices concerning a nation's leadership and broad policy direction. This, in turn, requires a free media, a high degree of transparency in government and decisionmaking, and the free flow of information and ideas. Intelligence operates according to entirely different principles: secrecy, need-to-know, and compartmentation of classified information.

(b) Democracies are typically suspicious of concentrated power and tend to devolve significant authority downward and outward toward provincial and municipal authorities. But intelligence agencies concentrate and centralize both authority and access to secrets. Such concentration is the natural concomitant to the overriding need to secure sensitive information and systems.

(c) Democracies are rooted in the rule of law, not personalities, and that law in turn is based on broadly held values in the society. The Justice Department took Microsoft to court under the anti-trust laws in response to a long-held American value judgment that the excessive concentration of corporate power is deleterious to public well-being. Intelligence, by contrast, often requires special exemptions under domestic law, and regularly involves violating the law of other countries. In most countries, and at most times, intelligence has been a ruthless business that, in the end, recognizes only the law of success and survival, and one measure of merit: will it work?

(d) Although not specifically enshrined in the U.S. Constitution, privacy has, over time, also assumed the status of a basic right. But when an individual becomes an employee of the CIA, he or she largely forfeits such rights vis-à-vis the intelligence community. A condition for employment is a 'full scope' polygraph, designed to probe and lay bare the most private behavior and attitudes. An agency employee is subject to being repolygraphed at various intervals, and someone who becomes the subject of a security investigation may have his/her bank records and other normally confidential data examined. CIA employees, present and former, are obligated to 'clear' writing for publication in advance with the Agency to assure that no classified information is being revealed.

(e) Finally, democracy, at some fundamental level, requires a degree of mutual trust among citizens, and between citizens and the government. Within the intelligence world, the price of security is vigilance, and with vigilance goes an engrained suspicion concerning the motives and activities of co-workers. Had those who worked with Aldrich Ames, Robert Hanssen or Jonathan Pollard been more distrustful, those agents of foreign powers would presumably have been detected much sooner.

This adds up to a dilemma. Can a democracy maintain an effective, capable intelligence service without doing violence to the norms, processes, and institutions of democracy itself? An affirmative answer is not guaranteed. Arguably, during much of the Cold War, no other nation, not even Great Britain, established effective, independent oversight of its intelligence services. In a parliamentary system, the fusing of legislature and executive creates a funda-mental structural impediment to effective legislative oversight of executive intelligence entities. In the United States, however, with its almost unique separation of powers, legislative oversight is, at least in principle, feasible. Feasible does not mean workable. Obvious and difficult questions exist as to whether an institution dedicated to free debate and wide-open public access can ever be a reliable custodian of the nation's most sensitive secrets. At the same time, congressional oversight is notably and particularly important in the case of intelligence, given its clandestine nature. The press and other watchdog organizations cannot provide the depth of public scrutiny of the Intelligence Community that they can of other government departments.

The Senate and House Intelligence Committees, while engaged in the same generic enterprise, have brought their own distinct approaches to aspects of oversight. The focus here will be primarily, though not exclusively, on the Senate experience in the past two decades.[1]

Oversight background

The history of U.S. intelligence oversight can be conveniently divided into four time periods: 1946–1975, 1976–1980, the 1980s, and the 1990s to the present.[2]

The early years: 1947–1975

The origins of congressional oversight of intelligence necessarily coincide with the enactment into law of the National Security Act of 1947. Prior to World War II, the U.S. had little real national intelligence capability. Instead, the State Department foreign service gathered and assessed information according to the gentlemanly rules prevailing in a world dominated by British and French diplomatic practice. But under the exigencies of World War II, the U.S., in the form of a new Office of Strategic Services (OSS), plunged into the cold waters of clandestine intelligence. When it became clear that the world war would be succeeded by a global cold war, Congress created, among other instrumentalities, the Central Intelligence Agency. This in turn generated a question: how would Congress oversee this new, secret entity?

The initial answer – and one that prevailed for nearly three decades – was to vest oversight authority in subcommittees of the Armed Services Committees of the House and Senate. In practice, real authority was sharply restricted to the chairman and a handful of key members on each committee. For most of this period, the key figure was the powerful chairman of the Senate Armed Services Committee, Senator Richard B. Russell (D., Georgia). But as America geared up to prosecute the Cold War, Senator Russell and his colleagues had far bigger fish to fry than intelligence. Because they supported the CIA and trusted its leadership, actual intelligence oversight was minimal at most. Oversight usually took the form of a meeting between senior intelligence officials and Senator Russell and a few colleagues in his office. The main agenda item was the intelligence budget; agreement was typically reached with little difficulty. Often an entire year would pass without a single Armed Services Subcommittee meeting on intelligence matters. In sum, 'oversight' hardly existed, and what there was occurred outside the purview of most of the Congress and the public.

These *de minimis* arrangements were due, not to any foot dragging on the part of CIA officials regarding consultation or testimony, but rather to aversion on the congressional end. A leading member of the Committee, Senator Leverett Saltonstall (R., Massachusetts) commented at the time: 'It is not a question of reluctance on the part of CIA officials to speak to us. It is a question of our reluctance, if you will, to seek information and knowledge on subjects which I personally, as a member of Congress and as a citizen, would rather not have.'[3] It was all very cozy, clubby, informal, and unsystematic. In dominating the process, Senator Russell protected the fledgling intelligence agency from less friendly congressional intrusion. Periodic attempts by the Senate Foreign Relations Committee to assert even partial oversight over CIA activities were rebuffed, as were efforts by Senate Majority Leader Senator Mike Mansfield (D., Montana) to establish a freestanding intelligence oversight committee modeled on the Joint Committee on Atomic Energy.

By the early 1970s, however, the era of minimal oversight was coming to an end. Senator Russell died in 1971. In 1973, the press published reports of apparent CIA involvement in a coup overthrowing the democratically elected government of Salvador Allende in Chile. Media coverage of the Vietnam War generated reports of controversial CIA programs in Vietnam and at home. In October 1974 the *New York Times* reported that the CIA and FBI had engaged in illegal intelligence operations against the antiwar movement in the United States. Meanwhile, the cumulative effect of the war and the simultaneous Watergate break-in scandal seriously undercut the traditional congressional deference enjoyed by the President in national security matters – including intelligence. The dikes built by Senator Russell against assertive congressional oversight of intelligence gave way in a flood. In 1974, the Congress passed the Hughes–Ryan Amendment to the Foreign Assistance Act, which, for the first time, set a legal requirement that the President formally authorize any covert action. Specifically, the President had to 'find' that a covert action was 'important to the national security of the United States.' The Amendment also required that the President report 'in a timely fashion, a description and scope of such operation' to the 'appropriate Committees of the Congress.'[4]

In 1975, Congress created two special investigatory committees, the Church Committee in the Senate and the Pike Committee in the House, with broad authority to examine intelligence activities across the board. In a five-volume public report after extensive hearings, the Church Committee documented a pattern of misconduct by intelligence agencies, and called for the creation of a committee for continuing congressional oversight. The Pike Committee reached a similar conclusion, but its formal report was never officially released to the public.

In May 1976, the Senate created its Select Committee on Intelligence (SSCI), and in July of the following year, the House established the House Permanent Select Committee on Intelligence (HPSCI). The modern era of intelligence oversight was born.

Institutionalizing oversight: 1976–1980

Among their first acts, both committees claimed exclusive jurisdiction within Congress over the Hughes–Ryan legislation. The most sensitive intelligence programs would thus be overseen only by the SSCI and HPSCI.

The concept involved in creating the oversight committees was straightforward enough. For congressional oversight to work, the number of committees and members involved would have to be carefully circumscribed. If every member of Congress could claim the right of intelligence oversight, secrecy would be impossible. But jurisdiction, i.e., 'turf,' is hard won on Capitol Hill. Even after establishment of the SSCI and HPSCI, six other committees (the Senate Panels on Armed Services, Appropriations, Foreign Relations, and their counterparts in the House) continued to claim varying degrees of intelligence oversight jurisdiction. Only with the passage of the Intelligence Oversight Act of 1980, after months of negotiations with the Carter administration, was the exclusive jurisdiction of the two Intelligence Committees codified. This legislation, which became Title V of the National Security Act of 1947, established, 'consistent with the constitutional responsibilities of the President,' specific reporting requirements for the heads of all the intelligence agencies.

Among these were the need to keep the two intelligence committees 'fully and currently informed of the intelligence activities of the United States;' to report 'significant anticipated intelligence activities' to the committees; to provide prior notice of covert actions, or notice in a 'timely fashion' if prior notice was not given; and to report violations of law and 'significant intelligence failures,' again, in a timely fashion. Finally the law retained the Hughes–Ryan requirement of presidential findings for covert action programs.[5] The Act also specified that these reporting requirements would be limited to just two committees, the SSCI and the HPSCI.

Equally important, the actual flow of intelligence information – assessments, reports, briefings, and testimony – rapidly increased in the late 1970s. By 1980, Congress had become a major consumer of intelligence. The oversight committees had established their jurisdiction. Gradually earning the grudging respect of the Intelligence Community for their custodianship of sensitive intelligence, the committee staffs developed an expertise in a variety of program areas, including counterintelligence, reconnaissance systems, budget, geographic analysis, and covert action.

As a consequence, the Intelligence Community has found itself, rather uncomfortably, somewhere between the executive and legislative branches of the government, with statutory obligations to both.[6] On numerous occasions CIA officials have responded to congressional demands for intelligence with information and analysis that has undercut prevailing administration policy.

Despite the 1980 Act, and an Executive Order supporting it, the actual ground rules concerning exactly what intelligence would be provided to Congress and under what specific circumstances, evolved through negotiations between the oversight committees and the Intelligence Community. These understandings developed through agreement and practice rather than legislation and regulation. For example, the committees, in principle, claimed an unhindered right to all intelligence information, without exception. In practice, however, the committees generally refrained from seeking certain very sensitive intelligence (e.g., the actual identities of recruited agents) as unnecessary to effective oversight. By 1980 these 'rules of the road' were largely in place and the process of intelligence oversight had become effectively institutionalized.

1980s: The golden age

The decade of the 1980s, viewed in retrospect, may fairly be described as the apogee of intelligence oversight, as far as the Senate is concerned. In this period the flow of intelligence information to Congress continued to rise, despite the palpable hostility to the entire oversight process evinced by President Ronald Reagan's first DCI, William J. Casey. By 1988, the CIA was annually conducting same 1000 briefings for Congress, transmitting over 4000 documents, and hosting over 100 visits by congressional members and staff at intelligence facilities in the U.S. and overseas. By mid-decade, a fair degree of mutual trust and respect animated these institutional interactions. Most senior Intelligence Community officials had come to realize that the oversight committees were the best and most effective friends the Community had on Capitol Hill. The combination of Senator David L. Boren

(D., Oklahoma) and William S. Cohen (R., Maine) as the SSCI's Chairman and Vice Chairman worked easily, mastered the often arcane substance of intelligence, and had no obvious political axes to grind. The professional staff, many of whom had come from positions in the Intelligence Community, was highly competent, often expert, and entirely apolitical.

A highlight of this period was an SSCI report to the Congress on whether the Intelligence Community could adequately verify Russian compliance with the Intermediate Nuclear Forces (INF) Treaty of 1987. The Senate's decision on ratification rested substantially on that question. A young, relatively junior staff member named George J. Tenet largely wrote the SSCI's highly detailed report to the Senate. Drawing upon the resources of the Intelligence Community, the report was a dispassionate distillation of the Community's analytical judgment and technical capabilities.

The newly robust oversight process was severely tested by the Iran–Contra affair. The initial phase of the SSCI's probe into possible U.S. support for the Nicaraguan anti-Sandinista Contras was largely frustrated by witnesses who refused to appear (e.g., Admiral John Poindexter and Colonel Oliver North), and those who dissembled and misled congressional investigators. Professor James Currie, a former SSCI staff member, cites one notable example:

> On 28 November 1986, the SSCI sent a letter to President Reagan informing him that the committee would begin an investigation of the Iranian initiative and the diversion of funds. As part of that investigation, Alan Fiers testified under oath on 9 December. . . . [I]n response to a question from SSCI Minority Staff Director Eric Newsom about the financial condition of the contras, Fiers responded, 'We have some general ideas of the amount of funding that they get, and no idea of where it comes from and how they process it.' He went on to say that 'Insofar as where that money came from, how they got it, and how they accounted for it, we don't have specific intelligence.' None of these statements were true.[7]

In time, however, the story broke wide open and Fiers ended up giving lengthy and riveting public testimony in which he detailed the Intelligence Community's role in the affair.

In sum, the system of oversight that had prevailed in the 1980s, though imperfect, was by far the most ambitious and effective ever established in a democratic polity. How did it work? First, through congressional authority. The powers of the oversight committees included the following:

- Legislate on all matters relating to the Intelligence Community from covert action reporting requirements, to the authorities and responsibilities of the DCI, to the CIA pension fund.
- Authorize the Intelligence Community budget for action by the full Senate after referral to the Senate Armed Services Committee.
- Investigate allegations of criminality, intelligence 'failure,' and/or waste, fraud, and abuse.
- Monitor CIA and other Community operations and programs, including audits of expenditures.
- Determine what intelligence capabilities imply for major decisions and issues facing the Senate – e.g., to judge administration claims that specific arms control agreements can be effectively verified or monitored for compliance.

- Confirm (Senate only) the most senior Intelligence Community officials as a precondition to assuming their appointments.[8]
- Receive prior notification of contemplated covert actions after the President has signed a finding but before operations have commenced.
- Access all sensitive Intelligence Community information and programs, including the authority to task Intelligence Community officials to supply such information through printed reports, letters, testimony and briefings.

If oversight is to function effectively, Congress generally, and the oversight committees specifically, must assume a set of reciprocal obligations. Most basic, Congress must demonstrate that it can and will protect classified information. To this end committee staffs are vetted through a full FBI field investigation. Members of Congress are deemed, by virtue of their election, to have met all the requirements for a security clearance. Sensitive materials are handled by means, and according to standards, that meet or exceed those of the Intelligence Community. The committees work within secure facilities that meet all the technical requirements set by the Intelligence Community. Every serious assessment during the 1980s of the problem of 'leaks' of classified material into the public domain concluded that the sources were predominantly, if not overwhelmingly, in the Executive Branch – including the Intelligence Community itself, not the oversight committees. During the same period, there were no serious allegations that a foreign intelligence service had penetrated the committee staffs.

The covert action dilemma

'Covert action' poses a special challenge to oversight. Covert actions involve intelligence programs that go beyond collecting and analyzing intelligence to actually affecting events. By their very nature, they carry with them a much higher political risk, as the Iran-Contra relationship demonstrated, than normal intelligence activities. Consequently, the oversight committees have tended to spend a disproportionate amount of time and effort on these programs which, in budgetary terms, are often of minor significance.

The formal procedures of oversight require that covert action programs come to the committees for review after authorization by a presidential finding. Congress has no authority to veto a covert action, but through the annual authorization bill it may deny funds for its implementation – a power that has been used. A DCI would be very ill-advised to proceed with a covert action in the face of clear disapproval from the oversight committees.[9] All members of the oversight committees, plus a restricted number of 'compartmented' staff, are normally authorized to attend a covert action hearing, whether on an existing or a newly authorized program. But, if the DCI judges a covert action to be extraordinarily sensitive, he may ask the chairmen of the two committees to restrict attendance to just themselves, their vice chairmen, plus the Senate Majority and Minority Leaders and the House Speaker and Minority Leader – the 'Gang of Eight.'

This restriction in participation, seldom invoked, has to date not been a source of significant controversy. But the timing of oversight review has. The Intelligence Oversight Act of 1980 and the Executive Order that preceded it call for a new presidential finding to be submitted to the oversight committees 'in a timely manner.' Congress has made it clear on several occasions that it regards 'timely' as within 48 hours from the President's signature on the finding. During the prolonged tug-of-war between the branches of government over Iran–Contra, the Reagan White House held fast to its position that the Constitution permitted the President to defer covert action notification to the Congress indefinitely if he felt circumstances so warranted. Congress did not concur with this assertion but was in no position to do anything about it. In the end, the executive and legislative branches agreed to disagree on the matter.

Relative nonpartisanship

As another basic requirement of effective oversight the committees must adopt a nonpolitical approach to their responsibilities. For important periods since its inception, the SSCI has been that great rarity – a genuinely nonpartisan Senate committee. The chairman from the majority party and the vice-chairman from the minority acted, in effect, as cochairmen. Behind the committee's sealed doors, out of sight of the press and public, members conducted their business as colleagues, not partisans. Professional staff was typically selected with no reference to political affiliation. An invisible observer in the committee room during this period, not knowing one senator from another, would have been unable to tell who was a Republican and who was a Democrat. This was remarkable in a partisan-crazed institution like the Senate.

Having served on the staffs of both the SSCI and the Senate Foreign Relations Committee during this period, I found the contrast between the two committees instructive. Foreign Relations continually operates in the public spotlight. A member appearing at a committee hearing looks upon an audience that includes a large press table and a phalanx of television cameras. Virtually every word uttered in that environment is chosen for its political effect. But the same member entering the SSCI hearing room faces no media or audience, except for committee staff and the few Intelligence Community witnesses providing testimony. With no gallery to play to, conversation among panel members assumed the tone of colleagues addressing issues that, for the most part, had few political ramifications.

Finally, the Intelligence committees have always had to recruit and retain highly professional, expert, nonpartisan staff. The SSCI staff during the 1980s met these criteria. In many instances, staff members had developed more expertise in key areas (e.g., counterintelligence programs) than their Intelligence Community counterparts. SSCI staff frequently had longer experience with a subject area than did the IC personnel, who were routinely subject to fairly frequent transfers to new responsibilities.

A notable example of staff influence involved the SSCI's chief budget officer, Keith Hall who came to the committee from the Office of Management and Budget with a prior background in Army intelligence. (He later became Director of the National Reconnaissance Office.) On more than one occasion, the committee listened to a DCI's formal budget presentation, backed by the assembled expertise of the Intelligence Community, regarding a choice among major, highly technical (and expensive) satellite systems. But, having considered the DCI's recommendation, the SSCI chose instead to adopt an alternative recommendation from Hall and his three or four-member staff. This reflected nothing more than the members' extraordinary confidence in the expertise of the committee staff. Senior IC officials did not always like those decisions, but they generally respected the staff judgment that lay behind them.

The quality of the SSCI staff in the 1980s and early 1990s is validated by the remarkable number of very senior Intelligence Community positions that these same individuals came to occupy in the 1990s. A partial list includes:

Director of Central Intelligence

CIA Inspector General
CIA Director of Congressional Affairs
CIA Deputy Executive Director
Director, National Reconnaissance Office
Chief of Staff, Office of the DCI (formerly) and CIA Director, Resource Management
    Directorate of Operations (currently)
Director, Intelligence Programs, National Security Council
Deputy Assistant Secretary of Defense (Intelligence)
Deputy Director, Center for Information Technology Operations
Inspector General, NRO
Deputy Staff Director, NRO Commission

To find a comparable example of the staff of a single congressional committee ascending to so many of the most senior positions of a major executive agency would be very difficult. It certainly has no precedent in the history of the U.S. or any other intelligence community.

1990s To the present: A dark age

The 1980s represented a signal achievement in creating an effective oversight system, but signs of trouble began to appear not long into the next decade. They were a reminder of just how difficult and tenuous intelligence oversight in a democracy really is.

The first indications that the system was vulnerable occurred in 1991 when Robert M. Gates was nominated by President George H. W. Bush to succeed William Webster as DCI. Gates was very well known to the SSCI, which would conduct his confirmation hearing. He had been Deputy Director for Intelligence (DDI) and Deputy Director for Central Intelligence (DDCI) under DCI Casey, and was again DDCI under Webster. The Reagan administration's original choice to succeed Casey, his 1987 confirmation hearing became instead a lightning rod for growing Senate concerns and questions regarding the Iran–Contra affair – a problem whose contours were then just becoming visible on Capitol Hill. Rather than prolong an increasingly difficult and potentially rancorous hearing process, Gates withdrew his name from consideration. In his place the administration nominated, and the SSCI confirmed, Webster, a former Director of the FBI. Judge Webster had no Iran–Contra baggage, and enjoyed a reputation as 'Mr. Clean' – a highly valued quality after what many considered the dubious adventurism of the Casey era. Placing a high value on good relations with Congress Webster was determined to be forthcoming in response to oversight requirements. Because his nearly four-year tenure as DCI set a new standard in comity between the branches of government, intelligence oversight had reached its full flowering.

Gates redux

Robert Gates had been a frequent and effective interlocutor between the Intelligence Community and Congress, appearing regularly as the senior administration witness at budget and other oversight hearings. He demonstrated an impressive mastery of detailed substantive material, allowing him to testify at length on complex programs, with little reliance on notes or support staff in the room. In addition, he conveyed to the committee members an understanding of how Congress works, and a general posture of support for the entire oversight enterprise.

When Gates's nomination was forwarded to the SSCI following Webster's retirement in 1991, there was a general expectation in both in the administration and the committee that his hearing would progress fairly rapidly and successfully toward confirmation. Some unfinished business concerning Iran–Contra remained but that was taken care of when Alan Fiers gave lengthy public testimony detailing CIA support for the Contras. His account, while compelling and detailed, did not tarnish Gates to any significant degree. That left one other matter to be addressed – persistent but unconfirmed allegations that the CIA under Casey and Gates had distorted some key intelligence analysis to fit the prevailing views of the White House. In short, it was said (by whom was not clear) that intelligence had been 'politicized.'

The charge was serious because it went to the heart of the entire intelligence enterprise. The value of intelligence to senior policymakers and to the nation rests to a critical degree on the confidence that the process is not corrupt – that intelligence collectors and analysts speak truth to power, however unpalatable it might be at any one time. During the Vietnam War, the Intelligence Community – to its great credit – continued to tell the White House bad news that President Lyndon B. Johnson did not want to hear.

Intelligence reporting and analysis might or might not be correct, but they must always be honest. If the integrity of the process and product is ever compromised, intelligence will become less than worthless because it will then be unreliable and misleading. Even the suspicion of distortion could be enough to gravely weaken this essential component of national security.

Nevertheless, prior to the Gates nomination, allegations of Casey-era manipulations had received scant attention, in either the oversight committees or the press. Consequently, the committee staff assigned to investigate them began with the assumption that the charges had little substance. That assumption was quickly challenged. As the investigation developed, the SSCI staff came into contact with former CIA analysts who provided detailed support for the allegations. Some of them provided dramatic testimony, first in secret and then in public, before the committee. Indications also increased that numerous veteran, currently serving, analysts shared the concern over politicization but, for understandable reasons, were reluctant to come forward on the public record. But six or seven then-current CIA analysts did come forward at considerable potential risk to their careers.[10] Many analysts recall that work in the DI ground to a near halt in one office after another as analysts gathered around television screens broadcasting the open hearings. Nothing comparable has happened before or since. Suddenly and surprisingly, the nomination appeared to be in serious jeopardy. Under heavy pressure from Gates himself, the Bush White House reacted by informing Republican members of the committee that the President would 'go to the mat' for Gates, and wanted his nomination confirmed at all costs.

This was a crucial moment in the history of intelligence oversight because the SSCI's GOP members responded by rallying behind Gates as a matter of political loyalty and obligation. Some committee Democrats responded in kind. For the first time in a decade, the SSCI's proceedings were being heavily influenced by partisan politics. The tendency was strongly accentuated by the committee's decision to conduct largely public hearings on the Gates confirmation.

The proceedings did not become entirely partisan because the chairman, Senator Boren, supported Gates's confirmation. Despite public professions of neutrality, Boren worked hard behind the scenes on Gates's behalf throughout the hearings. Ultimately, the nomination was saved, due largely to Boren's support and Gates's far-reaching pledges to take congressional views heavily into account during his tenure as DCI. Thus, more than any of his predecessors, he became a creature of the Congress. The *New York Times* noted the irony: 'In an administration that has shown its disdain for what it considers Congressional meddling in national security issues, Mr. Gates will be the first director who is directly beholden to Congress. He has vowed to resign rather than jeopardize that relationship should differences emerge between the executive branch and the CIA.'[11]

For Gates there was one more irony. George H. W. Bush lost the subsequent (1992) presidential election and Gates, despite his obvious desire to stay on, was not retained by the new Clinton administration. Gates thus served for only little more than a year in the job that he had won at such heavy cost.

Greater conflict at hand

The Gates hearing proved to be not an anomaly but a harbinger. President Bill Clinton tapped R. James Woolsey, a widely respected, Washington-based attorney with conservative foreign policy views, as his DCI. Senator Boren's tenure as chairman of the SSCI ended with the 103rd Congress in January 1993. Senator Dennis DeConcini (D., Arizona) succeeded him for a two-year term (1993–1994). DeConcini, who lacked Boren's accumulated expertise on intelligence matters, faced one overriding task: to reduce the post–Cold War intelligence budget in rough correspondence with ongoing reductions in the Defense budget. From DeConcini's standpoint, the political and bureaucratic pressures on the budget were irresistible. The issue was not whether to cut, but where and by how much. He badly needed a DCI who would work closely with him to make the necessary reductions as thoughtfully as possible.

Instead, Woolsey repeatedly demanded that the Intelligence Community budget be *increased*, and fought DeConcini at every turn. Relations between them deteriorated to the point where every matter of committee business became an issue or dispute. Consequently, Woolsey's brief tenure as DCI was, from an oversight perspective, a disaster. Senator DeConcini compounded the difficulties by selecting as SSCI staff director an old friend from Arizona with no background or interest in intelligence. George Tenet, Senator Boren's last staff director, had moved to the National Security Council (NSC) staff. The new staff director made it clear that he had little regard for his job, and conducted himself accordingly.

Nevertheless, some positives can be noted. After a rocky beginning Senator DeConcini and his Vice Chairman, Senator John W. Warner (R., Virginia) developed a solid, cooperative working relationship. Relations between committee staff and the Intelligence Community remained generally positive and professional. This was largely due to the fact that the staff director essentially ceded his responsibilities to his deputy, who performed effectively.[12]

DeConcini's successor as chairman was Senator Arlen Specter (R., Pennsylvania) for the two-year term (1995–1996). Specter demonstrated far more interest in his ongoing presidential candidacy than in trying to strengthen the fabric of intelligence oversight. As a presidential aspirant, Specter was keenly interested in media/press coverage. Consequently, he initiated what was, by SSCI standards, a large number of public hearings, whereas past practice had been to conduct the vast majority of the committee's business *in camera*. Senator Specter did select a capable and experience staff director, who tried to do what he could but, with an inattentive, publicity-hungry chairman, his effectiveness was limited.

By the time the chairmanship of the committee passed to Senator Richard C. Shelby (R., Alabama) in January 1997, the committee's oversight capabilities had already been crippled. Most of the professional staff from the Boren era had left and been replaced, not by intelligence professionals, but by individuals selected for their political loyalties. Shelby, who brought to the chairmanship no demonstrated expertise in intelligence, selected a staff director with a narrow technical background and no real understanding of what made oversight work – or fail. Under his management, the replacement of expertise with partisanship on the staff, and with it the 'dumbing down' of the committee, proceeded apace. Equally important, a change of climate took hold. In place of an attitude that valued cooperation across political party and institutional divisions, a new 'us vs. them' mindset became dominant. For the GOP majority, the committee came to be viewed as a club to wield against the Clinton administration. This change becomes evident when comparing, for example, the SSCI's report on intelligence verification of the INF Treaty in the late 1980s with the committee's report on U.S. vulnerability to ballistic missile attack (regarding possible abrogation of the ABM Treaty) in the late 1990s.

Even more than the congressional norm, the SSCI reflects its chairman. Unlike most other committees, no subcommittee chairmen share the load with the chairman or act as a counterweight to his views. Moreover, the SSCI's rules effectively give the chairman full power over the hiring, firing, and organization of the staff. All staff members are under the control of the staff director selected by the chairman.[13] This means, among other things, that bipartisanship can exist only as a gift from the chairman and the majority.

From the beginning, Senator Shelby treated the SSCI as no different than any other committee, i.e., as an instrument of partisan politics.[14] Consequently, under his chairmanship the SSCI became a highly partisan body in its approach to oversight. And Shelby became a frequent presence on television, generally assuming the role of harsh critic of the Clinton administration. Still more important, partisanship took over the committee's internal workings, with staff now formally designated as majority and minority, and members acting in a largely partisan capacity. Comity and even communication between Republican and Democratic staff largely broke down. Whereas in past years, political distinctions within the staff were nonexistent, now they became pervasive. The effect was exacerbated by the obvious personal animus Senator Shelby felt for the current DCI, George Tenet. The origins and motivations for Shelby's attitude are unclear, but the reality is not. By contrast, Representative Porter J. Goss (R., Florida) has consistently and publicly affirmed his high regard and support for Tenet. When George W. Bush assumed the presidency in January 2001, Shelby recommended that Tenet be replaced, whereas Goss endorsed his retention.

Negative responses to partisanship

The cumulative effects of these changes in chairmanship were accentuated by changes in the membership of the committee. During the 1990s the Senate leadership on both sides of the aisle began appointing senators to the committee for political reasons rather than for reasons of their experience, judgment, or stature in the national security arena. The committee membership of the 1980s included such heavyweights as Democrats Sam Nunn (Georgia), John Glenn (Ohio), Lloyd M. Bentsen (Texas), and Ernest F. Hollings (South Carolina), along with Republicans Warren Rudman (New Hampshire), William Cohen, and John Warner. In the 1990s a number of more junior, inexperienced and often very partisan senators (several of them having just moved over from the House) became members.

Partisanship is, of course, part of the Senate's very fabric. Nearly all committees function to a greater or lesser degree along partisan lines. Moreover, partisanship can give impetus to effective oversight, forcing the executive to confront issues it would rather avoid. A partisan edge may be required to uncover waste in the Department of Agriculture, or a disregard for congressional intent at the Department of Energy, or instances of taxpayer abuse at the Internal Revenue Service (IRS). But intelligence is qualitatively different from most executive functions. The information that is its product and lifeblood is too sensitive, and the potential consequences of failure are too horrific to be treated like data on public housing at the Department of Housing and Urban Development (HUD). In short, partisanship and intelligence oversight simply won't mix. Rigorous intellectual integrity is the coin of the intelligence realm. The only intelligence community worth having is one that calls the facts and their implications without heed to the political or related consequences. This standard, though high and hard, is a necessary one.

In addition, the relationship between oversight and the quality of intelligence product is not always simple or even direct. As oversight comes to reflect partisan pressures, specific pieces of high-profile analysis with controversial implications for policy may well become a target. Meanwhile, the vast majority of day-to-day analytical products will be unaffected. But when the process is perceived to be vulnerable to political manipulation in even one or two instances, the entire intelligence *oeuvre* will rapidly lose credibility. Put bluntly, the moment policymakers (or senators) conclude that intelligence is being trimmed to fit the policy or political winds, the intelligence agencies might as well be closed down.

Furthermore, in the immediate post–Cold War years the CIA was a wounded institution. Budget cuts, personnel reductions, a rapid succession of short-tenure DCIs (including a failed nomination), two of its own (Aldrich Ames and Harold Nicholson) revealed as Communist spies – all exacerbated a pervasive sense of disorientation as the overriding anti-Soviet mission evaporated. The Agency badly needed the help of congressional oversight committees that were highly professional and at the top of their game. The last thing intelligence professionals needed was overseers levying competing political demands and using the intelligence product in games of political gamesmanship.

The intelligence agencies themselves take it as axiomatic that their budgets, programs, and analysis should not be political issues. So, when one of the oversight committees begins to approach its responsibilities in a partisan manner, demanding this and criticizing that to score political points, the agencies do not know how to respond. When they believe or know that the information they provide will be misused, the volition that oversight ultimately depends upon begins to erode. A perception that the oversight committees are irresponsible will in time inevitably engender a temptation to stonewall, evade, and deceive on the part of intelligence officials. At a minimum, the Intelligence Community stops seeing the committees as partners, but rather as entities to avoid if at all possible. This has already happened.

Implementation of partisanship

The disquieting transformation of the Senate Intelligence Committee was put on public display during the 1997 confirmation hearings for Anthony Lake as DCI. Dr. Lake, President Clinton's first National Security Adviser, was nominated by the White House to succeed John Deutch as DCI. The confirmation hearing before the SSCI quickly became a political circus. The vitriolic, partisan exchanges among committee members during the public portion of the hearings were without precedent in its history. Chairman Shelby initially demanded that the raw files compiled during the FBI's background security investigation of Lake be made available to the committee (rather than the FBI-prepared summaries as in the past) and to the entire Republican membership of the Senate. No prior SSCI chairman would have even considered tossing the committee's most sensitive business (not to mention highly personal data on a nominee) into the lap of a party caucus.

The political environment has aggravated certain of the SSCI's long-standing structural liabilities. One often cited by Gates is the inattention and nonparticipation of most members. Senators have multiple committee assignments and, under the best of circumstances, have difficulty giving adequate time and attention to any one of them. In the case of the Intelligence Committee, the problem is compounded by two factors: (1) the often arcane and technical quality of the subject matter, and (2) the closed nature of the committee proceedings, which mean that a senator sees little or no political payoff for the time and effort expended on the panel. Consequently, only two or three members tend to be present at any given time, even in important hearings. This changes, of course, on those occasions such as the present when the committee holds public hearings.

Another structural problem involves membership turnover. The authors of the statute establishing the SSCI feared that its members would be 'captured' by the Intelligence Community, and thereby lose their independence and objectivity. Members were therefore limited to a maximum term of eight years. The result, as Gates and many others have noted, is that a senator barely has time to master the substance of intelligence before his or her committee term is up. In the House, the problem is even more acute, with HPSCI members limited to six years of service.[15] But House members have the compensating advantage of far fewer committee assignments. The effect of both turnover and inattention is a reinforcement of the staff's critical role and quality.

An additional development has further eroded the committee's effectiveness. The SSCI's relationship with the Senate Armed Services Committee is unique. As is well-known, the authorization bill for the Intelligence Community for security purposes, is imbedded within that for the Defense Department. Similarly, the intelligence authorization bill in the Congress is incorporated within the larger defense authorization. So, instead of going directly to the Appropriations Committee, the budget authorization determined by the SSCI goes to the Armed Services Committee. In the Boren era, the chairman of the Armed Services Committee was Sam Nunn. Boren and Nunn had close working and personal relationships, and under Nunn the Armed Services Committee largely kept hands off the intelligence authorization.

A similar situation existed with the Appropriations Committee where Senator Robert C. Byrd (D., West Virginia) held sway. Close cooperation extended from the chairman to other members of the three committees and to their staffs. For the SSCI, this was crucial because the far more powerful Armed Services and Appropriations committees can, if they choose, effectively override the SSCI and dictate outcomes. The essential cooperation and camaraderie that characterized relations among the three committees during the Boren–Cohen era continued largely intact under DeConcini, but began to break down under Specter, and largely disappeared under Shelby. The growth of partisanship diminished the SSCI's reputation and standing within the Senate as a whole. As a consequence, the intelligence agencies know they are dealing not only with a far more partisan SSCI, but a far weaker one as well.

The symptoms of the SSCI's deterioration are not hard to detect. One involves an increasing trend toward legislative micromanagement. In recent years, a number of SSCI-mandated Congressionally Directed Actions (CDAs), requiring a variety of often detailed administrative initiatives, has grown steadily. Along with the CDAs has come a lengthening list of obligatory reports, many of them required annually, about intelligence programs. A debatable but fair generalization is that the quality of interaction between an oversight committee and an executive agency is in inverse proportion to the number of required CDAs and reports. The inevitable consequence is the dwindling respect for the committee and its staff within the Intelligence Community.

Hopeful signs

Ironically, the extent to which oversight still works with regard to the Senate occurs because so many of the senior officials of the Intelligence Community come from the SSCI. To a person, they believe in the importance of congressional oversight, and have continued to act on that belief even as the Senate committee lost viability. DCI Tenet continues his effort to make oversight work. But this is obviously a very short-term situation. As new incumbents without a Capitol Hill background assume relevant senior posts on the panel, the current anomalous Community-led oversight will certainly fade.

Any overall judgment on the current state of oversight should note that the HPSCI – which has had a history of being more partisan and considerably less effective than the SSCI – has performed very creditably in the last five years under the chairmanship of Congressman Goss. It is surely no coincidence that Goss is a former CIA career intelligence officer.

In June 2001, the SSCI, like the rest of the Senate, underwent a sudden power shift, passing unexpectedly from Republican to Democratic control. Senator Bob Graham (D., Florida) became the new chairman. It is too early to judge whether he will have any lasting success in arresting the committee's downward trajectory. He has not attempted the key task of replacing the political spear-carriers on the committee staff with professionals actually knowledgeable about intelligence and dedicated to expert, nonpartisan oversight. The reason is surely pragmatic – to do so would precipitate a major battle within the committee. Forcing a changeover in key staff assignments would be a pyrhhic victory, given the likely political costs and the short time remaining on his chairmanship.

Congressional collaboration

The SSCI, working jointly with the HPSCI, has taken one important initiative with potentially enduring consequences. In February 2002 the two oversight committees announced a joint inquiry into the 11 September 2001 attacks and possible attendant intelligence failures. To carry out the inquiry, the committees established a single investigational staff, to be organized and run by a director, and supporting both oversight committees separate from their existing staffs. The director was to be selected by the leadership of the two committees, but would in turn have full authority to select the staff of the inquiry. According to the Senate Historian's Office, the creation of such a unified (vice joint) investigation serving both House and Senate is apparently unique in congressional history. The selection of a director was both critical – and difficult. Ultimately the choice was L. Britt Snider, until recently the CIA's Inspector General, and before that the SSCI's General Counsel. Snider, in turn, quickly assembled a staff of experienced professionals with impressive credentials.

In announcing the launching of the joint investigation, both Senator Graham and Representative Goss struck a note of objectivity and bipartisanship. Graham stated: 'I have no interest in simply looking in the rear view mirror and playing the "blame game" about what went wrong from an intelligence perspective. Rather, I wish to identify any systemic shortcomings in our intelligence community and fix these problems as soon as possible.' Snider set a firm target date for completion of the inquiry and the release of a report of findings by the end of the calendar year 2002. That would be a Herculean undertaking, given the vast quantities of material to be reviewed, including 400,000 FBI documents alone.

The potential importance of the report can hardly be exaggerated. It could provide a critical part of the historical record of the 11 September attacks. In that sense, its only counterpart would be the inquiry following Pearl Harbor. Still more important, an understanding of intelligence failures and vulnerabilities could be critical in preventing future attacks of this or greater magnitude.

The Intelligence Community evidently took the inquiry very seriously, and viewed it with considerable trepidation. At the same time, full community cooperation was and is the sine qua non for a successful outcome. From all evidence, that cooperation was forthcoming – perhaps, in large part, because senior IC officials trusted Snider, whose reputation for professionalism and integrity was unassailable. But, suddenly, on 26 April Snider resigned without comment. Committee sources would say only that there had been an issue over a 'personnel' decision involving the investigative staff. The circumstantial evidence strongly suggested that Snider and the staff were subjected to the same partisan political pressures that have so damaged Senate oversight in recent years.

Subsequently, however, James Risen of *The New York Times* reported that

> the leaders of the joint House-Senate panel forced . . . Snider . . . to resign after they learned that he had hired a C.I.A. officer who was the subject of a counterintelligence investigation. C.I.A. officials had told Mr. Snider that the employee was under scrutiny because of problems that had surfaced in a polygraph examination. . . . Mr. Snider did not immediately inform the committee leadership when he learned of the inquiry, and crucial lawmakers were angered after they somehow found out on their own. . . .[15]

Risen also reported that Snider's close association with DCI Tenet, begun when they worked together on the SSCI staff a decade ago, had raised some doubts among critics about his ability to 'aggressively investigate the agency's performance in the months leading up to the attacks.'[16] Senator Graham nevertheless praised Snider for assembling a professional staff and playing a very significant role in the panel's progress.[17]

Risen concluded: 'Some members want a look back that assigns blame for the intelligence failure culminating on Sept. 11. Others want to look forward and propose reforms in the government's counterterrorism operations.' Senator Graham and Congressman Goss, he writes, 'generally seem inclined to make the panel forward-looking. But Senator Shelby has made it clear that he believes Mr. Tenet's tenure at the C.I.A. should be scrutinized to determine if he should be held accountable for the intelligence failure before Sept. 11.'[18]

Subsequently Senator Graham clearly viewed the inquiry and its report as the legacy of his chairmanship. It might have been even more. A credible, nonpolitical, and persuasive report could constitute a critical first step toward rebuilding effective oversight. But stripped of the credibility provided by Snider's involvement, the odds against its success lengthened markedly. A high-profile debacle was narrowly averted largely due to two developments. First, Snider personally persuaded the remaining joint inquiry staff not to resign in an act of sympathetic protest, and Senator Graham and Rep. Goss found an able replacement in the person of Eleanor Hill, whose background and personality were remarkably similar to Snider's. A former Inspector General of the Department of Defense with substantial prior experience on Capitol Hill, most notably as Chief Counsel to the Senate Governmental Affairs Subcommittee on Investigations (a post once held by Robert Kennedy), she succeeded in maintaining the momentum of the ongoing staff work, and handled the pressures of the subsequent public hearings with a steady professionalism.

Another issue arising out of the 9/11 investigation dramatically highlighted the problematic complexity of relations between the oversight committees and the executive branch. On 19 June 2002 CNN reported the content of highly classified testimony by the Director of the National Security Agency before the two committees. This produced an angry reaction from the White House. The circumstances of the leak strongly suggested its emanation from the SSCI. A chagrined committee leadership immediately called for an FBI investigation of members and staff to affix blame. This was a critical moment in the history of oversight. Citing Constitutional separation of powers, the oversight committees had in the past effectively declared themselves off limits to FBI security investigations.[19] Staff members are vetted through routine FBI field investigations prior to hiring, but they are not subjected to a polygraph as are employees of the CIA and other executive intelligence agencies. But, given the explosive environment in this most recent case, the FBI was invited to question members and staff. Several members found this development highly unsettling – particularly since it came at a time when the committees (through the joint inquiry) were investigating the FBI's performance prior to 9/11.

The FBI interviewed all thirty-seven members of the House and Senate oversight committees and some sixty staff members. As the next step, the FBI asked seventeen senators to turn over their phone records, appointment calendars, and schedules that would reveal contact with the media.[20] Senator Graham announced that he would comply, but it remains unclear to what extent other senators did so. FBI interviewers also asked their subjects if they would submit to a polygraph. If implemented, an FBI polygraph of congressional members and staff would represent a complete breach of a historic firewall.

Those familiar with the FBI know that the Bureau dislikes investigations of leaks, because they so seldom produce a conclusive outcome. This investigation was no exception. Although still nominally ongoing by late 2002, the FBI had not tried to actually conduct any polygraph examinations, and the firewall remained partly, but not wholly, breached.

Restoring an institutional asset

In sum, the U.S. system of intelligence oversight by Congress has proven to be a viable solution to a tricky problem. But the system requires a very special set of conditions to work. These include, on the IC side, a recognition that oversight is not only a legal requirement, but if done properly, an essential institutional asset. The Intelligence Community must be ready and willing to support, not resist, oversight. On the congressional side, the list of requirements is longer: (1) nonpartisanship; (2) an expert professional staff; (3) a competent, experienced staff director; (4) a chairman (hopefully supported by other members of the committee), who has mastered the substance of major issues and programs; and (5) a good working relationship among the oversight, Armed Services, and Appropriations committees.

Clearly, under present circumstances, Senate-conducted intelligence oversight no longer measures up to these threshold requirements. Whether it can be restored to viability, or whether the damage is irreparable, remains open to question.

References

1 The author's personal experience primarily involved the Senate where he was a professional staff member (1984–1992) and Deputy (Minority) Staff Director. He was hired by a Republican Chairman and for most of his tenure with the committee was the 'designee' of another Republican. However, neither Senator (nor the committee staff director) inquired concerning the author's political views or affiliation – which is as it should be in a nonpartisan environment.
2 L. Britt Snider developed this organization of the historical record in his monograph, *Sharing Secrets with Lawmakers: Congress as a User of Intelligence* (Washington, DC: Center for the Study of Intelligence, February 1997).
3 Quoted in Ibid., p. 2.

4 Section 662 of the Foreign Assistance Act (22 U.S.C. 2422).

5 S. Res. 400, Sec 11. Text in *Legislative Oversight of Intelligence Activities: the U.S. Experience*, Report prepared by the Select Committee on Intelligence, October 1994, p. 35.

6 The 'Intelligence Community' is a collective noun referring to the various executive branch intelligence agencies of the U.S. government. S. Res. 400 gives the SSCI oversight and authorization jurisdiction over the following: '(A) The Central Intelligence Agency and Director of Central Intelligence. (B) The Defense Intelligence Agency. (C) The National Security Agency. (D) The intelligence activities of other agencies and subdivisions of the Department of Defense. (E) The intelligence activities of the Department of State. (F) The intelligence activities of the Federal Bureau of Investigation . . . (G) Any department, agency, or subdivision which is the successor to any agency named in clause (A), (B), or (C). . . .'

7 James T. Currie, 'Iran-Contra and Congressional Oversight of the CIA,' *International Journal of Intelligence and CounterIntelligence*, Vol. 11, No. 2, Summer 1998, p. 198.

8 DCI, DDCI, General Counsel, Inspector General, Deputy Director for Community Management.

9 If a new covert action is funded by a reserve release (as many are initially), the committees are technically 'notified' of the release. While the administration typically does not use the reserve until the committees (including Appropriations) have cleared off, the law permits it to do so. A continuing covert action program, though, has to be funded in the annual authorization, and here the committees have denied funding on occasion.

10 The SSCI in the person of Chairman Boren extracted a specific pledge from Robert Gates that as DCI he would not take adverse action against these analysts because of their testimony. During Gates's subsequent brief tenure as DCI the pledge was, to my knowledge, honored.

11 Elaine Sciolino, 'Senate Approves Gates by 64–31, to Head the C.I.A.,' *The New York Times*, 6 November 1991, A23.

12 For example, two high profile issues that had real potential for partisan exploitation – the Aldrich Ames spy case and controversial expenditures by the NRO on its new headquarters complex – were both handled in a professional and essentially nonpartisan fashion by the SSCI.

13 The committee, virtually since its inception, has operated under an informal 'designee' system whereby members of the committee can select a staff member who will serve as their particular resource on the committee. These designees can be political or professional depending on the requirements or nonrequirements established by the chairman.

14 For a very different assessment of Senator Shelby's tenure, see Gregory C. McCarthy, 'GOP Oversight of Intelligence in the Clinton Era,' *International Journal of Intelligence and CounterIntelligence*, Vol. 15, No. 1, Spring 2002, pp. 26–51.

15 The term limitation has usually, but not always, been rigidly applied. Senator Specter successfully persuaded the Republican Leader, Senator Robert J. Dole (R., Kansas), to allow him leave the committee for two years to stop the clock on his tenure – and to enable him to rejoin the committee and assume the chairmanship for his remaining two years. Senator Mike DeWine (R., Ohio) has negotiated an analogous arrangement. Senator Graham was granted an extra two years by the Democratic Leader, Senator Thomas Daschle (D., South Dakota), to allow him to assume the chairmanship when Senator Charles Robb (D., Virginia), who had been next in line, was defeated for reelection.

16 James Risen, 'Reason Cited for Ousting of Terror Inquiry's Director: Staff Member's Security Problem Is Blamed,' *The New York Times*, 9 May 2002, p. A34.

17 Ibid.

18 Ibid.

19 There is general agreement among legal experts that in the event of a criminal investigation, Congressional claims based on the separation of powers would have to give way.

20 Dana Priest, 'Probe of Hill Leaks On 9/11 Is Intensified,' *The Washington Post*, 24 August 2002, 1.

M.C. Ott, 'Partisanship and the Decline of Intelligence Oversight.' *International Journal of Intelligence and Counterintelligence* Spring 2003, 16/1, pp.69–94.

19 The British experience with intelligence accountability

Mark Phythian

This article assesses the British experience with intelligence accountability through an analysis of the principal mechanism that exists to provide for it – the parliamentary Intelligence and Security Committee. It discusses the context within which oversight proposals emerged, the debate surrounding the nature of the new oversight body, and assesses the performance of the Committee over the first decade of its existence. It concludes that while the Committee has secured some important advances with regard to the accountability of the intelligence and security services, there are nevertheless significant limitations and weaknesses, many of which were evident in the Committee's 2003 investigation and report into pre-war intelligence on Iraqi WMD. In this context, the debate as to whether the oversight body should have select committee status, discussed at length in the article, remains highly relevant.

This article assesses the British experience with intelligence accountability through a consideration of the principal mechanism that exists to provide for this – the Intelligence and Security Committee (ISC). In discussing the British experience with intelligence accountability we are looking at a country whose principal internal security and external intelligence organizations – the Security Service (MI5) and the Secret Intelligence Service (MI6) – trace their origins back to 1909, but whose peacetime existence was only formally acknowledged in the late 1980s and early 1990s. Then, in the wake of a succession of intelligence-linked exposés and in the context of the end of the Cold War and the intrusion of European law into the domestic polity, the Conservative governments of Margaret Thatcher and John Major finally introduced legislation formalizing their existence.

The emergence of oversight

A string of revelations and allegations during the 1970s and 1980s created a momentum for greater accountability of the security and intelligence agencies, albeit one that lagged behind similar debates in the US, Canada and Australia. The motor driving these concerns was the widespread belief on the Left that in guarding against domestic subversion, MI5 was monitoring and interfering with legitimate political dissent. Left-wing critics argued that MI5 saw its primary allegiance as being to the Crown rather than the elected government of the day. There were suspicions that this extended to undermining Labour governments, reinforced by the revelations contained in former MI5 officer Peter Wright's memoir *Spycatcher*.[1] There were other dimensions to the damage done to the reputation of the security and intelligence services during this period. The public exposure in November 1979 of Sir Anthony Blunt, Surveyor of the Queen's Pictures and pillar of the establishment, as a former Soviet spy, was quickly followed by the Prime and Bettaney espionage cases, all of which provided fertile ground for Wright's claim that former MI5 director-general Sir Roger Hollis had been a Soviet spy. By the time of Paul Foot's 1989 book, *Who Framed Colin Wallace?* – at its core an account of the 'cowboy' era of military intelligence in the laboratory that was Northern Ireland in the early 1970s, it seemed that there was a reservoir of security and intelligence intrigue and scandal that was in no danger of running dry.[2]

While all of this created heightened parliamentary concern, the existence of what Tony Geraghty has termed the 'very public war' in Northern Ireland served as a disincentive for government to act.[3] When Parliament did probe, former ministers were hardly reassuring. For example, when former Prime Minister Jim Callaghan gave evidence to the Treasury and Civil Service Committee in 1986 and was asked if he was satisfied that the agencies were sufficiently accountable, he replied:

> I am not sure what its accountability is to Parliament, I am not sure about ministers. I find it a difficult question to answer, I really do. They are run . . . as separate departments. They are not in the Minister's office, as it were, not in his headquarters. There is, therefore, all the difficulty of physical separation. When the Minister has to up sticks to ask questions and go somewhere else, that makes for remoteness. There is not immediate day to day closeness. Some Ministers do not want to know a lot: Home Secretary or Foreign Secretary, Prime Minister, others want to know a great deal about what is going on. I am going to give you a very unsatisfactory answer, I do not know. I am certain there must be a very high degree of responsibility among those who serve in MI5 or MI6 because they have great powers . . . and I think the ethos of those particular services is probably as important as the degree of accountability that you can visit upon them. I am very, very mixed up about this, I do not think I can help you with this.[4]

The most pressing impetus to act from the British government's perspective (although it did not concede this at the time) arose from the impact of European law on the British polity, in particular the European Convention on Human Rights (ECHR). Having fallen foul of this in 1984, the government enacted the Interception of Communications Act the following year. When former MI5 officer Cathy Massiter revealed that future Labour government ministers Harriet Harman and Patricia Hewitt had been placed under surveillance as a consequence of working for the National Council for Civil Liberties, at that time classed by MI5 as a subversive organization, they prepared to take their case to the ECHR. The prospect of further adverse rulings led to the 1989 Security Service Act.

This established MI5 on a legal footing. It created a Commissioner, 'a person who holds or has held high judicial office', who would review the Home Secretary's exercise of his powers in signing warrants allowing for interference with private property, and produce an annual report for the Prime Minister who would lay it before Parliament after removing any material considered 'prejudicial to the continued discharge of the functions of the Service'. The Act also created a three-member Tribunal to investigate complaints about MI5 from the public which, like the Commissioner, had access to MI5 records and personnel. The Tribunal would (in conjunction with the Commissioner where allegations of property interference were involved) establish whether MI5 had conducted investigations into a complainant and, if so, establish whether the grounds for doing so were reasonable. If the Tribunal found against MI5 it could order that any records relating to the complainant be destroyed, further investigations ended, and compensation paid. Out of over 100 cases investigated by the Tribunal in its first three years of operation, it did not find for the complainant in a single case. Nevertheless, the Commissioner, in his 1992 annual report, suggested that the very existence of the Tribunal had acted as a spur to MI5 adopting a more cautious approach to warrants and surveillance.

In mid-1992 Prime Minister John Major, then embarked on a wider 'open government' drive, broke with tradition by admitting that MI6 actually existed and undertaking to put it on a statutory footing. Briefings to journalists at this time suggested that parliamentary scrutiny of the services was unlikely to be a feature of this opening. However, when the Intelligence Services Bill was unveiled in 1993, tacked on to the end was provision for a form of parliamentary scrutiny of MI5, MI6 and the Government Communication Headquarters (GCHQ).

Why did Major move to introduce an oversight body at this time? There is no doubt that the end of the Cold War created a political space that made this possible. At the same time as this left politicians feeling bolder about removing some of the secrecy surrounding MI5 and MI6, it also affected these organizations' own view of the desirability of a limited degree of accountability. There was a general expectation that the end of the Cold War would bring with it a peace dividend, with clear implications for defence budgets. The intelligence agencies could expect to face similar pressure. In this context, it was felt that agreement to some form of scrutiny was necessary in retaining public confidence and protecting the UK intelligence budget (in 1992, £185 million). Moreover, the more perceptive intelligence managers may have appreciated that if oversight was increasingly inevitable, it should be accommodated rather than resisted. After all, scrutineers could also become advocates. They faced in addition the prospect of a future Labour government seeking to introduce more far-reaching reforms than the agencies were comfortable with – the Labour Party's 1983 election manifesto had spoken in terms of the 'now widespread concern about our security services' and committed a future Labour government to introducing legislation that provided for oversight by a select committee, a prospect which must have caused some concern in the agencies. Reinforcing such arguments in favour of cooperation would have been the feedback from foreign counterparts subject to oversight, offering reassurance that it could be accommodated.

Moreover, in searching for a post-Cold War raison d'être, MI5 had assumed the lead role in combating terrorism in Northern Ireland, a role previously occupied by the Metropolitan Police Special Branch, and as such was under some pressure to make itself as accountable for its part in this as the police had been. At the same time, allegations continued to emerge that strengthened the case for oversight – for example, those emanating from the Scott Inquiry into the arms-to-Iraq affair, and concerning the role of MI5 during the 1984–85 miners' strike. Finally, MI6 reportedly took a more relaxed view of the prospect of oversight than MI5, on the basis that its operations abroad were likely to be of less concern to MPs than the domestic operations of MI5, which carried with them greater concerns over civil liberties. Crucially, legislating from a position of relative strength, rather than being driven by some scandal, allowed the government and agencies to control the agenda. A key dimension of this was the idea, to quote Foreign Secretary Douglas Hurd, that 'the past is another country' and not one that the oversight body would be invited to explore.[5]

The Intelligence Services Bill

The Intelligence Services Bill included provision for the creation of a committee of six parliamentarians (in the event, increased to nine – the only alteration made to the draft bill), hand-picked by the Prime Minister, who would meet in closed session and produce reports for the Prime Minister, who would lay them before Parliament after removing material considered prejudicial to the activities of the agencies. Hence, it was accountable to the executive and only through the executive was it accountable to the legislature. This arrangement would be a continual source of soul-searching and debate as to whether the committee should not be a select committee of Parliament, directly accountable to the legislature. To coincide with the introduction of the Bill, the head of MI6, Sir Colin McColl, made an unprecedented public appearance to welcome the move towards greater accountability, but also reassure former, current and prospective agents that: 'Secrecy is our absolute stock in trade. It is important to the people who work for us and risk their lives that we remain a secret service. When the Central Intelligence Agency went open in the 1970s it worried a lot of their people. I want to send our people a signal that we are not going to open everything up.'[6]

McColl may have welcomed the Bill, but the Labour opposition did not, arguing for scrutiny by a parliamentary select committee rather than the proposed hybrid. As Jack Cunningham, leading for the opposition, put it:

> it is proposed that the committee should not report to Parliament but to the Prime Minister. I do not regard that as parliamentary scrutiny or oversight, because the Prime Minister has the right to veto sections of its report – I call it prime ministerial oversight and scrutiny. If we are to have an effective parliamentary watchdog to oversee such matters and to probe and scrutinise, it should report to Parliament. It cannot legitimately be called a parliamentary committee unless it does so.[7]

Future members of the ISC were amongst those who expressed concern over the proposed form of oversight. Labour MP John Gilbert called it 'far more timid than necessary'. He was one of several MPs who could not see that the government had made the case for not granting the proposed oversight committee select committee status, arguing that the existing select committee practice of 'sidelining' (i.e. removing) sensitive material would apply. The advantages to the government, it was argued, lay in being in control of the timing of publication of the report and that the proposed committee would not have the same powers as a select committee to send for persons and papers. As future ISC member Allan Rogers put it: 'The committee will be a charade, a pretence at accountability.'[8] In general, the opposition made it clear that, while voting for the Bill, they favoured select committee status. It would be two years later, with the increasing likelihood that they would form the next government, before the Labour Party began to distance itself from its earlier enthusiasm for genuine parliamentary oversight.

In response to fears that the proposed committee would be toothless, William Waldegrave closed the debate by emphasizing the powers that it would possess:

> The committee will be involved in very secret areas that have never before been shared with others outside the Secretary of State's responsibilities . . . The committee will not only deal with high-level policy in a broad-brush way; it will be able to examine the actual tasking, the money and the organisational structures. The committee will be fully trusted, and fully inside the secret wall. I believe that the result, while it will not establish within the House the parliamentary accountability that . . . we believe would be extremely difficult to organise, will be to spread the reassurance that senior, trusted people on both sides of the House share the secrets of the services, and have a formidable power to cause trouble for the Government. Somebody asked earlier where the teeth

were. The teeth consist of the fact that the committee . . . will have the right not to publish stuff that would damage national security – which it would not want to do – but to write a report saying, 'We believe that things are not being handled properly, and that Ministers are not responding properly.' No Government . . . would want to risk such criticism.[9]

The intelligence and security committee under Tom King, 1994–2001

Nevertheless, the Committee would first of all have to discover that things were not being handled properly, and there remained concerns about its ability to do so. The final Intelligence Services Act stated that the ISC's requests for information would not be met if that information was deemed 'sensitive' (and 'sensitive' was broadly defined), or because the Home or Foreign Secretary 'determined that it shall not be disclosed'. As with the 1989 Act, a Commissioner and Tribunal were created. The separate Tribunals have since been supplanted by a single Tribunal under the terms of the Regulation of Investigatory Powers Act (RIPA) 2000, introduced to keep pace with advances in European law. In his brief annual report, the Commissioner registers the number of warrants issued in a confidential annex, while openly recording the number of complaints investigated by the Tribunal, and the number upheld following investigation, usually none.

The ISC's first chairman was former Conservative Secretary of State for Defence and Northern Ireland Tom King, and the committee featured a Conservative Party majority. Its first report was an 11-paragraph interim report published in May 1995, stating that: 'In general terms, we have been encouraged by the openness of the intelligence "insiders" that we have come into contact with thus far, and in particular by the helpful approach of the Heads of the Agencies themselves.'[10] In an 11-paragraph report, the inclusion of the preambular 'In general terms' was not without significance. In terms of the Committee's approach, the report noted that it would 'concentrate on major issues rather than, for example, be drawn into every individual intelligence item of current excitement – unless they are of such significance and relevance as to merit exceptional consideration and report to you'. The framing of the Committee's interpretation of its mandate inevitably involved a tussle over the question of investigating allegations of past abuses. An attempt by Allan Rogers to raise the question of the agencies' relationship with Soviet defector Oleg Gordievsky, in the context of his contemporaneous allegation that former Labour Party leader Michael Foot was regarded by the KGB as an 'agent of influence', were defeated inside the Committee, with Lord Howe echoing Douglas Hurd's earlier intervention and arguing that the ISC should not involve itself in 'political archaeology'. However, in the US, Canada and Australia the question of past abuses or scandals was amongst the first to be investigated by the newly-formed oversight committees. Having decided that the 'past is another country' and interpreted its mandate as involving broad, strategic policy questions, in its first years of operation the ISC focused on the implications for the agencies of the changed post-Cold War world. Its second report, nine paragraphs long, concerned the decision to move MI5 into the fight against organized crime. Its first annual report was completed in December 1995 and published in March 1996.

There is no doubting the industry of the individual committee members in getting to grips with their task, or the learning curve they faced. This first annual report revealed what became a pattern of at least weekly meetings and of visits to the agencies and abroad (although the agencies have always stressed the limited utility of overseas experiences with accountability, instead emphasizing the unique character of MI5 and MI6). On the basis of its early experiences the ISC felt able to reassure the Prime Minister that it considered its structure appropriate to the task. However, it would not be long before it requested the addition of an investigative capacity to assist it in its work.

One fundamental early aim of the ISC was to establish the confidence of the agencies themselves. King would subsequently allude to the initial Australian experience with intelligence oversight, wherein what he termed the 'awkward squad' was selected to sit on the oversight body, and consequently enjoyed little cooperation from the agencies. The ISC sought to reassure the agencies that any information they shared with committee members would be handled securely. In return, the ISC was keen that, in turn, the agencies:

> Understand our needs and are sufficiently frank and open with a new oversight body with whom they have previously not had to relate. These mutual concerns must be met if the Committee is to command the confidence of parliament and the public. This is an essential foundation for our work, particularly if we were at any time required to deal urgently with some specially sensitive or difficult issue.[11]

In comparing the US intelligence agencies' legal obligation to keep their oversight committees informed of their activities with the UK agencies' much more limited legal obligation to respond to requests from the ISC for information, the report later observed that the ISC 'does expect to be kept properly and promptly informed'. How fully the ISC succeeded in this area is an open question. Nevertheless, it is worth noting that this expectation represented something of an attempted expansion of its role – the Act was silent here. Similarly, its first annual report adopted an expansive interpretation of its financial oversight remit, arguing that this extended to, 'the clear responsibility to ensure that the Agencies have access to adequate resources for the tasks they are asked to undertake',[12] and not just how cost-effectively such resources were used.

The second annual report, for 1996, was completed in December 1996 and published in February 1997. This reported that the Committee had faced the first challenges to its decision to focus on major issues rather than feel obliged to address each and every controversy that might arise, in allegations concerning Menwith Hill and, separately, the alleged surveillance of a meeting between MPs and members of Sinn Fein inside the Palace of Westminster. Having asked the agencies about these matters, 'we received . . . categorical assurances, which we accept, that the stories were without foundation'.[13] Having no wider investigatory capability, it had little option but to do so.

The third annual report was completed at the end of July 1998, a full 19 months after the previous one, the intervening period being disrupted by the election of a Labour government in 1997 and the subsequent reorganization of the ISC to reflect political retirements and the parliamentary dominance of the Labour Party. Tom King remained as Chair of the Committee, reflecting the desire of the Labour government to reassure the agencies that the 1983 election manifesto was long forgotten. With this new membership the ISC came to see itself as having more of a public education role, opening its third annual report with a lengthy overview of the recent history of the agencies and the evolving nature of the threats they countered. It assured Prime Minister, Parliament and the public that these new challenges were 'real enough' and not 'invented to justify the Agencies' continued existence', as some critics had asserted, and, moreover, that 'intelligence and security capabilities cannot be turned on and off like a tap. To meet their responsibilities, they must be maintained, and funded in a sustainable way'.[14] To some extent, the ISC was becoming involved in advocacy on the agencies' behalf.

Having taken an interest in the agencies' internal procedures, the now Labour-dominated ISC returned to these in the wake of the August 1997 revelations of MI5 officer David Shayler, soon to be joined by those of former MI6 officer Richard Tomlinson. Frustrated by what he saw as an antiquated approach to management in general and personnel issues in particular, Shayler had gone public when he failed to secure what he felt was a fair hearing of his grievances internally. Amongst his revelations, Shayler disclosed the names of a few people on whom MI5 kept personal files, extending to the man to whom they were account-able, Home Secretary Jack Straw, and including other Cabinet members, thereby reviving an issue of particular sensitivity on the Labour Left. He was also to allege that MI6 had been involved in a plot to assassinate Libyan leader Colonel Gaddafi. The ISC responded by returning to the question of personnel policies, vetting and internal security at relative length.[15] However, it refused to meet or take evidence from Shayler and showed no interest in investigating his allegations of an assassination plot.

The Shayler revelations did, however, lead to a renewed interest in the issue of MI5's files. In its 1997–98 report the ISC confirmed that MI5 held approximately 250,000 hard copy personal files, with a further 40,000 held on microfiche, and outlined the process of opening, storing and classifying these files – the first time this had been done. Concerned at Shayler's ability as an MI5 officer to call up the files of any politician or celebrity that took his fancy, the ISC recommended that access should be restricted to those 'with a clear need to see them' and be accompanied by a detailed audit trail indicating who had seen any file, when and for what purpose.

From the vantage point of the late 1990s, of even greater concern than MI5's historic maintenance of such an extensive number of personal files was the question of the destruction of those files. The ISC was able to bring considerable light to bear on MI5's approach to file retention/destruction. It revealed that until 1970 MI5 had a policy of weeding and destroying files. However, this had affected its ability to pursue a number of espionage cases. Hence, the policy shifted from destruction to microfiching. However, the ISC revealed that in 1992, MI5 'reconsidered its files policy again in the light of the changing nature of the threat with the end of the Cold War and the decline in the threat from subversion'. As a result, MI5 began reviewing and destroying personal files on a case by case basis, destroying, and concealing, aspects of its own history in the process. As ISC member Yvette Cooper argued:

> I accept that only the Security Service can make the operational decision whether it still needs to retain a file and continue to use it, but, once the service has decided that it does not need it, there is an historical – not operational – decision to be made. History is not an operational decision. There is absolutely no reason why only the Security Service should be capable of deciding whether something has historical significance for the future. In fact, for the sake of the credibility of history, someone other than the Security Service should make that decision.
>
> It is controversial stuff. We have all heard the allegations about the monitoring of so-called subversives in the 1970s and 1980s. For all I know, none of it may have happened. On the other hand, all sorts of outrageous things may have happened. The point is that future generations have a right to know what happened and how the organs of the state behaved. They have a right to be able to learn from that and to know that what they are looking at is the entire record. They need to be confident about that. For the sake of credibility, it should not be the Security Service that decides that. Future

historians should never be able to say that the service was given a licence to write its own history.[16]

By the time the ISC investigated the issue 110,000 files, the 'vast majority' of which related to subversion, had either been destroyed or marked for destruction. The ISC found that: 'Ultimately, the judgement in respect of the review and destruction of individual files is made solely by the Security Service', and recommended that, 'some form of independent check should be built into the process, particularly in respect of files relating to subversion'.[17]

In sum, the 1997–98 report suggested a more assertive ISC, possibly a consequence of having developed greater self-confidence, possibly a consequence of its changed composition, most likely a combination of the two. Having initially reassured Prime Minister and Parliament that its structure was well suited to its task, the ISC had by this point become aware of the fact that it had no investigatory capability of its own, and without this it could not 'make authoritative statements on certain issues'. Hence, it argued that an investigatory arm would, 'reinforce the authority of any findings that we make, and be an important element in establishing public confidence in the oversight system'.[18]

Two innovations followed from this report: firstly the government began the practice of producing a published response; secondly, it granted an annual parliamentary debate on the reports. In its first response, the government rejected the ISC's proposal that some form of independent check should be built into the process by which MI5 files were reviewed for destruction. It also asserted that access to files was already restricted and subject to audit arrangements, raising the question of why the ISC, assumed to have access to information on such processes, made the recommendation in the first place. It also seemed to resist the introduction of an investigative arm.

There are two further noteworthy dimensions to this response. Firstly, while the ISC was reporting to the Prime Minister on its oversight of the agencies, in formulating its response, the government was clearly working closely with the intelligence agencies in framing their joint rejection of certain of the ISC's proposals. In other words, government had established the ISC to oversee the agencies, but joined forces with the agencies to reject recommendations arising from this oversight. The response found in favour of the agencies and their continued information monopoly rather than in favour of greater openness and accountability. Secondly, the timing of the government's response was significant. One of the weaknesses of the ISC structure highlighted in the debates over the Intelligence Services Bill had been that the executive would dictate the timing of publication. Here, a report that was published after a 19-month gap had to wait a further three months for a government response and parliamentary debate. Hence, Parliament was unable to debate the 1997–98 annual report until November 1998.

Parliamentary debate served to highlight concerns about the ISC on the part of its own members and the House of Commons in general. For example, it quickly exposed concerns about the implication for select committees' ability to oversee matters that now fell under the remit of the ISC. In practice, the existence of the ISC could allow government to justify a refusal to disclose information to select committees – as, indeed, it would on several occasions in the future, most significantly over the highly sensitive question of intelligence and the case for war in Iraq.

Debate also kept the question of the desirability of a move towards select committee status alive. Allan Rogers referred to the ISC's own, 'strong debates on the possible adoption of a Select Committee style for our proceedings'. Fellow ISC member Dale Campbell-Savours did not believe that oversight is fully credible while the Committee remains a creature of the Executive – and that is what it is. The problem at the moment is that the Committee considers its relationship with the Prime Minister more important to its operation than its relationship with Parliament. I strongly dissent from that view and find the arguments in favour of Select Committee status utterly overwhelming.[19]

One reason why a narrow majority of ISC members came to believe that select committee status was unnecessary was that they saw an alternative route – further evolution of the ISC, and in particular the idea that an investigatory arm should be established. As Yvette Cooper, one of the most articulate advocates of expanded oversight, argued:

> At the moment, information is provided by agency chiefs and by Ministers at their discretion, which raises a difficult point: how can we have proper oversight if the very people whom we are supposed to be overseeing are determining what information we get? That severely jeopardizes the Committee's ability to pronounce with authority on important intelligence issues. Credibility demands knowledge and knowledge demands the power to verify – the power to check what is going on. Until now, the ISC has not had that power, and that reduces its credibility in the public mind, as well as in Parliament's mind.
>
> None of that means that I suspect the agencies of any wrongdoing; it means simply that we on the Committee lack the ability to pronounce with confidence that all is well. We cannot come to the House, put our hands on our hearts and say that all is well, because we do not have the power to know.[20]

By the time the ISC produced its 1998–99 report (in August 1999), the government had consented to the appointment of a single Investigator, despite some agency unease at the prospect. The Investigator, whose terms of reference were dictated by the Prime Minister rather than the ISC, occupied an interesting position, further inside the 'ring of secrecy' than ISC members from whom he could well be obliged to withhold information. Before providing a report on an issue for the ISC, the Investigator was required to consult with the agency involved, 'so as to allow the Head of the Agency to detemine whether any particular material should be withheld from the Committee'.[21]

In its 1998–99 annual report there was further evidence of ISC assertiveness. It argued that it should be granted access to the confidential annexes to the reports of the two Commissioners created to investigate warrants in relation to interference with property and complaints referred to them by the Tribunals where the Tribunal did not uphold a complaint but nevertheless felt that an agency's conduct was unreasonable. On the question of MI5's personal files, its recommendations had contributed towards the creation of a degree of external scrutiny to help ensure that historically valuable documents were not being destroyed. However, the Committee learned that during the period in between the Home Secretary undertaking to review the issue and the announcement that there would be external scrutiny in future, rather than suspend file destruction, MI5 destroyed a further 3,000.[22] It also continued its campaign to bring greater transparency to the question of the agencies' budgets, and expanded its focus on weapons of mass destruction (WMD), sounding a cautionary note as to the utility of control regimes and treaties, and advocating a more proactive approach on the part of MI6 to tracking and frustrating would-be proliferators. In its response the government refused to make the confidential annexes to the Commissioners' reports available to the ISC on the basis that they fell within the category of information defined as 'sensitive' in the 1994 Act. It also continued to resist the ISC's attempts to bring greater transparency to the question of agency budgets, and rejected the notion that it placed too much faith in control regimes and treaties when it came to countering the spread of WMD, although its subsequent policy towards Iraq suggested it rapidly lost this faith.

The timing of the report's publication and the government's response was again tardy in the extreme. A report completed in August 1999 was only published in November 1999, the government's response being published at the end of January 2000, and the parliamentary debate finally being held in June 2000, almost a year after the report was completed and just two months before the subsequent annual report was presented to the Prime Minister. The delay in publication, response, and scheduling meant that this 'annual' debate was held a full 20 months after the previous one.

While the ISC was established as a self-tasking body, in September 1999 it agreed to the government's request to investigate the policy and procedures employed by the agencies in their handling of information acquired through Soviet defector Vasili Mitrokhin and the events that culminated in the publication of the first volume of his account of Soviet espionage, co-authored with the agencies' favourite academic, Christopher Andrew.[23] This was also interesting in that it was made clear on establishing the ISC that 'the past is another country'. Now, the ISC was being invited to investigate those parts of that country where it could be helpful to the government. Central to this case were issues of agency accountability to ministers and the degree to which ministers were kept informed about espionage issues. The key case was that of Melita Norwood, code-named HOLA, whom the Mitrokhin papers allowed to be identified as a Soviet spy as long ago as 1992, but MI5 effectively decided against prosecuting. In 1999, when the first volume of the *Mitrokhin Archive* was about to be published, MI5 asked for an opinion on a possible prosecution, only for the Attorney General to advise that a court would be likely to view such a prosecution as an abuse of process, given that no action had been taken when Norwood's identity had first become known. The ISC concluded that:

> it was a serious failure of the Security Service not to refer Mrs Norwood's case to the Law Officers in mid 1993. This failure to consult the Law Officers resulted in the decision whether or not to prosecute Mrs Norwood effectively being taken by the Security Service. The Committee is concerned that the Service used public interest reasons to justify taking no further action against Mrs Norwood, when this was for the Law Officers to decide. We also believe that the failure of the Security Services to interview Mrs Norwood at this time prevented her possible prosecution.[24]

In a report highly critical of aspects of MI5's performance, the Committee also said that the Norwood case should have been kept under review between 1993 and 1998 and not allowed to 'slip out of sight'. That it did represented 'a further serious failure'. MI5 Director General Sir Stephen Lander would subsequently refer to this ISC report as representing a 'public kicking' for the agency.[25]

The government had needed to be seen to launch some kind of investigation into the Mitrokhin/Norwood affair. The ISC was the ideal vehicle, given that original documents would remain within the 'ring of secrecy' and not be made public as was likely under alternative forms of inquiry. However, the ISC had made clear that in order to undertake the investigation it needed full access to information, including the normally sacrosanct advice to Ministers, a development that caused some concern within MI5. As the ISC reported, 'Although there was some delay in reaching agreement about the papers, the request was eventually met in full'.[26] This access would further embolden the Committee. At the same time, however, despite working to achieve a high level of mutual trust with the agencies, the Committee was never informed of the Mitrokhin/Norwood issue, even after a decision had been taken to publish the *Mitrokhin Archive*. Hence, while this episode demonstrated that the ISC was not afraid to criticize the agencies, and that it was increasingly self-confident, it also left hanging questions about the degree of accountability it was achieving, thereby affecting public confidence in it.

The 1999–2000 report continued to provide evidence of assertiveness and the beginning of the emphasis that the ISC would henceforth give to the failure of the Prime Minister to regularly convene the Ministerial Committee on the Intelligence Services (CSI), responsible for approving the National Intelligence Requirements, and which would enable senior ministers to take a collective strategic view of the challenges and priorities in the fields of security and intelligence. On investigation, the ISC discovered that this had not met at all since 1995, and that the civil service committee that shadowed it, the Permanent Secretaries' Committee on the Intelligence Services, had met just three times. The ISC was clear on this issue:

> We believe that there should be a clear recognition and demonstration of the lines of responsibility and authority for these important Agencies. We recommend that CSI should meet, under your Chairmanship, at least annually to approve the National Intelligence Requirements and endorse or approve the Agencies' budgets.[27]

It also returned to the question of access to the confidential annexes to the reports of the Commissioners, and the government's decision to refuse their request, giving a clear warning that this refusal was compromising the Committee's ability to carry out its oversight function: 'it is still important for us to see the classified annexes to be able to establish the corrective action that the Agencies have introduced following the Commissioners' identification of errors and thus fulfil our statutory requirement to oversee the Agencies' administration processes'.[28]

Its analysis of the intelligence contribution to the 1999 Kosovo campaign was so heavily redacted as to be without meaning. Elsewhere, it advocated greater intelligence resources be applied to combating drugs trafficking and tobacco smuggling, and expressed concern at the scale of illegal immigration. In its response, published in December 2000, some four months after the report was submitted, the government accepted the ISC recommendation that the CSI should meet annually. However, it maintained its refusal to allow the ISC access to the annexes to the Commissioners' reports.

The ISC produced an interim report in March 2001, in anticipation of the calling of a general election, marking the final contributions of a majority of the Committee, including chairman Tom King. The report once again criticized the government over the failure of the CSI to meet, despite a government commitment that it would do so, leading the ISC to reiterate that it believed that, 'it is important for the senior cabinet ministers to be properly briefed on the overall performance of the Agencies and we repeat our recommendation that CSI meets at least annually to review this'.[29] Elsewhere, it reiterated its disappointment in the government's refusal to publish fuller agency budget figures (in its response the government again declined), and continued to press for the creation of an employment Tribunal capable of hearing the grievances of agency staff to prevent the emergence of further Tomlinsons and Shaylers, something over which the government continued to drag its feet. It again asked the government to reconsider its refusal to grant access to the Commissioners' confidential annexes, and the government again declined. In sum, the picture that emerged at the end of the Tom King era was of a Committee which had worked hard to establish itself, had evolved its own terms of reference, had gained a significant degree of trust from the agencies, had been critical of both government and agencies on occasion, and had probed government repeatedly in an attempt to secure access to a full range of information. And yet, in the nature of its responses, its handling of the reports, responses and debates, the government inevitably had the upper hand. Nevertheless, emboldened by its access to material and ability to demonstrate a safe pair of hands over the Mitrokhin affair, the ISC concluded this phase of its development by suggesting a further evolution, in which the past was not necessarily 'another country'. It concluded the interim report by warning:

> One of the characteristics of the intelligence and security field is the frequent, often sensational but unsubstantiated reports that appear in the media. The Committee takes an interest in such matters and seeks to determine which require action by the Committee. A case in point is the allegation of support for a plot to overthrow Colonel Gaddafi. We intended to report to you on this matter but are not yet fully in a position to do so. We believe that the Committee's Report on the Mitrokhin Archive demonstrated our competence in this area, providing an objective view of events with conclusions and recommendations for future work and any necessary changes.[30]

This would represent a significant expansion of the ISC's role, and it remained to be seen whether the significant personnel changes in the wake of the 2001 general election would affect this determination.

The ISC under Ann Taylor, 2001–05

Following the 2001 general election, the government appointed a new ISC in August comprising five new members and chaired by one of these, Ann Taylor, a former Labour Chief Whip. It produced its first annual report in May 2002, covering the security and intelligence environment in the aftermath of the attacks of 11 September 2001 (9/11). In it the ISC again pointed to the fact that the CSI had still to meet, although the Prime Minister had convened ad hoc meetings of a similar composition after 9/11. On the question of the 9/11 attacks, a significantly redacted section of the report showed that, prior to 9/11, Afghanistan had not been a high priority for the agencies. As the Foreign Secretary, Jack Straw, told the ISC, 'the West [had] essentially walked away from Afghanistan, we are trying to get it back'.[31] A joint summit of US and UK intelligence agencies had spent time discussing Osama bin Laden prior to 9/11, but he remained a 'hard target' for the agencies, with a specific lack of intelligence on his thinking:

> A JIC [Joint Intelligence Committee] assessment in July 2001 suggested that UBL [Usama bin Laden] organised attacks were in their final stages of preparation. While US or Israeli interests were the most likely targets, UK interests were at risk, including from collateral damage in attacks on US targets. This lack of intelligence access to a notably hard target meant that the UK and the US did not know who was going to carry out the attacks, how the attacks were going to be mounted or where the attacks were going to take place. Up to that point the West had not foreseen suicide attacks taking place on the USA mainland and certainly not that the attacks would result in some 3,000 deaths, including the single greatest loss of UK citizens' lives to terrorist attack.[32]

Was this an intelligence failure? The Committee was guardedly ambivalent. The agencies had recognized that there was a 'pressing need' to gather intelligence on bin Laden and ministers had been told that this was in hand; a July 2001 JIC paper had correctly assessed that planning for attacks on Western targets was in the final stages, although it did not present this as a 'stark warning' of a threat to the UK; the conjunction of these facts and bin Laden's track record, 'could have warned all concerned that more urgent action was needed to counter this threat'. It concluded that, with hindsight, 'the scale of the threat and the vulnerability of Western states to terrorists with this degree of sophistication and a total disregard for their own lives was not understood'.[33] The government's response, drawn up with agency input, defended the agencies' record in relation to the threat from Al Qaeda, declined to make a commitment to follow the ISC's strong and repeated recommendation that the CSI meet at least annually, and continued to refuse to allow the ISC access to the confidential annexes to the Commissioners' reports. At this point, the ISC threw in the towel on the question of access to the annexes. If it believed, as it said it did, that access to these was necessary for it to fulfil its mandate, it now appeared to be settling for partial fulfilment of that mandate.

In October 2002 the ISC was asked by the Foreign Secretary to undertake an inquiry into the adequacy of warnings prior to the Bali bombings of that month which killed 190 people, including 24 Britons. Its report was critical of the threat assessment produced by MI5. It concluded that MI5 made a 'serious misjudgement' and failed to 'assess the threat correctly' in not raising the threat level from 'significant' (the third highest level on a six-point scale) to 'high' (the second, behind 'imminent'). At the same time, it reassured Parliament and public that, on the basis of the available intelligence, the attacks could not have been prevented. However, the implication was clear: MI5's threat assessment had been wrong. The ISC also suggested the addition of a further level between 'significant' and 'high' to, 'allow the threat to be better described for the recipients of the Security Service assessments'. As in response to the previous annual report, the government's response included a staunch defence of the agencies and a rejection of the ISC's conclusion that the threat level should have been higher at the time of the bombings. Nevertheless, it also revealed that, as a result of a Security Service review rather than ISC recommendations, 'threat level definitions have been reworked to give greater definition between levels, to make them more informative to customers and to better support the selection of appropriate protective measures'.[34] Similarly, it revealed the establishment of the Joint Terrorism Analysis Centre (JTAC), an evolution from the multi-agency Counter-Terrorist Analysis Centre established after 9/11.

The ISC's 2002–03 annual report was published in June 2003, in the wake of both the 2003 Iraq war and the controversial case for war presented to the public by Prime Minister Tony Blair and senior Cabinet members. Again, it took up the fact that the Prime Minister had declined to convene a meeting of the CSI despite the repeated strong recommendations of the Committee, offering its opinion that 'CSI Ministers are not sufficiently engaged in the setting of requirements and priorities for secret intelligence, nor do they all see the full capability of intelligence collection'.[35] Bizarrely, the government's response was to agree 'that CSI has an important function especially in relation to the resourcing and future prioritization of the Agencies' work, and should meet when appropriate to consider this work'.[36] In reality, the Prime Minister had given no indication that he attached any importance whatsoever to either the CSI or the ISC's continual highlighting of its failure to meet. However, on 18 December 2003, some eight years after its previous meeting, the CSI finally met, although it was not to be the beginning of the regular series of meetings that the ISC strongly recommended.

The Committee reported separately, in September 2003, on the question of pre-war UK intelligence on Iraq's WMD, which had been fundamental to the Prime Minister's case for war in Iraq. In March 2001, Tom King had warned that 'we must remember that intelligence can be wasted, ignored – especially if it does not accord with the prejudices and preconceptions of the person on whose desk it falls – used for the wrong purposes or misdirected. The Committee exists to monitor those matters and to try to ensure that mistakes are not made'.[37] The corollary of this was that intelligence could be exaggerated. This was the charge levelled at Prime Minister Tony Blair in relation to his case for war with Iraq. This also represented the kind of controversial issue that for some observers would represent a litmus test of the ISC's ability to hold the agencies to account and deal objectively with an issue of great political sensitivity. How would the ISC respond to this?

The ISC sought 'to examine whether the available intelligence, which informed the decision to invade Iraq, was adequate and properly assessed and whether it was accurately reflected in Government publications'.[38] It did not consider the decision to go to war *per se*. It reported four months later that, based on the intelligence it had seen, 'there was convincing intelligence that Iraq had active chemical, biological and nuclear programmes and the capability to produce chemical and biological weapons'. At the heart of the controversy over pre-war intelligence on Iraq was a dossier produced by Downing Street in September 2002 and containing intelligence cleared by JIC chairman John Scarlett.[39] In its 2002–03 annual report, the ISC had noted this and said that it 'supports the responsible use of intelligence and material collected by the Agencies to inform the public on matters such as these'. The question here, then, was how far this represented responsible use of the material, and how far it informed the public as opposed to misled them. However, the ISC did not rise to the challenge, offering no commentary on evidence that the political case was in advance of the intelligence case for war. For example, in a draft of Tony Blair's Foreword to the dossier, it was acknowledged that there was no threat of nuclear attack on the UK, but this had been excluded from the published version. This denied the public available reassurance, removed an opportunity to bring some context to bear, and served to heighten the sense of threat posed by Iraq. In a tame criticism, the ISC contented itself with observing that: 'It was unfortunate that this point was removed from the published version of the foreword and not highlighted elsewhere.'[40]

The government's response was a further stage in the presentational game that had begun in earnest with the September 2002 dossier itself. It emphasized those aspects of the ISC report that appeared to support its conduct over the production of the dossier, and rejected its criticisms. For example, with regard to the charge that the dossier was misleading, its response was that:

> the dossier did present a balanced view of Iraq's CBW capability based on the intelligence available. The dossier made clear (paragraph 14, page 16) that the withdrawal of the United Nations Special Commission (UNSCOM) had greatly diminished the ability of the international community to monitor and assess Iraq's continued efforts to reconstitute its programmes. It also noted (paragraph 13, page 16) that UNSCOM was unable to account for significant quantities of agents, precursors and munitions.[41]

But the government could not have it both ways. Either – as this and the objective record both suggested – the intelligence picture on Iraq was characterized by a significant degree of uncertainty, or, as Tony Blair wrote in his Foreword to the dossier, it was known that

Iraq represented a 'current and serious threat to the UK national interest'. The ISC was dissatisfied with the government's response, as it 'emphasised only four key conclusions while either rejecting or failing to address fully many of our other conclusions and recommendations. We regard this as extremely unsatisfactory . . . Our dissatisfaction was increased by the Government's decision to allow such little time for parliamentary debate' on its Iraq and annual reports.[42] As a result, the government response to the 2003–04 annual report began a practice of responding to each of the ISC's conclusions individually. However, it did not deal directly with the core question, simply stating, 'we regret that the Committee found [the] response unsatisfactory'.[43] This did not amount to effective oversight. Key questions had gone unanswered, and the ISC had effectively run out of options in the face of the government's refusal to engage with it. Its investigation had been limited, its findings dismissed by government, and its credibility damaged.

Moreover, it emerged that, although the ISC had stated that it had seen all JIC assessments on Iraq produced between August 1990 and September 2002, and the eight produced in the period October 2002 to March 2003, in fact eight had been withheld – five from the former period, three from the latter. While the Committee was 'satisfied that knowledge of them would not have led us to change the conclusions, including those that were critical, in our Report',[44] earlier access would have allowed it to include further material, and their conclusions would have been more securely rooted in a fuller picture.

Read in the context of the steady spread of democratic oversight of intelligence in the last 30 years, one thing is very striking about ISC reports published before 2005 – the complete absence of explicit reference to human rights. In 2005, however, the ISC reported on an issue at the heart of the 'global war on terror': the treatment of those detained in Afghanistan, Guantánamo Bay and Iraq. Paying careful attention to its own boundaries, the ISC investigated any involvement in or witnessing of abuse by intelligence personnel, the adequacy of training as to what to do if it was witnessed, and when ministers were informed of any concerns. Its report rehearsed the relevant conventions on treatment of prisoners, noting that the US did not regard those detained in Afghanistan as covered by them. The substance of the report was taken up with cases in which intelligence personnel reported their concerns at the treatment of detainees by US personnel, found that these were relatively few (less than 15 out of over 2,000 interviews witnessed), criticized the lack of training of staff in Convention matters before deployment to Afghanistan, Guantánamo and Iraq, and noted that when concerns were expressed to US authorities, these were inadequately followed up.

Overall, the report does not provide adequate oversight; certainly the actions of UK soldiers lie within the remit of the Defence Select Committee and the ISC noted that a number were court-martialled, but the Committee did not even explore the issue that soldiers might have 'prepared' detainees for interrogation as US evidence shows. The ISC noted widespread concern about the use of information obtained under torture and briefly noted the pragmatic and principled arguments but did 'not attempt to answer these difficult questions'. Instead they quoted at length the Foreign Secretary's utilitarian justification for using such information if necessary. Moreover, just as revelations on Iraq subsequent to the ISC investigation left its conclusions there looking thin, so too ongoing revelations about the involvement of UK intelligence personnel in the handling and interrogation of detainees have raised questions about the reliability of this investigation.

Conclusions

In its 1997–98 annual report, the ISC recognized that:

> It is vital that public confidence is maintained in the Agencies. At times of grave national threat, their value is readily accepted. At other times, in the face of a bungled operation or security lapse, public confidence can be very fragile. That is the inevitable consequence of operating within the 'ring of secrecy', which prevents a more balanced public view of their activities and their value. The public must therefore be confident that there is adequate independent scrutiny and democratic accountability on their behalf, by people within that 'ring of secrecy'.[45]

How far has the ISC succeeded in providing this? In attempting to answer this, other questions need to be considered: what was the government's purpose in creating the ISC? Was it to provide accountability, or give the appearance of accountability and thereby satisfy growing demands for some form of accountability? Fundamentally, the ISC was set up to serve the executive, and that is what it does. Even disagreements between the ISC and executive, or examples of ISC assertion, serve the executive as they confirm the appearance of accountability and thereby dampen demands for more far-reaching accountability, or the introduction of legislative accountability through a select committee of the House of Commons.

Who guards the guardians? This question needs to be adapted slightly to ask: to whom are the oversight committee accountable? Members are accountable to the Prime Minister, and beyond this to themselves collectively and individually. There is no *parliamentary* accountability. This is significant in that the ISC has proved itself unable to be overly critical of executive failures. It can adequately monitor the financial and administrative dimensions of the agencies on behalf of the executive, but not the actions of the executive on behalf of the legislature. Part of the oversight function should be to do precisely this.

Any assessment of the ISC must consider areas of omission as well as commission. For some observers, the real test for the ISC would come when it was faced with a scandal of comparable gravity to those that had been revealed in the years prior to its establishment. While the question of politicization of intelligence has emerged as an area of central concern in the post-9/11 environment, it is an issue for which the ISC has shown no appetite. Appointed by the executive, reporting to the executive, and holding membership at the pleasure of the executive (in the majority of cases, also the party leader), it has failed to explore the question of executive responsibility.

There are other areas of omission, for example, regarding the Shayler allegations – particularly relating to his allegation that MI6 was involved in a plot to assassinate Libyan leader Muammar Gaddafi. Despite the fundamental nature of the allegations, despite some support within the ISC for undertaking an investigation, and despite the fact that Foreign Secretary Robin Cook had been willing to see the ISC investigate the lesser matter of possible Foreign Office connivance in breaking an arms embargo on Sierra Leone, the ISC has failed to address the issue and thereby offer the public the reassurance of which it spoke in its 1997–98 annual report. Issues relating to Northern Ireland have been largely absent from the ISC's published record but, in the light of the Stevens Inquiry report, continue to cause concern. Questions that the case of Katharine Gun might have raised about tasking and policy regarding espionage aimed at the UN Secretary General have been avoided.

Despite the advances made by the ISC, particularly in the years up to 2001, as it stands, the scope of intelligence accountability in the UK lags behind that of other Western democracies. It even lags behind that of the emerging eastern European democracies, such as Romania and Poland – as the ISC themselves have acknowledged. A significant component of it should be parliamentary debate, a dedicated opportunity for ISC members to speak in the chamber and offer the reassurances that their oversight function is being carried out to their satisfaction and amplifying areas of concern identified in their reports. However, full parliamentary debate was slow arriving. There was no set debate on the reports until 1998, before the events of 9/11 they were poorly attended, the early debates were held after a significant time had elapsed from the production of the relevant annual report, and when ISC members were critical of the government's response or failure to respond to specific issues they were effectively ignored.

Oversight of intelligence, whoever carries it out, is inescapably political and those conducting it must remember that they are engaged in contests of power in which the stakes are high. Shortly after the ISC was established, Peter Gill suggested that a significant indicator of its political will would be 'the struggles that take place over access to information. If there are no such battles then we would be justified in concluding that the ISC has failed to challenge central information control'.[46] There have been too few of these in the post-9/11 era – the Committee proudly records in the preface to its annual report that it has agreed all government redactions from its annual reports. An oversight committee might be expected to contest at least some of these. This state of affairs suggests a committee too deferential to the executive and too willing to accept deletions. The key area of contest with the executive – over access to the confidential annexes to the Commissioner's report – was conceded. To rebuild public and parliamentary trust post-Iraq, the ISC needs to engage in these contests over information.

There are additional limitations or weaknesses that must be considered in any assessment of the ISC. Given the environment in which it must operate, a strong chairman is essential, and in this respect it is worth noting that the elements of role enhancement mentioned in this article essentially took place under Tom King's chairmanship. It can be too easily distracted by events, particularly as it is capacity-limited and needs to choose its subjects for inquiry very carefully. In this respect, its decision to dispense with the services of its Investigator – after praising his work in successive annual reports – is very disappointing. It was clearly a reaction to his public comments concerning the Blair government's case for war in Iraq. The Committee needs to expand its investigatory and staff base rather than remove it in response to pressure, real or perceived, from agencies or executive. Moreover, there is a very real sense in which, post-9/11, the ISC's definition of its role has come to focus more on intelligence management and concern that the agencies are adequately funded at the expense of legislative oversight of the executive branch.

On a more positive note, the ISC was tasked with performing intelligence from scratch, with no more guidance as to how to go about this in practice than that provided by the bare bones of the 1994 Intelligence Services Act. It has put considerable flesh on these in the years since, expanding its remit in the process. In practice, it has also taken an interest in operational matters, despite these falling outside its remit – for example, in investigating issues relating to the Kosovo campaign, WMD proliferation, Sierra Leone, and the Mitrokhin affair. Moreover, it has introduced significant accountability with regard to the agencies' finances, previously an area of limited transparency even at ministerial level. Indeed, until 1994 there was no external auditing of the agencies' accounts. It is also undoubtedly the case that the very existence of the ISC has given the agencies cause to reflect on proposed actions in advance of undertaking them. King at one time referred to 'a tendency now within the agencies to ask what the Intelligence and Security Committee would think if they embarked on a certain course of action' and suggested that this 'could be used in the future against Ministers who want intelligence in areas that the agencies do not think fall within their remit'.[47]

Does the ISC represent a first step on the road to fuller accountability, or the best feasible balance between competing demands? During parliamentary debate on the Intelligence Services Bill MPs were divided on this point. Yet it seems inevitable that the ISC of 1994 will come to be seen as having represented a first step on the road to accountability. As such, in the wake of the division and distrust engendered by the government's presentation of its case for war in Iraq, the time is ripe for a further step, so that accountability structures retain the confidence of the public they are designed to reassure. In June 2000 ISC member Dale Campbell-Savours told the House of Commons: 'The arguments about whether the ISC is a Select Committee will simply be cast aside by history. The process is inevitable; it will happen.'[48] However, the treatment of Dr David Kelly, who committed suicide after a particularly fierce grilling by the Foreign Affairs Committee, has meant that any agency enthuasiasm for such a development has been extinguished for now. Nevertheless, it remains a necessary step for the achievement of the fullest feasible degree of accountability.

Notes

The author would like to thank Peter Gill for his comments on an earlier draft of this article.

The author would also like to thank the Praeger publishing house for allowing this article to be published here as well as in the work edited by Loch K. Johnson, *Strategic Intelligence*, 5 vols. (Westport, CT: Praeger 2007).

1 Peter Wright, *Spycatcher: The Candid Autobiography of a Senior Intelligence Officer* (New York: Viking 1987).
2 Paul Foot, *Who Framed Colin Wallace?* (London: Macmillan 1989).
3 Tony Geraghty, *The Irish War: The Military History of a Domestic Conflict* (London: HarperCollins 1998) Ch.4.
4 Richard Norton-Taylor, 'Tories block inquiries into spying past', *The Guardian*, 27 March 1995.
5 *New Statesman*, 12 December 1986, p.7.
6 John Willman, 'Secret Service Open to Scrutiny', *Financial Times*, 25 November 1993.
7 *Hansard*, 22 February 1994, col.171.
8 *Hansard*, 27 April 1994, col.351.
9 *Hansard*, 22 February 1994, col.240.
10 *Interim Report of the Intelligence and Security Committee* (ISC), Cm 2873, May 1995, para.8.
11 ISC, *Annual Report 1995*, Cm 3198, March 1996, para.7.
12 Ibid. para.37.
13 ISC, *Annual Report 1996*, Cm 3574, para.6.
14 ISC *Annual Report 1997–98*, Cm 4073, November 1998, Foreword.
15 Ibid. paras.24–38.
16 *Hansard*, 2 November 1998. col.612.
17 ISC *Annual Report 1997–98* (note 11) para.50.
18 Ibid. para.69.
19 *Hansard*, 2 November 1998, cols.596, 618.
20 Ibid. col.610.
21 *Government Response to the Intelligence and Security Committee's Annual Report 1998–99*, Cm 4569, January 2000, para.34.
22 ISC *Annual Report 1998–99*, <http://www.archive.official-documents.co.uk/document/cm45/4532/4532.htm> 2 February 2007, para.79.
23 Christopher Andrew and Vasili Mitrokhin, *The Mitrokhin Archive: The KGB in Europe and the West* (London: Allen Lane 1999). 'The SIS regarded Professor Andrew as a safe pair of hands [who] was

also security cleared and had signed the Official Secrets Act.' ISC, *The Mitrokhin Inquiry Report*, Cm 4764, June 2000, para.46.

24 Ibid. para.34.

25 Sir Stephen Lander, 'The Oversight of Security and Intelligence', speech at Royal United Services Institute, London, 15 March 2001.

26 ISC, *Mitrokhin Inquiry Report*, para.8.

27 ISC *Annual Report 1999–2000*, Cm 4897, November 2000, para.19.

28 Ibid. para.35.

29 ISC *Interim Report 2000–01*, Cm 5126, March 2001, para.15.

30 Ibid. para.34.

31 ISC *Annual Report 2001–02*, Cm 5542, June 2002, para.54.

32 Ibid. para.63.

33 Ibid. para.65.

34 *Government Response to the Intelligence and Security Committee Inquiry into Intelligence, Assessments and Advice prior to the Terrorist Bombings on Bali 12 October 2002*, Cm 5765, February 2003, para.10.

35 ISC, *Annual Report 2002–03*, Cm 5837, June 2003, para.56.

36 *Government Response to the Intelligence and Security Committee's Annual Report 2002–03*, Cm 5838, June 2003, para.10.

37 *Hansard*, 29 March 2001, col.1149.

38 ISC, *Iraqi Weapons of Mass Destruction – Intelligence and Assessments*, Cm 5972, September 2003, para.11.

39 On this, see Mark Phythian, 'Hutton and Scott: A Tale of Two Inquiries', *Parliamentary Affairs* 58/1 (January 1995) pp.124–37; Peter Gill and Mark Phythian, *Intelligence in an Insecure World* (Cambridge: Polity 2006) esp. Ch.7.

40 ISC, *Iraqi Weapons of Mass Destruction*, para.83.

41 *Government Response to ISC Report on Iraqi Weapons of Mass Destruction – Intelligence and Assessments*, Cm 6118, February 2004, para.13.

42 ISC *Annual Report 2003–04*, Cm 6240, June 2004, para.87.

43 *Government's Response to the Intelligence and Security Committee's Annual Report 2003–04*, Cm 6241, July 2004, para.P.

44 ISC, *Annual Report 2003–04* (note 37) para.146.

45 ISC *Annual Report 1997–98* (note 11) Foreword.

46 Peter Gill, 'Reasserting Control: Recent Changes in the Oversight of the UK Intelligence Community', *Intelligence and National Security* 11/2 (April 1996) p.328.

47 *Hansard*, 29 March 2001, col.1149.

48 *Hansard*, 22 June 2000, col.512.

Mark Phythian, 'The British experience with intelligence accountability', *Intelligence & National Security* 22/1 (2007) pp.75–99.

THE PROBLEMS OF OVERSIGHT AND ACCOUNTABILITY

Further reading: Books and reports

W. Michael Reisman and James E. Baker, *Regulating Covert Action, Practices, Contexts and Policies* (New Haven: Yale University Press, 1992).

Hans Born, Loch K. Johnson & Ian Leigh, (eds.) *Who's Watching the Spies? Establishing Intelligence Service Accountability* (Dulles, VA: Potomac 2005).

Hans Born & Ian Leigh, *Making Intelligence Accountable: Legal Standards and Best Practice Oversight of Intelligence Agencies* (Oslo: Publishing House of the Parliament of Norway 2005).

Peter Gill, *Policing Politics: Security Intelligence and the Liberal Democratic State* (London: Frank Cass 1994).

Peter Gill and Mark Pythian, *Intelligence in an Insecure World* (Cambridge: Polity 2006) chapter 8.

Glen P. Hastedt, (ed.) *Controlling Intelligence* (London: Frank Cass 1991).

Michael Herman, *Intelligence Power in Peace and War* (Cambridge: Cambridge University Press, 1996).

R. Jeffreys-Jones, *The CIA and American Democracy* (New Haven CT: Yale University Press, 3rd Ed 2003).

Loch K. Johnson & James J. Wirtz, *Intelligence and National Security: The Secret World of Spies* (NY: Oxford University Press, 2nd ed 2007) chapters 28–31

Sherman Kent, *Strategic Intelligence for American Foreign Policy* (Princeton: Princeton University Press, 1949).

Harold Hongju Koh, *The National Security Constitution: Sharing Power After the Iran-Contra Affair* (New Haven: Yale University Press, 1990).

Walter Laqueur, *World of Secrets: The Uses and Limits of Intelligence* (NY: Basic Books, 1985).

Mark Lowenthal, *Intelligence: From Secrets to Policy* (Washington D.C.: CQ Press, 3rd Ed 2006), chapter 10.

Lawrence Lustgarten & Ian Leigh, *In From the Cold: National Security and Democracy* (Oxford: Oxford University Press, 1994).

Abram N. Shulsky and Gary J. Schmitt, *Silent Warfare: Understanding the World of Intelligence* (Dulles, VA: Brassey's Inc., 2002) pp.131–58.

Further reading: Essays and articles

L. Britt Snyder, 'Congressional Accountability and Intelligence after September 11,' in Jennifer E. Sims, and Burton L. Gerber, (eds.) *Transforming U.S. Intelligence* (Washington, DC: Georgetown University Press, 2005) pp.239–58.

William J. Daugherty, 'Approval and Review of Covert Action Programs since Reagan.' *International Journal of Intelligence and Counterintelligence* 17/1 (2004) pp.62–80.

P Gill, 'Evaluating intelligence oversight committees: The UK Intelligence and Security Committee and the 'war on terror', *Intelligence & National Security* 22/1 (2007) pp.14–37.

Peter Gill, 'Reasserting Control: Recent Changes in the Oversight of the UK Intelligence. Community', *Intelligence and National Security* 11/2 (1996) pp.313–31.

Peter Gill, 'Symbolic or Real? The Impact of the Canadian Security Intelligence Review Committee, 1984–88?', *Intelligence and National Security* 4/3 (1989) pp.550–75.

Anthony Glees & Philip H.J. Davies. 'Intelligence, Iraq and the Limits of Legislative Accountability during Political Crisis,' *Intelligence and National Security* 21/5 (2006) pp.848–883.

M. Head, 'ASIO, Secrecy and Lack of Accountability', *E-Law: Murdoch University Electronic Journal of Law*, 11/4 (December 2004).

A. Hulnick, 'Openness: Being Public About Secret Intelligence.' *International Journal of Intelligence and Counterintelligence* (1999), 12/4, pp.463–483.

L Johnson, 'The CIA and the Question of Accountability', *Intelligence and National Security* 12/1 (1997) pp.178–200

L. Johnson, 'Accountability and America's Secret Foreign Policy: Keeping a Legislative Eye on the Central Intelligence Agency', *Foreign Policy Analysis* 1/1 (2005) pp.99–120.

S.F. Knott, 'The Great Republican Transformation on Oversight', *International Journal of Intelligence and Counterintelligence* 13/1 (2000) pp.49–63.

H. P. Lee, 'The Australian Security Intelligence Organisation: New Mechanisms for Accountability', *The International and Comparative Law Quarterly* 38/4 (1989) pp.890–905

Lawrence Lustgarten, 'Security Services, Constitutional Structure, and the Varieties of Accountability in Canada and Australia,' in Philip Stenning (ed.), *Accountability for Criminal Justice* (Toronto: University of Toronto Press 1995) pp.162–184.

Lawrence Lustgarten, 'Accountability of Security Services in Western Democracies,' in Dennis Tollborg (ed.), *National Security and the Law: The Gothenburg Symposium 1997* (Gotborgs: Centrum for Europaforskning, Gotborgs Universitet, 1997) pp.53–79.

F.F. Manget, 'Another System of Oversight: Intelligence and the Rise of Judicial Intervention,' *Studies in Intelligence* 39/5 (1996) pp.43–50.

M.C. Ott, 'Partisanship and the Decline of Intelligence Oversight,' *International Journal of Intelligence and Counterintelligence* 16/1 (2003) pp.69–94.

Mark Phythian, 'Still a Matter of Trust: Post-9/11 British Intelligence and Political Culture', *International Journal of Intelligence and CounterIntelligence* 18/4 (2005) pp.653–81.

Mark Phythian, 'The British experience with intelligence accountability', *Intelligence & National Security* 22/1 (2007) pp.75–99.

Roy Rempel, 'Canada's Parliamentary Oversight of Security and Intelligence,' *International Journal of Intelligence and Counterintelligence* 17/4 (2004) pp.634–54.

K.G. Robertson, 'Recent Reform of Intelligence in the UK,' *Intelligence and National Security* 13/2 (1999) pp.144–59.

Frederick A.O. Schwarz, 'The Church Committee and a New Era of Intelligence Oversight,' *Intelligence and National Security* 22/2 (2007) pp.270–297.

Matthew B. Walker, 'Reforming Congressional Oversight of Intelligence.' *International Journal of Intelligence and Counterintelligence* 19/4 (2006–7) pp.702–720

Geoffrey R. Weller, 'Oversight of Australia's Intelligence Services', *International Journal of Intelligence and CounterIntelligence* 12/4 (1999) pp.484–503.

R. Whitaker, 'The Politics of Security Intelligence Policy-making in Canada: I 1970–84', *Intelligence and National Security* 6/4 (1992) pp.649–68.

R. Whitaker, 'The Politics of Security Intelligence Policy-making in Canada: II 1984–91', *Intelligence and National Security* 7/2 (1992) pp.53–76.

R. Whitaker, 'The "Bristow Affair": A Crisis of Accountability in Canadian Security Intelligence', *Intelligence and National Security* 11/2 (1996) pp.279–305.

The journal *Parliamentary Affairs* also devoted much of issue 58/1 (2005) to essays on the Hutton enquiry.

Essay questions

- 'Serious abuses are almost always uncovered by whistleblowers, journalists and freebooting researchers. Accountability committees only examine things that do not need examination.' Discuss.
- 'The first rule of a secret service is that it should be secret. Democratic control is incompatible with this.' Discuss.
- Compare and contrast the systems of accountability employed by at least two English-speaking states. [Possibilities include UK, US, Canada, Australia and New Zealand]
- Consider the structure and functions of the UK Intelligence and Security Committee. Comment on its effectiveness and suggest ways in which it might be improved.

20 Domestic intelligence and civil liberties

Kate Martin

Since September 11, domestic intelligence authorities and technical capabilities have been expanded to fight terrorism. There are calls to substitute an 'intelligence' paradigm for a 'law enforcement' paradigm in domestic counterterrorism efforts and proposals to establish a new domestic intelligence agency. While better information and analysis is needed to fight terrorism, there is reason to fear that transforming domestic counterterrorism primarily into an intelligence matter is unlikely to appreciably increase security, but will seriously threaten civil liberties. This article outlines an alternative approach that will serve to obtain the intelligence necessary to prevent catastrophic attacks without compromising civil liberties.

The terrible attacks of September 11 have been described as the worst U.S. intelligence failure since Pearl Harbor.[1] In their wake Congress and the Bush administration have expanded domestic intelligence powers and shifted institutional responsibilities for intelligence gathering inside the United States. There are now calls for further changes, including proposals to create a new 'domestic intelligence agency.'

While there is a general consensus that better information and analysis is needed to fight terrorism, there is reason to fear that many of these changes – in particular, transforming domestic counterterrorism primarily into an intelligence matter and expanding the legal authorities for 'domestic intelligence' – are unlikely to appreciably increase security, but instead will threaten civil liberties. An intelligence-centered approach ignores the continuing importance of law enforcement measures to disable potential terrorists, increases the potential for serious abuses of power, and does not address the real problems highlighted by the intelligence failures before September 11. This article will outline an alternative approach that would serve to obtain the intelligence necessary to prevent catastrophic attacks without compromising civil liberties.

Civil liberties risks inherent in domestic intelligence

Domestic intelligence activities – the secret collection of information by a government on its own citizens and residents – have always posed a serious threat to individual liberty and to constitutional government. (On the other hand, intelligence gathering to assess the vulnerabilities of domestic infrastructures, one of the tasks of the new Department of Homeland Security, does not pose risks to civil liberties.) There is virtually no domestic intelligence agency, including MI5 in Great Britain, untainted by scandal, political spying and dirty tricks, activities that threaten not only individual rights, but the proper functioning of democratic government. In 1976, the Church Committee documented and catalogued the abuses committed by the FBI, CIA and other intelligence agencies against

Americans: violations of and lack of regard for the law; overbroad domestic intelligence activity; excessive use of intrusive techniques; use of covert action to disrupt and discredit domestic groups; political abuse of intelligence information; inadequate controls on dissemination and retention of information about individuals; and deficiencies in control and accountability.[2]

Risks to civil liberties are inherent in the very nature of domestic intelligence. This is because intelligence necessarily operates in secret and, as a result, it is exceedingly difficult to subject intelligence activities to the checks and balances that the Framers of the Constitution understood as essential to prevent abuses of power. Secrecy operates to make congressional oversight less vigorous than usual, even though it is needed in this case to compensate for the lack of the usual forms of public scrutiny over government activity. In addition, the Executive Branch has been very successful in arguing that judicial review of intelligence activities should be extremely deferential and limited, even when constitutional rights are at stake.[3] Perhaps the greatest barrier to strong oversight and accountability is the always-present notion that the interest served by the intelligence agencies – national security – is of paramount concern and always outweighs other interests. While the overriding importance of national security may be true as a general proposition, what is required in any specific situation is an analysis of the competing interests at stake.

The 'wall' between law enforcement and intelligence

Since September 11, government officials have frequently cited the existence of a 'wall' between law enforcement and intelligence as the main reason the CIA and FBI didn't find the September 11 hijackers. They claim that legal obstacles prevented law enforcement and intelligence agencies from sharing vital information about suspected terrorists. The Justice Department made this argument when it sought the repeal of key safeguards against abuse of surveillance authorities as part of the Patriot Act. But this 'wall' metaphor is inaccurate and the existence of legal barriers to sharing information is highly exaggerated. Such talk is used to obscure bureaucratic failures of coordination and communication between the FBI and CIA, as well as inside each agency.

The term 'wall' is shorthand for reforms adopted following the Church Committee revelations of intelligence abuses to implement fundamental principles limiting government surveillance of Americans. Those reforms proceeded from the recognition that there are important consequences for individuals depending on the government's purpose in initiating surveillance; in particular whether it intends to use the fruits of its surveillance against the individual to prosecute and jail him. The reforms incorporated the teaching of the Fourth Amendment, which states that the best protection against abuse of surveillance powers is to require the government to have some indication of criminal activity before investigating an individual. This principle also reflects the understanding that the essence of liberty is to be left alone by one's government. Accordingly, the government is limited as to when it can act against its citizens, and therefore may only punish individuals for acts, not thoughts. Moreover, requiring some criminal predicate for government investigations helps protect citizens from being targeted based on dissent, religion, or ethnicity, and helps to ensure that surveillance and intelligence are not used for political purposes. Foreign intelligence gathering, the collection of information that policymakers need concerning the capabilities and intentions of foreign governments and groups, however, is not linked to a criminal predicate. The distinction between the two – investigating possible wrong-doing by individuals and spying on foreign powers – is the fundamental rationale for separating the functions of law enforcement and intelligence agencies.

Indeed, to protect civil liberties and guard against the creation of a Gestapo-like agency, the CIA's original charter, the 1947 National Security Act, prohibited the agency from exercising any 'police, subpoena, law-en-forcement powers, or internal security functions.' But this early attempt to prevent the CIA from spying on Americans was not enforced through any law or oversight mechanism, and in fact the intelligences agencies did engage in widespread political spying. The Defense Department's description of how DOD intelligence and counterintelligence units came to spy on Americans in the 1960s and 1970s is instructive:

> What had occurred was a classic example of what we would today call 'mission creep.' What had begun as a simple requirement to provide basic intelligence to [military] commanders [in the United States] charged with assisting in the maintenance and restoration of order, had become a monumentally intrusive effort. This resulted in the monitoring of activities of innocent persons involved in the constitutionally protected expression of their views on civil rights or anti-war activities. The information collected on the persons targeted by Defense intelligence personnel was entered into a national data bank and made available to civilian law enforcement authorities. This produced a chilling effect on political expression by those who were legally working for political change in domestic and foreign policies.[4]

The reforms undertaken since the 1970s to prevent such abuses have been misunderstood as creating a so-called 'wall' between law enforcement and intelligence. In particular, the rules governing surveillance and retention of data on Americans, along with the efforts to confine the CIA to intelligence-gathering overseas, have been faulted.

In fact, there were separate authorities written to govern law enforcement and foreign intelligence investigations in the United States, but those authorities did not erect a 'wall' between the two. In particular, since 1978, wiretapping to investigate crimes has been governed by one federal statute, while the Foreign Intelligence Surveillance Act (FISA), governs wiretapping agents of a foreign power inside the United States for the purpose of gathering foreign intelligence. Similarly, the Attorney General's Guidelines governing FBI activities, written by Attorney General Levi in 1976 and since amended, provided one set of rules for criminal investigations and another for gathering foreign intelligence relating to espionage or international terrorism inside the United States. These authorities allowed the government much wider latitude in gathering information about Americans and keeping it secret for foreign intelligence purposes. This latitude is greater than that which is allowed for law enforcement purposes. They also provided much less judicial oversight in the gathering of information for foreign intelligence purposes than for criminal investigations.

The post-Church Committee reforms also attempted to enforce the original intent of the CIA's charter by severely limiting the agency's domestic operations. New regulations confined the CIA largely to gathering foreign intelligence abroad regarding the intentions and capabilities of foreign powers for policymakers. The FBI was given both law enforcement and intelligence responsibilities inside the United States, specifically for counter-espionage and international terrorism investigations using FISA and other authorities.

This difference in functions is important from the standpoint of civil liberties. The CIA acts overseas, in secret, and its mission includes violating the laws of the country in which it is operating when necessary. It is charged with collecting information overseas without regard to individual privacy, rights against self-incrimination, or requirements for admissibility of evidence. It is also tasked with carrying out covert actions to influence events by whatever means the President authorizes. The agency gives the highest priority to protection of its sources and methods. In contrast, the FBI's law enforcement efforts involve the collection of information for use as evidence at trial, and its methods and informants are quite likely to be publicly identified. Perhaps most significantly, law enforcement agencies, unlike intelligence agencies, must *always* operate within the law of whatever jurisdiction in which they are operating.

Similarly, there are important differences between government investigations for foreign intelligence purposes and those for law enforcement purposes. The constitutional concerns for Fourth Amendment due process and First Amendment rights of Americans and others located inside U.S. borders do not extend to aliens overseas and thus place fewer restrictions on government activity abroad than at home. (An intelligence agency collecting information overseas for use by policymakers has less opportunity to improperly use that information against individuals than does a police agency working with prosecutors.) While the task of foreign intelligence is to learn as much as possible to provide analyses to policymakers, deep-seated notions of privacy rooted in the Constitution limit the information the government may collect and keep about Americans.[5]

Recognizing the difference between law enforcement and intelligence objectives is especially important in terrorism investigations – both to protect civil liberties and to ensure effective investigations. Terrorism, unlike organized crime for example, raises problems concerning the intersection between protected First Amendment rights and alleged criminal activity. It is always difficult to investigate planned terrorist activity without targeting those who may share the religious or political beliefs or the ethnic backgrounds of the terrorists, but do not engage in criminal activity. It is easier for an agency to identify those who share the political goals or religious fanaticism of terrorists than to identify and locate those actually plotting harm. It is therefore crucial to structure bureaucratic rules and incentives to discourage investigations based on political and religious activities and to require focusing on finding actual terrorists. An important means for doing this is to require agencies to focus on criminal activity, which encompasses all terrorist plotting and financing, rather than authorizing an intelligence approach that absorbs all available information about thousands of individuals in the hope of finding something useful.

Indeed, for years before September 11, there was disagreement between civil libertarians and the Justice Department over whether its 'intelligence' investigations of terrorism – of right-wing militias and anti-abortion groups, for example – ranged too far in targeting First Amendment-protected activity. Civil libertarians argued that rules that require investigations to be tied to some reasonable indication of planned terrorist activity not only serve to protect against government abuse of individual liberties, but also help to focus bureaucratic resources on true threats.[6]

While the pre-September 11 framework assumed differences between law enforcement and intelligence, everyone, including the civil liberties community, always recognized the necessity of effective coordination between the intelligence community and law enforcement to fight terrorism.[7] Indeed, for all the talk of a 'wall,' the pre-September 11 legal regime acknowledged that terrorism – like espionage, and to a lesser extent international narcotics trafficking – is both a law enforcement and intelligence matter. Much work had been done on the legal issues raised by the necessity of close coordination between agencies whose job is to collect critical intelligence by illegal spying abroad if necessary, and by agencies seeking to prosecute individuals within a system of law. The original drafters of the FISA in 1978 specifically provided for a situation in which foreign intelligence gathering uncovers evidence of a crime warranting prosecution. In addition, the long-standing concerns of the intelligence community about exposing sources and methods in criminal prosecutions were addressed by crafting procedures to reconcile the need for secrecy and the constitutional requirements of public trials and disclosure of relevant evidence.[8] (The only prosecution derailed by these requirements in the Classified Information Procedures Act was one of a CIA officer charged with lying to Congress in the Iran Contra affair.[9])

Better coordination or substituting 'intelligence' for 'law enforcement'?

Despite the recognition of the need for coordination between law enforcement and intelligence, there have been many difficulties and failures of communication and planning among agencies. Some difficulties are bound to arise when more than one agency has counterterrorism responsibilities. Such expected difficulties were further compounded by bureaucratic rivalries and perhaps incompetencies.

The September 11 attacks dramatically highlighted these problems. But since then, there has been inadequate consideration of how to increase the necessary cooperation United States and collaboration between agencies operating overseas and those operating in the and between foreign intelligence gathering and criminal prosecutions. Instead, both Congress and the Bush Administration have resorted to a rhetorical demand for more 'intelligence' and blamed the 'wall' for whatever agency failures contributed to the attacks. But the most serious pre-September 11 failures – the CIA's lack of a timely warning to the FBI that two known associates of Al Qaeda were in the United States, the FBI's lack of follow-up to the Phoenix memo, as well as other mistakes – were not caused by any of the safeguards imposed after the 1970s on national security surveillance.[10] Nothing in the pre-September 11 law prevented the CIA from informing the FBI that the suspected terrorists had entered the United States, and nothing would have prevented the FBI from pursuing them.

Instead of focusing on this truly difficult, yet essential task of coordination, many have simply argued that there needs to be a shift from a law enforcement paradigm to an intelligence paradigm with a focus on preventing rather than solving crimes. This formulation, however, is based on faulty assumptions, and substitutes rhetoric for analysis. As the FBI points out, it has always been in the business of preventing terrorist attacks and it had some notable successes before September 11, such as the foiled plot to blow up the Holland Tunnel in New York in 1993. Rather than pose a falsely rigid dichotomy between law enforcement and intelligence, it is necessary to examine how intelligence information is actually used in counterterrorism.

The first use of 'intelligence' information is to identify and locate individuals involved in planning terrorist acts. This information must then be used to prevent the attack, in ways that are legally permissible (for the purposes of this discussion) inside the United States. Potential terrorists found in the United States may be placed under intensive surveillance. They may be apprehended if there is probable cause that they are engaged in criminal activity, have been in the past, or are in the United States in violation of the immigration laws. They may be arrested not only for plotting terrorism, including attempt or conspiracy, but for any crime or visa violation. The government may also attempt to turn them into informants on their associates (with or without arresting them). Ultimately, in order to disable individuals from future terrorist activity, they have to be arrested and prosecuted. Such 'prevention' through prosecution has remained one of the government's major anti-terrorism tools even since September 11. Such an approach focuses on individuals involved in planning criminal activities and ultimately relies on law enforcement authorities.[11]

The talk of re-focusing domestic anti-terrorism efforts as an 'intelligence' activity, rather than a law enforcement effort using intelligence information, raises the disturbing specter of a different approach to prevention. The methods used by the CIA and foreign intelligence agencies to 'disable' terrorists – predator drones shooting missiles at a car crossing the desert; turning individuals over without any legal proceedings to intelligence services infamous for coercive interrogations; or indefinitely detaining individuals incommunicado without any legal process – have never been deemed constitutional or appropriate to use against individuals in the United States. Even absent military hostilities, overseas intelligence methods include disruption of groups and harassment of individuals using agent provocateurs, blackmail or other means, which would be illegal in the United States.

While the morality and legality of employing such methods overseas was debated before September 11 and depends in part on the particular circumstances, (such as the existence of an armed conflict) no reasonable voices advocated their use domestically.[12] But since September 11, the rhetoric of intelligence and prevention has already been invoked to justify measures that were virtually unthinkable before. The President ordered the military detention of two U.S. citizens and one non-citizen arrested in the United States without charge or trial as 'enemy combatants.' They are being denied access to legal counsel and held incommunicado, on the grounds that it is necessary to do so in order to interrogate them for 'intelligence' purposes. One of the key justifications for the President's November 13, 2001 order authorizing secret military detention and trial of suspected 'terrorist' aliens is the need to protect intelligence sources and methods. The Justice Department defended its refusal to release the names of hundreds of individuals who were jailed after the attacks but were never charged with terrorism by claiming the names were part of a larger intelligence 'mosaic.'[13] There is every reason to fear that the Administration's insistence on describing the domestic counterterrorism task as an 'intelligence' one is a back door effort to construct a new approach that would allow the use of 'intelligence' and military methods against individuals, including citizens, found in the United States and fully protected by the Constitution.

The U.S. Patriot Act and other surveillance measures

The push to expand domestic intelligence authorities began within days of the September 11 attacks, long before any examination of whether insufficient surveillance powers had played any part in the pre-September 11 failures. In the Patriot Act, Congress and the Bush administration first repealed the most important check against abuse of FISA surveillance, and then required wholesale sharing of information on Americans with the CIA with virtually no safeguards.

In seeking the Patriot Act, the administration complained that FISA barred the sharing of information with prosecutors and law enforcement investigators. They asked Congress to repeal its fundamental requirement that FISA's secret and extraordinary procedures be used only when the government's primary purpose is to collect foreign intelligence. Before September 11, it was understood that if the government started out with the primary purpose of making a criminal case against an individual, it must use the criminal surveillance authorities, not FISA.[14] In the Patriot Act, the administration sought to allow the use of FISA's extraordinary powers when the government targets an individual for criminal prosecution or otherwise.

Contrary to the administration's assertion, however, there was no statutory prohibition on sharing information prior to September 11, and FISA information had been used in many criminal cases. To the extent that the administration believed that legal rather than bureaucratic obstacles existed to sharing information, Congress could have adequately addressed the problem simply by providing that FISA information could be shared with law enforcement personnel, a provision proposed by Senator Leahy and included in the final Act (section 505). But Congress went much further and acceded to the administration's request to repeal the requirement that foreign intelligence gathering be the primary purpose when initiating FISA surveillance.

In doing so, Congress simply ignored that FISA authorizes broader surveillance on less probable cause of criminal activity than is authorized by the Fourth Amendment in criminal investigations. Moreover, FISA contains many fewer safeguards against abuse because there is no post surveillance check on either the legality of the initial warrant or on how the surveillance was conducted. Americans targeted by FISA wiretaps or searches of their homes are never told of those searches unless they are subsequently criminally indicted and the government tries to use the fruits of the searches against them. Even then, unlike with a criminal warrant, there is no opportunity for an adversarial judicial review of the adequacy and legality of the search, because the original application for a FISA warrant, unlike a criminal warrant application, is always withheld from the target.[15]

The Patriot Act also increases the domestic intelligence authority of the CIA. It gives the Director of Central Intelligence a role in identifying which Americans to target for FISA wiretaps and secret searches. It requires that vast amounts of information gathered on Americans by criminal investigators be turned over to intelligence agencies, but fails to enact any safeguards on the use or dissemination of this information. In particular, the Patriot Act requires the Attorney General to turn over to the Director of Central Intelligence all 'foreign intelligence information' obtained in any criminal investigation, including the most sensitive grand jury information and wiretap intercepts. Over the objections of civil liberties groups and some Democratic senators, the administration refused to limit this mandatory sharing to information related to international terrorism or to intelligence officials with counterterrorism responsibilities. Instead, the Act requires the Justice Department to give the CIA *all* information relating to any American's contacts or activities involving any foreign government, organization, or individual, and sets no standards or safeguards for use of this information. Such an approach will be counter-productive in identifying useful information for counterterrorism purposes. Its only purpose would seem to be to facilitate the construction of a vast intelligence database on Americans.

Following the Patriot Act, in May 2002, the Attorney General amended the guidelines governing FBI criminal investigations inside the United States to eliminate the requirement that the FBI must be investigating a past or planned crime or criminal conspiracy before it may collect information on the lawful political or religious activities of Americans. (This requirement had not applied to FBI 'foreign intelligence' investigations.) Thus, the FBI is now authorized to go into mosques and churches without identifying themselves, and collect information on Americans worshipping there. On the slightest hint of a connection to a foreign church or government, the FBI is required to share that information with the CIA, which is free to include it in any secret databases.

Total information awareness: Data-mining as counterterrorism

In addition to changes in the law since September 11, massive efforts are underway to increase government data-mining capabilities. These efforts are also rooted in an intelligence paradigm rather than a law enforcement one.

In addition to attempting to recruit informants in terrorist groups, there are two fundamentally different strategies that can be used to identify and locate dangerous individuals in the United States and their sources of financing. One approach, based on an 'intelligence' paradigm, is data-mining: the 'suspicion-less investigation' of large groups of people, through the use of linked computerized databases, pattern analysis software like the Total Information Awareness program, and the creation of a 'terrorist profile.'

The alternative approach, based on a 'law enforcement' paradigm, is both more effective and much less threatening to individual privacy and liberty. It involves following the leads from the voluminous information the government possesses about actual terrorists. Today, the U.S. government knows the identity of thousands of individuals associated with al Qaeda.[16] (Indeed, it knew the identities of many of them even before September 11, including at least two of the hijackers.) It has seized scores of documents, computer hard drives and other information from terrorists in Afghanistan and around the world. According to press accounts citing official sources, the government is obtaining important information from interrogating individuals held in captivity. Effective counterterrorism requires following every one of those leads, by tracing the associates, contacts, and activities of each one of those individuals, as well as all of their financial transactions and their travel records. It requires using all available databases and technological resources to follow the leads, including the most intrusive kinds of surveillance where authorized. This is obviously an enormous job, requiring resources, patience, analysis, and thoroughness. It is made more difficult and time consuming because much of the information is likely to be located overseas, in a language other than English. Nonetheless, it is likely to be the most effective means of preventing terrorist attacks.

Such an approach could be used to investigate all the individuals who traveled to Afghanistan before September 11, when the Taliban and al Qaeda were running training camps there, and to follow up on their associates and activities. It would require reading and analyzing the volumes of information seized from the first World Trade Center bombers, reportedly untouched by the FBI before September 11.

Following leads based on individualized suspicion tied to a person's activities and contacts would likely have uncovered, at least in part, the network of September 11 conspirators. Using such an approach before September 11, the FBI could have followed up on the infamous Phoenix memo by looking at various students in flight schools, investigating their backgrounds and associations, and probing their connections with legitimate airlines. Before September 11, the FBI and CIA knew two of the hijackers as suspected terrorists who had attended an al Qaeda meeting in Malaysia. The CIA knew that those individuals successfully entered the United States and the agency eventually informed the FBI. Neither agency put out an all-points bulletin to locate the men.

But the current effort to increase technological capabilities to electronically access data about the details of everyone's life, and to examine all this data looking for 'potential terrorists,' is tied to an intelligence rather than law enforcement approach. There is a push to create a comprehensive networked system that would include linked databases containing a biometric identifier for all individuals and virtually all available information about them.

The Defense Department's controversial Total Information Awareness program, renamed Terrorist Information Awareness (TIA) is typical; it views entire communities rather than specific individuals as potentially suspect.[17]

In fact, the government, and in particular the intelligence community, already has access to vast amounts of information that could be included in any such database. The Patriot Act gave the FBI the authority to secretly subpoena any private database on individuals simply on the assertion that such database is needed 'to protect against international terrorism or clandestine intelligence activities.'[18] This was followed in May 2002, by an order from the Attorney General authorizing the FBI to use commercial data mining services to access commercial databases, which contain myriad details on hundreds of millions of Americans, including credit histories.[19] Apparently the FBI does so regularly.[20] In 2002, Congress also required airlines to provide the government with departure and arrival manifests for all passengers, including U.S. citizens, information that can now be used to create a permanent database of all overseas travel by Americans.[21] Moreover, in the course of several programs to interview non-citizens from Middle Eastern countries, the Department of Justice has collected the names and addresses of all those in the United States in contact with the interviewees, including their American family and friends, even when there is no suspicion of any terrorist link.[22] That information can now be used to create a database of Americans' contacts with non-citizens.

Having accessed and linked all these databases, intelligence agencies will then be able to use some anonymous algorithm in a program like TIA to conduct pattern analysis to generate a list of 'potential terrorists.' It is not known whether the algorithm would use religion or ethnicity, or names or national origin as a proxy for religion, as criteria to generate lists of suspicious individuals meriting further scrutiny. It is not known whether the algorithm would use the neighborhood in which known terrorists lived as a criterion in the same way that the FBI did when it arrested an individual who applied for a drivers' license at the same office as one of the hijackers.[23]

It is useful to contrast how this data-mining approach might have been employed before September 11 with the more targeted 'law enforcement' approach. Various government officials have spoken about following the pattern of financial transactions by the September 11 hijackers to identify additional suspects. The data-mining approach would presumably look at money transfers from various countries in the Middle East to individuals in the United States. Even if it were limited to transfers through particular banks, or perhaps through Germany, the analysis would undoubtedly generate thousands of hits, most of which, upon further scrutiny, would turn out to involve innocent people making innocent transfers. As we have seen, the other approach, based on individualized suspicion, would require looking at the particular individuals and accounts used to fund the hijackers and the accounts of those who knew the hijackers. It would mean following every lead and using all available data analysis techniques on the data that would be gathered in this way. While perhaps harder in certain respects, the likelihood of generating useful information is much greater than in the case of the more general data-mining, pattern analysis approach.[24]

While the data-mining paradigm is unlikely to yield useful information, its costs are enormous. It requires scarce federal budget dollars and even more scarce human resources, including limited but crucial translation capabilities. Spending such limited resources for such limited benefits increases the risk of missing the real terrorists, at the same time that it generates massive amounts of information about all Americans or all immigrants, particularly Arabs and Muslims. Building this kind of technological capability will fundamentally alter the relationship between Americans and their government. And it is very difficult, if not impossible, to enact laws or build oversight mechanisms strong enough to protect against abuses. As Senator Sam Ervin recognized in 1974:

> Government has an insatiable appetite for power, and it will not stop usurping power unless it is restrained by laws they cannot repeal or nullify. There are mighty few laws they cannot nullify . . .

> Each time we give up a bit of information about ourselves to the Government, we give up some of our freedom. For the more the Government or any institution knows about us, the more power it has over us. When the Government knows all of our secrets we stand naked before official power. Stripped of our privacy, we lose our rights and privileges . . .

> One of the most obvious threats the computer poses to privacy comes in its ability to collect, store, and disseminate information without any subjective concern for human emotion and fallibility.[25]

At the time the Framers wrote the Fourth Amendment, individual privacy was protected by the law and by the technological limitations on the part of the government to know what was said in the privacy of the home or to retain and catalogue information. When the government comes to possess unlimited capabilities to gather and process information on everyone, the law is a thin reed to protect our privacy and to resist the enormous pressure within the government to misuse the information for political or other purposes.

A new domestic counter-intelligence agency: The right solution?

These questions of law enforcement versus intelligence lie at the heart of another proposal: as part of its mandate to examine the causes of the September 11 attacks, Congress has charged the National Commission on Terrorist Attacks to consider the wisdom of creating a new domestic intelligence agency without law enforcement responsibilities. Many argue that a new agency is needed because of the concern that the FBI cannot be adequately reformed to meet future terrorist threats.

The institutional weaknesses of the FBI are outside the scope of this article. But it is clear that instead of increasing security, a domestic intelligence agency as currently proposed is likely to pose significant dangers to open government, individual privacy, and civil liberties. A new intelligence agency will not address the existing 'hand-off' problems of sharing information collected overseas and information collected domestically and will only exacerbate the difficulty of coordination between intelligence and law enforcement. Information collected by the CIA will still have to be shared in a timely manner with the new domestic agency and those responsible for prosecuting terrorists in the United States. In addition, the FBI and the Justice Department will now have to deal with a new agency collecting information to be used in such prosecutions. Such coordination is crucial because, even though the Bush administration claims dangerous new powers to indefinitely detain individuals outside the criminal justice system, most of the successes claimed by the Justice Department in its war against terrorism have consisted of criminal prosecutions of alleged terrorists.

If a new agency is needed, a better model would begin with the recognition that law enforcement authorities ultimately must be used against terrorists found in the United States. Thus, any new agency should be constructed primarily as a law enforcement rather than intelligence agency, devoted solely to – and ultimately responsible for – counterterrorism. The agency should be authorized to use existing domestic intelligence authorities, grounded in the law, like FISA, and to obtain all other relevant intelligence information from other agencies, including information collected overseas. An agency constructed on this model could bridge the overseas/ domestic divide by operating both abroad and at home, and would eliminate the 'hand-off' problem between intelligence and law enforcement. Such an agency could appropriately be housed in the Department of Justice, but not in an intelligence agency or under the Director of Central Intelligence.

If a new agency is established, it should assume all of the FBI's current counterterrorism responsibilities and perhaps certain responsibilities now resident in other domestic agencies as well. The transfer of responsibilities from the CIA and other overseas intelligence agencies would be more complicated, but should be based on the premise that efforts to apprehend individual terrorists (outside the field of active military operations) should presumptively be carried out within the framework of the criminal law and thus be transferred to the new agency. The new agency, because it has extensive law enforcement responsibilities, should not be permitted to act illegally. Overseas covert actions, on the other hand, which are by definition illegal where carried out, would still need to be solely the province of the CIA and other intelligence agencies.

The creation of a new agency would of course involve many difficulties, not the least of which is the likelihood that, for political reasons, the FBI would never be forced to surrender its counterterrorism responsibilities. In the end, such a proposal may not be better than leaving counterterrorism with the FBI. The crucial point is to insist that anti-terrorism efforts in the United States be focused on identifying and apprehending individuals planning and financing terrorist acts against Americans. The alternative approach, building an intelligence capability directed at all Americans and divorced from law enforcement, is a less effective way to fight terrorism, and a grave danger to civil liberties.

Notes

1 Following an investigation by the intelligence committees of the Congress, 'Joint Inquiry Into Intelligence Community Activities Before and After the Terrorist Attacks of September 11, 2001,' Report of the U.S. Senate Select Committee on Intelligence and U.S. House Permanent Select Committee on Intelligence (December 2002) 'Joint Inquiry Report', <www.gpoaccess.gov/serial-set/creports/911.html>, Congress established the National Commission on Terrorist Attacks upon the United States to investigate the circumstances surrounding the attacks, and make recommendations. Its report is currently due in May 2004. See <www.9–11commission.gov>.

2 See The Final Report of the Select Committee to Study Governmental Operations with Respect to Intelligence Activities, United States Senate (Church Committee), Book II: Intelligence Activities and the Rights of Americans, <www.aarclibrary.org/publib/church/reports/book2/contents.htm>.

3 See for example: *Snepp v. United States*, 444 U.S. 507 (1980); *CIA v. Sims*, 471 U.S. 159 (1985); compare *New York Times Co. v. United States*, 403 U.S. 713 (1971) and *Webster v. Doe*, 486 U.S. 592 (1988).

4 U.S. Department of Defense web site, Office of the Assistant to the Secretary of Defense (Intelligence Oversight) <www.dtic.mil/atsdio/mission.html>.

5 But the effort to blur the distinction between law enforcement and intelligence responsibilities began before September 11. In 1996, Congress amended the 1947 National Security Act to assign the CIA law enforcement responsibilities for the first time, authorizing the CIA to undertake the illegal collection of information overseas for the sole purpose of making a criminal case against a foreigner in a U.S. court.

6 When Congress first criminalized material support of terrorism, it prohibited the initiation of investigations of such crimes based solely on First Amendment-protected activity. This protection was repealed in the 1996 Anti-Terrorism and Effective Death Penalty Act, leaving the FBI free since then to open investigations based purely on protected speech and religious activities.

7 See, for example, Kate Martin's 24 September 2001 testimony before the Senate Select Committee on Intelligence on the Legislative Proposals in the Wake of September 11, 2001 Attacks, including the Intelligence to Prevent Terrorism Act of 2001, available at <www.cnss.org/kmtestimony0924.pdf>.

8 See for example, the 1980 Classified Information Procedures Act and the Joint Task Force on Intelligence and Law Enforcement Report to the Attorney General and Director of Central Intelligence (Richards/Rindskopf Report) May, 1995.

9 See *United States v. Fernandez*, 913 F.2d 148 (4th Cir. 1990).

10 See the Joint Inquiry Report.

11 Counterterrorism investigations, unlike foreign intelligence efforts focused on the legal activities of foreign governments in the United States, are always concerned with crimes, because all planning and involvement in terrorist activities is criminal.

12 While international human rights law provides many of the protections recognized in the Bill of Rights and is not limited by national borders, its applicability to intelligence activities in times of emergency or war is less developed and outside the scope of this discussion.

13 See *Center for National Security Studies v. Department of Justice*, 331 7.3d 918 (D.C. Cir), cert. pending (2003).

14 But see *In re: Sealed Case No. 02–001*, Foreign Intelligence Surveillance Court of Review, 18 November 2002, <http://www.cnss.org/FISCR_opinion.pdf>.

15 The Patriot Act and subsequent legislation also expanded the scope of personal information, which the government could seize in secret. See for example, section 215 authorizing secret seizures of library records and commercial databases.

16 The Attorney General has described 'a database of thousands of known terrorists. The operations of the U.S. military in Afghanistan have allowed us to expand that database considerably . . . now we have a sizable database of fingerprints of known terrorists.' Attorney General Prepared Remarks on the National Security Entry-Exit Registration System, 6 June 2002. <www.usdoj.gov/ag/speeches/2002/060502agpreparedremarks.htm>.

17 While Congress voted to cut off funds for the original TIA program, the data-mining software and research tools were simply transferred to different, undisclosed agencies. 'Washington in Brief,' *The Washington Post*, 26 September 2003.

18 Section 215 added this authority to the FISA; it is best known for authorizing the secret seizure of library records.

19 See Fact Sheet on Attorney General's Guidelines: Detecting and Preventing Terrorist Attacks, 30 May 2002.

20 Glenn Simpson, 'Big Brother-in-Law: If the FBI Hopes to Get the Goods on You, It May Ask ChoicePoint – U.S. Agencies' Growing Use of Outside Data Suppliers Raises Privacy Concerns,' *The Wall Street Journal*, 13 April 2002.

21 Federal Register, Vol. 68, No. 2, 3 January 2003, Proposed Rule to implement section 402 of the Enhanced Border Security and Visa Entry Reform Act of 2002 (Pub. L. 107–173).

22 Memorandum for All United States Attorneys, All Members of the Anti-Terrorism Task Force from the Deputy Attorney General re: Guidelines for the Interviews Regarding International Terrorism, 9 November 2001. In late 2002 and 2003, as part of the National Security Entrance and Exit Registration System, non-citizens were also required to give the names and contact information of individuals they knew in the United States a U.S. Department of Justice Special Registration Worksheet.

23 See 'A Deliberate Strategy of Disruption; Massive, Secretive Detention Effort Aimed Mainly at Preventing More Terror,' *The Washington Post*, 4 November 2001.

24 Of course, at some point, the two approaches – one focused on collecting information relevant to criminal activity and one seeking to collect all information and looking for suspicious patterns – overlap.

25 Introductory Remarks of Senator Sam J. Ervin on S. 3418, Legislative History of the Privacy Act of 1974 S. 3418. (Public Law 93–579), Committee on Government Operations United States

Senate and the Committee on Government Operations House of Representatives Subcommittee on Government Information and Individual Rights, 1 May 1974.

Reprinted with permission Kate Martin, 'Domestic Intelligence and Civil Liberties', *SAIS Review* 24/1 (2004) pp.7–21.

21 High policing in the security control society

James Sheptycki

This article considers the nature and practice of high policing in the security control society. It looks at the effects of the new information technologies on the organization of policing-intelligence and argues that a number of 'organizational pathologies' have arisen that make the functioning of security-intelligence processes in high policing deeply problematic. The article also looks at the changing context of policing and argues that the circuits of the security-intelligence apparatus are woven into, and help to compose, the panic scenes of the security control society. Seen this way, the habits of high policing are not the governance of crisis, but rather governance through crisis. An alternative paradigm is suggested, viz.: the human security paradigm and the paper concludes that, unless senior ranking policing officers the 'police intelligentsia' adopt new ways of thinking, the already existing organizational pathologies of the security-intelligence system are likely to continue undermining efforts at fostering security.

Introduction

'This information is top security. When you have read it, destroy yourself.

Marshall McLuhan'

Elsewhere in this, the inaugural issue of *Policing; a journal of policy and practice*, scholars have considered the concept of 'high policing', its historical genesis and import for practical policing. The concept represents what was, for a considerable period, an analytical and research backwater in Police Studies. Some time ago, other scholars observed that high policing 'is a subject which government would prefer academics and others should ignore' (Thurlow, 1994, p. 1) and it was noted, even a longer time ago, that the vocabulary for talking about high policing (internal security, national security, intelligence gathering, etc.) is euphemistic, its 'meaning has been ravaged, reduced to disembodied buzz words' (Donner, 1980, p. xv). At the millennium, things seemed to change. The pace of organizational transformation in policing institutions (and every other major social institution) was ramped up as a result of the so called information revolution (Castells, 2000) and policing scholars saw a resulting shift in policing vocabulary with the introduction of new terms such as 'strategic' and 'pro-active', together with 'intelligence-led policing' (Maguire, 2000). Scholars coined the term 'surveillant assemblage' to describe the concatenation of surveillance technologies and techniques that are currently deployed in the governance of individuals and populations (Haggerty and Ericson, 2000).

It is not implausible to suggest that there has been a revolution in intelligence affairs, brought about by a variety of causes: the rise of 'postmodern' society, the crosscurrents of economic, social, cultural and political 'globalization', and the 'information revolution'. One of the key anxieties of our age has to do with the pervasive sense of insecurity that exists amidst, and in spite of, the multiplication of tactics and techniques for ensuring security. The irony is that the undeniable increase in surveillance and security practices is only congruent with the multiplication of insecurity and fear. This is the paradox of the security control society and it lies at the heart of the politics of policing surveillance. The almost endless possibilities for dissassembly and reassembly of information into intelligence – via techniques of data-mining – intensify this paradox because the purpose is not merely *cura promovendi salutem* (concerned with the promotion of public safety or public good) but also with *cura advertendi mala futura* (concerned to avert future ills) (cf. Sheptycki, 1998). Furthermore, in the transnational state system where governance transcends national jurisdictions and simultaneously valorizes the national security function, there are no confident and clear lines of political accountability, so the responsibility for globally defining the public good and any future ills that may impact upon it is left in the shadows (Loader, 2002; Sheptycki, 2004). It is also the case that the technologies of surveillance underpinning the revolution in intelligence affairs have both 'panoptic' and 'synoptic' qualities (Mathiesen, 1997). They enable both the few to watch the many and the many to watch the few, and this has a number of outcomes, sometimes discussed in terms of the viewer-voyeur society, or the society of the spectacle. The paradox ensures that the spectacle is one of security control, and, *a fortiori*, the way that it is played out tends to be punitive and vengeance-oriented (cf. Haggerty and Ericson, 2006).

Understanding the revolution in intelligence affairs potentially offers a way out of the paradox of the security control society. Critical analysis may allow for the possibility to intervene and undercut the conditions that foster it. However, it has to be recognized at the outset, that crime and security intelligence processes are politicized. Globally, we are in the midst of a transformation of the architectures of policing (Sheptycki, 2007; Walker, 2000). In tandem with the redesignation of serious and organized crime as matters of national security concern, the declaration of a world-wide war on terrorism has powerfully reshaped – and is reshaping – the policing apparatus. These tropes have accompanied the establishment of new supraordinate policing institutions – for example, the Serious and Organized Crime Agency in the United Kingdom and the Department of Homeland Security in the United States – and increasingly, the entire ambit of state-based policing activities have acquired the hallmarks of high policing. In the current climate of fear, academics who concern themselves with policing practice will have to work very hard to cultivate critical awareness, especially among senior police officers, if the conditions that underpin the security control paradox are to be undermined.

Inside the machine

Some time ago, and considerably prior to the supposed watershed marked by 9/11, scholars studying the changing morphology of European police institutions observed that the secretive and élitist ethos of the security services was gaining ground and worried that 'the ideal of a transparent, rule governed and politically neutral [police] system would become no more than a remote possibility' (Anderson *et al.*, 1995, p, 175). A veil of secrecy has been cast over increasingly large parts of the policing apparatus, making it more difficult for academics to gain research access in order to gauge the nature and efficaciousness of the new intelligence-led policing paradigm (ILP) (Sheptycki, 2007). Lack of transparency retards the development of a critical perspective on contemporary high policing, a perspective which is essential because, as advocates of ILP have noted, 'the paradigm shift to an intelligence-driven model needs a reality check' (Christopher, 2004, p. 190). Fortunately, in the United Kingdom at least, there has been enough empirical research relating to these transformations so as to allow for such an analysis (e.g. Cope, 2004; Gill, 2000; Innes and Sheptycki, 2004). This is crucial because, although changes in the broader societal context of policing undoubtedly shape the current predicament, it may also be the case that the method of responding to that predicament is, itself, part of the problem. In confronting the security control paradox, it is essential to have a view of the inside workings of the policing machine.

At a very fundamental level, the advent of new information technologies is driving drastic changes in the architecture of policing. The information revolution challenges a very basic premise of bureaucratic institutions – to which police agencies certainly conform – and that is their classic pyramidal structure. The literature on the social significance of information technologies defines IT broadly. The concept includes computers, obviously, but extends to include the entire array of machines for collecting, storing, analysing, duplicating, and disseminating information (Castells, 2000). Empirical observation confirms the significance of all of these technologies; they tend to erode information hierarchies and supplant them with networks. I realized this some time ago when interviewing undercover police officers working cross-border between the Netherlands and Belgium (Sheptycki, 2002, p. 84). I naively asked my interviewees about the difficulties I thought they might be experiencing due to the fact that they were from different national police agencies which used different radio equipment and communications protocols. They laughed and assured me that, with their newly acquired cell phones, they could be in touch with any number of colleagues in any number of locations irrespective of jurisdiction and without need of their centrally controlled radio systems. Many theorists of the information society argue that networked organizations are organizationally superior to hierarchically organized ones and this may, indeed, be the case generally (Zuboff, 1988). However, some organizations – particularly policing-type organizations – aggressively work to impose hierarchical models of information flow onto the naturally emerging networks. Irresistible force meets immovable object and a number of organizational pathologies arise (Sheptycki, 2004a, 2004b).

Among professionals directly concerned with policing intelligence, one of the most often mentioned organizational pathologies is that of 'information silos' – a concept which reflects the significance of the tension between hierarchical models and networked thinking. In information silos there is only one direction for information to flow and that is up. This contributes to another organizational pathology that professionals recognize: 'linkage blindness'. Loosely speaking, because information is constrained to flow in bureau-cratically defined pyramids – each with different governmental objects (e.g. drugs, illegal immigrants, illegal firearms, stolen property, terrorist cells, etc.) policing agents frequently fail to link bytes of information coursing in the veins of their intelligence systems and turn them into meaningful intelligence. Recognizing these organizational pathologies leads to mission failure and wishing to avoid accusations of incompetence, *ad hoc* task forces and intelligence centres are frequently formed. One example of this is the special intelligence-led policing squads dedicated to the pursuit of outlaw motorcycle gangs that have been constituted in a number of police institutions in Europe, Scandinavia, and North America. Crime attributed to such groups is very often high profile and notorious and it would be widely seen as a dereliction of duty if policing bodies failed to do something about it (Sheptycki, 2003). However, and despite any well-advertized *tactical* successes that may be scored, the multiplication of *ad hoc* special task forces and intelligence centres undermines attempts to refine a reliable and valid *strategic* intelligence picture. The result is a failure of the intelligence process, but one that remains hidden behind public announcements regarding the successes of the special task forces. The extent of the failure to form a strategic view is practically incalculable, but a thought experiment is suggestive. Compare and contrast the harm due to crimes against the environment and those due to intellectual property theft (admittedly a difficult empirical question) and ask, on balance, how much harm is attributable to phenomena that fall under these rubrics and how much policing resource is presently devoted to preventing them? Police executives know that a considerable portion of policing resource is now devoted to the latter concern, but that very little is devoted to the former. Aware of the serious harm that results from eco-destruction and the sad future that will surely follow, this thought experiment ought to provide a sense of the magnitude of failure in the current strategic intelligence view of police agencies in countries with advanced economies.

There are several more organizational pathologies that could be mentioned, but two are especially important, these are the continuing problem of 'intelligence gaps', and the difficulties that arise from 'compulsive data demand'. Intelligence gaps exist for any number of reasons: inappropriate allocation of intelligence acquisition resources, hierarchical information flows, failure to report or record information to name only the most obvious. Such gaps exist at the same time that organizations are becoming equipped with new technologies which allow for the amassing and storage of inconceivably huge amounts of data, some of it held by private sector operators and sold to police and security intelligence organizations on a contractual, for profit, basis. So equipped, policing organizations compulsively demand ever more data in wanton pursuit of the chimera of 'total information awareness'. Because compulsive data demand and intelligence gaps continue to exist side-by-side, intelligence systems are invariably awash in low-grade 'noise' – information with little practical value – and intelligence officers find themselves struggling to overcome problems of 'information overload'. In one of my field interviews, an intelligence analyst likened the task of analysing the tens of thousands of suspicious financial transactions coming to his unit to 'drinking from a fire hose' (Sheptycki, 2004c, p. 17).

Because of these many organizational pathologies, the functioning of the security intelligence process is deeply problematic. The structural basis of policing intelligence processes is at odds with itself. Within policing institutions, the reaction of agents to the possibilities of the information revolution has been to unwittingly act so as to preserve the already existing principals of hierarchical organization. The all-too-often unremarked organizational pathologies result in the failure of strategic vision. Moreover, while intelligence processes are not strategic, the tactical successes may be rather capricious, as evidenced by the many 'false positives' and other intelligence failures that plague the intelligence system, as the case of Maher Arar amply demonstrates (http://www.maherarar.ca and mms://media.osgoode. yorku.ca/afterarar). The effort to impose information hierarchy onto communications networks is not an instinctive reaction by police professionals, but rather is a result of the embeddedness of their subculturally learned ways of thinking. It is the inability of a subculture based upon crime fighting and the status concerns of a rank-structured bureaucracy to grasp the significance of networked thinking and to change itself that has brought about the range of organizational pathologies briefly discussed above. Thus hobbled, large-scale policing and security intelligence systems offer few safeguards against overt politicization of the intelligence process, save the integrity of the individual personnel who give it life. Articulated within an increasing climate of fear and insecurity, these pathologies undermine the credibility and the efficaciousness of the entire enterprise even while they feed on the increasing sense of panic.

The changing context of policing

Intelligence-led policing is a transnational phenomenon (Ratcliffe, 2004). Looking inside the global police security intelligence system, so to speak, it is apparent that there is a deep structural disjuncture between information hierarchies and information networks and that this has given rise to a number of organizational pathologies. These have undercut to an unmeasured, but nevertheless significant, extent both the strategic effectiveness and legitimation of the intelligence process. At the same time, massive societal changes – themselves partially driven by the IT revolution – are also taking place. A variety of concerns may be raised, but chief among them are the various processes of trasnationalization. National societies are no longer what they once were when modern state structures (and their attendant policing and security apparatuses) were being put in place at the dawn of modernity. Transnational corporations, the transnational capitalist class and the cultural ideology of consumerism have been put forward as the three fundamental building blocks of globalization (Sklair, 2001), and criminological analysis suggests the resulting system as inherently criminogenic (Pearce and Woodiwiss, 1993; Sheptycki and Wardak, 2005; Woodiwiss, 2005).

Popular explanations regarding globalization and crime seldom display any awareness of the systemic or structural bases of transnational crime. Instead they usually focus on a welter of different diasporic communities – cultural others who are easily labelled even if they are poorly understood. Such communities, it is true, provide the basis of identities that are transgressive of national boundaries and therefore potentially enriching of the realms of human experience. Globally and locally, diasporic communities have differing degrees of political influence, but it is necessary to be cautious before unreservedly advocating their enhanced and equal influence, for example, under the rubric of multi-culturalism. Of course, we must guard against the view that the Outsider is somehow inimical to peace, order and good government. However, it is also true that diasporic communities provide the basis for the transnational reproduction of social conflict in diverse settings and that the detrimental influence of these conflicts has been cross-regional and world ordering.[1] Admitting the difficulties of policing conflicts that have gone transnational due to the dispersal of diasporic communities is not the same thing as giving in to the anxious excesses of purveyors of theories that relate to a global terrorist-organized crime 'nexus' or 'continuum' (Shelley *et al.*, 2005). It does, however, lend a sense of urgency to thinking about how, under conditions of transnationalization, to authorize and render accountable normatively robust policing (Goldsmith and Sheptycki, 2007)

Even more fundamental than multiculturalism, is the deracination of self-identity formation in the contemporary wired world. Echoing Richard Sennett (1998), it is possible to say that, as traditional bases for self-identity formation have faded, people have come to mystify their own condition. Absent the traditional sources of self-identity, people increasingly mold the sense of self narrowly – on the basis of their limited personal experience – and on the basis of cultural information sources; the mass media and the Internet. Margaret Thatcher famously said that 'there is no such thing as society, only individuals and families' – an obvious overstatement – and yet, societal atomization has long been clearly recognizable in the evergrowing occupation, dispossession, and reter-ritorialization of everyday life by the abstract grids, geometries and routines imprinted onto social life by globalized capitalism and the transnational-state-system, leading people to increasingly seek refuge in privatized and narcissistic existences (Sennett, 1977).[2] Crucially, the atomization of the basis of self-identity is happening simultaneously with the transnationalization of social life. The feeling grows that the relevance of the nation-state as the linchpin of governance, the font of sovereignty and the basis of good social order is increasingly tenuous even while state-based bureaucracies – especially those devoted to policing in its broadest sense – strive to impose authority transnationally and to secure legitimacy for doing so. Perhaps this recalls 19th century efforts to police and order the shifting populations of Europe (Deflem, 1996, 2002) and perhaps it gives rise to a sort of 'Westphalian fatalism' wherein, by imputation, state-based police authorities are said to hold an 'in-the-final-instance' authority over the governance of insecurity (Loader and Walker, 2007. It certainly brings to mind Emile Durkheim's caution that 'a society made up of a boundless dust-heap of unrelated individuals whom an overdeveloped state tries to hem and hold in, is a true sociological monstrosity' (quoted in Baltzell, 1989).

Seldom remarked, and yet crucial to contemporary policing scholarship, should be recognition of the *dual* connection between the intelligence process and the new mediated forms of self-identity formation found on the Internet and through the mass media. The intelligence process is connected to these media through various surveillance practices, ranging from monitoring the news media through to the stealthy monitoring of Internet use, and even satellite tracking, that much is obvious. But there is a second, less well studied, connection. This is manifest in the idiom of intelligence analysts as 'open source intelligence' – a term which refers to the entire gambit of publicly available sources of information including both the old-fashioned newspaper and the weblog. Intelligence analysts use a variety of intelligence sources in their research – for example, technical surveillance, or clandestine human sources, as well as information from 'open sources'. Some of the results of their analyses seep out into the public realm with the potential to become yet another byte of open source intelligence. Herein lies the institutional basis for a spiraling information feedback loop. Swedish criminologist Janne Flyghed (2002) has argued that the expansion of security measures has come through the depiction of imminent danger of dramatic proportions based on scant empirical evidence. He argues that repeated references to insecurity threats, based on unattributed 'intelligence sources', produce a popular false consciousness of impending danger linked to perceptions of non-specific and diffuse, but nonetheless serious threats. These threats are often the results of intelligence reports (leaks) and are based upon knowledge (intelligence) that is difficult to independently verify. The circuits of the security intelligence apparatus are woven into, and help to compose, the panic scenes of the security control society.

All the while, the background to the emergent security control society is a scene of intense global political and economic restructuring. The rise to prominence of global neo-liberalism, which has given free reign to mighty torrents of hot capital, is hollowing out the capacities of local state governance and policy is increasingly being set at the transnational level and is therefore largely unaccountable. Transnational governance, such as it is, resides in the shadowy world of the Bilder-berg Group, the Trilateral Commission and the Wolfsberg Group, as well as in somewhat more well known transnational entities such as the UN, G8, OECD, WTO, World Bank and the IMF. Apart from its less than democratic basis, the institutional fragmentation of contemporary transnational governance results in repeated failures to turn concerns for the global common interest into practical action (Ericson and Stehr, 2000; Held and McGrew, 2002). These institutions of transnational governance appear as background factors in most analyses of transnational policing and security, but policing institutions, only some of which are transnational themselves, form part of the fragmented terrain of transnational governance. Furthermore, looked at in the context of the transnational condition, the unaccountability and lack of transparency in the function of high policing exacerbates the ungovernability of the global system (Held, 1995, pp. 113–120).

The information revolution has given rise to electronic money (Weatherford, 1997) and interpenetrated illicit and licit markets in every conceivable commodity circle around the globe (Ruggiero, 2000). This further exacerbates the symptoms of impoverishment and economic polarization characteristic of neo-liberalism (Young, 1999) especially in what the Spanish sociologist Manuel Castells referred to as the 'black-holes of global capitalism' (Castells, 1998, pp. 74–82, 164). The 'global South' finds itself segregated inside the heartlands of the metropolitan countries, while beleaguered outposts of prosperity, sitting amidst surrounding seas of impoverishment, continuously fortify themselves with the latest security devices (Caldeira, 2001; Davis, 1992, 2006). From top to bottom and all around the world, the foundational assumptions about relationships between the individual, the social and the institutions of governance are rapidly changing. All of this provokes anxiety. The rapid pace of change gives rise to the thought that governance is impossible, that ungovernability is only to be expected, and all of the potential of high policing is thus expended in a vain attempt to impose a vision of transnational order.

Conclusion

What are we to make of this? That is to say, given this understanding: what is to be done? This is obviously a huge question and one that is difficult to answer within the confines of a short article. However, it is possible to suggest that part of the answer, but by no means all of it, lies within the ambit of the policing *intelligentsia*. Critical scholarship can help policing elites to recognise the limitations of their subculturally defined worldview and shrug it off as an instance of bad faith. By doing so, the Mandarins of high policing stand a chance of throwing off the organizational pathologies that plague the institutions of policing. And anyway, these subcultural means and ends emanate ultimately from the doctrine of national security, a clearly outdated notion for a globalizing world and one which should be replaced by a much more general understanding of human security.

Human security – the freedom from fear and the freedom from want – should be elevated to the new watchwords and the doctrine of individual human rights should be its worldwide code of practice (Goldsmith and Sheptycki, 2007; see also: http://www.humansecurity.info/). The practitioners of high policing must think of themselves as human beings first and foremost and act on the basis of their common humanity and in the interests of the global commonweal, rather than on the basis of narrowly prescribed institutional choices. By itself, this is not enough to ensure a better future, since so much depends on individuals in all walks of life confronting their own choices instead of simply being swept along by the – often trivial – circumstances of their momentary lives. Collectively and globally, there must be an authentic conversation about the possible futures for mankind and the planet that does not privilege the already established practices of power habitually watched over and nurtured by the doyens of global high policing. While it would be wrong to say this would, by itself, guarantee a better future, it remains the case that a likely first step to ending the present security control paradox would be if the individual practitioners of high policing themselves openly and transparently contributed to the global collective conversation about genuine human security by speaking truth to power.

Notes

1 I am thinking here of the shadowy underworld of Miami Cuban exiles – a good example of a diasporic community whose political clout is felt locally in Miami and transnationally through their

influence in Washington DC. A number of people in this community have been involved in various terrorist plots and attacks over the past four decades or more. Possibly the most notorious incident is the bombing of Cubana Flight 455 on October 6 1976. On that day, two time bombs planted by several Cuban exiles exploded killing 73 people. One of the perpetrators of the attack, Luis Posada Carriles, was arrested but subsequently escaped custody in Venezuela and eventually fled, via Panama, to the United States. The case gained some renewed notoriety in April 2005, when a new warrant for Posada's arrest in connection with the bombing was issued by Venezuela under the government of Hugo Chávez. In September 2005, a US immigration judge ruled that Posada should not be deported to either Cuba or Venezuela because he might be subject to torture.

2 Although Sennett certainly does not mention it, here one thinks of online pedophiles, sex tourists, and cyber bullying.

References

Anderson, M., den Boer, M., Cullen, P., Gilmore, W.C., Raab, C., and Walker, N. 1995. *Policing the European Union; Theory, Law and Practice*, Oxford: Oxford University Press.

Baltzell, E.D. 1989. *Philadelphia Gentlemen; the Making of a National Upper Class*, New Brunswick, USA: Transaction Publishers.

Caldeira, T.P.R. 2001. *City of Walls*, Berkley and Los Angels: University of California Press.

Castells, M. 1998. *The Information Age, Volume 3 The End of the Millennium*, Oxford: Basil Blackwell.

Castells, M. 2000. 'Materials for an Exploratory Theory of the Network Society.' *British Journal of Sociology* 51(1): 5–24.

Christopher, S. 2004. 'A Practitioner's Perspective of UK Strategic Intelligence.' In Ratcliffe, J.H. (ed.). *Strategic Thinking in Criminal Intelligence*, Annadale NSW: The Federation Press; 177–193.

Cope, N. 2004. 'Intelligence-Led Policing or Policing-Led Intelligence?.' *British Journal of Criminology* 44(2): 188–203.

Davis, M. 1992. *City of Quartz*, London: Vintage.

Davis, M. 2006. *Planet of Slums*, New York: Verso.

Deflem, M. 1996. 'International Policing in 19th Century Europe.' *International Criminal Justice Review* 6: 36–57.

Deflem, M. 2002. *Policing World Society*, Oxford: Oxford University Press.

Donner, F. 1980. *The Age of Surveillance; The Aims and Methods of America's Political Intelligence System*, New York: Alfred A. Knopf.

Ericson, R.V., and Stehr, N. (eds). 2000. *Governing Modern Societies*, Toronto: University of Toronto Press.

Flyghed, J. 2002. 'Normalising the Exceptional.' *Policing and Society* 13(1): 23–41.

Gill, P. 2000. *Rounding up the Usual Suspects; Developments in Contemporary law Enforcement Intelligence*, Aldershot: Ashgate.

Goldsmith, A., and Sheptycki, J.W.E. 2007. *Crafting Transnational Policing: State-building and Police Reform Across Borders*, Oxford: Hart.

Haggerty, K.D., and Ericson, R.V. 2000. 'The Surveillant Assemblage.' *The British Journal of Sociology* 51(4): 605–622.

Haggerty, K.D., and Ericson, R.V. (eds). 2006. *The New Politics of Surveillance and Visibility*, Toronto: University of Toronto Press.

Held, D. 1995. *Democracy and the Global Order; From Modern State to Cosmopolitan Governance*, Cambridge: Polity Press.

Held, D., and McGrew, A. 2002. *Globalization/Anti-Globalization*, Cambridge: Polity Press.

Innes, M., and Sheptycki, J. 2004. 'From Detection to Disruption: Intelligence and the Changing Logics of Police Crime Control in the United Kingdom.' *International Criminal Justice Review* 14: 1–24.

Loader, I. 2002. 'Policing, Securitization and Democratization in Europe.' *Criminal Justice* 2(2): 125–153.

Loader, I., and Walker, N. 2007. 'Locating the Public Interest in Transnational Policing.' in *Crafting Transnational Policing*, A. Goldsmith and J. Sheptycki (eds.) Oxford: Hart Publications (forthcoming).

Maguire, M. 2000. 'Policing by Risks and Targets; Some Dimensions and Implications of Intelligence-Led Crime Control.' *Policing and Society* **9**(4): 315–336.

Mathiesen, T. 1997. ' "The Viewer Society; Michel Foucault's "Panopticon" Revisited" ' *Theoretical Criminology* **1**(2): 215–235.

Pearce, F., and Woodiwiss, M. 1993. *Global Crime Connections*, London: MacMillan.

Ratcliffe, J. (ed.). 2004. *Strategic Thinking in Criminal Intelligence*, Annandale NSW: The Federation Press.

Ruggiero, V. 2000. *Crime and Markets*, Oxford: Oxford University Press.

Sennett, R. 1977. *The Fall of Public Man*, New York: Alfred Knopf.

Sennett, R. 1998. *The Corrosion of Character: The Personal Consequences of Work in the New Capitalism*, New York: W. W. Norton.

Shelley, L., Picarelli, J.T., Irby, A., Hart, D.M., Craig-Hart, P., Williams, P., Simon, S., Addullaev, N., Stanislawski, B., and Covill, L. 2005. *Methods and Motives: Exploring Links Between Transnational Organized Crime and International Terrorism*, Washington, DC: US Department of Justice (unpublished research report Award No. 2003-IJ-CX-1019) available at http://www.ncjrs.gov/pdffiles1/nij/grants/211207.pdf.

Sheptycki, J.W.E. 1998. 'Policing, Postmodernism and Transnationalisation.' *The British Journal of Criminology* 38(3): 485–503.

Sheptycki, J.W.E. 2002. *In Search of Transnational Policing*, Aldershot: Ashgate.

Sheptycki, J.W.E. 2003. 'The Governance of Organised Crime in Canada.' *The Canadian Journal of Sociology* 28(3): 489–517.

Sheptycki, J.W.E. 2004. 'The Accountability of Transnational Policing Institutions: The Strange Case of Interpol.' *The Canadian Journal of Law and Society* 19(1): 107–134.

Sheptycki, J.W.E. 2004a. 'Organizational Pathologies in Police Intelligence Systems; Some Contributions to the Lexicon of Intelligence-Led Policing.' *The European Journal of Criminology* 1(3): 307–332.

Sheptycki, J.W.E. 2004b. *Review of the Influence of Strategic Intelligence on Organized Crime Policy and Practice*, London: Home Office Research Development and Statistics Directorate, *Special Interest Paper* No. 14.

Sheptycki, J.W.E. 2007. 'Police Ethnography in the House of Serious and Organized Crime.' In Henry, A., and Smith, D.J. (eds). *Transformations of Policing*, Aldershot: Ashgate.

Sheptycki, J.W.E., and Wardak, A. (eds). 2005. *Transnational and Comparative Criminology*, London: Taylor and Francis.

Sklair, L. 2001. *The Transnational Capitalist Class*, Oxford: Blackwell.

Thurlow, R. 1994. *The Secret State: British Internal Security in the Twentieth Century*, Oxford: Basil Blackwell.

Walker, N. 2000. *Policing in a Changing Constitutional Order*, London: Sweet and Maxwell.

Weatherford, J. 1997. *The History of Money*, New York: Three Rivers Press.

Woodiwiss, M. 2005. *Gangster Capitalism*, New York: Carroll and Graf Publishers.

Young, J. 1999. *The Exclusive Society*, London: Sage.

Zuboff, S. 1988. *In the Age of the Smart Machine: the Future of Work and Power*, Oxford: Heinemann.

Reprinted with permission from James Sheptycki, 'High Policing in the Security Control Society', *Policing* 1/1 (2007) pp.70–79.

PROBLEMS OF SURVEILLANCE AND CIVIL LIBERTIES

Further reading: Books and reports

F.H. Cate, *Privacy in the Information Age* (Washington DC: Brookings Institute 1997).

D. Cohen & J. Wells, (eds.) *American National Security and Civil Liberties in an Era of Terrorism* (London: Palgrave 2004).

W. Diffie & S. Landau, *Privacy on the Line: The Politics of Wiretapping and Encryption* (Cambridge MA: MIT Press 1998).

A. Etzioni, *The Limits of Privacy* (NY: Basic Books 1999).

A. Etzioni, & JH Marsh, eds. *Rights vs. Public Safety After 9/11: America in the Age of Terrorism* (Lanham MD: Rowman & Littlefield Publishers, 2003).

S. Field & C. Pelser (eds.) *Invading the private: state accountability and new investigative methods in Europe* (Aldershot: Dartmouth 1998).

Simon Garfinkel, *Database Nation: The Death of Privacy in the 21st Century* (NY: O'Reilly & Associates Inc. 2000).

David Garrow, *The FBI and Martin Luther King* (New Haven MA: Yale University Press 2001).

P.B. Heymann, *Terrorism, Freedom and Security* (MIT Press, Cambridge, MA 2003).

Philip B. Heymann & Juliette N. Kayyem, *Protecting Liberty in an Age of Terror* (Cambridge, MA: MIT Press, 2005).

Richard Hunter, *World without secret: business, crime, and privacy in the age of ubiquitous computing* (Wiley 2002).

R. Leone & G. Anrig (eds.), *The War on Our Freedoms: Civil liberties in an age of terrorism*, (NY: Public Affairs 2003).

D. Lyon, *The Electronic Eye: The Rise of the Surveillance Society* (Minneapolis: University of Minnesota Press, 1994).

D. Lyon, *Surveillance After September 11* (Cambridge, United Kingdom: Polity Press 2003).

D. Lyon, *Surveillance Studies: An Overview* (Cambridge: Polity, 2007).

C. Norris & G. Armstrong, *The Maximum Surveillance Society: the rise of CCTV* (Oxford: Berg 1999).

J Rosen, *The Unwanted Gaze: The destruction of privacy in America* (NY: Random House 2000).

M. Sidel, *More Secure Less Free? Antiterrorism Policy and Civil Liberties after September 11* (Ann Arbor. University of Michigan Press 2004).

W.G. Staples, *Everyday surveillance: vigilance and visibility in postmodern life* (Lanham, MD, Oxford: Rowman & Littlefield Publishers, 2000).

William G. Staples, *The Culture of Surveillance: Discipline and social control in the United States* (NY: St. Martin's Press, 1997).

Frank Webster, *Theories of the Information Society* (Routledge, London 1995) especially chapter 4 on Giddens.

Reg Whitaker, *The end of privacy: how total surveillance is becoming a reality* New (NY: New Press, 1999).

Further reading: Essays and articles

Louise Amoore, 'Biometric borders: Governing mobilities in the war on terror', *Political Geography* 25/3 (2006) pp.336–351.

C. Bell, 'Surveillance Strategies and Populations at Risk', *Security Dialogue* 37/2 (2006) pp.147–65.

M. De Rosa, 'Privacy in the Age of Terror', *The Washington Quarterly* 26/3 (2003) pp.27–41.

M. Elvins, 'State Surveillance and New Information Technology in the European Union' in P Wilkin (ed.) *Communication and global social change* (London: Palgrave 2003).

Robin Evans, 'Bentham's Panopticon: An incident in the social history of architecture,' *Architectural Association Quarterly* 3/2 (1971) pp.21–37.

C. Gearty, 'Terrorism and Human Rights', *Government and Opposition* 42/3 (2007) pp.340–62.

P. Gill, 'Defining Subversion: The Canadian Experience since 1977,' *Public Law* 617 (1989) pp.617–636.

Peter Gill, 'Not Just Joining the Dots But Crossing the Borders and Bridging the Voids: Constructing Security Networks after 11 September 2001' *Policing and Society* 16/1 (2006) pp.27–49.

Michael Levi & David Wall, 'Technologies, Security, and Privacy in the Post-9/11 European Information Society', *Journal of Law and Society* 31/2 (2004) pp.194–220.

Kate Martin, 'Domestic Intelligence and Civil Liberties', *SAIS Review* 24/1, (2004), pp.7–21.

Gary Marx, 'Some Concepts that May be Useful in Understanding the Myriad Forms and Contexts of Surveillance', in L.V. Scott and P.D. Jackson (eds.) *Understanding Intelligence in the 21st Century* (London: Routledge 2004), pp.78–98.

Mark Poster, 'Databases as discourse, or Electronic Interpellations,' in D. Lyon and E. Zureik

[Eds.] *Computers, Surveillance and Privacy*. (Minneapolis: University of Minnesota Press, 1996) pp.175–192.

Ken Roach, 'The World Wide Expansion of Terrorism Laws after September 11,' *Studi Senesi* 116 (2004) pp.487–524.

K.G. Robertson, 'Intelligence, Terrorism and Civil Liberties', *Conflict Quarterly*, 7/2 (1987) pp.43–62 also in P. Wilkinson & AM Stewart (eds.) *Contemporary Research on Terrorism* (Aberdeen: University of Aberdeen Press, 1987).

Shlomo Shpiro, 'No Place to Hide: Intelligence and Civil Liberties in Israel', *Cambridge Review of International Affairs* 19/4 (2006) pp.629–48

Thomas Mathieson, 'The Viewer Society: Foucault's Panopticon revisited' in *Theoretical Criminology* 1 (1997) pp.125–134.

Jennifer Sims, 'Intelligence to counter terror: The importance of all-source fusion', *Intelligence and National Security*, 22/1 (2007) pp.38–56.

Lee S. Strickland, 'Civil Liberties vs. Intelligence Collection: The Secret Foreign Intelligence Surveillance Act Court Speaks in Public.' *Government Information Quarterly* 20/1 (2003) pp.1–12.

H.E. Ventura, J. Miller, J. Mitchell and M Deflem, 'Governmentality and the War on Terror: FBI Project Carnivore and the Diffusion of Disciplinary Power,' *Critical Criminology* 13/1 (2005) pp.55–71.

Essay questions

- How far can civil liberties be reconciled with the security demands made by the modern surveillance state after 11 September 2001?
- Do technological societies and knowledge-based economies naturally produce 'states of surveillance', or do such new developments actually help us to curb excessive surveillance by the state?
- To what extent are security, democracy, affluence and privacy compatible in developed democratic states in the twenty-first century?
- 'If citizens demand transparency of the state, then the state is entitled to demand transparency of its citizens.' Discuss.

22 Ethics and intelligence after September 2001

Michael Herman

This essay argues that the ethics of intelligence might be in need of a new paradigm. In the past the place of intelligence has been determined by ideas of national sovereignty, threats and interstate competition. The growth of wide co-operation against common targets such as terrorism offers the hope of a legitimised activity, with some recognised international standards, similar to law enforcement. Intelligence's ethics are hardly international society's greatest problem. Yet events have confirmed that intelligence is everywhere as a major national attribute, and an increasingly significant factor in international relations. Intelligence has to adjust to an increasingly co-operative system of states, perhaps with bigger changes. Hopefully, there will be opportunities for practitioners and academics to join together to explore a concept of 'ethical intelligence' and where its implications point.

Perhaps there is no need to mix intelligence and ethics. The *Times* took a strictly realist view some years ago that 'Cold War or no Cold War, nations routinely spy on each other', and the British Security Service's official handout takes the view that 'spying has been going on for centuries and as nations emerged they began spying on each other and will probably always do so'.[1] Some would say that that is all that need be said. Intelligence is information and information gathering, not *doing* things to people; no-one gets hurt by it, at least not directly. Some agencies do indeed carry out covert action, which confuses the ethical issues, but this is a separable and subsidiary function; thus the British Joint Intelligence Committee is emphatically not a covert action committee.

Yet, even as information gathering, intelligence carries an ethical baggage with it, or – to be more accurate – a baggage of unworthiness. This dates back at least two centuries, when Kant condemned espionage as 'intrinsically despicable' since it 'exploits only the dishonesty of others',[2] and its modern version was illustrated in the judgement of two respected British academics in the 1990s that it was all 'positively immoral', apart 'from certain extreme cases'.[3] This baggage owes a lot to the visceral dislike of espionage, and to intelligence's role of internal surveillance, but the distaste ranges wider. David Kahn, the doyen of the history of codebreaking, concluded that as an activity it is 'surreptitious, snooping, sneaking . . . the very opposite of all that is best in mankind'. It was justified in defence, but 'when a nation is not threatened, it is wrong for it to violate another's dignity by clandestine prying into its messages'. Views are further confused by the media's penchant for describing all intelligence collection as 'spying', producing a kind of guilt by association. Thus GCHQ, the British SIGINT centre, is always described as 'the Cheltenham spy centre', which it certainly is not.

Recent events have given intelligence a more favourable image, but there is still a world-wide distrust of it, from liberal, anti-American, anti-authoritarian and other standpoints. There is still some feeling that its activities are internationally improper, unbefitting for example the ethical dimension of foreign policy announced by the new British Labour Foreign Secretary in 1997. To at least a swathe of liberal opinion, there still is a much bigger question mark against it than for the general run of government service.

So there is a real issue. Intelligence exists as a government institution and cannot be disinvented. But is it to be encouraged internationally, in the way governments accept the value of statistics, meteorology, epidemiology and other knowledge specialities as important inputs to national and collective policy making? Are its practitioners members of a valued profession? Or is it like nuclear weapons, which most people dislike and seek to limit, even if they disagree about what else to do about them? It may be part of the international game, but is it a necessary evil to be discarded eventually for an intelligence-free world; or should it remain, perhaps with its rules improved?

This paper outlines these issues as they seemed in the decade after the end of the Cold War, and discusses how far the events of the new century have changed them. It limits itself to three of intelligence's aspects. First, it bases itself on its roles and rationales: what is expected of it, not its historical record of successes and failures. Second, it treats it as the essentially national activity that it will remain as far as can be foreseen; it does not consider the scope for developing it as an international institution, building on precedents such as the blue-helmeted tactical intelligence units that have featured in some UN operations, and the U-2s and UAVs under UN control for UNSCOM and UNMOVIC. Third, it concentrates on the familiar English-speaking, to some extent 'Western' system, and does not discuss others, such as Russian, Chinese and Arabic intelligence; this is an ethnocentric treatment, but is all that can be done in the present state of intelligence studies. For intelligence within these parameters, then, what ethics can be held to apply?

What ethics?

Ethics fuse ideas of personal morality and social utility; on the one hand the dictates of good conscience, and on the other accepted standards (or ideals) of human intercourse and the social consequences if they are flouted. Cheating at cricket is condemned at one level because it is intrinsically dishonest, and at another because the game has no point if players do not play to common rules.[4] States' international activities are judged by similarly complex morality. The second element   the societal *consequences* – often pre-dominates; thus the Argentine invasion of the Falklands was condemned internationally for trying to settle a dispute by force, as anti-social behaviour in the modern society of states, even though not deeply offensive in purely humanitarian terms. Yet states' actions are also regularly judged by a morality deeper than rules of a game. In an extreme case, the bombing of Dresden is criticised (rightly or wrongly) for its inhumanity, irrespective of law, custom and precedent. At a more prosaic level, states' international reputations include ethical-like judgements of reliability and consistency, or duplicity and untrustworthiness.

International law draws on both these elements, though often partially and imperfectly. It legalises some things, prohibits others and says nothing about others. Nothing is prohibited for intelligence by the laws of war, except the torture of prisoners. A similar lacuna applies over most peacetime information gathering; states have no inherent rights of privacy against other states. Some peacetime collection has been palpably illegal, such as the violations of Soviet airspace and territorial waters in some Western operations, but the illegality was in the collectors' presence and not their intelligence purpose.

Nevertheless, there are some traces of a legal recognition of information gathering as an activity. The Law of the Sea excludes information gathering as a purpose covered by legal rights of innocent passage through territorial waters.[5] The International Telecommunications Union Convention of 1973 provided for the secrecy of international communications, though the small print left governments with escape clauses.[6] The 1961 Vienna Convention specified diplomacy's purpose of collecting information by *lawful* means, but left these tantalisingly unexplained. The US–Soviet SALT and ABM agreements of the 1970s and a succession of more recent and wider agreements, notably the Comprehensive Test Ban Treaty, recognised National Technical Means (the euphemism for technical intelligence collection) for verifying arms control, provided that the (undefined) 'recognised principles of international law' applied to their operation. And its customary element – 'that informal, unwritten body of rules derived from the practice and opinions of States'[7] – is developed aspirational and normative directions.

This paper does not seek to unpick these various constituents of international legitimacy.[8] Its main emphasis is on intelligence's observable international effects; in crude terms, whether it is good or bad for international society, using the commonsense yardsticks whether it promotes or discourages responsible government behaviour, good inter-state relationships, the minimisation of tension, co-operation for internationally valuable purposes, and the avoidance of war.[9] But this 'consequentialist' approach does not exclude the more absolute views of Kant and his successors. 'Moral conduct means acting within a constraining framework of principles that are independent of consequential considerations.'[10] Legitimacy with any real force 'embodies, rules, values, and shared purposes that create some sense of felt obligation'.[11] Nor can the hints of international law be ignored altogether. The three elements make up the elements of the ethical balance sheet attempted here.

The twentieth-century position

Intelligence up to the end of the twentieth century was then, as it still is, a dyad of two overlapping functions: collecting and producing information by special means; and acting as government's expert on its own particular subjects, drawing on overt as well as covert sources. In both functions it has been characterised as 'telling truth to power'. The idea of 'truth' in any absolute sense is open to argument, but crediting intelligence with a professional ethos of truthfulness – or at least attempting it – is less controversial.

On that basis I argued some years ago that intelligence did not raise first-order ethical questions akin to those of war and peace; but that it did raise some. At that time I put forward three propositions that bore on them.[12] First, governments drawing on a professional standard of intelligence knowledge tended to behave as more responsible members of international society than those that had to manage without it, or chose to do so – less ignorant, less insensitive and (I would now add of democratic states) less impetuous.[13] This was a general effect, though specific cases could also be adduced in which intelligence had been deliberately used to underpin specific stability producing, conflict reduction arrangements, as in arms control, or some of the US mediation efforts in the Middle East and south Asia. There was indeed a contrary line or argument that criticised intelligence as an institutionally distorting prism, with vested interests in 'worst case' views of the world or in reinforcing governments' preconceptions; but it seemed that the historical record of Western intelligence did not bear this out in any consistent way. Intelligence is liable to be wrong, but underestimates threats as often as exaggerates them.

Second, much of intelligence's information gathering still followed the well-established pattern of targeting other states. By and large this caused no observable problems for inter-state relations. Just occasionally, indeed, the United States and the Soviet Union had accepted and co-operated with the other's intelligence collection against them as a means of verifying arms control.[14] But some of the intelligence collection was particularly intrusive and could be perceived as a mark of hostility, reinforcing its target's perceptions of threat or tension. Examples from the Cold War were Western overflights of the Soviet Union, the position of diplomats and embassies in providing cover for covert collection (and also as the targets of intelligence operations directed against them), and above all the sheer scale of Russian espionage. Even outside a context of threats, intrusive collection of these kinds implied a disrespect for the target governments, an international equivalent of a two-fingered gesture.

None of this had ceased with the end of the Cold War. Russia and the West moved towards better relationships, yet more espionage cases between them seemed to hit the headlines than before. It was difficult not to believe that intrusive collection when detected or suspected was an obstacle to close relations and collaboration between states, even if it was not one of the major ones.

Third, however, a newer category of collection had expanded after the end of the Cold War, directed not at what the nineteenth century would have called other 'civilised' states, but at an increasing number of different targets: non-state and quasi-state entities of many kinds, including terrorist organisations; the varied actors involved in situations of breakdown and suffering, typically wars within states rather than between them; and the so-called rogue states, outside the pale as far as the main club of states was concerned. Targeting of this kind did nothing to produce friction among the civilised state community, and indeed usually supported international collaboration between them in good causes.

So intelligence knowledge got good ethical marks, but the effects of its collection were variable. Some of it against other states could still be seen as producing its own version of the security dilemma. What intelligence was produced, reduced irresponsible and ignorant national behaviour and on balance made the world better; but some of the activities pro-ducing it made the world marginally worse. So before September 2001 there already seemed scope for developing an intelligence variant of medieval Just War doctrine for such activities. By extension, the criteria of restraint, necessity and proportionality might be applicable to intrusive interstate collection rather as it applies to the violence of war.[15]

At the same time, however, the extension to the newer, post-Cold War non-state and pariah-type targets pointed in a different direction. Absolutists might still have reservations about some of the methods used, but consequentialists judging observable effects could feel that there need be no inhibitions about their effects on international society; indeed quite the reverse, where considerations of international security and humanitarianism were among the motives. The present writer's sympathy was with the view that, on such targets and in such circumstances, *almost* any methods of collection were justified, short of gross violations of human rights.[16] The scope for 'Just Intelligence' seemed quite wide.

Of course this was a simplification. The newer, post-Cold War targets were only new in scale and not in kind; collection against terrorism dated back at least 30 years. As for the purposes served by targeting them, no causes are unambiguously good or have universal international support. International society is itself not just a well-defined club of respect-able states, with clear divisions between them and other targets outside it. The difference between intrusive and non-intrusive collection is equally a matter of degree; the seriousness of intrusion is anyway in the eye of those intruded upon, as in the way the French and

European Parliaments worried greatly before September 2001 about the English-speaking countries' Echelon system for collecting international communications, despite the fact that its big dishes pointed into the heavens and were not pointed at any particular group of states. There were no general criteria of acceptability and unacceptability.[17]

Nevertheless, distinctions could reasonably be drawn between the three effects: those of intelligence knowledge, intrusive collection on respectable states (in the extreme case, 'spying on friends'), and collection against the other, newer targets, including support of counter-terrorism and other international good causes. How far have they now been modified by the events of 2001 and 2002?

Changed status

The main change has been the dramatic increase in intelligence's own importance after September 11, 2001. A trend in that direction had begun earlier; after intelligence budgets had been reduced as part of the peace dividend at the end of the Cold War, they were already being restored to cope not only with terrorism but also with the requirements of the 1990s for support of multi-lateral and international peace enforcement and humanitarian operations, and for intelligence on WMD proliferation, sanctions evasion, drug trafficking and the other emerging targets of the decade. Governments were already adapting them-selves to what seemed an increasingly unstable world, and to the information revolution within it both in the information available and in governments' ability to collect and process it. Intelligence as a whole was growing again and was no longer quite such a deniable activity.

Nevertheless, before September 11, it was still not seen as a defence against an overarch-ing and common threat. The Western military interventions of the 1990s had been interven-tions by choice, and international terrorism and other threats were still seen as peripheral ones, slightly remote. Terrorists struck at US citizens overseas but not at home. I could argue that intelligence would become increasingly variegated, flexible and opportunistic. In terms of Britain's survival it is now less vital than during the Cold War, but probably more useful . . . British intelligence's national importance therefore needs to be judged mainly in rather general contexts: public assumptions about foreign policy and defence; long-standing expectations of intelligence as a strong card in government's hand; the links between intelli-gence and the transatlantic political relationship.[18]

The events of September 11 and what followed radically altered this position. As in the Cold War, intelligence's main target has become once again a major and widely shared threat – except that it is now actual, and not potential. In the Cold War, intelligence was helping governments to avoid war; now it is actively involved in fighting one, seeking to save lives and defend national security in the most literal sense, in an asymmetrical contest whose nature gives it a special importance. Whatever reservations were expressed about the US declaration of a 'war on terrorism', the wartime metaphor fits intelligence's current status rather well. Apparently reliable reports in January 2003 that since September 11, 2001, 100 terrorist attacks have been thwarted world-wide and 3,000 suspects detained in 100 coun-tries (including Britain) leave little doubt about its seriousness.[19] The current prominence of Iraq and North Korea has reinforced the effect. Major decisions now seem to turn particu-larly on what intelligence is able to discover on the intentions and capabilities of highly secretive targets.

So its budgets are increasing everywhere, and hardly a day passes without its appearance in the news. President Bush mentioned it 18 times in his National Security Strategy of

20 September 2002, almost as frequently as military power and over twice as often as diplomacy.[20] Prime Minister Blair waxed eloquently about intelligence in January 2003; it was 'Britain's first line of defence against terrorism'.[21] Most Western countries have amended existing legislation to give it greater scope and reduced restrictions. Intelligence is confirmed as a major attribute of national soft (or semi-soft) power.[22] All nations except the smallest in the world's near-200 states will soon develop its institutions if they do not have them already. The Security Council's Resolution 1373 on terrorism mandated exchanges on it; the first mandate of this kind.[23] All this has given intelligence some new legitimacy, though this by no means unambiguous. The UN mandate is still for 'information exchanges', and not intelligence.

Events have also had two other related effects. One is to re-emphasise the importance of covert collection and the secrecy needed to protect it. In the years after the Cold War ended commentators could argue that in an increasingly open world intelligence's emphasis would shift away from collection and towards analysis: there would be more emphasis on 'intelligence-as-information', drawing on more open source material, and less on 'intelligence-as-secrets'.[24] On this view a liberal could expect that intelligence would become rather less mysterious and 'special', and eventually rather more like a normal information service such as government statistics; more open and unspectacular, and attracting less media curiosity and hype.

This now seems very dated. Already by the end of the 1990s the pendulum was swinging back some way towards the older view. Operations in the former Yugoslavia had demonstrated the importance of secret collection, even in situations with media coverage. Now, as in the Cold War, intelligence's main obstacle is the secrecy of intensely difficult targets. Analysis remains important everywhere. But counter-terrorism puts a renewed emphasis on intrusive collection – particularly the human agent, but also eavesdropping on national and international communications – accompanied by rapid investigation and operational use. Dame Stella Rimington's claim in 1994 that the security forces in Northern Ireland were by then frustrating four out of every five attempted terrorist attacks had earlier illustrated the cumulative but unspectacular significance of successful pre-emptive warning.[25] As in any war, intelligence's value in a counter-terrorist campaign is sometimes less to high-level decision taking than in nitty-gritty tactical use. Intelligence as a whole is again 'special', secret, an object of great public curiosity: all characteristics that a few years earlier could be felt to be on the wane.

The other, apparently contradictory effect has been to make it at the same time more international. In itself this was also nothing new. Even before September 11, the CIA already had liaisons with some 400 foreign intelligence, security and police organisations.[26] By comparison, the Russian FSB (the internal security part of the old KGB) was similarly claiming to have 'around 80 missions representing the special services of 56 countries' working permanently in Moscow, and formal agreements with '40 foreign partners in 33 countries'.[27] Up to UNSCOM's withdrawal in 1998, up to 20 nations are said to have passed information to it on Iraqi sanctions busting and weapons development.

But September 11 brought a great boost to this 'internationalisation'. Despite being an intelligence superpower, the United States cannot meet all its counter-terrorist requirements itself. Almost every nation is able to supply some unique intelligence on global terrorism, from its local records and local human and technical sources. The United States accordingly developed a set of new or deeper counter-terrorist relationships, and Britain followed suit. The Blair–Putin statement after their meeting of 20–21 December 2001 confirmed that 'co-operation on intelligence matters has been unprecedently close' and announced an

Anglo-Russian agreement to set up a new 'joint group to share intelligence'. The Security Service, necessarily the most domestically oriented of the British agencies, had over 100 links with foreign intelligence and security services in 2002.[28] In the United States the Presidential message of September 2002 formally confirmed the objective of co-ordinating closely with allies for common assessment of the most dangerous threats.

This internationalisation has not been completely centred on the US hub or the English-speaking communities. The European Union for its part developed its 'anti-terrorist roadmap' for European action, including common measures for improving databases on individuals, making more information available from public electronic communications, and the establishment of a new group of heads of security and intelligence agencies to meet regularly.[29] There have been similar regional agreements elsewhere. Thus in southeast Asia the Philippines, Cambodia, Indonesia, Malaysia and Thailand have signed anti-terrorist agreements, most recently under the influence of the Bali atrocity.[30] In the United Nations, the new British-chaired Counter-Terrorism Committee initially declared one of its aims to be 'to establish a network of information-sharing and cooperative action'.[31]

Of course US influence predominates, and its intelligence community is no doubt influenced by the conflicting tugs in all US policy making between unilateralism and multilateralism. But intelligence is one subject on which the United States needs some foreign help, and this will tend to underpin the world-wide trend, which seems to be towards increased intelligence collaboration, sometimes between unlikely allies including the former Cold War antagonists. Equally striking have been the public demands of the chief of UNMOVIC in the winter of 2002–03 for more national intelligence inputs to the Commission's investigation of Saddam Hussein's WMD programme: demands on behalf of the United Nations which earlier would have been put very discreetly or not at all.

This is all a considerable shift. Despite all its bilateral and multi-lateral foreign liaisons, intelligence was previously regarded as still an essentially separate, eremitic national activity. It is now becoming an increasingly important international network in its own right, in the world of ever-growing inter-governmental co-operation. The effect on its ethical balance sheet is twofold. It narrows the area to which the security dilemma applies; yet simultaneously sharpens the dilemma where it does.

Anything goes?

The last two years have increased the credit balance for intelligence knowledge. Its recent importance is obvious enough in the general run of world events, particularly over Iraq; and above all there is its wartime-like importance in counter-terrorism. Events are also emphasising the importance of professional qualities throughout its whole process of collection, evaluation, assessment and distribution. At a national level, both the CIA and British agencies seem to have acted as governments' consciences over Iraq. The CIA has kept a low profile in the divisions between hawks and doves in the US Administration, but there have been some press reports of its protests over exaggerations at policy level over the evidence of Iraqi contacts with al-Qaeda.[32] In Britain, whatever misjudgements intelligence may have made, even those most opposed to action against Saddam Hussein have not suggested that it has wilfully tailored its product to fit government policy.

This importance of standards spreads well beyond the English-speaking communities and applies to intelligence's internationalisation. The era of increased intergovernment co-operation increases the need not only for intelligence exchanges, but also for professionalism in handling it. Exchanges of information for international action are of only limited value without some corresponding international growth of depoliticisation and the pursuit of truthfulness in producing and interpreting them.

This importance of knowledge and standards might seem to increase the dilemma of results versus collection methods, yet in one way its scale is reducing. More intelligence is now targeted for objectives shared by the 'civilised' international community, and not on the community itself. On international terrorism alone, the British SIGINT organisation – by far the largest of the national agencies – was officially stated to be devoting 30–40 per cent of its total effort to the post-September 11 crisis, and it would be surprising if this has subsequently decreased greatly; and to this should be added all the (relatively) newer targets discussed earlier, such as counter-proliferation and the pariah states, outside the 'respectable' parts of the international system.

To conclude that literally 'anything goes' on such targets may still be an exaggeration. As Sir Michael Quinlan pointed out some years ago, covert collection carries some moral debits even in good causes. Secrecy fits awkwardly into the accountability of open democracies; and intelligence has now become more secret again. More international co-operation on terrorism means consorting with politically dubious foreign bedfellows. Espionage may involve normally reprehensible activities or associations (though its agents may equally be motivated by high principles). Nevertheless on collection against this class of target the events of the last two years have tipped the balance further against substantial ethical restraints, such as those on whose account the US Executive, Congress and media are said to have knocked the stuffing out of CIA's HUMINT in the 1990s. If the wartime metaphor fits counter-terrorism, it implies relatively few moral restrictions on information gathering on its targets. To repeat the opening of this paper: information gathering is not action to which separate ethical criteria must be applied.

Spying on friends?

Yet on some other targets the last two years have at the same time sharpened the ethical dilemma. If intrusive 'spying on friends' formerly increased the problems of inter-state friction in a rather general way, now it also poses particular difficulties for the increased international collaboration now developing. Even if terrorism took up 30–40 per cent of GCHQ's effort after September 11 and the other 'newer' targeting was substantial, sizable resources were still presumably devoted to the older-style coverage of other states, excluding the pariahs; and probably still are. Relatively few of these states are actually 'friends'; most inter-state relationships are somewhere on a long scale between the extremes of friendship and enmity, and have conflicting elements anyway. But the likelihood remains that, despite the growth of international consultation and collaboration on common causes, significant intelligence is still collected to defend or advance purely national interests; for example, helping governments to get the best deal they can in the welter of trade, economic, financial and other negotiations that make up international society's daily substance. Some of this intelligence – perhaps not a large part – is produced by means which the targets would consider to be intrusive. Can this targeting really be squared with the governments' simultaneously seeking closer intelligence collaboration in common causes?

Governments' increasing transparency gives additional force to this old dilemma. Covert collection does not upset anyone if it remains truly covert, but it is now harder than it used to be for governments anywhere to keep secrets for long; most of them leak out sooner or later. And democratic foreign policies are now more influenced than formerly by mass opinion formers who react strongly to finding spies under the national bed; more strongly than the worldly wise diplomats who previously accepted intrusive intelligence as part of the game, provided as little was said about it as possible. Modern democracies are easily insulted, even if not significantly threatened, and do not take easily to hushing up the detection of foreign spies. They have correspondingly tender consciences about their own methods, and demand a corresponding Caesar's wife-like standard over their own governments' clean hands and international legality.

It still cannot be proved that revelations of 'spying' (in its extended popular sense) really matter. The cases in Moscow and Washington in the 1990s and the related expulsions of diplomats did not prevent a gradual development of US – Russian understanding; no-one can judge whether they delayed it. It has recently been claimed that CIA used its Russian opposition numbers to plant devices to detect emissions from the North Korean nuclear weapons programme sometime in the 1990s,[33] so it may be that intelligence co-operation can continue to co-exist with spying on each other. But this is to be doubted in the long term. It is difficult to believe that the extended Anglo-Russian intelligence exchanges announced in December 2001 would survive a cause célèbre connected with a large undeclared Russian intelligence presence in the London embassy; or vice versa.

So intelligence as a booming world institution still has a doubtful reputation. If it were a multi-national corporation it might ask 'do we need to clean up our act?' But it would be too much to ask any state to engage again in the kind of unilateral disarmament that the US Secretary of State undertook to close the American codebreaking 'Black Chamber' in 1929 with the feeling that 'gentlemen don't read each others' mail'.[34] Neither is the United Nations likely to endorse any covert collection methods, even for the information whose exchanges on terrorism it mandates. The ethical dilemma over intelligence of this kind can only be reduced by inter-governmental reciprocity.

Customs and understandings

This would not be breaking completely new ground. Collection has not been conducted against other states in peacetime in a spirit of short-term realism; there has often been some restraint. This has been neither strong nor widespread enough to be a recognised international norm, assuming that a norm is rather stronger and more widely shared than an attitude.[35] But intelligence's networks of liaisons and alliances have had the result that some countries do not conduct operations of any kind against each other. The Britain–United States–Old Commonwealth community is the normally quoted example, but there may be other areas of tacit abstention; some or all of the Scandinavian countries, for example. Israeli intelligence was reputed not to collect against the US government until the disastrous Pollard case in the 1980s. Close intelligence liaisons do not necessarily rule out all mutual targeting, but probably limit the use of the most potentially embarrassing methods. But understandings about restraint are tacit or tightly held. The only recent public declaration was the agreement between Russia and the new Confederation of Independent States around it to foreswear operations against each other, shortly after the break-up of the Soviet Union. There must be doubts whether its effect was ever more than cosmetic.

Some restraint has also been exercised against adversaries. The British overflights of the Soviet Union were conducted in the first half of the 1950s because President Eisenhower was not prepared to authorise the US Air Force to mount them. Subsequently the position was reversed when Anthony Eden refused authorisation for such operations, including American U-2 flights from British bases. British peripheral flights around the Soviet Union, though entirely legal, remained subject to ministerial approval throughout the Cold War, as were more genuinely covert collection operations. All depended on the circumstances of particular cases, including the risk of being found out. But at least in the West there was some recognition of intelligence's provocative quality, perhaps entwined with considerations of governments' international and national images and older ideas of national 'honour'. It would be interesting to know whether the authors of the new British government's 1997 foreign policy statement had intelligence in mind when including 'respect for other states' as a principle, returning full circle to Kant's principles of international morality.[36]

In the decade after the end of the Cold War there were some indications of tentative moves towards restraint, perhaps in reaction to the spy cases of the period. Russia was reported to have pressed the UN Secretary-General in 1998 for an international treaty banning information warfare.[37] A Russian spokesman had denied in 1996 that there were any agreements with the United States about high-level penetration agents,[38] but the possibility of mutual US and Russian reductions was raised, apparently from the US side, in July 1999 in Washington discussions between the US Vice President and the Russian Prime Minister of the day, and remitted for further examination.[39] Reducing the scale of Russian espionage in Britain was said similarly to have been raised by Blair with Putin at a one-to-one meeting in March 2001.[40] The idea of 'intelligence arms control' had had some slight airing before September 11, 2001.

Now it has additional relevance. Not only is there the increased need for closer intelligence collaboration, but there are also the practical resource issues raised by the scale of counter-terrorism and the other newer requirements. Ever since the end of the Cold War 'intelligence arms control' would have been of mutual benefit to Russia and the United States, both intensely concerned at the threat of foreign espionage; it would also have benefited Britain, though London has in practice seemed rather less anxious about foreign espionage threats. Now the benefit would be even greater, freeing intelligence resources for deployment on counter-terrorism, instead of mutual espionage and all the defensive counterintelligence and counter-espionage it necessitates. Smaller intelligence powers might also be influenced by the example of restraint in inter-state targeting by larger ones.

The only actual pointer in this direction has been Putin's announcement in late 2001 of his intention to close the large Russian interception station on Cuba, long a source of Congressional opposition to closer US–Russian relations, as well as the similar station at Cam Rahn in Vietnam. The announcement was welcomed by President Bush at the time as 'taking down relics of the Cold War and building a new, cooperative and transparent relationship for the twenty-first century',[41] though there has been no obvious reciprocity.[42] It might be significant that in December 2001 the annual Russian end-of-year summary of detected espionage cases pointed less than on previous occasions to US and British complicity.[43] On the other hand a British media article in late 2002 claimed that 'Russia was engaged in a massive expansion of espionage in Europe and North America', and that the Russian intelligence presence in the London embassy had increased from one in 1991 to 33.[44] So intelligence restraint may not yet be on the international agenda; though it is unlikely to be publicised even if it ever is.

A new intelligence paradigm?

Perhaps what is needed is a new paradigm. Intelligence's place has been determined historically by ideas of national sovereignty, threats and interstate competition. Despite alliances and exchanges, one state's gain in knowledge has been seen basically as another's defeat in information protection. Yet September 11 and the counter-terrorist campaign link with other events of recent years to produce a mood for new ideas. Intelligence could be seen no longer as primarily an element in states' competition with others, but as a means of co-operation for shared objectives against common targets: a legitimised activity, with some recognised international standards similar to those of other professions, such as law enforcement. Michael MccGwire has written of the possibility of a 'paradigm shift' in the concept of national security, taking a paradigm to be 'the mixture of beliefs, theory, pre-conceptions and prejudices that shapes ideas of how the international system works, gener-ates expectations and prescribes appropriate behaviour', and argues for an international rather than a national view of security.[45] A revision of the mental framework for intelligence might be part of some much larger process of that kind.[46]

This may seem pie-in-the-sky, yet states can change their working assumptions radically. In the nineteenth century the Red Cross owed its development to a private initiative which caught on and moved governments;[47] and the Hague Conference of 1899 and its contribu-tions to the laws of war originated in an unexpected initiative from the Tsar, possibly from reading a book on future war.[48] Sir Michael Howard reminded us before 2001 that, until the eighteenth-century enlightenment, war between states 'remained an almost automatic activ-ity, part of the natural order of things'.[49] 'If anyone could be said to have invented peace as more than a mere pious aspiration, it was Kant.'[50] The changing view of military power provides another analogy. Armies are still national, but John Keegan argued in 1998 that democracy's professional soldiers are now also international society's check upon violence; 'those honourable warriors who administer force in the cause of peace'.[51] *Mutatis mutandis*, the twenty-first century may bring us to see intelligence in that light.

So intelligence's ethics are at least worth consideration. They are not international soci-ety's greatest problem. The ethical issues they pose are Second Division and not First Division ones. Yet events have confirmed intelligence everywhere as a major national attrib-ute, and an increasingly significant factor in international relations amid the Information Revolution of which it is part. It cannot now be handled entirely in a mood of old-fashioned realism; and indeed never has been. The idea of ethical foreign policy got a bad press when given political salience in Britain in 1997, but was in reality a statement of the obvious. Intelligence has to fit into the ethics of an increasingly co-operative system of states, perhaps with bigger changes in thinking than have previously seemed possible. I hope that there will be opportunities for practitioners and academics to join together to explore a concept of 'ethical intelligence', and where its implications point.

Notes

I am grateful to Sir Michael Quinlan and Toni Erskine for their comments on earlier drafts of this paper.

1 *MI5: The Security Service* 4th edn (London: The Stationery Office 2002), p. 15. It shows 14.4 per cent of the service's resources as allocated to counter-espionage.

2 H. Reiss (tr. H.B. Nisbet), *Kant: Political Writings* (Cambridge: Cambridge University Press 1991), pp. 96–7.

3 L. Lustgarten and I. Leigh, *In from the Cold: National Security and Parliamentary Democracy* (Oxford: Clarendon Press 1994), p. 225. This work concentrates on intelligence's domestic aspects, but incidentally provides ethical criticism of foreign intelligence.

4 Cricket in fact has 'laws', which interestingly have traditionally included observing the 'spirit of the game', and in recent years have attempted to codify it.

5 The relevant law on maritime collection is *United Nations Convention on the Law of the Sea 1982,*

articles 19 and 29. 'Innocent passage' excludes 'collecting information to the prejudice of the defence or security of the coastal state' (19.2 (c)).

6 Details in the author's *Intelligence Power in Peace and War* (Cambridge: Cambridge University Press 1996), p. 89.

7 Michael Byers, 'Terrorism, the Use of Force and International Law after 11 September', *International Relations*, 16, 2 (August 2002).

8 For modern legitimacy, see Andrew Hurrell, ' "There Are No Rules" (George W. Bush): International Order after September 11', *International Relations*, 16 (August 2002).

9 For the idea of international society I draw on David Armstrong, 'Globalization and the Social State', *Review of International Studies*, 24, 4 (October 1998).

10 Terry Nardin, 'International Pluralism and the Rule of Law', *Review of International Studies*, 26, Special Issue (December 2000), p. 100.

11 Hurrell, 'There Are No Rules', p. 189.

12 Set out in M. Herman, *Intelligence Services in the Information Age: Theory and Practice* (London: Frank Cass 2001), Ch. 13.

13 It has recently been argued that decision takers have varied attitudes to risks that produce different but equally 'rational' decisions over possible gains and losses; in situations of equal uncertainty, some are risk-averse and others risk-acceptant (Barry O'Neill, 'Risk Aversion in International Relations Theory', *International Studies Quarterly*, 45, 4 (December 2001)). But intelligence's role is to provide both classes with accurate calibrations of uncertainty and risk.

14 This has continued. 'On 24 August 2001 the last 450 US Minuteman missile silos earmarked for destruction under SALT I were destroyed. The detonation of explosives turns the silos into 90-foot craters, which are then filled with rubble, capped and left for 90 days to allow Russian satellites to verify their elimination.' (Vertic *Trust and Verify*, 100 (January–February 2002).)

15 For the idea of 'Just Intelligence', see Michael Quinlan, 'The Future of Covert Intelligence' and M. Herman, 'Modern Intelligence Services: Have They a Place in Ethical Foreign Policies?', both in Harold Shukman (ed.), *Agents for Change: Intelligence Services in the 21st Century* (London: St Ermin's Press 2000), pp. 68, 307–8. But note that Just War theory starts from the premise that war is quite special in the ethical problems its raises.

16 Set out, for example, in Herman, *Intelligence Services in the Information Age*, pp. 211–12.

17 But there are sometimes tacit yardsticks of what is acceptable and unacceptable even between antagonists. During the Cold War the Russian Commander of the Soviet Forces in East Germany protested that the British Military Mission had gone too far; one collection operation had gone beyond recognised '*razvedka*' (reconnaissance) to an unacceptable degree of '*shpionazh*' (espionage). I am grateful to Colonel Roy Giles for this example.

18 M. Herman, *British Intelligence towards the Millennium* (London: Centre for Defence Studies 1997), pp. 64–5.

19 Richard A. Serrano and Greg Miller, '100 Terrorist Attacks Thwarted, U.S. Says', *Los Angeles Times*, 11 January 2003.

20 There were 23 references to military forces, and seven to diplomacy.

21 Address to House of Commons Liaison Committee, 21 January 2003.

22 Compare Nye's definition of soft power as the ability 'to get others to want what you want' (Joseph Nye, 'The New Rome Meets the New Barbarians', *The Economist*, 23 March 2002).

23 The Security Council in that Resolution decided that 'all states shall . . . take the necessary steps to prevent the commission of terrorist acts, including by provision of early warning to other States by exchange of information' (2(b)). Various parts of item 3 'called upon' states to exchange terrorist information to prevent the commission of terrorist acts.

24 Gregory F. Treverton, *Reshaping National Intelligence for an Age of Information* (Cambridge: Cambridge University Press 2001), *passim*.

25 S. Rimington, Richard Dimbleby Lecture, *Security and Democracy* (London: BBC Educational Developments 1994), p. 9.

26 Treverton, *Reshaping National Intelligence*, p. 137.

27 Article by FSB Director N. Patrushev, Russian National Information Service, 20 December 2001.

28 *MI5: The Security Service*, p. 26.

29 Summary in *Statewatch*, 11, 5 (August–October 2001).

30 Details from *Straits Times*, 16 January 2003.

31 Sir Jeremy Greenstock (Chairman), press conference 19 October 2001 (http://www.un.org/Docs/sc/committees/1373).
32 The *Guardian*, 10 October 2002.
33 James Risen, *New York Times*, 20 January 2003. This was however denied by a spokesman for the Russian SVR the following day.
34 Note however that the actual words were the speaker's rationalisation 17 years later: see correspondence in *Intelligence and National Security*, 2, 4 (October 1987).
35 But norms do not have to be universally accepted. For discussion see Vaughn P. Shannon, 'Norms Are What States Make of Them: The Political Psychology of Norm Violation', *International Studies Quarterly*, 44, 2 (June 2000), especially pp. 294–6.
36 Nardin, 'International Pluralism and the Rule of Law', p. 97 n.
37 *Sunday Times*, 25 July 1999, p. 21.
38 *Nezavisimaya Gazeta*, 22 November 1996.
39 Russian accounts of the press conference refer to 'total mutual understanding' having been reached on 'one sensitive topic', and existing agreements 'to work in a fairly correct sort of way' (FBIS and BBC translations of 28 and 29 July 1999 items).
40 *Sunday Times*, 25 March 2001.
41 Details from the Association of Former Intelligence Officers Weekly Notes October 2001 (www.afio.com/sections/wins).
42 The Russian Foreign Ministry suggested that the United States should close down 'the radar station in Vardoe (Norway)'. (Gordon Bennett, *Vladimir Putin and Russia's Special Services* (Sandhurst: Conflict Studies Research Centre 2002)), p. 69.
43 Ibid., p. 24.
44 *Jane's Intelligence Review*, 3 December 2002.
45 Michael MccGwire, 'The Paradigm that Lost its Way' and 'Shifting the Paradigm', *International Affairs*, 77, 4 (2001), and 78, 1 (2002). The quotation is from the first, p. 649.
46 A changed framework for intelligence would involve changes for covert action, on similar lines.
47 Pam Brown, *Henry Dunant: The Founder of the Red Cross* (Watford: Exley 1988).
48 Geoffrey Best, 'Peace Conferences and the Century of Total War: The 1899 Hague Conference and What Came After', *International Affairs*, 75, 3 (July 1999), p. 622.
49 M. Howard, *The Invention of Peace: Reflections on War and International Order* (London: Profile Books 2000), p. 13.
50 Ibid., p. 31.
51 Concluding words in J. Keegan, *War and Our World* (London: Hutchinson 1998), p. 74.

Reprinted with permission from Michael Herman, 'Ethics and Intelligence after September 2001,' *Intelligence and National Security* 19/2 (2004) pp.342–358.

23 Ethical guidelines in using secret intelligence for public security

Sir David Omand

Pre-emptive intelligence is seen as key to enabling the state to counter terrorism without alienating the minority communities from whom the terrorists hope to gain support. The international nature of jihadist terrorism is placing increasing demands on intelligence agencies to co-operate with new partners overseas and to extend their range of methods, human and technical, to acquire such intelligence. This pressure is creating ethical dilemmas for the agencies at a time when the methods of secret intelligence and their impact on individual rights are the subject of public controversy. This article discusses the implications of the requirement to produce and share actionable high-value intelligence, and suggests a set of ethical guidelines for the British intelligence community. These guidelines aim to help sustain public confidence in intelligence work and in the directions in which this work must develop in order to generate the pre-emptive intelligence needed for public security.

Introduction [1]

The growth of jihadist terrorism poses risks to public security of a type and scale not previously encountered, and is a threat that will persist for some years to come.[2] Emergency responses will no longer do, and there needs to be a well thought-out long-term strategy that commands public understanding and support and reduces the risk to Britain's national interests, whilst allowing people to go about their normal business freely and with confidence (Omand 2005–2006). Good intelligence has to be seen as the necessary (if not sufficient) basis for such sustainable success against terrorism. But the efforts of governments to generate that vital intelligence are raising ethical dilemmas for Western intelligence communities. The British intelligence agencies are already governed by a mixture of statutory provisions and internal regulation. This article attempts to make explicit the principles that lie – or ought to lie – behind such regulation, in the hope that this may illuminate future debate on where limits should be placed on the scale and type of intelligence-gathering used in pursuit of greater public security.

Lessons from experience

An act of terrorism is an ultimate act of communication: to intimidate the target population, to rally supporters and to inspire recruits. It can also be intended to lead governments to over-react and create the conditions for revolutionary consciousness among the uncommitted. A key assumption in this article is therefore that sound strategy to counter terrorism will involve upholding and promoting the freedoms and human rights, including the right to the rule of law, that are at the heart of what has to be defended from the terrorists. The hard-won British experience in past campaigns is that compromising our values in the hope of quick knockout blows against the terrorists is self-defeating. A clear example was the use in 1971 of internment coupled with 'deep interrogation' techniques[3] by British authorities in Northern Ireland, which produced limited intelligence at the cost of a propaganda disaster that turned many in the community against the authorities. Heavy-handed security measures, such as house-to-house searches or undue use of 'stop and search' powers, impact on the innocent and ill-intentioned alike. Similarly, well-intentioned steps taken for public protection can quickly come to appear to target whole communities, and thus can become themselves radicalising factors among those whom terrorists hope to recruit.

Experience also teaches us that intelligence is often the only source of the early indications that can lead to the uncovering of terrorist networks. Good pre-emptive intelligence enables counter-terrorist operations to be designed and focused on legitimate targets without dislocating the normal life of the community: in terms of state action, enabling the bludgeon to be replaced by the rapier. Of course, as we have been forcibly reminded recently, secret intelligence is only one of many contributions to the situational awareness of government. It is rarely decisive, is often ambiguous and fragmentary and is sometimes wrong.

We should also recognise that the tactical capabilities of terrorist and international criminal networks, such as counter-surveillance and secret methods of communication and financing, are improving, potentially frustrating conventional law enforcement. The reasonable expectation is that intelligence agencies will be able to use their special skills and advanced techniques to penetrate and disrupt these networks.

It is no surprise therefore that as the current jihadist threat has grown, governments have been active in taking steps to generate more actionable intelligence, and encouraging their agencies to develop new liaisons with a wide range of countries, including some with very different security and intelligence traditions from Britain's.[4] Governments know that they are expected to deliver public safety through pre-emption, and not just enable effective police investigation and prosecution after the event. The British experience is that the public has shown itself to be resilient and indeed stoical in the face of terrorist attacks or attempted attacks. There is public recognition of the need to manage the risks involved in tackling terrorism but, regrettably, expectations of the level of protection governments can offer are probably still unrealistically high. We know from experience that intelligence coverage can never be expected to be complete and that there will inevitably be further casualties in a long campaign. The intelligence community also knows all too well that, despite their many successes, when terrorists do get through under the security radar, the accusation will be that this was because of a failure of intelligence.

The global spread of the jihadist brand of terrorism is an additional factor putting greater demands on the intelligence community than in the past. We should not be surprised that the international nature of the terrorist threat blurs traditional distinctions between the domestic space, occupied by police and domestic security services, and 'overseas' space, the preserve of secret services. When achieved, active inter-agency operational cooperation across national/international boundaries is a powerful asset against the terrorists, and in that respect, of course, the United Kingdom is very fortunate. The established international connections of British intelligence agencies are also proving invaluable, but some governments' responses to this legitimate need for better pre-emptive intelligence are themselves generating ethical concerns. Dilemmas are arising over what are legitimate methods to apply in collecting and using intelligence against terrorists. There are signs that sections of the public are becoming concerned at what is allegedly being done in their name by secret agencies involved in the so-called 'war on terror'.

Four dilemmas facing the British intelligence community

Let me describe four areas where such dilemmas arise for intelligence activity. First, we have seen intelligence used to direct a combination of overt military force and covert means to strike at known locations of terrorist activity overseas. These operations seek to discover and then disrupt terrorist planning, training and logistics pipelines, and to disable terrorist leadership.

Some of these counter-terrorist operations raise fundamental questions about the use, outside the battlefield, of intelligence to guide military or covert action against terrorists. We have seen 'targeted killing' by United States forces, for example by precision-guided air strike, following determination by the US President that the individual terrorists concerned may be killed if they are located and capture is not feasible.[5] The Israeli government is currently defending its policy of extra-judicial killing before its Supreme Court.[6] The legal issues arising over how military rules of engagement permit such pre-emptive lethal force are considerable. Should such activity be confined to recognised and declared war zones and be prohibited elsewhere? What degree of intelligence confidence ought to be required before strikes are launched? What are ethically acceptable rules for assessing risks of collateral deaths when the fight is thus pursued within populated areas? The UK intelligence community does not engage in assassination; is it therefore acceptable to pass actionable intelligence on to a country whose rules of engagement for dealing with terrorists are different? And what is to be done with those captured as part of counter-terrorist operations overseas? What methods are ethically acceptable for detaining and interrogating those captured, or returning suspects to third countries that wish to interrogate them in relation to allegations of involvement in terrorism?

Secondly, Western governments are, reasonably, helping to develop the security and intelligence capability of governments elsewhere that are also suffering from terrorism. But what if these countries are themselves suspected of ill-treatment of suspects? The present British policy is to accept information from any source that bears on Britain's major interests, at the same time as all reasonable steps are taken to promote overseas British views about acceptable interrogation methods. But can we sustain the position that British intelligence information should be passed to other countries if that information might lead to action by others that would be considered unacceptable by the UK?

Thirdly, at home, governments have increased the overall resources allocated to security and intelligence work[7] and emphasised its importance. The British Security Service will, for example, by 2008 be double the size it was before 9/11. I sense considerable public support for this in the UK. At the same time, however, there has been vigorous opposition to aspects of counter-terrorist legislation designed to assist the security effort. Opponents suggest that such legislation is disproportionate – a suggestion that is allied to concerns that Britain's counter-terrorism strategy risks long-term erosion of fundamental aspects of the rule of law.[8] It has been argued that the present situation, although dangerous, does not constitute a threat to the life of the nation which would justify derogation from human rights provisions.[9] Means are held to matter here as well as ends.

Finally, in seeking to sharpen the effectiveness of their intelligence establishments, governments are exploiting the latest information technology. These technical methods are proving particularly valuable in providing first clues to the existence of covert networks, but their very effectiveness is rubbing up against feelings of invasion of individual privacy, and worries over the wider uses to which such information might be put. For example, the US administration is facing legal challenge to the steps it has taken, controversially using war powers, to harness the capability of information technology to search large volumes of personal internet communications and financial transactions. We must expect the intelligence value of such methods to increase further, while the costs of these technologies continue to fall. Similar dilemmas arise in some European countries – for example, over the increasing use of closed-circuit surveillance cameras, already very widely used in the UK. I note in passing, however, that particularly in the light of the various inquiries after 9/11, there is a renewed US emphasis on building up the capability to generate high-value human intelligence, which was relatively neglected in the US during the long Cold War. This marks a reversal of the arguments of the 1970s against human intelligence (humint) in favour of investment in 'national technical means'.[10]

The case for thinking ethically about secret intelligence

The realm of intelligence operations is a zone where the ethical rules that we hope govern our private conduct as individuals in society cannot fully apply. Finding out other people's secrets is going to involve breaking everyday moral rules: the equivalent of reading others' mail; listening at and peeping through keyholes; deliberately encouraging indiscretion; inciting breaches of confidence; as well as masquerading as what you are not. In addition, effectiveness against global networks requires cooperation with secret services overseas; and such liaisons will include countries whose methods one might regard as crude and ethically doubtful. Intelligence collection against terrorist and criminal networks also increasingly involves the use of modern information technology to sift through large quantities of personal information. This raises issues of individual privacy and distaste for state prying.

Yet, even the United Nations has accepted the value of intelligence in combating terrorism (Herman 2004). A dirty business such as war can have its ethical guidelines[11] and, for the UK, it is certainly not the case that *inter arma silent leges* (Cicero). My thesis is that the public would value reassurance that there can also be ethical guidelines for intelligence, and that they are applied by UK agencies in countering terrorism. Such an understanding may become essential to securing public support in the UK, and agreement at a European level, for necessary future developments in intelligence collection and their use in reducing terrorism-related risk. A similar argument could no doubt be mounted in respect of the threats from proliferation of weapons of mass destruction and from the growth of serious organised crime.

We hit an immediate difficulty here over how an informed public debate can be conducted on these issues when much remains classified or sub judice and much of what is reported is the product of media speculation. Of necessity, intelligence methods are only going to be able to be fully effective in uncovering terrorist networks if the terrorists have imperfect knowledge of one's techniques. A truly informed public discussion about the details of contemporary intelligence sources and methods is thus hard to have.

But if government cannot responsibly give the public a full explanation of the inwardness of some of the proposals for counter-terrorist measures, then the public must be invited to consider only the general principles motivating these measures and take quite a lot of the detail on trust.

Such trust in the ethics of intelligence collection, and trust in the integrity of all those involved in the intelligence community, is still problematic after the controversy over the use of intelligence in the run-up to the war in Iraq and over the conduct of some current counter-terrorist operations.

It would not be a complete answer, but it would help if the public could recognise the extent to which members of the intelligence community do, as part of their everyday professional life, follow a set of ethical norms set firmly within the framework of human rights. I believe that this is the case already, implicitly, in line with both statute law and the internal instructions of the various agencies. I want to explore here how one might go about trying to set down the ethical principles that should guide intelligence activities.

A set of guidelines for the consideration of intelligence activity

Sir Michael Quinlan has reminded us in a recent lecture (2006) of the relevance of the just war tradition to discussion of contemporary security dilemmas: the tradition specifies the conditions that ought to be satisfied if war is to be justly undertaken – *jus ad bellum*, in the accepted shorthand – and the constraints and prohibitions that ought to be observed in the conduct of war – *jus in bello* (Walzer 1977).

In modern intelligence agencies, we have very powerful capabilities for personal intrusion, for acquiring private information and for triggering action. We need to be clear about the purposes – the potential targets – for which government should acquire such capabilities, about what Quinlan would invite us to think about as *jus ad intelligentiam*. And we need to establish what limitations society should place on the methods to be employed before these capabilities are unleashed, *jus in intelligentia*.

I would suggest six guidelines to govern the development, targeting and maintenance of national intelligence capability (*jus ad intelligentiam*) and the methods to be used in specific types of case (*jus in intelligentia*). I shall briefly explore some of the issues that arise in considering intelligence activity under each of these headings, hoping both to reassure as to the extent to which such guidelines are already implicitly incorporated into legislation or into the prevailing ethos within the British intelligence community, and to point to areas of potential or actual difficulty. The six guidelines are:

1 There must be sufficient sustainable cause.
2 There must be integrity of motive.
3 The methods to be used must be proportionate.
4 There must be right authority.
5 There must be reasonable prospect of success.
6 Recourse to secret intelligence must be a last resort.

First guideline: There must be sufficient sustainable cause

This is a check on any tendency for the secret world to encroach into areas that are justified neither by the scale of potential harm to national interests if no action is taken, nor by the advantage to be secured. If intelligence capability is to be developed and maintained, there has to be a sufficiently compelling purpose that can then be reflected, in British usage, in an approved set of intelligence requirements.

With such considerations in mind, in the legislation that placed the intelligence agencies on a statutory footing, the UK Parliament limited the purposes for which intelligence activities are allowed. Thus, for example, the functions of the Secret Intelligence Service (SIS) and Government Communications Headquarters (GCHQ) are legally restricted to being exercisable only:

(a)   in the interests of national security, with particular reference to the defence and foreign policies of Her Majesty's Government in the United Kingdom; or

(b)   in the interests of the economic well-being of the United Kingdom; or

(c)   in support of the prevention or detection of serious crime. (Intelligence Services Act 1994)

From time to time, intelligence operations may produce as a by-product interesting information on matters that would never have justified the operation by itself. Where minor (and thus possibly unfunded) requirements are thus met, that is a bonus for the policymakers working on those subjects, but it is important to recognise that the intelligence agencies can only operate within their statutory functions.

The underlying logic behind framing the first guideline is to seek the assurance that the intended class of intelligence target must be capable of doing real damage either to the interests of the nation or to the lives and livelihoods of its citizens. This still leaves room for judgement about what is sensible within these limits in terms of priorities. In a recent lecture, Quinlan (2005) has given the example of finding out the bottom-line of overseas government X in an impending negotiation about tariffs on trade in cabbages. Like Quinlan, I find it hard to suppose that the damage to national economic well-being of a poor outcome in such a case would justify that target as an intelligence requirement (even if there was no alternative open sources of information available, guideline 6, and the methods proposed were non-intrusive, guideline 3, and non-risky, guideline 5). But, in practice, given the demands of unarguably high-priority work within the legal limits on the functions of secret agencies, considerations regarding the allocation of scarce resources are likely to operate as a major constraint well before ethical prohibitions may come into play.

Meeting this guideline is not just about the ability to grasp immediate advantage, but should also be about ensuring that the development and deployment of such intelligence capability are likely to further national strategic objectives in the longer term. In the British system, approved requirements for collection within this definition are drawn up annually by the Joint Intelligence Committee and submitted to ministers along with strategic guidelines for the development of future capability. Intelligence capability does, however, take considerable time to develop, whether in terms of recruiting networks of agents or of developing technical means. Much development therefore has to take place in anticipation of need, a characteristic that intelligence shares with national defence.

Whilst describing legitimate purposes, it is important to recognise that intelligence agencies do not just collect intelligence; they also support covert action on behalf of government. This is clearly legitimate, with examples recommending this interpretation including the use of back channels to persuade a country like Libya to renounce its WMD programmes, or the initiation of a 'sting' against terrorist groups seeking to buy surface-to-air missiles. But covert action can also involve trying to follow in the dark policies that a government cannot admit to pursuing in the light. Covert policies usually get exposed eventually and can be highly controversial, generating scandals such as the US Iran–Contra affair. As with Wotan's attempts to bypass the treaties engraved on his spear-point, attempts to use controlled proxies to surreptitiously achieve ends that are not publicly admissible or lawful can end in Wagnerian disaster. The major issues raised by such covert operations are largely about the conduct of foreign policy by non-diplomatic means, and not about the ethics of intelligence collection itself. That is a debate for another occasion, though if there is international mistrust of intelligence agencies, some of that stems from controversy over their part in past covert activity rather than over collection itself. For present purposes, I want to focus on intelligence collection and assessment for public protection and actions that can only take place because of the knowledge given by such secret intelligence. In that sense, even intelligence assessment involves actions that are susceptible to ethical scrutiny (Erskine 2004).

Second guideline: There must be integrity of motive

As writers of spy fiction like to remind us, this can be a world where all is not what it seems, and case-officers can become lost in a 'wilderness of mirrors'.[12] Are the motives of all concerned in a proposed operation what they appear? And is there integrity in the recruitment of human sources, who must be convinced that their identity and their interests will be protected?

Following this guideline should involve assurance that there is proper concern with the integrity of the whole system throughout the intelligence process, from collection through to the analysis, assessment and presentation of the resulting intelligence. For there is certainly one ethical norm that should apply to all intelligence work, that is, integrity in presenting the results to customers for intelligence. Whatever the arts of deception (the 'tradecraft' in the jargon), the reader must have complete confidence in the integrity of the system that delivered the intelligence. The greatest sin for an intelligence officer, as for the scientist, is to betray the integrity of professional method. The results must not be massaged to fit prejudices or prevailing orthodoxics, or to avoid offending the prevailing political climate. Negative results must be reported as well as positive scoops, and every result must have the error estimate and the degree of reliability associated with it. Such issues were central to the independent review (the Butler Inquiry) set up by the British government in 2004 into intelligence on WMD. One key finding by Lord Butler's Committee was that there had been weaknesses in the effective application and resourcing of validation procedures to scrutinise human intelligence sources,[13] and that this helped explain the problems of unreliable or questionable intelligence on Iraqi WMD. All of this is setting a very high standard, but assurance of integrity of the workings of the intelligence community has to remain at the heart of the profession of intelligence.

I would highlight one particular application of this guideline that is essential to building public trust in the use of intelligence for public protection. When and how should secret intelligence about terrorist activity be revealed to the public? In this situation, to have public trust in the integrity underlying one's motive is essential. We should expect to be given public warnings related to threats that are being uncovered by intelligence when such warnings would enable the public to take action that would reduce the risk to themselves and their interests. The warnings of threats overseas given on the Foreign and Commonwealth Office website are a good example of this. We already have assurances from ministers that these warnings will be given. But we should remember that the best chance of reducing the risk to the public is to follow the leads and uncover the whole conspiracy. Counter-terrorist operations require police and intelligence staff alike to keep significant nerve as they manage the risks involved. They have to be trusted to have the protection of the public – now and in the future – as their sole motive, and not considerations of media presentation or political climate.

These days, governments are too often accused of having hidden agendas, not least in their presentation of the terrorist threat to the public. Any guidelines for the intelligence community must make clear that there is no possibility of political authority being misused. In what is probably the most sensitive area for the UK, the Security Service's

intelligence-gathering at home, unlike most areas of government,[14] the minister is not statutorily personally responsible and therefore cannot give operational directions. The authority
to direct domestic operations is vested directly in the director general, and not ministers,
precisely in order to avoid any perception that ministers are misusing the power of their
office for political or personal purposes. As part of 'right authority' (guideline 4), the secretary of state is, however, accountable to Parliament (that is, may be held to render an
account rather than be held personally responsible) for the operations of the Service. Since
the director general is appointed by the secretary of state, this provides a counter-balancing
mechanism for ultimate democratic control.

Third guideline: The methods to be used must be proportionate

This guideline is perhaps the most fundamental for those managing and approving
intelligence operations. Is the likely impact of the proposed intelligence-gathering operation, taking account of the methods to be used, in proportion to the seriousness of the
business at hand, for example, by intruding no more than necessary into the private affairs of
others?

Within the impact of a humint intelligence operation, I include the nature of the agent
recruitment and inducements, the physical risks involved and the moral hazard to agent and
handler alike – particularly where participating informants are being run. These are matters
that are largely governed in the UK by internal regulation within the intelligence community
rather than by statute. There are some important issues not covered in legislation. For
example, how far should the state go in indemnifying its officers from the consequences of
their actions when on duty? If we take the use of force, in terms of proportionality, there are
no special rules, only the criminal law and the common law doctrine of minimum force. We
have seen this doctrine tested in the courts in Northern Ireland, holding members of the
security forces accountable under the ordinary law and liable to prosecution after, say, a
shooting by a soldier at a roadblock. No one has 007 status.

Nor do agents have 'get out of jail' cards. The ethics of so-called 'participating informers'
merit a separate discussion.[15] It is hard to avoid the taint of having colluded in criminal acts
when well-placed agents in a terrorist or serious narcotics-trafficking organisation are likely
to have engaged in criminal activity or have blood on their hands. Yet, it is precisely such
agents that are likely to be the key to the pre-emptive intelligence needed for public safety.
Great care is taken by UK agencies in the supervision of those concerned in such operational activities (Maguire and John 1995), and it may be that at some point legislation
may be needed to protect those engaged in running such agents and to clarify their legal
standing – but I do not pretend that such law would be at all easy to construct.

When assessing proportionality under this guideline for technical intelligence operations,
the impact must also be judged in terms of the extent of intrusion into personal affairs or
family privacy. In this area, there is full legislative coverage in the UK. The Regulation of
Investigative Powers Act 2000 (RIPA), for example, already embodies the principle of proportionality through differing levels of request and approval. In other words, the test for
those approving bugging and eavesdropping operations is of minimum necessary intrusion,[16]
comparable to the common law doctrine of 'minimum necessary force'.

Most of the ethical problems associated with legislation to counter terrorism, including
facilitating intelligence-gathering, centre on how one might balance individual categories of
rights, such as the right to life and to be protected by the state from threats to oneself and
one's family and the right to privacy of personal and family life, for the circumstances in

question. There is an obvious danger that security concerns are somehow thought to trump human rights, with any immediate security gain given automatic primacy. It is a balancing act within rights that should be sought under this guideline, and not a trade-off between rights and something called 'security'.

It is also a balancing act to ensure that the long-term impact of the methods chosen for proposed operations is properly assessed, along with immediate gains. Governments will always want to apply utilitarian judgements in their balancing act. Governments will find doing so easier if they ensure that strategic as well as tactical considerations are included – thus avoiding the obvious trap of desirable immediate security benefits for the majority justifying actions that may disproportionately affect a minority. A current example is the debate over airline passenger profiling.[17]

Fourth guideline: There must be right authority

The issue here is whether it can be demonstrated that sensitive intelligence-gathering activities have a proper authorising process at a sufficiently senior level, and with accountability within a chain of command. Additionally, proper oversight must come from outside the intelligence community, and there must be a robust mechanism whereby any individual issues of conscience or concern within the community can be raised without fear while preserving secrecy. This oversight is necessary if public confidence is to be preserved.

The most sensitive area is probably that of domestic surveillance. For this category of intrusive operations, the UK public can, I hope, take reassurance in the fact that the relevant Act – RIPA 2000 – carefully calibrates both those who may request intrusive operations and the level of seniority of those approving them. Because the secretary of state is at the apex of approval for authorising the most intrusive operations, the secretary and the key officials in the department are given insight into the day-to-day activities of the agencies. At the same time, as I have explained, the statute has safeguards against political interference in operations. A very British constitutional settlement.

There is insufficient recognition of the extent of judicial oversight over the activities of the UK intelligence community. A senior judge is appointed as Intelligence Services Commissioner under RIPA 2000 to keep under review the issue of warrants by the secretary of state that authorise eavesdropping and interference with property, as well as the use by the Security Service of covert human intelligence sources.[18] In addition, RIPA 2000 provides for another senior judge to act as interception of communications commissioner with responsibility to keep under review the issue of interception warrants by the secretary of state.[19]

More generally, for the oversight of the expenditure, administration and policy of the secret intelligence agencies, Parliament has legislated to create the cross-party Intelligence and Security Committee (ISC), membership of which is to be drawn from both Houses of Parliament (Intelligence Services Act 1994). The ISC works within 'the ring of secrecy' throughout the course of an investigation, and is granted access to senior agency staff and to classified information. The ISC is, therefore, in practice in a position to provide Parliament with informed reassurance on the ethical standards being applied and to draw attention to issues it uncovers.

Fifth guideline: There must be reasonable prospect of success

Intelligence operations carry risks. Before approval is given, there has to be a judgement that the impact, if the operation were to be exposed, is acceptable. Even if the purpose is valid (guideline 1) and the methods to be used are proportionate to the issue (guideline 3), there needs to be a hard-headed assessment of risk to the operatives, to future operations of that nature and to institutional reputations. And the authorising authority has to weigh the risks of unintended consequences, or of political or diplomatic damage, if the operation were exposed, and judge them acceptable – including applying the golden rule 'do unto others as you would be done by'.

Since the infamous Commander Crabb affair,[20] it has been the practice in the UK that the Foreign Office must be consulted about operations by any of the agencies where there are risks of diplomatic damage so that officials, or in major cases the foreign secretary, can judge whether to authorise the operation. This practice is widely known and we have to accept that intelligence activity, if discovered, will be assumed to have been carried out in the name of Her Majesty's Government. Britain has thereby reduced the force of any complaint it might make over other nations caught conducting comparable intelligence operations against it. Whatever the public diplomacy, the practice of espionage is widespread, including the use of diplomatic immunity, and is not going to change. The 'golden rule' in such circumstances is therefore worth following as a guide.

Sixth guideline: Recourse to secret intelligence must be a last resort

In one sense, of course, collecting open information and, where justified, secret intelligence should always be the first resort of government, and armed force the last resort. I include this guideline, however, as a reminder that, for any individual line of intelligence-gathering, it has to be asked whether there is no reasonable alternative way of acquiring the information from less sensitive or non-secret sources, thereby avoiding all the possible moral hazards and trade-offs that collecting secret intelligence may involve. Secret intelligence is also expensive and makes demands on very scarce human resources. On those grounds alone, even without invoking ethical considerations, secret intelligence should not be sought if there are open ways of obtaining the information needed.

In framing ethical guidelines, do hard cases make bad law?

The British approach to legislation governing intelligence-gathering and the management of these ethical issues by the heads of the agencies has helped the UK intelligence community to build up a powerful ethos of compliance, with strict control over operational activity up their chain of command and political authorisation of sensitive activities. Ethical guidelines of the kind I have outlined are both a summary of the rules being followed and a reminder in hard cases of the tests to be applied. They are also rules that we should be encouraging other nations to follow. In the end, however, guidelines cannot be more than that. We have to recognise the difficulty of the decisions and balancing acts we expect from government, and trust to the individual judgements and conscience of those concerned.

Some might fear that over-emphasis on ethical codes will lead to over-cautious decisions, and perhaps unjustified whistle-blowing, by individuals within the intelligence community not in possession of the wider picture of all the considerations in any particular operational circumstance. I would argue that this risk is already with us. Better to recognise it and re-emphasise to staff that if they have concerns about ethical compliance, they have ready and confidential access to the 'staff counsellor', a senior figure appointed to the UK intelligence agencies as an individual of independent status, but experienced in the realities of the secret world and available in confidence to all staff as a source of wise counsel. Such an easy avenue for staff to air concerns in private will become even more important as the public, and no doubt agency staff and their families, increasingly debate ethical issues concerning intelligence activity.

Another objection that might be raised is that hard cases might arise where the public might be put at extreme risk through intelligence staff being forced to follow ethical guidelines. Balancing acts such as those implicit in the guidelines are, however, familiar in common law; consider, for example, the use of minimum force. Even the right to life is not absolute under the law.

Would similar application of the proportionality principle then mean that any method, however extreme, would be justified for gathering intelligence on the most serious of threats, provided the right hoops were gone through? What solution are we to give consistent with these proposed guidelines when faced with, for example, the often-quoted (so far hypothetical) conundrum of what is to be done with the captured terrorist believed to know the location of the nuclear device about to explode? Should the guidelines be interpreted to mean allowing torture, or allowing coercive means that might amount to 'cruel, inhuman or degrading treatment'[21] (methods currently prohibited to UK agencies)? Can it be argued that extreme circumstances (hundreds of thousands of lives at stake) would justify such means to extract the information from the suspect?

I think not. There is one absolute norm that has international recognition, and that is the prohibition on torture.[22] Such a firm rule cannot have a force majeure let-out clause, to be invoked when the stakes are high without vitiating the role of ethical guidelines. It is not necessary, and indeed it is harmful overall, to try to produce as part of a code of ethics a 'strict necessity' let-out. Such a let-out clause would allow the code itself to be set aside when the stakes are high enough, either in the view of the officers directly concerned or of their superiors – including ministers. We cannot have ethical guidelines that cease to apply when they are most needed.

There is another argument that allows us to continue the exercise of crafting ethical guidelines without being derailed by having to cover the hardest cases or 'ticking bomb' scenarios. We have to recognise that individuals still retain the freedom to guide their own actions as free moral agents. If they choose to operate outside their guidelines – just as if a soldier in Northern Ireland had individually chosen to open fire in extremis, outside 'the Yellow Card' that contains the essence of their rules of engagement – they know they will be answerable at law. They should know that if they survive, they will have to justify their actions before both the court of public opinion and their own conscience. If they had decided to play outside the rules then they would have to face the possible legal consequences. Equally, and importantly in the hypothetical case of the terrorists with a nuclear weapon, the individuals concerned would also have to justify any inaction. They would not be entitled and should not expect to be allowed to use the secrecy of their profession to evade accountability. Nor could they mount 'a Nuremburg defence' of following orders, since there is no duty to follow an unlawful order. In the unlikely event of having to face such a scenario, in which hundreds of thousands of lives were at stake from the ticking bomb and there was such a chance of preventing it, I would expect senior ministers to tell the security authorities that they must justify to Parliament and to a court any action that the officers felt to be necessary to secure the vital information and prevent disaster. That would not, I emphasise, make an unlawful order lawful. However, armed with such a 'letter of comfort', the individuals concerned might well trust the prosecuting authorities and – if it came to it – the courts, to recognise in mitigation the public interest in their actions in extremis. But what they could not have under the sort of ethical guidelines I suggest is pre-emptive legal absolution. Hard cases make bad law, and we should not build our ethical guidelines on the extreme case.

That is not to say that sufficient national peril might justify the suspension of some non-absolute rights, presuming proper derogation from international obligations. This was the case for the UK in 1939. But in following the approach outlined here, we have to insist that the justification for the measure will be sustainable in terms of the strategy being followed. In the eyes of most Americans, 9/11 was a war-like emergency, justifying the detention measures taken. Some years further on, the balance of argument for the strategic justification for the detention facilities at Guantanamo Bay and elsewhere[23] fails. It can be seen more clearly that the methods used initially carried a high price in terms of strategic loss when set against the immediate security gains. One approach that has been explored by American jurists is to have 'war zones' designated in which rules of engagement would be set that would allow the capture and interrogation of suspects using coercive methods and without legal process (Heymann and Kayyem 2005). Lethal force might also be authorised within such zones against terrorists identified by intelligence. Outside such designated war zones, such methods would be prohibited. The longer-term effect of that approach is harder to judge, but such an approach at least represents a recognition that a problem exists and attempts to resolve it within a legal framework.

Conclusion

When Admiral Stansfield Turner headed the Central Intelligence Agency in the 1980s, he offered some well-known guidance:

> There is one overall test of the ethics of human intelligence activities. That is whether those approving them feel they could defend their decisions before the public if their actions became public. (Turner 1986)

He qualified this remark by saying that he was not advocating a prior consideration of what the public would tolerate, in terms of assessing the public mood at the particular moment of decision. Instead, he was advocating the combination of readiness to stand up and be counted if exposure came, with personal conviction of the rationale you would then deploy. Implicitly, what is never justifiable under this doctrine is to undertake activities that one would be ashamed to defend openly, and which therefore rely only on the cloak of secrecy remaining intact.

The British approach to legislation and to the management of these ethical issues has helped UK agencies build up a powerful ethos of being highly effective yet (in part because) law-abiding. The British approach combines strict control over operational activity up the chain of command, political authorisation of sensitive activities that might have diplomatic repercussions, and appropriate mechanisms to prevent abuse of power and abuse of the secrecy of the intelligence world. The guidelines suggested in this paper are intended as both a public exposition of the approach that the UK is trying to follow, and a firm reminder of the tests to be applied in hard cases to come. For this is not an area where any complacency would be justified. There are dilemmas facing the intelligence community in responding to pressure for better pre-emptive intelligence for public security against terrorism. Opinion across the Islamic world and beyond has already been stirred by the handling of some of these issues, and additional seeds of future radicalisation may be being sown, including at home in Britain. Given that a struggle against terrorism must take place amongst the people, whose support is needed to sustain the campaign, this would be a high price to pay. That is what I have referred to as the sustainability part of the exercise. It is a hard test in realpolitik as well as in ethics.

Notes

1 Earlier versions of this paper were delivered at King's College London, Centre of International Studies (University of Cambridge), St Antony's College (University of Oxford) and the Royal Institute of International Affairs. I am grateful for the vigorous debate on these issues which followed, which has greatly informed this paper.

2 This is certainly the view of the United Kingdom security authorities, as set out in the White Paper, *Countering International Terrorism: the United Kingdom's Strategy* (Great Britain Cabinet Office and Great Britain Home Office 2006)

3 This was later found by the European Court of Human Rights to amount to brutal and degrading treatment: *Ireland v The United Kingdom* 5310/71 [1978] ECHR 1 (18 January 1978).

4 For example, the UK government has done this as part of its counter-terrorism strategy, CONTEST, see Great Britain Cabinet Office and Great Britain Home Office (2006). The French government has done this through the measures announced in the *Livre blanc sur la sécurité intérieure face au terrorisme* (Secrétariat général de la Défense nationale 2006).

5 See the full discussion of the United States experience in Heymann and Kayyem (2005) and in Byman (2006).

6 See the analysis in Kretzmer (2005).

7 In his speech at the Royal United Services Institute on 13 February 2006, Chancellor Gordon Brown highlighted that since 11 September 2001, an extra 16,000 police officers have been recruited across Britain, while another 6,000 have been employed by London's Metropolitan Police. By 2008, a further £75 million will have be allocated to the Metropolitan Police's counter-terrorist capability and a further £135 million invested in regional intelligence and investigation. Also, by that time, the Security Service will have doubled in terms of personnel. In total, there will be an investment of £2 billion a year, double what is presently (2006) spent.

8 For example, from the retired law lord, Lord Lloyd, who criticised the government's anti-terrorism laws for having 'sinister' constitutional implications while failing to improve public protection (*The Times*, 9 June 2006).

9 Lord Hoffman, House of Lords judgment in the case of *A and Others(Appellants) v the Secretary of State*, SESSION 2004–2005 [2004] UKHL 56, <http://www.bailii.org/uk/cases/UKHL/2004/56.html>.

10 E Drexel Godfrey, Jr (1978) argued for cutbacks in humint precisely because of the moral damage from covert operations and the then perceived superiority of technical intelligence.

11 As Queen's Regulations for the Army 1975 state (J7.121):

> It is the duty of all ranks to:
>
> (1) Abide by the law of armed conflict.
> (2) Do all in their power to prevent any breaches taking place.
> (3) Upon becoming aware of an allegation of any breach of the law of armed conflict, report the circumstances to their commanding officer.

12 The phrase comes from TS Eliot's 'Gerontion' (in Poems, 1920) and was used by James Jesus Angleton to describe the world of double and triple agents of the Cold War. The poem also expresses the counter-intelligence officer's dilemma: 'What will the spider do, suspend its operations, will the weevil delay?'

13 Review of Intelligence on Weapons of Mass Destruction, HC898, 14 July 2004.

14 Under the 'Carltona' principle, UK civil servants act using the authority of their minister, who therefore retains responsibility for their actions in his or her name.

15 Some of the legal issues arising from human rights legislation are discussed by Alistair Gillespie (2005).

16 A term used by the late Reginald Victor Jones (1989).
17 YouGov/Spectator Survey Results, 15 August 2006, <http://you.gov.uk/archives>.
18 The commissioner's annual report is presented to Parliament. See, for example, <http://www.official-documents.co.uk/document/hc0506/hc05/0548/0548.pdf>.
19 The commissioner makes annual reports on this. See, for example, Swinton (2004).
20 The Commander Crabb affair involved the botched and fatal frogman operation of 19 April 1956 to inspect the hull of the Soviet cruiser *Ordzhonikidze* in Portsmouth harbour which resulted in the resignation of the Chief of SIS.
21 Such as the six techniques of hooding, sleep deprivation, wall-standing, restrictions on food and water, and white noise that were banned by the UK following the adverse finding of the European Human Rights Court: *Ireland v United Kingdom*, 5310/71 [1978] ECHR 1 (18 January 1978).
22 This norm was recognised in the Convention against Torture and Other Cruel, Inhuman or Degrading Treatment or Punishment, 10 December 1984, 1465 UNTS 85.
23 See, for example, the judgement in the House of Lords in December 2004 that the requirement of imminence is not expressed in Article 15 of the European Convention or Article 4 of the International Covenant on Civil and Political Rights, but has been treated by the European Court as a necessary condition of a valid derogation. It is a view shared by the distinguished academic authors of the Siracusa Principles on the Limitation and Derogation Provisions in the International Covenant on Civil and Political Rights, who in 1985 formulated the rule: 'The principle of strict necessity shall be applied in an objective manner. Each measure shall be directed to an actual, clear, present, or imminent danger and may not be imposed merely because of an apprehension of potential danger.' *A and others (Appellants) v Secretary of State for the Home Department Session 2004–2005* [2004] UKHL 56.

References

Brown, G (2006) 'Securing Our Future', speech at the Royal United Services Institute, London, 13 February

Brown, Lord (2004) 'Report of the Intelligence Services Commissioner 2004', presented to Parliament by the Prime Minister pursuant to Section 60(4) of the Regulation of Investigatory Powers Act 2000, <http://www.official-documents.co.uk/document/hc0506/hc05/0548/0548.pdf>, accessed 27 August 2006

Byman, D (2006) 'Do Targeted Killings Work?', *Foreign Affairs*, 85:2, 95–111

Erskine, T (2004) 'Moral Agents and Intelligence Gathering', *Intelligence and National Security*, 19:2, 359–381

Gillespie, AA (2000) 'The Legal Use of Participating Informers', *Web Journal of Current Legal Issues*, 5, <http://webjcli.ncl.ac.uk/2000/issue5/gillespie5.html>, accessed 27 August 2006

Godfrey, ED Jr (1978) 'Ethics and Intelligence', *Foreign Affairs*, 56:3, 624–642

Great Britain Cabinet Office and Great Britain Home Office (2006) *Countering International Terrorism: the United Kingdom's Strategy, Cm 6888*, White Paper (London)

Herman, M (2004) 'Ethics and Intelligence after September 2001', *Intelligence and National Security*, 19:2, 342–358

Heymann, P and Kayyem, J (2005) *Protecting Liberty in an Age of Terror* (Cambridge, Massachusetts: MIT Press)

Intelligence Services Act (1994) <http://www.opsi.gov.uk/acts/acts1994/Ukpga_19940013_en_1.htm>

Jones, RV (1989) *Reflections on Intelligence* (London: William Heinemann)

Krezmer, D (2005) 'Targeted Killing of Suspected Terrorists: Extra-judicial Executions or Legitimate Means of Defence?', *European Journal of International Law*, 16:2, 171–212

Maguire, M and John, T (1995) *Intelligence, Surveillance and Informants: Integrated Approaches* (London: Home Office)

Omand, D (2005–2006) 'The Use of Strategy', *Survival*, 47:1, 107–116

Quinlan, M (2005) 'A Policymaker's View of Intelligence', lecture at the University of Wales, Aberystwyth, 3 November

Quinlan, M (2006) 'The Just War Tradition and the Use of Armed Force in the Twenty-First Century', annual lecture of the War Studies Department, King's College London, 25 January

Secrétariat général de la Défense nationale. (2006) *Livre blanc sur la sécurité intérieure face au terrorisme* (Paris: La documentation Française)

Thomas, S (2004) 'Report of the Interception of Communications Commissioner 2004', presented to Parliament by the Prime Minister pursuant to Section 58(6) of the Regulation of Investigatory Powers Act 2000, <http://www.archive2.official-documents.co.uk/document/deps/hc/hc883/883.pdf>, accessed 27 August 2006

Turner, Admiral Stansfield (1986) *Secrecy and Democracy* (London: Sidgwick & Jackson)

Walzer, M (1977) *Just and Unjust Wars* (New York: Basic Books)

Reprinted with permission from Sir David Omand, 'Ethical Guidelines in Using Secret Intelligence for Public Security', *Cambridge Review of International Affairs* 19/4 (2006) pp.613–28.

INTELLIGENCE AND ETHICS

Further reading: Books and reports

Jan Goldman, (ed.), *Ethics of Spying: A Reader for the Intelligence Professional* (Lanham, MD: Scarecrow Press 2005).

Peter Gill and Mark Pythian, *Intelligence in an Insecure World* (Cambridge: Polity, 2006).

Michael Herman, *Intelligence Power in Peace and War* (Cambridge: Cambridge University Press, 1996).

J. Kish, *International Law and Espionage* (The Hague: Kluwer Law International 1995).

Loch K. Johnson & James J. Wirtz, *Intelligence and National Security: The Secret World of Spies* (NY: Oxford University Press, 2nd ed 2007), chapters 29–30..

R.V. Jones, *Reflections on Intelligence* (London: Heinemann 1989) pp.35–57.

Walter Laqueuer, *World of Secrets: The Uses and Limits of Intelligence* (NY: Basic Books, 1985).

Mark Lowenthal, *Intelligence: From Secrets to Policy* (Washington D.C.: CQ Press, 3rd Ed 2006) chapter 12.

James Olson, *Fair Play: The Moral Dilemmas of Spying* (Washington DC: Potomac 2006).

Further reading: Essays and articles

John Barry, 'Covert Action Can Be Just.' *Orbis* 37/3 (1993) pp.375–390.

Charles Beitz, 'Covert Intervention as a Moral Problem,' *Ethics and International Affairs* 3 (1989) pp.45–60.

Lincoln P. Bloomfield,. 'The Legitimacy of Covert Action: Sorting Out the Moral Responsibilities,' *International Journal of Intelligence and Counterintelligence* 4/4 (1990) pp.525–537.

David Canon, 'Intelligence and Ethics: The CIA's Covert Operations.' *Journal of Libertarian Studies* 4/2 (1980) pp.197–214.

Robert D. Chapman, 'Lies, Torture, and Humanity.' *International Journal of Intelligence and Counterintelligence* 20/1 (2007) pp.188–194.

H Cohen & R Dudai, 'Human Rights Dilemmas in Using Informers to Combat Terrorism: The Israeli-Palestinian Case'. *Terrorism and Political Violence* 17/4 (2005) pp.229–243.

William E. Colby, 'Public Policy, Secret Action' *Ethics and International Affairs* 3 (1989) pp.61–71.

Paul G. Ericson, 'The Need for Ethical Norms,' *Studies in Intelligence* 36/5 (1992) pp.15–18.

Toni Erskine, ' "As Rays of Light to the Human Soul?" Moral Agents and Intelligence Gathering,' *Intelligence and National Security* 19/2 (2004) pp.359–381.

Angela Gendron, 'Just War, Just Intelligence: An Ethical Framework for Foreign Intelligence,' *International Journal of Intelligence and Counterintelligence* 18/3 (2005) pp.398–434

E. Drexel Godfrey, 'Ethics & Intelligence.' *Foreign Affairs* 56/3 (1978) pp.624–642. [Note also the response by Arthur L. Jacobs, 'Comments & Correspondence,' *Foreign Affairs* 56/4 (1978) pp.867–875.]

Dorian D. Greene, 'Ethical Dilemmas Confronting Intelligence Agency Counsel,' *Tulsa Journal of Comparative & International Law* 2 (1994) pp.91–108.

Michael Herman, 'Intelligence Services and Ethics in the New Millenium,' *Irish Studies in International Affairs* 10 (1999) pp.260–261.

Michael Herman, 'Modern Intelligence Services: Have They a Place in Ethical Foreign Policies' in, Harold Shukman (ed.) *Agents for Change: Intelligence Services in the 21st Century* (London: St. Ermin's 2000) pp.287–311.

Arthur S Hulnick & David W. Mattausch. 'Ethics and Morality in United States Secret Intelligence,' *Harvard Journal of Law & Public Policy* 12/2 (1989) pp.509–522.

William R Johnson, 'Ethics and Clandestine Collection,' *Studies in Intelligence* 27/1 (1983) pp.1–8.

John, S.J. Langan, 'Moral Damage and the Justification of Intelligence Collection from Human Sources,' *Studies in Intelligence* 25/2 (1981) pp.57–64.

Kent Pekel, 'Integrity, Ethics, and the CIA: The Need for Improvement,' *Studies in Intelligence* (1998) pp.85–94.

David L. Perry, 'Repugnant Philosophy: Ethics, Espionage, and Covert Action,' *Journal of Conflict Studies*, 15/1 (1995) pp.92–115.

Tony Pfaff & Jeffrey Tiel, 'The ethics of espionage', *Journal of Military Ethics* 3/1, (2004) pp.1–15.

Sir Michael Quinlan, 'Just Intelligence: Prolegomena to an Ethical Theory.' *Intelligence and National Security* 22/1 (2007) pp.1–13, also in Peter Hennessy (ed.), *The New Protective State* (London: Continuum 2007) pp.97–122.

Gregory F. Treverton, 'Covert Action and Open Society.' *Foreign Affairs* 65/5 (1987) pp. 995–1014.

Gregory F. Treverton, 'Imposing a Standard: Covert Action and American Democracy,' *Ethics & International Affairs* 3 (1989) pp.27–43.

Richard R. Valcourt, 'Controlling U.S. Hired Hands.' *International Journal of Intelligence and Counter-intelligence* 2/2 (1988) pp.163–178.

Essay questions

- Can espionage form part of an ethical foreign policy?
- 'Although espionage can be ethical, it can never be moral'. Discuss.
- How far would you accept the contentions of authors like Philip Knightley and James Rusbridger that secret agencies are, by their nature, corrupt and self-serving?
- How useful is the concept of 'Just War' as an ethical benchmark for both foreign intelligence and covert action?

24 Can the torture of terrorist suspects be justified?

Maureen Ramsay

This article discusses allegations of the widespread use of torture on terrorist suspects and evidence that the US administration authorised and condoned its use. Its main focus is the subsequent and misplaced academic debate which concedes that torture in certain catastrophic circumstances is morally permissible in order to prevent a greater evil. It challenges arguments for 'principled' torture, whether by juridical warrant or by advocating retaining an absolute ban while excusing extra legal torture and finds them equally flawed. It disputes the general acceptance by both that if the stakes are high enough, torture can be justified on consequentialist grounds. It concludes that the debate about whether torture is permissible is conducted within a narrow narrative framework which both obscures the purpose of torture and sets up false and misleading choices between respect for human rights and averting terrorist threats.

The terrorist attacks of 11 September 2001 portrayed by government officials as an assault on American values and civilisation have provoked an abandonment of the very values that supposedly inform a civilised way of life. The US administration has betrayed the cause of the protection of basic human rights and fundamental freedoms in the name of national security and counterterrorism. The starkest, most graphic illustration of this is manifest in the images which have become emblematic of America's response to their war on terrorism: those broadcast in the dehumanised images of shackled, hooded, caged men in Guantanamo Bay and the trophy photographs of pyramids of naked men, publicly humiliated and abused at Abu Ghraib.

The first section of this article refers to the documentary evidence that has come to light demonstrating how in the aftermath of 11 September 2001 torture and other forms of ill-treatment became America's policy and practice. But the main focus of this article is the subsequent and misplaced academic debate which countenances the breaking of the deepest and most fundamental liberal taboo by considering the possibility that torture is in some circumstances justified. These circumstances are those analogous to the hypothetical ticking bomb scenario, where the torture of a terrorist suspect to find the location of a bomb set to explode is justified as the lesser evil. The second and third sections consider two different types of proposals for 'principled' torture under these circumstances. It argues that both Derschowitz's proposal for advance juridical approval by a torture warrant and opposing views which advocate the retaining of an absolute ban while excusing 'off the books' torture are equally flawed. Despite their claims to the contrary, neither proposal succeeds in demonstrating that it would limit the amount of torture permitted, increase accountability, hold those responsible for unjustified acts to account or leave the norm against torture untarnished. The fourth section disputes the general acceptance by both that if the stakes are high enough, torture can be justified on consequentialist grounds. Counterproductive consequences themselves undermine any argument which attempts to excuse or sanction the torture of terrorist subjects. Given that the counterproductive effects of torture are well known, the next section addresses the question of why torture continues to be used and what is wrong with torture independent of its negative consequences. Conceptions of what is inherently wrong with torture focus on the morally perverted power relations between the torturer and victim. These accounts suggest that in addition to extracting information, the purpose of torture is to dominate and dehumanise the victim, to break the individual and collective will to resist. From this view, torture is not merely a morally questionable way to extract information to save multiple lives. The article concludes that the debate about whether torture is morally permissible is conducted within a narrow narrative framework which not only obscures the purpose of torture and the distinctive kind of wrong that characterises torture, but also sets up a polarised and misleading choice between respect for human rights and averting terrorism threats.

US revision of the absolute prohibition against torture

International law separates illegal practices into two categories: torture and cruel, inhuman or degrading treatment. The *UN Convention against Torture and other Cruel, Inhuman or Degrading Treatment* states that:

> The term torture means any act by which severe pain or suffering whether physical or mental, is intentionally inflicted on a person for such purposes as obtaining from him or a third party information or confession, punishing him for an act he or a third person has committed, or is suspected of committing, or intimidating or coercing him or a third person, or for an reason based on discrimination of any kind, whether such pain or suffering is inflicted by or at the instigation or with the consent or acquiescence of a public official or other person acting in an official capacity.[1]

The Convention bans torture absolutely: 'No exceptional circumstances whatsoever, whether a state of war, internal political instability or any kind of public emergency, must be invoked as a justification for torture.'[2] The Convention does not define 'cruel, inhuman or degrading treatment or punishment', but requires signatories to 'undertake to prevent such practices'.[3] The *UN Declaration of Human Rights*, the *International Convention of Civil and Political Rights*, the *European Convention for the Protection of Human Rights and Fundamental Freedoms*, and the *Geneva Convention* all prohibit both torture and cruel, inhuman or degrading treatment at all times.

News reports, reports by the International Red Cross, human rights groups, testimony from victims, former US intelligence officers and several investigations reveal that the methods used by US interrogators at Bagram Air Base in Afghanistan, at Guantanamo Bay and at Abu Ghraib in Iraq violate the prohibition on torture and other forms of ill-treatment enshrined in international law. Allegations of prisoner abuse began to emerge shortly after Bush launched his war on terror. As early as December 2002, *The Washington Post* reported that US agents at Bagram used interrogation techniques euphemistically named 'stress and duress' and 'torture lite'. According to that article these techniques included stress positions – prisoners were kept standing or kneeling for prolonged periods chained to the ceiling with their feet shackled, kept naked or hooded, and subjected to 24 hour bombardment with lights and sleep deprivation. It was also alleged that terrorist suspects were 'rendered' to interrogation centres in Jordan, Egypt, Morocco and Syria, countries known to engage in torture. Interview with current and former government officials have confirmed that the CIA holds terrorist suspects incommunicado in secret locations around the world.[4] Under the *Geneva Convention* it is illegal to ask another party to torture prisoners and illegal for the US to gather information gained as a result of torture.

The International Committee of the Red Cross (ICRC) reported on methods of physical and psychological coercion that were used in a routine and systematic way to extract information from prisoners in Iraq[5] and according to press reports warned the US government that these methods were 'tantamount to torture'.[6] These methods included:

- Hoodings, sometimes in conjunction with beatings
- Handcuffing resulting in skin lesions and nerve damage
- Beatings with hard objects, slapping, punching and kicking
- Parading detainees naked sometimes with women's underwear on their heads
- Handcuffing naked prisoners to the bars of completely empty, dark cells for several days
- Hooded exposure to loud music, noise and prolonged exposure to the heat of the sun (127° F)
- Threats of ill-treatment and reprisals against families, of execution and transfer to other countries.

The Fay Investigation into Abu Ghraib detainee abuse revealed that detainees were slapped, kicked, punched, beaten with chairs and brooms, threatened and terrified by dogs, routinely and repetitively subject to total isolation and light deprivation, exposed to extremes of heat and cold, deprived of sleep, denied food and water and subjected to sexual abuse and humiliating and degrading treatment.

The practices at Abu Ghraib focused the world's attention because the images were caught on camera, but they merely freeze a moment in a grim catalogue of routine brutal acts which continue to emerge in press reports from all corners of the war on terror.[7]

Those directly responsible for the practices at Abu Ghraib were held to account, though they were depicted as isolated incidents, as 'acts of brutal and purposeless sadism, representing deviant behaviour',[8] and were described by both Bush and Rumsfeld as 'abuse' rather than torture or cruel, inhuman or degrading treatment.[9] However defined, the techniques used at Abu Ghraib were neither an aberration nor isolated cases. They were the predictable effects of a deliberate attempt by the Bush administration to eliminate legal restraints on permissible means to extract information from detainees. Other commentators and organisations have demonstrated this by cataloguing and analysing evidence from documents produced within the Bush administration.[10] These include letters, internal memos and reports defining the status of prisoners to circumvent the protection of the *Geneva Convention* and to deprive suspected terrorists of their rights. They include evidence from official decisions on what interrogation techniques could be legally applied to avoid international and domestic prohibition on torture, the suggestion that cruel, inhuman or degrading treatment was permissible and the redefinition on what counts as torture.

This process began with a memo from the then White House Counsel, now Attorney General, Alberto Gonzales to Bush in January 2002. Gonzales announced a revision of established norms: 'The war on terror is a new kind of war . . . this new paradigm renders obsolete Geneva's strict limitation on questioning of enemy prisoners and renders quaint some of its provisions.'[11] Gonzales referred to Bush's decision that the Geneva Convention against coercive interrogation did not apply to members of Al Qaeda and the Taliban, who were determined 'unlawful combatants' rather than deserving protection as prisoners of war. According to Gonzales this redefinition of the status of prisoners would free US interrogators and make prosecution for war crimes less likely. The prospect of interrogation practices outlawed by the Geneva Convention being applied to those considered to be outside the law was compounded when, on 2 December 2002, Rumsfeld authorised a number of interrogation techniques for 'unlawful combatants' in Afghanistan and Guantanamo 'as a matter of policy'.[12] These included 20-hour interrogations, hooding, isolation, stress positions, sensory deprivation, exploiting phobias, dietary 'adjustment', removal of clothing and religious items, forced grooming and the use of dogs. On 15 January 2003, Rumsfeld rescinded and revised these techniques[13] and in April 2003 issued a further memo in which he did not rule out any interrogation method and allowed for additional techniques to be requested on a case by case basis.[14]

A now infamous memo (since repudiated by the Administration) from Attorney General Bybee to White House Counsel Gonzales had virtually ensured that such interrogation practices could not be defined as torture.[15] Bybee legitimised these methods by narrowly redefining torture as physical pain equivalent to 'serious physical injury such as organ failure, impairment of bodily function or even death'. According to Bybee, only the most extreme acts are impermissible, lesser acts of cruel, inhuman or degrading treatment did not violate the UN Convention, which reserves criminal penalties solely for acts of torture. Moreover, Bybee further argued that the President as Commander in Chief could override the prohibition on torture and, if authorised by the President, interrogators could escape prosecution by the Justice Department. Bybee added that if prosecuted for torture, interrogators might escape criminal liability by presenting a necessity defence or self-defence justification. Interrogators could violate the prohibition on torture if they believed it necessary as a lesser evil to prevent a direct or immanent threat to the US and its citizens.

Referring to and contradicting this document, the UN High Commission for Human Rights stressed that 'there can be no doubt that the prohibition on torture and cruel, inhuman and degrading treatment is non-derogable under international law'.[16] The UN Special Rapporteur on Torture condemned the use of the necessity defence and the methods approved, saying that 'the jurisprudence of both international and regional human rights mechanisms is unanimous in stating that such methods violate the prohibition on torture and ill treatment'.[17] Human Rights Watch report that the US itself had denounced the same methods as torture when used by other countries.[18]

Though the policies approved for Al Qaeda and the Taliban were not intended to apply to Iraq, whose detainees come under the protection of Geneva, the same methods migrated to Iraq and were sanctioned by senior commanders. In August 2003 Major General Geoffrey D. Miller, commander at Guantanamo, visited Baghdad to 'Gitmoise' the Iraqi system. Lieutenant General Sanchez (then Commander of US Forces in Iraq) issued three different policy memos on the treatment of prisoners in Iraq to put pressure on them for information about insurgent activity. Sanchez authorised interrogation techniques at Abu Ghraib which included elements of the Guantanamo policy and Special Operation Force Policy in Afghanistan.[19] Harsh methods were approved which deviated from standard operating procedures and international norms protecting the basic rights of prisoners and led to confusion about what methods were authorised.

The so-called 'abuses' at Abu Ghraib were not simply the result of deviant behaviour by a few rogue elements. They were just one example of what has become a systematic practice. They were the product of a morally degraded climate created by the institutional approval of the US government for overriding international prohibition on the treatment on enemy combatants; its redefinition of torture and legally permissible treatment and its necessity justification for obtaining intelligence in the context of the war on terrorism.

Since 11 September 2001 the Bush administration has pursued a blatant consequentialist end justifies the means policy. Political imperatives to maintain national security have taken priority over legal constraints and moral considerations. Subsequently, legal, political and moral philosophers have taken up the debate about what means can be justified in the war on terrorism.

The academic debate on torture

Even those who agree that torture is inherently morally wrong and generally counterproductive concede that in certain catastrophic circumstances an absolute ban on torture is morally indefensible. The notorious hypothetical 'ticking bomb' situation is taken as illustrative of a catastrophic circumstance that may justify torture. Here the person under interrogation knows the location of the bomb set to explode endangering thousands of lives and refuses to divulge the information necessary to remove or defuse the bomb.

Many commentators acknowledge that the ticking bomb situation is improbable and artificial but believe that it needs addressing because since 11 September leaders have used this scenario as a narrative framework and as a justification for modifying prohibitions on international law regarding torture as well as a justification for curbing civil liberties more generally.

The argument begins with the assumption that an absolute ban on torture is practically and morally untenable. It sets unrealistic standards which cannot hope to be met in catastrophic circumstances where there is a concrete and imminent danger to be avoided. Parry argues that torture may be a legitimate option, the lesser of two evils in rare circumstances.[20] Posner agrees that 'only the most doctrinaire civil libertarian would deny that if the stakes are high enough, torture is permissible' and that anyone who doubts this should not be in a position of responsibility.[21] This is echoed by Gross, who argues that even if we support an absolute ban, we would still not want those responsible for our security to be strictly bound by similar constraints.[22] Elshtain similarly suggests that in circumstances where we believe that a suspect might have vital information, it is preferable to act with harsh necessity. To condemn torture is to lapse into pietistic rigour in which moral purity is ranked over all other goods.[23] Even Shue entertains the possibility that torture may be justified in rare situations.[24] These writers, though, are unwilling to legalise torture. Gross argues that in exceptional circumstances public officials must step outside the legal framework and act extra-legally and be ready to accept the legal ramifications of their actions, with the possibility that extra-legal actions may be legally (if not morally) excused ex post.[25] Posner agrees that the legal prohibition should be left in place 'with the understanding that it will not be enforced in exceptional circumstances'.[26] We should trust the executive to break the rules when the stakes are high enough and enable officials to obtain political absolution for their illegal conduct.

Shue compares this approach to civil disobedience justifications in that anyone who thinks torture is the least available evil can justify their act morally in order to defend it legally. The torturer must convince their peers in a public trial that all necessary conditions for the permissibility of the actions are met. Shue concludes that in this situation 'we would expect a judge to suspend the sentence'.[27]

In contrast to this position, Derschowitz argues that as a matter of undeniable fact torture is currently being employed without accountability and would be used in a ticking bomb situation. He argues that if the use of torture is justified in a ticking bomb situation, rather than allowing it to take place off the record in violation of existing law and subject to punishment only if discovered, it would be normatively better to advocate advance juridical approval by a torture warrant.[28] When torture is the only means to avoid catastrophic loss of life 'a sterilised needle under the fingernails may be the option that a government should adopt'.[29]

Both those who advocate retaining an absolute ban while allowing for ex post justification and those who argue for pre-sanctioned torture claim that their respective proposals would decrease or limit the amount of torture permitted on suspects and increase accountability. For Derschowitz, this is because a torture warrant would not be issued unless executive officers and judges agree. They are both unlikely to authorise warrants without compelling evidence as to their necessity. Visibility and accountability are increased as there is official documentation and record of applications and outcomes, and judges and executive officers can be held to account for excesses.[30] Derschowitz claims that it is better to control and regulate torture with accountability, record keeping, standards and limits, than to denounce torture but to tolerate extra-legal actions. Similarly, those who support an absolute ban while allowing for ex post justification claim that this would limit the amount of torture practised. This is because of the prospects of public disclosure of means which may be later judged unnecessary.[31] Scarry argues that given the costs of acting extra-legally, the risk of facing criminal proceedings, civil suits, loss of liberty, prosecution and moral condemnation, the would-be torturer must test the situation and be confident that the person to be tortured has the required information.[32] Gross claims that ex post ratification limits torture and does not set a precedent because the interrogator acts as an autonomous moral agent, rather than an agent from the hierarchical institution he serves.[33] Thus, the proposal emphasises an ethic of responsibility for the individual public official and the public in general. It requires transparency, accountability and publicity and this limits the choice of methods permissible. Government agents must give reasons ex post to justify their conduct. Society as a whole decides whether to hold agents to account for the wrongfulness of their actions or whether to approve them retrospectively. If they are judged abhorrent or unjustified, the agent is required to make legal and political amends. If not, officials are able to obtain political absolution for illegal conduct and may be rewarded or commended for their actions.[34]

Both proposals for an absolute ban while allowing for ex post justification and Derschowitz's torture warrant have similar disadvantages. Neither proposal guarantees to limit the amount of torture permitted against suspects, increases accountability, transparency or publicity or leaves the norm against torture untarnished. Opponents of Derschowitz's pre-sanctioned torture argue that it is unclear whether the institutional structures that issue warrants would minimise torture or limit it to ticking bomb situations. Judges rely on information from officials who seek warrants. As Kreimer notes, current experience with search warrants suggests that even when the stakes are low, officials seeking warrants embellish the truth to serve the perceived ends of law enforcement. Therefore, we might suppose that officials in pursuit of anti-terrorist goals would be inclined to 'sex up' applications for warrants.[35] Posner argues that Derschowitz exaggerates the significance of the warrant as a check on executive discretion. The warrant system may make officials more careful when seeking to secure the warrant, but not necessarily more truthful.[36] Moreover, Kreimer argues that judges too would be under pressure to do anything possible to avoid a terrorist catastrophe.[37] In these circumstances it seems likely that warrants would be issued in cases where there are speculative benefits which fall short of the certainty required by the ticking bomb justification for torturing terrorist suspects.

Scarry argues that Derschowitz credits the torture warrant system with powers of accountability and documentation that it does not have. Cases of torture that take place when officials fail to apply for a warrant remain undocumented. There is a record of those cases where torture has been agreed by juridical warrant, but by means of the warrant the person who tortures has been released from the constraints against torture and so from accountability. Therefore the warrant results in an unknowable amount of illegal instances of torture that cannot be recorded and the torturer is not held to account, and a knowable number of legal instances that because warranted are unlikely to be reviewed or revoked.[38] Despite these objections by those who favour an absolute ban while allowing for possible ex post ratification, it is not clear that their proposal fares any better in these respects.

It may seem plausible that the fear of public disclosure and the prospect of punishment would make interrogators reluctant to torture in cases short of the ticking bomb. But if interrogators are constrained only by prudential calculation about the likelihood of public ratification or disapproval, then they would also have good reason to avoid being found out rather than not to torture or, if found out, like those who seek torture warrants, to embellish the case for justification to avoid condemnation.

This argument leaves the ultimate judgment about whether the torture was justified to a judge or to a jury of peers. But the judge and jury will be operating under the same pressures with regard to security as judges under the warrant system, so that the criteria for absolution will not necessarily correspond to the criteria for justifications for torture in a ticking bomb scenario. It would seem that there would be unequivocal grounds for condemnation of the torturer who acts on weak evidence, careless miscalculation or gratuitous cruelty. But a judge and jury might refrain from convicting such an interrogator if the coercive methods they used did in fact avert some catastrophic event, or indeed if it did not. This possibility is likely given the culture of leniency and military impunity that currently surrounds prosecutions for actual abuses that could not be justified by a necessity defence. Despite mounting evidence of ill-treatment, not one US agent has been charged with torture under US law, a small number of mainly low-ranking soldiers have been court marshalled and in over 70% of official actions taken in response to substantiated allegations of abuse, those committing them have received non-judicial or administrative sentences.[39]

Moreover, the argument that the prospect of public approval or disapproval increases accountability and lessens incidents of torture assumes that the torturer is brought to trial in the first place. Given the dilatoriness of investigations into allegations of torture; the official failure by the Army Prosecuting Authorities to bring prosecutions in relation to deaths in custody; the lack of official detection procedures and the refusal of access to Human Rights Commission to investigate cases; the rendering of detainees to secret destinations where torture is rife; and the accidental nature of many of the revelations of abuse in the war on terror, it is certain that much torture remains secret and unaccountable. Consequently, the system of absolute prohibition which sanctions 'off the books' torture results, like the torture warrant system, in an unknowable amount of illegal instance of torture that cannot be condemned or approved and where the torturer cannot be held to account. It also results in a knowable number of illegal instances that may be warranted ex post, but for reasons which are not justified on the ticking bomb rationale and so does not hold those responsible for unjustified acts to account.

The legal prohibition on torture with a possible justification after the event undermines rather than reinforces responsibility and accountability in another sense. It places disproportionate responsibility on the actual perpetrators of the illegal acts. It leaves the decision to torture to individual interrogators. It places trust in their judgment and relies on their willingness to break the rules and to violate morality on our behalf when they deem torture to be necessary in a particular case.

The abuses at Abu Ghraib, and the torture cases there and in Afghanistan and Guantanamo demonstrate what happens when we trust intelligence agents and interrogators to act unlawfully or when they act with the understanding that legal penalties will not be enforced. Insisting that interrogators act as autonomous moral agents rather than agents of the hierarchical institution they serve supposedly guards against setting a precedent. But this has the disadvantage of making individual interrogators the only actors that are held to account, if indeed they are. In the war on terror the moral autonomy of those who carried out the abuse is questionable given the pressure for actionable intelligence to save lives and divert terrorist attacks. Though the actual interrogators are directly responsible for the methods used, indirect and ultimate responsibility lies precisely in those hierarchical institutions whose policies progressively and systematically corroded the prohibitions on the use of torture. A system which advocates responsibility and accountability of the actual perpetrators of torture does nothing to tackle the problem of ascribing responsibility for the results of political decisions or to challenge the official Bush administration policy which condoned and overlooked the abuse or to hold them to account.[40]

The advantage of ex post justification over pre-sanctioned torture is thought to be the moral inhibition which remains in place under the former. Kreimer argues that under the warrant system torture is an ever present option because there is no physic cost in seeking it; officials off-load moral responsibility to a judge. This institutionalises torture and saps the force of norms that restrain potential torturers. If torture is permitted it is increasingly difficult for officials under pressure to refrain from torture. Those who resist lose their moral stature. There is no norm of civilised behaviour in place to refer back to.[41] In contrast, the norm remains in place when officials engage in torture in defiance of absolute prohibition. Proponents of this view claim that allowing exceptions to the prohibition does not thereby sanction or legitimise torture. Torture remains a tactic which is forbidden, though there are moments when the rule prohibiting it may be overridden. The norm remains, though the rule may have been broken.[42] Parry writes that 'in theory we can admit to an exception to universal prohibition, without undermining the values that gave rise to that prohibition',[43] and according to Gross, ratification ex post 'does not cancel or terminate the general duty not to torture'.[44] But it is hard to see how this can be so.

Ex post justification excuses torture in individual cases. The torturer is pardoned if, all things considered, he did the right thing in utilitarian terms. It is hard to avoid giving some legitimacy to torture unless acts of torture are prosecuted as strict liability offences. Once a necessity defence is available to interrogators to justify particular acts of torture, then this inevitably undermines the norm that torture is wrong in itself, regardless of the good consequences particular acts may promote. Justifying torture as the right thing to do in utilitarian terms subordinates the values that gave rise to prohibition to consequentialist calculation. The rule, the moral prohibition against such acts, has in effect been cancelled or annulled. It is as though torture in some circumstances ceases to be morally wrong.

Walzer's dirty hands

There are more nuanced and complex positions which recognise the moral costs involved in means–end calculation. Walzer, in his classic essay about the dilemma of dirty hands, highlights the paradox of actions which are morally justifiable, but despite this morally wrong. He argues that 'a particular act of government may be exactly the right thing to do in utilitarian terms and yet leave the man who does it guilty of a moral wrong'.[45] Walzer accepts that consequentialism is necessary in politics, but resists the conclusion that prudential calculation exhausts the content of moral judgment. The politician who breaks moral rules in order to achieve a good end is nevertheless guilty of a moral crime.

On this view success in achieving political ends could sometimes justify torture, but no political end could cause torture to cease to be morally wrong. This seems to more adequately capture the idea absent from a straightforward necessity defence of torture, that whatever the good consequences of such methods, a moral wrong has been done. The question remains as to whether this view leaves the norm prohibiting torture in place.

Walzer asks how we should regard the leader who authorises torture in the ticking bomb situation by discussing three views of dirty hands, Machiavellian, Weberian, and Camus's in *Just Assassins*. According to Walzer, the Machiavellian view of the political actor who must do terrible things is that he simply throws away morality for the good results that will be achieved. For Weber, this political actor is a tragic hero, who is horribly aware that he is doing bad in order to achieve good and that in doing so he surrenders his soul. On the Machiavellian view of dirty hands the moral norms prohibiting torture and the moral costs involved in violating them are simply set aside. In the Weberian view the moral norms and costs are acknowledged solely within the confines of the individual's conscience.

Camus's good men with dirty hands are assassins, who having killed are prepared to die and will die by execution. Execution is self-punishment and expiation for the moral costs involved in achieving their just ends. Hands are washed clean on the scaffold. For Walzer, this is the most attractive view of the moral costs involved in consequentialist action. It is also the most promising way to view the claim by those who admit exceptions to the universal prohibition on torture, that although the rule has been broken, the norm has been preserved. Although there is no executioner in the wings waiting to administer punishment, this view of moral costs requires us to imagine a punishment that fits the crime and so to examine the nature of the crime. This refers us back to the moral code, the norm which has been violated. Walzer argues that if we could enforce moral sanctions against the perpetrator we could 'honour the man who did bad in order to do good, and at the same time we could punish him. We could honour him for the good he has done, and we could punish him for the bad he has done.'[46]

Walzer's interpretation of Camus's view, though, is also an inadequate view of the moral costs of doing wrong and the moral standard that has been violated unless moral and legal sanctions are enforced against the torturer whether or not good ends are achieved, as the just assassins execution implies. But if this is the case, then Walzer's claim that the politician should be punished for breaking a moral rule sits uncomfortably with his view of the necessary and justified use of immoral means and his view of the politician who should be honoured for doing what he had to do in the circumstances. This dual judgment pulls in opposite directions. If a politician who breaks the moral rule against torture in a ticking bomb situation acts rightly on the whole, as Walzer claims, then it seems disingenuous for citizens, judges, or philosophers who agree the means are necessary and justified, to punish the politician who does the evil on their behalf, for their benefit and with their tacit approval. Conversely, if just assassins and ticking bomb torturers ought to be punished, then this implies that the action required such an abandonment of principle that is was unjustified regardless of the good consequences and that the politician acted wrongly.

It is difficult to fuse together the conflicting judgments that the action was both right and wrong and to make sense of the idea that we should simultaneously honour and condemn the politician for the same deed. It is equally difficult to imagine what it would actually mean in practice to punish politicians for the use of immoral means and at the same time reward them for the ends these achieved.

Walzer's solution to the problem of preserving the norm against torture while allowing exceptions fails because the moral rule prohibiting torture is only reaffirmed after it is overthrown. Moral costs and moral standards are only counted after the event in the private or public guilt or punishment of the perpetrator. Since the means adopted are decided on consequentialist criteria, the moral duty not to torture is removed from the heart of the dilemma and only resurfaces in the post mortem. Walzer writes as if the problem of dirty hands were simply a matter of trying to discover some form of social recognition and public sanction for the necessary wrong that politicians do. His solution seems to sanction immoral actions as long as those who commit them are punished. Expiation and punishment after the event have the paradoxical consequence that torture can be justified as long as it is acknowledged as wrong.

Those who support exceptions to the universal prohibition on torture claim that the norm remains in place and those who would engage in torture are restrained by the moral costs of their actions. They are more likely to hold on to their integrity, be guided by the norm, and be disinclined to resort to torture when confronted with difficult dilemmas. This may be so if there is an absolute rule against torture with no exceptions. If the ticking bomb scenario is accepted as an exception, in these circumstances recognition of moral norms will do nothing to prevent their sacrifice. Acknowledging the wrong that is done cannot have any moral significance if this moral sense, this norm of civilised behaviour, is ultimately overridden by utility considerations. The difficulty in keeping a place for moral standards, for retaining the norm and duty not to torture, results from a general acceptance that torture in ticking bomb situations is justified on consequentialist grounds. When this is so, then absolute moral principles are bound to play a subsidiary role.

Consequentialist arguments against torture

To be convincing, any consequentialist defence of torture as a legitimate option in rare circumstances whether by warrant or extra-legal justification would have to show at least the following. One, that the general societal harm did not outweigh the particular benefits of the legitimated torture, two, the certainty that torture would be confined to exceptional cases and, three, that torture works. Each of these conditions cannot be guaranteed. Even if in a particular case there are apparent benefits, approval of torture may have long term and systematic implications which outweigh those benefits. As the most powerful country in the world the US's dilution of the absolute ban on torture undermines the rule of law and acts as a dangerous precedent for government behaviour worldwide. Loosening the prohibition on torture makes it difficult to condemn its use elsewhere when it is justified on the same criteria. Governments from Israel to Uzbekistan, Egypt to Nepal defy human rights and international humanitarian law in the name of national security and counterterrorism. Authorising or excusing torture undermines the values of freedom and democracy that the war on terror is supposedly intended to promote. Revelations of torture and systematic ill-treatment of prisoners have intensified the crisis in American relations with the Muslim world and acted as a rallying cry to a new generation of terrorists. Accepting torture as a solution to the problem of diverting terrorist acts prevents us from examining and redressing the regularly stated Muslim grievances that inform the context in which their actions take place. The slow fuse that lit the London bombs has been ticking relentlessly since Blair signed up to Bush's war on terror and there were authoritative warnings by security services that the invasion of Iraq would increase the risk of terrorist attacks on Britain.[47] The same fuse lit by injustices in the Middle East sparked the September 11 attacks and is kept burning by images of shock and awe in Baghdad, the destruction of Fallujah, the hooded, chained prisoners at Guantanamo, the human pyramids of naked, twisted bodies at Abu Ghraib and the bloodbath that is the new Iraq.

Even if torture is only authorised in special cases, there is the danger that whatever necessary conditions are specified, the practice becomes entrenched. If the state authorities sanction or excuse torture in exceptional circumstances, there is good reason to believe that the concept of necessity will become elastic and that torture will spread and be used in circumstances which are not so legitimated. Both past and present cases bear this out. From 1987 the torture of Palestinian suspects in Israel was justified by citing the ticking bomb argument. However, according to Human Rights Watch:

> Israeli forces rarely if ever were able to identify a particular suspect with knowledge about a particular bomb set to explode imminently. Rather they ended up applying the scenario metaphorically to justify torturing virtually every Palestinian security detainee – thousands of people – on the theory that they might know about some unspecified future terrorist activity.[48]

American Prospect reports that a decade later one study showed that 80% of Palestinians in custody and another that 94% were subject to torture during that period.[49] Neither are the current instances of torture and ill-treatment in Afghanistan, Guantanamo and Iraq confined to cases that could be justified by the ticking bomb argument. The US authorities claim that they have obtained information about Al Qaeda and related terrorist networks from interrogations.[50] But harsh interrogation methods have been applied to a large number of detainees who certainly have no specific knowledge of imminent catastrophic attacks compatible with ticking bomb justifications. Erik Saar, a translator in interrogation sessions at Guantanamo reported that a great many prisoners had no terrorist links and that little worthwhile intelligence information had been gained there.[51] A coalition forces military intelligence officer told the ICRC that an estimated 70–90% of prisoners in Iraq had been arrested by mistake.[52] Moreover some cases of ill-treatment do not even occur during interrogation sessions. Abuse by British forces at Camp Breadbasket was inflicted on looters as 'punishment', and some abuses were carried out at Abu Ghraib 'just for the fun of it', for the sadistic amusement of the guards.[53] Recent investigations of widespread human rights violations by counter-insurgency forces in Iraq reveal a ghost network of secret detention centres, evidence of the use of violent interrogation techniques including hanging by the arms in cuffs, burnings, beatings, electric shocks, arbitrary arrests, extra-judicial executions and claims that serious abuse has taken place within the Iraqi government's own Ministry of Interior under the noses of US and UK officials.[54] Reports that torture is increasingly prevalent in the new Iraq suggest that Iraq is implementing a policy of institutionalised torture as a general counter-insurgency measure. Thirty years ago Amnesty International wrote that:

> History shows that torture is never limited . . . As soon as its use is permitted once, as for example, in one of the extreme circumstances like a bomb, it is logical to use it on people who might place bombs, or on people who might think of placing bombs, or on people who defend the kind of person who might think of placing bombs.[55]

For torture to be justified in a ticking bomb situation, it must be the case that those who authorise or use it have good reason to believe that torture will produce accurate actionable information. But torture is a notoriously unreliable way of obtaining information. Langbein, writing about the history of torture concludes: 'Against the coercive force of the engines of torture, no safeguards were ever found that could protect the innocent and guarantee the truth. The agony of torture created an incentive to speak, but not necessarily to speak the truth.'[56]

The lesson from history is that it is not possible to guarantee that the information generated under torture is reliable. Even people who practise torture deny its efficacy as an interrogation tool. A recently declassified memo written by an FBI official in Guantanamo states that extreme coercion produced 'nothing more than the FBI got by using simple interrogation techniques'.[57] The most recent version of the US Army Intelligence field Manual (FM35–52) states that 'experience indicates the use of prohibited torture is not necessary to gain the cooperation of interrogation sources', and that it is a poor technique which yields unreliable results. Counter-terrorist officials have even complained that US ill-treatment of detainees at Guantanamo and elsewhere has actually hindered the gathering of intelligence from informants who might otherwise have provided information.[58] Since the counterproductive effects of torture are well known, we might ask why governments continue to practise it and why academics continue to debate circumstances when it may be used.

What is inherently wrong with torture?

Investigation as to what is wrong with torture, independent of its bad effects, may throw some light on why torture is practised and how academics obscure the purpose of torture when they debate its justification as a way of extracting information to save multiple lives in a ticking bomb context. What is inherently wrong with torture is captured by the Kantian idea that torture violates physical and mental integrity and negates autonomy, humanity and dignity, coercing the victim to act against their most fundamental beliefs, values and interests.[59] For Shue, it is that fact that the victim is powerless before unrestrained conquerors that accounts for the particular disgust torture evokes. Torture violates the prohibition of constraint against the defenceless.[60] For Parry, torture demonstrates the end of the normative world of the victim and expresses the domination of the state and the torturer. The torturer and the victim create their own terrible world of over-whelming vulnerability and total control with potential escalation that asserts complete domination. Torture is world destroying in its ability to invert and degrade ideas of agency, consent and responsibility.[61]

Sussman argues that there is a distinctive kind of wrong that characterises torture that distinguishes it from other kinds of violence or physical and psychological harm. What is wrong with torture is not just that torture enacts an asymmetrical relation of complete dependence and vulnerability so that the victim acts against his or her own choices and interests. Nor is it just the profound disrespect shown to the humanity and autonomy of the victim as an extreme instance of using a person as a means to an end they would not reasonably consent to. Torture involves a systematic mockery of the moral relations between people. It is a deliberate perversion of the value of dignity and an insult to agency. Agency is turned on itself. The torturer forces the victim into a position of colluding against himself, so he experiences himself as simultaneously powerless (a passive victim) yet actively complicit in his own debasement. Torture is not just an extreme form of cruelty, but an instance of forced self-betrayal where the torturer pits the victim against himself, as an active participant in his own violation.[62]

These accounts focus on what happens when torture takes place, rather than the bad consequences of torture or what specific practices constitute torture. What constitutes torture here is not defined by the severity or intensity of pain, but rather by the logic of the morally perverted structure of the relationship between the torturer and victim. If what is inherently wrong with torture is the mockery of moral relations, the asymmetrical relationship of power and defencelessness it enacts which degrades agency, humanity and dignity; which coerces the victims to act against their choices, beliefs, values and interests, then it could be that this is precisely why it is used. The explanation of what torture is, is connected to the point and purpose of torture.

Within a ticking bomb situation, the motive for torture is the need to extract information, but Parry argues that this is not its only purpose.

> . . . the impulse to torture may derive from identification of the victim with a larger challenge to social order and values. This possibility takes on greater salience amid claims that the threat of terrorism requires aggressive self defence in the post September 11 world . . . when the social order is threatened especially by people seen as outsiders or subordinates, torture may function as a method of individual and collective assertion that creates perhaps an illusory sense of overcoming vulnerability through the thorough domination of others.[63]

Parry points out US interrogation practices take place against a background of terrorism which has created a sense of vulnerability and social upheaval. Given this, it is plausible to suggest that in addition to seeking information from suspects, torture has been used to assert and confirm the unconstrained power of the US, to degrade and dehumanise the enemy, to force the silencing and betrayal of their beliefs and values, to signify the end of their normative world. It would not be surprising to learn that torture has been used as a method of total domination and social control, not only over the prisoners in the cages of Guantanamo, or the cells in Afghanistan and Iraq, but over those communities hostile to US power, to intimidate and to break their collective will to act in accordance with their own beliefs, values and interests.

If the impulse to torture is as much about instantiating power relationships as it is about extracting actionable, credible information, then this may explain, though it could never justify, why the US resorted to torture in its war on terrorism. Such an explanation is necessary especially given that counterproductive consequentialist considerations undermine arguments which excuse or sanction the torture of terrorist suspects for alleged intelligence benefits. Such an explanation fits given that the vast majority, if not all cases of torture and cruel, degrading and inhuman treatment since September 11 could not be justified by the belief that the suspects held vital information that could divert imminent catastrophic attacks. Torture and other forms of ill-treatment have become the norm rather than an exception in rare circumstances. Yet, despite this, torture continues to be debated as if it were merely a morally questionable way to extract information and as if it was this purpose which requires defending.

Conclusion

The conclusion of this article is that we need to reaffirm the absolute prohibition on torture in all circumstances without exception and to reaffirm the most basic of all principles, respect for human dignity. Since 11 September 2001 leaders have breached these principles and created a narrative framework which subjugates fundamental human rights and basic protections to the imperatives of national security. Necessity justifications for torture' and ill-treatment fit into this framework, as does the climate of fear which promotes public indifference towards the treatment of detainees. So too does academic discussion which takes the ticking bomb scenario as its paradigm. This is so whether like Derschowitz they claim that it would be better to legally authorise torture or whether they stress the importance of legal prohibition while sanctioning 'off the books' torture.

Most commentators acknowledge that the unrealistic scenario of the ticking bomb situation has no correspondence with the thousands of cases that actually occur. The 'perfect' torture situation assumes omniscience, that the torturer is certain that the suspect has crucial information to prevent imminent catastrophe, that the device will destroy thousands of people, that the suspect will reveal accurate information under torture.[64] But it is the ticking bomb situation they address when discussing justifications for torture and this artificially restricts the debate. Arguments for principled torture whether by advance permission or through retrospective forgiveness talk within a framework that by forcing a choice between security and individual rights inevitably finds torture acceptable as the lesser evil. Those who advocate absolute prohibition in these circumstances are regarded as utopian, naïve and irresponsible. But it is utopian, naïve and irresponsible to assume that a defence of limited torture in a hypothetical 'ideal' situation of imminent catastrophe, perfect knowledge and accurate cost–benefit analysis will not migrate to and be distorted in actual judicial or policy or individual interrogator's decisions in less ideal, less calculable circumstances. Moreover, conceptualising the problem within the confines of the ticking bomb's stark choices obscures what is wrong with torture and the fact the torture may be practised for purposes of control and domination and for purposes that fall short of preventing imminent catastrophe and cannot be justified by such purposes. Discussing torture within the context of this extreme security threat reconfigures our instinctive disgust for torture, substituting a respect for human dignity with an accommodating, excusatory response to abuse. The polarised choice between security and individual rights falsely suggests that measures to strengthen security necessarily involve the sacrifice of human rights and liberties; and, conversely, that in this new kind of war, championing those rights as absolute irresponsibly involves weakening security. This restricted and misleading choice not only undermines the values prohibiting torture, but discourages stepping outside this framework and exploring alternative ways of gaining information and other policies to improve security which do not involve violations of human rights. It helps perpetuate the illusion that the success in fighting the war on terror is dependent on the quality of intelligence and is not dependent on political action or the foreign policy of western governments. In doing so, it diverts attention away from the conditions in which the perceived need for torture arises and which themselves are in need of moral scrutiny and rectification. Given this, it would be less utopian, more realistic and responsible to change those aspects of international relations that ferment terrorism and the situations in which the need for torture arises, rather than accepting the inevitability of torture in some circumstances and trying to find criteria to justify its use.

Though we cannot be sure of the true motivations of the terrorists, we can be sure that violations of human rights and intelligence gathering through torture will not extinguish the threat they pose. Academics, by setting the argument for torture within the polarised and narrow focus of the ticking bomb, give credibility to those who have a vested interest in perpetuating the vain hope that it will.

Notes

1 UN Convention Against Torture and Other Cruel, Inhuman or Degrading Treatment pt.1, art.1 (1984), available at http://www.un.org/documents/ga/res/39/a39ro46.htm.

2 Ibid., art.2 para.2.

3 Ibid., art.16 para.1.

4 See *The New York Times*, 8 March 2005 and http://hrw.org/reports/2005/US0405.

5 Report of the International Committee of the Red Cross (ICRC) reprinted in M. Danner, *Torture and Truth: America, Abu Ghraib and the War on Terror* (London: Granta Books 2005), pp.241–270.

6 *New York Times*, 30 November 2004, p.A1.

7 See, for instance, details of abuse and sexual torture of prisoners at Guantanamo in *The Observer*, 8 May 2005, reports of detainee deaths in custody in Iraq in *The Washington Post*, 19 April 2005, reports of repeated incidents of mistreatment, abuse and beatings by US soldiers on Afghan suspects in the *New York Times*, 20 May 2005, a list of detention and interrogation practices alleges to have been authorised by the US in Amnesty International Report, *Guantanamo and Beyond?* AMR 5/1063/2005, 13 May 2005, available at http://www.web/amnesty/org/library/Index/ENGAMR510632002, Appendix 3.

8 The Schlesinger Report, reprinted in Danner (note 5) pp.321–394.

9 See Rumsfeld's interview with David Frost BBC TV, Department of Defense news transcript 27 June 2004 and the President's Statement on the UN International Day in Support of Victims of Torture, 26 June 2004.

10 See, for example, Danner (note 5); K.J. Greenberg and J.L. Dratel, *The Torture Papers: The Road to Abu Ghraib* (Cambridge: Cambridge University Press 2005); S. Strasser (ed.), *The Abu Ghraib Investigations* (USA: Public Affairs LLC, Perseus Book Group 2004); Human Rights Watch Report, *The Road to Abu Ghraib*, June 2004, available at http://www.hrw.org/reports/2004/USA0604; Amnesty International Report, *Human Rights Denied: Torture and Accountability in the War on Terror*, 27 October 2004, available at http://www.web.amnesty.org/library/Index/ENGAMR511452004.

11 Memo for the President from Alberto R. Gonzales re Application of the Geneva Conventions on POW to the Conflict with Al Qaeda and the Taliban, Draft, 25 January 2002, reprinted as Memo 7 in Greenberg and Dratel (note 10) pp.118–121.

12 Memo 11 to Rumsfeld from William J. Haynes re Counter-Resistance Techniques, 27 November 2002, approved by Rumsfeld 2 December 2002, reprinted as Memo 21 in Greenberg and Dratel (note 10) p.237.

13 Memo to General Counsel of the Dept of Defense from Rumsfeld re Detainee Interrogations, 15 January 2002 reprinted as Memo 22 in Greenberg and Dratel (note 10) p.238.

14 Memo to Commander, US Southern Command from Rumsfeld re Counter Resistance Techniques in the War on Terror, 16 April 2003, reprinted as Memo 27 in Greenberg and Dratel (note 10) pp.360–365.

15 Memo to Alberto Gonzales from Jay Bybee, Office of Legal Counsel, Dept of Justice re Standards for Interrogation, reprinted as Memo 14 in Greenberg and Dratel (note 10) pp.172–217.

16 Security under the Rule of Law, Address of Louise Arbor, UN High Commission for Human Rights to the Bienn. Conf of the Int. Comm of Jurists (Berlin), 27 August 2004.

17 Report of the Special Rapporteur on Torture and Other Cruel, Inhuman or Degrading Punishment or Treatment, Forty-ninth Session of the General Assembly, UNDocA/59/3249, 23 August 2004.

18 See 'US State Department Criticism of "Stress and Duress" Around the World', *A Human Rights Backgrounder*, April 2003, available at http://www.hrw.org/press/2003/04/stressnduress.htm.

19 See The Schlesinger Report: Final Report of the Independent Panel to Review DOD Detention Operations, August 224, reprinted in Greenberg and Dratel (note 10) pp.925–926.

20 J.T. Parry, 'Escalation and Necessity: Defining Torture at Home and Abroad', in S. Levinson (ed.), *Torture: A Collection* (Oxford: Oxford University Press 2004), p.60.

21 R.A. Posner, 'The Best Offense', *New Republic*, 2 September 2002, p.28.

22 O. Gross, 'The Prohibition on Torture and the Limits of the Law', in Levinson (note 20) p.238.

23 J.B. Elshstain, 'Reflections on the Problem of "Dirty Hands" ', in Levinson (note 20) pp.87–88.

24 H. Shue, 'Torture', in Levinson (note 20) p.17.

25 Gross (note 22) pp.240–241.

26 R.A. Posner, 'Escalation and Necessity: Defining Torture at Home and Abroad', in Levinson (note 20) p.298.

27 Shue (note 24) p.59.
28 A.M. Derschowitz, *Why Terrorism Works: Understanding the Threat, Responding to the Challenge* (New Haven, CT: Yale University Press 2002), pp.131–163.
29 Ibid., p.144.
30 Ibid., pp.152–153, 158–159.
31 Gross (note 22) pp.244–245.
32 E. Scarry, 'Five Errors in the Reasoning of Alan Derschowitz', in Levinson (note 20) p.283.
33 Gross (note 22) p.242.
34 Ibid., p.241; see also Posner (note 26) p.298.
35 S.F. Kreimer, 'Too Close to the Rack and Screw: Constitutional Constraints on Torture in the War on Terror', *University of Pennsylvania Journal of Constitutional Law*, 6 (2003), pp.146–147; see also Scarry (note 32) p.286.
36 Posner (note 26) p.296.
37 Kreimer (note 35) p.148; see also Scarry (note 32) p.286.
38 Scarry (note 32) pp.287–288.
39 See Amnesty International Report (note 7), Appendix 3.
40 There have been at least ten official military investigations into Abu Ghraib; responsibility has stopped at a handful of enlisted army recruits.
41 Kreimer (note 35) pp.156–157.
42 Elshtain (note 23) p.83.
43 Parry (note 20) p.160.
44 Gross (note 22) p.247.
45 M. Walzer, 'Political Action and the Problem of Dirty Hands', *Philosophy and Public Affairs*, Vol.2, No.2 (1973), p.161.
46 Ibid., p.179.
47 The Intelligence and Select Committee Report (ISC) on 11 September 2003 revealed that on 10 February 2003, a month before invasion of Iraq, the Joint Intelligence Committee (JIC) warned Blair that military action in Iraq would increase the terrorist threat and that Blair overruled this warning. Text of ISC report available at http://www.online.gov.uk/Root/04/00/89/06/04008906.pdf. *The Guardian*, 18 July 2002 reported the publication of a paper by an independent think-tank on foreign affairs, the Chatham House Organisation, which claimed that there is no doubt that UK involvement in wars in Afghanistan and Iraq contributed to terrorist attacks in London.
48 http://www.hrw.org/press/2001/11/tortureQandAhtm#laws.
49 *American Prospect*, 4 February 2005, see also *The Guardian*, 18 October 2003.
50 See http://www.defenselink.mil.news/Mar2005/d20050304.info.pdf.
51 *The Observer*, 8 May 2005.
52 *New York Review of Books*, 12 May 2004.
53 *The Washington Post*, 24 May 2004.
54 *The Observer*, 3 July 2005.
55 Report on Torture, Amnesty International, 1973.
56 H.H. Langbein, 'The Legal History of Torture', in Levinson (note 20) p.97.
57 *The Guardian*, 14 May 2005.
58 *The Guardian*, 18 July 2005, 19 July 2005.
59 See for example E. Scarry, *The Body in Pain* (New York: Oxford University Press, 1985), pp.27–59.
60 Shue (note 24) p.50.
61 Parry (note 20) p.153.
62 D. Sussman, 'What's Wrong with Torture?', *Philosophy and Public Affairs*, Vol.33, No.2 (2005), pp.4, 13, 14, 22, 30.
63 Parry (note 20) p.152.
64 See especially Scarry (note 32) pp.281–285.

Reprinted with permission from Maureen Ramsay, 'Can the torture of terrorist suspects be justified?', *The International Journal of Human Rights* 10/2 (2006) pp.103–19.

TORTURE AND ASSASSINATION

Further reading: Books and reports

M. Bagaric & J. Clarke, *Torture: When the Unthinkable Is Morally Permissible*, (NY: State University of New York Press 2007).

Bruce Berkowitz, *The New Face of War: How War Will be Fought in the 21ˢᵗ Century* (NY: Free Press 2000) pp.119–34.

R. Crelinsten & A Schmid (eds.), *The politics of pain: Torturers and their masters* (Boulder, CO: Westview 1995).

M. Danner, *Torture and Truth: America, Abu Ghraib, and the War on Terror* (London: Granta Books 2005).

Alan M. Dershowitz, *Why Terrorism Works, New Haven* (New Haven: Yale University Press 2002).

Karen J. Greenberg (ed.), *The Torture Debate in America* (NY: Cambridge University Press 2006)

Karen J. Greenberg & J. Dratel, *The Torture Papers: The Road. to Abu Ghraib* (Cambridge: Cambridge University Press 2005).

M. Benvenisti (ed.), *Abu Ghraib: The Politics of Torture* (Berkeley, CA: North Atlantic Books 2004).

Stephen Grey, *Ghost Plane: The Untold Story of the CIA's Secret Rendition* (London: Hurst 2006).

Michael Ignatieff, *The Lesser Evil: Political Ethics in an Age of Terror* (Princeton, NJ: Princeton University Press 2004).

J. Jaffer & A. Singh, *Administration of Torture: A Documentary Record from Washington to Abu Ghraib and Beyond* (NY: Columbia University Press 2007).

M. Lazreg, *Torture and the Twilight of Empire: From Algiers to Baghdad* (Princeton, NJ: Princeton University Press 2007).

Sanford Levinson (ed.), *Torture: A Collection* (NY: Oxford University Press 2004).

C. Mackey & G. Miller, *The Interrogators: Inside the Secret War Against al Qaeda* (NY: Little, Brown, 2004).

Alfred W. McCoy, *A Question of Torture: CIA Interrogation, from the Cold War to the War on Terror* (NY: Metropolitan Books, 2006).

T. Paglen & A.C. Thompson, *Torture Taxi On the Trail of the CIA's Rendition Flights* (NY: Melville House Publishing, 2006).

D. Rejali, *Torture and Democracy* (Princeton: Princeton University Press 2007).

Kenneth Roth, Minky Worden & Amy D. Bernstein (eds.), *Torture: Does it Make Us Safer? Is It Ever OK?: A Human Rights Perspective* (NY: Human Rights Watch 2005),

E. Saar, *Inside the Wire : A Military Intelligence Soldier's Eyewitness Account of Life at Guantanamo* (New York: Penguin, 2005).

S. Strasser, *The Abu Ghraib Investigations: The Official Reports of the Independent Panel and Pentagon on the Shocking Prisoner Abuse in Iraq* (New York: Public Affairs 2004).

Michael Walzer, *Arguing About War* (New Haven, CT: Yale University Press, 2004).

Tom Williamson, *Investigative Interviewing: Rights, research, and regulation* (NY: Willan Publishing, 2006).

Further reading: Essays and articles

F. Allhof, 'Terrorism and Torture', *International Journal of Applied Philosophy* 17/1 (2003) pp.105–18.

Thomas E Ayres, ' "Six Floors" of Detainee Operations in the Post-9/11 World', *Parameters*, 35/3 (Autumn 2005) pp.3–53.

Mirko Bagaric and Julie Clarke, 'Not Enough Official Torture in the World? The Circumstances in Which Torture Is Morally Justifiable,' *University of San Francisco of Law Review* 39 (2005) pp.581–616. [see reply by Rumney below]

Alex Bellamy, 'No pain, no gain? Torture and ethics in the war on terror', *International Affairs* 82/1 (2006) pp.121–48.

B. Berkowtiz, 'Is Assassination an Option', *Hoover Digest* 2002, 1 at – http://www.hoover.org/publications/digest/4477731.html

Ruth Blakeley, 'Language, policy and the construction of a torture culture in the war on terrorism', *Review of International Studies* 33/1 (2007) pp.373–94.

Mark Bowden, 'The Dark Art of Interrogation,' *Atlantic Monthly*, 292/3 (2003) pp.51–76.

R.J. Bruemmer, 'The Prohibition on Assassination: A Legal & Ethical Analysis,' in Hayden B. Peake and Samuel Halpern (eds.), *In the Name of Intelligence: Essays in Honor of Walter Pforzheimer* (Washington, DC: NIBC Press 1994) pp.137–165.

Daniel S Byman 'Time to Kill? Assassinations and Foreign Policy,' 85/2 *Foreign Affairs* (2006) pp.95–111.

Jeffrey Claburn', 'Public Constraints on assassination as an Instrument of U.S Foreign Policy', *International Journal of Intelligence and Counterintelligence* 7/1 (1994) 97–109.

R. Crelinsten, 'The World of Torture: A Constructed Reality,' *Theoretical Criminology* 7/3 (2003) pp.293–318.

Alex Danchev, 'Accomplicity: Britain, Torture, and Terror,' *The British Journal of Politics and International Relations* 8/4 (2006) pp.587–601.

Alan M. Dershowitz, 'Reply: Torture Without Visibility And Accountability Is Worse Than With It,' *University of Pennsylvania Journal of Constitutional Law* 6 (2003):326. [reply to Kriemer, see below]

Alan M. Dershowitz, 'The Torture Warrant: a Response to Professor Strauss', *New York Law School Law Review* 48 (2003) pp.275–294 [reply to Strauss, see below]

Steven R. David & Yael Stein, 'Israel's Policy of Targeted Killings,' *Ethics and International Affairs* 17/2 (2003) pp.111–126.

K. Eichensehr, 'On the Offensive: Assassination Policy Under International Law', *Harvard International Review* 25/3 (Fall 2003)

ML Gross, 'Fighting by other means in the Mideast: a Critical Analysis of Israel's Assassination Policy', *Political Studies* 51/2 (2003) pp.350–68 [see the reply by Statman below].

David Forsythe, 'United States Policy toward Enemy Detainees in the "War on Terrorism', *Human Rights Quarterly* 28/2 (2006) pp.465–491.

G. Hook & C. Mosher, 'Outrages Against Personal Dignity: Rationalizing Abuse and Torture in the War on Terror', *Social Forces* 83/4 (2005) pp.1627–1646.

Richard Jackson, 'Language, policy and the construction of a torture culture in the war on terrorism', *Review of International Studies* 33/1 (2007) pp.353–371

B.M. Johnson, 'Executive Order 12,333: The Permissibility of an American Assassination of a Foreign Leader' *Cornell International Law Journal* 25/2 (1992) pp.401–436.

Asa Kasher & Amos Yadlin, 'Assassination and Preventive Killing', *SAIS Review*, 25/1 (2005) pp.41–57.

Seth Kreimer, 'Too Close to the Rack and the Screw: Constitutional Constraints on Torture in the War on Terror,' *University of Pennsylvania Journal of Constitutional Law* 6 (2003) 278 [see reply by Dershowitz above]

D. Krezmer, 'Targeted Killing of Suspected Terrorists: Extra-judicial Executions or Legitimate Means of Defence?', *European Journal of International Law* 16/2 (2005) pp.171–212.

Catherine Lotrionte, 'When to target leaders', *The Washington Quarterly* 26/3 (2003) pp.73–86.

Alfred W. McCoy, 'Cruel Science: CIA Torture and U.S. Foreign Policy', *New England Journal of Public Policy*, 19/2 (2005) pp.1–54.

Assaf Meydani, 'The Interrogation Policy of the Israeli General Security Service: Between Law and Politics', *International Journal of Intelligence and CounterIntelligence* 21/1 (2008) pp.26–39.

Assaf Meydani, 'Security and Human Rights Policy: Israel and the Interrogation Case of 1999', *Contemporary Security Policy* 28/3 (2007) pp.579–96.

Eric Patterson & Teresa Casale, 'Targeting Terror: The Ethical and Practical Implications of Targeted Killing,' *International Journal of Intelligence and Counterintelligence* 18/4 (2005–2006) pp.638–652.

John T. Parry, 'What Is Torture, Are We Doing It, and What If We Are?' *University of Pittsburgh Law Review* 64 (2003) pp.237–262.

Jeffrey Richelson, 'When Kindness Fails: Assassination as a National Security Option,' *International Journal of Intelligence and Counterintelligence* 15/2 (2002) pp.243–274.

Adam Roberts, 'Torture and Incompetence in the "War on Terror" ', *Survival* 49/1 (2007) pp.199–212.

Bruce A. Ross, 'The Case for Targeting Leadership in War,' *Naval War College Review* 46/1 (1993) pp.73–93.

Philip N.S. Rumney, 'Is Coercive Interrogation of Terrorist Suspects Effective? A Response to Bagaric and Clarke,' *University of San Francisco of Law Review* 40 (2006) pp.479–513 [see Bagaric and Clarke above].

H. Schue, 'Torture', *Philosophy and Public Affairs* 7/2 (1978) pp.124–43

M.N. Schmitt, 'State-Sponsored Assassination in International and Domestic Law,' *Yale Journal of International Law* 17/2 (1992) pp.609–685.

Jerome Slater, 'Tragic Choices in the War on Terrorism: Should We Try to Regulate and Control Torture?', *Political Science Quarterly* 121/2 (2006) pp.191–215.

Daniel Statman 'The Morality of Assassination: A Response to Gross' *Political Studies* 51/4 (2003) pp.775–779. [see Gross above]

Marcy Strauss, 'Torture'. *New York Law School Law Review*, 48/1&2 (2004) pp.201–274 [see reply by Dershowitz above]

T. Ward, 'Norms and Security: The Case of International Assassination,' *International Security* 25/1 (2000) pp.105–33

T. Ward, 'The New Age of Assassination', *SAIS Review* 25/1 (2005) pp.27–39.

Patricia Zengel, 'Assassination and the Law of Armed Conflict,' *Military Law Review* 131 (1991) pp.23–55.

Peace and Conflict: Journal of Peace Psychology, 13/4 (2007) is a special issue of eight essays focusing on torture.

Essay questions

- Can an ethical case ever be made for the use of torture during interrogation?
- Given that we have transparently failed to prevent torture in many democratic countries since 1945, is Dershowitz right to suggest that we must, at the very least, seek to regulate it?
- Can an ethical case ever be made for assassination?
- 'Where countries like the United States, Israel and former Soviet Union have attempted assassinations, the effects have always been unpredictable and often negative'. Discuss.

Part 4

Intelligence and the new warfare

Intelligence is regarded as a Cinderella service . . . War is, in fact, the Fairy Godmother who changes Cinderella into the Princess.

Rear Admiral Edmund Rushbrooke (DNI)[1]

SUMMARY

Covert action

The term 'covert action' is often misunderstood. A covert action might well be defined as an operation carried out in such a way that the parties responsible for the action are able to distance themselves from it. The action, and especially its results, might be plain for all to see, however the perpetrators must be able to maintain plausible deniability. The emphasis is placed on concealment of identity of the sponsor, rather than on concealment of the operation itself. Covert actions might be political, psychological, economic or para-military in nature but the factor they have in common is the intention to intervene and actively change something. This is contrast to intelligence gathering, which is often rather passive. By contrast, because intelligence gathering tends to be more passive, its operations might reasonably hope to remain hidden, or 'clandestine', for a long period of time, perhaps even forever. Although the terms 'covert' and 'clandestine' are sometimes used interchangeably this is erroneous, since their meanings are quite different. The terminology for covert actions varies from country to country. In the UK, covert action is often termed 'special operations' or in France an 'action operation'.

Covert actions are most often performed in the place of overt military operations because the latter would embarrass the perpetrator or break the law in a specific country. They have also been employed by Prime Ministers and Presidents as a private foreign policy option that allows them the pursue possibilites that are independent of the rest of the bureaucracy, or else highly unpopular with a large political constituency. To this extent they may be illegal in the country which has initiated them. The Iran-Contra episode in the 1980s offers a text-book case of an illegal operation which resulted in an officer from the National Security Council, Admiral Richard Poindexter, being sentenced to six months in jail.

Covert operations are also employed in situations where openly operating against a target would be politically or diplomatically risky, or be counterproductive to the overall purpose of the mission. In the case of enemies, there may be a range of issues regarding violation of neutrality, perhaps concerns over military strength, the presence of treaties, laws, moral principles, or else a simple aversion to negative media attention. Operations may be conducted with, or even directed against, allies and friends to secure their support or to influence or to secretly assist their own policy against a common enemy. For example, the UK conducted a range of high-risk political influence operations in the period before December 1941 intended to help draw the United States into the Second World War. Covert action is often disliked by those engaged in traditional human espionage activity, since it is thought to attract unwelcome attention and may result in the exposure of collection networks.

Intense media interest in covert action has resulted in a presumption that this is normally military or para-military in nature. Certainly some of the most ambitious covert operations have been of this kind, including a mercenary army of some 40,000 soldiers maintained by the CIA in Laos during the Vietnam War. Paramilitary operations do commonly involve training, support and advice to military forces in another country, or else secret support for an insurgency, often termed 'pro-insurgency'. Support for the Mujahhedin against the Soviet occupation in Afghanistan during the 1980s is perhaps the best known example. Political action is less visible, but no less common and typically involves advising or funding a political group in another country. Propaganda can also constitute covert action if the source of the broadcasts is disguised, often being termed 'black propaganda'. Economic disruption and sabotage also falls within the realm of covert action.

The growth of counter-terrorism has seen a range of covert action directed against individuals, including the kidnapping or assassination of key terrorist figures. Israel has been prominent in advocating these types of measures. Such activities are high-risk and frequently go wrong, with serious political consequences. This was illustrated in September 1997 by Mossad's embarrassing botched attempt to assassinate the senior Hamas figure, Khaled Meshal, in Jordan using operatives equipped with a poison spray and carrying Canadian passports. Covert action, more than any other secret service activity, tends to reflect national style. The UK has been inclined to opt for lower key special operations, often termed 'disruption', while leaving specialist military units to undertake more kinetic activities. During the Cold War, the Soviet Union developed an exotic range of covert action for use in both war and peace, which they termed 'active measures'. They devolved particular roles to their Eastern Bloc allies. The East German Stasi specialised in extending security support to the leaders of Third World regimes while Bulgaria specialised in assassination.[2]

Whatever their national style, the common theme of covert action is relative unsecrecy. They rarely remain covert for very long. Indeed, the idea of secret armies and silent warfare is something of a contradiction in terms. The other abiding problem is control. The sorts of figures who practice covert action are temperamentally unhappy with formal chains of command. Moreover, covert action normally involves co-operation with local partners be they political groups or tribal organisations. These groups are relatively easy to train, fund or arm, but once they become strong they are often resistant to taking orders. During the Cold War the CIA funded many cultural groups as part of its information war with the Soviet Union. Historians continue to debate whether the CIA was able to 'call the tune', simply because it paid the piper. Increasingly historians have concluded that this was not the case.[3]

Deception and military operations

In the modern military context, intelligence is increasingly associated with broader concepts such as information dominance and the 'Revolution in Military Affairs' or 'RMA'. RMA is a catchall phrase that denotes what many see as a fundamental change in the nature of warfare, driven by new technologies. Advances in command, communications and intelligence have been amongst the most important and are leading to significant changes in military doctrine and in how operational military forces are structured. Although originating in Russia, the more recent thinking on RMA has also borrowed from modern business methods, which emphasise flat hierarchies and flexible teams that communicate laterally.

RMA also reflects politics as well as technology. Many anticipated that the end of the Cold War would issue in a period of relative peace, but in reality, defence departments was confronted with an increasing need for expeditionary forces, beginning with the Gulf War of 1990–1. This has altered the priorities of the military intelligence machine. During the Cold War, high-grade military intelligence was often about 'estimates' and support for policy-makers in national capitals. Now the emphasis has shifted to a forward-leaning posture, pushing intelligence down to the operational and tactical level. The current challenge is to create a single information battlespace within which high-grade intelligence from national assets can be fed seamlessly to soldiers on the front line. This in turn is changing the way in which intelligence is organised and indeed classified. However, the varied extent to which countries have, or have not, embraced these changes can create difficulties for intelligence sharing within a military coalition.

An important area where intelligence and information can exert a pivotal effect over military operations is deception. Intelligence and deception are not synonymous. However intelligence is an essential part of deception. Intelligence is important in planning deception, since it is necessary to ascertain at the outset what the enemy is pre-disposed to believe. It is important in mounting a counter-intelligence effort to feed enemy intelligence with false information to create and sustain the deception. Finally, intelligence is important in detecting whether the enemy has 'taken the bait', or else whether they have rumbled the deception. Deception is not limited to the military sphere. During the Cold War the Soviets mounted a vast deception campaign as part of its political warfare programme. Deception can also form part of the game of espionage and counter-espionage between human intelligence services, often referred to as the 'wilderness of mirrors'.

The classic example of a successful strategic deception plan is the cover for D-Day invasion of Normandy in 1944, codenamed FORTITUDE SOUTH. Alongside this plan there were other major deceptions, including false invasions in the western Mediterranean, an invasion of France from the Bay of Biscay and even a fictive plan for the invasion of Norway. FORTITUDE SOUTH sought to persuade the Germans to believe what they already thought was most likely, namely that the invasion of France would happen at the Pas de Calais. This was the shortest distance across the English Channel and was an area that was well provided with harbours. In reality, Allied forces were mostly located in Devon and Dorset ready to attack the Normandy coast. Therefore an entirely false military formation had to be built up in Kent to sustain the German belief that Calais was the target. This was the mythical First U.S. Army Group led by the well-known General Patton.

Elaborate efforts were undertaken to deceive Axis intelligence. The Allies had to ensure that German photo-reconnaissance would support the notion of an attack on Calais. False airfields and storage depots were constructed. Enemy signals intelligence also needed to be deceived, so signals officers created a volume of radio traffic that suggested that an Army Group was gathering in Kent. Exercises were recorded and then re-played over the airwaves. On the eve of D-Day, enemy radars had to be deceived by dropping aluminium chaff from aircraft to make it appear that large numbers of ships were heading for Calais.[4]

Perhaps the most impressive aspect of the deception campaign was the use of double agents. Partly because of Allied dominance in the area of signals intelligence, all the German spies in the UK had been caught, and more importantly were known to be caught. In some cases they had been 'turned' to assist in the deception. The elaborate business of orchestrating the output of these double agents was the work of Twenty Committee (XX) or the 'Double Cross' Committee. The best known operative was the legendary double agent 'Garbo', whose false reporting reached Hitler. Garbo was awarded an Iron Cross for his 'heroic' efforts. The D-Day deception is suggested here as a useful case study because it underlines the demanding nature of strategic deception operations. They require the sophisticated integration of intelligence, counter-intelligence and operational planning at all levels together with excellent security discipline.

Intelligence and counter-insurgency

Although intelligence has long been held to be central to effective counterinsurgency operations, remarkably little has been written about intelligence and low intensity conflict in the abstract. In part, this may be an auspicious sign. While intelligence is important in an optimised counter-insurgency campaign, it should also be seamlessly integrated with other aspects of governance, including military operations, policing, psychological warfare, relief aid and civil development. Notwithstanding this, for the student of intelligence, the literature on counter-insurgency is dominated by descriptive case studies and is hard to navigate.

Intelligence in support of counter-insurgency might be said to provide two main functions. The first is operational and consists of locating an enemy that relies upon elusiveness as a central tactic. As General Frank Kitson once remarked, in all low intensity conflict, 'the problem of defeating the consists very largely of finding him'.[5] However, to talk of locating the enemy is perhaps too simplistic. The ability to find the enemy is also essential if the government forces are to create a virtuous cycle of victory. Finding the enemy permits the use of minimum force and offers the option of carefully targeted operations that do not aggravate the mainstream population. This in turn leads to better co-operation from the local population, which provides more intelligence. As a cycle of victory gather momentum there should also be surrenders by the insurgents, providing one of the most promising accelerators for government forces. Surrendered enemy personnel or SEPs are not only likely to be good sources if intelligence, but also good pyswar-operators. In some conflicts, SEPs have been 'turned' and used as covert counter-forces. In other words intelligence, special operations and psywar must be closely integrated to make use of local resources. This even extends to the enemy rank and file themselves.

Intelligence also serves a strategic function. The insurgency must be understood in its complete political, social and economic context. In the absence of a stable civil environment and its normal accoutrement of press and elections, quite often intelligence provides the best means by which commanders can understand the mood of the populace, the local environment and the strategy of the insurgents. Moreover, success and failure in insurgency is hard to evaluate. Famously, in Malaya during the early 1950s, both the guerrillas and the government forces simultaneously believed they were losing the war. Ironically, the more successful a counter-insurgency campaign becomes, the harder it is to draw to a conclusion because the declining density of guerrillas renders them yet harder to find. In the closing stages of a counter-insurgency, intelligence is important in locating the last remnants of the enemy and quite often in facilitating an agreement that terminates the conflict.

All low intensity conflicts – including peacekeeping – share certain common characteristics. Although counter-insurgency and peacekeeping might look different in a text-book, on the ground they can often look disturbingly similar, as they did in Bosnia and in Somalia. The British Army found the transition from Northern Ireland to peacekeeping in Bosnia relatively straightforward because in both environments they understood the high value of tactical intelligence collection by human beings. Large proportions of 'straight' military forces were devoted to intelligence and even during mundane operations each soldier was regarded as an intelligence collector. Small and seemingly insignificant changes in the local environment were often important indicators. Most modern conflicts are now what Rupert Smith has termed 'war among the people' and for that reasons, while highly technical forms of intelligence have a contribution to make, human intelligence remains prominent in the realm of low intensity conflict.[6]

Intelligence for peacekeeping and peacemaking

Peacekeeping operations, whether conducted under auspices of the United Nations, or by regional organisations such as the Organisations of Africa Unity, are now regarded as essential to the stability of the emerging world order. Peacekeeping operations that are directed by the United Nations constitute the second largest global military effort, only being eclipsed by that of the United States. In other words, the United Nations is the second most important military power in terms of its day-to-day operations. Yet it has no serious independent intelligence capability. In the early 1990s, the idea of United Nations intelligence activity was regarded by some with amusement or disdain. Intelligence support for United Nations activities is now regarded as a serious issue.

Intelligence for peace has a part to play at three different levels. First, effective intelligence support can greatly assist peacekeeping and all operational aspects of conflict resolution. Such support for a peacekeeping force can often be provided by the troop contributing nations. However, while regional alliances such as NATO enjoy sophisticated sharing arrangements, the problems of distributing intelligence amongst a kaleidoscopic coalition of peacekeepers can be difficult. Historically, as in the Congo in the 1960s, commanders of peacekeeping operations have often developed their own local ad hoc intelligence capability. In the 1990s, the former Yugoslavia presented a steep learning curve, both in terms of the problems of sharing and the difficulties that some partner nations had in reconciling United Nations duties with anything as unseemly as espionage.[7]

Second, in the wake of conflicts, the United Nations may well depend on intelligence support from states to monitor cease-fires, agreements on decommissioning weapons or to serve commissions designed to investigate war crimes. The UNSCOM Commission that investigated the scale of Iraqi WMD in the 1990s was dependent upon, and some have alleged worked in conjunction with, the intelligence communities of the major powers. More dramatically the International Criminal Tribunal for the Former Yugoslavia at the Hague has boasted an investigations department staffed largely with former military and police intelligence officers. Although specific in function, this unit is in effect a focused United National intelligence unit. In its efforts to apprehend war criminals it has had to worked closely with the intelligence services and special forces of NATO.

Third, and most controversially, the Secretary General of the United Nations, together with with its senior officers, require strategic intelligence support. In the 1990s, the United Nations found it necessary to develop an analytical capability at its New York headquarters. A number of countries on the Security Council seconded intelligence officers to the bur-geoning Situation Centre. For much of the 1990s the United Nations boasted a SitCen and an Information and Research Unit. It mostly served UN decision-makers but also assisted various multinational forces. Although closed down in 1999, reportedly because it leaked, many regard it as a useful indicator of how the UN might develop in the future.

Perhaps the least known role of intelligence services is that of direct peacemaker. Intelligence officers have long offered a back channel through which adversaries may talk to each other when they do not wish to be seen doing so. Intelligence officers provided a means by which Britain could talk to Nazi Germany after September 1939 and through which a possible peace was explored. During the Cold War, the United States often took a CIA officer to major international conference to talk to Chinese communist delegation behind the scenes, because non-recognition made open dialogue difficult. More recently, intelligence officers have been important in facilitating peace talks with terrorist organisations, including the IRA and several Middle East groups. Intelligence organisations have been successful in making contact with non-state groups and perhaps, as fellow field operators, they enjoy more credibility than a diplomat in bow tie.[8]

Notes

1 Rushbrooke makes these remarks in NID, Vol.42, 'HMS Anderson and Special Intelligence in the Far East', p.12, ADM 223/297, PRO.
2 Christopher Andrew and Vasili Mitrokhin, *The Mitrokhin Archive II: The KGB and the World*, (London: Allen Lane, 2005), pp.434, 437, 454–5, 459.
3 Hugh Wilford, *The Mighty Wurlitzer: How the CIA Played America* (New Haven: Yale University Press, 2007).
4 Roger Hesketh, *Fortitude – The D-Day Deception Campaign* (London: St Ermin's Press, 1999).
5 Frank Kitson, *Low Intensity Operations; Subversion, Insurgency, Peacekeeping* (London: faber & faber, 1971), p.95
6 Richard J. Aldrich, 'From Ireland to Bosnia: Intelligence Support for UK Low Intensity Operations', in Ben de Jong, Robert Steele and Wies Platje (eds.) *Peacekeeping Intelligence: Emerging Concepts for the Future* (Oakton: OSS International Press, 2003), pp.73–100.
7 Cees Wiebes, *Intelligence and The War in Bosnia 1992–1995* (Munster: Lit Verlag 2003).
8 Len Scott, 'Secret Intelligence, Covert Action and Clandestine Diplomacy', *Intelligence and National Security* 19/2 (2004) pp.322–34.

25 Covert action and the Pentagon

Jennifer D. Kibbe

The White House and the Pentagon have designated the military's Special Operations Command as the lead organization in the 'war on terror'. As the military has become more involved in fighting terrorism since 9/11, special operations forces have become increasingly active in the covert, or unacknowledged, operations that have traditionally been the CIA's bailiwick. This article examines the turf battles caused by the Pentagon's new covert profile, as well as its ramifications for congressional oversight.

The attacks on 11 September 2001 brought about a number of changes in the United States' national security outlook, not the least of which was a renewed willingness to consider covert action as a policy option. During this same period, the single most significant change in the military services has been the expansion, in both size and responsibility, of its special operations forces. The concurrence of these two trends has led to a blurring of the distinction of whether or not military units are conducting covert operations and raises important questions about congressional oversight. The Quadrennial Defense Review issued by the Pentagon in February 2006 stated unequivocally that special operations forces would be leading the 'war on terror', making it that much more important to understand the issues raised by potential military involvement in covert action.

Covert action is defined in US law as activity that is meant 'to influence political, economic, or military conditions abroad, where it is intended that the role of the United States Government will not be apparent or acknowledged publicly'.[1] Covert actions are, thus, legally distinct from clandestine missions: 'clandestine' refers to the tactical secrecy of the operation itself, 'covert' refers to the secrecy of its sponsor. Although most often associated with the assassination of leaders or the overthrow of a government, the category of covert action can include a wide range of activity, from propaganda and disinformation to political influence operations, economic destabilization, and paramilitary operations. Historically, the Central Intelligence Agency (CIA) has been the main agent of US covert action, but the growth of special operations forces since 2001 has raised new questions about who is best suited for conducting covert operations and stirred debate over congressional versus executive control of covert action.

Evolution of SOCOM

The military's unconventional warfare operations, whether covert or clandestine, are part of the US Special Operations Command (SOCOM), a relatively new command that has now been designated as the leader in the US war against terrorism. Although their roots can be traced to various World War II forces, including the Office of Strategic Services (OSS), air commandos, Scouts and Raiders, American special operations forces were first really built up in Vietnam as a result of President Kennedy's interest in using the Green Berets to conduct unconventional warfare. However, these forces were somewhat resented by the regular troops and officers, who felt that the armed forces' conventional training and approach to warfare had always been good enough before and that there was no need to introduce any sort of 'special' forces. Thus, when the end of the war in Vietnam led to severe budget cuts, every one of the armed services drastically cut its special operations units.

The event that caused the pendulum to swing back the other way again was the failed mission to rescue the American hostages in Iran in 1980. Because the US had no standing counterterrorist task force, the necessary personnel and equipment were drawn from the various services, leaving a significant gap in overall coordination. When two aircraft collided in the desert outside Tehran, eight members of the operation died and the rest were forced to turn back without attempting to rescue the hostages, leaving behind three intact heli-copters to boot. Within weeks, a commission had been formed to review the failed operation and determine how to improve the US's ability to run such operations in the future. The Holloway Commission, named for its chair, Chief of Naval Operations Admiral James Holloway, emphasized the uncoordinated nature of US special operations, as well as the lack of any independent review of the operational plans and the poor intelligence support. The commission's recommendation of the creation of a Counterterrorist Joint Task Force was adopted and implemented over the next several years.[2]

The early 1980s saw increased funding for special operations forces, an expansion in personnel and the creation of the Joint Special Operations Command (JSOC, pro-nounced 'jay-sock'), whose goal was to provide increased coordination. The first real operational test of the improvements was Operation Urgent Fury, the 1983 invasion of Grenada. Special operations forces, including SEALs (Sea, Air, Land), Rangers and members of Delta Force, were directly involved in seven of the operation's eight targets, of which only two were fully successful. Three of the operations were costly failures, with special operations forces incurring heavy casualties as a result of poor planning, coordin-ation, and intelligence.[3]

The failures at Grenada fueled a new round of calls for reform, and not just of special operations forces. This time, however, those interested in reform included some on Capitol Hill. This round of investigations eventually resulted in the Department of Defense Reorganization Act of 1986, also known as the Goldwater–Nichols Act, which substantially strengthened the power of the Chairman of the Joint Chiefs of Staff and the unified combatant commanders (the commanders of the various regional theaters). The element of the Goldwater-Nichols Act that most affected special operations, though, was the subsequent Nunn–Cohen Amendment that, most importantly, established the US Special Operations Command. Although SOCOM was established as a supporting command, meaning that it could not plan or execute its own independent operations and could only operate in support of other commands' operations, the new legislation still represented a significant step forward in the coordination and enhancement of special operations forces. The Nunn–Cohen amendment also specifically laid out in law, for the first time, the types of missions that would be included under the rubric of special operations: 'Direct action, strategic reconnaissance, unconventional warfare, foreign internal defense, civil affairs, psychological operations, counterterrorism, humanitarian assistance, theater search and rescue, [and] such other activities as may be specified by the Secretary of Defense.'[4]

In the four major conflicts involving the US since Grenada (the invasion of Panama, the

Gulf War, the Afghanistan War and the Iraq War), special operations forces have proven to be increasingly effective and useful.

Special operations forces today

Special Operations Command is comprised of both units that conduct overt or 'white' operations, and those that conduct 'black' operations, including both covert and clandestine missions. Those involved in white special operations include Army Special Forces (Green Berets), most Ranger units, most of the Navy SEALs, two Marine Special Operations Battalions (newly created in late 2005), and numerous aviation, civil affairs, and psychological operations units. These white special operators are largely involved in training selected foreign forces in counterterror, counterinsurgency, and counternarcotics tactics, helping with various civil government projects, and disseminating information to foreign audiences through the mass media. The black operators fall under JSOC, which commands the elite units of each service's special operations forces, including 1st Special Forces Operational Detachment-Delta (Delta Force), Naval Special Warfare Development Group (DEVGRU, or SEAL Team 6), the Air Force's 24th Special Tactics Squadron, the Army's 160th Special Operations Aviation Regiment and 75th Ranger Regiment, and a highly classified Intelligence Support Activity team (known as ISA, or more recently as Gray Fox, although its name changes frequently). These units (also known as special mission units) specialize in direct action operations such as hunting terrorists and rescuing hostages. While it is generally understood that these units exist, the Pentagon does not officially acknowledge them.

Throughout his term, one of Secretary of Defense Donald Rumsfeld's chief priorities was to transform the military from a large conventional force built to face another superpower into a leaner, and more flexible and agile force capable of fighting the less conventional conflicts that have dominated the post-Cold War period. While his desire to expand special operations was part of that original overall goal, it received a huge boost when, at the beginning of the war in Afghanistan, the military's special operations units had to rely on CIA operatives to establish links to the Northern Alliance fighters. By all accounts, Rumsfeld was incensed and became determined to build up the Pentagon's special operations capabilities to eliminate any future dependence on the CIA.

That determination has gradually led to significant increases in funding, personnel, and authority for special operations forces. The Fiscal Year (FY) 2007 defense budget called for special operations funding to grow to $5.1 billion, approximately $1 billion more than the previous year and double the amount allocated to it in 2001. The 2006 Quadrennial Defense Review, the Pentagon's main planning document for the next four years, aimed to increase special operations troops, which numbered about 50,000 at the beginning of 2006, by 14,000 through 2011, at a cost of nearly $28 billion. (Note that of the 50,000 current special operations forces, only approximately 10,000–13,000 are 'trigger-pullers', i.e. those in the field involved in operations. The remainder are support and administrative staff.)

Beyond the actual numbers, Rumsfeld also effected several substantive changes in the way SOCOM is run. First, he replaced those leaders of SOCOM who were, in his estimation, too cautious about the command's assuming a more aggressive role in the war on terror. He also significantly increased SOCOM's authority by changing it from a supporting to a supported command, meaning that it could now plan and execute its own missions (if authorized by the Secretary and, if necessary, the President). This change gave SOCOM a considerable amount of increased flexibility, since it meant the chain of command now went directly from SOCOM to the Secretary, without having to go through a regional unified command (Southern Command, for example). This change could also be seen as giving the Secretary increased control over special operations. Cutting out the regional commands, however, also presents an increased risk that special operations units may plan missions without taking sufficient account of possible regional repercussions.

In March 2004, after an intensive bureaucratic struggle, Rumsfeld was successful in his campaign to install SOCOM as the leader of the war on terror, ahead of the conventional forces whose leaders he perceived as too tentative. President Bush signed the new Unified Command Plan 2004, which designated SOCOM as the 'lead combatant commander for planning, synchronizing, and as directed, executing global operations' in the war on terror (although it did leave the regional commanders in charge of counterterrorism operations in their own theaters).[5]

An amendment to the defense authorization bill in October 2004 represented a further step along SOCOM's road to independence as Congress granted its forces the authority, for the first time, to spend money to pay informants, recruit foreign paramilitary fighters, and purchase equipment or other items from foreigners. Previously, only the CIA had been authorized to disburse such funds, meaning that special operations forces had had to rely on the CIA to provide the funds for various operations.

One other significant step in the special operations forces' rise to prominence came in January 2006 when JSOC's headquarters was raised from a two-star to a three-star command, thus giving its chief more authority and influence in dealing with other military officers.

There is little doubt that Rumsfeld's vision for SOCOM was a long-term one. Indeed, in presenting the 2006 Quadrennial Defense Review to the press in February 2006, Rumsfeld described its emphasis on developing special operations forces as a necessary component of US preparation for what he called the 'long war' ahead against extremism. The review not only calls for significant increases in forces, but also for increased training of conventional troops in 'irregular' operations, such as counterinsurgency and stabilization operations, thus freeing up special forces operators for 'more demanding and specialized tasks, especially long-duration, indirect and clandestine operations in politically sensitive environments and denied areas'. In addition, the document states that for direct action, special operations forces 'will possess an expanded organic ability to locate, tag and track dangerous individuals and other high-value targets globally'.[6]

Also in February 2006, General Peter Pace, Chairman of the Joint Chiefs of Staff, reportedly signed a new, classified counterterrorism strategy that orders the Defense Department to undertake a broad campaign to find and attack or neutralize terrorist leaders, their havens, financial networks, methods of communication and ability to travel. According to the *New York Times*, the strategy document specifies that the effort to defeat terrorism requires 'continuous military operations to develop the situation and generate the intelligence that allows us to attack global terrorist organizations'.[7]

Another major facet of SOCOM's burgeoning role is its wide geographic scope. In the five years since 9/11, special forces operations have been reported in the Philippines, Malaysia, Georgia, Colombia, Indonesia, Pakistan, Yemen, Algeria, Morocco, Mauritania, Niger, Mali, Chad, Nigeria, Somalia, Ethiopia, Djibouti, Yemen, and Jordan. While most of the reported operations are of the white variety, usually involving counterinsurgency and counterterrorism training of indigenous forces, there is little doubt that, with the Pentagon's stated goal of hunting down terrorists, black special operators are or will be active in many of the same countries.

Special Operations Command's growth in size, scope, and influence raises the questions of whether it is conducting any covert operations and of the degree and adequacy of congressional oversight of its activities.

Legal requirements

Congress first tried to assert control over covert action in the mid-1970s, in reaction to revelations of US involvement in the coup against Salvador Allende in Chile and assassination attempts against Fidel Castro. The Church Committee in the Senate and the Pike Committee in the House each conducted investigations that led to the establishment of permanent intelligence committees in both houses of Congress. The Iran–Contra scandal in the Reagan administration, however, highlighted important gaps in the new congressional oversight requirements. In response, Congress adopted more stringent provisions in the 1991 Intelligence Authorization Act, which is still the governing legislation on congressional oversight requirements. The Act codified two requirements for any covert (unacknowledged) action. First, there must be a written presidential finding, which cannot be issued retroactively, stating that the action is important to US national security. Second, the administration must notify the intelligence committees of the action as soon as possible after the finding has been issued and before the initiation of the operation, unless 'extraordinary circumstances' exist, in which case the President must fully inform the committees 'in a timely fashion'.[8]

The other significant feature of the 1991 Intelligence Authorization Act is that, in response to the Reagan administration's use of the National Security Council staff to conduct covert action in connection with Iran–Contra, it expressly applied the requirements to 'any department, agency, or entity of the United States Government'. In other words, Congress no longer assumed that only the CIA could or would conduct covert operations and it asserted its right to oversee those operations, no matter what agency was conducting them.

The law also included, however, a few designated exceptions to the definition of covert action. Under the most significant one, 'traditional . . . military activities or routine support to such activities' are deemed not to be covert action and thus do not require a presidential finding or congressional notification. While the act itself does not define 'traditional military activities', the conference committee report presenting the legislative history states that the phrase is meant to include actions preceding and related to hostilities which are anticipated to involve (conventional) US military forces or where such hostilities are ongoing, whether US involvement in the action is made public or not, as well as any military action where the US role is apparent or to be acknowledged publicly.[9]

It is the interpretation of the 'traditional military activities' exception that has caused considerable controversy as the Bush administration relies increasingly on special operations forces in the war on terror. Covert operations conducted by special operations forces during wartime clearly do not require a presidential finding and congressional notification. The definition leaves a gray area, however, around the interpretation of the word 'anticipated'. It is most commonly thought of in the literal sense of 'preparing the battlespace' (i.e. for conventional troops) and, in fact, the conference committee report of the 1991 law defines 'anticipated' hostilities as those for which operational planning has been approved. Defense Department officials, however, have explained that under the Pentagon's interpretation, the language could refer to events taking place 'years in advance' of any involvement of US military forces. Critics contend that the Bush administration has been eager to shift more covert activity from the CIA to the military precisely because they see it as giving them more of a free rein.

The administration's view of the 'traditional military activities' exception helps explain the emphasis in the new classified counterterrorism strategy on the 'continuous military operations' that are required 'to develop the situation' to allow the US to attack global terrorist organizations.

But the Pentagon's interpretation of the word 'anticipated' raises an obvious and important question: in prosecuting the war on terrorism, when special operations forces conduct an unacknowledged operation in a country where US troops are not already present, how can they prove that it is in anticipation of involvement of the regular armed forces later on, and thus not a covert action that requires a presidential finding and congressional notification (particularly if it occurs 'years in advance')?

An even trickier question is who will ask them to prove it? Legally, the ultimate arbiters of what does and does not constitute covert action are the House and Senate intelligence committees, which exert a type of veto through their control of the intelligence authorization process. However, there are several loopholes in this set-up. First, if it is a special operations mission, funding authorization in the Senate shifts to the Armed Services Committee (in the House, it remains with the Intelligence Committee). Second, in both houses, the armed services committees have ultimate control over the intelligence authorization process in any case, since they must sign off on intelligence authorization bills before they go to the full House and Senate for votes. As one Senate Armed Services Committee staffer described the relationship, 'we prevail because they're subordinate to us'. Third, most appropriations for intelligence activities are included as a classified section of the defense appropriations bill, meaning that the real control over the intelligence purse lies with the defense subcommittees of the House and Senate appropriations committees, thus creating a three-way split between the authority to determine whether it is a covert action and budgetary control. Finally, the fact of the matter is that congressional committees only know about those operations that the administration tells them about. In the tradition of Rumsfeld's 'unknown unknowns' they cannot ask questions about operations that they do not know exist.

Beyond the technicalities of arguing the meaning of the word 'anticipated', the Bush administration has made an even broader claim regarding its use of the military to conduct what would be called covert action if it were conducted by the CIA. Having defined the broad post-9/11 strategic environment as a 'war on terror', administration officials argue that anything the government does to prosecute the fight against terrorism is part of a 'war' and thus, legitimately is a 'traditional military activity'. A variant of this argument stems from Senate Joint Resolution 23, the authorization to use force granted by the Congress in response to the 9/11 attacks. That resolution authorizes the President

> to use all necessary and appropriate force against those nations, organizations, or persons he determines planned, authorized, committed, or aided the terrorist attacks that occurred on September 11, 2001, or harbored such organizations or persons, in order to prevent any future acts of international terrorism against the United States by such nations, organizations or persons.[10]

Thus, according to some legal experts, the resolution grants the President virtually unlimited authority, as long as he 'determines' that a particular target has some connection to Al Qaeda.

Finally, some Pentagon lawyers have interpreted the post-9/11 landscape even more broadly. Bush does not even need the resolution's authority, they contend; because of the attacks, anything he does in the fight against terrorism can be seen as a legitimate act of self-defense, and thus a 'traditional military activity'.

'Special activities'

Another aspect of the increasing overlap of covert action and special operations forces, and the implications of that overlap for congressional oversight, concerns several individual programs that suggest the Pentagon is conducting covert operations under headings other than 'traditional military activities'. The Department of Defense has defined a category of so-called 'special activities' with four characteristics. These are activities which are: (1) conducted abroad; (2) in which the US role is not apparent or acknowledged; (3) that do not include the collection or production of intelligence; and (4) which are not diplomatic activities.[11] It is difficult to obtain precise information about such 'special activities', but they are conducted under some presidential authority, such as executive orders, and do entail some degree of congressional notification, although it is impossible to know how many and which members that includes. What is clear is that they are not conducted under the covert action requirements of the law and do not involve notification of whole committees, whether intelligence or armed services. The relevant question is, whatever they are called, are these operations subject to effective oversight?

Another overlapping category that includes unacknowledged operations is that of 'special access programs', or SAPs. Special access programs, established by Executive Order 12958, are sensitive programs that impose 'need-to-know and access controls beyond those normally provided for access to confidential, secret, or top secret information'.[12] This 'beyond top secret' designation is to be established only upon an agency head's determination that: (1) the vulnerability of, or threat to, specific information is exceptional; and (2) the normal criteria for determining eligibility for access are not deemed sufficient to protect the information.[13]

The standard reporting requirement for Pentagon SAPs is that the congressional defense committees be given 30 days' notice before the program is initiated. However, the Bush administration has effectively nullified this requirement since January 2002. In various executive orders and presidential signing statements accompanying defense legislation, President Bush has included language claiming that the Supreme Court 'has stated that the President's authority to classify and control access to information bearing on national security flows from the Constitution and does not depend upon a legislative grant of authority'. As a result, he states that while in most situations the 30-day advance notice can be provided, 'as a matter of comity, situations may arise, especially in wartime, in which the President must promptly establish special access controls on classified national security information under his constitutional grants of the executive power and authority as Commander in Chief of the Armed Forces'. The statements then make plain that the executive branch will interpret the reporting requirements 'in a manner consistent with the constitutional authority of the President'.[14]

There are three categories of special access programs: (1) acknowledged programs, which are unclassified; (2) unacknowledged programs, which are classified but reported to Congress in the same form as acknowledged SAPs; and (3) waived programs, where the classifying agency head waives the standard reporting requirement. Waived SAPs are only orally briefed to the so-called 'Gang of Eight'; i.e. the chair and ranking (minority) members of both the Senate and House intelligence (or armed services) committees, and the House and

Senate majority and minority leaders.[15] The controversial program involving the National Security Agency (NSA)'s program of warrantless domestic surveillance that surfaced in late 2005 was one such waived SAP (which was ruled unconstitutional in August 2006 by US District Judge Anna Diggs Taylor).

Army documents that came to light in early 2006 as a result of the ongoing Freedom of Information Act lawsuit brought by the American Civil Liberties Union against the Defense Department regarding the abuses at Abu Ghraib prison highlight the risks involved in special operations forces being both involved in the war on terror and covered by SAPs. These documents confirm that a special operations unit known as Task Force 6–26 (also known as Task Force Omaha) has been implicated in numerous detainee abuse incidents in Iraq. Moreover, one Army file details how an Army Criminal Investigation Command investigator looking into claims that a detainee captured by Task Force 6–26 in Tikrit, Iraq, was stripped, humiliated, and physically abused until he passed out, was unable to continue the investigation because the unit was part of an SAP. The report notes that the 6–26 members used fake names during the interrogation and that 6–26 'also had a major computer malfunction which resulted in them losing 70 percent of their files; therefore, they can't find the cases we need to review'. The report concludes that the investigation does not need to be reopened, noting that 'Hell, even if we reopened it we wouldn't get anymore information then [sic] we already have'.[16]

There exists yet another process that provides for the protection of classified information. Known as Alternative or Compensatory Control Measures (ACCMs), these are a way of applying 'need-to-know' restrictions on information to, in essence, compartmentalize a program. According to a Navy directive, ACCMs are to be used in situations where need-to-know restrictions are deemed necessary but SAP controls are not warranted.[17] These measures are distinct from SAPs in that, while they provide the same internal security standards, they do not need the formal approval of the agency head and they do not have to be reported to Congress. Since 9/11, hundreds of ACCMs have been established to compartmentalize information regarding a range of sensitive activities, from special operations in specific countries, to intelligence collection and processing programs, to various war planning contingencies.[18]

One indication of the potential for abuse of ACCMs arose in an internal Navy audit conducted in 2005. The audit reportedly found that secrecy was being used to restrict congressional, Defense Department, and internal access to potentially controversial or even illegal activities.[19] As a result of the audit's findings, the Navy's new directive on ACCMs states that: 'The use of ACCM measures shall not preclude, nor unnecessarily impede, congressional, Office of the Secretary of Defense, or other appropriate oversight of programs, command functions, or operations.'[20]

There have been indications that some members of Congress are becoming uncomfortable with the Pentagon's increasing independence in the area of unacknowledged operations. In June 2005, the House Permanent Select Committee on Intelligence's report on the 2006 Intelligence Authorization Act stated the committee's belief 'that it does not have full visibility over some defense intelligence programs' that fall outside of specific budget categories.[21] Speaking to the press, Representative Peter Hoekstra (R-MI), the chair of the House committee, expressed his concern that the Pentagon was trying to hide activities such as information operations programs, including electronic warfare, psychological operations and counterpropaganda programs from both the newly-created Director of National Intelligence and Congress.[22]

Periodically, information about some previously unknown program will reach the public eye and a few members of Congress will express their concern about whether the Pentagon is evading oversight restrictions. They often issue calls for hearings, which may or may not be held. Momentum for developing more robust congressional oversight of special operations, however, tends to be derailed by a combination of factors. Often, the Pentagon sends representatives to Capitol Hill for either closed-door briefings or closed hearings in which they explain how they are not violating the covert action restrictions because they do not, by their definition, conduct covert action (unless an individual operative is on assignment to the CIA). Rather, they explain, they are conducting 'traditional military activities' or 'special activities' and they have complied with the relevant notification requirements (as interpreted by the administration).

Another factor working against congressional efforts for a larger role is the underlying antagonism between the intelligence and defense committees, and their respective sense of ownership of their particular issues. The concerns raised by today's special operations invariably involve both committees, and will not be addressed adequately until this fundamental issue of turf-sharing is resolved. And, in addition to the turf problem, there is the structural impediment that brings in the defense subcommittees of the appropriations committees as yet another congressional player.

Members' motivation to increase their oversight role also tends to wither in the face of Congress' traditional reluctance to go up against the Pentagon in a time of war. Finally, while members on both sides of the aisle have voiced concern about the oversight issue, since 2000 it has more frequently been expressed by what was until recently the Democratic minority which, of course, opened it up to partisan debate and power struggles, struggles the minority usually lost. With their new congressional majorities, the Democrats have promised to strengthen oversight, but their ability to overcome the obstacles to reform remains to be seen.

Issues beyond congress

The expansion of special operations forces into the realm traditionally occupied by the CIA's covert operators has created several other controversies beyond those in Congress. The first involves the question of who is better suited to conduct such operations, whatever they are called. Pentagon officials contend that the CIA is not responsive enough to the military's needs, that it is too risk-averse, and that it is simply too small to meet the global terrorist challenge. The CIA has approximately 700–800 covert operators, compared to the roughly 10,000–13,000 special operations forces. On the other hand, their relative sizes are not as askew as these numbers seem to indicate. Of that total, no more than 2,000 are JSOC black operators, i.e. directly comparable to CIA operatives. Moreover, according to many analysts, the difference in size of the overall organizations is a significant advantage for CIA operators. Having much less bureaucracy to deal with, they can do things faster, cheaper and with more flexibility than special operations forces – the main reason, the CIA's advocates contend, that the agency was able to have men on the ground at the beginning of the Afghanistan war quicker than the military. Even though this has clearly been one of the Pentagon's priorities in enacting its SOCOM reforms, most analysts still believe that the CIA continues to retain an advantage in speed and flexibility.

The CIA also has the advantage of experience: it has been conducting this type of operation for a long time and thus has case officers stationed at embassies throughout the world who have built up an extensive network of contacts that the military simply does not have. In addition, conducting operations where the role of the US is unacknowledged means, by definition, operating out of uniform. If captured, therefore, a special operations soldier is in an inherently different position than a conventional one. Whereas the latter is covered by international legal mechanisms such as the Geneva Conventions, which govern the conduct of war and the treatment of prisoners, a special operations soldier will have no such recourse. People who join the CIA's operations division are aware of and accept the risk that, if captured, they will essentially be completely on their own and that their country will not acknowledge them. Soldiers, however, join with a different set of expectations. They generally assume that if they fight for and defend their country, Washington will do its best to protect them if they are captured. While many special operations soldiers knowingly accept that risk, analysts point out that it is a dangerously slippery slope. Once some contingent of US military personnel is left without protection, they argue, that endangers the protection of all military personnel serving abroad, and could damage troop morale as well.

Many CIA and JSOC operators oppose the Pentagon's emphasis on moving special operations forces into the unacknowledged realm for precisely these reasons. There was, for instance, considerable opposition among special operations forces themselves to the 9/11 Commission's recommendation of moving all paramilitary responsibilities to SOCOM. Furthermore, these critics argue, JSOC's direct action units do not have the training for covert action operations and if they do undertake the training required, that will detract from their readiness for their traditional, highly specialized missions, such as hostage rescue, close-quarters combat and dealing with weapons of mass destruction. While there are other personnel capable of conducting covert action (i.e. in the CIA), if special operations forces are distracted from their traditional missions, there is no one else who can take their place, leaving the US vulnerable in certain situations.

One final issue that arises in weighing the relative advantages of CIA unacknowledged operations versus those conducted by special operations forces stems from the differences in mission planning procedures between the two organizations. Traditionally, CIA covert operations are developed by an operational planning group, and then subjected to several levels of approval within the agency. After receiving the CIA's approval, the proposal is then reviewed by the deputies' committee at the National Security Council (NSC), and possibly by the principals themselves, before being passed on to the President. Military operational planning, however, is conducted quite differently. Because its primary mission is combat, the military has full authority to make its own operational decisions with no input from outside agencies. A military black operation, therefore, is planned completely within the Pentagon and approved by the Secretary. This insulated decision-making system raises obvious diplomatic risks in a situation where special operations forces are conducting unacknowledged operations in a wide range of countries with which the US has a variety of relationships.

There has also been increasing concern that the military is running its own unacknowledged operations without even notifying the 'country team' in the relevant location; i.e. the CIA station chief and the ambassador. As Chief of Mission, the ambassador has traditionally had authority over all US government personnel and activities in a country, meaning that no US personnel could operate there without the ambassador's approval, while the CIA station chief has been in charge of coordinating any intelligence operations in the country. In March 2006, the *New York Times* revealed the existence of 'military liaison elements' (MLEs), small teams of special operations forces (some just two or three people) that had been placed in embassies in various countries in Africa, Latin America and Southeast Asia with which the US was not at war and with which it had friendly relations, to gather intelligence and 'prepare for potential missions to disrupt, capture or kill' terrorists.

According to the *Times*, some of these MLEs had, at least initially, been operating without the knowledge of the country team.[23] Such completely independent special operations not only run the risk of embarrassing the US diplomatically, but if the CIA were conducting an operation in the same area and the operators were unknown to each other, they could conceivably perceive each other as the enemy, a situation known as 'confliction'. In an attempt to resolve the confliction issue, in October 2005 the administration designated the CIA's Directorate of Operations as the new National Clandestine Service (NCS), and put it in charge of coordinating all overseas human intelligence activities, no matter what agency they were conducted by. As evidenced by the continuing MLE dispute, however, that step proved not to have enough bureaucratic punch to resolve the problem.

The MLE issue was merely the latest, and most concrete and public, symbol of the larger problem that had been brewing in the administration's counterterrorism ranks since the early days after 9/11, when President Bush framed his response to the attacks in strongly militaristic terms and dubbed it the 'Global War on Terror'. As Rumsfeld pushed ever harder for more authority and independence, both the CIA and the State Department challenged what they saw as the Pentagon's usurpation of their authority in its unilateral expansion of its counterterrorism mission. Resolving these turf battles (and the numerous others engendered by the war on terror) was the primary goal of a contentious two-year-long review designed to specify each agency's responsibility and the lines of division between them. The review finally resulted in the adoption of the classified National Security Presidential Directive (NSPD) 46 in March 2006. The directive designated the National Counterterrorism Center (NCTC, created by the intelligence reform legislation and housed under the Director of National Intelligence) as the entity responsible for ensuring that each agency sticks to the 'lanes in the road'. However, as frequently happens when negotiations are particularly difficult, the most contentious issues were left to be worked out later in annexes negotiated among the agencies involved.[24]

One of the most contentious issues was precisely this issue about how much independence the Pentagon should have in conducting operations in countries with which the US is not at war. Eventually, the level of animosity over the MLEs got to the point that then-Deputy Director of Intelligence Michael Hayden had to step in and pressure the two sides to come to some sort of agreement. The result was a memorandum of understanding in which the Pentagon and the State Department agreed that ambassadors would be informed of all military activity in their countries and given the opportunity to object.[25]

Another controversy triggered by the Pentagon's increasing covert profile concerns the rising level of discomfort within the special operations forces themselves about the direction their expansion is taking. Their fear is that all the attention is being focused on direct action (especially 'man-hunting') to the exclusion of SOCOM's other main missions, including unconventional warfare, civil affairs work, foreign internal defense, and information operations. As historian Max Boot of the Council on Foreign Relations explained in a June 2006 congressional hearing, SOCOM has become:

> very focused on direct action, on rappelling out of helicopters, kicking down doors, taking out bad guys. . . . Making real progress against Islamist terrorism is going to require accomplishing much more difficult and much less glamorous tasks, such as establishing security, furthering economic and political development and spreading the right information to win hearts and minds. . . . Above all, it will require working with the indigenous allies who must carry the bulk of the burden.[26]

In other words, it will require precisely the sort of tasks carried out by the 'white' special operators who have been receiving short shrift in the administration's 'war on terror'.

While there has been a gradual realization of the importance of unconventional warfare, Pentagon critics fear that the way SOCOM's leadership is currently structured all but guarantees its continued heavy reliance on direct action. They point to an imbalance in SOCOM's leadership ranks where the direct action segments of the community (i.e. Rangers, 160th Special Operations Aviation Regiment, and the JSOC units) are over-represented and the significantly larger numbers of special operators who perform other 'white' functions are underrepresented.[27]

One final question critics raise revolves around the actual difficulties involved in expanding special operations forces. The Pentagon has called for a significant increase in special operations soldiers by 2011. However, the whole point of special operations forces is that they are the best of the best and are put through much more rigorous and thorough training than conventional soldiers. Many analysts have questioned SOCOM's ability to produce that many more operators, particularly when its training infrastructure is already under stress as a result of increased training loads ever since 9/11. The command has revamped some of its training to make it more efficient and get more done in less time, but the fact remains that the high level of training for special operations requires a considerable amount of time and many question whether the Pentagon's push for increased numbers will result in compromising the quality of the resulting forces. More-over, in many ways it is easier to train a black special operator than a white one. The former needs training only in physical skills that can be quantifiably measured. The latter, however, also needs extensive education in language and culture, which can be very time-consuming. Thus, the worry is that under pressure to increase numbers, SOCOM will meet those targets by turning out proportionally more black operators, thus furthering its emphasis on direct action.[28]

Commission recommendations

In its final report, the National Commission on Terrorist Attacks upon the United States (9/11 Commission) stepped squarely into the debate over who is better suited to be leading the covert battle against terrorism. The Commission recommended that 'Lead responsibility for directing and executing paramilitary operations [i.e. missions of a significant size], whether clandestine or covert, should shift to the Defense Department. There it should be consolidated with the capabilities for training, direction, and execution of such operations already being developed in the Special Operations Command.'[29] In response, President Bush asked the Pentagon and CIA to study the Commission's conclusion and come up with a joint recommendation. Although many assumed that, because of the Pentagon's political muscle and Rumsfeld's expressed goals, it was a foregone conclusion that the Pentagon–CIA study would agree with the Commission's recommendation, in fact they ended up rejecting it, as did the President.

When the Commission on the Intelligence Capabilities of the United States Regarding Weapons of Mass Destruction (Silberman–Robb Commission) issued its recommendations in mid-2005, it reportedly included a classified recommendation that also would have given the Pentagon greater authority to conduct covert action.[30] Once again, though, the White House rejected the recommendation. While this would seem to run counter to the Pentagon's moves to expand special operations in the years since 9/11, in the context of the definitional issues explained above it appears likely that, in fact, the Pentagon does not want more control of covert action. It has the greatest freedom of action in the present system whereby the CIA conducts covert action per se and is thus subject to more formal congressional oversight, while the Pentagon can continue conducting its special activities, SAPs and ACCMs, with minimal, sometimes nonexistent, oversight.

Conclusion

The question of the military's involvement in unacknowledged operations is shaped by four main factors. First is the Pentagon's broad vision of SOCOM's role in the 'long war' against terrorism. Second is the geographic expansion of special operations forces, in terms of the number of different countries in which both black and white operators are present. A third facet of the issue is the Pentagon's definition of unacknowledged operations as either 'traditional military activities' subject to no congressional notification requirements, or as 'special activities' with more lenient notification requirements than the covert action conducted by the CIA. In addition, the military has the special categories of SAPs and ACCMs which restrict information even further. Finally, there are the indications that some past SAPs have led to highly controversial policies, including renditions (the practice of seizing suspects in one country and delivering them into custody in another country), covert media influence operations in Iraq and Afghanistan, and the direct evidence of the involvement of Task Force 6–26 in interrogations at Abu Ghraib. The military's role in unacknowledged operations is an increasingly complex issue and it remains to be seen how Congress will serve the twin goals of protecting the United States from terrorism and ensuring that there is sufficient accountability to the public.

Notes

1 50 U.S.C. § 413(b)(e).
2 Susan L. Marquis, *Unconventional Warfare: Rebuilding Special Operations Forces* (Washington, DC: Brookings Institution Press 1997) pp.72–3.
3 Ibid. pp.91–2.
4 Nunn-Cohen Amendment to the 1986 Defense Reorganization Act, 10 U.S.C. § 167.
5 Statement of Vice Admiral Eric T. Olson, U.S. Navy Deputy Commander United States Special Operations Command Before the Senate Armed Services Committee Subcommittee on Emerging Threats and Capabilities, 5 April 2006, p.3.
6 *Quadrennial Defense Review Report*, United States Department of Defense, 6 February 2006, <http://www.defenselink.mil/qdr/report/Report20060203.pdf#search=%222006%20quadrennial%20defense%20review%22> (last accessed 24 August 2006).
7 Thom Shanker, 'Pentagon Hones Its Strategy Against Terrorism', *New York Times*, 5 February 2006, p.16.
8 50 U.S.C. § 413(b)(e).
9 H.R. Conf. Rep. No. 166, 102d Cong., 1st Sess., reprinted in 137 *Congressional Record*, No. 115, H5904–06 (daily ed. 25 July 1991), pp.5905–6.
10 S.J. Res. 23, 107th Cong., 1st sess. (18 September 2001), *Authorization to Use Military Force*, <http://frwebgate.access.gpo.gov/cgi-bin/getdoc.cgi?dbname=107_cong_public_laws&docid=f:publ040.107.pdf> (last accessed 3 September 2006).
11 Author interview with military analyst William Arkin, 28 February 2006.
12 US Marine Corps Oversight Division, <http://hqinet001.hqmc.usmc.mil/ig/Oversight%20Division.htm> (last accessed 3 September 2006).
13 Executive Order 12958, *Classified National Security Information*, 17 April 1995, <http://www.fas.org/sgp/clinton/eo12958.html> (last accessed 3 September 2006).
14 See George W. Bush, Defense Bill Signing Statement, 10 January 2002, <http://www.whitehouse.gov/news/releases/2002/01/20020110-8.html>, and most recently George W. Bush,

President's Statement on Signing of H.R. 2863, the 'Department of Defense, Emergency Supplemental Appropriations to Address Hurricanes in the Gulf of Mexico, and Pandemic Influenza Act, 2006', 30 December 2005, <http://www.whitehouse.gov/news/releases/2005/12/20051230-8.html> (last accessed 24 August 2006).

15 William M. Arkin, 'S&M at the Congress', Early Warning Weblog, *Washington Post*, 21 December 2005, <http://blog.washingtonpost.com/earlywarning/2005/12/sm_at_the_congress.html> (last accessed 24 August 2006).

16 Annex B105, Excerpt from Army Criminal Investigative Command Investigation Number 0213-2004-CID259-80250. Full record available at <http://www.aclu.org/projects/foiasearch/pdf/DOD044418.pdf> (last accessed 24 August 2006).

17 Chief of Naval Operations, 'Alternative or Compensatory Control Measures Policy Change Notice and Data Call', 3 October 2005, <http://www.navysecurity.navy.mil/documents/information/safegrd-accmpolicy.pdf#search=%22navy%20directive%20accm%22> (last accessed 24 August 2006).

18 William M. Arkin, 'More Compartmented Programs', Early Warning Weblog, *Washington Post*, 13 January 2006, <http://blog.washingtonpost.com/earlywarning/2006/01/more_compartmented_programs.html> (last accessed 26 August 2006).

19 Ibid.

20 Chief of Naval Operations, 'Alternative or Compensatory Control Measures Policy Change Notice and Data Call', 3 October 2005.

21 House Report 109–101, *Intelligence Authorization Act for Fiscal Year 2006*, 109th Cong., 1st sess., 2 June 2005.

22 Douglas Jehl, 'Republicans See Signs That Pentagon is Evading Oversight', *New York Times*, 29 September 2005, p.20.

23 Thom Shanker and Scott Shane, 'Elite Troops Get Expanded Role on Intelligence', *New York Times*, 8 March 2006, p.1.

24 Jim Hoagland, 'Terror Turf Wars: Bush's Secret Blueprint, Stalled by Infighting', *Washington Post*, 16 April 2006, p.B2. See also Major Michael T. Kenny, *Leveraging Operational Preparation of the Environment in the GWOT*, US Army Command and General Staff College, 15 May 2006.

25 Karen DeYoung, 'A Fight Against Terrorism – and Disorganization', *Washington Post*, 9 August 2006, p.A1.

26 Testimony of Max Boot, *Assessing U.S. Special Operations Command's Missions and Roles*, Hearing of the Terrorism, Unconventional Threats and Capabilities Subcommittee of the House Armed Services Committee, 29 June 2006.

27 Sean D. Naylor, 'More than Door-kickers', *Armed Forces Journal*, March 2006; Linda Robinson, 'Men on a Mission', *U.S. News & World Report*, 11 September 2006.

28 Testimony of Max Boot, *Assessing U.S. Special Operations Command's Missions and Roles*, Hearing of the Terrorism, Unconventional Threats and Capabilities Subcommittee of the House Armed Services Committee, 29 June 2006.

29 *The 9/11 Commission Report: Final Report of the National Commission on Terrorist Attacks Upon the United States* (New York: W.W. Norton 2004) p.415.

30 Douglas Jehl, 'White House Is Said to Reject Panel's Call for a Greater Pentagon Role in Covert Operations', *New York Times*, 28 June 2005.

Jennifer D. Kibbe, 'Covert action and the Pentagon', *Intelligence and National Security* 22/1 (2007) pp.57–74.

COVERT ACTION

Further reading: Books and reports

Peter Bergen, *Holy War Inc: Inside the Secret World of Osama Bin Laden* (London: Weidenfeld & Nicolson 2001) pp.45–83.

B. Berkowitz & A.E. Goodman, *Best Truth: Intelligence in the Information Age* (New Haven CT: Yale University Press 2000), pp.124–46.

Richard A. Best & Andrew Feickert. *Special Operations Forces (SOF) and CIA Paramilitary Operations: Issues for Congress* (Washington, DC: Congressional Research Service, Library of Congress, 6 Dec. 2006). http://www.fas.org/sgp/crs/intel/RS22017.pdf.

Steve Coll, *Ghost Wars: The Secret History of the CIA, Afghanistan, and Bin Laden, from the Soviet Invasion to September 10, 2001* (NY: Penguin, 2004).

John K. Cooley, *Unholy Wars: Afghanistan, America and International Terrorism*. (London: Pluto Press 1999).

Diego Cordovez & Selig S. Harrison. *Out of Afghanistan: The Inside Story of the Soviet Withdrawal*. (Oxford: Oxford University Press 1995).

William J. Daugherty, *Executive Secrets: Covert Action and the Presidency* (Lexington KY: University Press of Kentucky, 2006).

Roger Z. George and Robert D. Kline (eds.), *Intelligence and National Security Strategist: Enduring Issues and Challenges* (Washington, DC: National Defense University Press, CSI, 2004), chapter 39, pp.509–15.

Roy Godson (ed.), *Dirty Tricks or Trump Cards: US Covert Action & Counterintelligence* (Washington DC: Brasseys 1995).

A.E. Goodman, *The Need to Know: The Report of the Twentieth Century Fund Task Force on Covert Action and American Democracy* (NY: Twentieth Century Fund Press, 1992).

Stephen Hosmer, *Operations against Enemy Leaders* (Santa Monica, CA: Rand, 2001).

Loch K. Johnson & James J. Wirtz, *Intelligence and National Security: The Secret World of Spies* (NY: Oxford UP, 2nd ed 2007).

Stephen Kinzer, *Overthrow: America's Century of Regime Change from Hawaii to Iraq* (NY: Times Books, 2006).

Kurt Lohbeck, *Holy War, Unholy Victory: Eyewitness to the CIA's Secret War in Afghanistan* (Washington DC: Regnery Gateway 1993).

Mark Lowenthal, *Intelligence: From Secrets to Policy* (Washington D.C.. CQ Press, 3rd Ed 2006), chapter 8.

Abram N. Shulsky and Gary J. Schmitt, *Silent Warfare: Understanding the World of Intelligence* (Dulles, VA: Brassey's Inc., 2002) pp.73–98.

Michael Smith, The Inside Story of America's Most Secret Special Operations Team (London: Weidenfeld and Nicolson 2005).

Gregory F. Treverton, *Covert Action: The Limits of Intervention in the Postwar World*. (NY: Basic Books 1987).

Further reading: Essays and articles

Richard B. Andres, Craig Wills & Thomas E. Griffith, 'Winning with Allies: The Strategic Value of the Afghan Model', *International Security* 30/3 (2005/06) pp.124–60.

Bruce D. Berkowitz & Allan E. Goodman, 'The Logic of Covert Action,' *The National Interest* 51/1 (1998) pp.38–46.

Colin Gray, 'Handfuls of Heroes on Desperate Ventures: When do Special Operations Succeed?', *Parameters* 29/1 (1999) pp.2–24.

Thomas H. Henriksen, 'Covert operations, now more than ever', *Orbis* 44/1 (2000) pp.145–156.

Loch K. Johnson, 'On Drawing a Bright Line for Covert Operations.' *American Journal of International Law* 86/2 (1992) pp.284–309

Jennifer D. Kibbe, 'The Rise of the Shadow Warriors', *Foreign Affairs* 83/2 (2004) pp.102–115.

Peter Dale Scott, 'The CIA's Secret Powers: Afghanistan, 9/11 and America's Most Dangerous Enemy', *Critical Asian Studies* 35/2 (2003) pp.233–258. http://socrates.berkeley.edu/~pdscott/d294.html

Todd Stiefler, 'CIA's Leadership and Major Covert Operations: Rogue Elephant or Risk-Averse Bureaucrats?' *Intelligence and National Security* 19/4 (2004) pp.632–654.

M. Smith, 'The United States' Use of Exiles in Promoting Regime Change in Cuba, 1961 and Iraq, 2002–3', *Small Wars and Insurgencies* 15/1 (2004) pp.38–53.

Essay questions

- 'Political hesitancy was the main limit on the effectiveness of covert action in the 1980s and 1990s.' Discuss.
- To what extent can international and national law regulate covert action?
- To what extent does covert action provide US Presidents with a foreign policy that is beyond congressional accountability or democratic control?
- 'Sooner or later, most covert actions result in serious blowback'. Discuss with regard to Iran in the 1950s or Afghanistan in the 1980s.

26 Netcentric warfare, C4ISR and information operations

Towards a revolution in military intelligence?

John Ferris

This essay examines the role of intelligence within the concept of a 'revolution in military affairs' (RMA). Current American military doctrine assumes that information is transforming the nature of war and can provide 'decision superiority' over any enemy and unprecedented flexibility of command. Central to this process is the use of new forms of information technology in order to fuse into systems that once were split into 'stovepipes'. It considers the increasing integration of strategic, operational and tactical levels and the way in which this might interplay with information operations and deception. It reviews the performance of these new ideas against the background of recent campaigns in Kosovo, Afghanistan and Iraq.

No military forces ever have placed such faith in intelligence as do US military forces today. The idea of a 'revolution in military affairs' (RMA) assumes that information and the 'information age' will transform the knowledge available to armed forces, and thus the nature of war. This faith is central to US doctrine and policy. Joint Visions 2010 and 2020, which guide strategic policy, predict forces with 'dominant battlespace awareness', and a 'frictional imbalance' and 'decision superiority' over any enemy. The aim is unprecedented flexibility of command: the ability to combine freedom for units with power for the top, and to pursue 'parallel, not sequential planning and real-time, not prearranged, decision making'.[1] Officials have created new concepts about intelligence and command. They hope to pursue power by using new forms of information technology in order to fuse into systems matters which once were split into 'stovepipes'. These concepts include netcentric warfare (NCW), the idea that armed forces will adopt flat structures, working in nets on the internet, with soldiers at the sharp end able to turn data processing systems at home into staffs through 'reachback', real time, immediate and thorough inter-communication; C4ISR (command, control, communications, computers, intelligence, surveillance and reconnaissance; loosely speaking, how armed forces gather, interpret and act on information); the 'infosphere', the body of information surrounding any event; and 'IO' (information operations), the actions of secret agencies. The aim is to realise the RMA, by creating a revolution in military intelligence. This paper will consider how far those ideas can be achieved, and how attempts to do so will affect the nature of power, intelligence and war in the twenty-first century. Progressives and revolutionaries debate the details of these issues (conservatives need not apply). The Marine Corps' draft doctrine on IO denies that technology can solve all problems and defends its 'timeless fighting principles'. Army doctrine too gives C4ISR a Clausewitzian cast, judging that it can 'reduce the friction caused by the fog of war' and help impose one's will on the enemy. But it also concludes that 'achieving accurate situational understanding depends at least as much on human judgment as on machine-processed information – particularly when assessing enemy intent and combat power . . . [U]ncertainty and risk are inherent in all military operations.'[2] But these judgements represent the cautious end of the spectrum of US military thinking about the future of warfare. Revolutionaries, conversely, assume C4ISR will function in a system precisely as a person sees the world, turns data to knowledge and acts on it. Enthusiasts believe armed forces can comprehend an enemy and a battle perfectly, and act without friction. David Alperts, a leading Pentagon figure in NCW, holds that

> we will effectively move from a situation in which we are preoccupied with reducing the fog of war to the extent possible and with designing approaches needed to accommodate any residual fog that exists to a situation in which we are preoccupied with optimizing a response to a particular situation ... we will move from a situation in which decision making takes place under 'uncertainty' or in the presence of incomplete and erroneously [sic] information, to a situation in which decisions are made with near 'perfect' information.[3]

All sides in this debate assume intelligence will have great power. They take its triumphs for its norms. Thus, in 1995, the USAF chief, General Fogleman, discussing ULTRA and FORTITUDE, said, 'Throughout history, soldiers, sailors, Marines and airmen have learned one valuable lesson. If you can analyze, act and assess faster than your opponent, you will win!' Unless, of course, the enemy is stronger or smarter or luckier.[4]

The military exponents of Information Warfare (IW) assign unprecedented weight to intelligence in war. In 1995 George Stein wrote 'Information warfare, in its essence, is about *ideas and epistemology* – big words meaning that information warfare is about the way humans think and, more important they way humans make decisions ... It is about influencing human beings and the decisions they make.' Colonel Szafranski spoke of '*targeting epistemology*'.[5] Faith in intelligence and IO underlies Command and Control Warfare, the main form of operations the United States plans to fight a version of blitzkrieg which seeks 'to deny information to, influence, degrade, or destroy' the enemy's 'information dependent process', so to shatter its ability to perceive and command.[6] Revolutionaries advocate a higher mode of war, Rapid Decisive Operations (RDO), which will open with the pursuit of a 'Superior Information Position (Fight First for Information Superiority)' and become 'knowledge-centric':

> The creation and sharing of superior knowledge are critical to RDO ... Decision makers, enabled by study, judgment, and experience, convert information into knowledge and situational understanding, which is the key to *decision superiority* [original emphasis] – the ability to make better decisions faster than the adversary ... IO are the information equivalent of manoeuvre and fire ... In planning for effects-based operations, *knowledge* is paramount.[7]

The revolutionaries conceptualise war as game and strategy as shooting. They assume that to be seen is to be shot, to be shot is to be killed, and to be fast is to win. As USAF planner and theorist Colonel John Warden wrote, 'a very simple rule for how to go about producing the effect: do it very fast ... the essence of success in future war will certainly be to make everything happen you want to happen in a very short period of time – instantly if possible'.[8] These tendencies are reinforced by the routine use of the 'OODA cycle' (Observe, Orient, Decide, Act), devised by strategic theorist Colonel John Boyd to describe all conflict on all levels of war, with the aim usually defined as moving through the cycle faster than one's opponent. Wiser heads urge that this gain in time be used to think more rather than simply act faster. Boyd's model, derived from his reflections on his experience as a fighter pilot in the Korean War, is a good means to conceptualise one-on-one combat. It is less useful for war. In a boxing match, speed may equal victory; in strategy, cries of 'faster! harder!' produce premature ejaculation. Focus on the OODA cycle, 'sensors to shooters', 'one shot one kill' weapons and the idea that armed forces can act almost without friction on near perfect knowledge, has led to a fetishisation of speed and the tacticisation of strategy.

These ideas frame much thinking about intelligence. The assumption is that intelligence will be an engine fit for a fine-tuned, high-performance, machine – reliable, understood, useful, usable and on-call. One can learn exactly what one wants to know when one needs to do so, and verify its accuracy with certainty and speed. The truth and only the truth can be known. It is further assumed that intelligence will show what should be done and what will happen if one does. According to this line of thought, action taken on knowledge will have precisely the effect one intends, nothing more or less.

Intelligence experts in the military academic complex have attacked these ideas. Williamson Murray notes that a key to Rapid Decisive Operations, the idea that 'Operational Net Assessment' will turn knowledge to power by constantly updating and fusing all data on everything related to a war, ignores every known problem in intelligence. At a strategic level, says Murray, net assessment rarely did more than bean counting. It usually fell victim to worst-or best-case assessments and mirror-imaging. Achieving Operational Net Assessment would require 'a revolution in the culture of intelligence'. Such a revolution would entail a 'move away from the search for the predictive to an emphasis on a broader, intuitive understanding of potential opponents' – from a focus on collection and technology to an emphasis on the importance of foreign languages, culture and history. Michael Handel argued that intelligence, once undervalued, has become oversold. 'If it sounds too good to be true', he briefed officers, 'maybe it is'.[9] In their doctrine, too, all US services treat the relationship between intelligence and operations carefully and well.[10]

The Pentagon expects normal intelligence to be as good as it ever has been, more central to planning and operations, and to be transformed along with every other element of power. In January 2003, the Chairman of the Joint Chiefs of Staff, General Myers, noted that,

> we have always tended to have this situation where intelligence people are in one stove pipe and the operators in another and we are real happy if they talk together. When today's world requires that they be totally integrated . . . you can't have an intel pod, throw it over a transom to an operator and say, here's what we know. This has got to be continuous, 24/7 sort of relationship and synergistic to the point where operations help with intel and vice versa.[11]

Some months later, commenting on Operation Iraqi Freedom, the Pentagon's Director of Force Transformation, Admiral Cebrowski, noted that,

> the intelligence analysis problem, where we have all of these intelligence sources, and they all produced their products and reports and fed databases, all of which are stove-piped. The analysis functions are similarly stove-piped. Essentially, we have an intelligence community that is organized by wavelength . . . But it needn't be that way. It could be more like this, where your intelligence is organized around the demand functions of warning, force protection, and warfighting intelligence, where you have

data mediation layers that are able to pull together all source information, plot it geo-spatially, and generate the kinds of displays in which a senior leader's question can in fact be answered at very, very high speed.[12]

Cebowski advocated 'a new demand centred intelligence system'. He argued that since 1970 intelligence had become unbalanced. The quantity of information had risen exponentially, and the power of analysis only in a linear fashion, while specialists alone collected, processed (and hoarded) material from each source. This caused both overload and strangulation. Too much information was available, too little used and even less co-ordinated, because it was divided into watertight pots defined not by function but source. Never was all the data on any topic brought together. Agencies collected what they did because that was what they did; the customer was forgotten. So to solve these problems, material from all sources should go to an 'Information Dominance Center' (IDC) for analysis characterised by 'Continuous merge . . . Megadata, All Source, Open Source and Geospatial Data, Dynamic Collection, Visualisa-tion'. This idea, like that of Operational Net Assessment, assumes analysts can constantly gather, analyse, synthesise, fuse and update intelligence from all sources on all aspects of an enemy in real time and make it useful to decision makers. This rolling product would be returned to agencies and to an office of an Under Secretary of Defense Intelligence, with three analytical–operational functions, 'Warning, CI/ Force Protection and War-fighting intelligence'.[13]

At first glance, such a body might solve the problems caused by uncoordinated single source agencies, but not that of information overload in analysis, unless one assumes that to centralise and automate and computerise information must transform its nature. This is precisely the assumption upon which much new thinking about 'operational net assessment' and 'knowledge-centric warfare' is based. As its name indicates, the IDC is intended to unleash the power of information: to bring intelligence into the information revolution, and vice versa.

Here, as often in the debates over the RMA and intelligence, vague language and jargon obscure a clash between ideas and agencies. Advocates of the RMA view the intelligence services which survived the Cold War as legacy forces, industrial age dinosaurs, muscle-bound and clumsy, too focused on technique, security, secrecy and the source of their collection as against the material it provides; too divided in acquiring their evidence and presenting their analyses; too reluctant to disseminate their data; providing too much useless information; too little able to answer key questions fast and accurately. In the Cold War, American intelligence focused on supporting millions of soldiers in a world-wide competi-tion against a peer, with the trump suit being the collection of data on strategic issues through technical means. In the information age, the focuses are terrorists or expeditionary forces. To meet these needs, the revolutionaries want intelligence services to become nimble, to simplify their techniques and reduce their emphasis on them, to alter their priorities and their focus on one source; to cease being monopolists of knowledge and oracles of assess-ment; to distribute their material widely and freely, to fuse it constantly in a rolling fashion, to cooperate in assessment with each other and the military in ad hoc teams, and to emphasise broad strategic or political issues less and military operational ones more, to provide less but better information. Advocates of the RMA see the attack on the Twin Towers as illustrating the flaws in US intelligence, but their criticisms are more fundamental. They want a revolution in military intelligence.

These ideas have political consequences which are intended even if they are unspoken. If an IDC is created, one analytical bureau, a military one, reflecting its aims and means, will handle all information from all sources, and dominate analysis in the intelligence community. If Operational Net Assessment is practiced, power in analysis will move from Washington to theatre commands. All this will revive demarcation disputes between collectors and customers over priorities and between the military and the Central Intelligence Agency (CIA) in analysis. Again, the problems in US intelligence can be solved by many means, not merely those proposed by advocates of the RMA. Intelligence services can adapt to the times; they do so all of the time. Without transforming or detracting from other work, refined 'push' and 'pull' techniques should let them flexibly and immediately meet the needs of each of the five divisions in an expedition, a good thing in itself. However, such reforms (even more those in the revolutionary programme) raise the danger that intelligence will be militarised and tacticised. Junior commanders always want to control intelligence, more than ever in an era of C4ISR and expeditionary forces; yet such steps threaten to erode the advantages of critical mass or centralisation.

Another problem is that the rise of precision weapons and the idea of intelligence, surveillance and reconnaissance (ISR) further blurs the boundary between target acquisition and intelligence. Somehow, in moving from C3I to C4ISR, 'computers' have eaten qualities once assigned to 'command' while 'intelligence' has diminished, as an idea connoting 'to think' slips into one meaning 'to sense'. After Afghanistan, one intelligence officer noted 'As weapons [systems] become more "intel centric" the importance of ISR increases proportionately . . . Think of Intel as a modern gun director', while Myers said bombs 'can be used like bullets from a rifle, aimed precisely and individually'.[14] When considering C4ISR, it is tempting to focus on the aspects most easily changed, machines, and to assume improvements to them must in turn raise the performance of the human aspects of command and decision. It is similarly tempting to believe solutions to one set of problems (target acquisition) will solve another (net assessment). In fact, one can improve every technological aspect of C4ISR without aiding any of the human ones, possibly even harming their performance. The same action can help target acquisition and harm net assessment. These pressures bolster the tendency in US intelligence to focus on technology.

Some revolutionaries hold that only nonhuman means can allow a C4I and NCW system to work. Contributors to the *Air Force 2025* project, which framed the USAF's policy on these matters, predicted a C4ISR system with the self-awareness of a man, or a god. According to these theorists, the future of battlefield command will be characterised by 'a series of intelligent microprocessor "brains" . . . all-knowing, all-sensing' and 'an intelligence architecture with human-like characteristics . . . [which will] . . . simultaneously sense and evaluate the earth in much the same way you remain aware of your day-to-day surroundings'. One concludes that: 'Future generations may come to regard tactical warfare as properly the business of machines and not appropriate for people at all.'[15] Against this pressure is the cry for 'HUMINT'. But this takes many forms. Many people call for a change in the culture of intelligence; others stress the need for human intelligence. Meanwhile, soldiers define 'HUMINT' vaguely, taking it to mean everything from cultural awareness or linguistic knowledge, to a focus on humans as sources of information and for subversion, to paying some attention to humans, or to anything but technology. Beneath the debate on intelligence is an inchoate struggle between emphasis on humans and reliance on machines.

Many of these ideas about intelligence are naive or misguided. Thus, C4ISR has solved only some problems of command and changed none of its conditions. As ever, the issue is how much information a system contains, how fast and flexibly it circulates, and how well it is used. In communications, intelligence and decision making, more or faster is not necessarily better; the value of multiplication depends on what is being multiplied; changes in quantity cause changes in quality, sometimes for the worse. Outside of fairy tales, rarely is intelligence self-evident and easy to use. The advocates of a revolution in military intelligence cannot achieve exactly what they intend. Still, their actions will have consequences. They may cause a revolution, even if it is not the one they plan. The RMA is the greatest matter affecting intelligence today, and its success depends on how far intelligence really can be transformed.

Ideas on these issues have affected US intelligence services, most notably those most closely linked to the military. Since 1995 these services have focused increasingly on serving C4ISR, especially by improving their databases, links with customers and reachback. The Defense Intelligence Agency (DIA) aims to provide 'Fused, Tailored Intelligence Essential to Battlefield Dominance' and 'Dominant Battlespace Intelligence for the Warfighter'. Similarly, among the five 'Core Competencies' in the National Security Agency's (NSA) 'National Cryptologic Strategy for the 21st Century' is the ability to 'ensure dominant battlespace knowledge through [the] integration of cryptology with joint operations'. The precise objective is to 'anticipate warfighter intelligence needs – on time, anywhere, at the lowest possible classification'.

> 3 Integration of cryptologic support to enable policy makers to promote stability and thwart aggression. NSA seeks to . . .

> (b) Work with policy customers to improve interoperability and ensure that intelligence can be tailored to meet customer needs.
> (c) Expand 'pull' dissemination capabilities to enable customers to initiate real time requests to improve crisis support.
> (d) Work with the I[ntelligence] C[ommunity] to create interactive databases that will enable searches for information gathered by members of the IC.

In Afghanistan during 2002 (and no doubt, Iraq in 2003), NSA personnel, 'integrated with the combatant commander staffs . . . ensured field commanders and others had access to NSA operations and crisis action centres; developed a collection system that supports military forces abroad' and co-ordinated reachback. On 17 October 2002, the NSA's Director, Michael Hayden, said, 'As we speak, NSA has over 700 people not *producing* SIGINT but sitting in our customer's spaces *explaining* and *sharing* SIGINT'. The National Imagery and Mapping Agency (NIMA), too, deployed 'the Target Management System Network', giving its 'customers direct access to targeting support and navigation data from the NIMA precise point database'.[16] By January 2003, NIMA and NSA exchanged personnel and combined imagery, geospatial and signals intelligence at the point of first production, before it was sent to consumers.[17] After Operation Iraqi Freedom, the director of the CIA praised 'the seamlessness, fusion, speed and quality of what is being provided on the battlefield' and held this proved his organisation must transform like other intelligence services.[18] These agencies all aim to distribute normal intelligence better than the best performance ever hitherto achieved. Though they are reforming rather than transforming, this pressure may reinforce the military's role in intelligence and the latter's tendency to focus on technology, technique and tactics, despite the rhetoric about the need to develop human sources and cultural awareness.

Meanwhile, the intelligence community began to enter the information age. By 2001 the US government had several web-based but enclosed intelligence intranets, linked to the military's 'SIPRnet' (Secret Internet Protocol Router Network), a self-contained internet gated from the conventional one. Intelligence and government agencies were joined to 'Intelink Intranet', which had further subsections. The latter included 'Intelink Common-wealth' (between US, Australian, British and Canadian agencies); 'Intelink-SCI' for the 'top-secret, compartmented intelligence level'; 'Intelink-S', an 'SIPRnet at the secret level' for military commands; and connections between the main intelligence agencies and their consumers, like the CIA's 'Intelink PolicyNet' and the DIA's 'Joint Intelligence Virtual Architecture', a web-based interactive system which joined 5,300 analysts world-wide for normal work and reachback. These nets were supported by steadily improving collection, search and analysis functions which, the head of the Joint Military Intelligence College noted, must allow 'mining of data not only of what the analyst knows is important but also of – while unthought-of by the analyst – what might be of importance'.[19] By 2003, the agencies were beginning to deploy an 'Intelligence Community System for Information Security system' (ICSIS), with secure gateways for the transfer of messages between net-works of different security classifications.[20] The inability of the CIA, the NSA and the Federal Bureau of Investigation to coordinate their databases before the attack on the Twin Towers shows the limits to this work, but one should not over-generalise from that failure. Even on 10 September 2001, intelligence databases on traditional military and diplomatic matters probably were linked fairly well. No doubt they have been made to work rather better since.

These steps were in pursuit of greater visions. The 'Strategic Investment Plan for Intelligence Community Analysis' noted that by 2007,

> the agencies aimed to achieve a virtual work environment enabled by collaborative and analytic tools, and interoperable databases . . . the breaking down of barriers and the sharing of databases of critical and common concern . . . [a system] that connects databases across the IC and a security framework to allow analysts to share knowledge and expertise and link them to collectors, consumers, allies, and outside experts . . . Efforts and electronic tracking and production systems to capture and make available intelligence 'products' that can be recovered and reused by customers and other analysts (knowledge warehouses).

The aim was to create the 'secure and classified sub-set' of the infosphere, 'the intelsphere, which is the virtual knowledge repository of authoritative intelligence information, relevant reference material, and resources used to store, maintain, access and protect this informa-tion'. The strategic investment plan noted that the DIA had taken the lead 'in developing the concepts underpinning knowledge management in order to provide full battlespace visualization to warfighters and military planners', but all military intelligence providers 'are automating their request, tasking, and response systems – at both the front and back ends – to serve a scattered and diverse constituency', and creating

> an integrated electronic production environment. The large organizations, for example, are making strides, albeit somewhat uneven, in tracking customer requests and in recording and capturing production flow, an effort that will become increasingly critical if we are to develop common 'knowledge warehouses' that are easily accessible to our customers and to each other.

To this system must be allied search techniques which would sidestep information overload, and 'reveal connections, facilitate analytic insights and deductions and streamline search by prioritizing information, automatically populating databases, and integrating data'. The ultimate aims of the strategic investment plan were threefold. First, to integrate national intelligence analysis from multiple sources with the timely reporting of tactical sensors, platforms and other battlefield information. Second, to provide customer, user and producer interfaces so that organisations at all levels (national–allied/coalition–theatre–tactical) have access to digital data that each can retrieve and manipulate. Third, to use advanced models, architectures, automated metrics/management tools and authoritative production templates within a collaborative environment to dynamically assign, prioritise, track and measure the operations/intelligence infosphere content.

By 2010, the intelligence community hopes to have 'a dynamic knowledge base . . . fully accessible from anywhere at any time by authorized users . . . Knowledge base linkage to collectors with information needs/gaps automatically identified'.[21] In a similar vein, the Army's Deputy Chief of Staff for Intelligence held that in the 'knowledgecentric' army,

> analytic operations will be executed collaboratively in a distributive environment with extensive use of virtual-teaming capabilities. Analysts at every level and in multiple locations will come together in virtual analytic teams to satisfy unit of action and employment intelligence requirements. Each analyst will have access to the entire body of knowledge on the subject at hand and will draw on interactive, integrated, interoperable databases to rapidly enable understanding. Communities of analytic interest will create and collapse around individual issues. The commander forward will be supported by the entire power of the formerly echeloned, hierarchical, analytic team.[22]

No doubt, some of this is mere rhetoric, a political response to pressure, while much that matters remains unsaid. Collectors and analysts fear the uncontrolled distribution of their best material, or that such a transformation in practices might degrade their work. According to Bruce Berkowitz (an academic with an intelligence background, seconded to the CIA during 2001–02) at that time its Directorates of Intelligence (DI) and Operations (DO), had incompatible databases. Each DI analyst had one computer linked to their own, poor, database, another to the internet, neither to other official systems. 'The CIA view is that there are risks to connecting CIA systems even to classified systems elsewhere.' Merely to send intranet e-mail to intelligence officers outside the agency was difficult. Few CIA computers were linked to the SIPRnet – though models which could receive but not send messages were quickly being introduced. The CIA disliked Intelink because it could not control dissemination of the documents which it provided to this database. It did 'post almost all of its products on CIASource, a website maintained on the Agency's network that is linked to Intelink' to which few outsiders had access. As a result, no-one outside the agency had much electronic access to CIA material. In order to study any topic, DI analysts had to search separate databases including the DI system, Intelink, and the internet. They often simply ignored the latter two. 'When it comes to it', Berkowitz notes,

> the CIA's approach is not 'risk management' but 'risk exclusion'. All this had cultural causes and consequences. Access by outsiders to CIA data threatened its hierarchical system of assessment and quality control, while by making technology a bogey-man rather than an ally, the CIA is reinforcing the well-known tendency toward introversion among most DI analysts.[23]

This critique was accurate for the time, but changes seem to have occurred since. The CIA now claims to be creating secure but flexible inter-agency databases and intranets, including the ICSIS (which had languished since 1998) and a browser-based system allowing document sharing and e-mail.[24]

In 1999, NSA Director Hayden had two teams investigate the NSA. Both condemned its culture and especially its rejection of the internet. The internal team noted 'we focus more on our own "tradecraft" than on our customers, partners, and stakeholders'. It advocated the NSA's 'transformation ... from an industrial age monopoly to an information age organization that has entered the competitive market place', embracing 'the Internet as a force-multiplier ... a means of creating numerous virtual centers of excellence with colleagues around the world'. The external team held that the NSA must be re-centred around the internet, and overcome its 'culture that discourages sending bad news up the chain of command ... a society where people were afraid to express their own thoughts'. It also called for changes in institutional culture. It observed that the 'NSA generally talks like engineers' and that '[it] will talk about the technical parameters of constructing a watch, describing gears and springs, when the customer simply wants to understand that we have just developed a better way to tell time. Even more important, NSA needs to learn to communicate what the ability to tell time might mean to a customer.'[25] Advocates of the information revolution view both the CIA and NSA as anal and ossified, unable to grasp the need to provide fast, flexible, fused material. Such criticisms have force. Yet, as Hayden noted, the NSA 'is a very conservative, risk-averse organization' because these characteristics, along with 'consistency and thoroughness and care', fit the Cold War.[26] They also suit any intelligence agency which dislikes error or insecurity.

But the rhetoric of transformation obscures the key issue – who gets what from whom? It is easy enough to produce good intelligence or co-ordinate analysts, or push material effectively in a crisis, or send fused information fast from Washington to a theatre command, or from there to an aircraft or unit commander. These are standard problems with school solutions: reachback, tailoring, fusion and pull techniques are old hat, they do not require transformation. To give thousands of people access to the databases of secret intelligence services, and to use them as they wish, however, is unprecedented. It gives intelligence services cause to fear for their security and tradecraft and the integrity of their data. There are concerns to be balanced. The question is, how?

Since 1995, the intelligence agencies have learned how better to push their product to the military, which have honed their means to pull it. Reachback is a reality, and will, in turn, reshape reality. Already, it has magnified the power of intelligence. Colonels can tap data from the centre to solve problems in the field and guide immediate strikes; junior analysts at home can warn sergeants at the sharp end of danger or promise just ahead. Yet in all fairy tales, curses accompany blessings. Search engines augment analysis but they cannot replace analysts. If intelnets work as advertised, collectors can more easily distribute their product and analysts find the material they want. Correlations can be made, expected or unexpected, and actions will be aided. Everyone will receive far more data than ever before – perhaps too much. So, to justify their existence, intelink agencies will stock 'knowledge factories' such as the projected IDC with reports in mass, many trivial, some competitive, all well-advertised. Analysts will be swamped in sites, losing their way down hot-linked detours. Analysis will be constipated by the quantity of information and by conflicts of interpretation and of interest. Need and politics will keep security restrictions in being, often blocking users precisely from the material they need or hiding all the best evidence.

This situation calls for education in intelligence and its pathologies, and the creation of a new culture for assessment and use. If this is achieved, analysts and engines will just be able to prevent the increased mass of detail from adding more friction to general decision making, while making great gains in two areas: when one knows what one wants to know, the answers will come with unprecedented power and speed; and the chances for discovery by serendipity will rise. If this aim fails, more will mean worse.

Again, by making intelligence more central than ever before, the United States has made C4ISR the centre of gravity for its power as well as its greatest vulnerability. All of this has also increased the importance and the difficulty of security. SIPRnet is the richest treasure ever for espionage, and intelink agencies are its crown jewels, which will shine the brighter the better intelligence is fused and distributed. In principle, the 'intelsphere' is walled from enemies but accessible to friends, who communicate with freedom. But if this firewall collapses, that web-based communication will become the equivalent of plain language traffic over wireless. If an enemy penetrates the 'intelsphere', it will have more chances than ever before to gather intelligence on you or to pirate intelligence and to use it as its own. It will also gain unprecedented ability to corrupt one's own data. The danger of penetration, indeed even the suspicion that databases are insecure, is the Achilles heel of the 'intelsphere'. If soldiers cannot trust the security of the 'intelsphere', how will they act on it? One successful corruption of information, producing one failure in the field, might cripple the machine or the trust on which it relies. A virus may be little more damaging than the fear of one.

Thus, as ever, security will trump flexibility. Databases are most easily defended when they are accessible only to regulated computers. SIPRnet, however, is easily accessible – anyone capturing intact any one of thousands of vehicles in Operation Iraqi Freedom in theory could reach any database linked to it. And penetration is common. In 2001, 16,000 attempts were made to enter the US Navy computer networks, 'of which 400 gained entry, and 40 traveled the networks'.[27] This danger will limit the significance of intelligence easily reached through SIPRnet, and force intelligence agencies to shelter their best material behind secure gates or else on separate intranets. The 'intelsphere' must stand apart from the 'infosphere', while still being linked to it through secure and flexible procedures, which allow information to be pushed from the top and pulled from below, and more co-ordination between databases, and between analysts and users. These links may be more rich, thick, flexible and fast than ever before, or alternately below the standards of 1944 or even 1918. Everything depends on the relationship between the techniques of cyber attack and defence. At worst, C4ISR may follow the classic downward spiral of C3I over radio, where jamming and the need for security sapped most of its flexibility and power.

The mechanisation of intelligence and command has also transformed the dilemma of security. The new killer applications are spies to steal information and cyberwar to corrupt databases. The key danger from hackers is the threat not of an ULTRA but of a nuclear strike on data. An agent in place, conversely, could betray one's entire database of intelligence and command. In the Cold War, sergeants turned spies pillaged storehouses of paper secrets; now, a Walker family could loot 'knowledge warehouses', or corrupt them; and already this has happened. During 1985–2000, the mid-level counter-intelligence officer and traitor, Robert Hanssen, raided FBI computer systems, including 'thousands of searches' on its Automated Case Support (ACS) database in 1999–2001. He sold Soviet/Russian intelligence much material from many agencies on US strategy, estimates and agents in Moscow, devastating US espionage, as well as monitoring information on himself. The FBI concluded its ACS system had elementary security problems – officers posted secret material which should not have been there, and failed to monitor people who accessed material they did not need to know. These problems had been known since ACS's inception in 1995, and ignored – they continued after Hanssen's treachery was discovered, and still did so in August 2003![28]

Had an 'intelsphere' existed, Hanssen would have inflicted even more damage than he did. Cyber defence must be geared to handle every possible enemy everywhere all of the time; and its strength will be defined by the weakest link of an 'intelnet'. For the United States, mercenary hackers rather than hostile nations may be the greatest problem for decades – at least until the rise of a peer competitor. Other states, meanwhile, will have to reckon with peers, or superiors. US authorities recognise these threats and have taken action to meet them. Thus, in 2002, a 'layered cyber-defense system' protected the Defense Information Infrastructure, combining 'local DoD intrusion detection systems' with an NSA-controlled 'computer network defense intrusion detection system . . . a network of sensors that are strategically placed within the DoD infrastructure, providing analysts the capability to iden- tify anomalous cyber activities traversing the network'. The Pentagon hosts annual cyberwar competitions which, in 2003, included 'a so-called rogue box in each network that the red team could use to simulate insider attacks'.[29] Though no US headquarters ever may feature signs reading 'He who uses the computer is a traitor!', this will happen to smaller states. The electron is a weapon. You can use it, but so may your enemy.

Compared to C4ISR and NCW, the concept of information operations is less novel and less problematic. It describes its subject better than any extant term, like 'covert action'. IO embrace many 'disciplines' – deception, operational security, electronic warfare and psycho- logical operations, but also civil and public affairs (public and press relations). Initially, the latter were added to IO to meet the Army's distinct problems with peace keeping, but the relationship has grown to include political warfare, both defensive and offensive. During the campaign in Afghanistan, in order to inoculate its media against hostile IO, the Pentagon briefed journalists about the techniques of Serb and Iraqi propaganda and press manipula- tion, or 'enemy denial and deception'.[30] This concern shaped its media policy during the 2003 war in Iraq, and also led to the short-lived 'Office of Strategic Influence' of 2002, a military organisation established to shape international media coverage. Due to bad pub- licity, that office closed a day after its existence was announced – and no doubt reopened the next under a new title. That US doctrine about IO fuses in one category matters once treated as 'black' (psyops) and 'white' (public relations) and regards their combined practice as normal presents problems for journalists, the public and the military itself. With the significant exception of Computer Network Attack (CNA), IO are less a matter of old wine in new bottles than new labels on old bottles. Functions which intelligence officers once might have conducted in a General Staff, perhaps with operations, security and signals personnel in secondary roles, are now treated as a combat arm, controlled by the senior Operations officer, with intelligence personnel first among equals of specialist elements. This rise of Operations and decline of Intelligence is marginal and reasonable. IO are oper- ational matters, but they require a close relationship with intelligence and other elements. The basic doctrine for IO is sound, and close to the best practices of the best practitioners of two world wars. IO should be controlled by an officer directly responsible to a commander, guided by a small 'cell' of specialists, able to provide expertise and liaison. They should be deliberately organised in an ad hoc manner, cut to fit the cloth; the various 'disciplines' of IO should be 'fused'; not merely coordinated, but combined.[31]

Thus, US doctrine on deception regards all aspects of intelligence as force multipliers, to be integrated into every aspect of planning and operations. It defines sound principles: 'centralised control'; 'security'; 'timeliness' in planning and execution; 'integration' of deceit with an operation; and, above all, 'focus' and a clear objective, aiming to influence the right decision makers and to affect their actions. The overall aim is therefore to treat the manipu- lation of intelligence and ideas merely as means to an end. In order to achieve these ends, practitioners must understand their foe's psychology. They must 'possess fertile imaginations and the ability to be creative'. They must also pass a story through many sources which an adversary will find believable, ideally by reinforcing its expectations. Finally, they must fuse intelligence, psychological warfare and operations security with deception. This doctrine is powerful, but it has weaknesses which stem from the roots of its strength, the influence of the British tradition of deception. The campaigns of 1943–44 which culminated in FOR-TITUDE stem from so many unique circumstances that they are a poor guide to the average. To treat them as normal is to assume deception is precise and predictable, that one will have edges equivalent to ULTRA and the 'double cross system', while the enemy's intelligence is castrated. These are tall assumptions. Again, 'focus' and 'objective' are fine principles: but in order to make key decision makers act as one wishes, one must know who they are, what they expect, how to reach them and how to know whether one has succeeded. This is not easy. Deceivers wrestle with uncertainties and pull strings they hope are attached to levers in a complex system they do not understand. Deception rarely has just the effect one wants and nothing else. The unintended cannot be avoided. American doctrine urges that this difficulty and others be resolved through risk assessment. But this is to mistake a condition for a problem. Reason is good, war games are fun; but when assessment concludes, risks will remain.[32]

IO doctrine has been easier to write than to test. US experience with its components since 1989 ranged in quality from poor (Somalia) to decent but uninspired (Panama; the 1991 Gulf War; Kosovo). In 1998, one IO colonel with experience in Bosnia and at Fort Leavenworth, Craig Jones, noted 'much confusion remains – IO is still many different things to many different people'. This was because it lacked measures of effectiveness. 'A commander has the right and the responsibility to ask his IO staff officer this simple question: "How do we know this IO stuff is helping me achieve my overall objectives?".' Between the conception of the idea and 2003, the US military had no experience with IO in war, except in Kosovo, where Serbs matched Americans; its theory was drawn from history, where good examples did abound, some still better than Operation Iraqi Freedom. The theory was good – the problem was praxis. In 2000 the IO Franchise, Battle Command Battle Lab, at Training and Doctrine Command, admitted the need for basic studies on IO in war, including 'good, reliable means' to assess its impact. 'Intelligence doctrine addressing IO remains to be produced, and training remains concentrated on the traditional functions of locating and identifying opposing forces', with 'intelligence products . . . designed to support force-on-force, kinetic, lethal engagements'. Again, in 'numerous Army Warfighter Exercises . . . attrition-focused command and staff training exercises', time was too short 'to employ the less tangible aspects of IO in a manner that would influence the operation', and to understand their value and limits. A division or corps headquarters had just hours 'between receipt of mission to course of action selection, allowing as much time as possible for coordination, synchronization, and orders production', and one at theatre level 'out to 120 hours and beyond'. Deception and psyops, however, might take months to work. 'The most important aspect of IO at the tactical and operational levels is execution', yet how far could division or corps staffs 'effectively integrate and execute all elements of IO into their decision-making processes, given the time constraints common to tactical operations?' If not, how should IO be organised? Historical experience, incidentally, including that from Iraq in 2003, suggests deception and psyops can work well even within a month from their start. It also indicates that a theatre-level headquarters should handle these matters for subordinate commands. Again, how should old disciplines like electronic warfare be adapted to fit new technology, IO and the information age?[33]

Even experts were unsure how to apply IO. It was practised only in exercises, peace keeping, and Kosovo, all experiences with limits. Bosnia illuminated IO's use in peace keeping but not in war, and perhaps provided some counter-productive lessons: a directing committee of 20-plus members possibly is too bureaucratic for operations. In 2000, reflecting on experience with IO in divisional work at the Exercise and Training Integration Center, one IO analyst, Roy Hollis, noted 'All too often, IO is associated with rear area or force protection operations only . . . This is only a part of what IO is capable of doing, and we have to unlearn this.' Since 'many staffers do not fully understand or appreciate the value of IO', without effective 'IO staff huddles', 'strong leadership' from the IO officer and a supportive Chief of Staff, 'the staff will focus on what they already know and give minimal attention to Information Operation requirements'. Personnel 'lacked actual subject matter expertise in the various disciplines or elements, plus intelligence support, that make up Information Operations', and spent too much time in too many meetings.[34] Amateurishness and bureaucracy are common problems in military intelligence; but for IO, a focus on form may turn revolution into a checklist. Until 2003, these problems characterised US efforts to apply their IO doctrine.

Properly handled, IO are powerful tools, but they do not necessarily work as one hopes. And they can also be used by one's adversary. Defence matters as much as attack; it is simply more difficult. The power of IO will be multiplied in an unpredictable way by the rise of a new discipline. Unclassified material rarely refers to Computer Network Attack but the topic has not been ignored, simply treated with secrecy, just as armies did deception and signals intelligence between 1919 and 1939. One USAF intelligence officer notes 'offensive IO weapons . . . remain shrouded in limited-access programs'. The Joint Chiefs of Staff's doctrine on IO discusses CNA in a classified annex. In 2000–01, the USAF sponsored research into specialist 'Cyber-Warfare Forces', 'potential targeting issues' and 'how to mitigate or minimize collateral damage effects'. This research will consider how CNA might affect 'the full-spectrum of Information Attacks'. It will also consider how to create and fuse new 'broadly defined multi-disciplinary activities, such as: cyber-based deception, Electro-Magnetic Interference (EMI), Web Security, Perception Management'.[35] The Pentagon's Command and Control Research Program describes CNA as 'a rapidly evolving field of study with its own concepts and technology'.[36] Anyone able to employ a hacker for love or money can hope to gain from CNA, while attack somewhere is easier than defence everywhere. The entry costs are small, the potential payoff large, and the consequences uncertain. Sooner or later some state will let slip the bytes of cyberwar, with uncertain effect. CNA may revolutionise IO by incapacitating computer systems, or replacing true data with false; or it may prove Y2K revisited. A first strike may be so advantageous that it creates an imperative to move first, adding a new twist to deterrence. Even when not used, CNA creates, one veteran noted, 'built-in paranoia' – the need to fear that hostile states or non-state actors are attacking and to react on that assumption to anything which looks like a threat.[37] This is doubly the case as CNA may be indistinguishable from accident, its authors are undetectable and it can inflict mass destruction (consider the consequences of wrecking the computers controlling air traffic control at Heathrow Airport, or of a nuclear power plant). So too, the nature of CNA power is unknown: 'How do you measure IO power?', asks the USAF's Institute for National Security Studies; 'How would one calculate Correlation of Forces à la past Soviet/Russian approaches?'; what are the 'units of IW force' or their structure 'e.g. squadrons of IW computers'?[38] These are imponderables at the centre of all thinking about IO as a force multiplier.

At the same time, IO are a known commodity; not so, C4ISR and NCW. How will reachback, intelnets, an IDC or 'knowledge warehouses' affect the normal working of intelligence, and its use in crises or operations? Certainly, they will not end uncertainty, but instead create new kinds of uncertainty. They will increase what Michael Handel called 'Type B uncertainty' – the problem of decision making in a context of too much and too constantly changing information.[39] Uncertainty is not just about what is seen, but how we see; not merely what we know, but how we know that we know what we know. It is a problem of too few facts, but also too many. It is a condition linked to problems. The problems can be eliminated. But attempts to end one problem often create another. A condition of uncertainty is that one can never solve all problems at any one time. One merely chooses which problems to avoid and which to embrace. This condition must be endured. One can increase one's certainty and reduce that of an adversary. The resulting gains may be great. But none of this is easy to achieve. When facing a serious foe, uncertainty will remain sizable. Even against a weak enemy it can never vanish. Chess players, knowing their foe's dispositions, remain uncertain about his or her intentions and the clash of their own strategies. C4ISR and 'Dominant Battlespace Knowledge' (DBK) will increase uncertainty precisely through the way they reduce it; they will have the same effect with friction. In time of routine, they will provide more data than a general needs. In time of crisis they will produce less intelligence. How far will the ability to collect and process information under routine circumstances affect ideas of what intelligence can do when it matters? Will such a routine not merely hide pathologies and paradoxes and make them even more debilitating when they strike, when it matters most? How will a machine accustomed to relying on the receipt of facts in hosts react when deprived of them? How will information junkies behave when thrown into cold turkey – just when battle starts?

A fluid but hardened information and command system will not be easy to achieve. The aims must be to simplify the flood of data and direct it where needed, so avoiding the classical problem with satellite imagery, which is that one knows what to look for only after the start of a crisis. It will be hard to gain full access to data about known unknowns and impossible even to know what questions to ask about unknown unknowns. Nor can such systems work unless doctrine and training prepares people to use them. Still, one can reduce these new forms of uncertainty through old-fashioned means. One must start by putting intelligence in its place. It does not make or execute decisions, people do. More fundamental issues, such as their education, intuition, doctrine, character, courage, openness of mind, wisdom, attitudes toward risk, determine how information of all kinds is understood and applied. Moreover, knowledge is only as useful as the action it inspires. Decision makers should listen to intelligence, yet they must remember that intelligence cannot answer every question. They cannot wait for the last bit of information to be received and for data processing to make their decisions. They must know when to act without intelligence or knowledge – that is why they are leaders. Soldiers need to know well enough so that they can act well enough when they must, and to understand when that moment is, nothing more and nothing less.

The key questions are: what information is essential? When and how does one know that one has sufficient information to act upon? All shades of opinion recognise that C4ISR and DBK have magnified problems like information overload, micromanagement and the fruitless search for certainty. A range of solutions have been proposed, all related to changing the culture of command. Units must be able to operate in harmony without command, through some new version of 'marching to the sound of the guns' (what the revolutionaries term 'swarming'). Commanders must learn to act when they have a good enough picture of events – even when this picture is imperfect and new information is arriving – and to understand when they have achieved that condition. Sometimes this process is called 'to opticise'. Clausewitz termed a similar process the 'imperative principle'.[40] When combined, these means have power but they also have limits. They can solve many problems of command, perhaps most of them, but not all. C4ISR will be a function of a complex system manned by many people. It will suffer from all of the things natural to both humans and complex systems, including uncertainty, friction, unachieved intentions, unintended consequences, unexpected failures and unplanned successes.

Operation Iraqi Freedom provides the first serious test of these ideas. But using it as a case study is not straightforward. Care must be taken in extrapolating from this unbalanced war. At the time of writing, data on the role of intelligence in the conflict is limited, if indicative. To a rare degree, this operation was intelligence driven. US authorities aimed to apply their doctrine and concepts, to follow all best practices, and to harness these matters to command and control warfare (C2W). The success of C4ISR and IO was overwhelming at the operational level but mixed at the strategic–political ones. In other words, the system was better at action than calculation, at target acquisition than knowledge. Everything based on machines achieved unparalleled power, all things focused on humans were mediocre, with the exception of IO. Authorities got Iraqi politics wrong. They exaggerated their ability to topple Saddam Hussein's regime through subversion, they overestimated its possession of weapons of mass destruction, and they misjudged the difficulties of post-conflict occupation. These failures stemmed from policy makers, but such errors are a fact of life. C4ISR has changed neither net assessment nor the politicisation of intelligence. Coalition intelligence worked better in military spheres, if less so on the more difficult issue of quality as opposed to quantity. Its picture of the enemy order of battle and tactical characteristics was good. It appreciated fairly well the strength needed to destroy its foe, though it overrated the enemy's quality. In technical terms these may have been major errors. Yet such mistakes are probably unavoidable and, in this case, they were of minor practical import. The Coalition could hardly have attacked with fewer forces than it did, or any earlier than it did. Even seasoned analysts had grounds for uncertainty about Iraqi capabilities, and thought it safer to believe some units were mediocre instead of all being bad. Nonetheless, the First Marine Division noted,

> we remained largely ignorant of the intentions of enemy commanders . . . This short-coming was especially critical as much of the war plan was either based on or keyed to specific enemy responses. When the enemy 'failed' to act in accordance with common military practice, we were caught flat-footed because we failed to accurately anticipate the unconventional response. This was primarily due to a dearth of HUMINT on the enemy leadership. In trying to map out the opposition's reactions we were largely relegated to our OSINT sources and rank speculation based on our own perceptions of the battlefield to make our assessments . . . Our technical dominance has made us overly reliant on technical and quantifiable intelligence collection means. There is institutional failure to account for the most critical dimension of the battlefield, the human one.[41]

C4ISR multiplied some forms of power more than others. At theatre level, reachback worked, national agencies distributed intelligence well, and a near-NCW system existed (all of which is common at this level). The theatre commander, General Franks, noted generals had 'much more precise technology-based information' than ever before.[42] This multiplied the ability to direct centralised firepower, and for aircraft to learn of targets of opportunity and to conduct interdiction. Airpower was directed with unprecedented speed, power, precision and reach. It mattered more to ground warfare than ever before, perhaps as much as did ground forces. Web-based air tasking orders let officers change missions at will. Fleeting chances which once would have been lost in the shuffle led to precise strikes.

Little, however, seems to have changed below the corps level in land warfare. The Marine Division faced every standard problem of bottlenecks and overload in information, and the failure of every technique touted to manage them. It often 'found the enemy by running into them, much as forces have done since the beginning of warfare'.[43] Failings in distribution at the national and theatre level, along with Frank's praiseworthy efforts to avoid over-centralisation of command, meant that regimental and divisional commanders often took the key actions on the ground without access to intelligence. Frank was cautious in sending orders or information to his subordinates, leaving them the initiative, at the price of often dividing intelligence from operations.

IO, meanwhile, were conducted with more skill and energy than the US military has shown for decades. Deception aimed to pin the Iraqi forces in Kurdistan, by drawing attention to the possibility of a Turkish front, and then to indications the war could not start until the Fourth Division was redeployed to Kuwait. This campaign was creative, though its effect is hard to determine. IO attempt to mobilise civilians in Iraq miscarried, but the Coalition had more success with a 'fused' attack on enemy epistemology. This approach involved the destruction of command and communication targets, and more. The air attacks on Saddam, and the claims they rested on reports from agents in Baghdad, were publicised, to shock his subordinates. His trust in his officers, and their mutual confidence, was sapped by announcements that the Americans were subverting Iraqi officers, and systematically contacting via e-mail those with access to computers. This effort, combining psyops, deception and a human form of cyberwar, manipulated the characteristics of a Stalinist regime and a paranoid political culture, with effect.

Operation Iraqi Freedom demonstrates a new standard for conventional war. How far this success can be repeated is unsure – NCW, C4ISR and IO worked less well in Kosovo. So one-sided was this war that intelligence served primarily for target acquisition rather than ONA. If ONA was practised, it failed, raising questions about the validity of 'Rapid Decisive Operations' as a workable concept. C4ISR, IO and NCW worked as planned because Coalition forces had the initiative and followed their plan, while the enemy was passive, overwhelmed, unable to strike Coalition forces or C4ISR. Had the Iraqis jammed communications, they would have broken most of the Coalition's enhanced power in intelligence and precision of attack or its command. Could this near-NCW system work in complex operations against an able and aggressive enemy? In Afghanistan and Iraq, after all, precise strikes often have failed, showing they work only when the machine performs without friction. Any friction yields failure and no system can always be perfect. An enemy which fights by its own rules, such as light infantry willing to die or to steal away in silence, has caught US forces at a disadvantage. What straws can be pulled from this wind?

NCW or C4ISR will not revolutionise events on the strategic level of war, or the strategic–diplomatic dimensions of peace, which are dominated by human rather than technological matters. Often they will affect these areas in counterproductive ways, by increasing confusion in and between levels of command for example. The US Navy's 'Global 2000' war games tested the application of NCW. It found both the power of C3I and its classic problems multiplied. With every member of the net able to post and edit notes, information overload paralysed command. Officers had so much data that they could make little use of any of it. Bad coin drove out good. One witness questioned the validity of 'visions of a command-and-control structure akin to the civilian internet . . . that the natural creativity, spontaneity, and adaptability of war fighters can be unleashed by freedom from constraint analogous to that of the civilian Internet in commercial settings'.[44] Experience in the Kosovo campaign led Air Commodore Stuart Peach to sombre conclusions. He observed that 'the drive to streamline procedures and handle ever more data has had an important side effect; airmen have become driven by process not strategy'. Hence, 'in reality, theory, doctrine and practice collide with process. Airmen claim one thing (centralized command and decentralized execution) and in fact practice another (centralized command and centralized execution).' The result was that 'refining the process of airspace control orders, air tasking orders and air task messages became the performance criteria, rather than creative and bold operational ideas or campaign plans'.[45]

According to one USAF officer, during this campaign the Supreme Allied Commander Europe, 'had in his office a terminal that allowed him to view what Predator unmanned aerial vehicles in the air were seeing'. Once, when Wesley Clark viewed three vehicles he thought tanks, 'he picked up a telephone, called the joint forces air component commander, and directed that those tanks be destroyed. With a single call, based on incomplete information, all the levels of war, from strategic to tactical, had been short-circuited.'[46] Similarly, during March 2002 in Afghanistan, officers in superior headquarters at home and abroad bombarded commanders with questions and advice based on live pictures transmitted from Predators in flight.[47] A case of friendly fire in that month showed that information overload, friction between layers of command and inexperienced personnel, had swamped the USAF's premier operational command, in western Asia. So much information was available that USAF squadrons could not circulate much material in ATOs to their pilots, while staff officers would not change their procedures, ensuring confusion between all layers of command.[48] The system processed and circulated far more information faster than ever before, but in this high tempo environment, the need to spend just 30 seconds in retrieving data could produce tragedy. It is so fast moving, fragile and complex that system errors are inevitable even without an enemy; the only questions are how often, at what cost, and crucially, how much an enemy will multiply them.

C4ISR and NCW sometimes will revolutionise tactics and operations where, all too often, friction at the systematic level has reduced the value of intelligence. The problem has always been that one actor has had information another might have used but did not receive in time to act, or that knowledge available in time could not be used with effect; failures by any one cog prevent the whole machine from working well, or at all. In conventional war, NCW and C4ISR may ensure that every cog of the machine works well at the same time, reducing friction to the lowest level possible. All national intelligence assets will focus on giving every unit every chance to exploit every fleeting opportunity; one's forces will be used for asking for or receiving such information and using it instantly, and well. In 1917, British signals intelligence constantly located U-Boats, prompting immediate air or surface strikes, which failed because units were slow and their ordnance weak. By 1943, intelligence on U-Boats was little better but allied forces far more able to kill. In 1944–45, allied air forces, using the cab rank system, could strike any target reported immediately, if not accurately; in the 2003 Iraq war, aircraft launched instant, precise and devastating strikes based on information acquired ten minutes earlier by headquarters 10,000 miles away. C4ISR and NCW will raise the bar on the best use of intelligence, and the frequency of optimum uses, in conventional war. It will multiply any form of firepower relying on rapid, precise and long-distance strikes. Perhaps this system would fail against a serious enemy or a real war, but for whom is this a concern? The point is not just one of transformation, or the quality of forces, but also one of quantity, or one's power relative to one's enemy. When Americans draw lessons from Iraq, they can apply them to a special case of conventional conflict pitting a giant against a dwarf. Other states must think of war as a whole.

Little will change where equals engage, or the weaker side evades one's strength or strikes one's C4ISR, or against guerrillas. If NCW fails in any instance on which it is relied, disaster will be redoubled because of that reliance. And fail NCW ultimately must, in part and in whole. If successful, it will force one's adversaries to find solutions by evading its strength and exploiting its weaknesses. NCW will always be convenient when one's enemy chooses to be foolish or weak (or foolish *and* weak). But not all enemies will make such poor choices and it would be foolish to assume that they will. A smart but weak foe may refuse any game where you can apply your strengths, and play instead by his own rules. Terrorism is an obvious case in point. A tough and able foe might turn the tables by attacking any precondition for NCW and then by imposing a different set of rules. The Revolution in Military Affairs has changed many things, but not everything. It has multiplied American strengths but not reduced American weaknesses. It has increased the value of high technology and firepower in conventional war but the basic nature of war is otherwise unchanged. As a result, where these things have always mattered, they now matter more than ever. But where they have not, nothing has changed. Iraq shows that the United States will aim to practice intelligence, command and war at a higher level than ever achieved before. When it can play to its strengths, it will succeed.

Notes

I am indebted to the late Michael Handel for discussions on these topics.

1 'Joint Vision 2010' and 'Joint Vision 2020', www.dtic.mil/doctrine.
2 Marine Corps Combat Development Command, Draft 'Information Operations', 25 September 2001, USMC, Doctrine Division Home Page; FM 100–6, 27 August 1996, 'Information Operations', www.adtdl.army.milcgi-bin/adtl.dll; FM 3-0, Operations, 14 June 2001, 5.75, 6.38, 11–47.
3 David Alperts, 'The Future of Command and Control with DBK', in Martin C. Libicki and Stuart E. Johnson (eds), *Dominant Battlespace Knowledge* (Washington, DC: NDU Press 1995).
4 General Ronald Fogleman, speeches, 25 April 1995, 'Information Operations: The Fifth Dimension of Warfare', *Defense Issues*, 10/47, www.defenselink.mil/speeches/1995 and 'Fundamentals of Information Warfare – An Airman's View', 16 May 1995, www.af.mil/news/speech/current.
5 George Stein, 'Information Warfare', *Airpower Journal* (Spring 1995), Richard Szafranski, 'A Theory of Information Warfare, Preparing for 2020', *Airpower Journal* (Spring 1995), emphasis in original.
6 Joint Pub 3–13.1, *Joint Doctrine for Command and Control Warfare (C2W)*, Joint Chiefs of Staff, 7 February 1996.
7 Department of Defense, *Transformation Planning Guidance*, April 2003, APP 4, 'Joint Concept Guidance, www.oft.osd.mil/; US Joint Forces Command, *A Concept for Rapid Decisive Operations, RDO Whitepaper*, J9 Joint Futures Lab, 2.3, 4.1, 4.3.1.3.
8 Colonel John A. Warden III, 'Air Theory for the Twenty-first Century', *Aerospace Power Chronicles, 'Battlefield of the Future': 21st Century Warfare Issues* (1995).
9 Williamson Murray, 'Transformation: Volume II', in Williamson Murray (ed.), *Transformation Concepts for National Security in the 21st Century* (Carlisle, PA: Strategic Studies Institute 2002). pp. 10–17. The US Army War College, September 2002; an untitled briefing paper by Michael Handel, copy in my possession, c. 2000. These papers offer fundamental critiques of assumptions about intelligence in the RMA; cf. John Ferris, 'The Biggest Force Multiplier? Knowledge, Information and Warfare in the 21st Century', in Wing Commander Alistair Dally and Ms Rosalind Bourke (eds), *Conflict, The State and Aerospace Power: The Proceedings of a Conference Held in Canberra by the Royal Australian Air Force, 28–29 May 2002* (Canberra: Aerospace Centre 2003), pp. 149–65.
10 Cf. n. 2, 6 and 30.

11 Defense Writers' Group, 22 January 2003, interview with General Richard Myers.

12 Arthur Cebrowski, speech to the Heritage Foundation, 13 May 2003.

13 Arthur Cebrowski, 17 June 2003, 'The Path not taken . . . Yet', www.oft.osd.mil/.

14 Briefing Paper by Joe Mazzafro (2002), 'Operation Enduring Freedom, Intelligence Lessons Learned, An Unofficial Quick Look', JWAD Mini-Symposium, 7 May 2002, www.max-well. af.mil/au/awc/awcgate/awc-lesn Jim Garamone, 'Myers says Joint Capabilities, Transformation Key to 21st Century War', American Forces Information Service, 5 February 2002, www.defenselink.mil/news/Feb2002/n020520002_200202054.

15 'Preface', '2025 In-Time Information Integrations System (I3S)', 'The Man in the Chair: Cornerstone of Global Battlespace Dominance', 'Wisdom Warfare for 2025', *Air Force 2025*, 1996, www.au.af.mil/au; Thomas K. Adams, 'Future Warfare and the Decline of Human Decisionmaking', *Parameters* (Winter 2001–02).

16 *Vector 21, Defense Intelligence Agency Strategic Plan, 1999–2000*; www.loyola.edu/dept/politics/milintel; NCS-21 (*National Cryptological Strategy for the 21st Century*), www.nsa.goc/programs/ncs21/index.; Director of Central Intelligence, *The 2002 Annual Report of the United States Intelligence Community*, 1.03, www.cia.gov/cia/publications/Ann_Rpt_2002/index.; 'Statement for the Record by Lieutenant General Michael V. Hayden, USAF, Director, National Security Agency/Chief, Central Security Service, Before the Joint Inquiry of the Senate Select Committee on Intelligence and the House Permanent Select Committee on Intelligence, 17 October 2002', www.nsa.gov/releases/speeches, emphasis in original.

17 Dan Caterinicchia, 'NIMA, NSA increasing collaboration', *Federal Computer Weekly*, 30 January 2003.

18 Dawn S. Onley, 'Success in Iraq due to Better Info Sharing, Tenet Says', *Government Computer News*, 11 June 2003.

19 *Vector 21, Defense Intelligence Agency Strategic Plan, 1999–2000*; Frederick Thomas Martin, *Top Secret Intranet: How US Intelligence Built Intelink, the World's Largest, Most Secure Network* (New York: Prentice Hall 1998); speech by A. Denis Clift, President, Joint Military Intelligence College, at Yale University, 27 April 2002, 'From Semaphore to Predator, Intelligence in the Internet Era', www.DIA.MIL/Public/Testimonics/statement06; 'Joint Intelligence Virtual Architecture JIVA', www.fas.org/irp/program/core/jiva.

20 Dawn S. Onley, 'Intelligence Analysts Strive to Share Data', *Government Computer News*, 28 May 2003.

21 ADCI/AP 2000–01, 'Strategic Investment Plan for Intelligence Community Analysis', www.cia.gov/cia/publications/pub.

22 Lt. Gen. Robert W. Noonan, Jr, and Lt. Col. Brad T. Andrew, Retired, 'Army Intelligence Provides the Knowledge Edge', *Army Magazine* (April 2002).

23 Bruce Berkowitz, 'The DI and "IT", Failing to Keep Up with the Information Revolution', *Studies in Intelligence*, 47/1, (2003), www.cia.gov/csi/studies/vol47/no1/article07.

24 Wilson P. Dizzard III, 'White Houses Promotes Data Sharing', *Government Computer News*, 28 June 2002 and Onley, 'Intelligence Analysts Strive to Share Data'.

25 *External Team Report, A Management Review for the Director, NSA*, 11 October 1999; *New Enterprise Team (NETeam) Recommendations, The Director's Work Plan for Change*, 1 October 1999, www.nsa.gov/releases/reports.html.

26 Richard Lardner, 'Leadership streamlined, chief of staff created, NSA Chief Pushes Ahead with Overhaul of Agency's Culture, Operations', inside *Defence Special Report*, 16 October 2000.

27 Charles L. Munns, 'Another View: Navy's Network Services Buy Pays Off', *Government Computer News*, 3 July 2003.

28 Office of the Inspector General, The Department of Justice, 'A Review of the FBI's Performance in Deterring, Detecting, and Investigating the Espionage Activities of Robert Philip Hanssen', 14 August 2003, www.usdoj.gov/oig/special/03-08/index.

29 Director of Central Intelligence, '2002 Annual Report'; William Jackson, 'Cyberdrill Carries Over to Real War', *Government Computer News*, 19 May 2003.

30 'Background Briefing on Enemy Denial and Deception', 24 October 2001, www.defense-link.mil/news/Oct2001/t10242001_t1024dd.ht.

31 Joint Chiefs of Staff, Joint Pub 3–58, *Joint Doctrine for Military Deception*, 31 May 1996 (under revision as of time of writing, June 2003); Joint Pub 3–54, *Joint Doctrine for Operations Security*, 24 February 1997; Joint Pub 3–13, Joint Doctrine for Information Operations, JCS, 9 October 1998; Joint

Publication 2-01.3, 24 May 2000, Joint Tactics, Techniques, and Procedures for Joint Intelligence Preparation of the Battlespace.

32 John Ferris, 'The Roots of FORTITUDE: The Evolution of British Deception in the Second World War', in T.G. Mahnken (ed.), *The Paradox of Intelligence: Essays in Honour of Michael Handel* (London: Frank Cass 2003).

33 Center for Army Lessons Learned (CALL) 2 October 2000, Information Operations Franchise, Research Project Proposals 4, 5.9, 10 and 12, www.call.army.mil/io/research.

34 CALL, 'The Information Operations Process'; 'Tactics, Techniques and Procedures for Information Operations (IO). Information Operations, Observations, TTP, and Lessons Learned. www.call.army.mil/io/ll.

35 Research Topics proposed by INNS, 25 July 2000, 'Information Operations (IO) 5.16', Computer Network Warfare, 'Information Operations (IO) 5.23, and 5.29; and Air Force Materiel Command, 8.28.01, 'Effects Based Information Operations', www.research.max-well.af.mil/js_Database; Colonel Carla D. Bass, 'Building Castles on Sand, Underestimating the Tide of Information Operations, *Aerospace Power Journal* (Summer 1999).

36 'CCRP Initiatives', Office of the Assistant Secretary of Defense Command, Control, Communications and Intelligence, 26 September 2001, www.dodccrp.org.

37 Dan Caternicchia (2003), 'DOD forms cyberattack task force', *Federal Computer Weekly*, 10 February 2003.

38 Research Topics proposed by INNS, 25 July 2000, IO 5.48 and IO 5.24.

39 J.R. Ferris and Michael Handel (1995), 'Clausewitz, Intelligence, Uncertainty and the Art of Command in Modern War', *Intelligence and National Security*, 10/1 (January 1995), pp. 1–58.

40 Ibid.

41 'Operation Iraqi Freedom, 1st Marine Division, Lessons Learned, 28 May 2003'; accessible from the website of the *Urban Operations Journal*, Operation Iraq Freedom, AARs, Observations, Analyses and Comments.

42 Joseph L. Galloway, 'General Tommy Franks Discusses Conducting the War in Iraq', 19 June 2003, Knight Ridder Washington Bureau, www.realcities.com/mld/krwashington/6124738.h.

43 'Operation Iraqi Freedom, 1st Marine Division, Lessons Learned, 28 May 2003'; ibid.

44 Kenneth Watman, 'Global 2000', *NWCR* (Spring 2000). For a more optimistic reading of this exercise, and others, cf. Network Centric Warfare, Department of Defense Report to Congress, 27.7.01, pp. E-24, www.c3i.osd.mil/NCW/.

45 Air Commodore Stuart Peach, 'The Airmen's Dilemma: To Command or Control', in Peter Gray (ed.), *Air Power 21: Challenges for the New Century* (London: Ministry of Defence 2001), pp. 123–4, 141. A US Army observer, Timothy L. Thomas, offered similar views in 'Kosovo and the Current Myth of Information Superiority', *Parameters* (Spring 2000).

46 Major William A. Woodcock, 'The Joint Forces' Air Command Problem – Is Networkcentric Warfare the Answer?', *Naval War College Review* (Winter 2003), p. 46; the words are Woodcock's, but his source is Michael Short, the Joint Air Force commander in Kosovo.

47 Anthony H. Cordesman, *The Lessons of Afghanistan, Warfighting, Intelligence, Force Transformation, Counterproliferation, and Arms Control* (Washington, DC: Center for Strategic and International Studies 2002), pp. 63–4.

48 Verbatim Testimony of Colonel David C. Nichols and Colonel Laurence A. Stutzreim, Tarnack Farms Enquiry. 1.03, www.barksdale.af.mil/tarnackfarms/rosenow.

Reprinted with permission from John Ferris, 'Netcentric Warfare, C4ISR and Information Operations: Towards a revolution in Military Intelligence? in L.V. Scott and P.D. Jackson, eds., *Understanding Intelligence in the Twenty-First Century: Journeys in Shadows*, (London: Routledge 2004), pp.54–77.

INTELLIGENCE, DECEPTION AND MILITARY OPERATIONS

Further reading: Books and reports

Bruce Berkowitz, *The New Face of War: How War Will be Fought in the 21ˢᵗ Century* (NY: Free Press 2000).

Donald C. Daniel & Katherine L. Herbig, *(eds.) Strategic Military Deception* (NY: Pergamon 1982).

Roger Z. George and Robert D. Kline (eds.), *Intelligence and National Security Strategist: Enduring Issues and Challenges* (Washington, DC: National Defense University Press, CSI, 2004), parts VIII & X, pp.359–417 & 459–517.

R. Godson & James J. Wirtz, (eds.) *Strategic Denial and Deception: The Twenty-First Century Challenge* (New Brunswick NJ: Transaction 2002).

Michael Herman, *Intelligence Power in Peace and War* (Cambridge: Cambridge University Press, 1996).

Michael Herman, *Intelligence Services in the Information Age* (London: Frank Cass 2001) chapter 3.

Thadeus Holt, *Allied Military Deception in the Second World War* (NY: Scribners 2005).

Klauss Knorr & Patrick Morgan, *Strategic Military Surprise* (New Brunswick: Transaction Books 1983).

Barton Whaley, *Stratagem: Deception and Surprise in War* (Boston: Artech House 2007).

Further reading: Essays and articles

Bowyer J. Bell, 'Toward a Theory of Deception,' *International Journal of Intelligence and Counterintelligence* 16/2 (2003) pp.244–279.

Stephen J. Cimbala, 'Mainstreaming Military Deception,' *International Journal of Intelligence and Counterintelligence* 3/4 (1989) pp.509–535.

J. Ferris, 'The Intelligence-Deception Complex', *Intelligence and National Security* 4/4 (October 1989) pp.719–34.

Michael Handel, 'Intelligence and Deception', in J. Gooch and Amos Perlmutter (eds.) *Military Deception and Strategic Surprise* (NY: Frank Cass 1982), pp.122–54.

Michael Handel, 'Surprise and Change in International Politics,' *International Security* 4/4 (1980) pp.57–85.

Michael Handel, 'Intelligence and Military Operations,' *Intelligence and National Security* 5/2 (1990) pp.1–95.

Michael Handel, 'Intelligence and the Problem of Strategic Surprise,' *Journal of Strategic Studies* 7/3 (1984) pp.229–281.

Michael Handel, 'Technological Surprise in War,' *Intelligence and National Security* 2/1 (1987) pp.1–53.

Richard J. Hueur, 'Strategic Deception and Counter-Deception', *International Studies Quarterly* 25/2 (1981) pp.294–327.

W. Nolte, 'Keeping Pace with the Revolution in Military Affairs', *Studies in Intelligence* 48/1 (2004).

Hank Smith, 'Intelligence and Afghanistan 2001–2' in Jennifer E. Sims & Burton L. Gerber, (eds.) *Transforming U.S. Intelligence* (Washington DC: Georgetown University Press, 2005), pp.162–80.

J.G. Stein, 'Military deception, strategic surprise, and conventional deterrence: a political analysis of Egypt and Israel, 1971–73', *Journal of Strategic Studies* 5/1 (1982) pp.94–121

Essay questions

- What were the main ingredients in the success of the D-Day deception Campaign?
- How are the proliferating communication technologies of the twenty-first century likely to change the business of denial and deception?
- Discuss the place of intelligence within the Revolution in Military Affairs.
- What are the main impediments to a forward leaning military intelligence posture?

27 Securing the globe

Peter Gill

Significant shifts have been underway in security intelligence agencies and processes since the 11 September 2001 attacks in the United States. Whereas the previous quarter of a century had seen a considerable democratization of intelligence, the article examines whether UK and US government responses risk the re-creation of 'security states'. Changes since 9/11 in law, doctrine, the intelligence process – targeting, collection, analysis, dissemination and action – and oversight are considered and it is concluded that there is a danger of the rebirth of independent security states.

> On present trends, the common response to this range of conflicts will be one of regaining and maintaining control, rather than addressing root causes ... the process is one of keeping the lid on dissent and instability – 'liddism' – by means of public order control that will, when necessary, extend to the use of military force.[1]

> While we'll try to find every snake in the swamp, the essence of the strategy is draining the swamp.[2]

This paper considers how post-9/11 developments can be interpreted in terms of earlier analyses of security intelligence. It is often asserted that 'everything' changed on 9/11 ... well, did it? Analysis needs to consider carefully what is shifting and what is not. As such, this paper reflects ongoing work: much of the post-9/11 architecture of security intelligence now seems to be in place but what the impact of its new policies will be is less certain. First, a simple typology developed some time ago has been adapted and is deployed to provide some basic benchmarks for characterizing security intelligence agencies; second, some of the main legal, doctrinal, organizational and practice developments in security intelligence structures and processes are described and, third, some conclusions are drawn as to the main direction in which security intelligence agencies seem headed.

A typology of security intelligence agencies

Ten years ago, in a comparative study of security intelligence agencies in North America and UK, I wrote:

> the state–society relationship should be seen not in terms of a two-person game, but as a n-person game dominated by strategic practices of information control and power as between various agencies operating at different levels of the state ... The two main concepts within which these practices might be summarised are autonomy and penetration. The first incorporates those processes by which secret state agencies resist the

encroachment of other state agencies and citizens, while the second covers the variety of techniques by which the secret state carries out its surveillance and supervision of other agencies and society in general.[3]

Autonomy is thus shorthand for agencies' bureaucratic power within their parent states. This has two dimensions: first, the extent to which they are subject (or not) to direction and control by ruling groups and, second, to oversight by external institutions, including assemblies, citizens and media. Penetration also summarizes two key dimensions of security intelligence: information gathering and what security policies (arrest, disruption, rendition etc) are conducted.[4]

Although these concepts were developed in the context of a study of liberal democracies, there seems no reason in principle why they may not be used more widely. For example, with respect to national security, states have been classified along a spectrum from democratic *via* 'national securitism' to 'garrison'[5] where a key element of classification is the extent of the autonomy of police, security and military agencies from 'normal' political processes. Similarly, the capacity of agencies to 'penetrate' society is in inverse relation to the enjoyment of privacy and other rights that are definitive in determining the presence or absence of democracy.

Combining the variables of autonomy and penetration gives us a typology of security intelligence agencies. This enables us to 'plot' the location of agencies and thus to compare them or note shifts in time. The 'zones' in Figure 1 are labelled[6] in such a way as to indicate (at lower left) a 'domestic intelligence bureau' that is subject to ministerial control and democratic oversight, on the one hand, and is limited by legal constraints in the extent to which it

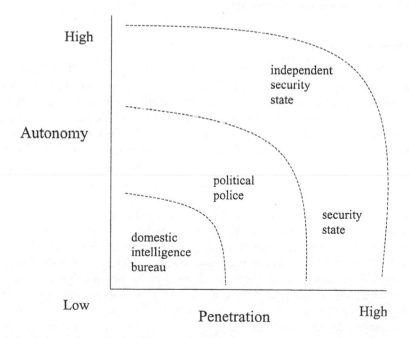

Figure 1 A typology of security intelligence agencies.

can gather information and, perhaps more importantly, act on the information it gathers. An example of an agency approximating to this type is the Canadian Security Intelligence

Service (CSIS), whose statutory mandate is limited to providing the government with intelligence and security advice. That is, it may not *act* as, for example, can the UK Security Service (MI5). The fact that MI5 receives less specific ministerial direction than CSIS and is empowered to *protect* security (for example, indulge in disruptive operations) makes it a good example of a 'political police' agency. At the outer end are agencies that might be described as 'security states' in which democratic control of the agency is absent and they have the power not only to gather information as widely as resources permit but also to act, for example, to arrest, imprison and, possibly, kill people. 'Independent security states' are those agencies that are not only immune from external oversight but also develop their own policies and practices independent of the ruling groups. Another way of putting this would be to describe agencies towards the lower left as essentially 'defensive', becoming more aggressive/offensive as they move up and to the right.

For the purposes of this paper, the main focus will be on internal US and UK agencies. This classification system is primarily applicable to internal security agencies: foreign intelligence agencies (by definition) break the laws of other states in seeking information and deploying covert operations. Therefore attention is focused on the US Federal Bureau of Investigation (FBI) and the UK Security Service but we must note the limits to an *institutional* approach to this question. In both countries, other internal law enforcement agencies (for example, police, immigration), intelligence agencies (even if they are primarily concerned with foreign intelligence) and private sector agencies interact in security *networks*. Further, one of the more significant post-9/11 developments has been the apparent convergence of what have traditionally been seen as separate intelligence disciplines such as 'security' and 'law enforcement'). Thus, one would want ideally to generalize about the autonomy and penetration of domestic security *networks* rather than single *agencies* but to achieve this task systematically is beyond the scope of this article.

Agencies prior to 9/11

First, where were these agencies before 9/11 in terms of the typology? The FBI has been characterized as shifting (in terms of Figure 1) upwards and to the right in the 1950s as it became the (more or less) respectable vehicle for liberal anti-communism in the US. It then continued on towards becoming an independent security state as J. Edgar Hoover built upon his autonomy from both Presidential control (with a slight blip 1961–63) and congressional oversight to develop the Bureau's own illegal counterintelligence (COINTELPRO) programmes to disrupt the social movements of the 1960s. From 1970 onwards, increasing evidence emerged as to the Bureau's behaviour and, after Hoover's death in 1972, it became enmeshed in the Watergate scandals so that by 1976 fresh controls were put in place with the aim of returning the FBI to its former status as domestic intelligence bureau.[7]

The lack of any UK equivalent of the US Freedom of Information Act (FOIA) and the fact that Security Service file releases still do not go much beyond the Second World War mean that we do not have the same detailed knowledge on which to base a classification of MI5. However, it is possible to track the main changes in the post-war period: until 1989 there was no statute covering any aspect of the Service's operations,[8] minimal ministerial control and no oversight at all, thus autonomy was high. The Service engaged in similar counter-intelligence operations to disrupt the trades union and unilateralist movements and has been centrally involved in counter-terrorist operations in Northern Ireland and the UK. Thus, it would be reasonable to describe the Service then as occupying a space toward the 'independent security state' zone. A combination of factors since the late 1980s (including pressures from decisions of the European Court of Human Rights and the collapse of the USSR) combined to reduce the autonomy of the Service and the *breadth* of its penetration into society may also have diminished even if its capacities certainly did not. Thus the greater integration of MI5 into governmental policy making since 1989 suggests 'political police' to be a more appropriate characterization.

Whether scandal or democratization (and sometimes both together) have been the main impetus for change, the main emphasis of reforms has been on increasing the legality and propriety of security intelligence operations. Although in some cases attention was paid also to the issue of obtaining effective security intelligence,[9] the overall direction of change was to the better control and accountability of agencies whose past activities had been dominated by the surveillance of political opponents rather than genuine security threats.

Agencies since 9/11

But since the 11 September 2001 attacks in New York and Washington, DC, the debates around security intelligence have shifted to the contemplation of 'intelligence failure' and how future threats can be averted. This repeats the historical pattern in which concern regarding *propriety* has increased following scandals while intelligence 'failures' such as 9/11 give rise to increased concern with *efficacy*. In this atmosphere it is easy to see how the democratic gains of the last 30 years might be swept away in the naïve belief that agencies 'unhampered' by oversight requirements might somehow be more efficient and effective.

It is a mistake to view efficacy and propriety as being in a zero (constant) sum relationship such that gains in one are outweighed by losses in the other. Rather, they should be viewed as being in a non-zero (variable) sum relationship such that both can be improved. This is not to say that there is no tension between the two: it is quite easy to see how, in the short run, the ability to conduct surveillance of an individual or group may be reduced by the requirement to follow procedures that seek to protect privacy but, in the longer term, such procedures are required if a state is to be entitled to call itself democratic. Such procedures should be designed in order that, even in the short term, the invasion of privacy is proportionate to the alleged threat but also to prevent it being directed at the wrong person or conducted in such a way as to amount to intimidation. Thus legal rules themselves may contribute to efficacy as much as to propriety.

Legal changes

New statutes have been passed: in the US the PATRIOT Act 2001 and in the UK the Anti-Terrorism, Crime and Security Act 2001. Each of these extends the legal powers of governments to carry out surveillance and act against individuals and groups identified as terrorist or, especially in the case of the UK, engaged in other serious crime. In US cities, too, police are seeking the reversal of restrictions imposed on their ability to surveille political groups and demonstrations, for example in New York the *Handschu* case.[10] In the UK it is clear that the Government still believes it lacks adequate powers to deal with those planning terrorist attacks, for example, in April 2004 Home Secretary David Blunkett announced plans for civil court orders to be taken out against those in contact with named suspects. Disobedience to the order would be a criminal offence, subject to imprisonment. Blunkett was quoted to the effect that 'It is intended to deter people from hanging around the fringes of undesirables'.[11] Understandably directed at the recruitment of young men to fundamentalism, it is very hard to see how this could be enforced without aggravating the very disaffection it is intended to discourage.

In the US another restriction enacted as a result of the abuses of intelligence was the 'firewall' placed between information generated for intelligence purposes and that used as evidence in law enforcement. Since the 1970s the increasing co-operation between military, intelligence and law enforcement agencies in the targeting of organized crime and the increased use of tactics of disruption (rather than arrest and prosecution) had already put pressure on this division. In the wake of 9/11 that pressure has increased tremendously: this can be seen clearly from the dispute over the use to be made of information obtained through wiretaps authorized by the special court established by the Foreign Intelligence Surveillance Act (FISA). After a series of court decisions the special appellate panel of the Foreign Intelligence Court of Review upheld the PATRIOT Act's grant of increased powers so that prosecutors would be permitted to use information obtained from FISA-authorized inter-ceptions in the prosecution of those accused of terrorism.[12] Ironically, this decision came shortly after it was revealed by the Senate Judiciary Committee that in 75 warrant applica-tions, mainly during the Clinton administration, the FBI and Justice Department had misled the FISA as to the actual existence of the 'firewall': information gathered from intelligence taps was used freely in bringing criminal charges.[13]

Doctrinal changes

But it is not just legal rules that have been re-written; probably the most dramatic assertions of power have been those in the military field, especially the extension of the traditional right of national self-defence to encompass pre-emptive attacks. However, in some respects 9/11 should be seen as an accelerator of changes towards more aggressive deployment of intelligence rather than a shift in direction: the Executive Order first signed by President Ford in 1975 prohibiting US agencies from engaging in assassinations of foreign leaders has been interpreted by Presidents at least since Bush Senior as not applying to 'terrorists'. But a Presidential 'finding' after 9/11 reinforces this by authorizing the CIA to kill what are described as 'high-value targets' in the al-Qaeda leadership such as they did in the Yemen in November 2002.[14]

There is also evidence of a shifting balance towards pre-emption in internal security. An abiding dilemma for security agencies is, having identified and located targets, whether to maintain surveillance in the interests of developing intelligence (and/or evidence) while risking the perpetration of an attack or whether to intervene earlier to disrupt/arrest/interrogate and risking the cutting-off of the information flow. 9/11 has shifted this balance clearly towards the latter because of the heightened fears of weapons of mass destruction (WMD) attacks (however fanciful some of these may be). For example, after an informant told MI5 of a plot to release cyanide gas on the London underground and the Service consulted with Downing Street, six people were arrested in North London.[15] Nine Algerians were arrested in December 2002 and charged under the Terrorism Act 2000 for an alleged plot to attack New Year celebrations in Edinburgh. Twelve months later all charges were dropped.[16] FBI officials have been quoted to the effect that they have resurrected the COINTELPRO tactics widely used during the 1960s, for example, exploiting rivalries within groups and using disinformation to convince some that others are informers.[17]

As has been the case with anti-terrorist legislation prior to 9/11, the impact of the new legislation must be measured more in terms of arrest, detentions and interrogations than prosecutions and convictions. Researchers at Syracuse University examined federal prosecution data and found that by September 2003, of 2,000 'terrorism-related' cases in which charges were preferred the government obtained 879 convictions of which 184 were said to involve 'international terrorism'. Yet 80 of these defendants were not sentenced to jail and 91 received 12 months or less, raising serious questions as to the nature of the 'terrorism'.[18] In the UK, of the 527 people arrested under terrorism legislation since 9/11, there have been 97 terrorism charges, 289 people have been released without charge, 99 have been charged with other criminal offences and 54 have been handed over to the Immigration Service.[19] How many of these charges will result in convictions remains to be seen. UK police stop and search powers were also increased, first under the Terrorism Act 2000 and second under the Anti-Terrorism, Crime and Security Act 2001,[20] and are being used extensively, though with a very low arrest rate compared with stop and search under general crime legislation. Thirteen per cent of Police and Criminal Evidence Act searches resulted in arrests but only 1.2 per cent of those were under terrorism powers and the majority were not for terrorist offences.[21] Therefore pre-emption, preventive detention[22] and disruption are the order of the day, strongly implying a shift towards more aggressive penetration by the agencies.

Organizational

In the US itself a major manifestation of the Presidential need to be seen to be in control is visible in the plans to reorganize security intelligence structures. In the short term these shifts will reduce the autonomy of agencies by reasserting centralization in order, it is hoped, to increase agencies' ability to penetrate society in pursuit of the war on terror. Legislation has been passed to create a new Department of Homeland Security (DHS). This proposal seems to have been guided by two main arguments: first, that the 'failure' of 9/11 was largely a failure to *co-ordinate* intelligence and security and, second, that a grand political gesture was required to convince the US public that 'something is being done' to improve security. Thus the plan is based on the strategy of combining previously disparate security organizations in the apparent belief that improved hierarchical co-ordination will improve matters.

This strategy might well be criticized (for example, hierarchical forms of organization are infamously poor at effectively developing and disseminating accurate information) but the main opposition to the plan in Congress was less about its wisdom *per se* than directed towards accompanying Presidential assertions of power that are certainly indicative of a shift towards a 'security state'. For example, the executive wanted to exempt the DHS both from access to information rules with respect to 'critical infrastructure' information and from whistleblower protection.[23] Consistent with an earlier Presidential order barring unionization for over 500 employees in parts of the Justice Department, DHS employees will enjoy fewer employment rights than elsewhere in the federal government.[24]

The original White House proposal did not give much prominence to intelligence co-ordination. Finally the Act established a division for 'Information Analysis and Infrastructure Protection'. Its analyses and warnings will be developed from a combination of products passed by the CIA and FBI and information gathered by, for example, border guards and secret service personnel who are now to be within the new department. Another new agency is also aimed at overcoming the fragmentation problem. The Terrorist Threat Integration Center (TTIC) started work in May 2003, providing all-source analysis of terrorist threats. It is initially located at CIA HQ in Langley but will eventually be located elsewhere together with the Director of Central Intelligence's (DCI) Counterterrorist Center (CTC) and the

FBI's Counterterrorism Division. The Director will report to the DCI. The TTIC will develop its own database and be able to direct collection and analysis by other intelligence community agencies and networks. A recent letter from heads of CIA, FBI, TTIC and DHS has sought to allay continuing Congressional concern that post-9/11 changes have not improved the possibilities of co-ordinating counter-terrorism analysis in the US but it is difficult to read it in any way other than that these changes have increased the possibilities for confusion. The TTIC, CIA and CTC now all have analytical responsibilities regarding international terrorism while FBI's Counterterrorism Division and DHS share analytical work for domestic terrorism.[25] On top of this, of course, are the myriad of interagency groups seeking to co-ordinate across the broader and highly fragmented law enforcement community at federal, state and local levels.[26]

The FBI remains outside the DHS apart from its critical infrastructure component that will be transferred. But the FBI itself has not escaped from reorganization efforts: CIA personnel were deployed to advise the Bureau on establishing its Office of Intelligence.[27] This is to be responsible for implementing the new intelligence strategies within the Bureau including intelligence units within each field office[28] and, through Joint Terrorism Task Forces, with state and local law enforcement, the Intelligence Community and TTIC.[29] However, this and increasing the proportion of agents working on counter-terrorism have not satisfied all that the Bureau can transform itself from 'law enforcement' into 'domestic security intelligence' agency.

Regular reports have appeared of the frustration of senior government officials at the alleged failure of FBI field offices to be more aggressive in developing human and technical sources against possible terrorist targets and to share information.[30] A partially declassified audit of the FBI's capacities in this respect was published in December 2003. Noting that the main problems identified after 9/11 had been the chronically inadequate communications and information technology (CIT) system and inability of the Bureau to conduct all source analysis, it identified some progress in CIT acquisition and the recruitment and training of analysts but made further recommendations.[31] There is clearly a debate underway in Washington DC and the 9/11 Commission (see below) as to whether the US should separate the security intelligence and law enforcement functions as Canada did in 1984 and as characterizes the separation of police and security service in the UK.[32]

What remains unclear is the cumulative effect of these changes: while the FBI develops its own intelligence capacities, technological infrastructure[33] and devotion to counter-terrorism, parts of its organization are re-located in multi-agency initiatives such as TTIC and fresh counter-terrorism players enter the field. Also, what of the impact on other investigations of threats to public safety and security other than 'terrorism'? With almost 26 per cent of field agents now assigned to counter-terrorism investigations, many white collar, fraud, corruption and drugs investigations languish, if they were ever started.[34]

Intelligence process: targeting, gathering and warehousing

Rearranging the organizational chairs is a common governmental reaction to security or policy failure but, although by no means new, the 'big idea' for addressing fragmentation is the development of data warehouses.[35] But the construction of ever-larger databases, data warehousing and data-mining, though of great significance in intelligence, cannot 'solve' intelligence problems without a process of targeting, careful evaluation of information and human analytical skills. (Indeed, arguably, the problem becomes ever greater as the proportion of information that is actually *analyzed* reduces.) Targets will include known individual names, groups, addresses etc. and also the search for unknown 'names' *via* profiling. There has been controversy for years in the US regarding profiling because doing so on the sole basis of ethnicity is unlawful yet post-9/11 surveillance operations have clearly concentrated on Arab-Americans, immigrants from the Middle East and especially from Iraq in the lead-up to war.[36] There is also much demand for new systems for security purposes, for example the Transportation Security Administration is seeking to develop a system[37] based on a ware-house of public and private databases (banks, credit agencies, car licences etc.) in order to classify air passengers at one of three 'risk' levels.

But the most hair-raising proposal has been for 'Total Information Awareness' (TIA), a Pentagon research project that sought to provide what might be described as a 'wet dream for Big Brother'. TIA sought to bring together in 'ultra-large all-source information reposi-tories' a number of existing CIT programmes – identifying links from message traffic and open source data, collaborative tools for humans and machines to 'think together', language processing for non-linguists, identification of predictive indicators of terrorist attacks, bio-metric identification technologies and exploiting 'non-traditional data sources to enable early detection and warning of a bio-terrorist event'.[38] Presumably the last of these referred to the 'pre-cogs' who were a rather critical link in the predictive chain featured in the film 'Minority Report'! Publicity of the TIA generated enough opposition for Congress to attach a provision to an appropriations bill preventing the programme from being directed against Americans and restricting the research without consultation with Congress,[39] but even chan-ging the name of the project to 'Terrorism Information Awareness' could not stave off opposition and the programme was closed by Congress in September 2003.[40] However, it would be naïve to suppose that such research initiatives are not continuing.

In addition to mining existing databases, however, the continuous search for new informa-tion is reflected in changes in the law or, in some cases, executive assertions that previous law does not apply. The clear purpose of the detention without trial in the US of two US citizens and 1,200 noncitizens is to gather information; whether people are ever placed on trial is a subsidiary consideration. Further, this has led not only to US agencies cooperating abroad with agencies long associated with human rights abuses, for example, Pakistan but also to transferring individuals arrested in one country to others such as Jordan, Egypt and Morocco where torture is an established part of interrogation procedures. Transnational information exchange is one thing, brokering the use of torture is another.[41] US officials have acknowledged that the official cause of death for two detainees at Bagram air base was homi-cide, their death certificates referring to 'blunt force injuries'.[42] More recently, major contro-versy has erupted in the US at the publication of pictures of serious abuse of Iraqi prisoners at the Abu Ghraib prison. An army report into allegations, conducted by Major General Taguba, was compiled in February and March 2004 and, having now found its way into the public domain, makes clear that not only was the abuse systematic but also that it was carried out under the tutelage of military intelligence officers with a view to obtaining information:

> between October and December 2003 . . . numerous incidents of sadistic, blatant, and wanton criminal abuses were inflicted on several detainees. This systemic and illegal abuse of detainees was intentionally perpetrated by several members of the military police guard force.[43]
> . . . I find that Military Intelligence interrogators and other US Government Agency's interrogators actively requested that MOP guards set physical and mental conditions for favourable interrogation of witnesses . . . I find that personnel . . . were directed to change facility procedures to 'set the conditions' for MI interrogations.[44]

However, Europeans cannot feel much moral superiority: the UK Special Immigration Appeals Commission (SIAC) has ruled that evidence obtained against detainees by means of torture will not necessarily be deemed to be inadmissible,[45] while the Italian Chamber of Deputies has just approved a legal amendment to the effect that only repeated use of violence by police would constitute torture.[46] UK military investigators are also examining allegations of prisoner abuse by British troops in Iraq at the time of writing.[47]

Less coercive but still open to abuse of power by agencies is the recruitment of informants. The widespread interviewing of Arab-Americans and migrants from the Middle East follows a long-established practice in which security agencies use immigration status as a lever for recruitment. Reportedly, the FBI is seeking improved HUMINT by incorporating University Police officers onto joint terrorism task forces. Given the history of FBI disruption of student groups in the 1960s, this led to some protests.[48]

Regarding TECHINT, in both the US and Europe executives are seeking improved access to electronic data. For example, the European Union has amended its 1997 Directive on Privacy so that the obligation of communications service providers to erase traffic data is deleted and they can retain data for 12–24 months.[49] Documents obtained through the FOIA in the US show that under the PATRIOT Act there is increased use of 'national security' letters under which banks, ISPs, telephone and credit companies etc. can be compelled to hand over customers' records. Prior to the Act the Government had to show 'probable cause' (comparable with 'reasonable suspicion' in the UK) but now they do not and companies are prohibited from telling anyone of the disclosure.[50] In the UK the Regulation of Investigatory Powers Act (RIPA) 2000 already included similar powers. The EU and USA also agreed an information exchange agreement between Europol and US agencies that arguably excluded the normal EU data protection provisions.[51]

More generally, in the wake of 9/11 the EU sought to respond by implementing more rapidly proposals that were already within the policy making process, for example, the common arrest warrant, and introducing others that had been on the shopping list of member agencies for some time. After the terrorist attacks in Madrid on 11 March 2004 the European Council issued a declaration and revised plan of action for member states to pursue. The strategic objectives are: to enhance international efforts to combat terrorism; to reduce terrorists' access to finance; to maximize EU and member state capacity to prevent, detect and prosecute terrorists; to enhance the security of transport and borders; to enhance capabilities to deal with the consequences of attacks; and to address the factors contributing to support for and recruitment into terrorism.[52]

Intelligence process: analysis, dissemination and policy

Arguably, too much of the Congressional and media discussion since 9/11 has centred on the search for pieces of information that would, it is assumed, have enabled the 9/11 attacks to be predicted and then prevented. If not the search for the 'smoking gun' then perhaps the search for the 'smouldering datum'! Given what is known about the *modus operandi* of those carrying out the attacks, it is extremely unlikely that such a piece of information exists. Nor was it just a case of the system failing 'to join the dots' between pieces of data so that warning could have been provided though this starts to get closer to the real failure of US intelligence: the failure of processing and analysis.[53] Analysts have always been the poor relations of gatherers within intelligence communities: they enjoy neither the reputation for 'derring-do' associated with HUMINT nor the capacity to generate large profits for equipment suppliers associated with TECHINT. Certainly there *were* failures in gathering prior to

9/11, for example, the failure of the FBI and CIA[54] to develop human sources at home and abroad. But the US intelligence 'community' was already awash with data and it is far from clear that increasing the flow further will enhance the ability to prevent further 'failures'.

The analytical process is fraught with structural problems that cannot be explored in detail here, for example, 'groupthink' and 'mirror-imaging' and the failure to find the weapons of mass destruction that the Western intelligence agencies were apparently convinced still existed in Iraq in 2002 has brought about unprecedented private and public soul-searching. In January 2004 David Kay resigned as head of the Iraqi Survey Group – whose job it was to search for evidence of WMD in Iraq – and in subsequent Congressional testimony[55] admitted that intelligence agencies had failed to recognize that Iraq had all but abandoned its efforts to produce large quantities of chemical and biological weapons after 1991. An institutional post-mortem had actually already started: by August 2003 George Tenet, US Director of Central Intelligence had commissioned internal reviews of tradecraft and the work leading up to the October 2002 National Intelligence Estimate (NIE). Tenet acknowledged that close examination was needed of the extent to which factors such as the history of deception and denial by Saddam Hussein and the very absence of information in key areas, especially after 1998, contributed to a failure to test prevailing assumptions. 'We did not have enough of our own human intelligence', said Tenet, commenting on the risks inherent in information from defectors and indirect information from partner agencies.[56] Early reports of the findings of the House and Senate Intelligence Committees indicate that they, too, found that the CIA relied too much on circumstantial, outdated intelligence and TECHINT.[57]

But perhaps the central controversy regarding the invasion of Iraq has been the apparent politicization of analysis. Both Kay and Tenet denied that CIA analysts had been subjected to political pressure in the run-up to the October 2002 NIE but others have argued otherwise. Kenneth Pollack, a CIA analyst for the Persian Gulf who worked later for the National Security Council (NSC) under Clinton, disputes that the strength of the October 2002 NIE can be put down solely to political pressure because it reflected what the agencies had been saying for some years. However, Pollack does acknowledge that the Office of Special Plans (OSP)[58] set up in the Pentagon was an attempt to manipulate intelligence. Ironically, given the soul-searching now underway in the CIA into its failure to test assumptions, it was the very fact that it *did* question the assumptions of the case for links between Iraq and al-Qaeda that frustrated Defense Secretary Rumsfeld, Under-Secretary Wolfowitz *et al.* So the OSP was created to find evidence of what they believed to be true: that Saddam Hussein had close ties to al-Qaeda and WMD that threatened the region and potentially the US. A particular aspect of the OSP's search for new intelligence was its reliance on Ahmad Chalabi and the Iraqi National Congress, that subsequently became the core for the regime installed after the invasion.[59]

In the UK a Defence Intelligence Staff (DIS) document was leaked to the BBC contradicting Government claims regarding the Iraq–al-Qaeda link.[60] It should be noted that DIS documents do not normally leak in this way and it could only have indicated frustration among intelligence personnel at their work being ignored or misrepresented as it was in the Government's infamous 'dodgy' dossier published in January 2003, most of which consisted of a plagiarized academic article.[61] In the UK the controversy took a tragic turn in July 2003 with the suicide of Dr David Kelly, a leading expert on chemical and biological warfare, in the wake of a BBC broadcast, for which Kelly was the alleged source, to the effect that the Government had knowingly lied in its September 2002 dossier. The Government sought to deal with the controversy by appointing Lord Hutton, a House of Lords judge, to enquire into the circumstances surrounding the death of Dr Kelly.[62] This actually became the third enquiry during the summer 2003 into the Iraq issue: the House of Commons Foreign Affairs Committee (FAC)[63] and the Intelligence and Security Committee (ISC)[64] provided the others. Each had different terms of reference and *modus operandi* and reached slightly divergent conclusions.[65]

In brief, Hutton absolved the Government from blame for just about everything, though was able to do so only by adopting a highly restricted view of what the public would have understood by 'sexing up'. But if the Government took great comfort from this, the predominant press and political reaction was that Hutton was a 'whitewash' and the Government responded a few days later with the appointment of yet another inquiry, to be headed by Lord Butler, that itself became rapidly enmeshed in disputes over the narrowness of the terms of reference. Simultaneously, in the US political pressure had grown steadily and to such an extent that the President, also, was obliged to institute an inquiry he did not want. Bush announced the establishment of a Commission on the Intelligence Capabilities of the United States Regarding Weapons of Mass Destruction[66] with broadly similar terms of reference to the Butler inquiry, that is, they are to compare the state of pre-invasion intelligence with the findings of the Iraqi Survey Group but are also to explore the more general problems involved in gathering intelligence with respect to WMD. Whereas Butler is to report in July 2004, Robb/Silverman will only do so in March 2005, safely after the Presidential election.

Now, some of the arguments regarding politicization of the intelligence on Iraq may seem somewhat tangential to the central issue of whether domestic security agencies are becoming more autonomous and penetrative but there is a significant link. If analytical failures (whether wilful or not) as occurred with respect to Iraqi WMD reinforce government propensities to pursue more aggressive security policies, including the targeting of suspect populations, then any general trend towards a 'security state' is reinforced. If analysis is actually misused for political purposes, then the possibilities for democratic control of intelligence are seriously damaged.

Further damage has been caused by intelligence agencies which have been the perpetrators of misinformation strategies and not just their victim at the hands of Iraqi defectors. Briefing Congress on Iraq's WMD capacity in September 2002 George Tenet (CIA Director) claimed that Iraq had attempted to buy uranium oxide from Niger. The claim reappeared in one of the UK Government's Iraq dossiers and Bush's State of the Union message before the International Atomic Energy Authority (IAEA) in Vienna demonstrated that the documents on which the claim was based were fakes. The finger seems to point to MI6 as a possible perpetrator.[67] Similar strands appear elsewhere: giving evidence to the ISC, David Kelly, just before his suicide, explained in answer to a question from the Chair, Ann Taylor, that within the DIS he liaised with the 'Rockingham cell' that serviced the weapons inspectors in Iraq.[68] This DIS group had the role, according to Scott Ritter, the former weapons inspector, of using intelligence from the United Nations (UN) inspectors in order to sustain in public the claims that Iraq was not in compliance with UN resolutions while ignoring ambiguous or contrary findings.[69] That a similar (if not part of the same) operation had been run by MI6 – Operation Mass Appeal – in the late 1990s was reportedly confirmed.[70]

But there are other dissemination issues apart from that of political manipulation: in the wake of 9/11 the FBI departed from usual practice by circulating a 'watch list' outside of government to banks, car rental, travel and other companies. For some time the Bureau circulated up-dates and corrections but then stopped. But in the meantime it had lost control of who had the list; it appeared on several internet sites and consequently it has proved virtually impossible for those incorrectly identified to have themselves removed from the list.[71]

Another key issue regarding dissemination that is just noted here, there being insufficient space to discuss it in detail, is 'warnings'. Since the perceived 'failure' to predict the 9/11 attacks, the US agencies have, not surprisingly, shown greater readiness to provide warning intelligence to political executives. We have seen varying practices in what they do with it: a tendency in the US to publicize vague warnings that make it very difficult for people to know how to respond (other than stocking up on bottled water and masking tape) while in the UK warnings have been fewer and more specific. On 30 April 2004 the Security Service re-launched its website to include a broad variety of threat assessments and protective security information.[72]

Secrecy, external oversight and 9/11[73]

If 9/11 has produced clear tendencies among political executives to reestablish the agencies' autonomy and capacities for penetration then the role for democratic oversight becomes even more crucial if a wholesale descent into 'national securitism' is to be prevented. The dominant source of the historical autonomy of security intelligence agencies is secrecy. The process of democratization observable since the 1970s saw a number of modifications to the traditional claim of absolute secrecy, for example, freedom of information legislation that normally exempted 'national security' but which provided space in which the agencies' claim of secrecy could be contested and the introduction of oversight bodies whose members enjoyed some degree of access to operational files – the 'brain' of any agency.

In general, the more counter-terrorism is viewed as 'war' then the greater the emphasis given by executives to 'secrecy' (both as counter-intelligence and as an essential prerequisite for 'surprising' enemies). There are several areas in which the US executive has sought to reduce the flow of information: in a memo to federal agencies Attorney General Ashcroft encouraged resistance to freedom of information requests – not in relation to security but more broadly in relation to 'institutional, commercial and personal privacy interests'.[74] The Homeland Security Act seems to have reinforced this tendency by encouraging companies to share with government information about infrastructure that might be vulnerable to attack but in such a way that, if they do so voluntarily, then the same information can be kept secret from, say, environmental regulators and the public in general.[75] The general increase in governmental secrecy in the US in the wake of 9/11 is not restricted to the federal level: almost half of state legislatures have passed exemptions to their FOI laws regarding the availability of information on government buildings, utility plants and other areas considered vulnerable to terrorism.[76]

Legislative and other committees

Democratic control of intelligence requires external review or oversight and this is likely to be provided primarily by specialist committees either *inside* national legislatures, for example, the Intelligence Committees of the US Senate and House of Representatives and the joint committees made up of members of both houses in the UK and Brazilian Parliaments or *outside* such as the Security Intelligence Review Committee (SIRC) in Canada and the Committee for Monitoring of Intelligence, Surveillance and Security Services in Norway. The other potential oversight institution at this level is judges who, in some countries, are involved in the authorization of warrants for intrusive surveillance and more episodic review may be provided by cases heard in courts, but there is insufficient space to deal with this here.

Before UK and US committees inquired into intelligence with respect to Iraqi weapons in 2003, they had investigated the intelligence failure of 9/11. The Joint Inquiry into 9/11 established by the two Congressional intelligence committees has been critical of attempts by the Executive to deny them access to information, for example, the refusal by the FBI to make available for testimony an informer and his handler[77] and that of the Director of Central Intelligence to declassify references to the Intelligence Community providing information to the White House.[78] For those more familiar with Parliamentary regimes, this denial is probably less surprising. For example, in the Canadian Security Intelligence Service Act 1984 Cabinet documents are explicitly excluded from the general rule that SIRC has access to all information (s.39) and in the UK the Minister is the Intelligence and Security Committee's gatekeeper to intelligence files containing 'sensitive' material.[79]

In the struggle for information control in the US the executive has also complained about the leaking of information from House and Senate Intelligence Committees regarding National Security Agency (NSA) interception of two 'warning' messages on 10 September 2001 that were not translated until 12 September. In the face of these complaints, the committee chairs requested a FBI investigation of the leaks.[80] Thus the answer to the question 'who guards the guards who guard the guards' is . . . 'the guards'!

The primary effort of the Congressional committees has been the investigation of the 9/11 'failure' – and some have criticized a relative lack of concern with the Government's legal responses.[81] A report of the Subcommittee on Terrorism of the House Intelligence Committee noted the lack of HUMINT in the CIA and poor dissemination to other agencies; that FBI counter-terrorism was hindered by decentralization and the culture of 'crime-fighting'; and that the NSA needed to be more proactive in information gathering.[82] The joint inquiry by the two Intelligence Committees identified seven areas of investigation including: evolution of the terrorist threat to US and the Government's response; what the Intelligence Community (defined as 14 agencies) knew prior to 9/11; what the Intelligence Community has learnt since 9/11 about perpetrators and clues to explaining the failure; what has emerged about systemic problems impeding the Community; how the Intelligence Community interacts with each other and the rest of the Government in countering terrorism. The overall 'factual' finding was that:

> for a variety of reasons, the Intelligence Community failed to capitalize on both the individual and collective significance of available information that appears relevant to the events of September 11. As a result, the Community missed opportunities to disrupt the September 11 plot by denying entry to or detaining would-be hijackers; to at least try to unravel the plot through surveillance and other investigative work within the US; and, finally, to generate a heightened state of alert and thus harden the homeland against attack.[83]

The Report also itemized 20 'systemic' findings, including: that US intelligence was neither well-organized nor equipped to meet the counter-terrorist challenge; that the foreign intelligence agencies paid inadequate attention to the potential for an attack in the US; that the FBI was unable to identify and monitor effectively the extent of al-Qaeda and other terrorist activity in the US; that the US lacked funding, relevant technology and linguistic capacities; that analytical capacity was inadequate and that there were serious problems with information sharing both within the intelligence community and between it and government authorities.[84] Yet these extensive reports have not stilled criticisms that the oversight performance of the intelligence committees has deteriorated.[85]

By comparison with the extensive external inquiries in the US, that in the UK has been minuscule. The 2001–02 Annual Report of the Intelligence and Security Committee[86] identified some resource pressures in the Security Service, Secret Intelligence Service and Defence Intelligence Staff (para. 61), referred to a Joint Intelligence Committee July 2001 assessment that al-Qaeda attacks were in the final planning stages but that timings, targets and methods were unknown (para. 65); noted the redeployment of staff post-9/11 (paras. 67–9) and the increased Security Service resources in collection and dissemination (para. 72) but, significantly, said nothing about analytical deficiencies. Finally, it noted the lack of linguists (para. 77).

It is important to note the significant methodological differences between these reviews, largely but not entirely determined by the availability of staff. The US Joint Inquiry team had 24 researchers divided into five investigative teams that interviewed officials, reviewed documents and submitted questionnaires not only at the FBI, CIA and NSA but also other departments.[87] Staff reviewed almost 500,000 pages of documents, conducted 300 interviews and participated in briefings and panel discussions involving 600 officials from the intelligence agencies and elsewhere.[88] The UK effort, by comparison, was hampered from the start by the fact that half of the nine-person committee (including the Chair) was newly appointed after the 2001 election. The members themselves 'took evidence' over the year from 37 witnesses (ministers, heads of services and other officials) and made 'visits' to the agencies. But what might properly be described as 'investigative' work fell to the single investigator who was tasked to carry out five investigations during the year, none of which appear to have concerned 9/11.[89] The conclusions drawn by the ISC appear to have been based entirely on briefings from agency heads; at least, there is nothing in the Report to lead one to suppose otherwise. What is especially worrying about the ISC approach is that one can read all their reports since 1995 without finding a single reference to human rights issues. Rather, their overriding concern is with management and efficiency issues.[90]

The concern of senior members of the Joint Congressional Inquiry at what they described as inadequate co-operation from the executive branch led them to endorse the establishment of a separate Commission of Inquiry into 9/11.[91] This idea had been growing in strength for some months, was supported by the families of victims of 9/11 and the House of Representatives had voted to support the idea in July 2002. The White House had opposed the move, saying it would distract the agencies from their primary tasks but then changed its mind.[92] However, it was only after further wrangling between White House and Congress that agreement was reached in the last session before Congress adjourned in 2002 and Thomas H. Kean, former Republican Governor of New Jersey was appointed to head the ten-member National Commission on Terrorist Attacks Upon the United States.[93] Similarly to the experience of the Congressional Inquiry, the Commission has struggled with persistent obstruction from the Executive to providing documents and making key personnel available for testimony[94] but when it did hold public hearings with, *inter alia*, Attorney General John Ashcroft, former FBI Director Louis Freeh, CIA Director George Tenet and National Security Advisor Condoleezza Rice in mid-April 2004 they were questioned vigorously on the basis of the Commission's initial findings itemizing the lack of preparedness throughout the US counter-terrorism architecture.[95]

Conclusion

It is clear from the foregoing that there has been an overall shift towards higher 'penetration' as the agencies themselves and their political masters seek to respond to the widespread perception of 9/11 as a major intelligence 'failure'. However, the heightened political and public interest in the agencies' activities has put them under an unaccustomed spotlight and some of the organizational shifts in the US are clearly aimed at better integrating them within organizational and informational networks, thus, in the short run, arguably reducing their autonomy. Whether this persists in the longer term remains to be seen; it is entirely possible that political attention will wane, at which point the agencies might regain autonomy. If at the same time external oversight bodies adopt a hands-off approach, for example, not wishing to be seen to hinder the 'war on terror', then autonomy is further enhanced. If that happens, then, combined with their increased penetrative powers, we may well see the rebirth of 'independent security states'.

The political consequences of this are clear: a return to the targeting of groups of people on the grounds of their ethnicity or affiliations may be inevitable but it should be checked with equal energy by external oversight bodies in order to guard against abuse of power. If 'liddism' was rightly criticized for its shortsightedness in viewing security conflicts[96] then we should be profoundly concerned that security intelligence strategies based on a more aggressive 'drainism' can only aggravate matters.

Notes

An earlier version of this article was presented to the Security and Intelligence Studies Group Panel on Developments in Global Policing and Security at the Annual Conference of the Political Studies Association, University of Leicester, 14–17 April 2003. This version was completed in May 2004 and there is no discussion of subsequent developments.

1   P. Rogers, *Losing Control: Global Security in the Twenty-First Century* (London: Pluto 2002) p.102.
2   Paul Wolfowitz to NATO Ministers Meeting, September 2001.
3   P. Gill, *Policing Politics: Security Intelligence and the Liberal Democratic State* (London: Cass 1994) p.83.
4   I have wondered whether we might substitute the less masculinist term 'surveillance' that, as A. Giddens defines it in *The Nation-State and Violence* (Berkeley: U. of California Press 1985) pp.181–92, similarly incorporates the two variables of information gathering and 'supervision' or discipline, but this term is used so widely by social and political theorists to discuss governance *in general*, there might actually be benefits to sticking with penetration in order to characterize the more *specific* governance practices of security agencies.
5   J.A. Tapia-Valdes, 'A Typology of National Security Policies', *Yale Journal of World Public Order* 9/10 (1982) p.17.
6   These labels were originally used by W.W. Keller, *The Liberals and J. Edgar Hoover* (Princeton: Princeton UP 1989) and adapted by Gill, *Policing Politics* (note 3). Recent discussions with Ken Dombrowski have helped me to refine the typology.
7   Keller, *The Liberals* (note 4). More generally on US intelligence reform see L.K. Johnson, *A Season of Inquiry: The US Senate Intelligence Investigation* (Lexington: University Press of Kentucky 1985) and K.S. Olmsted, *Challenging the Secret Government: The Post-Watergate Investigations of the CIA and FBI* (Chapel Hill: University of North Carolina Press 1996).
8   With the slight exception of the Interception of Communications Act 1985 that placed previous procedure for obtaining ministerial warrants on a statutory footing.
9   For example, D. McDonald, *Commission of Enquiry Concerning Certain Activities of the RCMP* (Ottawa: Minister of Supply and Services, especially Second Report, 1981).
10   *Washington Post*, 29 November 2002. On the *Handschu* case see P. Gill, *Rounding Up the Usual Suspects* (Aldershot: Ashgate 2000) pp.107–8.
11   *The Observer*, 11 April 2004.

12 *New York Times*, 1 August 2002; 24 November 2002.

13 *New York Times*, 23 August 2002. Yet note the observation that different cultures between law enforcement and intelligence organizations resulted in cautious interpretations of what could and could not be shared so that the wall became 'very high'. G. Treverton, 'Terrorism, Intelligence and Law Enforcement: Learning the Right Lessons', *Intelligence and National Security* 18/4 (2003) pp.121–40.

14 *New York Times*, 15 December 2002; *LA Times*, 11 January 2003.

15 *Sunday Times*, 17 November 2002.

16 *Statewatch*, 13/6 (November–December 2003) pp.2–3.

17 *Washington Times*, 11 April 2002.

18 *LA Times*, 8 December 2003; 21 December 2003.

19 *Independent*, 30 April 2004.

20 C. Walker, *Blackstone's Guide to the Anti-Terrorism Legislation* (Oxford: Oxford UP 2002) pp.147–49.

21 *Statewatch*, 13/6 (November–December 2003) pp.16–17.

22 The US Department of Homeland Security announced on 13 April 2004 that immigrants detailed in terrorism investigations would no longer be held indefinitely without evidence. *LA Times*, 14 April 2004.

23 *Washington Post*, 17 July 2002; 24 February 2002; *New York Times*, 27 June 2002.

24 *New York Times*, 16 January 2002; WP, 21 November 2002.

25 Letter to Senators Susan Collins and Carl Levin, 13 April 2004 <www.fas.org/irp>, accessed April 2004.

26 A snapshot of these in the US is provided in Gill, *Rounding Up the Usual Suspects* (note 10) pp.40–54.

27 Testimony of Robert S. Mueller III, Director FBI, before the Senate Select Committee on Intelligence and the House Permanent Select Committee on Intelligence, 17 October 2002.

28 Most of which now include also CIA agents – *Washington Post*, 23 October 2002.

29 FBI National Press Office Release, 3 April 2002 <www.fas.org/irp/news/>.

30 For example, *Washington Post*, 16 November 2002; *New York Times*, 21 November 2002; 2 December 2002; 6 March 2003.

31 Office of the Inspector General, Audit Division, *The FBI's Efforts to Improve the Sharing of Intelligence and Other Information*, Report 04–10, December 2003, Washington DC: Department of Justice.

32 For example, see *Washington Post*, 16 November 2002; *New York Times*, 15 April 2004. See also House Permanent Select Committee on Intelligence and the Senate Select Committee on Intelligence, *Report of the Joint Inquiry into Intelligence Community Activities Before and After the Terrorist Attacks of September 11, 2001*, December 2002, declassified version pp.349–53.

33 As part of its technology up-grade the FBI is developing its own counter-terrorism database (Terrorism Intelligence and Data – TID) storing information from state and local agencies, DEA, ATF and joint terrorism task forces <www.govexec.com/news/index> (story dated 3 April, accessed 7 April 2003). How this will relate to the database to be developed by TTIC is unclear.

34 For example, *Washington Post*, 3 March 2003.

35 Constructing warehouses has been made technically possible by XML (Extended Markup Language) software that enables previously separate databases to be 'merged' *via* a universal language.

36 For example, *New York Times*, 6 October 2002.

37 Computer Assisted Passenger Pre-Screening II (CAPPS II) <www.ired.com/news> (accessed 7 April 2003).

38 <www.darpa.mil/iao/programs.htm> (accessed March 2003).

39 *New York Times*, 12 February 2003.

40 <www.wired.com/news/privacy/0,1848,60588,00.html?tw=wn_story_related> 25 September 2003 (accessed 7 May 2004).

41 See also *Washington Post*, 1 November 2002; *Guardian*, 24 January 2003; 5 March 2003.

42 *Independent*, 7 March 2003.

43 *Hearing: Article 15–6 Investigation of the 800th Military Police Brigade*, Part One – specific findings of fact, para. 5 <www.globalsecurity.org/intell/library/reports/2004/800-mp-bde.htm> (accessed 6 May 2004).

44 Ibid. para. 10.

45 *The Guardian*, 30 October 2003.

46 *Independent*, 23 April 2004. For cases in both North America and Europe see Human Rights Watch, *'Empty Promises': Diplomatic Assurances No Safeguard against Torture*, Report D1604, April 2004 <www.hrw.org/publications>.

47 For example, *The Guardian*, 7 May 2004.

48 *Washington Post*, 25 January 2003.

49 *Statewatch* 12/3–4 (2002) p.1.

50 <www.aclu.org/SafeandFree> 24 March 2003.

51 *Guardian*, 20 December 2002; *Statewatch*, 29 November 2002, press release.

52 Accessed at <www.statewatch.org/news> 26 April 2004. Statewatch also provides its own 'score-board' on the extent to which the post-Madrid counter-terrorism plans are actually directly relevant. It concludes that almost half of the proposals are more to deal with crime in general and surveillance. Violent crime cannot be simply separated from other crime but it is important to retain an analytical distinction between 'terrorism' and 'organized crime' and to check the propensity of states and police/security agencies to take advantage of security scares to legislate measures that may actually have little to contribute to public safety.

53 For example, R. Whitaker, 'A Poor Bargain', *New Scientist* 174, 29 June 2002, p.26.

54 In particular, see R. Baer, *See No Evil* (New York: Crown Publishers 2002).

55 This can be accessed at <www.nsarchive.org> in the Saddam Hussein Sourcebook.

56 Remarks as prepared for delivery by DCI George Tenet at Georgetown University, Washington DC, 5 February 2004.

57 *Washington Post*, 30 January 2004.

58 K.M. Pollack, 'Spies, Lies and Weapons: What Went Wrong', *The Atlantic Monthly* (January/February 2004).

59 S.M. Hersh, 'Selective Intelligence', *The New Yorker*, 6 May 2003; K. Kwiatkowski, 'The New Pentagon Papers', *Salon*, 10 March 2004.

60 BBC News on-line, 5 February 2003.

61 Most of the dossier was copied without acknowledgement from Ibrahim al-Marashi, 'Iraq's Security and Intelligence Network: A Guide and Analysis', *Middle East Review of International Affairs*, 6/3 (September 2002) .

62 Lord Hutton, *Report of the Inquiry into the Circumstances Surrounding the Death of David Kelly C.M.G.*, 2004. The Report, most of the evidence submitted to it and transcripts of the hearings are accessible at <www.the-hutton-inquiry.org.uk>.

63 House of Commons Foreign Affairs Committee, *The Decision to go to War in Iraq*, Ninth report of Sessions 2002–03, vol. 1, HC 813-I, July 2003.

64 Intelligence and Security Committee, *Iraqi Weapons of Mass Destruction – Intelligence and Assessments*, Cm 5972, September 2003.

65 The Iraq inquiries are discussed in a more detailed study by the present author: 'The Politicisation of Intelligence: Lessons from the Invasion of Iraq', in H. Born *et al.* (eds), *Who's Watching the Spies? Establishing Intelligence Service Accountability* (Washington DC: Brassey's Inc. forthcoming) .

66 Executive Order 13328, 6 February 2004.

67 S. Hersh, 'Who Lied To Whom?' *The New Yorker*, 31 March 2003.

68 Hutton, *Report*, (note 62) para. 112.

69 TV interview with Amy Goodman, 30 December 2003, transcript in *Security and Intelligence Digest*, Intel Research, PO Box 550, London SW3 2YQ.

70 N. Rufford, 'Revealed: How MI6 Sold the Iraq War', *The Times*, 28 December 2003.

71 *Wall Street Journal*, 19 November 2002.

72 <www.mi5.gov.uk>.

73 A more thorough discussion by this author of the impact of 9/11 on oversight is *Democratic and Parliamentary Accountability of Intelligence Services after September 11th*, Working Paper 103, Geneva Centre for Democratic Control of Armed Forces, January 2003. <www.dcaf.ch/publications/Working_Papers/103.pdf>.

74 *San Francisco Chronicle*, 6 January 2002; *Guardian*, 6 March 2002.

75 *Washington Post*, 10 February 2003.

76 *USA Today*, 3 April 2003.

77 *New York Times*, 6 October 2002.

78 E. Hill, *Joint Inquiry Staff Statement*, Part I, House Permanent Select Committee on Intelligence and Senate Select Committee on Intelligence, 18 September 2002 <www.fa-s.org/irp/congress/2002_hr/091802hill.html>.

79 For example, P. Gill, 'Reasserting Control: Recent Changes in the Oversight of the UK Intelligence Community', *Intelligence and National Security*, 11/2 (April 1996) pp.313–31.

80 *Washington Post*, 21 June 2002.
81 Editorial 'Silence on the Hill . . .', *Washington Post*, 5 January 2004.
82 Report of the Subcommittee on Terrorism and Homeland Security, *Counterterrorism Intelligence Capabilities and Performance Prior to 9–11* (Washington DC: House Permanent Select Committee on Intelligence, July 2002).
83 Joint House/Senate Inquiry, *Report* (note 32) p.33.
84 Ibid. pp.33–117.
85 For example, see *Washington Post*, 27 April 2004.
86 Intelligence and Security Committee, *Annual Report 2001–2002*, Cm 5542, June 2002.
87 Hill, *Joint Inquiry Staff Statement* (note 78).
88 Joint House/Senate Inquiry, *Report* (note 32) p.2.
89 Intelligence and Security Committee, *Annual Report 2001–2002* (note 86) pp.5, 29–31.
90 Cf. also K.G. Robertson, 'Recent Reform of Intelligence in the United Kingdom: Democratization or Risk Management?' *Intelligence and National Security* 13/2 (1998) pp.144–58.
91 FAS Project on Government Secrecy, Issue 91, 19 September 2002.
92 *New York Times*, 21 September 2002.
93 *New York Times*, 17 December 2002. Initially it was announced that the Commission would be headed by Henry Kissinger. He shortly declined on the grounds that he was unwilling to disclose his international consulting clients as required by federal law.
94 For example, *New York Times*, 9 July 2003; 3 April 2004.
95 For example, *Washington Post*, 14, 15 April 2004. The staff reports and testimony are available at <www.9–11commission.gov> and reporting deadline is 26 July 2004.
96 Rogers, *Losing Control* (note 1) pp.101–18

Reprinted with permission from Peter Gill, 'Securing the Globe: Intelligence and the Post-9/11 Shift from 'Liddism' to 'Drainism', *Intelligence and National Security* 19, 3, (2004) pp.467–489.

INTELLIGENCE AND COUNTER-INSURGENCY

Further reading: Books and reports

Richard J. Aldrich, *The Hidden Hand: Britain, America and Cold War Secret Intelligence*. (London: John Murray 2001) chapters 12, 22, 25.

Dale Andrade, *Ashes To Ashes – The Phoenix Program and the Vietnam War* (Lexington MA: Lexington Books 1990).

Orrin Deforest & David Chanoff, *Slow Burn: The Rise And Bitter Fall Of American Intelligence In Vietnam* (NY: Simon & Schuster 1990).

Bruce Hoffman, *Insurgency and Counter-Insurgency in Iraq* (Washington DC: RAND, 2004).

Clive Jones, *Ministers, Mercenaries and Mandarins: Britain and the Yemen Civil War 1962–1965* (Brighton: Sussex Academic Press, 2004).

Thomas R. Mockaitis, *British Counterinsurgency, 1919–60*. (London: Macmillan 1990).

Mark Moyar, *Phoenix and the Birds of Prey* (University of Nebraska Press, 2008).

John A Nagl, *Learning to Eat Soup with a Knife: Counterinsurgency Lessons from Malaya and Vietnam.* (Chicago: University of Chicago Press 2005).

Jim Parker, *Assignment Selous Scouts: Inside Story of a Rhodesian Special Branch Officer* (Galago, 2006).

H.S. Rothstein, *Afghanistan and the Troubled Future of Unconventional Warfare* (Annapolis MD: Naval Institute Press, 2006).

Sam C. Sarkesian, *Unconventional Conflicts in a New Security Era: Lessons from Malaya and Vietnam* (Westport CT: Greenwood Press, 1993).

Jonathan Walker, *Aden Insurgency: The Savage War in South Arabia 1962–1967* (Staplehurst: Spellmount 2005).

Further reading: Essays and articles

Captain Christian H. Breede, 'Intelligence Lessons and The Emerging Canadian Counter-insurgency Doctrine', *Canadian Army Journal* 9/3 (2006) pp.24–40.

Lester Grau, 'Something Old, Something New: Guerrillas, Terrorists and Intelligence Analysis', *Military Review* (August 2004) pp.42–9.

Christopher C. Harmon, 'Illustrations of "learning" in counterinsurgency', *Comparative Strategy*, 11/1 (1992) pp.29–48.

Brian A. Jackson, 'Counterinsurgency Intelligence in a "Long War" The British Experience in Northern Ireland', *Military Review*, (January-February 2007) pp.74–85.

K. Jeffery, 'Intelligence and Counter-Insurgency Operations' Some Reflections of the British Experience, *Intelligence and National Security* 2/1 (1987) pp.118–50.

Paul Kan, 'Counternarcotics Operations within Counterinsurgency: The Pivotal Role of Intelligence', *International Journal of Intelligence and Counterintelligence* 19/4 (2006) pp.586–599.

David Kilcullen, 'Counterinsurgency *Redux*', *Survival* 48/4 (2006) pp.111–130

Schlomo Gazit & Michael Handel. 'Insurgency, Terrorism, and Intelligence' in Roy Godson (ed.) *Intelligence. Requirements for the 1980s: Counterintelligence*, (Lexington Mass: Heath, 1986), pp.125–47

Karl Hack, 'British Intelligence and Counter-Insurgency in the Era of Decolonisation: The Example of Malaya.' *Intelligence and National Security* 14/2 (1999) pp.124–155.

Bruce Hoffman, 'Insurgency and Counterinsurgency in Iraq', *Studies in Conflict and Terrorism* 29/2 (2006) pp.103–121.

Kyle Teamey and Jonathon Sweet, 'Organizing Intelligence for Counterinsurgency', *Military Review* (September-October 2006) pp.24–9.

Clive Jones, ' "A reach greater than the grasp": Israeli intelligence and the conflict in south Lebanon 1990–2000', *Intelligence and National Security* 16/3 (2001) pp.1–26.

Charles D. Melson, 'Top Secret War: Rhodesian Special Operations', *Small Wars & Insurgencies* 16/1, (2005) pp.57–82.

Kevin O'Brien, 'Counter-Intelligence for counter-revolutionary warfare: The South African police security branch 1979–1990', *Intelligence and National Security* 16/3, (2001) pp.27–59.

Richard Popplewell, 'Lacking in Intelligence: Some Reflections on Recent Approaches to British Counter-insurgency, 1900–1960.' *Intelligence and National Security* 10/2 (1995) pp.336–352.

Simon C. Smith, 'General Templer and Counter-Insurgency in Malaya: Hearts and Minds, Intelligence, and Propaganda.' *Intelligence and National Security* 16/3 (2001) pp.60–78.

Essay questions

- Why were the British so slow to learn the lessons of intelligence in the context of counter-insurgency?
- What intelligence lessons might we draw from the insurgencies in Rhodesia and South Africa?
- What have proved to be the main intelligence challenges of the campaign in Afghanistan since 2002?
- Should police, military or civil intelligence formations predominate in a counter-insurgency campaign?

28 Intelligence and UN peacekeeping

Hugh Smith

This article reviews the problems and prospects for Intelligence support for UN peacekeeping operations. It agrees that the development of UN intelligence will be shaped by a small group of Western nations with the required experience and global capabilities. Technical intelligence in particular is likely to reinforce the dominance of Western powers. This may evoke an adverse reaction from the majority of its members outside the club. The development of an intelligence function by the UN is required but will have to overcome many political constraints. OM the long term however, UN intelligence might have a certain life of its own. States are losing control over the creation and transfer of information, just as they have lost, to some degree, their monopoly over the means of violence and their ability to regulate national economies.

An old United Nations (UN) hand once observed that 'the UN has no intelligence'. Putting aside the deliberate ambiguity of this remark, it is certainly true that the UN does not collect, process and disseminate intelligence in the directed and comprehensive way that major powers do as a matter of course. The UN is reluctant even to use the word 'intelligence', preferring the term 'information' in order to avoid the usual connotations of subterfuge and secrecy.[1] 'Intelligence' also implies the existence of enemies or, at least rivals – a suggestion that the UN is naturally anxious to avoid. For these and other reasons that are discussed below, the role of, and need for, intelligence capabilities in peacekeeping operations is rarely debated in either UN documents or the public literature.[2]

Whatever terminology is used, the problem of determining what information is required, collecting and assessing this information, and disseminating the resultant intelligence is of growing importance to the UN in its peacekeeping activities. During the Cold War, peacekeeping was, by and large, a matter of monitoring agreements or stable cease-fires that had already been negotiated between the contending parties. Apart from the Congo operation (1960–64), peacekeepers were seldom directly involved in military action. While the UN would have liked better intelligence in its peacekeeping activities, it was able to get by with *ad hoc* and inadequate arrangements. The situation has changed markedly in recent years.

A second generation of peacekeeping operations has emerged in response to a wide range of difficult problems, particularly internal conflicts or the breakdown of law and order.[3] Peacekeepers are liable to find themselves in countries in which no government is in undisputed control, special order has broken down or is on the point of collapse, hostilities are actually under way or imminent and the use of force against UN personnel is a distinct possibility. In these circumstances, roles such as protecting humanitarian aid, disarming factions, monitoring fragile cease-fires, preventive deployment and negotiating agreements among reluctant players have made the requirement for good and timely intelligence overwhelming.

The need for intelligence is being increasingly felt both by the UN and by states contributing to peacekeeping operations. Particularly in more complex and fluid situations, intelligence will be crucial in achieving the goals of the mission laid down by the UN Security Council. Intelligence may also be important for the lives and well being of UN personnel on the ground. With more than 200 peacekeepers killed in 1993 alone, the greater hazards of contemporary peacekeeping have led governments to demand better intelligence both prior to making a commitment to an operation and during its deployment.[4] The anarchical or near-anarchical situations that have created this demand for improved intelligence, however, will also usually make such intelligence more difficult to obtain, keep current and disseminate effectively.

The UN must come to terms with intelligence. But the problems are not easily resolved. Traditionally, intelligence has been produced and used by a particular state for its own purposes. Much of the intelligence is gathered without the consent or even knowledge of the Target State. Intelligence, too, is normally retained under national control, although it may be shared with friendly governments – up to a point. In the UN, however, intelligence takes on a very different shape. It is gathered not in order to be used against enemies – the UN has no enemies of the kind that national intelligence thrives on – but for the purposes of the international community. It is gathered more openly than national intelligence and is unlikely to remain secure in the medium or long term.

The concept of 'UN intelligence' promises to turn traditional principles of intelligence on their heads. Intelligence will have to be based on information that is collected primarily by overt means, that is, by methods that do not threaten the target state or group and do not compromise the integrity or impartiality of the UN. It will have to be intelligence that is by definition shared among a number of nations and that in most cases will become widely known in the short or medium term. And it will have to be intelligence that is directed towards the purposes of the international community. Such a system is unlikely to emerge of its own accord. The UN needs to establish a clear conception of how it wants intelligence to develop in the context of peacekeeping – and perhaps also, of preventive diplomacy.

The need for intelligence

Intelligence is required at all levels and is needed in both the planning and deployment of peacekeeping. Strategic intelligence is obviously required to understand the political situation between the parties to a conflict prior to UN involvement and, once peacekeepers are deployed, to anticipate the political moves of governments or factions, especially if there is a risk of violence.[5] The fundamental importance of political intelligence is self-evident, for the UN is seeking to produce a desired political outcome. Information about the economy and society of the country will also be valuable.

Operational intelligence is required to plan the most effective deployment of resources and to carry out the UN mandate. It will be particularly important in fluid military and political situations. The ability to assess the level of armaments, and the movements, strategies, military potential of and likely threats to peacekeepers by the contending factions is obviously vital. The security or insecurity of transport and supplies is also crucial. In addition, there is the vast array of information that military forces need in order to deploy to and maintain themselves in a given country: terrain; weather; transport routes and their usability; water and electricity supplies; hospital and medical resources; risks from disease; communications facilities and local infrastructure. All of these may affect the viability of the mission in general.

Tactical intelligence is needed by troops on the ground to support peacekeeping activities, such as monitoring cease-fires or border areas and to alert personnel to potential dangers. The identification of breaches of cease-fires, unauthorised troop and weapon movements, the level of demobilisation and the existence of weapons caches can be critical to the maintenance of peace. Such tactical information is liable to pose difficult political problems for the UN and has the potential to take on strategic significance in delicate situations. The management of intelligence at the tactical level, moreover, can be influential in maintaining or losing the UN's credibility among the parties to the conflict. If intelligence is not deftly handled, it is easy for the organisation to gain a reputation for being slow to react and for gullibility and political partiality. At the tactical level, too, counter-intelligence may be necessary if there are elements hostile to the UN.

Current deficiencies and partial remedies

The existing structure of intelligence in peacekeeping operations is largely *ad hoc* at both the planning and deployment stages. The UN's inability to conduct adequate advance planning is one of the acknowledged defects of peacekeeping and is one of the areas currently being strengthened.[6] Some of the problems are inherent, such as the suddenness with which some crises arise, but a weakness is often the lack of relevant intelligence. In some instances, the UN is able to send fact-finding missions or reconnaissance and advance parties (as with the UN Advance Mission in Cambodia (UNAMIC)), but the scope of these missions is usually limited by a lack of time and resources. More often than not, the UN can provide only minimal information to peacekeepers before they are deployed.

In some instances, states are able to provide their own contingents with the necessary intelligence prior to deployment. Some countries will have extensive knowledge of the area concerned, especially if they have been a colonial power there or are regional neighbours. More likely, however, the contributing state will have had time or no connection with the area concerned. Most participants in peacekeeping operations find themselves operating well outside their area of direct military and political interest. Small and even middle powers simply cannot maintain accurate and current intelligence on every part of the world where they might be called upon to take part in peacekeeping operations.

On deployment, peacekeeping missions will establish some kind of headquarters that will have at least rudimentary facilities for receiving and processing what is called 'military information'. In most cases, the intelligence function must be built up over a period of time with the personnel that are available and can be spared from less pressing tasks. Even in major operations, such as the UN Protection Force (UNPROFOR), raw information often had to substitute for intelligence, at least in the early phases when collection plans were lacking and no capacity existed for processing the data gathered. The mixture of nationalities involved also makes for difficult communications as well as revealing national differences in operating procedures and significant variations in the level of training and expertise. There are also differences in attitude between the various nationalities. Some countries will reject the development of an intelligence capacity because they do not appreciate its significance, because they consider it inappropriate for the UN, or because they see their role as simply collecting data without providing analysis.

National contingents, of course, may partly overcome these problems by receiving intelligence directly from their own governments. Again, the ability of countries to do this varies and difficult situations may arise. Same contingents may be better supplied with intelligence than others or, more significantly, better supplied than the force commander. One

UNPROFOR commander, Lieutenant-general Satish Nambiar, for example, could not, as an Indian national, receive intelligence from North Atlantic Treaty Organisation (NATO) sources. In these circumstances, the principle of exclusive operational command by the UN may be undermined and the risk of contingents following orders only from their national authorities heightened.[7]

The ability of national contingents to collect and process intelligence within their area of operations will also vary. Some, perhaps most, will simply lack the resources, expertise and experience to conduct intelligence activities, while some may lack an interest in doing so. A number of countries, however, will incorporate an intelligence capacity into a contingent as a matter of routine. Their doctrine for national defence may also focus on the collection of information and the preparation of intelligence in low-level conflicts. Australia and Indonesia, for example, have concentrated on collecting intelligence for low-level conflicts, although for rather different reasons.

The pooling of intelligence in the course of peacekeeping operations is to be welcomed, but there are limitations. Such dissemination normally requires the approval of national headquarters and may require the sanitising of information. A further distinction may be drawn between intelligence that can be retained by other states and intelligence that can be shown to, but not retained by, other states.[8] Existing intelligence links among NATO countries and between the US and other states have proven particularly useful in allowing information to be shared among the countries concerned. In practice, too, contingents may use their own discretion in passing on information and informal networks will develop among some of the contingents.

In some circumstances, the force commander may be able to receive intelligence from a friendly nation that is not available to other national contingents. In the case of the UN Transitional Authority in Cambodia (UNTAC), for example, the Force Commander, Lieutenant General John Sanderson, was no doubt provided with intelligence not only by his own government in Australia, but also by the United States. From the military perspective, this is unlikely to cause problems since commanders are frequently privy to information that their subordinates are not. The problem is, rather, a political one. As an Australian, General Sanderson could receive intelligence from the US in a way that, for example, an Indian or a Brazilian force commander could not. Countries might thus be denied the command of peacekeeping operations because of their political alignment.

Against this background of partial, *ad hoc* arrangements, there will be intelligence failures, usually minor, but sometimes disastrous. An example was the attempt by US Army Rangers to capture General Aideed in July 1993. A carefully-planned raid was executed on a suspected hideout, only to discover that the building was the office of a UN agency.[9] This failure of intelligence was due in part to a refusal by US forces to share information with the UN. In the subsequent handover to the UN Operation in Somalia (UNOSOM II), by contrast, it was the UN that displayed initial reluctance to accept intelligence support from the United States, because of the organisation's distrust of military intelligence and of US intelligence in particular.[10]

In the face of this patchwork of capabilities and *ad hoc* arrangements, the force commander must do what he can to hold the intelligence function together. The idea of one state playing the lead role in intelligence has been suggested, but this is likely to run into the expected political objections unless one state is playing the lead role in the mission as a whole. In the case of UNPROFOR, the establishment of a headquarters was certainly assisted by a common NATO background, but this is not likely to be a frequent occurrence. In general, an improvement in intelligence capabilities is more likely to occur as part of a wider process of professionalising the military side of peacekeeping in areas such as planning, logistics, training, communications, and command and control.[11]

An important step in this direction was the creation in 1993 of a Situation Centre at UN headquarters to monitor peacekeeping operations. The Centre gathers and processes information from the field on a continuous and systematic basis. The Centre functions for 24 hours a day and seven days a week – a major improvement on the previous arrangements whereby UN headquarters was accessible to peacekeepers in the field for only five days a week from 9 am to 5 pm. With a staff of about 24, the Centre maintains two officers on duty at all times to receive communications from any UN peacekeeping operation.[12] The Centre produces reports on the major operations under way that are then forwarded to the UN Secretary-General, via the Under-Secretary-General for Peacekeeping, by noon each day or more frequently as required.

The Centre, however, does more than simply pass on information received from various transmissions to the UN Secretariat. The Centre has a research and information cell that interprets information received from the field and combines it with data obtained from a wide variety of other sources. The Centre is not a comprehensive intelligence unit, a command centre or a 'war room' (as some US Congressmen call it). It does, however, systematise data and has begun to provide an institutional memory.[13] The Centre is also going some way towards meeting the growing demand from the UN leadership and from contributing states for intelligence about ongoing operations. It is apparent that, once the benefits of timely and accurate intelligence are understood, both national and international decision-makers will tend to seek even more intelligence.

The UN's intelligence efforts in peacekeeping operations have thus been limited both in terms of planning and of conducting peacekeeping operations. Some improvements have been made, but the further development of intelligence capabilities raises a number of important issues that point to major constraints and possible inherent limits on what the UN can achieve.

Intelligence and the impartiality of the UN

The collection of information is a normal part of any operation involving military personnel. The value of locally gathered intelligence from civil disorders, tenuous cease-fires or armed factions has already been emphasised. But the collection of information is an activity that is fraught with political difficulties. The principal concern is that the collection of intelligence by the UN in the course of peacekeeping – whether it is operating within a state or between states – could be seen as compromising the organisation's traditional impartiality towards the contending parties.[14]

It is possible that one or more sides will be reluctant for the UN to acquire information about their activities. One reason for this, of course, is that a party to a conflict has something to hide. It may wish to conceal the fact that it has breached a cease-fire, has moved troops and weapons in contravention of an existing agreement, has evaded undertakings to demobilise forces or simply wishes to feed the UN with false information. It has been a common claim in the former Yugoslavia, for example, that attacks on civilians have been staged by the victim in order to win international sympathy and to denigrate the other side. Unless the UN has some idea of what is actually happening on the ground, it will find that its role as an impartial monitor may be politically compromised or revealed as ineffective.

It is possible, too, that all parties to the conflict will be suspicious of the UN in its gathering of information. Even if one side has scrupulously observed the terms of an agreement, it may still be anxious that information about its positions or activities will be leaked from the UN to its opponents. This is not an unreasonable fear. Some contingents in UNPROFOR, for instance, appear to have provided information, which was acquired through the UN, to the side the contingent favoured. The UN, moreover, normally ensures that its signals are non-secure.[15] This caused much anxiety, for example, for the Israelis during their presence in Lebanon since they feared that signals could be intercepted by their opponents. There may also be a concern that national contingents in a peacekeeping operation could collect information for their own purposes – whether for commercial or security reasons. Everything the UN does in a particular country, moreover, is liable to be observed and, perhaps, bugged by local factions.

In addition to organisational deficiencies and differences of approach, the means available to the UN to acquire reliable and timely information will vary from mission to mission. In some situations, the mere presence of observers and reports from the local population will be extremely useful. The value of patrol forces has also been frequently stressed by experienced peacekeepers.[16] Effective patrolling will potentially reduce risks to peacekeepers rather than expose them to danger. The scope for collecting human intelligence will, of course, depend on local conditions. In parts of Somalia, for example, a friendly population, freedom of movement of forces and support from non-governmental organisations provided favourable conditions.[17] A significant, but by no means total, limitation on the value of patrols may be the lack of knowledge of the local language.

Technical means of collecting information may also be available and appropriate. Where hostilities are under way, the widely taught techniques of crater analysis may reveal the locations of weapons and the origins of munitions employed. In the former Yugoslavia, aerial reconnaissance and mortar-locating radar's (*Cymbeline*) have also proved effective.[18] Aerial photography is often an attractive option, having the advantages that it is cheap, simple and – compared to satellite photography – requires little interpretation. It is also a capability possessed by over 50 states.[19]

There are limits, however, to these techniques. UN personnel may be refused total access to this technology on the grounds, for example, that there is a danger from snipers or mines, or that their safety cannot be guaranteed. The technical means of gathering information may suffer not only from a lack of the relevant resources, but also from inherent problems. Crater analysis, for example, will be less valuable when the same kinds of munitions are used by all sides in a conflict, which is the case, for example, in the former Yugoslavia (where most munitions come from a once-united national army) and Cambodia (where same weaponry dated back to the Second World War). Mines, too, are eminently difficult to track to their source. The use of a mortar-locating radar near Sarajevo by a Ukrainian detachment also ran into particular problems when both sides made it an object of attack and killed eight personnel.

Ideally, of course, clear and agreed rules for the UN to collect information – whether by human or technical means – will be established. But in practice, the UN will commonly be faced with numerous problems that place it squarely in the political arena: should the UN seek out the required information more vigorously and thus risk alienating one or more sides to a conflict? Should information collected about one party be made available to the other, which may happen surreptitiously in any case? Should the UN seek to ensure that information made public does not assist one side or the other? Is it consistent with impartiality for the UN to threaten to publicise information about, say, breaches of a cease-fire? Should the UN ever publicly denounce the offending side by, for example, the release of aerial photography as in the Cuban missile crisis of 1962? Should the UN admit its incapacity to determine who are the perpetrators of significant breaches of a cease-fire or of blatant attacks on civilians?

The political problems of intelligence become greater the more proactive the UN's role becomes. The intention may be to prohibit factions from deploying forces in prohibited areas or to push an offending party towards compliance with the terms of an agreement, but there is a risk that the effect will be to alienate or provoke the party concerned. If the UN is contemplating even more vigorous action, such as air strikes, the political impact will be even greater and the need for intelligence imperative. Clearly the possession of information is never a neutral fact. It makes the UN a player in the politics of the country concerned and it leaves the UN more dependent than ever on intelligence of the highest quality.

It is also important to remember that the UN will not necessarily be able to act on the information it has and that this, too, may carry political disadvantages. It may be clear to the world, for example, that the UN is aware of terrible events occurring before its very eyes, yet the organisation can only look on impotently. Erskine Childers recounts the bitter words of one Bosnian who looked up at a UN aircraft and said 'there goes the UN – monitoring genocide'.[20] In the case of the UN, knowledge also implies responsibility.

The security of UN intelligence

The security of UN intelligence – or, more accurately, the lack of security – is a political minefield and underlies some of the problems discussed in the previous section. Traditionally, intelligence is kept from hostile powers and is confined to those who need to know. Both of these principles are challenged by intelligence in UN operations. It must be reasoned that any information provided to the UN will sooner or later become public knowledge. There are inevitable political reasons for this release of information. A wide range of parties are interested in information relevant to peacekeeping. All of these parties – UN military personnel in the field, UN civilian and military staff; states participating in a peacekeeping operation, as many as 30 or 40 in a single mission; and members of the Security Council, the principal decision-making body for peacekeeping – have a claim upon this information. Peacekeeping does not involve security of information in the conventional sense.

The fundamental reason for the openness of UN intelligence is the fact that the organisation is international and its personnel are multinational. First, on the political level, states tend to have diverse interests in any peacekeeping operation. Once states acquire information that can promote their own interests, the temptation to exploit this information will be strong. Second, the loyalty of personnel working directly and indirectly for the UN will tend to lie, in the last analysis, with their own country. This is not to deny that many individuals can and do maintain a strong loyalty to the UN, but the security of information must always be in some doubt.[21] It is simply impossible to conduct security clearances on UN personnel, a situation which will be exacerbated as more personnel are assigned to intelligence tasks and the numbers of civilian staff and private contractors increase. Fears that the UN could not keep information secure and that UN staff had been infiltrated by supporters of Aideed, for example, apparently contributed to the failures of communication that led to the fire-fight that killed 18 and wounded 78 US soldiers in October 1993.

It can be legitimately asked: whose side are UN intelligence personnel on? The UN Situation Centre provides an interesting case study. In late 1993, the Centre comprised 24 staff, headed by a Canadian civilian with a Belgian Lieutenant-Colonel as deputy. A total of 16 different nationalities were represented – from Australia to Zimbabwe, Norway to

Pakistan, Jordan to Russia. It is to be expected that many of these personnel will be under instructions to report any significant information that goes through the Centre to their national authorities. In the most obvious case, staff who learn of an impending threat to their country's personnel in a peacekeeping force could hardly be expected to hold back such information from their government.

It is worth noting that as far as military personnel are concerned, it is US policy to instruct officers assigned to the UN to put the organisation before their country. This is not so much a conversion to internationalism on the part of the US, but rather the result of a long-term political calculation. The US hopes to avoid awakening suspicion of its motives while encouraging other states to contribute intelligence to the UN. The US can also afford to serve the UN first because its own intelligence sources and agencies are far more numerous and effective than those available to the UN. Most countries are not so fortunate.

Another factor contributing to the openness of UN intelligence is the transparency of peacekeeping operations, which are normally accessible to the world's media in a way that national military operations are not. Since peacekeeping operations are rarely as dangerous, and hence as inhibiting to reporters, as actual hostilities, peacekeeping operations tend to attract media attention.[22] The UN finds it very difficult to prevent reporters from moving around an operational area – the result of a lack of authority as well as a lack of resources – so that the media is often only limited in their access by the unavailability of transport. National contingents, moreover, may actively encourage the media to report on their activities. Peace-keeping operations are thus liable to be compromised, by, for example, the premature disclosure of movements, the revelation of problems and limitations on UN forces, or the exaggerated reporting of risks and casualties with a consequent undermining of morale.

Despite the many problems in the security of intelligence, there are two compensating factors. First, is the short lifespan of much intelligence. Once it becomes widely known, most intelligence ceases to be sensitive because the event has already occurred or relevant action has been taken. Provided that sources are not compromised, which is generally less of a problem in the case of the UN, subsequent disclosure is not necessarily undesirable. Second, is that the insecurity of intelligence is more likely to prove inconvenient than fatal. Most peacekeeping operations, most of the time, do not involve the use of force by or against the UN. Nonetheless, it is precisely in the most dangerous situations that secure intelligence is most needed.

Sources of information

The sources of information available to the UN are in principle as diverse as those open to states, although differences naturally exist. It is not expected, for example, that the UN will make use of spies or agents or resort to bribery and blackmail in its quest for information. Such covert information gathering is seen as contrary to the ethic of peacekeeping and as a breach of the sovereignty of the targeted nations. It also leaves all parties to a conflict suspicious of what the UN might know or what the UN might mistakenly believe about them. The subsequent revelation of covert activities would also prove highly embarrassing and counter-productive. Nonetheless, the UN may receive unsolicited information from all kinds of sources, including individuals and organisations. In some cases, national laws will have been broken by the informants. The UN Special Commission on Iraq, for example, received secret tip-offs, unsolicited documents and many other kinds of information about Iraqi weapons capabilities.[23] Such informal sources clearly require delicate handling.

The principal sources of intelligence open to the UN, however, are essentially 'above board'. This does not mean that they rely purely on the cooperation of the parties to a conflict, but that the methods of collection are overt. Indeed, there are many sources of information that can be turned into intelligence for peacekeeping purposes and access to them is perhaps the least of the difficulties surrounding UN intelligence. Nonetheless, each source has its own special characteristics.

Member-states

The UN can call upon any of its over 180 members to provide information and since the end of the Cold War there are signs that member-states are increasingly willing to respond. The intelligence-rich members of the UN – notably the US, Britain and France – have become significant participants in peacekeeping, while Russia has been actively supporting the UN in certain operations. Even if the major powers do not have personnel in a particular mission, they may well be willing to assist the operation by providing intelligence. At the same time, the contributions of middle and small powers should not be overlooked. There are many areas of the world that do not attract much attention from the major powers   Central Africa, for example – where neighbouring countries may be best placed to provide information for the UN.

In encouraging member-states to contribute intelligence for peacekeeping, the UN can take various approaches. One useful strategy is to play off one state against another. It can be argued that a UN operation should not rely on information provided by only one or two states and that other states should ensure that their data are also given to the UN. Another strategy is to establish permanent channels of communication with member-states. The Situation Centre, for example, has acquired a computer-based system for transferring information known as the Joint Deployable Intelligence Support System (JDISS).[24] This allows the Centre to talk to databases in other countries that have the same system, notably the US and one of two NATO countries. The interchange of information is, of course, closely controlled by each state, but the basis for greater collaboration has thereby been established.

The principle long-term approach must be to accustom States to sharing information and to establish confidence in the ability of the UN to use information effectively and discreetly. This will be greatly enhanced by political support at the highest level. In January 1993, for example, President Bush set out US policy:

> To the extent prudent, US intelligence today is . . . being used in dramatically new ways, such as assisting the international organisations like the United Nations when called upon in support of crucial peacekeeping, humanitarian assistance and arms control efforts. We will share information and assets that strengthen peaceful relationships and aid in building confidence.[25]

This sort of commitment, which can be maintained even if the US does not send personnel, is essential to help the UN price information out of national intelligence agencies that are unaccustomed to sharing information with international organisations.

The genuine difficulties that exist for member-states in providing information to an international organisation cannot be ignored, especially by an organisation that does not have effective security classification procedures or security practices. The UN has not needed such procedures and practices in the past and may, as suggested above, find it impossible to implement them fully. National agencies are, therefore, likely to retain their natural concern with compromising sources, national-security classification requirements, sensitivity towards neighbours and allies, third-party restrictions, information that has been illegally obtained and domestic political factors.[26] Giving away hard-won information goes 'against the grain'.

These same organisations, however, are also facing the challenge of diminishing resources. A number of governments, especially in the West, have come to see cuts in intelligence as part of the peace dividend. One consequence may well be less support for the UN, but an alternative response could be a search for new roles. Support for UN peacekeeping might prove an attractive budget-enhancing or, at least, budget-protecting option for national intelligence organisations.

Open sources

National sources of intelligence are not necessarily reliable or appropriate for the UN's needs. To reduce reliance on member-states, the UN can make use of open sources that are becoming increasingly varied and accessible. There are traditional public sources used by journalists, scholars and other investigators – books, journals, magazines, industry publications, government documents, legislative reports and records (notably the US Congressional Record), commercial registers, such as the Lloyd's Register of Shipping, and the data collected by institutions, such as the Stockholm International Peace Research Institute and the International Institute for Strategic Studies.

For current information, the most accessible open sources are television and radio networks. While CNN, for example, can arouse public concern over humanitarian issues, it is also invaluable in providing continuous information on many conflicts around the world and is keenly watched in the Situation Centre. There are also numerous national and international news services available and it is politic for the UN to subscribe to a wide range of these – if only to allay suspicions that it is reliant on one or two agencies identified with particular countries.

In recent years, the world information market has grown even wider as certain governments have sought to make money through the sale of information. Russia has opened its archives to raise hard currency, while the Central Intelligence Agency is also de-classifying material for sale. Satellite data are also increasingly available.[27] The Situation Centre already buys information from the French SPOT satellite, which has a resolution of 25 meters. A recent entrant to the satellite data market is Russia, which is reported to be willing to sell imagery with a resolution of two metres.[28] While low-resolution imagery is primarily of background value, the signs are that better-quality imagery will soon become readily available to the UN, as it will to any interested party.

Other international agencies

In principle, the UN has access to information from a great variety of international agencies and organisations that could be of relevance to peacekeeping. Its own specialised agencies, such as the World Health Organisation, the UN Educational, Scientific and Cultural Organisation, the International Labour Organisation, the Food and Agriculture Organisation and the UN Industrial Development Organisation, together with programs such as the United Nations High Commission for Refugees, the United Nations Development Programme and the United Nations Environment Programme, all gather information on population, health, economic development, refugees, educational and scientific programmes, and environmental issues for their own particular purposes. Outside the UN itself there are various international regimes dealing with such matters as nuclear non-proliferation, the control of chemical and biological weapons and the transfer of conventional arms and missile technology.

The use by the UN of information acquired by such organisations, however, raises problems of principle and practice. Data are provided by a state or collected by an agency for the purposes of that agency. Should such information be made available to the UN for peacekeeping operations (or any other purpose for that matter)? There is a risk that the integrity of an agency will be questioned and the flow of information to it compromised if it supplies information to other organisations – even the UN.

On the other hand, could information gathered by the UN in the course of peacekeeping be properly put to other purposes. In some instances, such a purpose may be directly related to the peacekeeping operation, for example war-crimes trials arising from a conflict in which the UN has been involved through peacekeeping. This may create a reluctance among states opposed to such trials to supply information to the UN. There is also the concern – manifest in the case of the former Yugoslavia – that the threat of war-crimes trials will cause local military and political leaders to resist a negotiated settlement. Further questions would arise over the transfer of information gained during peacekeeping to other international agencies for entirely unconnected purposes.

UN-owned sources

Apart from collecting information through its own officials and through peacekeeping forces on the ground, the UN can make use of its own technical means to gather data. This has already been done on a small scale in some peacekeeping operations in which UN forces have already made use of some fairly sophisticated technologies. Night-vision binoculars, for instance, have been used by peacekeepers in Lebanon, Kuwait and Western Sahara, although they are expensive at over $3,000 each and may be limited by ground haze. Attention has also been given to the prospect of the UN acquiring advanced technology for information gathering. At the top of the range of options for new technology are observation and communications satellites that would be owned and operated by the UN. These would certainly prove an expensive undertaking and a source of disputes over funding, the areas to be targeted, access to the data collected and the staffing of the agency.

There are more down-to-earth, less contentious technologies, however, that have a range of possible uses.[29] The Synthetic Aperture Radar, for example, can be employed to search for weapons caches under a jungle canopy and is potentially useful when peacekeepers have the responsibility of disarming factions in a civil war. Passive ground sensors can pick up vehicle movement and, in favourable conditions, human activity. Low-altitude drones, which are difficult to detect on radar and pose no risk to pilots' lives, could be of particular value when the UN is monitoring a cease-fire or contested territory and is constrained in its movements.

Some of these technologies, however, have drawbacks as means of collecting intelligence. Such technologies are liable to be expensive, to suffer technical limitations and to require skilled operation and interpretation. To secure maximum value from technical methods, moreover, the UN would need to develop a body of expertise among its own personnel or gain access to such expertise from member-nations. Both options pose difficulties. Nonetheless, the attractiveness to the UN of control over its own assets is likely to be high – primarily to reduce reliance on information provided by national governments that may not always be forthcoming. In theory, too, the wider use of such technology could reduce the cost of peacekeeping or allow the UN to use its limited manpower more effectively.[30]

Technology, of course, will never remove the need for other sources of intelligence. It cannot provide the political knowledge essential to peacekeeping. It cannot substitute for the operational and tactical intelligence that can only be obtained by human contact on the ground. Nor will technology fill the gap left by the UN's substantial inability – for practical and ethical reasons – to gather secret information by covert means. As with any other organisation that makes use of intelligence, the UN will have to combine its sources of information as best it can and exploit to the full those in which it has an advantage.

Institutionalising UN intelligence

The desirability of a coordinated and comprehensive intelligence capability in UN peace-keeping operations hardly needs demonstration. The barriers to developing such a capability are equally self-evident – the political sensitivity of acquiring and exploiting information, the lack of security of information and problems of access. Nonetheless, certain steps have been taken towards the development of an intelligence capability in some areas. How far can this process go? Can UN intelligence for peacekeeping be institutionalised?

One important factor will be the natural pressure for the UN to establish its own intelligence system, with its own means of collection, analysis and dissemination. It is a trend encouraged by the prospect of reduced reliance on national sources of intelligence and by the potential for the UN to gain access to data from other international agencies and to acquire its own information-gathering technology. The major Western powers appear to support such a development – or at least not to oppose it – but this is no doubt based on the assumption that the West will be able to retain a dominant role in any UN intelligence function.

A further pressure for the creation of a UN intelligence system is the attraction of preventive diplomacy, which requires a strong information base. This led to the establishment in 1987 of an Office of Research and Collection of Information in order to provide an early warning of conflicts and to suggest options for dealing with them to the UN Secretary-General.[31] The Office was abolished in 1992 following the reorganisation of the Department of Political Affairs, but the need for early warning still remains. Boutros Boutros-Ghali's *An Agenda for Peace*, published in 1992, asked member-states to 'be ready to provide the information needed for effective preventive diplomacy'.[32] In the following year, the UN Secretary-General pointed out that the UN had set up more fact-finding missions in 1992–93 than in any other year.[33] The thirst for information in the field of preventive diplomacy may thus provide a continuing basis for intelligence in peacekeeping.

Proposals have been made for the establishment of a permanent intelligence unit within the UN. The Australian Foreign Minister, Senator Gareth Evans, for example, has suggested that 'a group of professionals from various countries with expertise in intelligence . . . be recruited and approved by the Security Council'.[34] The group, it was suggested, would have access to classified information in order to provide independent advice to the Council. Several concerns exist about this and similar proposals. Could military or civilian officials sever their national connections and become genuinely independent? Would such impartiality be given credibility by member-states? There are also organisational difficulties. Could the UN provide adequate training for its staff or keep abreast of current expertise? How would the UN deal with the recurrent problems of recruiting high-quality staff while satisfying demands for national representativeness?

The institutionalisation of UN intelligence also raises questions about effectiveness. How efficient would such a bureaucracy be? A large and expensive organisation might produce little in the way of results, especially as far as peacekeeping is concerned. Such an organisation might also become prey to the defects common to intelligence agencies in general, such as rigidity, narrow views of the world or obsessive concern with secrecy. The organisation might also fall into the temptation of using agents and other covert means of information gathering – or be suspected of doing so. Any process of institutionalisation is liable to entrench undesirable as well as desirable features.

The task of establishing an effective UN intelligence function might be eased by the development of information centres based on regional organisations. Centres of this kind would gather data on a wide range of topics of concern to regional states. In Europe, for example, there are plans to establish a Western European Union Space Centre to collect and coordinate satellite data and make it available to member-states.[35] The function of this Centre would be to assist in the monitoring of arms-control agreements, regional crises, environmental change and other agreed purposes, but the relevance to peacekeeping is apparent. Proposals have also been put forward for the European Union to establish an intelligence organisation.[36]

In South-east Asia, there has been widespread discussion about confidence-building measures and transparency as part of a common effort to improve mutual security.[37] A regional data centre has been mooted and it would be a logical step forward for the states of the region. Centres of this kind would avoid the political difficulties entailed in establishing UN-owned agencies in a region, while being able to provide information to the UN for a wide range of purposes. Nonetheless, any agreement between a regional agency and the UN on how and when to provide information would entail a delicate balancing of interests

Prospects and pressures

It is apparent that any development of UN intelligence will be heavily shaped by a small group of Western nations. They, almost exclusively, have the knowledge, experience and global reach that is required. In the UN Situation Centre, for example, 17 of the 24 staff were drawn from Western Europe, North America and Australia and generally occupied the senior positions. Procedures in the Centre are based on Western practice, while English is spoken and used for all written reports. Any extension of the use of technology in intelligence gathering for the UN, moreover, would only reinforce the dominance of Western powers, both practically and symbolically.[38]

Such developments will serve to emphasise the hegemony of the major Western powers – in terms not of military power, but of information. Substantial reliance on Western intelligence by the UN could well produce an adverse reaction from the majority of its members outside the club. It is already a common complaint among Third-World nations that they provide the majority of peacekeeping personnel, but play relatively little part in the direction and management of peacekeeping operations. These complaints will only grow louder if the UN increases its reliance on Western powers for intelligence. The reality is, however, that it may have little other option.

The development of an intelligence function by the UN, if it is to occur at all, will have to observe these and other political constraints. It is not a matter primarily of financial and personnel resources, much less of technology. Nor will the future of intelligence in UN peacekeeping operations be determined by bureaucratic pressures, favourable as they may be, or by the growing desire for intelligence by the UN leadership. Nor will the domination of particular powers in itself produce an intelligence capacity. In the final analysis, it will be a matter of politics. The principal determinant will be the role of the UN relative to the interests of its members and the commitment members are prepared to make to the organisation.

Nonetheless, it might be supposed that intelligence could have a certain life of its own. States are losing control over the creation and transfer of information, just as they have lost, to some degree, their monopoly over the means of violence and their ability to regulate national economies. If we are entering the 'information age', greater opportunities may exist in the future for the UN to enhance its influence through peacekeeping, and other activities, by controlling and managing intelligence.

Acknowledgments

The author is grateful to a number of military personnel and civilian officials for helpful discussions on this topic. An earlier version of this paper was presented at a conference on 'Intelligence and Australian National Security Policy', held at the Australian Defence Studies Centre, Canberra, 25–26 November 1993.

Notes

1 Intelligence is a 'dirty word' according to the International Peace Academy, *Peacekeeper's Handbook* (New York: Pergamon Press, 1984), p. 39.
2 The topic is barely mentioned in the UN Secretary-General's report, *Improving the Capacity of the United Nations for Peace-keeping*, A/48/403, 14 March 1994. Some discussion is contained in International Peace Academy, *Peacekeeper's Handbook*, pp. 59–62, 120–21, which notes that 'the intelligence concept' may be required in certain future operations.
3 For discussions of the nature of contemporary peacekeeping, see John Mackinlay and Jarat Chopra, *A Draft Concept of Second Generation Multinational Operations 1993* (Providence, RI: Thomas J. Watson Institute for International Studies, Brown University, 1993); Cathy Downes, 'Challenges for Smaller Nations in the New Era of UN and Multinational Operations', in Hugh Smith (ed.), *Peacekeeping – Challenges for the Future* (Canberra: Australian Defence Studies Center, 1993), and 'Demobilization after Civil Wars', in IISS, *Strategic Survey 1993–1994* (London: Brassey's for the IISS), pp. 25–31.
4 For the British position, see British reply to the Secretary-General, *United Nations Peacekeeping* (London: HMSO, July 1993), pp. 4 and 7–8.
5 For an example of timely information passed to the UN Special Representative in the United Nations Transition Assistance Group (Namibia), see Margaret Thatcher, *The Downing Street Years* (London: Harper Collins, 1993), pp. 528–29.
6 The report of the UN Secretary-General, *Improving the Capacity of the United Nations for Peace-keeping*, pp. 36–37.
7 On the importance of this principle, see *ibid.*, pp. 25–27.
8 See Joint Chiefs of Staff, *Joint Doctrine for Intelligence Support to Operations* (Washington DC: Joint Publication 2–0, Joint Staff. 1993), pp. VII, 1–2.
9 Ruth Sina, 'Warlord Slips Through Wide Intelligence Net'. *The Australian*, 7 October 1993, p. 6.
10 Lieutenant-Colonel David J. Hurley, 'Operation Solace', *Defence Force Journal* (Australia), no. 104, January/February 1994, p. 33.
11 See the report of the UN Secretary-General, *Improving the Capacity of the United Nations for Peace-keeping*, pp. 28–39.
12 Staffed initially through the voluntary secondment of staff by member-states, an establishment of 15 has recently been approved. Supplementation by member-states will, therefore, still be needed.
13 Mats R. Berdal, 'Fateful Encounter: The United States and UN Peacekeeping', *Survival*, vol. 36, no. 1, Spring 1994, p. 46.

14 Mats R. Berdal, *Whither UN Peacekeeping?*, Adelphi Paper 281 (London. Brassey's for the IISS, 1993), p. 43.

15 *Ibid.*, p. 8. See also International Peace Academy, *Peacekeeper's Handbook*, pp. 39 and 120.

16 The scope for using patrols to collect information is emphasised in International Peace Academy, *Peacekeeper's Handbook*. pp. 105–14.

17 Lieutenant-Colonel Geoffrey Peterson, 'Human Intelligence and Somalia – A Cost Effective Winner for a Small Army'. *Defence Force Journal* (Australia), no. 104, January/February 1994, p. 37.

18 General Rose: 'Looking for a Return to Normality', *Jane's Defence Weekly*, 11 June 1994, p. 5.

19 Michael Krepon and Jeffrey P. Tracey, ' "Open Skies" and UN Peacekeeping', *Survival*, vol. 32, no, 3, May/June 1990, pp. 261–62 and 263.

20 'The United Nations in the 1990s: Restoring the Vision', a seminar at the Peace Research Centre, Australian National University, 26 August 1993.

21 The possibility also exists that UN personnel could use information for private gain and would be susceptible to blackmail or bribery.

22 On procedures for dealing with the media, see International Peace Academy, *Peacekeeper's Handbook*, pp. 76–78 and 340–42.

23 Remarks by Timothy T. Trevan, in United Nations, 'Disarmament – New Realities: Disarmament, Peace-building and Global Security', excerpts from panel discussions at a conference held at the United Nations, New York, 20–23 April 1993 (New York: United, Nations, 1993), p. 262.

24 Berdal, 'Fateful Encounter', p. 46.

25 George Bush, *National Security Strategy of the United States* (Washington. DC: White House, January 1993) p. 18.

26 In Bosnia-Herzegovina, for example, the UN command received no intelligence from national sources because of the lack of security and the reluctance of nations to supply intelligence. See Brigadier Roderick Cordy-Simpson, 'UN Operations in Bosnia-Herzegovina', in Smith (ed.), *Peacekeeping*, p. 106.

27 General Lewis Mackenzie indicated the potential value of satellite data when he remarked that 'Sarajevo cried out for things like satellite imagery'. Cited in Peter Saracino, 'Polemics and Prescriptions', *International Defence Review*, vol. 26, no. 5, May 1993, p. 370.

28 Bhupendra Jasani, 'The Value Of Civilian Satellite Imagery', *Jane's Intelligence Review*, vol. 5, no. 5, May 1993, p. 235.

29 Details are taken from Krepon and Tracey, 'Open Skies'; and William J. Durch, 'Running the Show: Planning and Implementation', in Durch (ed.), *The Evolution of UN Peacekeeping* (New York: St Martin's Press, 1993), pp. 69–71.

30 Krepon and Tracey, 'Open Skies', p. 251. This is disputed in a Canadian study. See Stephan B. Flemming, *Organizational and Military Impacts of High-Tech Surveillance and Detection Systems for UN Peacekeeping*, Project Report 535 (Ottawa: Operational Research and Analysis Establishment, Department of National Defence, 1992), p. 3.

31 Gareth Evans, *Cooperating for Peace: The Global Agenda for the 1990s and Beyond* (Sydney: Allen and Unwin, 1993), p. 65.

32 Boutros Boutros-Ghali, *An Agenda for Peace: Preventive Diplomacy, Peacemaking and Peace-Keeping* (New York; United Nations, 1992), p. 14.

33 Boutros Boutros-Ghali, 'Agenda for Peace – One Year Later', *Orbis*, vol. 37, no. 3, Summer 1993, p. 325.

34 Evans, *Cooperating for Peace*, p. 163. See also remarks by William Colby, former Director of Central Intelligence, in *Disarmament – New Realities*, pp. 254–55.

35 Jasani, 'Civilian Satellite Imagery', p. 235.

36 Jaap Donath, 'A European Community Intelligence Organization', *Defence Intelligence Journal*, vol, 2, no. 1, Spring 1993, pp. 15–33.

37 Desmond Ball, 'Arms and Affluence: Military Acquisitions in the Asia-Pacific Region', *International Security*, vol. 18, no. 3, Winter 1993/94, pp. 105–12.

38 Flemming, *Organizational and Military Impacts*, p. 9.

Reprinted with permission from Hugh Smith, Intelligence and UN Peacekeeping, *Survival* 36/3 (1994): 177–97

29 Intelligence and the International Security Assistance Force in Afghanistan (ISAF)

Joop van Reijn

The International Security Assistance Force (ISAF) mission in Kabul depended heavily on intelligence for its effectiveness. This essay describes the intelligence preparations that Germany and the Netherlands made prior to taking over the ISAF mission from Turkey as lead nations in 2003. It discusses both the specific intelligence and security problems of ISAF together with the interaction with national intelligence components of other contributing nations and local Afghan services.

Introduction

On 10 February 2003, the Headquarters of the First German Netherlands Army Corps (HQ 1GE/NL Corps) took over from Turkey, the command of the International Security Assistance Force (better known as ISAF) in Kabul, Afghanistan. During the preparations for the handover ceremony, an explosive device was detected and removed from the area where the ceremony was to take place. Later that day, two rockets exploded near the camp where the troops were based, forcing them to take shelter in the bunkers. These incidents were typical for the environment in which the two lead nations were to operate for the next six months. Nonetheless, the Headquarters' first situation report describes the overall situation that day in Kabul as quiet. Missions like ISAF depend heavily on effective intelligence. This article will review from an intelligence perspective how Germany and The Netherlands prepared for this mission as lead nations, how they operated and what can be said in terms of experiences and outcome.

The political situation in Afghanistan in 2003

Afghanistan is about two times the size of Germany. Important neighbours are Pakistan to the East, and Iran to the West. There is quite a variety of ethnic groups in the country. The Afghan population is about 29 million, ethnically divided over Pashtun (42%) in the South and East; Tajiks (27%) and Uzbeks (9%) in the North; and Hazara (9%) in the Midwest (and 13 % others). The two main languages are Dari (50%) – mainly spoken in the North and West, and Pashtu (35%) – mainly spoken in the South and East. About 80% of the population is Sunni Muslim[1]. An area particular worth mentioning are the so called Tribal Areas (N and S Waziristan) in the Southeast, on the Afghan/Pakistan border, where Pakistan authority and control are very limited. From the mid-nineties, Afghanistan was dominated by the fundamentalist Taliban regime, led by Mullah Omar. Internationally isolated, the regime provided hospitality to the terrorist Al Qaeda movement of Osama Bin Laden. Following the terrorist attacks in the United States in September 2001, the US, together with local Afghan opposition forces, united in the Northern Alliance, launched a military operation in

Afghanistan, operation Enduring Freedom. The objective was to remove the Taliban regime as well as the Al Qaeda leadership and powerbase in Afghanistan. The resulting *failed state* had to be rebuilt[2]. A broad based, multi-ethnic, politically balanced and freely chosen Afghan administration had to be formed. In the Bonn Agreement of December 2001, all the local parties and factions agreed on a road map for the future of Afghanistan. A Transitional Authority (TA) was formed, led by Hamid Karzai. Elections for a temporary government were to be held and a new constitution had to be formulated.

ISAF's mission in Kabul

Late December 2001, the UN adopted United Nations Security Council Resolution (UNSCR) 1386, which provided for an International Security Assistance Force. ISAF's mission was to provide a secure environment in and around Kabul for the Afghan TA and the UN, to be able to implement the Bonn Agreement. ISAF was not, however, a formal UN peacekeeping mission. Rather, it was an organisation of voluntary contributing nations, mainly European, operating under a UN-mandate[3]. The troops were organised in the so called Kabul Multinational Brigade (KMNB), and involved nations like the United Kingdom, France, Italy, Germany, Netherlands, Austria, the Scandinavian countries and some East-European countries as well. The size of the force was limited to around 5000 troops and a headquarters, provided by a lead nation, initially the United Kingdom and subsequently Turkey. Its area of responsibility was limited to Kabul and its direct vicinity, situated at 1800 meters altitude in a wide valley with a very high mountain range, the Hindu Kush, rising steeply to the North and with a mixed population of about 3 million people. Tasks of ISAF included ensuring a safe environment, rebuilding Afghan security institutions, operating Kabul International Airport (KIA – a Belgian responsibility) and generally improving the quality of life in the city[4].

In the fall of 2002, the governments of Germany and The Netherlands decided on a joint lead-nation role for ISAF. The German and Dutch decision to jointly assume the lead nation role in ISAF III was a logical step. Both nations contributed to the KMNB from the start. Germany was in command of the brigade as of March 2002. Further, a suitable Headquarters was available at short notice, HQ 1st GE/NL Corps in Münster, which had just qualified as a multinational High Readiness Force Headquarters for NATO[5]. On the intelligence side, a year earlier, both nations had gained valuable experience in Task Force Fox in Macedonia (FYROM) under Dutch command, working closely together and sharing intelligence capabilities and information.

Intelligence activity at three levels[6]

Preparing and executing a mission like ISAF requires intelligence activity at three different levels. At home, strategic intelligence support is given to the lead-nation governments for political decision making and direction. In Germany, this involved the *Bundes Nachrichten Dienst* (BND) for signals intelligence (SIGINT), human intelligence (HUMINT) and analysis, the *Amt für das Nachrichtenwesen des Bundeswehrs* or Bundeswehr Military Intelligence Centre (BMIC) for military intelligence and the *Militärische Abschirm Dienst* (MAD) for military security issues. In The Netherlands, all these intelligence roles were combined in a single organisation, the Defence Intelligence and Security Service (NL-DISS). This almost automatically put the NL-DISS in a co-ordinating role. As soon as it became clear (in the summer of 2002) that Germany and The Netherlands were considering making HQ 1st GE/NL Corps available as HQ ISAF, the BND and the NL-DISS bilaterally concluded that very close co-operation and sharing of intelligence was necessary in order to present the two governments involved with a single intelligence assessment, on which decision making could be based.

At the level of military headquarters, the operational level, intelligence support was required for translating political guidance into military direction, and for supporting the mission's political and military objectives. The *Einsatzführungskommando der Bundeswehr* or Bundeswehr Operations Command (BwOpsCmd) in Potsdam was appointed the Joint Commander. And his Intelligence Chief or J2 was tasked with providing operational intelligence and required capabilities to HQ ISAF. Inputs came from BMIC and NL-DISS. Remarkably, the BND did not involve itself at this level and, throughout the operation, never participated in any of the co-ordinating meetings in Potsdam. Here again, it was the NL-DISS which had to take the initiative for periodical co-ordination at the level of BwOpsCmd.

And finally at troop level, the tactical level, intelligence activity was required directly in support of military tasks and responsibilities. This was the responsibility of the J2 of HQ 1st GE/NL Corps, a German Colonel. In his staff, a separate J2X element, led by a Dutch LtCol, was responsible for counterintelligence, security and co-ordination of tactical human intelligence[7]. An MAD representative was part of this CI-element. At this level, fact finding missions in Afghanistan were conducted as early as Oct and Nov 2002, to assess the situation and required capabilities. A bilateral seminar on HUMINT was organised to improve mutual understanding. And prior to deployment, the NL-DISS organised a large scale co-ordinating meeting in December 2002 in The Hague, involving all German and Dutch intelligence services and all intelligence players at the military level of BwOpsCmd and HQ ISAF to ensure an effective intelligence structure.

As indicated earlier, HQ 1st GE/NL Corps was not just a bilateral affair, but already a multinational high readiness HQ. As HQ ISAF III, this was even more so, with 12 nations involved. Thus, also the J2 Staff was multinational in composition, around 20 staff from 9 different nations of which 50% were German, 20% Dutch, and 30% others, including non-NATO nations which were contributing troops to ISAF[8].

Intelligence structure

The first challenge was setting up an effective intelligence structure. Typically in crisis management, a seamless flow of intelligence is required between the various commandlevels involved in the operation. Hence, a secure communication system is required to pass highly classified intelligence easily up and down the chain of command. Preferably, the system should also be capable of distributing intelligence at tactical level within the command itself. For Germany and The Netherlands, a logical choice was to make use of existing NATO systems like BICES (Battlefield Intelligence Collection and Exploitation System). This however, generated long and arduous discussions about the involvement of non-NATO nations[9]. Pending the outcome of this debate, the German national system JASMIN was used as a back up. To this end, Dutch intelligence was given access to JASMIN.

A controversial element in this structure is the so called National Intelligence Cells, or NICs. When contributing to risky crisis management operations, governments are normally keen to receive information directly from the crisis area, rather than through a long (and possibly filtered) chain of command. Also, there should be a possibility to feed crucial national intelligence directly into the military operational process, when urgency so requires.

To this end, NICs are deployed, preferably co-located with the commanding headquarters. Germany and The Netherlands decided to co-locate their NICs and work closely together, so as to avoid any discrepancy in national reporting. In the GE-NIC, the BND, BMIC and MAD were represented, including a human intelligence capability. NL-NIC contained similar capabilities, including a tactical SIGINT capability.

The typical intelligence structure for this crisis management operation is given in figure 1. For a single nation, organising this effectively is already a challenge. However, ISAF was a truly multinational force, with an all-German military chain of command and two nations in the lead. For such an operation, setting up an effective intelligence structure becomes even more of a challenge. How did this structure work in practice? To answer this question, first a few words on intelligence requirements, then on the threat facing ISAF and then on actual intelligence work, i.e. sources, collection and assessment.

Intelligence requirements

For ISAF, intelligence requirements broadly fell into two categories. First, *intelligence* was required in support of the mission objectives and to establish situational awareness. What is the nature of the conflict and what are the effects on the ISAF mission? Second, *counterintelligence* was required for force protection. What are capabilities and intentions of the conflicting parties in harming ISAF itself?

To meet these requirements, six areas of interest were identified: political developments in Afghanistan and Kabul; the conduct of the warlords in and around Kabul, demobilising, disarming and re-integrating their troops (the so called DDR-process), the forming of local police forces and the Afghan National Army (ANA), the opposing forces and their actions against the Transitional Authority as well as against ISAF, and lastly actual threat warnings and attacks.

The security situation in Afghanistan in early 2003

The security situation in Afghanistan not only had an adverse effect on ISAF's mission, but also posed a threat to the security of the force itself. In wider Afghanistan, the indirect threat was the deep distrust amongst various ethnic groups; warlords like Ismael Khan, Mohammed Atta and Abdulrashid Dostum were a continuous challenge to the central government. They accumulated wealth from drugs trade (an estimated 2.8 billion dollar in 2003, 60% of the Afghan GNP[10]) and illegal arms trafficking, resulting in internal feuds and rivalry. Moreover, the Taliban was slowly recovering from the US attacks. In this, the Pakistan Intelligence Service (ISI), played a doubtful role, with Islamabad tolerating actions of Taliban in S and E of Afghanistan, aimed at soft targets like aid workers and local leaders and mullahs which supported the Karzai government[11]. Actually, that situation has not changed to date. The summer of 2005 was the most violent summer since 2001[12].

A more direct threat to ISAF in Kabul came from the fundamental Islam and was predominantly from Pashtun origin. The Hezb i Islami Gulbuddin (HiG) led by mr. Hekmatyar and the Taliban, which were vehemently resisting any foreign presence; and scattered elements of Al Qaeda. The presence of a large number of armed factions in the city was also a source of instability. Particularly, there were doubts as to loyalty of the Pathan leader Abdul Sayyaf, who controlled part of the city of Kabul.

Intelligence sources

At strategic level, the German and Dutch intelligence services kept a close watch on political developments and the overall security situation in Afghanistan and Kabul, using their regular sources. Particularly the BND's ample SIGINT production was an important asset, which was shared with the Dutch DISS. Both services then came to joint assessments, which were made available to the political and military level in Germany and The Netherlands. This remained so throughout the operation, with daily contacts by phone and weekly teleconferencing between BND and DISS. At the NL-DISS' initiative, the BMIC was also involved is this process. Additionally, monthly meetings were conducted at the political level in The Hague, with all ISAF nations involved. Obviously, these strategic intelligence assessments were also made available to the operational level at BwOpsCmd and HQ ISAF, in support of their situational awareness.

At the level of HQ ISAF, operational and tactical intelligence was essential for developing situational awareness. At the same time, there was a premium on effective counter intelligence for force protection. A wide range of collection means was used: intensive patrolling and special reconnaissance by KMNB both by vehicle and on foot throughout the city; the employment of field HUMINT teams, controlled by J2X at HQ ISAF; and also by technical means, such as tactical SIGINT, unmanned aerial vehicles (UAVs), notably the German Luna and Aladdin systems, and Dutch target acquisition radar to spot launch sites of incoming rockets (which happened quite frequently). And, of course, national intelligence was received through the NICs. Field HUMINT proved to be the most effective means, for which ISAF employed 7 teams altogether, 4 German, 1 Dutch, 1 Austrian and 1 Turkish team. Also, open source intelligence (OSINT) was critical for situational awareness. The performance of the technical means however, fell below expectations. Translation and analysis capacity for tactical SIGINT were grossly insufficient and the UAVs had difficulty staying in the air most of the time.

Of the many intelligence sources available to ISAF, the local Afghan services were an important one (figure 2^{13}). And there were quite a number of them in Kabul: the National Directorate of Security, the security directorates of the Ministry of Defence and the Ministry of the Interior, the Kabul City Police and the Kabul Garrison. Some of these were unreliable, notably the police and the garrison, because of corruption through lack of payment to their employees. Some were extremely effective, also in technical terms, using state-of-the-art commercial-of-the-shelf equipment, e.g. for tactical SIGINT. Tapping in on these sources was very useful, but also very time consuming, given the Afghan way of doing business. Also, harmonising their efforts was a challenge, to what end ISAF eventually managed to establish a co-ordinating platform, the Joint Security Co-ordination Centre (JSCC).

Other sources included the UN authorities, civil/military co-operation activities known as CIMIC, the Embassies of the nations involved and, sometimes, non-governmental organisations (NGO's). With many of these sources, ISAF established permanent liaison, although not all of the Liaison officers were intelligence trained, which reduced their effectiveness.

And lastly, there were the Americans engaged in operation Enduring Freedom (OEF). Obviously, ISAF established co-operative arrangements with the American CJTF-180, which after some initial problems with regard to the release of national intelligence, resulted in co-operation at an acceptable level. An American liaison officer was working in the J2 staff, and ISAF was eventually linked up to the US CENTRIX System, comparable with the German JASMIN system mentioned earlier.

Challenges[14]

The heart of the operational intelligence process is called CCIRM, the co-ordination of collection efforts and the management of information requirements. All collected information is subsequently processed, fed into a database, analysed and distributed in the form of Intelligence Summaries (Intsums) and counterintelligence reports (CIsums). The latter contained mainly threat warnings for possible or imminent attacks on ISAF, and were widely distributed over all the ISAF subunits. All in all some 150 Intsums and 65 CIsums were produced. For the rather small intelligence staff of ISAF III, this resulted in an ever increasing workload with which it could not effectively cope. In addition to the continuous problem of being overburdened, ISAF III encountered a number of intelligence related problems and issues, some of which serious.

The handover by Turkey as lead nation to HQ 1st GE/NL Corps was a total failure. Despite German and Dutch service contacts with Ankara, as well as the Corps own fact-finding missions in Kabul, the Turkish headquarters left Kabul without leaving an intelligence database or even a single contact with local services. Thus, situational awareness and force protection had to be built up from scratch, relying initially on national and American intelligence.

The situation in Afghanistan during German/Dutch lead-nationship was quite volatile. Throughout the country, there was a sharp increase in violent incidents and attacks, reaching a peak of 193 in April 2003, part of which was probably linked to the US offensive in Iraq. Also, the number of attacks on ISAF itself saw a marked increase, notably rocket attacks and the use of Improvised Explosive Devices. Against this background, the frequent use in ISAF Intsums of terms like "All quiet in Kabul" and "Nothing to report" was a source of considerable irritation at BwOpsCmd and in capitals, as they felt that they were left out of the picture. In reality, ISAF-CI was overburdened by a very large number of threat warnings, which had to be assessed. Later, ISAF-CI was reinforced by NATO, bringing in professional CI-capacity from Allied Command Europe, which somewhat mitigated the problem. Indeed, an analysis of the actual attacks on the force explains the nations' concern. Over a six-month period, 22 attacks were carried out against ISAF, resulting in 5 soldiers killed and 46 wounded, a number of which seriously. Here again, as in wider Afghanistan, there is a marked increase in April and May 2003, culminating in the suicide attack on a German troop convoy on 7 June 2003.

Eventually, towards the end of May, ComISAF *did* change his assessment of the situation, noting that security in ISAFs Area of Responsibility (AoR) was indeed deteriorating. Additionally, he sensed a risk of spill-over from outside the AoR, where the situation was volatile. In addition, he added a request to BwOpsCmd to give him more freedom of manoeuvre by expanding the AoR and carrying out cross-boundary operations. Logical as this may seem from a military point of view, his request was turned down by Berlin on the grounds that there was no significant and fundamental change in the security situation to justify such drastic measures. This assessment is questionable, given the record of threat warnings and attacks. However, in the light of the sensitive American/German political relations at the time (as a result of the war in Iraq) the response is perfectly understandable: both lead nations were keen on – at least visibly – keeping clear of American operations in Afghanistan.

The attack of 7 June 2003 casts light on another problem, which was the screening of locally employed Afghan personnel, or LEPs. ISAF employed 600 of them in the various camps. However German law, vehemently promoted by the MAD, prohibited effective screening of these people. As a result, there was no effective system of ID-card exchange for going in and out of the camps. In this, the MAD was supported by Berlin, much to the irritation of Com ISAF and the Dutch. Earlier on, following an incident on KIA, the NDS had already warned ISAF that some LEPs posed a security risk. Following the 7 June attack, ISAF conducted a large round-up under the LEPs, on the grounds that one of them may have given the tip-off for the troop convoy, as this was a somewhat out-of-routine movement. Mobile phones, voice recorders and digital cameras found on them were turned over to the *Bundeskriminalamt* for further investigation. But the fact that LEPs were admitted to the camps carrying this sort of equipment is in itself shocking. Eventually, in July 2003, a compromise was reached by delegating the screening of the LEPs to the local NDS (which was very good in doing so). In a subsequent second round-up, 8 Afghan LEPs were handed over to the NDS for further investigation. Nonetheless, for the larger part of ISAF's term in Kabul, the screening of LEPs was inadequate.

A continuous source of irritation between ISAF and the nations' capitals (and thus the national intelligence and security services) was the presence of the NICs. Most nations in ISAF had deployed NICs, of which only 4 were co-located with ISAF HQ, notably GE, NL, AUT and BE. The 5 others were part of their national contingent. ISAF felt that the NICs had little to contribute in terms of relevant intelligence, and were merely an uncontrolled information link tot capitals[15]. As a result, the NICs were largely ignored by ComISAF and his J2, even the ones who had co-located themselves with HQ ISAF and thus shown a willingness to co-operate. The NICs in turn, felt that their potential contribution to ISAF's intelligence effort was undervalued. Actually, in analysing ISAF's CI-reports, it becomes clear that national intelligence *did* generate a significant number of threat warnings as a basis for these reports. Whatever the truth, NICs are a fact of life in any crisis management operation, and ignoring them is thus not a solution to the problem.

Partly related to the NIC-issue was the lack of control over HUMINT activity. As stated earlier, ISAF-CI was directing 7 HUMINT teams. However, the actual number of national HUMINT teams operating in and around Kabul was higher than that. Some nations simply did their own thing as far as intelligence collection was concerned, hiding HUMINT capability in their NIC or in their national contingent. Apart from the sometimes poor quality of these national teams, this was indeed a potentially dangerous course of action. Sources can easily be compromised, source fatigue can emerge and the circulation of threat warnings gets out of control, as a single threat may pop up as five separate ones if reporting and assessment is not properly co-ordinated. Much to ComISAFs concern, this situation persisted throughout the deployment.

Last, but certainly not least, incompatibility of language, formats and databases remained a problem throughout ISAF III. Although formally at HQ 1st GE/NL Corps, English was the common language, at troop level this was not really the case given the multitude of nations involved. Additionally, there was no common standard for intelligence and incident reporting up the chain of command, as most nations simply used national formats. As a result, processing information from the various collection activities was very time consuming and crucial information might easily have been overlooked. As another example, the intelligence databases of HQ ISAF and HQ KMNB were incompatible, severely limiting automated data processing, apart from the fact that HQ-KMNB worked mainly in the German language. As late as July 2003, ComISAF issued orders to remedy these problems, largely to no avail. As this was not a NATO or a UN operation, his options for imposing anything at all in terms of procedures, were very limited.

NATO takeover

On 11 August 2003, Germany and The Netherlands handed over the lead-nation role in ISAF to NATO. Joint Forces Command HQ Brunssum in The Netherlands was appointed the Joint Commander, and Land Component Command HQ Heidelberg assumed command of ISAF in Kabul with a Canadian general in charge. Around the same time, Canada took over the command of the Kabul Multinational Brigade, bringing in around 1500 troops. This take-over of ISAF by a long standing political and military organisation like NATO immediately solved some of the problems that emerged under German/Dutch leadership, but by no means all of them.

First of all, connectivity was much improved by the use of NATO systems like CRONOS and BICES for force-wide reporting and dissemination of intelligence. And a single NATO database system called JOICE was deployed to Afghanistan. In addition, problems of language, formats and standards were settled by enforcing the use of NATO agreed procedures (laid down in NATO Stanags); analysis capability was reinforced, with the intelligence staff expanding from 24 to around 40 people. Analysis was supported by the use of adequate tools like Analyst Notebook. Also, professional CI and HUMINT capacity was brought in. All this resulted in a much more efficient intelligence process, which gave a noticeable increase in coherence of intelligence reporting up the chain of command. What remained, though, were political issues, such as ISAF's relationship to Operation Enduring Freedom; legal matters such as detention and interrogation policies; problems of continuity with the frequent rotation of HQs and staff; and technical issues, such as maintaining the integrity of systems and databases.

Last, but certainly not least, along with NATO came a solid system of force generation, which allowed ISAF to gradually expand and reach out beyond Kabul and its direct vicinity through the gradual establishment of Provincial Reconstruction Teams (PRTs) in a phased approach throughout Afghanistan. Initially teams were set up in the relatively quiet areas north of Kabul (Konduz, Baghlan and Mazar-i-Sharif) and subsequently also in the Northwest. NATO is currently at the brink of launching Phase III, establishing PRTs in the provinces Nimroz, Helmand, Kandahar and Uruzgan, supported by a multinational brigade size Reaction Force, requiring a significant step-up of the strategy and capabilities for intelligence, surveillance and reconnaissance for ISAF. To what extent NATO will be capable of meeting the additional challenges in the field of intelligence remains to be seen.

Assessment

As demonstrated, the challenges in the field of intelligence and security facing the lead nations and HQ 1st GE/NL Corps in its 6 months as HQ ISAF III, were significant. The intelligence effort made to counter these challenges was equally significant, resulting in overburdening of the intelligence staff in ISAF. A number of serious incidents occurred. And, particularly as regards the security of ISAF itself, adequate action was sometimes slow, resulting in unnecessary risks to the force.

A number of intelligence related issues during ISAF III have been discussed. Were they the result of ineffective German/Dutch intelligence co-operation in ISAF? The answer to that question is most likely 'no'. Under the circumstances of early 2003, the co-operation between German and Dutch intelligence organisations was good and effective, at both the political and military level. Mutual trust, transparency and lots of hard-work-put-in are the key words. Previous joint experiences, the resulting personal relations and thorough joint preparation, played an essential role, as did the long standing military co-operation between the two nations involved. Perhaps the only exception was a growing concern on the Dutch side over the security of the force, and irritation about the extremely slow German legal decision making.

Many of the problems that emerged in intelligence and security were quite typical for any crisis management operation in a multinational environment. Frictions in the chain of command were mainly an inner-German problem, rather than political problems between the two nations involved. Differences in perspective at the political and military level are quite common in any operation, but in this case were aggravated through lack of experience and political complications, notably the war in Iraq. NIC-problems are as old as multi-national operations themselves, and so are legal issues and differences in national attitude. The problems with procedures, language, reporting formats and communications were larger than they normally should be, but they were mainly the result of the incremental way in which ISAF was built up and the rather loose operational environment.

Germany and The Netherlands demonstrated that investing in a concept as the 1st GE/NL Corps is a worthwhile effort[16]. In ISAF III the two nations managed to work together effectively in the field of intelligence, building on mutual trust and long standing military relations. At the same time ISAF III made it clear, that multinational military cooperation in a crisis environment is not an easy task and requires determination and a willingness to bridge the gaps of tradition, culture, experiences and bureaucracy. Nonetheless, the German/Dutch lead-nationship of ISAF was a step forward on Afghanistan's long road to peace and stability.

Epilogue

Finally, the key question remains whether Afghanistan – with ISAFs backing – is now progressing towards a better functioning and more secure state. In a general sense, there is a gradual improvement. Pashtun/Tajik antagonism has gradually developed into a political process, with the central government in control. The struggle for power has descended to the regional level, with Hamid Karzai exercising a policy of "divide et impera" from Kabul. With the recent elections – both the system and the outcome–, a political process "Afghan style" is underway. At national level, the warlord problem is in control, with most of the former contenders for power in Afghanistan neutralised. In Kabul, and in the North and West, the security situation has improved, with the central government gradually gaining influence in the provinces. Disarming and reintegrating the various militias and illegally armed groups in those areas is largely successful. A process of nation building is in progress, albeit slowly.

On the downside, however, in the South and East, improvement is very limited. The year 2005 was the most violent one since 2001. Taliban strength is increasing, operating in larger groups and engaging in bolder and more brutal actions. Increasingly, the Afghan population itself is the target, such as local police, the ANA, and local leaders and mullahs supporting the central government. Increasingly, NGOs and troops engaged in OEF are being targeted, resulting in 10 NGO staff and over 70 US soldiers being killed in 2005 alone. There is also an increasing influx of foreign fighters, notably from Iraq, Uzbekistan and Chechnia. The counter narcotics program is largely a failure[17]. Although growing poppies is officially forbidden since 2002, drugs now provide for 55–60% of the GNP. Of the worlds production of heroin 85% comes from Afghanistan. The country's economic weakness and the damage of

25 years of war is its Achilles heel. The slow economic development provides insufficient alternative for the profits of drugs. Corruption at local level is on the rise, with criminal elements gradually gaining influence in local politics. Unfortunately, this process is aided by the recent election of Provincial Councils, with persons of dubious background (but with lots of money and influence) entering local politics.

On balance, there is no reason for great optimism *or* pessimism over Afghanistan's future[18]. The most likely scenario therefore is "muddling through", with ISAF's presence being required for many more years to come.

Notes

1 The CIA World Factbook 2005
2 Maloney, Sean M., Afghanistan: From Here to Eternity?', Parameters, US Army War College, Spring 2004, 7/8
3 Bertholee, R.A.C. (Bgen) and Tjepkema, drs. A.C. (Col retd), De ISAF missie in Kabul, Militaire Spectator, November 2003, page 3
4 UNSCR 1386, *Assist the Transitional Authority (TA) in maintaining security within the ISAF Area of Operations (AOR) so that the TA as well as the personnel of the UN can operate in a secure environment in order to enable the TA the build up of security structures in Afghanistan in accordance with the Bonn Agreement and as agreed in the Military Technical Agreement (MTA). . . .*
5 Kropman, LTC R.: 'ISAF III Experience', NATO Briefing UNCLAS, Autumn 2003, page 3
6 Based on authors' experiences as Director NL-DISS (until late December 2002)
7 The J2X was LTC R. Kropman, who also prepared the NATO briefing on ISAF Experiences. The author has had an extensive interview with LTC Kropman on ISAF III intelligence lessons learned.
8 Kropman, LTC R.: 'ISAF III Experience', NATO Briefing UNCLAS, Autumn 2003 page 6,8
9 Kropman, LTC R.: 'ISAF III Experience', NATO Briefing UNCLAS, Autumn 2003 page 5
10 Netherlands Defence Intelligence and Security Service: 'Annual Report 2004' The Hague May 2005, page 28
11 Haqqani, Hussein: De Taliban blijven actief zolang Pakistan dat uitkomt, Volkskrant 15 May 2005
12 AFP, AP, Reuters: Taliban lijden forse verliezen, Volkskrant 23 August 2005
13 Kropman, LTC R.: 'ISAF III Experience', NATO Briefing UNCLAS, Autumn 2003 page 11
14 Based on extensive interview with LTC Kropman, Spring 2005
15 Kropman, LTC R.: 'ISAF III Experience', NATO Briefing UNCLAS, Autumn 2003 page 33–34
16 Bertholee, R.A.C. (Bgen) and Tjepkema, drs. A.C. (Col retd), De ISAF missie in Kabul, Militaire Spectator, November 2003, page 10
17 Rubin, Barnett R., Hamidzada, Humayun and Stoddard, Abby: 'Afghanistan 2005 and Beyond: Prospects for Improved Stability Reference Document', Centre on International Cooperation, New York University, For the Clingendael Institute, April 2005, page 63–65
18 Maloney, Sean M.: 'Afghanistan Four Years On: An Assessment', Parameters, Autumn 2005, page 21, 31–32

Bibliography

Bertholee, R.A.C. (Bgen) and Tjepkema, drs. A.C. (Col retd): De ISAF missie in Kabul, Militaire Spectator, November 2003
Kropman, LTC R.: 'ISAF III Experience', NATO Briefing UNCLAS, Autumn 2003
Maloney, Sean M., Afghanistan: From Here to Eternity?', Parameters, US Army War College, Spring 2004
Maloney, Sean M.: 'Afghanistan Four Years On: An Assessment', Parameters, US Army War College, Autumn 2005
Netherlands Defence Intelligence and Security Service: 'Annual Report 2004' The Hague May 2005
Rubin, Barnett R., Hamidzada, Humayun and Stoddard, Abby: 'Afghanistan 2005 and Beyond:

Prospects for Improved Stability Reference Document', Centre on International Cooperation, New York University, For the Clingendael Institute, April 2005

Rubin, Barnett R.: 'Road to Ruin: Afghanistan's Booming Opium Industry', Centre on International Cooperation, New York University, October 7 2004

Joop van Reijn, 'Germany and the Netherlands in the Headquarters of the International Security assistance Force in Afghanistan (ISAF): An Intelligence perspective', in Beatrice de Graaf, Ben de Jong & Wies Platje (eds.) *Battleground Western Europe: Intelligence Operations in Germany and the Netherlands in the Twentieth Century* (Apeldoorn: Het Spinhuis 2007) pp. 217–33.

INTELLIGENCE FOR PEACEKEEPING AND PEACEMAKING

Further reading: Books and reports

Hesi Carmel (ed.), *Intelligence for Peace* (London: Frank Cass 2000).

David Carment & Martin Rudner (eds.), *Peacekeeping Intelligence: New Players, Extended Boundaries* (London: Routledge 2006).

Roger Z. George and Robert D. Kline (eds.), *Intelligence and National Security Strategist: Enduring Issues and Challenges* (Washington, DC: National Defense University Press, CSI, 2004).

Loch K. Johnson, *Bomb, Bugs, Drugs, and Thugs* (NY: New York University Press, 2000), 95–121

Ben de Jong, Wies Platje & Robert Steele (eds.) *Peacekeeping Intelligence: Emerging Concepts for the Future* (Oakton VA: OSS International Press 2003).

Klass van Walraven (ed.), *Early Warning and Conflict Prevention: Limitations and. Possibilities* (The Hague: Kluwer Law International 1998).

Cees Wiebes, *Intelligence and The War in Bosnia 1992–1995* (Munster: Lit Verlag 2003).

Further reading: Essays and articles

William E. Demars, 'Hazardous Partnership: NGOs and United States Intelligence in Small Wars', *International Journal of Intelligence and Counterintelligence* 14/2 (2001) pp.193–222.

A. Walter Dorn and David J.H. Bell, 'Intelligence and Peacekeeping: The UN Operation in the Congo 1960–64', *International Peacekeeping* 2/1 (1995) pp.11–33.

A Walter Dorn, 'The Cloak and the Blue Beret: Limitations on Intelligence in UN Peacekeeping', *International Journal of Intelligence and Counterintelligence* 12 (1998)

Bassey Ekpe, 'The Intelligence Assets of the United Nations: Sources, Methods, and Implications', *International Journal of Intelligence and CounterIntelligence* 20/3 (2007) pp.377–400.

Pär Eriksson, 'Intelligence in peacekeeping operations', *International Journal of Intelligence and Counter-Intelligence* 10/1 (1997) pp.1–18.

D. Hannay, 'Intelligence and International Agencies', in Shukman (ed.), *Agents for change. Intelligence services in the 21st century* (London: St Ermins' Press 2000, pp.179.

Paul Johnston, 'No Cloak and Dagger Required: Intelligence Support to UN Peacekeeping,' , *Intelligence & National Security* 12/4, (1997) pp.102–13. [see Quiggen response below]

T. Quiggen, 'Response to 'No Cloak and Dagger', *Intelligence and National Security* 13/4 (1998) pp.203–8

Sir David Ramsbotham, 'Analysis and Assessment for Peacekeeping Operations, *Intelligence and National Security* 10/4 (1995) pp.162–75.

Martin Rudner, 'The Future of Canada's Defence Intelligence', *International Journal of Intelligence and CounterIntelligence* 15/4 (2002) pp.540–564.

Len Scott, 'Secret Intelligence, Covert Action and Clandestine Diplomacy', *Intelligence & National Security* 19/2 (2004) pp.322–34.

Shlomo Shpiro, 'The CIA as Middle East Peace Broker?', *Survival* 45/2, (2003) pp.91–112.

H. Smith, 'Intelligence and UN Peacekeeping', *Survival* 36/ 3 (1994) pp.174–92.

Robert David Steele, 'Peacekeeping Intelligence and Information Peacekeeping', *International Journal of Intelligence and CounterIntelligence*, 19/3 (2006) pp.519–537

John D. Stempel, 'Covert Action and Diplomacy,' *International Journal of Intelligence and Counterintelligence* 20/1 (2007) pp.122–135.

Peter Wilson, The contribution of intelligence services to security sector reform, *Conflict, Security and Development* 5/1 (2005) pp. 87–107.

Essay questions

- Is a permanent UN intelligence agency desireable? If so, is it feasible?
- What kinds of intelligence support are required for peacekeeping operations?
- What was the nature of the main intelligence challenges that confronted peacekeepers in the former Yugoslavia in the 1990s?
- Examine the role of intelligence officers as clandestine peace brokers? What advantages and disadvantages do they carry?

30 Learning to live with intelligence

Wesley K. Wark

This essay argues that learning to live with 'the war on terror' will mean learning to live with intelligence. This acceptance will include, amongst its many aspects, the important role that technology has played in the collection and analysis of intelligence during the last century, not least the 'Open Source' revolution. These changes take the form of a permanent revolution, with the more recent shift to violent transnational actors prompting the re-evaluation of human intelligence against technical systems. It has also prompted a re-assessment of the vast Cold War intelligence alliances that have dominated the landscape since 1945. Most importantly, there have been changes in the way in which intelligence is used, not least the rise of 'public intelligence' to justify pre-emption. Public intelligence will require a new public outlook on intelligence. To achieve this, the future of intelligence requires a discovery of the past.

The key strategic and cultural issue of the Cold War was, as Stanley Kubrick suggested so deliciously, 'learning to live with ("love") the bomb'.[1] Everyone, from Pentagon planners, to spy fiction novelists, came up with fictional cures for the atomic dilemma, ranging from MAD (Mutual Assured Destruction) to James Bond. Fear of the bomb remains with us, although the nightmare scenarios are under revision. It is no longer nutters of the General Ripper variety, Frankenstein villains such as Ian Fleming's Dr NO, or the dread possibility of accidental or uncontrollable nuclear war between the superpowers, that preoccupies us. Since September 11, 2001, it is the twin threats of the proliferation of weapons of mass destruction, and the spectacle of future attempts at 'superterrorism' by Al Qaeda and other terrorist organizations of similar, unbounded malevolence.[2]

The events of September 11, 2001 are too recent and raw to have allowed for the generation of fictional cures, or even of fully-fledged strategic doctrines. But one thing seems clear. Learning to live with an open-ended 'war on terrorism' will mean learning to live with intelligence. We do not have a Stanley Kubrick to limn the possibilities, or tickle the dark side, but between these pages readers will find some of the best expert commentary on the future of intelligence.

Learning to live with intelligence means, among other things, grasping the role that technology has played and will continue to play in shaping intelligence practices and capabilities. Technology was a key driver in the intelligence revolution of the twentieth century. Its most obvious impact has been on the methods used to collect intelligence. Fundamental changes in communications, especially the advent of radio prior to World War I, opened up the possibility of 'real-time' intelligence.[3] The discipline of Sigint (signals intelligence) was born and flourished during World War I and remained the sometimes elusive jewel of intelligence for the remainder of the century. The Wright brothers' experiments in the sand dunes of Kitty Hawk, North Carolina eventually launched espionage into the air and gave intelligence collection an entirely new domain – eyes in the sky. Imint (imagery intelligence) developed historically in parallel with Sigint as a premier collection methodology.

But intelligence collection was not alone in being affected by the impact of technology. The classic intelligence cycle model identifies three essential stages in the production of finished intelligence – collection, assessment and dissemination. During World War II, experiments were undertaken with the presentation of intelligence to decision-makers, beginning with specialised maps and graphical charts for use in the 'war rooms' built for British and US leaders. This activity would spawn an on-going effort in the decades to come to fix the attention of leaders on intelligence's message through improvements to the style, visual impact, speed of delivery, and compression of reporting. In this domain, technology was an essential assist to the allure and blight of intelligence, its tight security wrapping.

The dimension of the classic intelligence cycle that was slowest to be affected by technological change was assessment. Although the concept of the interdisciplinary evaluation of raw intelligence and the use of collective expertise to provide for intelligence judgements was first articulated with the creation of the British Joint Intelligence Committee in 1936, it was not until the widespread use of desktop computers beginning in the 1980s that the analytical function of intelligence was fundamentally affected.

The computer revolution, followed by the Internet revolution, changed the ways in which intelligence data could be stored and retrieved, and altered the nature of interactions between individual analysts and analytical groups within intelligence agencies. The Internet revolution, in particular, opened up the prospect of 'open source' (unclassified, publicly accessible) intelligence as a vital tool. Fast access to a global stockpile of knowledge, assisted by increasingly sophisticated search engines, has transformed the nature of intelligence assessment and fundamentally altered its traditional reliance on secrets. The 'open source' revolution has also led to a previously unthinkable privatisation of assessment, with a plethora of private sector companies offering expertise in global risk analysis, often for a hefty fee.

Technology, as it affects the domain of intelligence as much as elsewhere, can, of course, be a double-edged weapon. Technological advances bring with them sometimes hidden costs and dangers; they can also generate inappropriate expectations. A parlour game among literary friends on a dark and stormy night in Switzerland led Mary Shelley to pen the classic tale, *Frankenstein, or the Modern Prometheus*.[1] It is always needful to be on the lookout for the Frankensteinian impulse and the monstrous birth in the application of technology to intelligence. But talk of Frankenstein might seem fanciful in the context of technology's seeming role as a beneficent deliverer of solutions to knowledge problems. Technology has delivered 'real time intelligence', a historical breakthrough; it has vastly broadened the conceptual lens through which information is collected and assessed; it has facilitated the processing and delivery of knowledge to decision-makers. Where be monsters?

They lie in wait in various corners of our experience and imagination. One is that technology's contemporary bounty has come to threaten the integrity and quality of the intelligence process itself. For much of its modern existence, intelligence services trafficked in scarcity. Secrets were hard to acquire; truly valuable secrets were a rare commodity. Certainly there were historic periods during which technology helped unleash a flood of intelligence. The most notable example was during the glory days of Ultra in 1943 and 1944, when Allied Sigint played a vital role in military victory on multiple fronts, on land in Normandy, at sea in the culmination of the vicious Battle of the Atlantic, and in the air in the prosecution of the bomber offensive and the blunting of Hitler's secret weapons offensives.[5]

But at some undefined point during the Cold War, the technological tide turned, once and for all, and the normal conditions of intelligence scarcity were replaced by the opposite problem of an increasing surfeit of intelligence, often generated through high-tech collection systems.

'Information overload' is now a common problem for all major intelligence systems. What Roberta Wohlstetter observed as a central problem explaining intelligence failure at Pearl Harbor in 1941, namely the difficulty of distinguishing true 'signals' from the ambient 'noise' in which they are embedded, now truly defines the twenty-first century intelligence challenge.[6]

What has changed since Pearl Harbor is the sheer volume of both signals and noise. As the mass of raw intelligence grows, it spawns worrisome problems for intelligence warning, analytical failures, and politicisation and manipulation of data and assessments by decision-makers. If 'cherry picking' has to be the norm inside intelligence communities, because of informational plenty, what resistance can there be to cherry picking of the intelligence pro-duct by political decision-makers intent on confirming pre-conceptions and finding support for policies determined on grounds other than that of intelligence judgements?

A second dilemma created by the stunning advances in technological intelligence collec-tion has been its tendency to distort and channel the overall intelligence effort. The advent of Sigint and Imint, and their increasing sophistication, introduced an inevitable, if not necessarily examined, hierarchy of intelligence products, with the high-tech and most expen-sive systems valued at a premium and more 'old fashioned' methods of intelligence collec-tion discounted. There remains good reason to value the Sigint product and the imagery that modern satellite, spy plane and drone systems can produce. The future of these systems may well be impressive. But to the extent that their allure has led to a devaluing of traditional agent reporting, or even a failure to fully appreciate the value of open source material, then intelligence communities have lost their balance.

The events of September 11 and the war on terrorism have led to much public specula-tion about the decline of operational capabilities in the field of agent penetration and reporting and a call for the re-invention of a key intelligence collection discipline, human intelligence or Humint. Humint is, by nature low-tech; its tools are human beings and their capacities. Humint lacks the 'real time' potentiality of other collection methods; its product frequently lacks the apparent clarity of information drawn through the technological spec-trum. Yet it is an indisputable part of the intelligence function and there may be many future questions, especially in the realm of counter-terrorism operations, which cannot be answered without a highly capable system for agent reporting.

In this regard, technology's strengths have reminded us of technology's weaknesses. There are secrets into which the aerial spy, the sensor, or the technological listener cannot fully penetrate.

Technology has also profoundly shaped intelligence power.[7] The cost and sophistication required to sustain technological advances in intelligence collection have led to a great concentration of intelligence power, which became manifest in the second half of the twentieth century. At the beginning of the modern intelligence revolution, just before 1914, intelligence capabilities were the preserve of a handful of European Great Powers. There-after, the idea of intelligence as a tool of statecraft was slowly exported until the practice became globalised and more or less universal, at least in the form of domestic security agencies. Paradoxically, the globalisation of intelligence did not create the conditions for the diffusion of intelligence power, but rather the reverse.

This was thanks to a growing technology gap between have and have-not states. Those that could afford some or all of the high-tech intelligence systems were the haves; those that could not, were the have-nots. In contemporary terms, the technology gap, combined with post-Cold War geopolitical realities, has created an unprecedented situation in which a single nation state, the United States, has emerged as an intelligence super, or hyper, power. The rest of the world struggles to avoid relegation to the status of intelligence have-not.

There may be an 'imperial' condition to deal with in the emergence of such a terrific concentration of intelligence power. Imperial intelligence, if that is what the United States suffers, or may suffer from in future, is a condition in which arrogance and insularity of judgement can easily flourish. The informal checks and balances built into traditional intelligence alliances, in which participating states had the capacity to challenge the intelligence judgements of an ally, could easily be lost in a new imperial system.

Equally, the shared sense of political objectives and the shared vision of threats that can be an outcome of intelligence alliances, the by-product of the intimate sharing of secrets and the reliance on burden-sharing in the global accumulation of intelligence, could be at risk. The most remarkable of all intelligence alliances is that which links the Anglo-Saxon powers, the United States, Britain, Canada, Australia and New Zealand. This alliance was first fashioned during World War II and was sustained throughout the Cold War and post-Cold War eras. It has reason to be concerned about its future. A certain imbalance of power always existed within this secret alliance, at least since 1945; now the imbalance is huge, casting the various rationales for the alliance into doubt.

The high cost of true intelligence power, especially imposed by technological collection systems, has also had the effect of forcing choices and distorting the intelligence capabilities of many states below the first-rank powers. Canada is a prime example of a state with global interests and a need for wide-ranging intelligence that felt compelled, because of limited resource allocations, to make historic choices about its intelligence capacities. These choices have proved hard and deterministic. At the onset of the Cold War period, the Canadian authorities decided to put their technological eggs in one basket, by creating a Sigint agency to function within an alliance setting.[8]

This decision, in turn, shaped both future resource allocation (heavily favouring collection at the expense of assessment and other intelligence functions) and the fundamental structure of the overall Canadian system. Struggling to create a functioning Sigint capacity, and favouring it, the Canadian authorities decided to eschew the creation of any foreign intelligence service along CIA or SIS lines.

A fourth technological 'monster', lurking alongside those of information overload, structural distortions within intelligence systems, and the imposition of concentrated power, is the shapeless phantom of expectation. Technological systems seem to hold out the promise of the perfectibility of intelligence. Multi-spectral intelligence delivered in real-time offers a vision of the transparency not just of the 'battlespace', but ultimately of conflicts and threats in general. Much of this thinking has been driven by speculation regarding the so-called 'revolution in military affairs' (RMA) and the impact that new sensor systems, new 'smart' weapons, and new methods of command and control will have on the future of war.

Several commentators in this collection reflect on the expectations delivered by RMA futurists. Perhaps no-one is closer to the mark than Nick Cullather, who is scathing about the 'infantilism' of many of these technological visions of the future of war.[9] The pursuit of 'perfect' intelligence is just another manifestation, though no less dangerous, of the general faith in technological progress to solve the world's problems. In the specific case of intelligence, technology is seen as a powerful tool to overcome secrets and penetrate what is hidden. In reality, technology is of strictly finite utility in tackling the classic intelligence dilemma of the complexity and unpredictability of events.

Indeed, technology has contributed to the problem by increasing the scope of complexity and helping fuel unpredictability. To create a powerful, technologically-driven intelligence system in the hope of solving complexity and resolving unpredictability has a Frankensteinian edge. The solutions, partial ones, lie elsewhere. They are to be found, especially, in the quality of intelligence assessment, which calls on very human capacities for local knowledge, wise judgement, imagination, intuition, and the courage of conviction.

In thinking about the future of intelligence, all the evidence before our eyes suggests that technology will continue to be a driver of change. In this case, predicting future developments as a form of continuity with the past seems a safe bet. The prediction also means that technological change will continue to be a double-edged weapon, with some Frankensteinian possibilities. The detailed ways in which new technological systems will contribute to the power of intelligence collection is beyond our capacity to imagine. But intelligence perfectibility will be forever elusive. The power of technologically driven change to corrupt systems and practices will remain.

Learning to live with intelligence means more than just grappling with the genie of technology. It also means learning to live with 'Orwell', more precisely with the infiltration of a nightmare vision of the national security state into popular consciousness.[10] George Orwell's dystopian novel, *Nineteen Eighty-Four* is rightly celebrated for warning us about many things, including the dangers of a debased collective mentality, the tenuousness of our grasp on history and private memory, the shaping influence of propaganda, the appetite for power for its own sake, the threat of a world plunged into eternal conflict between warring blocs. But the warning that Orwell, perhaps unintentionally, planted most deeply in the popular imagination, was a warning about the powers of state surveillance. 'Orwellian' conveys above all a picture of telescreens, thought police, the Ministry of Truth, and the 'really frightening one,' the Ministry of Love. 'BIG BROTHER', Orwell, eternally reminds us, 'IS WATCHING YOU.'[11] Orwell, writing in 1949, fixed a fear in our minds about what intelligence could become.

It is both a salutary fear and an exaggerated one. Salutary to the extent that Orwell reminds us of the potential abuses that a too-powerful intelligence system could inflict on civil society – abuses against truth and against civil liberties. But the Orwellian vision is exaggerated (as it must be to fulfill the demands of dystopian creation) in that few intelligence services have ever come appreciably close to possessing the capabilities of Orwell's Oceania troopers (perhaps the East German Stasi was a partial exception). More importantly the Orwellian vision lent itself to misunderstanding. It was not the Thought Police and the apparatus of surveillance that created the totalitarian political system of *Nineteen Eighty-Four*. Rather the system created the surveillance.

This is an important but little understood lesson about the place of intelligence in society. Intelligence services need their potential power held in check by cultural mores, traditions, laws, and systems of accountability and review. Yet intelligence services have to be seen as products of the society in which they function, not as exotic 'rogues'. Learning to live with Orwell means appreciating the Orwellian warning for what it is, essentially a dark signal about what can go wrong when a society loses its hold on history and memory and falls into the hands of a doctrine of absolute power for its own sake.

Learning to live with Orwell means having a healthy fear of the abuse of power, but not succumbing to an automatic distrust, or any kind of fearful caricature, of the role of intelligence services in the state. Learning to live with Orwell, means the need for citizens to recognize intelligence as a critical component of international statecraft and an important foundation of the night watchman state.

Orwell's *Nineteen Eighty-Four* was not, of course, an argument for the Thought Police. But neither was it an argument against intelligence services. Orwell himself recognized the need for vigilance against fanaticism and enemies of the state.[12] He had seen such things at work firsthand during the Spanish Civil War, and feared their coming to Britain under fire during World War II, and under pressure during the Cold War.[13] But thanks in part to the penetration of an Orwellian vision, as well as to other popular culture manifestations, we have inherited an automatic distrust of the intelligence function. The future of intelligence depends in part on 'Orwell' loosening his grip on our imagination.

The diminution of 'Orwell', a codeword for the fear of intelligence, will be a necessary condition for the success of a revolutionary change now unfolding in the practice of intelligence. Looking back, the twentieth century may be seen as the age of 'secret intelligence.' This age was born at the intersection of two needs – the need to uncover, in a rapidly destabilising Europe prior to 1914, the secret military plans, equipment and deployments of the enemy; and the need to protect one's own military secrets from discovery by foreigners.

Intelligence practice, for most of the remainder of the twentieth century was focused on penetrating secrets and protecting secrets. There were, to be sure, some conscious and famous lapses, such as the public use of British Sigint decrypts to denounce Bolshevik perfidy on several occasions in the 1920s, and the presentation to the United Nations of classified U-2 photographs revealing the Soviet deployment of long-range ballistic missiles to Cuba in October 1962. But for the most part, secrecy ruled.

The twenty-first century may prove, by contrast, the age of 'public intelligence'. Events and doctrine both give weight to this possibility.[14] In the aftermath of the terrorist attacks of September 11, governments in Britain and the United States in particular, have felt compelled to make public their intelligence in support of decisions on war and peace. The trend began with the release of a British government dossier linking Al Qaeda and its bases in Afghanistan to the September 11 assault. The trend accelerated in the Fall and Winter of 2002/3 as the governments of Tony Blair and George Bush prepared themselves for a controversial war on Iraq. In September 2002, the British government led the way by releasing a Joint Intelligence Committee assessment of the threat posed by Iraq's weapons of mass destruction programmes. The document carried a preface by the British Prime Minister that stated:

'It is unprecedented for the government to publish this kind of document. But in the light of the debate about Iraq and Weapons of Mass Destruction, I want to share with the British public the reasons why I believe this issue to be a current and serious threat to the UK national interest.'[15]

The UK Parliamentary Intelligence and Security Committee, drawn from all parties, approved the concept of the release of the dossier. Its annual report for 2002–3 noted 'The Committee supports the responsible use of intelligence and material collected by the Agencies to inform the public on matters such as these.'[16] The Parliamentary committee did not alter its judgement about the principle of releasing intelligence into the public domain, even after finding some fault with the contents of the dossier itself.

These British straws in the wind were matched by public statements based on US intelligence. In October 2002, the US government released a declassified version of the CIA's National Intelligence Estimate (NIE) on Iraq's weapons of mass destruction (WMD). This estimate had been drawn up at the express request of the Senate Select Committee on Intelligence, suggesting an uneasy alliance of motives between the Congressional and Executive branches of government. The US NIE was later supplemented by the televised presentation made to the UN Security Council by Secretary of State Colin Powell in February 2003, surely the most dramatic public use of intelligence for the purposes of swaying domestic and global public opinion since the Cuban Missile Crisis, over 40 years earlier.

Underpinning at least the American use of 'public intelligence' in the run-up to the war against Iraq was a newly declared, and radical, statement of US strategy. In September 2002, the Bush White House released a document called the National Security Strategy.[17] Previous iterations of this strategy paper had been pro-forma exercises to meet an executive branch reporting requirement. The September 2002 document was something different. Its most controversial feature was its advocacy of a doctrine of pre-emption, designed to legitimate the exercise of military force against emerging threats to US security. It was billed as the proactive answer to September 11, in a new environment in which a fusion might occur between the new age's worst nightmares – terrorism, rogue states, and the proliferation of weapons of mass destruction.[18]

One feature that went generally unnoticed in commentary about the National Security Strategy was the onus placed on intelligence, and indeed on public intelligence. The document laid down three conditions for successful pre-emption, all of which had implications for the future performance of intelligence. The conditions included:

1. the requirement for good intelligence on, and early warning of, emerging threats
2. the need to build international coalitions on the basis of a shared conviction about emerging threats
3. the capacity to win pre-emptive wars quickly and with minimal casualties to friendly forces or civilian populations.

Cumulatively, these three conditions place an extremely heavy burden on intelligence, suggesting a degree of expectation about intelligence capabilities never before levied. The National Security Strategy paper concluded its discussion with a statement that when the pre-emption option is exercised, 'the reasons for our actions will be clear, the force measured, and the cause just'.[19]

Providing clarity, and proclaiming a just war, inescapably require the use of intelligence in the public domain. So, in a different way, does international coalition-building, especially when the intended partners and the arena for such activities exist outside the framework of traditional intelligence alliances, with their established circuitry for the passage of secret intelligence.

The Iraq War was the first test case for the strategy of pre-emption. Its long term outcome, impossible to foretell, and the growing evidence of badly flawed trans-Atlantic intelligence assessment about Iraq's WMD, may yet call the strategy into question. But at the time of writing there is no sign that the current US administration of George W. Bush intends to abandon it. Quite the contrary. Amid a worsening security situation in postwar Iraq, President Bush delivered a speech on 16 October 2003, in San Bernadino, California, on his way to an Asian summit. In that speech, Bush reiterated American determination to pursue a strategy of pre-emption, when circumstance demanded. The challenge for America, as Bush put it, was to 'show our motives are pure'. A display of 'pure motives' requires, of course, public intelligence.

If an age of public intelligence is upon us, it will demand a revolutionary change in the practice of intelligence and in the doctrine of secrecy. New attention will have to be paid to devising intelligence assessments designed for public consumption, as opposed to products shaped for intelligence's traditional government 'consumers'. While such forms of intelligence assessment are devised, great care will have to be given to protecting the role that intelligence traditionally plays in informing government decision-making on national and international security issues. Great care will also be required in protecting intelligence sources and methods – the lifeblood of intelligence work. New restraints will have to be devised to ensure that the intelligence product does not become completely politicised in its transit to the public audience, both domestic and foreign. As US scholar John Prados put it, 'what is there to prevent public intelligence from becoming public relations?'[20]

Integrity of intelligence reporting will be a huge issue. The quality and persuasiveness of intelligence judgements will face an enormous test, in the open and fractious marketplace of public debate. To persuade its new, and much more diverse audience, intelligence assessments will have to be very good indeed.

Finally, there will be a reciprocal onus on public consumers of intelligence to understand the nature of the intelligence product, both its strengths and its limitations.

If public intelligence is the radical future, its emergence will build on the technological enhancement and delivery of intelligence. Public intelligence requires display, precisely of the sort delivered by Colin Powell's address to the Security Council in February 2003, with its Sigint soundtrack, and its satellite imagery. Public intelligence is unthinkable without the technological infrastructure that supports a global media and global Internet.

Public intelligence has emerged in the context of an unprecedented and open-ended war on terrorism, with its attendant doctrine of pre-emption. Perhaps the political and strategic conditions that have given rise to it will disappear, and intelligence will return to the relative safety of its traditional doctrine of secrecy and its traditional role as a discrete provider of special information to government decision-makers. Such a reversal seems unlikely. More pertinent may be the issue of whether public intelligence will be restricted to the hopefully rare case of pre-emptive war, or whether it might, with time, become the norm.

Whether rare, or the norm, public intelligence will require a new public outlook on intelligence, one beyond, as suggested above, the habit of 'Orwell'. To achieve this, the future of intelligence requires a discovery of the past. For much of the twentieth century, intelligence had no usable past. Its failures were sometimes visible, but its general operations and practices were not. The evolution of intelligence 'power' remained obscure. A substantial literature on intelligence did not begin to emerge until the last quarter of the twentieth century. Writing on intelligence began from a relatively narrow base. It was sparked in the beginning by a historical fascination with newly released documentation on the impact of signals intelligence during World War II, the famous story of Ultra, and contemporary concerns about intelligence abuses, particularly in the conduct of covert operations.[21]

Since the mid-1970s, the literature on intelligence has grown exponentially and moved well beyond its original interests. Intelligence now has at least the outlines of a usable past, with a library of case studies, national histories, and synoptic studies waiting the reader. Two pioneering essay collections, both published 20 years ago, in 1984, helped point the way forward.

Christopher Andrew and David Dilks reminded us that intelligence was the 'missing dimension' in our understanding of critical policy-making decisions in the realm of international relations. The concept of the 'missing dimension' was both a rallying cry for new research and writing and a manifesto suggesting the overlooked significance of the intelligence process and input.[22]

Ernest May, in the same year, called our attention to two realities. In the opening essay of

Knowing One's Enemies, May explored the decision-making process of three European great powers in the crisis-filled years before 1914. His examination of how these states used their nascent intelligence capabilities suggested the significance both of political structures and of the phenomenon of bureaucratic feuding and competition.[23]

The message of both books was simple, but needful. Intelligence was important, pace Andrew and Dilks; intelligence practices were idiosyncratic and rooted in national political structures and cultural norms, pace May. The future of intelligence may well depend on a true digesting of such messages.

But intelligence's usable past remains under-exploited and unrealized, thanks to two phenomena.

One is the contrary motion of popular culture representation, which disinclines us from taking intelligence seriously, with its polarities of conspiracy theories and civilisation-saving, heroic adventure.[24]

The other is the curious unwillingness to learn lessons from history. Learning lessons from history is a different exercise from the practice of post-mortems, and after-action reports, which have been a part of the landscape since the British government set out to learn what went wrong during the South African War (1899–1902) and discovered that a good part of the difficulty resulted from poor intelligence.[25] In such studies, the focus is on the short term and on the case in hand. The business of learning lessons from history has to take a longer view, and look for the deeper patterns, not least in the mentality of intelligence practice, its unexamined inner 'culture'.[26]

There are various possible explanation for this failure of learning, ranging from the notion that the pace of change in intelligence has been so rapid, that historical lessons have no purchase, to the lack of interest on the part of intelligence communities themselves, steeped as they are in present concerns, to the failure of the literature itself to offer usable lessons, beyond the bleak one that intelligence failures are inevitable.[27] None of these explanations is fully plausible.

The failure to draw on a usable past may simply be a product of the lack of any sense of urgency about connecting intelligence's past to intelligence's future. But the elements of the future of intelligence suggested in this essay, whether in the realm of technological change, the adjustment of cultural vision, or the redrawing of a definition of the purpose of intelligence, cannot be appreciated without a sense of the past. That sense of the past must call attention both to things that must be overcome, and aspects of established intelligence practice that must be preserved or acknowledged as essential elements of continuity.

The essays to follow all hold visions of the future of intelligence that are disciplined by expert knowledge of intelligence's past. All prediction about the future of intelligence is, in this sense, a prediction about what mattered in the recent and more distant past. Certainly prediction, even through a historical rear-view mirror, is not easy. The history of this collection is proof of this. Many of the essays contained here were first envisaged as contributions to a conference organized by the Canadian Association for Security and Intelligence Studies on the theme of 'The Future of Intelligence'. The conference was held in Ottawa in the Fall of 2000. None of us predicted the near-term future of September 11. All of the essay writers returned to their subjects afresh in the aftermath of September 11. Still, it is hard to keep up with the future. Yet unless students and practitioners of intelligence can find a way to link past and future, we risk the fate of John Hollander's fictional agent, 'Cupcake'. Hollander's 'poetical, ineffective, meditative spy' ultimately found no way to live with intelligence.[28] His last message before going off the air conveys a paralysing fear of unintelligibility:

This transmission sent out on all frequencies,
Encoded uncommonly; the superflux
Here is no dross, though, and I have sat watching
Key numbers in their serial dance growing
Further apart, outdistancing their touching,
Outstretched arms.[29]

Notes

1 'Dr. Strangelove or: How I Learned to Stop Worrying and Love the Bomb,' dir. Stanley Kubrick. Columbia Pictures, 1963.
2 Useful reflections on the new reality of superterrorism include Lawrence Freedman (ed.), *Super-terrorism: Policy Responses* (Oxford: Blackwell Publishing 2002) and Walter Laqueur, *No End to War: Terrorism in the Twenty-First Century* (New York: Continuum 2003).
3 A point well made by Sir John Keegan in his *Intelligence in War: Knowledge of the Enemy from Napoleon to Al Qaeda* (Toronto: Key Porter Books 2003), Chapter 1.
4 Mary Shelley, *Frankenstein, or the Modern Prometheus* (Oxford UP/Oxford World's Classics, 1998 edition), introduction by M.K. Joseph. The novel was first published in 1817.
5 The best general survey of Sigint in World War II is, in my view, Stephen Budiansky's *Battle of Wits: The Complete Story of Codebreaking in World War II* (NY: The Free Press 2000). F.H. Hinsley's multi-volume official history, *British Intelligence in the Second World War* (London: HMSO 1979–90) remains indispensable for a full understanding of the development and application of Sigint.
6 Roberta Wohlstetter, *Pearl Harbor: Warning and Decision* (Stanford UP 1962). Wohlstetter's remarkable book remains the classic study.
7 For a broad ranging study, see Michael Herman's magisterial *Intelligence Power in Peace and War* (Cambridge: CUP/Royal Inst. for International Affairs 1996).
8 The Canadian Sigint agency was formally established in 1946, based on the remnants of its wartime efforts. It was first named the Communications Branch of the National Research Council (CBNRC). Following a media exposé, the name was changed to Communications Security Establishment (CSE) and it was transferred to the administrative control of the Department of National Defence. There is no full study of Canadian Sigint, but see the useful survey by Martin Rudner, 'Canada's Communication Security Establishment from Cold War to Globalisation', *Intelligence and National Security* 16/1 (Spring 2001) pp.97–128. For the early history of Canadian Sigint, see Wesley K. Wark, 'Cryptographic Innocence: The Origins of Signals Intelligence in Canada in the Second World War', *Journal of Contemporary History* 22/4 (Oct. 1987), pp.639–65.
9 See Nick Cullather, 'Bombing at the Speed of Thought: Intelligence in the Coming Age of Cyber War', in this collection.
10 There is much interesting work on the elevation of George Orwell to the status of prophet. See, in particular, John Rodden, *The Politics of Literary Reputation: The Making and Claiming of 'St. George' Orwell* (NY: OUP 1989).
11 George Orwell, *Nineteen Eighty-Four* [1949] (Penguin paperback edition, 1990) p.1.
12 In 1949, Orwell provided a list of 'crypto-communists' to the Foreign Office's Information Research Department. See Timothy Garton Ash, 'Orwell's List', *New York Review of Books* 50/14, 25 Sept. 2003, pp. 6–12. The original of Orwell's controversial list has now been released as FO 1110/189 in the British National Archives.
13 Recent work on Orwell includes a jaunty polemic by Christopher Hitchens, *Why Orwell Matters* (NY: Basic Books 2002) and two new biographies, Gordon Bowker, *George Orwell* (Boston: Little Brown 2003) and D.J. Taylor, *Orwell: The Life* (NY: Henry Holt 2003)
14 Greg Treverton has tentatively raised the prospect of intelligence serving a wider audience. See Gregory F. Treverton, *Reshaping National Intelligence for an Age of Information* (Cambridge: CUP/RAND 2001). For example, Treverton writes, on p.15 'Should intelligence primarily support military planning and operations? Or should it also serve the entire U.S. government – and, perhaps, the broader American society as well . . .?' My remarks push the argument further.
15 'Iraq's Weapons of Mass Destruction: The Assessment of the British Government', 24 Sept. 2002, available online at <www.pm.gov.uk>.

16 Cm 5837, quoted in Cm 5972, Intelligence and Security Committee, 'Iraqi Weapons of Mass Destruction – Intelligence and Assessments', Sept. 2003, p.4. Available online at <www.cabinet-office.gov.uk/reports/isc>.

17 Available online at the White House website, <www.whitehouse.gov>.

18 For one assessment see John Lewis Gaddis, 'A Global Strategy of Transformation', *Foreign Policy*, Nov./Dec. 2002. The article is available online at <www.foreignpolicy.com/issue_novdec_2002/gaddis.html>.

19 National Security Strategy, Chapter V, 'Preventing Our Enemies from Threatening Us, Our Allies, and Our Friends with Weapons of Mass Destruction', quote at p.16.

20 Remarks by John Prados during a session of the annual conference of the Canadian Association for Security and Intelligence Studies, Vancouver, British Columbia, 17 Oct. 2003.

21 Critical to the development of the literature on intelligence was the publication of the British official history of intelligence in World War II, written by a team of historians headed by the Cambridge don and Bletchley Park veteran, F.H. Hinsley. The more contemporary orientation of intelligence studies was sparked by the investigations and published reports of the US Congressional committees, especially the Frank Church committee, in the mid-1970s.

22 Christopher Andrew and David Dilks (eds.), *The Missing Dimension: Governments and Intelligence Communities in the Twentieth Century* (London: Macmillan 1984)

23 Ernest R. May (ed.), *Knowing One's Enemies: Intelligence Assessment before the Two World Wars* (Princeton UP 1984).

24 For some reflection on these polarities, see the introduction by Wesley K. Wark in idem (ed.), *Spy Fiction, Spy Films and Real Intelligence* (London: Frank Cass 1991).

25 For this story, see Thomas G. Fergusson, *British Military Intelligence 1870–1914: The Development of a Modern Intelligence Organization* (London: Arms & Armour Press 1984).

26 For a fine study of how historical lessons can influence thinking on foreign policy, see Ernest R. May, *'Lessons' of the Past: The Use and Misuse of History in American Foreign Policy* (London: OUP 1975).

27 The most powerful statement on the inevitability of intelligence failure is to be found in Richard Betts, 'Analysis, War and Decision-Making: Why Intelligence Failures are Inevitable', *World Politics* 31 (1978) pp.61–89. Betts reformulated his argument to focus on the events of Sept. 11, 2001, in an essay entitled 'Intelligence Test: The Limits of Prevention', in James F. Hoge and Gideon Rose (eds.), *How Did This Happen: Terrorism and the New War* (NY: Public Affairs/Council on Foreign Relations 2001), pp.145–61.

28 The description of 'Cupcake' is from a letter by Hollander to Noel Annan, undated, in my possession.

29 John Hollander, *Reflections on Espionage* (NY: Atheneum 1976), p.71. Hollander's long poem is a unique and wonderful reflection on intelligence, stimulated by the reading of Sir John Masterman's 1972 book on World War II deception operations, *The Double Cross System*. For an interview that I conducted with Hollander about his poem, see the special issue of *Queen's Quarterly*, 'The Future of Espionage' (Summer 1993) pp.351–4.

Reprinted with permission from Wesley K. Wark, 'Learning to Live with Intelligence', *Intelligence and National Security* 18/4 (Winter 2003) pp.1–14.

Some helpful web resources

- A web-site with additional materials and readings for this volume is available at –
  http://www2.warwick.ac.uk/fac/soc/pais/staff/aldrich/intel
- A web-site with excellent bibliographic resources is available at –
  http://intellit.muskingum.edu
- A very useful review of world intelligence agencies is available at – http://fas.org/irp

Index